Date Due

May 8 '57			
May 25 '59			
Feb 8 '60			
May 25 '61			
May 19 66			

THE DEVELOPMENT
OF MODERN EUROPE

◀ VOLUME II ▶

The Merging of European
into World History

BY

JAMES HARVEY ROBINSON

AND

CHARLES A. BEARD

Completely Revised and Enlarged Edition

GINN AND COMPANY

BOSTON · NEW YORK · CHICAGO · LONDON
ATLANTA · DALLAS · COLUMBUS · SAN FRANCISCO

D
209
.R8
1929
V2

21387
Feb. '46

The Athenæum Press

GINN AND COMPANY · PRO-
PRIETORS · BOSTON · U.S.A.

PREFACE

This volume, like the preceding one, is based upon our *Development of Modern Europe*, originally published in 1907 and 1908. A great part of it, however, is entirely new; for the twenty years and more which have elapsed since the book appeared have witnessed the most incredible and fundamental changes in the affairs of the world. It has proved a very difficult task to give some semblance of coherency to the multiform developments of our century—the most difficult task which has ever presented itself to the historical writer. In our effort to meet this problem we have arranged the matter topically in successive sections under distinct headings, each section being devoted to some particular phase of human interest. The chronological sequence, however, is never neglected, although subordinated to our effort to make clear leading issues, of which there are now a bewildering variety. The constant aim of the writers has been to put their readers in a position to follow intelligently the unfolding of the great human drama as it is reported from day to day and month to month.

C. A. B.
J. H. R.

CONTENTS

CHAPTER   PAGE

I. THE HERITAGE OF THE TWENTIETH CENTURY

General Retrospect 1
The National State and Democratic Ideas 5
The Technological Revolution 9
Conquest of Feudalism by Capitalism 10
Inherited Modes of Thought 13
Classical Political Economy : Laissez Faire 16
Ethical Criticism of Classical Economy 20
Utopian Socialism 21
Marxian Socialism 24
The Anarchist Scheme of Thought 27
German National Economy : State Socialism 29
Some Effects of Darwin's Theories 32
Tendencies at the Close of the Nineteenth Century 34

II. DEVELOPMENT OF GOVERNMENT IN THE NAME OF THE "PEOPLE" (1870–1914)

The Third French Republic 40
The German Imperial Constitution 46
Extension of the Suffrage and Cabinet System 51
Political Parties 55
Freedom of Press and Speech 57
Misgivings about Democracy 61

III. CONFLICTS OF DEMOCRACY WITH KINGS, PEERS, AND PRELATES

The Perdurance of Monarchy 64
Upper Chambers : Lords and Senators 66
Monarchy and Aristocracy in Central Europe 70
Democratic Struggles in Russia under Nicholas II 74
The Russian Duma 83
State and Church amid Democratic Tendencies 88
Religious Freedom in England 91
The Roman Catholic Church and Papal Infallibility 93
The Religious Conflict in Germany 95
Separation of Church and State in France 98

CHAPTER   PAGE

IV. THE GROWTH OF STATE ECONOMIC CONTROL

    Rise of Marxian Socialism in Germany and France 106
    Socialism in Great Britain 109
    International Socialism 110
    Social Legislation in England 111
    Later Phases of Social Reform in Great Britain 116
    State Socialism in Germany 122
    General Progress of Social Legislation on the Continent . . 125
    Growth of Protective Tariffs 127

V. PROGRESS OF IMPERIALISM

    New Phases of European Expansion 133
    New Means of Transportation and Intercommunication . . 136
    Missionary Activities and Imperialism 147
    Expansion of France 151
    Expansion of Germany and Italy 155
    Russian Expansion 160
    The Exploration of Africa 162
    Belgian Congo 168
    Morocco 170
    The British in Egypt 171

VI. THE BRITISH EMPIRE BEFORE THE WORLD WAR

    Advantages of Great Britain in Empire-building 175
    British India 177
    The Dominion of Canada 187
    The Australasian Colonies 191
    Growth of the British Empire in Africa 196
    British Imperial Federation 203
    The Irish Question 208

VII. THE NEW WORLD AND THE OLD

    Relation of American Civilization to European 222
    Economic Influences of the Americas on Europe 223
    American Diplomatic Relations 232
    Influence on Europe of American Political Events and Ideas . 241

VIII. THE AWAKENING OF THE FAR EAST

    Peculiar Position of China and Japan 248
    Early Relations of Europe with China 249
    How Japan became a World Power 256

CHAPTER PAGE

War between Japan and China and its Results 261
The Boxer Rising 265
Russo-Japanese War (1904–1905) 268
Revolution in China 271

IX. ORIGINS OF THE WORLD WAR

Sources of Information 274
Ancient Continental Grudges 277
Alsace and Lorraine 278
Problems of Southeastern Europe 281
Imperialistic Rivalries 285
Periodical "Crises" 289
The System of Secret Alliances 291
Rivalry in Armaments 296
Failure of the Peace Movement 299
The Balkan Wars 304
Fatal Floundering of Diplomats in July, 1914 311
So-called "War Guilt" 315

X. THE WORLD WAR. PART I

Novel Features of the War 321
Diplomacy and Secret Treaties 332
Propaganda 340

XI. THE WORLD WAR. PART II

First Phase of the War on Land (1914–1916) 348
War On and Under the Sea 356
Position of the United States during the Early Phases of the
    World War 361
Entrance of the United States into the War 364
The Russian Revolution; the Bolsheviki 367
Issues of the War 370
The World at War 379
Fall of the Hohenzollern and Hapsburg Dynasties; Close of the
    War 384

XII. A PERTURBING PEACE

The Peace Conference of 1919 390
The New Map of Europe 392
The Punishment and Crippling of Germany 403
Plight of Europe after the War 411

CHAPTER   PAGE

XIII. CHIEF FACTORS IN RECONSTRUCTION

The New Constitutions of Europe 415
Progress of Socialism and Communism 425
The Agrarian Revolutions 438
New Phases of the Old Conflict between Church and State . 443

XIV. DEMOCRACY IN CENTRAL AND WESTERN EUROPE

Germany and Austria as Republics 447
The Western Slavic States 454
France after the War 458
Great Britain and her Self-governing Empire 461

XV. STARTLING EXPERIMENTS IN GOVERNMENT

The Bolshevik Régime 470
Mussolini and the Fascisti 483
Disturbances in Southeastern Europe 497

XVI. GROWING INFLUENCE OF WESTERN IDEAS IN AFRICA AND ASIA

Africa after the War 504
The Turkish Republic—the Near East 514
Restless India 526
Republican China and the Far East 531

XVII. QUEST FOR INTERNATIONAL PEACE AND UNDERSTANDING

The Question of German Reparations 540
The World Court 547
Projects for Peace and Security 550
The United States and World Affairs 559
The League of Nations 564
Is War an Anachronism? 574

XVIII. NEW CONCEPTIONS OF THE WORLD WE LIVE IN

The Fundamental Rôle of Knowledge in Human Affairs . . 578
The Great Age of the Earth 584
The Theory of Evolution: Darwinism 587
The Study of Living Cells and its Results 594
Bacteria and the Germ Theory of Disease 598
The Constitution of Matter: Atoms and Molecules . . . 602

CONTENTS

CHAPTER   PAGE

XIX. NEW VIEWS OF MAN'S NATURE AND TRADITIONS

    Influence of Natural Science upon the Study of Man Himself .   608
    The Newer Aims of Historical Study   610
    The Perspective of Human Development   612
    The Comparative Study of Mankind and its Fruits   615
    Race Prejudice, Nations, and Nationalism   620
    The New Methods of Studying Mind   622
    Importance of Childhood; the Unconscious   624
    The Problems of Education   628

XX. THE STUDY OF MANKIND IN FICTION

    Historical Significance of Stories and the Drama   634
    The Problem of Evil   638
    Romanticism   643
    "The Quintessence of Ibsenism"   649
    H. G. Wells et Al.   655
    Epilogue   660

SUGGESTIONS FOR READING   i

INDEX   xiii

LIST OF MAPS

PAGE

Europe in 1914 (in colors) 42
The Suez Canal 140
The Partition of Africa (in colors) 154
European Advance in Asia, 1914 (in colors) 162
The British Empire, 1914 (in colors) 174
India and Farther India, 1914 179
India at the Sepoy Rebellion (in colors) 180
Australia and New Zealand in 1904 (in colors) 194
South Africa before the Boer War 197
Ireland, showing the boundaries of the Pale 212
South America (in colors) 226
The Far East (in colors) 250
Southeastern Europe, 1907 and 1914 (in colors) 306
Western Front, 1914–1917 348
Eastern Front, 1914–1917 349
Austria-Hungary, 1867–1918 (in colors) 352
German War Zone, February, 1917 365
Germany, showing losses after the World War 393
Ethnographic Map of Austria-Hungary before the World War . . 394
The Austrian Republic and the Hungarian Monarchy 395
Western Portion of Union of Socialist Soviet Republics 397
Yugoslavia 399
Greater Rumania 400
Europe after the Treaty of Versailles (in colors) 402
Irish Free State 467
Africa, showing Colonies and Mandated Territories (in colors) . . 508
Republic of Turkey 515
The Near East 518
Fifty-Kilometer Zone 554

THE DEVELOPMENT OF MODERN EUROPE

THE MERGING OF EUROPEAN INTO WORLD HISTORY

CHAPTER I

THE HERITAGE OF THE TWENTIETH CENTURY

GENERAL RETROSPECT

The colorful and multiform pageantry of outward events, with its personalities, glories, and tragedies, which crowds the years of the past three centuries, resolves itself, when viewed at a distance, into a few striking scenes and phases. Though the origins of governments, religions, laws, customs, and ideas about nature and mankind can be traced far back into the distant past, yet, owing to novel conditions, the most striking characteristics of our present civilization are the product of achievements wrought since the age of Elizabeth and Essex. In its political aspects the pageant includes three stirring revolutions, each accompanied by radicalism and followed by a reaction which in turn ebbed. The first of them was in England. It opened in 1603 with a contest between Parliament and James I, ran through years of discord, bringing in its train civil war, the execution of Charles I in 1649, a republic, leveling and communistic agitations, a dictatorship under Cromwell, the restoration of Charles II, the expulsion of James II in 1688, and the final triumph of the Parliament over the monarch. Looking upon the English as an excitable, unruly, and violent race, monarchists on the Continent congratulated themselves on the docility of their nations, and sought to keep out dangerous English ideas—to establish a quarantine against the contagion of fitful political fevers.

For nearly a century, while the new régime in England settled down to a steady course, all was fairly calm in the domestic politics of the western world. Then suddenly the British colonies in America, applying revolutionary ideas taken from the English upheavals of 1649 and 1688, rose in revolt against the government of George III. This war—in many significant aspects also a domestic revolution—ran through seven years and brought with it the still more leveling doctrines of Thomas Paine and Thomas Jefferson. For a time after 1783 it looked as if the familiar military despotism was destined to come, but the patriotism of Washington and the ingenuity of American statesmen avoided this outcome. So Europe was face to face with a republic—a revolutionary form of government, which, as Oliver Wendell Holmes later said, was a standing menace to all governments founded on different principles.

In the very spring when Washington was inaugurated first president of the United States, the king of France, Louis XVI, who had aided the American revolutionists and squared some old colonial scores with England, found himself in the presence of revolution at home. After all, it had been impossible to keep English revolutionary ideas out of his kingdom or to prevent new and disturbing views about man and nature from penetrating the intellectual circles of his realm. State, Church, and historic morals had been undermined by Voltaire, Diderot, Helvétius, Rousseau, and the other *philosophes*. Young army officers brought back from America leveling doctrines, and, as they danced in red-heeled shoes at the court, discoursed light-heartedly on the superior merits of democracies and republics. State constitutions drawn up by American revolutionists were translated into French and read in drawing-rooms and taverns. And when Louis XVI got into financial troubles in 1789 and called the Estates-General after a lapse of a hundred and seventy odd years, a storm burst. Historic privileges of the aristocracy and clergy were abolished. The king was forced to sign a constitution depriving him of his royal supremacy. Civil disorders ensued: Louis and his queen were sent to the scaffold; a republic was attempted; wars with neighboring monarchies broke out; one type of dictatorship followed another, until a military officer, Bonaparte, finding the French crown on the ground, as he said, picked it up with his sword. Once in power, he transformed the republic into an empire, conferring on himself the title of "Emperor"—the good old Roman name for the high war lord. For more than twenty years all Europe was at war. Fleet-footed revolutionary ideas, which had been spreading through Europe, were substantiated by arms as Napoleon invaded Holland, Italy, Austria, Spain, Germany, and Russia, overturning thrones, abolishing feudal privileges, and reducing the power of princes and clergy.

When the French emperor was overthrown at Waterloo in 1815, old Europe was, as it proved, beyond salvage. Resolutely statesmen of the conservative school, with their clerical allies, sought to restore as much as possible of the old régime and to seal revolutionary doctrines in the tomb. But at best they could get only a portion of the ruins to stand for a time. It was impossible to settle what could not be settled.

During the years of social peace (1815–1870), broken by two revolutions,—a slight affair in France in 1830 and a second and more general upheaval in 1848,—Europe was preparing to adopt nearly all the leading political ideas which had appeared to many so new and frightful in 1789. For instance, almost everywhere in western Europe the business classes, so despised by the ancient landed aristocracy, had by the middle of the century been admitted to a share in government.

During the period when these internal changes were taking place, a succession of wars between the respective governments of Europe greatly altered their relations to one another (Vol. I, pp. 86 ff.). The seventeenth century had scarcely

T

opened when the Thirty Years' War, centering mainly in German territory, spread devastation far and wide. After a brief interval of peace, established at Westphalia in 1648, the ambitions of Louis XIV and the over-sea enterprises of Spain, Holland, and England filled Europe anew with wars—first, little preludes; and then the grand conflagration known as the War of the Spanish Succession, which drew its weary length to a finish in 1713. Except for some brief wars and the notable encroachments of Frederick the Great at the expense of his neighbors, peace was kept, in a way, until 1754. In that year an Anglo-French conflict in the western wilds of Pennsylvania kindled flames that spread around the world in the Seven Years' War. Within little more than ten years after its close, the American Revolution opened another struggle, involving powers on both sides of the Atlantic; and then, exactly ten years after it came to an end,—namely, in 1793,—the wars of the French Revolution started and merged into the Napoleonic struggles which raged until 1815. At last a general peace was established, and, apart from "localized wars" such as the Crimean and the Franco-Prussian wars, Europe saw no more general conflicts until 1914. Underlying these two centuries and more of fighting were the pride of princes, with their lust for neighboring territory, their rivalry for world trade and colonies, and finally the passions of nations aroused on one pretext or another. Governments that were at each other's throats one year were the next year allied as bosom companions against former friends. Solemn treaties were made, only to be broken.

Into these agitations of western Europe the peoples of eastern Europe were gradually drawn. From the close of the seventeenth century, when Peter the Great visited Germany, Holland, and England to study their arts and sciences, Russia's interest and influence in Europe increased. Slowly the Bear turned from the Orient to the Occident, taking part in its wars and councils and receiving impacts from its revolutions. While this great branch of the Slavic race was joining the main stream of European events, another division to the south was shaking off the Turkish yoke imposed centuries before when the hosts of Islam swept as far west as the gates of Vienna. It was the peasants of Slavic Serbia who broke the Sultan's power in a desperate struggle for independence lasting from 1804 to 1817. The success of the Serbs was followed by a declaration of independence on the part of the Greeks in 1822, and by the steady disintegration of Moslem dominion. If it had not been for aid given to Turkey by England and France in the Crimean War of 1854–1856, Russia would probably have broken through the Dardanelles at the middle of the century and freed the rest of southeastern Europe from the rule of the Sultan. But the jealousy of the western nations prevented that consummation.

By this time two newly unified powers, Italy and Germany, were becoming prominent figures in the European scene. Through a long struggle under Sardinian leadership the divided and warring states of Italy were brought under a single sovereign; Austria was expelled from nearly all her ancient possessions in the peninsula, and at last, in 1870, Rome was wrested from the Pope by Italian troops and became the capital of the new kingdom. While King Victor Emmanuel was opening his first parliament early in 1871, the Germans under Bismarck's direction were, after their victory over France, completing their union by welding the North German Federation and the south-German states into a new empire.

THE NATIONAL STATE AND DEMOCRATIC IDEAS

When in January, 1871, the king of Prussia was proclaimed German Emperor in the old palace of Louis XIV at Versailles, a long chain of events stretching back into the Dark Ages was brought to a dramatic climax: the anarchy of the petty feudal principalities which had sprung up amid the ruins of the Roman Empire was at last completely subdued by national governments throughout Europe.

Looking far back through the welter of kingly wars, royal intrigues, international marriages, slippery diplomacy, and circumspect assassinations, we can see one great state after another rising slowly out of the chaos into which Europe fell after the decline of Rome, with the sword-bearing monarch as the center of the process. There they stood like political milestones scattered along the centuries: England, France, Spain, Russia, Italy, and finally Germany.

Although the last scenes in this grand drama were enacted in the age of steam and electricity, it is well to remember that the process began long before the machine age was ever dreamed of. Steam and electricity, like gunpowder, served to accelerate the operation, but they did not originate it. It had been fairly begun even before cannons were heard of; let us say, with the establishment of the Norman monarchy in England by the stark William the Conqueror who did Harold to death at the battle of Hastings in 1066. And the methods of this consolidation remained very much the same to the end: iron and blood, as in the beginning. If James Watt had never invented the steam engine, if Stephenson had never designed a locomotive, the process of unifying the feudal disruption would have gone forward to its logical conclusion. The outstanding political achievements of the nineteenth century were, in short, not vitally dependent upon factories and railways.

Although there was always a powerful war lord or monarch at the center of the state-making, his work was usually carried on with the aid of certain classes in the community, and he always had to reckon with resistance to his military and financial exactions. In this way were developed parliaments, ministers, and cabinets, which were in time subjected to more or less popular control and in some countries transformed into democratic institutions. In many parts of medieval Europe—Russia, the Scandinavian countries, several German states, Spain, France, and England, for example—parliaments came into being as princes called upon their subjects for money and arms. But these parliaments represented classes, or estates, not the people as individuals. In the *Cortes* of old Aragon sat clergy, great barons, minor barons, and burgesses of the towns. The first Estates-General convoked in France, in 1302, consisted of the higher clergy and nobility summoned in person, representatives of the lower clergy, and delegates from the towns—orders of society known collectively as the clergy, nobility, and third estate. In the Parliament of medieval England there were—in fact, whatever the theory—four estates: clergy, lay barons, landed gentry, and burgesses from the towns.

It is true that as a general rule these assemblies disappeared from the Continent as soon as the monarchs felt strong enough to dispense with the irksome necessity of consulting the taxpayers about royal expenditures. In England, however, Parliament escaped destruction and furnished a model and inspiration for the later popular efforts to control kings and princes in Europe. Moreover, in connection with the American and the French revolutions a radical change was made in the very idea of a parliament. Rousseau worked out a theory that sovereignty, or all political power, rightly belongs to the people, considered as individuals, not as estates. If the state, he said, consists of ten thousand citizens, then each of them has one ten-thousandth part of sovereign authority, and the will of the majority is law. "All men are created equal," ran the words of Jefferson's immortal Declaration of Independence—to wit, everyone should have his individual share in choosing those who conduct the affairs of state. Instead of classes—clergy, nobility, and *bourgeoisie*—there are to be only citizens.

Naturally this theory played havoc with the concept of parliaments as collections of estates. In the French Revolution the third estate—really the *bourgeoisie* and prosperous peasants—almost immediately swept aside the clergy and nobility and seized sovereign powers. Of course this third estate did not propose to give the vote to propertyless workingmen and laborers, but by announcing the doctrine of equality, so useful in its war on the clergy and the nobility, it started a movement that was destined to destroy the old class governments all around the world. Steadily and amid a great deal of turmoil, class parliaments or estates-general were supplanted more or less completely by parliaments elected by "free and equal heads."

With much fear conservatives on both sides of the Atlantic, Alexander Hamilton no less than Metternich, watched the sweep of this equalitarian doctrine over the face of Western civilization. Whenever possible they sought to block it. In setting up a parliament after the storm of 1848, the king of Prussia created a House of Lords representing the landed interests and an assembly so constituted that the richest subjects could elect two thirds of the members. The Austrian parliament established in 1861 was based frankly on class representation, and this system, with minor modifications, was retained until 1907. But the idea of complete equality, which ultimately included women as well as men, made headway everywhere, aided by the agitations of the proletariat, namely, the voteless working people of the industrial towns. In this way the popular or democratic side of the centralizing process was promoted and the great state system of nineteenth-century Europe was created—a leveling down, and consequent elimination of class lines and social distinctions in politics. And, as has been emphasized, all the prime ideas and institutions associated with democracy—representative government, extension of the suffrage, equality before the law, political parties, liberty of press and speech, individualism, and separation of State and Church —antedate the Industrial Revolution. They originated and developed in the age of agriculture, handicrafts, and general illiteracy. No doubt the printing press, railways, and the growth of cities accelerated their progress, but they would have advanced without these new engines of the modern age.

THE TECHNOLOGICAL REVOLUTION

Far removed from the spotlight in which kings, princes, bishops, diplomats, and politicians played their rôles with solemn ceremony, operations were going on which were to effect thoroughgoing alterations in the practice and persiflage of politics and to make the social and economic development of the twentieth century radically different from that of the nineteenth. To these operations and man's interpretation of them we must now give our attention. In 1769, the year in which Napoleon Bonaparte was born, James Watt secured his first patent for a steam engine; and when the little Corsican was carried away to St. Helena, Watt was still hard at work improving and turning out steam engines at Birmingham. During the tense years while Metternich was trying to hold Europe fast to the settlement of 1815, George Stephenson was manufacturing locomotives at Newcastle; it was in Metternich's fatal summer of 1848 that the English engineer passed from the world which he had done so much to alter. While the Reform Bill of 1832 was agitating all England, Samuel F. B. Morse was meditating on the possibility of transmitting information by electricity; during the span of his years, Gladstone, Disraeli, Bismarck, Cavour, and Napoleon III were the stars on the political stage. While Bismarck was discussing politics and morals in the language of Moses and the Old Testament, patient chemists were laboring in the laboratories at Giessen, Göttingen, Marburg, and Leipzig, helping to revolutionize man's knowledge of the material world and the industries by which he lives.

From the workshop and the laboratory the discoveries of the mind were carried to the four corners of the earth. In due time they began to destroy the world of fact in which the whole system of politics and political argument known to the nineteenth century had originated. By the side of the feudal landlords who had, with the aid of kings, governed western Europe since the break-up of the Roman Empire, there now appeared new competitors—business men—who increased in number, wealth, and power until they became the real directors of the political and economic drama. From the open countryside political power was transferred to the crowded city. For the limited productivity of agricultural land, technology substituted the apparently unlimited productive power of steam, electricity, and chemical processes. To the peasants, once likely to break loose and sack castles, technology added a huge urban working class which soon showed a similar tendency to make trouble for governing classes.

By technology the whole intellectual climate in which the masses lived and worked was revolutionized, slowly but inexorably. The old agriculturist, ignorant of chemistry and equipped with a few crude tools, was a victim of rains, floods, droughts, cattle plagues, insects, and declining fertility, and in times of distress he resorted to prayers, genuflections, and the exorcism of evil spirits. How different was the life of the machine man in the age of science! For him the area of everyday mysteries was greatly contracted. If his steam engine broke down, he knew that exact mechanical methods, not prayers to angry gods, would make it work again. If typhoid fever began to rage in his city, he relied on the chemist and bacteriologist, not the priest or medicine man. For him a vast mass of emotions, hopes, theories, omens, signs, and ceremonies ceased to have any meaning. Mysteries remained, no doubt, but not the homely mysteries of the barn lot, wheat field, and village churchyard.

CONQUEST OF FEUDALISM BY CAPITALISM

With this transformation wrought by technology came a revolution in the system of economy itself. For more than a thousand years Europe had been living under the régime of feudalism. The term is vague, no doubt, and even at its height the system was in process of change; but as a scheme of life it had fairly definite characteristics. Primarily it was a social structure in which the status or occupation of everyone was determined by birth or law. King, lord, bishop, priest, serf, tailor, baker, and tinker all had their status and duties. Under this system production was carried on to meet immediate needs or for local exchange at a "just price." The accumulation of great fortunes in capital or even modest savings were almost unknown—at least until world commerce disturbed the ancient routine of Europe. Feudalism was a fairly stable order of production for immediate use, in which all ranks had reciprocal responsibilities and obligations. The ethics of the Middle Ages, formulated by scholastic professors, was mainly concerned with working out the moral relations of the members of this fixed social order.

As technology swept into the field of industry, it was accompanied by the rise of a new system of production known for convenience as "capitalism." What is capitalism? It is not synonymous with capital goods, such as mines, machinery, and railways, for in that sense feudalism was capitalistic, in that it had accumulations of tools and materials used in production. Nor is capitalism synonymous with manufacturing; conceivably it might take over the whole scheme of agricultural economy. It is not the same as machine industry, because it had begun to flourish before machinery was extensively used in production of goods.

In contrast to the feudal order which it superseded, capitalism may be viewed as a system of production in which the primary object is *profit*. Unlike primitive agriculture and handicrafts, which produce for use or for local exchange at a just price, capitalism produces to sell on the most advantageous terms, that is, with the largest profit possible to the owners and directors. The area of its operations seems unbounded. While the amount of farm land in any particular country is limited, the area of capitalistic operations has no limits. Under the capitalistic system the amount of goods turned out, the amount of wealth that can be accumulated, the number of men and women who can be employed, seem capable of indefinite expansion.

More than this, the agriculture of a country is carried on within its geographical boundaries and under its flag, while the capitalists of a nation may operate throughout the world. Conceivably the capital of any particular nation invested in foreign countries might exceed in value the amount invested at home. In 1927, the Secretary of the United States Navy declared that the amount of American property abroad and on the high seas in that year was about equal to the total wealth of the country some fifty years before. Inevitably, like feudalism, capitalism developed its scheme of morals and reasoning. This was in itself a revolution in social thinking. In its essence capitalism is "rational"; that is, it is based not upon piety, mysteries, and supplications but on calculable factors which can be mirrored in the balance sheet: plant, buildings, machines, raw materials, hands, wages, prices, output, sales, profits, and surplus. Capitalists may pray for riches, but they expect no material help from the invocation of saints. Bookkeeping—or to use the technical word, accounting—can cover all capitalistic operations in mathematical terms, just as mathematics underlies all operations on the technological side.

Before the nineteenth century had drawn to a close, capitalism had become dominant over feudalism and agriculture throughout a large part of the Western world. The question now presents itself, How can we discover the point at which capitalism becomes dominant in any particular country? There is no easy answer. One measure is the money value of the instruments used in capitalistic production as contrasted with agriculture. Another measure is the number of men and women employed in capitalistic as against agricultural enterprises. A third is the influence exercised by the owners of capitalistic undertakings on the operations of government, domestic and foreign—an influence difficult to assess on account of its subtlety, but none the less real.

Judged by such standards, capitalism was conquering Western civilization at the time that the statesmen of the last half of the nineteenth century were playing their respective rôles with political ambitions inherited mainly from the long agricultural past. For convenience approximate dates may be set. For England, the year of capitalistic victory may be fixed as 1846, when free trade was established for the benefit of English manufacturers. The Revolution of 1848 in France, while it temporarily revealed the power of organized labor, crowned the *bourgeoisie* revolution of 1830 and marked the doom of landlords and clergy as the ruling element. By 1850 the value of the instrumentalities employed in capitalist undertakings in the United States had overtopped the value of the land; and in 1865 the armies of the Southern planters surrendered at Appomattox. In Germany capitalism did not get into full swing until after 1870, and this triumph was not politically recognized until after the collapse of Prussia in 1918.

INHERITED MODES OF THOUGHT

When this new Leviathan, capitalism, armed with technology, invaded the feudal world of guilds and agriculture, what was the intellectual climate in which thought about it had to be conducted? New facts do not automatically bring their appropriate interpretation. On the contrary, they must inevitably be considered at first in the light of prevailing ideas. Capitalism and technology ran like a sword into the old web of notions about the world, mankind, and politics. Of necessity they were considered in terms of inherited phraseology and logic; they had to be adjusted to the opinions, morals, creeds, laws, sayings, surmises, and guesses already current, no matter how relevant or irrelevant they might be. For example, the Declaration of the Rights of Man said that "men are born and remain free and equal in rights"; then it follows that a capitalist, with a million francs, sitting securely in his countinghouse, is the equal of a half-starved workman asking for employment at the factory gate. Was there in fact any appropriateness at all for capitalism in a system of rights designed to bring feudal lords and clergy down to the level of merchants and farmers? If any thinking was to be started in respect of the new economic order, a beginning had to be made by reconsidering inherited modes of thought.

Broadly speaking, three systems of thought were available at the opening of the nineteenth century for those who were attempting to apply their intelligence to the swift changes then in process. The first of them may be called for the sake of convenience the "fixed order of God." This was the scholastic pattern of words evolved during the Middle Ages as appropriate to a fixed social order in which each rank or class had its status, its duties, and its obligations. Naturally the fixed-order-of-God theory was most popular in feudal and Catholic countries, among feudal and clerical classes. More or less opposed to it, however, appeared another assortment of ideas, the "fixed order of *nature*," which was to be discovered by reason and was to bring happiness when understood and conformed to. By formulating the law of gravitation, Newton gave a great impetus to the development of this idea; and the French *philosophes*, in their war on the clergy and nobility, made constant use of it. Now this fixed order of nature, or natural law, was of necessity in essence mathematical, numerical, material, and flatly opposed to the system of sentiments associated with the divine order. For convenience it may be called the "system of natural reason." Though apparently opposed, in reality these two schemes of ideas had much in common; perhaps they were the obverse and reverse of the same thing. They were both essentially theological, definite, positive, unchangeable; they had no room for the tough facts of change that did not fit into their logic.

But the adherents of these two systems were always in trouble. Those who expounded the divine order were continually perplexed by the fact that the conduct of mankind by no means conformed exactly to the rules and regulations of the system. If they got some consolation from ascribing this nonconformity to perversity and sin, the fact still remained that the divine order, especially after the Protestant revolt, seemed to be elusive, when tested by human conduct and actual institutions. Nor were the philosophers who espoused the fixed natural order in any better case: human conduct simply would not conform to any purely numerical rules respecting pleasures and pains, profit and loss, gains and subtractions. Life, being organic, could not be entirely covered by reason, whether theological or scientific. On the whole, thinkers with old feudal predilections were more inclined to the scholastic scheme of thought, while mercantile and capitalist thinkers turned rather to the natural order of affairs. And this is not strange.

A third system of thought, opposed equally to the fixed order of God and the fixed order of nature, was a new philosophy which conceived of the world as endless change. Inevitably this also took various forms. Francis Bacon (Vol. I, pp. 13 ff.) had proclaimed the possibility of the continuous improvement of the lot of mankind on this earth by the attainment of knowledge and the subjugation of the material world to the welfare of the human race. This "idea of progress" was unknown to the Greeks and the Romans and foreign to the spirit and doctrines of early Christianity; but during the latter part of the eighteenth century and all through the nineteenth century it spread far and wide in Western civilization. Condorcet's sketch of the progress of the human spirit appeared in a beautiful translation in Philadelphia in 1796.

Taken up by the German philosopher Hegel, this notion of the world was worked out in an interpretation of history. With Hegel the truth is not a collection of ready-made dogmatic propositions respecting any fixed order, God's or nature's; it is in fact an endless chain of changes—of becoming and passing, and this chain reflected in the human brain is philosophy itself. But this everlasting flow of things, Hegel went on to say, is the progressive realization of the idea of God; underlying all the forms and changes of civilization is an infinite power working toward its aim, the "absolute rational design of the world."

Shortly after Hegel's death in 1831, this concept was given a very strange turn by the founder of modern socialism, Karl Marx. Admitting his debt to the German philosopher, Marx declared that he found Hegel standing on his head and that he turned him over, putting him on his feet. By this Marx meant that he found the cause of changes not in the ideas of God but in material circumstances—climate, soil, inventions, the economic struggle of classes, and similar material forces. Of this, however, we shall say more later (pp. 24 ff.); for the present it is essential to take note of the three general systems of philosophy with which the thinkers of the nineteenth century had to work when they began to speculate on the nature of the revolution brought about in human affairs by science, the steam engine, machinery, and capitalism.

Classical Political Economy: Laissez Faire

Taking a practical view of the scheme of things in which they found themselves, English economists studied the capitalist system in a naturalistic spirit; they sought to discover its "laws"—that is, to apply to it the philosophy of the fixed natural order. Appropriately enough the title of "the Newton of political economy" was given to Ricardo (1772–1823), the distinguished successor of Adam Smith, and with less justification it might have been conferred on John Stuart Mill.

Broadly speaking, the political economy of the classical school —the early nineteenth-century economists—laid down the "natural laws" of the business world. In brief form its philosophy ran as follows: Society is composed of individuals, each struggling to avoid pain and to secure pleasure-giving possessions. Where legal freedom of contract and of residence exists, the individual applies his talents and capital to the enterprise for which he is best fitted. Competition guarantees the survival of those who render economical services at the lowest price. The purchaser of goods knows what is best for himself and can avoid adulterations and frauds. Competition and rent regulate prices, profits, and wages, so that each productive factor in society—land, labor, and capital—obtains a reward fairly apportioned to its deserts. Pressure of population keeps wages near the cost of subsistence, and the unfailing improvidence of the poor assures an abundant and cheap labor supply. Everybody is the best judge of what is beneficial to himself and by trusting to his instincts and reason will find the place in society to which his merits entitle him. Attempts to control prices, wages, and the quality of goods are interferences with "natural laws," bound to fail and to injure those for whose supposed benefit they are made.

The freedom which works so perfectly within the state, continues the classical economist, works equally well among states; under a régime of free trade, each nation produces the goods for which it is best adapted by climate, resources, and skill; and a free exchange of goods among states results in the widest benefit for all, each party to every transaction receiving the most desirable goods at the lowest price. Attempts to build up industries by tariffs and bounties are efforts to make water run uphill. Bananas could be grown in hothouses at the north pole, but it is cheaper to import them from the warmer regions where they grow naturally, and so forth.

From this system of ideas it followed that there should be no interference with the freedom of capitalists to buy, manufacture, and sell. If private monopolies arise and attempt to control prices, they run contrary to natural law, and should be dissolved by the government. If trade unions make a similar attempt to control wages, they too violate natural law and should be dissolved. In short, it is the duty of the government to protect private property and to keep order, allowing the economic machine to function freely under its own momentum —the profit-making passion and the struggle for existence. If the government will keep its hands off business and not attempt to "improve" the condition of anybody by legislation, then everyone will be as happy and prosperous as he deserves to be. All this will flow from natural laws. Obviously, this is a scholastic-Newtonian scheme of thought, founded on a fixed-order assumption—not on the concept of eternal flow or change, either Hegelian or Marxian.

With a view to making this abstract scheme of thought clear to the poor and uneducated classes of England, a number of popular writers reduced it to its elements and adorned it with humble illustrations. By a series of stories relating how the merchants and manufacturers of England had risen from poverty to riches by hard and unremitting labors, Samuel Smiles tried to show what "any poor boy could do." This kind of thinking could be summed up in the trite saying, "There is always room at the top," to which an English miner once replied, "What we want is more room at the bottom." Besides indicating how individuals could mount the ladder to fame and wealth, popularizers of political economy developed a set of moral rules for those who had to hold the ladder for the fortunate climbers. In her tales for the common people, Hannah More made Ricardo's economics explicit for peasants, shepherds, and working people.

In one of these pious interpretations of the classical school of political economy, Miss More tells the story of a poverty-stricken shepherd in his own words. His house for himself, his wife, and eight children is a miserable hovel; but instead of being discontented with his lot, he exults: "How many better men have been worse lodged! How many good Christians have perished in prisons and dungeons, in comparison of which my cottage is a palace. The house is very well, sir; and if the rain did not sometimes beat down upon us through the thatch when we are a-bed, I should not desire a better." He is grateful that he can read the Bible; indeed, reading is becoming more common "through the goodness of Providence and the generosity of the rich." But the poor man will not read wicked books containing disturbing ideas. "When those men, I say, come to my poor hovel with their new doctrines and their new books, I would never look into them. . . . My own book told me—To fear God and honor the king—To meddle not with them who are given to change—Not to speak evil of dignities —To render honor to whom honor is due." In time this virtue was rewarded by an outburst of generosity on the part of a rich man who took delight in the shepherd's contentment with the station to which the Lord had appointed him; the shepherd was then able to move into a two-room cottage with a kitchen and was set to teaching his sound doctrines to the children of the village. Moreover, his laborious wife was induced to accept a warm blanket in spite of her fear that comfort in this world might deprive her of heavenly joys hereafter.

In Miss More's tales, the good workman never drank, never grumbled about long hours, never complained of low wages or unemployment, never read books likely to stir up discontent with the best of possible worlds, and was always grateful to God, the rich, and the parsons for the permission to live at all. She was especially devoted to "that beautiful hymn so deservedly the favorite of all children":

> Not more than others I deserve,
>   Yet God hath given me more;
> For I have food while others starve,
>   Or beg from door to door.

Thus theological sanction was found for the perfect world of the natural order revealed to the Newton of political economy, David Ricardo.

T

ETHICAL CRITICISM OF CLASSICAL ECONOMY

From many angles, however, the new system of political economy was brought under fire. A great deal of this criticism came from the advocates of the theory of the divine order. The Catholic Church, which flourished best in agricultural countries and had long been supported by landed endowments, could not be expected to accept the materialistic doctrines of classical economy and become reconciled to the natural science, utilitarianism, and pecuniary standards of that scheme of thought. When Pius IX made out his famous Syllabus of Errors in 1864, he listed among the serious mistakes the doctrine that "the Roman pontiff can and ought to reconcile himself to, and make terms with, progress, liberalism, and civilization as lately conceived" (see page 94). Idealizing the old feudal relations in which superior persons protected and subordinate persons served (at least theoretically), Catholic writers attacked the cold-blooded economy which enabled an employer to wash his hands of all responsibility to labor, even in times of industrial crises when thousands were on the verge of starvation. Here was one of the intellectual roots of Christian socialism.

In England this mode of thinking found eloquent exponents in Thomas Carlyle and John Ruskin. The former was really the philosopher of idealized feudalism. In his *Past and Present* he contrasted the beneficent order of the Middle Ages with the misery and starvation which he saw all around him in industrial England. In his life of Frederick the Great he praised the Prussian despot who talked loudly about "serving his people." Classical economics, democracy, *laissez faire*,[1] utilitarianism, and all the defensive theories of capitalism were to Carlyle sheer nonsense and hypocrisy. But his solution for the

---

[1] This term is derived from the advice of a French economist, Gournay, to Louis XV to refrain from government interference in the nation's business — *Laissez faire, laissez passer* (Let things take their course).

evils which he portrayed was vague—a kind of appeal for a new aristocracy of leaders who would protect and care for the humbler orders of society.

Carlyle's companion in criticism, John Ruskin, combined with his faith in a new feudalism a passion for the art of the late Middle Ages and their beautiful handicrafts. Besides, he was more definite in his solution for the problem of poverty and misery. The directing classes of every nation, he argued, were bound to promote its welfare. It is the duty of the soldier to defend it, the pastor to teach it, the physician to keep it in health, the lawyer to enforce justice, and the merchant to provide for it. To give the title of "captain of industry" to a manufacturer who lived on the fat of the land while his working people starved in a period of unemployment would have seemed to Ruskin sheer sacrilege. "As the captain of the ship," he said, "is bound to be the last man to leave his ship in case of wreck, and to share his last crust with the sailors in case of a famine, so the manufacturer in any commercial crisis or distress is bound to take the suffering of it with his men, and even to take more of it for himself than he allows his men to feel." In addition to requiring each class to do its full duty, Ruskin proposed that the state set up workshops, serve as a model employer, and manufacture honest goods at a fair price. In short, both Carlyle and Ruskin advocated a fixed order of society, headed by an aristocracy of virtue and dominated by the ideal of a just price and living wage rather than the competition for profits.

UTOPIAN SOCIALISM

To the same general type of thinking belongs the attack on classical economy which may be included under the head of Utopian socialism. It is instructive to remember that the very word itself is derived from the famous book *Utopia* ("Land of Nowhere"), written by Sir Thomas More, the devout Catholic statesman who perished in the reign of Henry VIII. This work described an ideal order of affairs, where everything was arranged as it should be, and men and women lived together in peace, plenty, and harmony.

Among the advocates of Utopian socialism was a descendant of an ancient feudal family, Comte de Saint-Simon, who had served in the American war of independence and was proud of calling himself a soldier of George Washington. Having been profoundly moved by the American experiment in democracy, Saint-Simon devoted himself to studying the problem of improving the lot of mankind. In the end he came to the conclusion that the solution lay in establishing an ideal Christian social order, and he entitled the book in which he expounded his system *The New Christianity*. In short, his scheme stemmed from the divine order; human affairs were to be arranged on Christian principles, and each group was to have its rights and duties. Goods were to be honestly made, prices were to be just, and wages fair. The direction of society was to be vested in the State.

While Saint-Simon was elaborating his plan for the regeneration of society, another Frenchman, Charles Fourier (b. 1772), was advocating a different remedy for poverty. He did not believe that the central government could possibly manage properly the great business enterprises necessary to human welfare; so he urged the formation of groups of families into what he called phalanxes, which should each contain about two thousand members. Each group was to own buildings and all the needful implements for the production of the necessities of life. The total product was to be divided up in the following manner: capital was to receive four twelfths, labor five twelfths, and the talent necessary for the proper management of the phalanxes and all their enterprises was to receive three twelfths. Fourier believed that in this way universal harmony would be produced. His profound confidence in his theory is illustrated by the fact that for years he was at his house at twelve o'clock to confer with any philanthropist who felt inclined to furnish the money to start the first phalanx. The awaited visitor never came, but nevertheless Fourier's theories won many sympathizers, especially in the United States, among men of no less insight than Horace Greeley, Charles A. Dana, and George William Curtis. The experiment of actually founding a species of phalanx was made in Massachusetts by the Brook Farm colony, of which several distinguished Americans were members for a time.

In England the first great exponent of Utopian socialism was Robert Owen (1771–1858), a successful manufacturer and a generous friend of the poor. Like Fourier, he believed that he had found the secret of the regeneration of mankind in the formation of coöperative groups owning and using for their own benefit all the means of production necessary for their common life. He wrote innumerable works and tracts, and preached his doctrine with untiring zeal; he even appealed to the crowned heads of Europe to take up his plan, and came to the United States to defend it before the House of Representatives. Several of his proposed colonies were actually founded in Great Britain and also in the United States (for example, at New Harmony, Indiana), but they failed for a variety of reasons. Nevertheless, Owen's writings and labors influenced the working classes in England, and it is to his inspiration that the beginnings of the great coöperative enterprises of England are largely due. It is probable, too, that we owe to Owen the word "socialism" (p. 114).

Fundamentally, Utopian socialism paralleled the underlying concept of the divine order idealized by the medieval theologians. All the Utopians insisted on the possibility of creating an ideal moral order out of the materials in hand. None of them ever surrendered to Ricardo's concept of the iron laws of economics. All their Utopias were small colonies combining handicrafts and agriculture, production for use and not for profit, minimum fair wages or allowances, and quality standards such as the old guilds were supposed to maintain. Not one of them was based on the system of world commerce and large-scale industry which flourishes under capitalism. It would be almost safe to say, therefore, that their schemes were in the last analysis derived from the idealized order of the scholastics and adapted to the state of technology at the opening of the nineteenth century.

In other respects the Utopians had much in common. Moved by the misery which they saw about them, they boldly condemned the system of society in which they lived and proposed a revolution which should remedy its evils. They did not, however, reckon with the great complexity of human nature or the respect for tradition which always stands in the way of change. They assumed that it would only be necessary to present a reasonable and beautiful theory of harmony and plenty in order to induce men to found a new social order. They all appealed to the upper classes for aid in realizing their schemes, and made no attempt to organize the great mass of workingmen into political parties for the purpose of getting control of the government and forcing it to forward their plans. Modern socialists look back, with some contempt, upon these Utopians as men who often had good ideas, but were, after all, mere unpractical and simple-minded dreamers.

MARXIAN SOCIALISM

Strangely combining the iron laws of the classical economists with the Hegelian idea of perpetual change, the German philosopher and agitator Karl Marx took socialism out of the realm of speculation and made it a movement to shake thrones and governments. Though Marx and his close friend and collaborator, Friedrich Engels, distinctly repudiated the theories of the Utopians, they nevertheless grew up in the age when Utopian socialism was in the air; they were familiar with its doctrines and knew personally many of its exponents. They also studied the classical economy of Adam Smith, Ricardo, and McCulloch. Ideas from these sources they worked into the Hegelian philosophy of everlasting change, producing a pattern of thought which exercised a profound influence on the course of ideas and of history itself. In fact, their argument drew strength from all three systems of thought available at the opening of the nineteenth century. From the iron laws of Ricardo they extracted iron laws of economy; from Hegel's philosophy they took the concept of inexorable change—change destined to make an end of capitalism as it had of feudalism; and from the Utopians they drew the concept of socialism as a kind of ideal state which was to follow the downfall of capitalism. The inevitable changes of the future would favor the great mass of mankind. Thus Marxism was at once a prophecy—based on the economic interpretation of history—of a future development and a promise of good things at the end.

Marx, the leader with whom this system of thought is associated, was born in 1818 in Trèves, reared in an enlightened home, and educated at the universities of Bonn and Berlin. He early decided upon the career of a university professor; but the boldness of his speech and his radical tendencies barred his way, and consequently he entered journalism. His attacks on the Prussian government led to the suppression of his newspaper in 1843, and the surveillance of the police caused him to migrate to Paris. He was, however, expelled from France by Guizot, and after some wanderings he finally settled in London, where he studied, agitated, and wrote until his death in 1883.

Throughout his life Marx wrote voluminously on history, philosophy, and current politics, and for a time he was a correspondent of the New York *Tribune* when it was under the management of Horace Greeley. His fundamental views on political economy were brought together in a large work of three volumes entitled *Das Kapital* ("Capital"), the first part of which appeared in 1867. This work is so widely circulated among socialist leaders that it is sometimes called the workingman's Bible, although it contains very few pages indeed that would enlighten a person seeking the cardinal doctrines of modern socialism which Marx laid down. These are to be found throughout his scattered writings and especially in the *Communist Manifesto* of 1847.

Marx differs fundamentally from the Utopian theorists— Saint-Simon, Fourier, and Owen—in repudiating the idea that socialism can be introduced by voluntary agreements among kindly disposed persons. He claims that the new order cannot be established artificially, but will nevertheless come as an inevitable result of the Industrial Revolution, which created capitalists and factory employees and introduced intense competition. "The history of all hitherto existing society," runs the *Communist Manifesto*, "is the history of class struggles. Freeman and slave, patrician and plebeian, lord and serf, guildmaster and journeyman, in a word, oppressor and oppressed, have stood in constant antagonism to one another and carried on an uninterrupted warfare, now secret, now open, which has in every case ended either in the revolutionary reconstruction of society at large or in the common ruin of the contending classes. . . . The modern society that has sprung from the ruins of feudal society has not done away with class antagonisms. It has but established new classes, new conditions of oppression, new forms of struggle in place of the old ones. Our epoch—the epoch of the bourgeoisie—possesses, however, this distinctive feature: it has simplified the class antagonisms. Society is more and more splitting up into two great hostile camps, into two great classes directly opposed to each other, bourgeoisie and proletariat."

In this struggle, Marx believed, the working class would win by uniting to overthrow the capitalist class, *not, however, by dividing up all property,*—which even to a socialist would seem sheer folly,—but by transferring ownership of productive capital to the state or nation as a whole, to be employed for the direct advantage of the people.

The very development of modern industry, Marx contended, favors the establishment of socialism. Wealth and industries are concentrating in the control of great companies, trusts, and corporations, which are managed from central offices and carried on by salaried employees and manual laborers, while the capitalist, he declared, is becoming only a stockholder, an idle drone drawing dividends earned for him by other men. Hence, argued Marx, the capitalist has become a mere owner of property, as useless as the feudal lords in the eighteenth century, who neither fought in the armies nor protected the peasants around their castles as their ancestors had done, but crowded about the court of the king, where they lived magnificently on revenues collected by their stewards from the poor people who tilled their estates. Marx therefore predicted that in time the capitalist's right of ownership will be abolished, and that the salaried employees of the great corporations will become the salaried clerks of the government when it takes over all the industries for the common good; thus socialism will be established.

THE ANARCHIST SCHEME OF THOUGHT

At the opposite pole from socialism, especially that of Marx, though often associated with it in the labor movement and in the popular mind, was the system of thought covered by the word "anarchy." Like all other political ideas, this too was very old. In ancient Greece the Stoic philosopher Zeno set forth the idea of a "free community" without any government at all. During the French Revolution opponents of the highly centralized authority were generally called "anarchists," and, in fact, some of them deserved the name, because they advocated the abolition of the national state and the federation of the thousands of towns and villages into one loosely united republic. While the revolution was in full swing, an English writer, Godwin, published two volumes entitled *An Inquiry concerning Political Justice*, in which he advocated a system of anarchy without employing the term to describe it.

As the nineteenth century advanced, the doctrine was taken up by the poverty-stricken son of a French cooper, Proudhon. Carrying the doctrine of *laissez faire* to an extreme, he declared that the State was not needed even to protect life and property, that it should be abolished entirely. He was convinced that if kings, parliaments, police officers, and other public authorities were swept away, the people, following the laws of their being, would form "naturally" free and happy associations. Indeed, Proudhon went so far as to say that the domestic questions of a nation could be solved by a bureau of statistics, and that international relations also were mere matters of trading arithmetic. The classical economists had declared that state interference, except to protect life and property, was an evil; Proudhon added that state interference in all forms was bad.

More violent in temper and methods, but cherishing the same hopes, was the Russian anarchist Bakunin, who appeared on the scene in western Europe during the upheaval of 1848. Although Bakunin coöperated with the Marxians in labor agitation, he did not share their views at all. "We wish the reconstruction of society and the establishment of the unity of mankind," he said, "not from above downward through authority, through socialistic officials, engineers, and public technicians, but from below upward through the voluntary federation of labor associations of all kinds emancipated entirely from the yoke of the state."

When examined closely this system of thought is found to contain three definite elements: the "natural order" of the English classical economists carried to a logical extreme, the equalitarianism of the Rousseau school, and the hatred of the State common in despotic countries where the State was personified in an absolute ruler—tsar, king, or kaiser. It did not reckon with technological advance and mass production.

The society forecast by it was a simple combination of agriculture and petty workshops exchanging their products locally. It took no account of international commerce and finance on a large scale. In the vision of the great novelist Tolstoy, anarchy symbolized simplicity, humble toil, brotherly love, and Christian virtues. In the minds of fanatics the ideal order was a distant goal, while the immediate task was the overthrow or assassination of absolute rulers and high state officials. Finding themselves often in prison with advocates of manhood suffrage, promoters of women suffrage, labor leaders, and socialists, anarchists made common cause against the governments which arrested and imprisoned them. For this reason anarchists were at first affiliated with the International Workingmen's Association founded in 1864, known as the "First International" (see page 110). It was on account of their direct opposition to the socialist goal that they were later expelled. But whether in or out of the official labor movement, anarchists, as the foes of government, were more feared by ruling persons in the nineteenth century than were the socialists—even the extremists among the latter who talked of attaining their ends by revolution. Especially in Slavic and Latin countries did they spread terror among state authorities, making a political furor all out of proportion to their numbers and the power of their ideas.

GERMAN NATIONAL ECONOMY: STATE SOCIALISM

Arising partly from fear of revolutionary movements and partly from economic conditions peculiar to Germany, there appeared still another type of thought about the new order of machine industry and capitalism—a type known as "state socialism." For various reasons the business classes of England had completely triumphed over the landed aristocracy by the middle of the nineteenth century. That aristocracy continued to exist, it is true,—it furnished leaders for politics and set the tone for English high society,—but it was outweighed in wealth and numbers by the rich middle class and, indeed, was largely recruited from bankers, cotton-spinners, brewers, soap-makers, and other enterprising capitalists who were "elevated" to the peerage. Isolated from warlike neighbors by the Channel and defended by the navy manned by volunteers, England needed no large standing army with its feudal heritage and feudal mentality. The dominant interest in England, therefore, was the business interest. Some members of the aristocracy did, no doubt, champion the rights of the laboring masses in the towns, partly through sympathy and partly to secure supporters against the capitalists, but as manufacturing encroached on agriculture coöperation between landed Tories and industrial workers against business men declined.

In Germany, on the other hand, social and economic conditions presented other facets. Wedged between Russia and France, instead of being isolated by water, Germany relied for defense upon a powerful standing army rather than a navy, and recruited her officers for this army largely from the landed aristocracy. English internal unity had been attained by iron and blood before the close of the middle ages; German unity was not attained until 1871. The survival of feudal monarchies, the necessities of defense, and the strength of the Prussian state, therefore, interposed many barriers to the free play of purely business interests—the increasing manufacture of goods to be sold at a profit. Now the feudal aristocracy, though it was as fond of money perhaps as was the *bourgeoisie*, was not engaged in constantly expanding profit-making industries. Its members had relatively small incomes as a rule; they were supposed to serve the government honestly at a low salary and to be content with decorations, titles, and social position. To the money-making ideal it opposed the ideal of the warrior—duty, obedience to superiors, sacrifice without pecuniary reward. English business men were called hucksters, and Prussian army officers heroes.

The center of this system was the Prussian state, that is, the Prussian king, his supporters among the landed aristocracy, and the great host of officials, high and low, all closely knit together in a political machine controlling the army, the police, and the agencies of government. Although the Prussian monarchy, like that of England and France, owed its original power to the sword, it had long been the custom of the Prussian king to speak of himself as the first servant of the state. In this contention there was some truth and some illusion.

At all events, the Prussian state was opposed to the dominance of business men in government, and it adopted the ancient Machiavellian scheme of maintaining its power by playing the capitalists and workingmen off against each other. And this operation was favored by certain peculiar circumstances. Threatened by socialism on the left, business men preferred to coöperate with the other propertied class, the landed aristocracy, rather than face revolution. They did not wish to overthrow this aristocracy, in the English or French fashion, if it meant an increase in the strength of Marxian socialism. Accordingly they rallied to the throne and the altar. Moreover, the competition of American wheat-growers and ranchers and the enactment of the McKinley tariff by the Congress of the United States in 1890 led German agriculturists and industrialists to make the same demand: protection of farm produce and manufactures. Hence the delay in the advance of Germany into a purely business state.

For these and other reasons German political economists never adopted the *laissez faire* doctrines so popular among the English. What was according to nature in England was not so in Germany. German political economy, especially as formulated by the two great leaders Wagner and Schmoller, fostered economic "nationalism," which meant protective tariffs rather than free trade. With a start of half a century English business men needed no protection, while their German competitors, far behind them in technology, clamored for high duties.

In respect to domestic affairs, German economists were inclined to increase rather than diminish the functions of government. Partly for military reasons the state built and operated the railways. On the whole, the state proved competent and honest; accordingly, reasoned the economists, it should carry out other large undertakings in the national interest. Being benevolent by tradition, the monarchy should show its solicitude in protecting the working classes against the poverty, sickness, and misfortune that accompanied industrial enterprise. The state, indirectly the people, should enjoy the revenues and profits accruing from the government's operation of railways, electric-light and gas plants, and other public utilities. Hence great sums of money that in England would have flowed into the coffers of capitalists were to be deflected into the public treasury. Such was the general structure of German state socialism, the development of which will be considered later (pp. 106 ff.).

SOME EFFECTS OF DARWIN'S THEORIES

The systems of thought which we have thus far considered were, it is apparent, in the nature of explanations and justifications for particular sets of circumstances and programs of reform. The divine order was satisfactory to the feudal landlord who wished his laborers to stay contented in the fields.

> God bless the squire and his relations
> And keep us all in our proper stations,

ran the refrain put into the mouth of a peasant by a satirical writer of old days. The natural order which forbade the State to interfere with economic affairs was highly gratifying to business men who wished nothing more ardently than to be let alone to do as they pleased. Likewise the heaven promised to workingmen by communist, socialist, or anarchist seemed quite "just and natural" to those for whose benefit the scheme was elaborated. Nor was the state socialism of the German economists less pleasing to the king of Prussia, his bureaucracy, and his supporting landlords. In short, all these patterns of thought look very much like "defense mechanisms," to use a term coined by modern psychologists.

It would scarcely be too much to say that all the thinking about human affairs that went on during the nineteenth century was colored more or less by one or more of these economic attitudes. Most of the thinkers were by origin or choice affiliated with one or another of the several economic orders, with landed proprietors, capitalists, or working people. None of them were disembodied spirits viewing earthly affairs from the heights of "pure reason."

Even in the biology of Darwin there were suggestions of the social conflicts. His father was of the middle class, a doctor, and his mother the daughter of a manufacturer. His wife was of similar origin, and the leisure which he enjoyed was secured by a modest fortune prudently invested. He owed one of his fundamental ideas, perhaps the most fruitful, that of "natural selection," to a political tract written to combat dangerous radical propaganda. To use his own words: "Having attended to the habits of animals and their relations to the surrounding conditions, I was able to realize the severe struggle for existence to which all organisms are subjected. . . . With my mind thus prepared I fortunately happened to read Malthus's *Essay on Population*; and the idea of natural selection through the struggle for existence at once occurred to me." And what was this *Essay* from which Darwin extracted this primary doctrine of his system? A scientific treatise written in a search for truth? On the contrary, it was a tract conceived in opposition to Godwin's theories respecting a happy anarchist society. It was an attack on the idea that substantial improvements could be made in the lot of mankind by projects for coöperation or government intervention. Its statistical and "scientific" garb was an afterthought.

Darwin helped to convince the English economists that their doctrines were rooted in nature and had the unanswerable support of biology. Darwin himself by no means ascribed the survival of the fittest to the results of mere physical strength, but his careless readers assumed that he had demonstrated in the animal kingdom a relentless "tooth and claw" struggle for survival, thus apparently lending sanction to the individualism of "sound political economy." The terrible warfare of each against all and all against each was a law running throughout creation. Hence socialistic efforts to soften this struggle were violations of an inexorable rule, bound to fail, to do more harm than good. It is true that Karl Marx carried the materialism of the Darwinian theory over into his system of thought and used it to prove that all social institutions were mere products of material circumstances. But it was the economists of the *laissez faire* school, rather than the socialists, who made the most effective use of Darwinism against state regulation of business. Taking the cue from this line of reasoning, certain of the anarchists demanded the abolition of state interference with property, under the guise of protection, and proposed to have a genuine individualistic conflict over the distribution of wealth, allowing the strongest and most cunning to reap the rewards of valor and virtue. Within a few years after the publication of Darwin's *Origin of Species* in 1859, his doctrines had begun to influence deeply all theories about human affairs. Not a few advocates of war saw in the grand conflict which broke out in 1914 a vindication of the Darwinian hypothesis, a bloody struggle for existence.

TENDENCIES AT THE CLOSE OF THE NINETEENTH CENTURY

Such in general were the economic and political movements and ideas which determined the broad lines of development in Europe as the nineteenth century wore into the twentieth. According to all outward signs, the democratic theory of politics

seemed destined to triumph everywhere, in spite of the misgivings in many quarters; even English aristocrats who helped
to enfranchise workingmen in 1867 called themselves "Tory
democrats." It seemed that every government was bound
to rest finally on the consent of the governed, and that popular sovereignty was to be exercised by means of a legislature
elected periodically by the people on the principle of universal suffrage, all adult men and women sharing alike. In
the legislature so chosen the political party commanding a
majority was to select the premier and cabinet officers and thus
to control the executive branch. If perchance for historical
reasons a second chamber, such as a house of lords, had survived the storms of the revolutionary movements, it was to be
abolished or at all events subjected to the will of the lower
house elected by the voters. From such a system it would follow naturally that the military arm of the government should
be controlled by the civilian population through a parliamentary check on the appropriation of funds for military purposes,
the size of the armies and navies created, the conduct of
diplomacy, and the declaration of war. Thus the military class
which had played such a prominent rôle in the history of
European states was to be brought under the direction of the
civilians—business men, farmers, peasants, working people
at large.

Since parliamentary government was of necessity party government, the democratic ideal assumed that the people would
have differences of opinion as to the policies and work of the
government, and that they should be permitted to discuss
issues freely and form political parties according to their beliefs and interests. Hence universal education, freedom of
press and speech, and the right of agitation were supposed to
be essential parts of the democratic order. Each minority
group in the country was entitled to win a majority to its views
if it could, and this would be impossible if the government or
party in power for the moment could suppress all opinion

T

hostile to its program and methods. Without a wide freedom of debate, popular government, it was argued, would be a solemn farce—a form without substance.

Concerned primarily with earthly or secular matters, liberal thinkers insisted that the government should not interfere with religion, but should leave it entirely to individual judgment. This ideal implied the separation of Church and State; that is, the government was not to give a monopoly or preference to any religious denomination, was not to compel citizens to attend any particular church, or tax them for its support. Thus each individual was free to choose his own religion or none at all, and each church was to be treated by the State as a private association of citizens for religious purposes. Conversely, no church was to be permitted to interfere with the business of government. No doubt it was difficult in practice to draw boundary lines between State and Church, but such in general was the liberal theory (see pages 88 ff.).

Supplementing this program of government was a system of individual rights. The members of the French National Assembly which began the work of revolution in 1789 were profoundly impressed by the things which they thought the government ought not to do, and they furnished a definite program in their Declaration of the Rights of Man. Continuing this tradition, liberals everywhere laid stress on the point that the government ought not to interfere with business and industry in any way. This was the theory of *laissez faire*, which we have already discussed.

Such was the general goal toward which Western civilization seemed to be moving in the closing decades of the century. Still it is necessary to add that all along a great many people strenuously opposed carrying the ideal to a logical extreme. Founders of the American republic, such as James Madison and John Adams, feared majority rule quite as much as they feared monarchy, and they sought to break the force of democracy by dividing the power of government among three departments—executive, legislative, and judicial. Everywhere in Europe, conservatives, taking a similar view of the populace, attempted to check democracy before it reached its logical goal. Even so great a liberal as John Stuart Mill was, as we shall see, afraid of the "tyranny of the majority," afraid that it would trample upon the rights of minorities if vested with full power.

Naturally, of course, the landed classes, wherever they maintained their economic supremacy, as in Russia, Hungary, and Prussia, fought hard to keep their ancient privileges and used the agencies of the state, especially the army and the police, to restrain the swelling forces of democracy.

Moreover, many checks were imposed on the application of the individualistic doctrines of the liberals. The growth of socialistic parties, the willingness of landed classes to aid workingmen in their contests with employers, the humanitarianism of Christian reformers, and the perdurance of ancient ideas of state benevolence made it impossible for governments to throw off all responsibility for the lot of the masses. For such reasons the advocates of *laissez faire* did not get very far toward the realization of their program of "anarchy plus the police constable." Indeed, they had scarcely shaken off the old restrictions imposed on economic undertakings by guilds and benevolent despotism before new restrictions devised by trade unions and democratic governments appeared. If, therefore, it seemed at the end of the nineteenth century that political democracy would win in the long run, it was not clear whether the democratic state was to be individualistic or socialistic.

Yet, without laying too much emphasis on either the hopes or the misgivings, it may be safely said that the points in the lines of development leading away from the fixed despotism of the Middle Ages toward the ideal goal set up by the nineteenth-century liberals furnish convenient marks from which to survey the political affairs of European countries between 1871 and the eve of the World War. The arrangement of the following chapters seems also justified by the fact that during the World War a great deal was said about the conflict between democracy and autocracy. Indeed, in President Wilson's eyes that struggle resolved itself into a "war for democracy," and as the war progressed English and French propagandists laid considerable emphasis on this objective. When the war closed, revolutions in central and eastern Europe resulted in constitutions which embodied democratic schemes of government long advocated by the liberal thinkers. Even the dictatorships established in Russia, Italy, Spain, and other countries used the democratic ideal as their point of departure—namely, as the type of government to be repudiated entirely. Hence, as civil engineers establish a fixed point, or surveyor's "bench mark," from which to triangulate a large stretch of territory, so it seems proper to take the ideal goal of the political liberal as the point from which to survey the course of European domestic history from the age of Bismarck to the World War.

In fixing this bench mark, it is well to recall that the political evolution of each European nation has been by no means a purely internal, or domestic, process. On the contrary, popular ideas originating in one country spread quickly to its neighbors; the English revolution of the seventeenth century furnished many of the ideas and arguments for the French revolution of the eighteenth century; and the latter set in motion agitations and wars which sent reverberations to the ends of the earth. The hostility of Austrian, Prussian, and English monarchs toward the French Republic helped to consolidate the power of the radicals in France and to make the revolution more intense and widespread than it would have been if the French had been permitted to work out their affairs in their own way. Once started, however, the French revolutionary propaganda wrought great changes in the opinions of European peoples from the Baltic to the Mediterranean. During the wars which followed, Napoleon did more to consolidate Germany than all the German kings since the Middle

Ages; in fact, this French conqueror made the unification of Germany possible at last, and by his harsh treatment of Prussia roused the Prussian people to a desperate national effort. In return, the Germans unwittingly helped the French republicans to do in 1871 what they had been trying to do for nearly a hundred years—namely, establish a republic. By the irony of history, the French, assisted by many allies, including the Russian autocracy of Nicholas II, repaid the debt in 1918 by making inevitable the overthrow of the Hohenzollerns, who had overthrown the Bonapartes. But that was not accomplished until the German armies had crushed Russia and rung out the doom of monarchy in Petrograd.

It has been the aim of this preliminary chapter to recall some of the striking phases of modern history, developed at much greater length in our first volume. At the same time it serves to furnish a program for this second volume, which falls into five rather distinct divisions: (1) The general trend of affairs within the several European countries before the war—Chapters II–IV. (2) The further merging of European history into world history through imperialism down to the World War—Chapters V–VIII. (3) The antecedents of the war and the war itself—Chapters IX–XI. (4) The aftermath of the war, the reconstruction of the various nations and the attempts to avoid future conflicts—Chapters XII–XVII. (5) The astonishing revolution in man's conception of himself and his world revealed by scientific research during the early twentieth century, and the reflection in literature of novel conditions, knowledge, and awakened criticism of human conduct and institutions—Chapters XVIII–XX.

We now turn to the great question of the relation of the governed to government as it was variously conceived and readjusted before the war. It seems appropriate to begin with France, which, as we saw in Volume I, wrote out, toward the end of the eighteenth century, a new program for mankind.

CHAPTER II

DEVELOPMENT OF GOVERNMENT IN THE NAME OF THE "PEOPLE" (1870–1914)

The Third French Republic

By decisively defeating the forces of Napoleon III, the Prussian armies brought the second French Empire to an end and accelerated the republican and democratic tendencies which, in spite of many checks, had been gaining in France since the fall of Napoleon I. As in every previous crisis, a minority of radicals came to the front in Paris, proclaimed a republic, seized power, and sought to strengthen their régime in every direction. Had they been given a free hand by the victors in the war, they might have established a republican dictatorship; but the Germans insisted that a general election should be held for the purpose of creating a lawful government with which final terms of peace could be made. And at that election, held in February, 1871, the great issue was war or peace, not the final constitution for France.

No direct referendum, therefore, was taken on the plan of government; nor was it easy to classify all the members elected to the National Assembly. Roughly speaking, about one third were republicans, and the remainder were monarchists, distributed among Bonapartists, Orleanists, and Bourbons. If these figures are to be taken as expressing the preferences of the French people, then about two thirds of them wanted a monarchy; the only reason why they did not reëstablish one was their inability to agree upon the family that was to have the crown. As Thiers tersely summed up the situation: "There is only one throne, and there are three claimants for a seat on it." For four years the Assembly debated the form of government intermittently without reaching a conclusion satisfactory to any one of the three monarchist factions.

In these circumstances (see Vol. I, pp. 486 ff.) the Assembly proceeded with the work of framing a plan of government, not by drafting an elaborate constitution, but by passing a series of laws. These separate laws, supplemented by later amendments, make up the constitution of the Third Republic, which consequently differs in many fundamental ways from all the previous French constitutions. It contains no reference to the sovereignty of the people; it includes no bill of rights enumerating the liberties of French citizens; and, indeed, it makes no definite provision for maintaining a republican form of government. It is, in fact, not a logically arranged and finished document; on the contrary, it bears throughout the marks of hasty compilation, designed, as it was, to tide the nation over a crisis until one of the contending parties in the Assembly should secure a triumphant majority. Nevertheless, despite the expectations of many who took part in its making, it has lasted longer and provided a more stable government than any other of the numerous constitutions France has had since 1789.

Under this new constitution the president of the French Republic occupies a position rather more like that of the king of England than that of the president of the United States. He is elected for a term of seven years, not by the people at large, but by the Senate and Chamber of Deputies meeting as one body in Versailles for the purpose. There is no vice president, and in case of the death or resignation of the president a new one is immediately chosen for the full term of seven years. The formal powers of the French executive are slight. He must select the cabinet from among the groups having a majority for the time being in the parliament, and the ministers thus chosen practically control his policy and appointments. He has no veto, but may return a measure to the Chamber and

Senate for reconsideration. The real head of the government is the prime minister, as in England.

The parliament consists of two houses, differing in this respect from the legislative bodies established in 1791 and 1848. The members of the Chamber of Deputies (612 in number in 1929) are chosen for a term of four years directly by the people, and every man over twenty-one years of age— unless he be in active service in the army—is permitted to vote. The 314 senators are distributed among the various departments or counties into which France (including certain colonies) is divided, and those assigned to each department are chosen for a term of nine years by a group of electors made up of local delegates and officials.

The parliament thus constituted is more powerful than the Congress of the United States. It not only elects the president, who is under the control of a ministry representing the majority in the chambers, but in joint session it may amend the constitution without the necessity of submitting the changes to the people for their ratification. There is no supreme court in France authorized to declare the measures of parliament unconstitutional, and the president cannot veto them. In short, the French parliament is for practical purposes a sovereign body.

Since this constitution was clearly designed to be provisional, it left the fundamental issue of a republic or monarchy to be decided in later party battles. At the first election, held in 1876, after the dissolution of the National Assembly[1] the republicans won an overwhelming majority in the Chamber of Deputies and enough seats in the Senate to give them the balance of power among the conflicting royalist factions. The Orleanist president, Marshal MacMahon, now found it impossible to work in harmony with the deputies, and in 1877 he dissolved the Chamber with the hope that, by meddling in the elections and manipulating the returns, he could secure at last a mo-

[1] Originally convened in 1871 to come to terms with Germany.

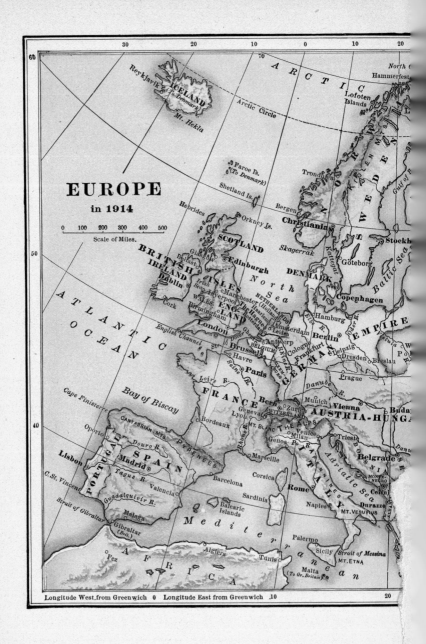

EUROPE

in 1914

0 100 200 300 400 500
Scale of Miles.

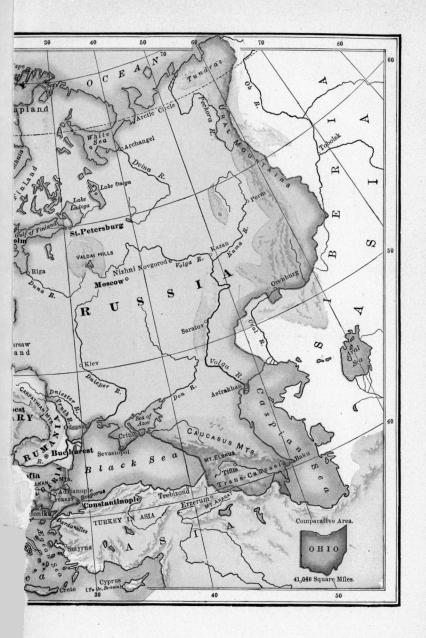

OCEAN

Cape

Lapland

Tundras

Arctic Circle

White
Sea

Archangel

Finland

Dvina R.

Lake Onega

Lake
Ladoga

Gulf of Finland

St.Petersburg

Ob R.

Pechora R.

URAL MOUNTAINS

Tobolsk

S I B E R I A

Perm

Riga

Duna R.

VALDAI HILLS

Nizhni Novgorod

Moscow

Volga R.

Kazan

Kama R.

Orenburg

R U S S I A

Saratov

Ural R.

Aral
Sea

rsaw
and

Kiev

Dnieper R.

Volga R.

Astrakhan

Don R.

Caspian Sea

CARPATHIAN MTS.

Dniester R.

Pruth R.

Odessa

Sea of
Azov

Crimea

CAUCASUS MTS.

RUMANIA

Bucharest

Sevastopol

MT.ELBRUS

Tiflis

Baku

Black Sea

Trans. Caucasia

R.

BULGARIA

BALKAN MTS.

Adrianople

Bosporus

Trebizond

Erzerum

MT.ARARAT

Constantinople

TURKEY

TURKEY IN ASIA

Dardanelles

Smyrna

A S I A

Comparative Area.

OHIO

41,040 Square Miles.

Crete

Cyprus
(To Gr.Britain)

narchical majority. This *coup d'état* failed. The new election ended in a victory for the republicans. Thus indorsed at the polls, they denounced the president's policy and refused to approve the budget that he presented. After continuing the struggle until 1879, MacMahon resigned and was succeeded by an unmistakable republican, Jules Grévy, who enjoyed the entire confidence of the Chamber.

Year by year the French Republic gained in the number of its adherents and in the confidence of the other powers of Europe. The death of the son of Napoleon III in 1879 was a fatal blow to the already declining hopes of the Bonapartists, and the death of the childless count of Chambord in 1883 left the legitimist faction without a head. A few Orleanists clung to their candidate, the count of Paris, until his death in 1894, but the elections of the preceding year, which resulted in the choice of only seventy-three royalist deputies—legitimists, Orleanists, and Bonapartists—had shown that France was at last committed to the republic, in spite of the active factions that continued to agitate for a monarchy.

Only twice since the formation of the republic has it been seriously threatened by political disturbances. The death of Gambetta in 1882 left the republicans without any distinguished leader, and they split up into many factions. Encouraged by this situation, a popular officer, General Boulanger, began courting the favor of the army and the workingmen in somewhat the same way that Napoleon III had done when he was planning to make himself master of France. As minister of war in 1886, Boulanger talked of avenging the defeat that France had suffered in the conflict with the Germans—always a popular theme—and he won some distinguished adherents by his denunciation of party divisions and corruption. He declared himself in favor of calling a National Assembly to revise the constitution and do away with the Senate and the presidency, but what his further plans were he did not explain. In 1889 he was reëlected to the Chamber of Deputies by a huge vote, and it seemed for a time that he might be able to gain sufficient popularity to enable him to get control of the government. His enemies, however, charged him with threatening the safety of the State, and he was tried and condemned to life imprisonment. He escaped from France, however, and in 1891 committed suicide, leaving his party to go to pieces. This episode served rather to discredit the monarchists than to weaken the republic.

France had scarcely settled down after the Boulanger episode when a singular incident rent the country into angry factions and aroused royalist hopes once more. In 1894 Captain Alfred Dreyfus, an Alsatian Jew in the French artillery service, was charged with having delivered to a representative of the German government "a certain number of confidential documents relating to national defense," which might enable Germany to undertake war against France. He was secretly tried by a military tribunal, condemned to life imprisonment, degraded from his rank, and sent into solitary confinement on the lonely Devil's Island off the coast of French Guiana.

Dreyfus had consistently protested that he was entirely innocent of the charge, and his friends began to work for a new trial. In 1896 Colonel Picquart, head of the detective department of the army, received information which led him to believe that the real offender was not Dreyfus but a Major Esterhazy. His superior officers, however, were determined that the Dreyfus affair should not be reopened, for fear, apparently, that something discreditable to the army might be unearthed. Colonel Picquart was accordingly removed from office; and his successor, Colonel Henry, at once charged him with having forged the evidence which had come to light in favor of Dreyfus. Esterhazy, after a farcical trial, was declared innocent.

These charges and countercharges now began to attract general attention and to arouse bitter feeling. The supporters of Dreyfus charged the army officers with intrigue and corruption; his opponents, on the other hand, appealed to the country in the name of the honor of the army. Churchmen attacked him as a Jew and as an enemy of Christian France. Government officials in general maintained his guilt, but many politicians, journalists, and prominent radicals declared their belief in his innocence and accused those in power of shielding criminal injustice. Monarchists cited the whole scandal as conclusive evidence of the failure of republican government. Thus the Dreyfus affair became a military, religious, and political question which created a sort of frenzy in France and awakened the interest of the whole civilized world.

The controversy reached a crisis in 1898, when the novelist Émile Zola published an article accusing all the officials connected with the trial and conviction of Dreyfus not only of wanton injustice but of downright dishonesty. Zola's charges greatly increased the excitement, and distinguished scholars and men of letters raised their voices in defense of Dreyfus. Zola was scarcely tried and condemned for his bold indictment[1] when Colonel Henry was himself imprisoned on the charge of having forged evidence against Dreyfus; later he was found dead in his cell, and this was construed as a confession of guilt. The reconsideration of the whole case could not be postponed any longer, and a new trial was ordered, which began at Rennes in the summer of 1899. This resulted in the condemnation of Dreyfus to ten years' imprisonment, but he was immediately pardoned by President Loubet. It was hoped that the credit of those who had originally condemned Dreyfus might in this way be saved, and yet no penalty be imposed on an innocent man.

Naturally enough, however, this did not satisfy Dreyfus, who wanted, not freedom as a pardoned criminal, but a judicial declaration of his innocence and a restoration to his former rank. Consequently his numerous friends and sympathizers continued to work for another hearing, and finally, in June,

[1] He escaped punishment by retiring to England.

1906, a third trial began in the highest court in France (the Court of Cassation). The following month the court quashed the verdict of the court at Rennes; the Senate and Chamber of Deputies concurred in a bill promoting Dreyfus to the rank of major; and on July 21, 1906, he was presented with the decoration of the Legion of Honor in the courtyard of the *École Militaire*, where twelve years before he had been degraded.

The affair was thus at an end, but the effects of the controversy on the political situation in France could not be undone. It produced an alliance, called the *bloc* (see page 56), among the republicans of all shades, including the socialists, for the purpose of reducing the political importance of the army and Church.[1] The army was republicanized by getting rid of many royalist officers, and the handful of monarchist agitators was thoroughly discredited. The Third Republic had ridden out a storm apparently stronger than ever.

THE GERMAN IMPERIAL CONSTITUTION

The war which had put an end to the Bonapartist empire in France served to entrench the Hohenzollern monarchy in Prussia and Germany; for the struggle with France had ended in the transformation of the North German Federation into the German Empire, and in the coronation of King William I of Prussia as the first German emperor. Measured by outward signs, little change was made by this action in the constitution of the Federation. In theory sovereignty continued to be vested, not in the emperor, nor in the people, but in the *Bundesrat*, or Federal Council, which was made up of the representatives of the twenty-two monarchies and three free cities included in the union. This arrangement was designed to avoid making the other German rulers subjects of the king of Prussia (Vol. I, p. 548). Nevertheless, the power of the Prussian monarchy

---

[1] The separation of Church and State in France will be discussed later (pp. 88 ff.).

and the Prussian ruling class in German affairs was decidedly increased by changes now made in the federation.

Under the constitution of the German Empire as it stood from 1871 to 1918, the emperor possessed important powers, both as king of Prussia and as German emperor. Since Prussia had about two thirds of the population, the political, economic, and military influence of its ruling monarch was predominating. In the Federal Council, Prussia had as many votes as Bavaria, Saxony, Württemberg, and Baden combined. As head of the German federation the emperor appointed and dismissed the chancellor—the directing minister—as well as other imperial officers. He was commander in chief of the army and navy, he selected and discharged diplomatic officials, and he took an active personal interest in the conduct of governmental business. Although he could not declare an offensive war without the consent of the Bundesrat, he could create a situation which made war inevitable, he could mobilize the army, and he could wage a war in defense of the country on his own authority.

The Bundesrat, like the Senate of the United States, represented the various states of the union, but its members were not free to vote as individuals. On the contrary, the delegates from each state had to vote as a unit according to instructions received from their respective governments on every question. Unlike the American system, the various states in the German union were not given equal representation in the Bundesrat: Prussia sent seventeen delegates, Bavaria six, Saxony four, Württemberg four, Baden and Hesse three each, Mecklenburg-Schwerin and Brunswick two each, and all the others one each.

The democratic element in the government was the *Reichstag*, or House of Representatives, which was established at the instance of Bismarck, not because he believed in popular rule, but because such a body was necessary to insure the loyalty of the people to the new union. The Reichstag consisted of about four hundred members distributed among the various states roughly according to their population. Every male citizen twenty-five years of age could vote for its members. The representatives were chosen for a term of five years, but the house could be dissolved at any time by the emperor with the consent of the Bundesrat.

The chief minister of the empire was the chancellor, who was appointed by the Kaiser, usually from among the Prussian delegates in the Bundesrat, and who could be dismissed by him at will without regard to the rise and fall of parties in the Reichstag. The chancellor was not bound by any resolutions or votes of the Reichstag; he was entirely at the command of the emperor, from whom alone he derived his authority. He presided over the Bundesrat, appointed the federal officers in the name of the emperor, and supervised the discharge of their duties. The departments of the empire, such as the foreign office, post office, and department of the interior, were simple bureaus under the control of the chancellor, and their heads were not ministers in the English sense, or cabinet officers in the American sense. They were not colleagues of the chancellor, but were responsible to him, not to the Reichstag; consequently the fate of political parties at elections did not affect their tenure of office.

In short, until the revolution of 1918 Germany did not introduce the cabinet system of government which prevailed in other countries of western Europe. The Kaiser exercised, through the chancellor, and in view of his position as king of Prussia, a power unrivaled by any other constitutional ruler of Europe; the general tone and policy of the government were materially influenced by his personal views and character, and the Reichstag served rather as a critic of, and check on, the government than as the directing force.

When German unity was finally achieved in 1871 by the formation of the empire, the new nation was very much in the position of the United States after the adoption of the Constitution in 1789. A federation had been entered into by states bound together by ties of a common race and language, but its permanence was by no means assured. The various German rulers were zealous in safeguarding their dignity and their own particular rights, and they were not altogether pleased with the preëminence assumed by the king of Prussia. Each commonwealth had its own traditions as an independent state, its own peculiar industrial interests, and its own particular form of government. Some were Protestant; others, Catholic. In some, agriculture predominated; in others, mining or manufacturing. Some wanted protective tariffs for grain; others, for textiles; still others wanted no tariff at all. Realizing that the new union might not bear the continued strain of these disruptive tendencies, the imperial government undertook to establish stronger national ties through the introduction of uniform laws for the whole German people, to supplant the diverse laws of the various commonwealths.

Leadership in this nationalizing movement fell naturally to Bismarck, chancellor of the empire and president of the Prussian ministry. Fortunately for him, the constitution conferred on the imperial legislature wide powers over matters which in the United States are reserved entirely to the states. The imperial parliament was authorized to regulate commerce and intercourse between the states and with foreign nations, to coin money, fix weights and measures, control the banking system, the railways, telegraph, and post office, besides other general powers. But, more than this, the federal government in Germany was authorized by the constitution to make uniform throughout the empire the criminal and civil law, the organization of the courts, and judicial procedure, whereas in the United States each state defines crimes, regulates the form of contracts, and so forth. In one important matter the two constitutions agreed—the citizens of each state were entitled to the civil rights of the citizens in all the other states.

The German parliament at once set to work to carry into effect the important powers conferred upon it. In 1873 a uniform currency law was passed, and the bewildering variety of coins and paper notes of the separate states was replaced by a simple system of which the mark (about twenty-five cents) was the basis. The new coins bore on one side the effigy of the emperor, and on the other the arms of the empire, "to preach to the people the good news of unity." Two years later the Prussian bank was transformed into a federal bank, and a financial center for the empire was established at Berlin. In 1871 a uniform criminal code was introduced; in 1877 a law was passed regulating the organization of the courts, civil and criminal procedure, bankruptcy, and patents; and from 1874 to 1887 a commission was busy drafting the civil code which went into effect in 1900.

As already indicated, the nature of the German imperial government depended on the institutions of Prussia as well as on the form of the federal constitution. Prussia, as we have said, had more than two thirds of the population of the empire. It was governed by a king, a house of lords, and a diet, or legislative assembly. Although the king had graciously granted his subjects a charter, in 1850, he still claimed to rule by divine right. The house of lords consisted of certain princes, landlords, and counts who held their seats by hereditary title, and a number of landlords, capitalists, and professional men whose appointment was approved by the king. In the diet, or lower house, the rich were equally powerful. Its members were elected by a curious indirect process. The highest taxpayers in the kingdom whose combined payments amounted to one third the total tax revenue chose one third of the members; the taxpayers who paid the next third chose the second third of the members; all the rest of the taxpayers, the overwhelming majority of the population, had to be content with electing the remaining third of the members. In short, Prussia was governed, according to law and in fact, by landed proprietors, capitalists, and the professional classes. The prime minister was appointed by the king and was responsible to him, not to the parliament. As a rule the same man served as chancellor of the empire and prime minister of Prussia, thus combining two high offices. He was generally a Prussian acceptable to the landed aristocracy and rich industrialists who governed the kingdom.

EXTENSION OF THE SUFFRAGE AND CABINET SYSTEM

Notwithstanding the conservative victory in Germany, the development of the Third French Republic on the basis of manhood suffrage gave an impetus to democratic tendencies. Scarcely a year passed between 1871 and 1914 without the adoption of a new constitution or the amendment of an old one, extending the range of popular government in some quarter of Europe. Where concessions were not made to democracy, agitations continued without abatement. After a brief experiment with a republic between 1873 and 1875, Spain established a constitutional monarchy and a parliament with one of its houses resting on a limited suffrage. By a law which went into force in 1882, Italy reduced the age limit of voters to twenty-one, cut down the tax qualification by one half, made other modifications, and increased the number of qualified voters from about six hundred thousand to more than two millions. Two years later the Liberal party in England, under Gladstone's leadership, gave the right to vote to agricultural laborers and widened the suffrage in the towns, adding about two million to the existing three million voters in the United Kingdom. In 1895 Italy again reduced the property qualifications of the right to vote, admitting at least one third of the adult males to a direct share in the government. Three years later Norway introduced universal manhood suffrage.

When the twentieth century opened, the democratic movement was still in full swing. The new Serbian constitution of 1903 created a cabinet system and a parliament of one house

T

elected by all adult males who paid an annual tax of approximately three dollars. After years of discussion, Austria, by her electoral law of 1907, conferred, with the hearty approval of Francis Joseph himself, the right to vote for members of parliament on all male citizens over twenty-four years of age. "It was the Emperor," says Redlich, "who indicated to the Austrian bureaucracy the path of democracy, nay, forced them to tread it." The same year Norway granted the ballot to women who paid taxes to a certain amount, thus enfranchising more than one half of them. Yielding at last to vigorous attacks on the limited suffrage and the three-class system long in vogue, the government of Prussia put through in 1910 a reform bill which made a few minor modifications in a democratic direction without satisfying any party. Liberals everywhere greeted it with scorn. "It is a declaration of war on the Prussian people," declared the socialist paper *Vorwärts*. It merely meant that the Prussian aristocracy was no longer so complacent in its seat of power. Across the border in Russia (see pages 83 ff.) the third *Duma*, or parliament (elected in 1907 under the Tsar's decree of 1905 creating a national assembly), was struggling to give some substance to its shadow of authority. Far away in Bosnia and Herzegovina, the Austro-Hungarian government provided a curious kind of parliament in which Catholics, Greek Orthodox, Moslems, and Jews, landlords, merchants, and peasants were to be represented. To the south the tiny kingdom of Montenegro was experimenting with manhood suffrage. Meanwhile the Young Turks, by threatening the aged Sultan with revolution, forced the establishment of a sort of constitution, and in 1908 a Turkish parliament was convened amid great hopes (see pages 305 ff.). Not to be outdone by her neighbors, Italy abolished in 1912 property qualifications for voters, while leaving a limited literacy test, and at one stroke increased the number of eligible voters to about nine millions. Democracy was on the march. When all the expectations of enthusiasts were fully discounted, it seemed that government of the people and by the people was making headway everywhere amid the decline of absolutism.

Running parallel with the extension of manhood suffrage was an agitation for woman suffrage. As we have seen (Vol. I, p. 347), Mary Wollstonecraft raised the issue during the first French revolution, and it kept cropping up in all parts of the Western world with the progress of democracy. A great woman's-rights convention held at Seneca Falls, New York, in 1848, proclaimed a new declaration of independence—for women. John Stuart Mill gave an impetus to the movement by publishing in 1869 a trenchant work, *The Subjection of Women*. In time the agitation bore fruit. In 1893 women were enfranchised in New Zealand, and a year later in South Australia. Shortly after the establishment of the new Commonwealth of Australia in 1901 full parliamentary suffrage was granted to women. In 1906 the women of Finland, and in 1907 and 1919 the women of Norway and Sweden respectively, were given the vote on certain conditions. Denmark took the same step in 1915.

In England a new and striking interest was given to the whole subject of woman's suffrage in 1905, when some of the leaders among the English women, particularly Mrs. Emmeline Pankhurst and her daughters, abandoned their peaceful methods of agitation and resorted to demonstrations of violence, which they assumed had been effective in the movement for manhood suffrage. In the winter of 1907–1908 the women suffragists organized demonstrations before the houses of cabinet officers and raided the House of Commons; and many of them, on being arrested, refused to pay their fines and were sent to jail. These disorders proved effective in centering attention on the demands of the women. Parliament, however, refused to pass any bill granting suffrage to women, and several years were spent in seemingly fruitless agitation. At the outbreak of the World War the militant party, under the leadership of Mrs. Pankhurst, announced that they would suspend agitation for the suffrage during the period of the war, and devote themselves unreservedly to the service of their country. And as we shall see, when that struggle was brought to a close women were given the ballot not only in England but also in many countries on the Continent and in the United States.

But if the democracy of any country was to be more than an empty form, it had to control the appointment, dismissal, and policy of the high officers of government—the premier and heads of departments, who, taken together, formed the cabinet. In England this control was effected by making these officers responsible to Parliament. Under that system (see Vol. I, pp. 505 ff.) the political party which mustered a majority in Parliament—in practice, the House of Commons—enjoyed the right to choose the prime minister and his colleagues. As long as they could command a majority, they remained in power. When they lost it they either resigned or appealed to the country in a new election, and stood or fell according to the results of the polling. In short, the majority of the voters—in some cases a mere plurality—decided who was to compose the government, and what its policies were to be. Such was the theory and practice of the parliamentary scheme. It was, as an American writer called it, "hair-trigger government," responding immediately to "the will of the people."

With the spread of democracy went the cabinet system. France adopted it definitely when the Third Republic was established. Italy took it over, in form at least. Spain incorporated it in her constitution of 1876. With the restoration of the Karageorgevitch line in Serbia in 1903, ministerial responsibility was proclaimed, and in practice the kingdom was governed by a cabinet which looked to the National Assembly, not the king, as the source of its authority. Although the constitution of Germany definitely provided that the chancellor was responsible to the emperor, the steady advance of democratic sentiment made it impossible for him to ignore the dominant parties in the Reichstag. "In Germany," said Chancellor von Bülow in 1906, "the ministers are not organs of the Parliament and of its temporary majority, but they are the entrusted representatives of the Crown." Nevertheless, the chancellor had to be careful in dealing with the majority in the Reichstag, and occasionally a minister was sacrificed to its will; for example, the secretary of state for the colonies, Herr Dernburg, in 1910. Among the planks of the Social Democratic party's platform was the demand for complete "parliamentary responsibility." Moreover, we now know from secret papers made public after the revolution of 1918 that the Kaiser was by no means the personal monarch which his speeches implied.

Political Parties

It is noteworthy that the form of parliamentary government was not always accompanied by the substance of democratic control. Its actual working depended upon the state of the political parties. From the inception of the cabinet system in England down to the close of the nineteenth century, two powerful political parties had alternately possessed a majority in the House of Commons—Tories and Whigs, later known as Conservatives and Liberals. It is true that the Irish members often insisted on acting independently, and that each of the old parties was frequently troubled with a threatened secession on the right or left wing; but in the main each cabinet rested on a solid parliamentary majority. Indeed, it was the very strength of the party which made the system work effectively. The king was always confronted by the choice between doing without money to carry on his government and accepting the cabinet which commanded the necessary votes in the House of Commons. Had there been five or six parties, none of them having a majority, he could have traded with them, played one group off against another, and, in fact, had a good deal to say about the selection of officers. Under the two-party system he had no choice; one of them always had a majority and was ready to take over the whole government.

On the Continent, however, the development of political parties ran along entirely different lines. Instead of two parties, each alternately commanding a majority, there were usually five or six or eight or ten, none of them possessing anything like a majority. In France, for example, the Chamber of Deputies consisted, after the election of 1910, of 113 Radicals, 150 Radical-Socialists, 72 Democratic Left, 75 Organized Socialists, 76 Progressionists, 34 Independent Socialists, 32 Action Liberals, 21 members of the Right, and 24 Independents. The German election of 1912 returned 110 Socialists, 90 Centrists, or members of the Catholic party, 44 National Liberals, 45 Conservatives, 41 Radicals, 18 Poles, 13 Free Conservatives, 11 Anti-Semites, 5 Alsatians, 4 Lorrainers, and representatives of four other minor groups, to say nothing of 6 free lances. Italy likewise had many parties, with the Constitutionalists, Radicals, Republicans, and Socialists in the lead.

As a result of such party divisions, cabinet governments on the Continent were either weak or instable, or both. Where no party could win a majority, it was necessary for each cabinet to be formed by combining two or more factions, usually including discordant elements. In such a case the tenure of a ministry was always precarious; for if any one of the groups upon which it depended for votes in parliament grew dissatisfied and withdrew, it had to resign or undergo a reconstruction. Between 1879 and 1910 there were at least thirty-six different ministries in France, and between 1890 and 1910 there were on the average about two ministries a year. Of course most of these changes were minor, the result of little party shifts here and there, and brought about no violent oscillation in government. Through it all there was a fair continuity of policy, and the system was defended on the ground that it permitted a gradual evolution and did not upset the country by making drastic changes every few years.

In monarchical countries like Spain, Italy, and Germany, however, the division of the people into many parties retarded the growth of democratic control which manhood suffrage was supposed to imply. The king of Italy, for example, finding it possible to trade with many parliamentary groups, was usually able to exert a great deal of influence on the selection of cabinet officers, even though he generally had to accept one or more powerful party leaders whether he liked them or not. It was a similar situation in Germany which enabled the Kaiser to retain many of his royal prerogatives. If any one of the political parties could have long commanded a solid majority in the Reichstag, he would have been compelled to choose a chancellor acceptable to it and thus in spite of himself introduce parliamentary responsibility.

FREEDOM OF PRESS AND SPEECH

Another popular feature essential to the successful working of democratic institutions was freedom of press and speech. If the voters were to have the right to turn out of office the party in power, if periodical elections were to be held for the choice of members of parliament, it followed that the people must enjoy the right to criticize the government in authority for the moment and to discuss the issues and candidates during political campaigns. While an absolute monarch, claiming to rule by divine right, might logically insist on punishing subjects who criticized him or his measures, a cabinet of party leaders dependent more or less on popular support could not take any such position without nullifying the whole system upon which their authority rested.

Inasmuch as England led in the development of parliamentary government, it was natural that she should also lead in promoting freedom of press and speech. As early as 1695 Parliament abolished government censorship of the press by refusing to renew an old law providing for this form of control over books and newspapers (Vol. I, pp. 76 ff.). However, in times of disturbance, the government adopted repressive measures, as, for instance, during the French Revolution and in 1819, when there was extensive popular agitation. Moreover, the stamp duties on newspapers and advertisements hampered the publication of cheap journals for the diffusion of political information among the masses and were systematically used by the government for this purpose. In 1819 the tax was extended even to leaflets and tracts, which had hitherto been allowed free circulation. The necessity of paying an eight-cent tax on each copy made the average price of a newspaper fourteen cents, while the price of the London *Times* was eighteen cents. In addition to these stamp duties there was a special tax on paper, which increased its cost about fifty per cent.

These "taxes on knowledge," as they were called, were attacked by those who advocated popular education, and also by the political reformers who wanted cheap newspapers through which to carry on their agitation. In 1830 a society was organized in London for the purpose of conducting a campaign against stamp duties. Some reformers openly defied the law by issuing political journals unstamped. *The Poor Man's Guardian* bore the motto "established contrary to law to try the power of right against might." The publisher of this journal adopted the ruse of sending waste-paper parcels out at the front door to engage the attention of the police while the regular copies were rushed out of the back door to be distributed to the public.

The laboring class was by no means alone in the struggle for a free press. Eminent men, such as Grote, the historian, and Bulwer-Lytton, the novelist, joined in the movement for the repeal of the obnoxious taxes. At last their labors were rewarded. In 1833 the tax on advertisements and in 1836 the stamp tax were reduced, bringing the price of most of the London papers down to ten cents each. Twenty years later the attacks of Cobden and Bright on the stamp duty and the tax on advertisements resulted in their entire abolition; and in 1861 the duty on printing paper was removed, thus giving England cheap newspapers, although special privileges in the form of low postal rates were not afforded to the newspapers as in the United States.

No less important to democracy than freedom of the press is the right of holding public meetings and criticizing the policy of the government. In common with all other European monarchies, England, in the sixteenth and seventeenth centuries, imprisoned, pilloried, and otherwise severely punished those who were bold enough to speak disrespectfully of the king and the government; and even after the Revolution of 1688 Parliament occasionally ordered the flogging or imprisonment of critics.

Moreover, on occasions when there was deemed to be some extraordinary public danger, special laws were directed against those who assailed the policy of the king and Parliament. In 1795 a Treasonable Practices Bill was passed, which made all adverse criticism of the government a high misdemeanor punishable by deportation to a penal colony for the second offense. This was followed four years later by a Corresponding Societies Bill, which suppressed political societies propagating reform doctrines, required the registration of all printing establishments, and even imposed penalties on lending books and papers for hire. Again, in 1819, when renewed agitation had frightened the government, six acts were passed subjecting public meetings, the press, and free speech to constant police surveillance.

The growth of the democratic spirit among the working classes, the numerical strength of the reform parties as demonstrated in the Chartist movement (Vol. I, pp. 497 ff.), and the utter impossibility of longer suppressing political discussion finally led the government to abandon the prosecution of political offenders. Freedom of discussion was therefore recognized in England as the rule for normal times, but, in the language of a distinguished lawyer, it was "little else than the right to write or say anything which a jury consisting of twelve shopkeepers think it expedient should be said or written."

In France the battle over freedom of press and speech continued throughout most of the nineteenth century. It is true that the press was declared free in 1789 and again in 1814, but the government constantly watched newspapers and punished editors who indulged in criticism distasteful to it. It was not until 1881 that the licenses previously required of those who wished to start publications were abolished; henceforward publishers were not forced to make deposits to insure respectful treatment of the government, and police courts were deprived of the right to try persons accused of defaming government officials. About the same time citizens were granted the privilege of holding public meetings freely on condition that they merely announced their intention to the authorities, and a law was passed permitting workingmen to form associations and to conduct meetings. Press and speech were now about as free in France as in England. However, if the government quit prosecuting editors, it did not cease to influence them by other methods, perhaps even more objectionable. Naturally, as in other countries, it enjoyed the support of the papers affiliated with the political parties in power at any given time. But it went beyond that; on various occasions it bribed editors by large grants of money from secret sources. From the revelations of the Russian archives, made public after the revolution of 1917, it appears that a number of the leading Paris papers, including *Le Temps*, *Le Figaro*, and *Le Radical*, received subsidies from Russian funds, disbursed under the supervision of the French premier. In such circumstances "freedom of the press" may be somewhat illusory.

Across the Rhine, in Germany, freedom in expressing opinion suffered many vicissitudes. The laws and practices relative to it varied from state to state. In the empire at large a rather generous liberty was allowed at first, but in 1878, after two

attempts had been made to assassinate the emperor, both unsuccessful, Bismarck forced through the Reichstag a law designed to suppress socialistic agitations of every kind. This
measure prohibited meetings, publications, and associations
having for their purpose the "subversion of the social order"
or the promotion of socialistic tendencies dangerous to the
public peace, and authorized the government to proclaim martial rule in any city threatened by labor disturbances. The repressive law remained in force for twelve years and completely
disorganized the socialist party as far as open participation in
national politics was concerned. It failed, however, in accomplishing its full purpose, for the socialists continued to form
local societies in spite of the precautions of the police, and to
spread their doctrines by means of papers smuggled in, principally from Switzerland.

After Bismarck was dismissed in 1890, repressive measures
were discontinued, and a wide freedom of press and public
assembly was established. Criticism of the emperor, *Majestätsbeleidigung*, was still an offense which frequently led to
imprisonment, but the discussion and agitation of public questions were generally tolerated. "We must start from the simple
thesis," wrote Heinrich von Treitschke near the end of the
century, "that the modern state requires the free public discussion of all social and political questions, and that the in-
discretions of a free press are less harmful than the danger
of the deep-rooted embitterment of men whose mouths are
closed." Yet, as in France, the government had its more or
less "official organs," which it controlled through influence if
not by money.

MISGIVINGS ABOUT DEMOCRACY

In recording this apparently "irresistible sweep of democracy," it is well to take note of the fact that many writers
who favored it cherished a great deal of skepticism respecting
the outcome of universal suffrage. As early as 1861, John

Stuart Mill, a sincere friend of democracy, in his work *Considerations on Representative Government* had, as we have seen, issued a warning against dangers ahead. "Looking at democracy in the way in which it is commonly conceived," he said, "as the rule of the numerical majority, it is surely possible that the ruling power may be under the dominion of sectional or class interests. . . . In all countries there is a majority of poor, a minority who, in contradistinction, may be called rich. Between these two classes, on many questions, there is a complete opposition of interest. . . . Is there not considerable danger lest the majority should throw upon the possessors of realizable property and upon larger incomes, an unfair share, or even the whole burden of taxation; and having done so, add to the amount without scruple, expending the proceeds in modes supposed to conduce to the profit and advantage of the laboring class?" To solve the problem he thus proposed, Mill suggested that the classes should be "balanced" in the government by adopting the principle of proportional representation, in the hope of introducing a moderate middle group into the legislature.

Later in the century a group of Continental writers—Leon Duguit and Charles Benoist in France and Albert Schäffle in Austria, for instance—attacked the basic idea of equality and alikeness underlying the democratic theory. Writers of this school said that in fact all men were not equal in mind, morals, or property, and that the assumption of equality was responsible for a great deal of folly and corruption in politics. The system, they argued, had brought into being the politician who had to treat the people as if they were all alike and of equal importance, when, in truth, he knew that they were composed of different classes and groups with conflicting interests. Only by deluding electors with slippery promises, catch phrases, and high-flown rhetoric could anybody hope to be chosen for parliament. And only a kind of oratorical windbag would ever engage in any such business. As a remedy for such evils, these new critics of democracy proposed that legislatures should represent, not heads, but groups: commerce, industry, landed property, the professions, and the industrial workers—in short, a sort of return to the representation of estates on the medieval model.

Accepting some of these theories at face value, a number of socialist writers attacked the democratic problem from another angle. They too said that there was an obvious contradiction between political equality and economic inequality; that a workingman and a millionaire were not equal merely because each had one vote. Their remedy was of course drastic: abolish the capitalist class and deprive everybody of property in capital goods; that would bring real equality! For the management of their socialistic state they proposed a kind of economic parliament composed of representatives of the great branches of labor—railways, mines, factories, and agriculture. Although many socialists thought that their scheme could be realized by converting voters and getting possession of the government by lawful election methods, others looked on democratic politics as merely a means of agitating, preliminary to a revolution by organized force. In either case, to the growing socialistic parties in Europe universal suffrage was not an end but a means to a more radical goal. These various views will be discussed more fully in Chapters XIII–XV.

For various reasons, therefore, shadows of doubt accompanied the advance of democracy into the twentieth century. It was almost as common to hear about the "failure of representative government" as about the failure of monarchical government. If nearly every year in the new century witnessed the extension of the suffrage in some country of Europe, it also beheld monarchs and houses of lords clinging to their old privileges, with no little support from the middle classes which had once been so critical of them, as well as from the people at large.

CHAPTER III

CONFLICTS OF DEMOCRACY WITH KINGS, PEERS, AND PRELATES

The Perdurance of Monarchy

After the suffrage had been widely extended, the party system developed, cabinet government introduced, and freedom of discussion legalized, there yet remained three ancient institutions that rested on medieval tradition, not on "the will of the people"—namely, monarchies, houses of lords, or upper chambers, and state churches.

Although it was said that in England the king reigned but did not rule, the statement is slightly exaggerated. It is true that no English sovereign after Queen Anne ventured to refuse to sign an act duly passed by Parliament; but the crown continued to be a conservative element in the English system. Historically associated with the landed aristocracy and the State Church, its sympathies were naturally against, rather than in favor of, the rising middle class, composed largely of Dissenters in religion, and millowners and shopkeepers in business. If Queen Victoria always yielded, often with bad grace, to the demands of the Liberal party led by Gladstone, she never surrendered the idea that she ruled by the grace of God, and on various occasions she exercised a decided influence on the course of affairs. Her son, Edward VII, though content to leave internal politics to party control, helped to shape foreign policy, read the important diplomatic notes sent and received, and took an active part in bringing about the Anglo-French entente which ended in the line-up against Germany (see pages 293 ff.).

64

On the Continent not a single great nation followed the example of France in establishing a republic in place of its monarchy, and in France itself that revolution was, as we have seen, the result of defeat in war rather than the deliberate choice of a majority of the voters. Among the smaller powers, Switzerland alone was governed under a kingless constitution, until Portugal became a republic in 1910. Spain tried a republic for two years, 1873–1875, only to give it up and return to the House of Bourbon. When in 1905 Norway declared her union with Sweden dissolved, the people were afraid to stand alone as a republic and elected Prince Carl of Denmark to rule over them as king, though it must be added that they were "given to understand" that a monarchy would be more acceptable than a republic to both England and Germany. Even the socialists, who were generally republicans in theory, gave less and less attention to agitations against kings, preferring rather to concentrate on their economic proposals. Whenever a new state was created in the Balkans—Greece, Rumania, Bulgaria, or Albania—the powers of Europe always insisted on establishing a monarchical form of government.

When the distinguished English historian H. A. L. Fisher came to America in 1910 to deliver the Lowell lectures on the republican tradition in Europe, he reported not progress for that cause but defeat. He said: "There can be no question that since 1870 the cause of republicanism has made no substantial progress in Europe. France is still the only great European republic, and the political history of France under her new régime has not been such as to invite imitation. The position of monarchies, which seemed so precarious in 1848, has been considerably, indeed, progressively, improved since the failure of that great and generous outburst of ill-calculated ideals. . . . The accepted formula of political progress seems, if we are to be guided by the recent examples of Russia and Turkey, to be constitutional monarchy rather than republicanism. The republican movement has done its work." Although within ten years this prophecy was utterly falsified by events in central and eastern Europe, it seemed to have in 1910 the hoary sanction of history. Monarchy was to stand as a make-weight against the prevailing of the people.

UPPER CHAMBERS: LORDS AND SENATORS

Equally important, and perhaps far more influential in practice, was the second of the three institutions founded on prestige rather than popular suffrage—namely, houses of lords, or upper chambers. In spite of the onrush of democracy, nearly everywhere in Europe in 1914 the branch of the legislature elected by the voters directly was checked, or counterbalanced, by a second chamber. Whether this chamber originated in the Middle Ages, as the House of Lords in England, or was newly created, as in France and Italy, it served as a brake on majority rule and was generally intended, as Sieyès said during the French Revolution, to extinguish the fires of Rousseau's popular sovereignty with the water of Montesquieu's separation of powers (Vol. I, p. 264). Two noteworthy exceptions to this rule were Bulgaria and Serbia, where the parliament consisted of a single house chosen by popular vote.

In many cases the upper chamber was in fact a house of lords and represented primarily the two ancient estates which had long shared with monarchs the power of government—namely, the nobility and the clergy. The British House of Lords, for example, consisted of the princes of royal blood, the peers of the United Kingdom (dukes, marquises, earls, viscounts, and barons), the "lords spiritual" (the two Anglican archbishops and twenty-four bishops), the Irish and Scottish peers (elected by their class), and four "law lords" appointed by the crown.[1] The great majority of these lords held their seats by hereditary right and were Conservative in politics.

[1] The number qualified to sit in the House of Lords varies. It was 654 in 1915, and about 740 in 1929.

As a legislative body the House of Lords enjoyed equal rights with the House of Commons, except that it was not supposed to originate money bills. It could and often did block measures passed by the lower chamber, and could be forced to give way only when the cabinet in power was strong enough to induce the king to threaten the creation of enough new peers to swamp the opposition. But this was drastic action and could be employed only on extraordinary occasions (Vol. I, pp. 509 f.).

The Austrian House of Lords (*Herrenhaus*) was formed on similar principles. It embraced in its membership princes of the imperial family, hereditary nobles, archbishops and bishops of princely title, and life members appointed by the emperor for distinguished services in Church, State, science, or art. In the other half of the dual monarchy—Hungary— the upper chamber, or Table of Magnates, as it was called, was almost identical in composition. Besides princes, counts, barons, and ecclesiastical dignitaries, it also contained a certain number of life peers named by the crown in recognition of services to State and Church.

When the French set about reconstructing their government after 1870, they could recall from their history certain experiments with a legislature of one house, notably under the constitutions of 1791 and 1848. In each case the chamber had had a brief and stormy career, and only the most radical thinkers were willing to try that plan again. But how was the upper house to be constituted? It was impossible to restore the Chamber of Peers, which had been established after the return of the Bourbons in 1815 and continued with slight modifications until the Revolution of 1848. It was equally impossible to continue the Senate set up under Napoleon III, which included cardinals, marshals, admirals of France, and members chosen for life by the emperor. The ancient nobility, of France, though still powerful, had been badly shaken by revolutions, and the high clergy had generally been associated with the monarchy, whatever its form.

T

Hence proposals to refashion the old house of peers seemed to be out of the question. Accordingly the National Assembly, in creating the constitution of the Third Republic, made a departure from precedents. It rejected the idea of a single legislative body, and likewise all schemes for a Chamber of Peers. It decided that there should be a strong upper house to check the democracy of the Chamber of Deputies, and that it should be composed, as we have seen, of members elected indirectly in the departments and colonies of France. Originally one third of the senators were elected for life by the National Assembly itself, but this provision was abolished in 1884, and the rule of election applied to all members. To give special strength to the upper house, it was arranged that the term of the senators should be nine years, and that only one third of them should retire at a time—that is, every three years.

Among all these houses of lords and senates, only one upper chamber, that of England, suffered any serious decline in power as the suffrage was extended. And that decline resulted from the attempt of the House of Lords to prevent the passage of the radical budget sponsored by the Liberals under the leadership of Herbert Asquith as premier and David Lloyd George as chancellor of the exchequer (pp. 120 ff.). When the bill came up from the House of Commons, the Lords rejected it by a vote of 350 to 75. Immediately the Liberals took up the gage thus thrown down to them. On December 2, 1909, Asquith moved in the House of Commons a resolution "That the action of the House of Lords in refusing to pass into law the financial provision made by the House for the services of the year is a breach of the Constitution and a usurpation of the rights of the House of Commons."

An appeal was then made to the country, and a new House of Commons was elected. Although the Liberal party found its numbers greatly reduced, it enjoyed the support of the Socialist, Labor, and Irish groups in endeavors to reduce the ancient powers of the House of Lords. When Asquith warned the Lords that unless they passed the proposed budget there would be another appeal to the country, they gave in, April, 1910. Still the general question of the powers of the upper house was not settled by this victory, and the war on the Lords' old right to reject measures passed by the Commons continued to be carried on in and out of Parliament. The death of King Edward VII (May, 1910) caused a brief truce, but the struggle was renewed in the succeeding autumn.

Shortly after the opening of the new Parliament in 1911 a bill designed to check the exercise of the veto power by the Lords was introduced in the Commons and passed by a good round majority. The measure was then sent to the House of Lords, and Asquith announced that he had received the consent of the new king, George V, to create enough new peers to insure its passage in case its Conservative opponents were able to defeat it. Thus intimidated, the upper house, on August 18, 1911, passed the Parliament Act, or the Lords' Veto Bill, as it was called, the leading provisions of which follow:

If any money bill—that is, a bill relative to raising taxes and making appropriations—is passed by the House of Commons and sent up to the Lords at least one month before the end of a session, and is not passed by the Lords within one month without amendment, the bill may be presented to the king for his signature and on being approved becomes a law, notwithstanding the fact that the Lords have not consented to it. Any other public bill passed by the House of Commons at three successive sessions and rejected by the Lords at each of the three sessions may likewise be presented to the king, and on receiving his approval becomes a law without the consent of the Lords. The veto bill also fixed *five* years instead of *seven* as the time which any parliament may last. That is, under the law of August 18, 1911, a new parliamentary election must be held at least every five years, although a dissolution may be brought about at any time by the cabinet.

Monarchy and Aristocracy in Central Europe

In central and eastern Europe no such reduction of the powers of the aristocracy as took place in England was possible, owing to the strength of the monarchy and the influence of the feudal classes in government. While Germany was under the direction of Bismarck—that is, until his resignation as chancellor in 1890—any triumph of popular government was unthinkable. "The question at issue," he said in 1862, "is not between conservative and liberal, but whether the régime in Prussia shall be monarchical or parliamentary. If necessary, parliamentarianism must be withstood by a period of dictatorship." Nor was he less dogmatic when he became chancellor of the empire. In the Reichstag the question was asked, To whom is the chancellor responsible? to the upper house? the lower chamber? the emperor? Bismarck ignored these inquiries. He was in power, and that was enough for him. And as a matter of fact, only a small minority of the Reichstag members ever voted in favor of making the new government parliamentary in form.

So things stood, substantially unchanged until two years after William II came to the throne. When the new emperor said to Bismarck that he wished to make the antisocialist law of 1878 milder to avoid "staining the first year of my reign with the blood of my subjects," the "iron chancellor" replied: "It is my duty, in virtue of my experience of these matters, to advise against the course you propose. Since the days of my entry into the government, the royal power has been steadily increasing. . . . This voluntary retreat would be the first step in the direction of parliamentary government, which might be convenient for the moment but would prove dangerous in the end."

In a few weeks Bismarck was practically forced to resign. But his going was no proof that William II intended to weaken the monarchy or to introduce parliamentary government. On the contrary, he was fond of making speeches in which he had much to say about the power God had given him; indeed, he seemed to be a stout adherent of that conception of kingship which Bossuet extracted from the Holy Scriptures and urged upon the willing Louis XIV (Vol. I, p. 51). On his accession the Kaiser expressed himself as follows: "Summoned to the throne of my fathers, I have taken up the reins of government, looking for aid to the King of kings. I have sworn to God to follow the example of my fathers and be to my people a just and firm ruler, to nurture piety and the fear of God, to cherish peace, and to be a helper of the poor and oppressed, and a faithful guardian of justice." To the army he said, "We belong together, I and the army; indeed, we are born for each other and we will act together, it matters not whether God wills peace or storm." And throughout his reign William continued to dwell upon the authority vested in him by God. If laughter and skepticism ran through the lower strata of the intellectual circles of Germany, the monarchy was solidly intrenched until the crash of 1918 shook the scepter from William's hands.

For a time it seemed as if William II proposed to conciliate the socialist party, although he could not possibly have had any real sympathy with its aims. The legislation against the socialists which Bismarck had inaugurated in 1878 (pp. 60 f.) was allowed to lapse in 1890, and they now carried on their agitation openly and with vigor and success. The emperor pledged himself to continue the social legislation begun by his grandfather, since he deemed it one of the duties of the State to relieve poverty, and declared that the welfare of the workingman lay close to his heart. He attempted to adjust strikes by arbitration, and in 1890 called together an international congress for the protection of labor, where he took occasion to make many lengthy addresses. Irritated, however, at his failure to check the expression of discontent on the part of the working classes, he grew angry and pronounced the Social Democrat as "nothing better than an enemy of the empire and his country." In 1894 he proposed a bill to stop the "virulent machinations" of the socialists; but this, like other measures aimed at the party, failed to pass the Reichstag. As time went on, the emperor said less about helping the workingman, and he watched with no little uneasiness the steady increase of the number of socialists, the most powerful party in Germany committed to democracy (p. 107).

The truth is that the German monarchy was historically associated with the landed aristocracy, and at the opening of the twentieth century great landholders were a striking feature of agriculture in Germany, especially in Prussia, the dominant state in the empire. In 1910 over one fifth of the cultivated land of the empire was in estates of more than 250 acres. In Bavaria and Baden such holdings occupied only 2 or 3 per cent of the area; but toward the north and east of Germany the proportion rose steadily, reaching in some regions more than 50 per cent of the total. Prussia had about 20,000 land-lords with 250 acres and more, and Prussia was the classical land of the Junker. "Whenever I sit among Prussian excellencies, the opposition between North and South Germany becomes strikingly clear. South German liberalism cannot cope with the Junkers; they are too numerous, too powerful, and have the monarchy and the army on their side," wrote Prince Chlodwig zu Hohenlohe-Schillingsfürst, in his journal, on December 15, 1898. In every Prussian province the commanding general and his family were at the head of social affairs; in that fixed class system every person had his place; it was a frozen order, and woe to all who neglected the code. At the apex was the king of Prussia, the German emperor. Conscious and proud of the fact that it had advanced the eastern frontier and had stood for centuries as a barrier to the Slavic flood, the *Junkertum* of the eastern half of Prussia refused to surrender to civilians and frock-coated bourgeoisie. "To fight the spirit of modern liberalism, the Prussian Junker feels himself justified by his conscience and before God. His battle has become a duty with him—therefore he is so dangerous," wrote Prince Philipp Eulenburg to his friend Holstein in 1897. Devotion to the traditions of war led the Prussian aristocracy to keep a firm hand on the army and insist upon its preparedness.

As time passed and Germany became increasingly capitalistic, the Junkers sank in the economic scale relatively, but were not conquered by the bourgeoisie. A number of reasons account for their ability to exercise an influence out of proportion to their financial strength: the Prussian monarchy and bureaucracy; social prestige; fear of Russia on the east; the growth of socialism, which frightened landlord and capitalist alike; and the Prussian class system of voting, which gave those who paid two thirds of the direct tax two thirds of the representatives in the Prussian Diet.

In Austria-Hungary the chance of subduing to democratic government the monarchy and the landed aristocracy dominant in the houses of lords was even less than in Germany. Apart from any personal popularity which the aged Francis Joseph may have enjoyed, the monarchy was the one bond of union which assured the supremacy of the German and Magyar elements in the state over the majority of South Slavs, Italians, Czechs, Slovaks, and other races in that miscellaneous empire. In the scale of great landlordism Austria-Hungary stood far ahead of Germany. On the eve of the war Austria had about 18,000 landed estates above 250 acres and 1733 above 2500 acres. Nearly one third of the land in Hungary was embraced in approximately 4000 estates of more than 1400 acres. If the landed aristocracy of these countries was more cultivated than that of Russia, it was no less dominant and belligerent. Representatives of that class were supreme in society and high politics—State, army, and Church. On no condition were they willing to surrender power to commoners in parliament or to see the prestige of the crown, which protected them, diminished by popular control over cabinets.

Democratic Struggles in Russia under Nicholas II

Among all the European countries in which the monarchy, Church, and feudal aristocracy resisted successfully oncoming democracy Russia of course stood first—and Russia was overwhelmingly agricultural from the Baltic to the Pacific. Of the total population, estimated at about 160,000,000 in 1910, nearly seven eighths, or, to be more precise, 138,000,000 in round numbers, were recorded as living in the country. In European Russia proper, exclusive of Poland, the State, the imperial families, and other governmental agencies owned, in the year 1905, 36 per cent of the land; peasants, 32.3 per cent; landlords, 23.7 per cent; 8 per cent was classified as unfit for cultivation. About the same time it was officially reported that 30,000 large landholders owned as many acres as did 10,000,000 peasant families.

When Nicholas II succeeded his father, Alexander III, in 1894,[1] at the age of twenty-six, there was some reason to hope

[1] It may not be superfluous to bring together at this point the names of the Russian rulers in recent times, since their autocratic position enabled them to play a more important rôle than monarchs of western Europe.

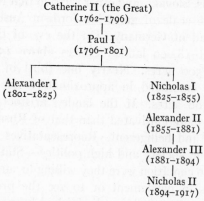

Catherine II (the Great)
(1762–1796)
|
Paul I
(1796–1801)
|
Alexander I   Nicholas I
(1801–1825)   (1825–1855)
|
Alexander II
(1855–1881)
|
Alexander III
(1881–1894)
|
Nicholas II
(1894–1917)

For the history of Russia before the accession of Nicholas II, see Vol. I, pp. 108 ff., 585 ff.

that he would face the problems of Russia in a progressive spirit. He had had an opportunity in his travels to become somewhat familiar with the enlightened governments of western Europe, and one of his first acts was to order the imprisonment of the prefect of police of St. Petersburg for annoying the correspondents of foreign newspapers.

But he soon dissipated the hopes of the liberals by saying: "Let it be understood by everyone that I shall employ all my powers in the best interests of the people, but the principle of autocracy will be sustained by me as firmly and unswervingly as it was by my never-to-be-forgotten father." Pobyedonostsev, Procurator of the Holy Synod, and other trusted advisers of Alexander III were retained in office, and it was clear that Nicholas would do all he could to keep Russia "frozen" so as to avoid the decay which he, like his predecessors, believed to be overtaking western Europe.

The censorship of the press was made stricter than ever, one decree alone adding two hundred books, including the works of Herbert Spencer, to the already long list of those which the government condemned.[1] A distinguished historian, Professor Milyoukov, was dismissed from the University of Moscow on the ground of his "generally noxious tendencies," and other teachers were warned not to talk about government. From the accession of Nicholas II on there was a steady increase in the number of people tried for attacking the government or offending its feelings. From 1500 in the year 1894, the number of persons involved in "political" cases reached a total in the single year 1903 of no less than 12,000, over half of whom were deprived of the ordinary protection afforded by the regular courts and were haled before special tribunals which were supposed to be in full sympathy with the Tsar's despotism. In this way the

---

[1] Among the books which the government prohibited in public libraries were the Russian translation of Mill's *Political Economy*, Green's *History of the English People*, Bryce's *American Commonwealth*, and Fyffe's *Modern Europe*.

bureaucracy[1] brought incalculable anxiety and suffering to thousands of innocent, law-abiding citizens, while doing little to discourage the violent agitators, who were relatively few in number. It may be noted that among the prisoners exiled to Siberia in the third year of Nicholas II's reign was a young lawyer, Vladimir Ilich Ulianov, later known as Lenin!

We must now trace the history of the terrible struggle between the Russian people and their despotic government which began openly in 1904. In 1902 an unpopular minister of the interior had been assassinated, and the Tsar had appointed a still more unpopular man in his place—namely, Venceslas Plehve—who was notorious for his success in hunting down those who criticized the government and for the vigor with which he had carried on the Russification of Finland. He at once declared that the existing discontent was due entirely to a handful of evil-minded agitators whom the police would soon catch. Plehve joined hands with Pobyedonostsev in the persecution of those among the Tsar's subjects who ventured to disagree with the doctrines of the Russian official church, to which every Russian was supposed to belong. The Jews suffered especially. There were massacres at Kishinev and elsewhere in 1903 which horrified the Western world and drove hundreds of thousands of Jews to foreign lands, especially to the United States. There is good reason to believe that Plehve actually arranged these massacres; he at least did nothing to prevent or discourage the atrocities.

Although it was not possible to organize political parties in the western sense to oppose the intolerable acts of the autocracy, there arose in Russia a number of more or less distinct groups bent on political and economic reforms. Of these groups the following were the most important.

---

[1] This word is commonly applied to governments in which the officials are not elected or controlled by the people and are free to interfere constantly in everyone's private affairs. The term is derived from the French *bureau*, the office in which an official transacts his business.

There were, first, the professional men, the university professors, the enlightened merchants and manufacturers, and the public-spirited nobility. These were not organized into a distinct party, but later came to be known as the Constitutional Democrats. They hoped that a parliament elected by the people might be established to coöperate with the Tsar and his ministers in making the laws and imposing the taxes. They demanded that all Russians should enjoy those rights which the French had in 1789 included in their Declaration of the Rights of Man: freedom of speech and of the press, the right to hold public meetings to discuss public questions, the abolition of the hideous police system, arbitrary imprisonment, and religious persecutions, and the gradual improvement of the condition of the peasants and workingmen through the passage of wise laws.

In the towns there grew up a socialistic party which advocated the theories of Karl Marx. It desired all the reforms advocated by the Constitutional Democrats just described, but looked forward to the time when the workingmen would become so numerous and powerful that they could seize the government offices and assume the management of lands, mines, and industries. This Social Democratic party believed that a constitutional assembly similar to the French Convention of 1792 should be summoned, and that the representatives of the people should freely decide what form of government Russia needed and wished. They advocated the abolition of village communities (Vol. I, pp. 595 ff.) as an outworn and cumbersome system which contributed to the misery of the peasant. Unlike the reformers next to be described, they did not believe in terrorism through murderous attacks upon unpopular government officials. Nevertheless, a number of Marxian socialists finally became convinced that little was to be expected from political agitation and that nothing short of a general uprising by the working classes would break the power of the autocracy.

The most conspicuous among the Russian agitators were those who belonged to the Socialist Revolutionary party. This was the successor to the People's Will party, which made war on the Tsar and his officials at the end of the reign of Alexander II (Vol. I, pp. 599 ff.). The Social Democrats, in the main, adopted the doctrines and policy of the German Social Democrats; the Socialist Revolutionary party was on the contrary a product of Russian conditions. It counted among its adherents many highly intelligent Russian patriots, who sought support among the peasants rather than among the workmen in the factories of the manufacturing towns. Like the Social Democratic party, it demanded a democratic form of government and the ownership by the people of railroads, mines, and industries of national importance. It urged, too, that the landlords should be forced to surrender all their land to the peasants, but instead of abolishing the village communities, it proposed to perpetuate them as an ancient and peculiar national institution of Russia which, if properly managed, would secure the greatest happiness and prosperity to the country people.

The Socialist Revolutionary party was well organized and was responsible for the chief acts of revolutionary violence which shook Russia at the opening of the twentieth century. It maintained that it was right to make war upon the government which was oppressing them and extorting money from the people to fill the pockets of dishonest officeholders. It selected its victims from the most notoriously cruel among the officials, and after a victim was killed it usually published a list of the offenses which cost him his life. Lists of those condemned to death were also prepared, after careful consideration, by an executive committee. The party did not practice, or in any way approve of, indiscriminate assassination, as was often supposed.

The more the police sought to stamp out protests against the autocracy, the more its enemies increased, and at last in

1904 discontent burst out in revolution. On February 5 of that year a war opened with Japan, due largely to Russia's encroachments in Korea and her evident intention of permanently depriving China of Manchuria (see pages 268 ff.). Russian Liberals attributed the conflict to bad management on the part of the Tsar's officials and declared it to be inhuman and contrary to the interests of the people. In March revolutionary manifestoes appeared, asserting that the Japanese were quite justified in their claims and urging that no intelligent Russian should help on the war in any way, either by contributions or enlistment.

In June the venerable Count Tolstoy issued a remarkable address to the Tsar, that "unfortunate, entangled young man" who was seizing other people's land and sending men to be murdered in its defense. The Russian Church was, he declared, giving a religious sanction and praying for the success of a war waged "in support of those stupidities, robberies, and every kind of abomination perpetrated in China and Korea by wicked and ambitious men now sitting peacefully in their palaces and expecting new glory, advantage, and profit from the slaughter."

In spite of the rising indignation Plehve continued, however, to encourage the police to break up scientific and literary meetings, in which disapprobation of the government was pretty sure to be expressed, and to send men eminent in science and literature to prison or to Siberia, until, on July 28, 1904, a bomb was suddenly thrown under his carriage by a former student in the University of Moscow, and the minister's career was brought to an abrupt close. The central committee of the Russian revolutionary socialists then issued an explanation and apology to "the citizens of the world," in which they explained that they were responsible for what they considered a righteous act in "executing" a man who was making war on all those who dared to think or who were striving for the freedom of Russia. They dis-

approved absolutely of a policy of terrorism in free countries, "but in Russia, where, owing to the reign of despotism,
no open political discussion is possible, where there is no re-
dress against the irresponsibility of absolute power throughout the whole bureaucratic organization, we shall be obliged
to counteract the violence of tyranny with the force of revolutionary right."

Disasters and revolt met the Russian government on every
hand. The Japanese continued to force back its soldiers in
Manchuria in a series of terrific conflicts south of Mukden.
In one long battle on the Shaho River sixty thousand Russians
perished. Their fleets in the East were annihilated, and on
January 1, 1905, Port Arthur fell, after one of the most terrible
sieges on record. Russian marines mutinied, reserve troops refused to go to the Far East and escaped to Austria or Germany
when they were not driven into the railroad trains at the point
of the bayonet. Crops failed, and starving peasants burned
and sacked the houses and barns of the nobles, arguing that if
the buildings were destroyed the owners could not come back,
and the police could no longer make them their headquarters.
But the Tsar lived in blissful indifference to the disasters. On
a day when news of a terrible defeat in the East reached him,
he entered this memorandum: "Had a stroll, killed one crow,
and went for a row on the Gatchina."

But his subjects could not be so cool. The war produced a
stagnation of commerce and industry, and strikes became common. Socialists in Warsaw marched about armed with knives
and revolvers and denouncing the war. Students in Moscow and
St. Petersburg shouted, "Down with autocracy!" "Stop the
war!" It became known that the government officials had been
stealing money that should have gone to strengthen and equip
the armies; rifles had been paid for that had never been delivered, supplies bought which never reached the suffering soldiers, and—most scandalous of all—high Russian dignitaries
had even appropriated the funds of the Red Cross Society for

aiding the wounded. Russia certainly seemed to be completely "thawed" by the end of 1904 and, as the Procurator of the Holy Synod had feared, was dissolving into anarchy.

With the hope of curing the unrest, the Tsar issued an imperial ukase on December 26, 1904, vaguely promising reforms, which he declared were under consideration and would be put into effect as soon as possible. But he was evidently still under the influence of the conservatives and showed no inclination to give up any of his powers. His proclamation failed, therefore, to stop agitation. On Sunday, January 22, 1905, a fearful event occurred. The workingmen of St. Petersburg, led by a certain Father Gapon, had sent a petition to the Tsar and had informed him that on Sunday they would march to the palace humbly to pray him in person to consider their sufferings, since they had no faith in his officials or ministers. They warned him that his advisers were bringing the country to ruin, and that money was wrung from the impoverished masses to be spent they knew not how. They urged the Tsar to "throw down the wall that separates him from his people" by immediately convoking an assembly which should include representatives even of the working classes. When Sunday morning came, masses of men, women, and children, wholly unarmed, with Father Gapon at their head, attempted to approach the Winter Palace in the pathetic hope that the "Little Father," as they called the Tsar, would listen to their woes. Instead, the Cossacks tried to disperse them with their whips, and then the troops which guarded the palace shot and cut down hundreds, and wounded thousands in a conflict which continued all day.

"Red Sunday" was followed by an outburst of strikes and by the organization of workers' councils, or "soviets," in the great industrial centers. Foremost among these councils was the St. Petersburg Soviet, in which Leon Trotzky was the leading figure. And among the observers of its sessions, sometimes from the gallery, was Lenin, now again in St. Petersburg in disguise, watching the drift of revolutionary opinion and taking notes on the conditions and demands of workingmen and peasants.

The day after Red Sunday all the leading lawyers and men of letters in St. Petersburg joined in the following declaration: "The public should understand that the government has declared war on the entire Russian people. There is no further doubt on this point. A government which is unable to hold intercourse with the people except with the assistance of sabers and rifles is self-condemned. We summon all the vital energies of Russian society to the assistance of the workingmen who began the struggle for the common cause of the whole people. Let shame overwhelm the names of those who, in these days of great and fateful struggle, oppose the people and join the ranks of their hangmen." The government replied by arresting a number of prominent writers, among them Maxim Gorky, the novelist; and General Trepoff, the younger, notorious for his brutality as head of the police of Moscow, was given full powers to restore order.

In meeting this crisis the conduct of the government, supported by the State Church and the army, was well-nigh incredible to foreigners. Its whole statesmanship consisted in making promises which it apparently had no intention of carrying out, and in imprisoning, torturing, exiling, or killing those whom it suspected of being its enemies. The authorities ordered Cossacks to disperse peaceful processions with their whips or commanded the troops to fire into helpless, unarmed crowds. Government officials deliberately organized massacres in the name of patriotism, religion, and order. They supplied Tartars with rifles to hunt down Armenians in the Caucasus, who were regarded as revolutionists, and organized the bands of roughs known as the "Black Hundreds" to represent the spirit of old Russia, and kill and maltreat those who favored reform and progress. Peasants, whom starvation drove to desperate measures, were flogged and tortured by hundreds.

In one village, where five men were beaten to death, a by-stander ventured to point out that the Tsar had abolished corporal punishment a year before. The officer in charge then ordered the Cossacks "to show that man whether corporal punishment has been abolished or not." Thereupon the unfortunate witness who had dared to protest was flogged into insensibility, and died subsequently on the way to a hospital.

THE RUSSIAN DUMA

Finding his oppressive measures of no avail in restoring peace, the Tsar so far yielded to the pressure of public opinion that on August 19 he promised to summon a *Duma*, or council, to meet not later than January, 1906. It was to represent all Russia, but to have no further power than that of giving to the still-autocratic ruler advice in making the laws. Against this trivial promise the intellectuals protested, and in October, 1905, working people brought still more powerful pressure to bear in a general strike. All the railroads stopped running; in the great towns the shops, except those that dealt in provisions, were closed; gas and electricity were no longer furnished; law courts ceased their duties; even apothecaries refused to prepare prescriptions until reforms should be granted.

The situation soon became intolerable, and on October 29 the Tsar announced that he had ordered "the government" to grant the people freedom of conscience, speech, and association, and to permit classes which had been excluded in his first edict to vote for members of the Duma. Lastly, he agreed "to establish an immutable rule that no law can come into force without the approval of the Duma, and that it shall be possible for those whom the people elect to enjoy a real supervision over the legality of the acts of the public officials."

The police and Cossacks, however, continued to attack peaceful gatherings, and Black Hundreds were organized by the government authorities in Odessa, Tiflis, Riga, and scores

T

of other towns to lead in massacres of the Jews. It was very easy to rouse the ignorant and fanatical masses to plunder and kill the representatives of a race they hated; and since the Jews were often revolutionists, the reactionary party could urge that attacks upon them were good proof of the general hostility of the Russian people to the reforms advocated by the liberals.

The strike had to be abandoned. But anarchy continued. In March, 1906, the Tsar issued a manifesto in which he explained how he proposed to convert his Council of the Empire into a sort of upper house to coöperate with the Duma and thus form a parliament for Russia somewhat similar to those of Western states. Half the members of the Council were to be appointed by the Tsar himself, and half to be chosen by various bodies, for example, the Synod of the Orthodox Church, the Academy of Sciences, the universities, the various bourses, or exchanges, and the nobility. All laws were to be approved by both houses before being submitted to the Tsar.

The elections for the Duma took place in March and April, and, in spite of the activity of the police, resulted in an overwhelming majority for the Constitutional Democrats. The deputies to the Duma assembled in no humble frame of mind. They came exasperated by the disasters of the war and the humiliations of the army and fleet, for all of which they held the ministers and the bureaucracy responsible; they were resolved to demand an account of the public income and expenditures, to punish fraud, hunt down and chastise the guilty, dismiss the corrupt, and purify the whole administration. They were determined, in a word, to give Russia an enlightened, liberal, and righteous constitutional government. Like the members of the Estates-General in 1789, they felt that they had the nation behind them. They listened stonily to the Tsar's remarks at the opening session, and it was clear from the first that they would not agree any better with their monarch than the French deputies had agreed with Louis XVI and his courtiers.

The first motion made in the Duma related to the freeing of those who had sacrificed their liberty for their country. In its address to the Tsar the assembly laid stress on the necessity of universal suffrage, and the abandonment on the part of the government of all its tyrannical habits. It also insisted that there was no hope of progress in regenerating the country so long as the upper house was under the Tsar's personal control, and his ministers were in no way responsible to the Duma. It recommended that all the land belonging to the State or the members of the royal house, as well as that of the churches and monasteries, should be turned over to the peasants on long leases. One of its members showed how the Tsar's ministers and their friends had been enriching themselves through the so-called Peasant's Bank. The Duma also discussed the organization of massacres by the police, of which a terrible example occurred in the middle of June. A bill abolishing capital punishment entirely was ardently discussed and finally passed.

Neither the Council of the Empire nor the Tsar's ministers would coöperate with the Duma in any of these measures, and on July 21 Nicholas II declared that he was "cruelly disappointed" because the deputies had not confined themselves to their proper duties and had commented upon many matters which belonged to him. He accordingly dissolved the Duma, as he had a legal right to do, and fixed March 5, 1907, as the date for the meeting of a new Duma.

The revolutionists made an unsuccessful attempt in August to blow up Premier Stolypin in his country house and continued to assassinate governors and police officials. The Black Hundreds, on the other hand, went on massacring Jews and liberals while the government established courts-martial to insure the speedy trial and immediate execution of revolutionists. In the two months, September and October, 1906, these courts summarily condemned three hundred persons to be shot or hanged. During the whole year some nine thousand persons were killed or wounded in connection with political activities of one kind or another.[1]

A terrible famine was afflicting the land at the end of the year, and it was discovered that a member of the Tsar's ministry had been stealing the money appropriated to furnish grain to the dying peasants. An observer who had traveled eight hundred miles through the famine-stricken district reported that he did not find a single village where the peasants had food enough for themselves or their cattle. In some places the peasants were reduced to eating bark and the straw used for their thatch roofs.

In October a ukase permitted peasants to leave their particular village community and join another, or to seek employment elsewhere. On November 25, peasants were empowered to become owners of their allotments and all redemption dues were remitted. This constituted a practical abolition of the system of ownership by village communities.

In accordance with the Tsar's imperial promise the second Duma met on March 5, 1907. It was speedily dissolved on account of its refusal to surrender a number of its members accused by the police of a plot to assassinate the Tsar. In order that the third Duma might be more docile than the first two, the Tsar and his ministers issued, quite unconstitutionally, a new set of regulations for the coming elections. Poland (see Vol. I, pp. 592 f.) was deprived of two thirds of its representatives, while those from the cities were so greatly reduced that only St. Petersburg, Moscow, Kiev, Odessa, Warsaw, Lodz, and Riga could send any deputies at all. The influence of the peasants, whom the government had found almost as radical as the workingmen of the towns, was also much diminished.

As a result of these unconstitutional measures, the third

[1] It is essential to recall these examples of the ruthless policy of the Tsar's government in judging the precedents it had set for the violence of the Bolsheviki, who were to be his successors.

Duma, which met on November 14, 1907, contained a much larger number of great landowners, retired government officials, priests, and other conservative members than the former assemblies. Nevertheless, on November 26, by a vote of 246 to 112, it declared the title "Autocrat" to be "no longer justifiable in the Russian State and incompatible with the system inaugurated by the manifesto issued by Emperor Nicholas on October 29, 1905."

During its term of five years the third Duma did little more than preserve the semblance of constitutional government. It did attempt to allay some of the unrest by establishing a system of insurance for industrial workers, it provided for the opening of more common schools under the control of the Orthodox Church, and it made a few minor concessions to the peasants. But it was powerless to stop the cruel guerrilla war between the masses and the police—accompanied by assassinations, executions, and banishments. Nor did it prevent the renewal of terrible pogroms, or massacres of the Jews. And when its term expired in 1912 the Russian government, in spirit and form, was not appreciably nearer to democracy than it was when Nicholas II was crowned.

The fourth Duma, chosen in 1912, also represented reaction rather than progress toward popular government. It is true that less than half its members belonged to the extreme right, but the majority was so split up into Octobrists, Progressists, Constitutionalists, Laborites, and Social Democrats that it was able to agree on little more than opposition to the autocracy, clergy, and bureaucracy. It was the fate of this Duma to last nearly to the end of the World War and, owing to the constant appeals made by the harassed government to the people to work, fight, and pay, it exerted a material influence over the selection and dismissal of cabinet officers. When in March, 1917, with unrest veering toward desperation, the Tsar dissolved the Duma, it defied his orders, continued its sessions, insisted on ousting the reactionary cabinet, demanded radical reforms, and in short transformed itself into a sort of revolutionary assembly. It hung on through the summer of that year, trying to steer Russia into a constitutional government, and was finally dissolved in the autumn on the eve of the Bolshevik revolution, which we will describe in a later chapter.

STATE AND CHURCH AMID DEMOCRATIC TENDENCIES

The increasing democratic control in European governments inevitably raised new questions as to the proper relation of the State to religious organizations. Neither Catholics nor Protestants at the time of the Protestant revolt contemplated the separation of Church and State and the granting of universal toleration to all religious denominations. In Catholic countries the State and the Church, though often engaged in quarrels over their respective rights and powers, continued their old relations; in Protestant countries the new Church was generally subordinated to the State and taken under its protection and patronage as a monopoly. However, as sects multiplied in number and doubts respecting the truth of the various religious dogmas increased, and the State gave more attention to economic and other secular matters, there came a demand for fundamental changes in the historic relations of the government and the Church in all countries, Protestant and Catholic alike.

These proposed changes included toleration for all religious denominations, the abolition of taxes and tithes for the support of religion, the exclusion of bishops and other clergy from houses of lords and other legislative bodies, and the abandonment of all favors hitherto shown to any church or denomination. Interested in the education of boys and girls for citizenship and for earning a livelihood, European governments, under popular pressure, began to build up independent school systems, and finally succeeded in breaking up the monopoly of education formerly enjoyed by the clergy. Since the children of all religious sects were educated at the same public schools, it became impossible to agree on any one form of religious instruction, and hence the schools tended to become purely secular, much to the alarm of the clergy. In time the State also insisted on passing laws respecting marriage, divorce, the willing of property, and other matters once left to the control of the clergy, thus raising disputes over practices to be allowed and over the fees to be paid for various services. At last the demand arose for the complete separation of Church and State. This meant, in general, that the government was not to take any part in the selection of bishops and other Church officials, was not to raise any money to pay them, and was to treat churches of all kinds as mere private associations, such as clubs, lodges, and fraternal orders.

However easy it was to formulate in theory, the proposal was difficult to carry out in practice, owing to the long association of Church and State throughout western Christendom. From early times the Church had been connected with monarchs; many heathen tribes were baptized when their rulers were converted; for centuries the clergy had preached obedience to kings and princes and had received gifts of money and land from them. To the pageantry of royal courts the clergy added color and dignity. Moreover bishops and high authorities in the Church were always to be found in the councils of monarchs, for they were great landed proprietors often richer than the secular lords. Indeed, the clergy as landholders formed a separate "estate" in each kingdom. When parliaments and councils were called they were entitled to a summons. As educated men they often held high office at the court of kings; Mazarin and Richelieu, both cardinals in the Church of Rome, were accounted among the greatest statesmen of the seventeenth century.

Associated with monarchs and with the secular feudal lords who supported monarchs, the clergy naturally had to bear some of the brunt of the attacks made on monarchy and land-lords by the middle classes rising to power and by the peasants bent on getting rid of the burden of tithes and feudal dues. No one could tell where the contest over property left off and differences over religion began. If those hostile to clerical power, always in a minority at the beginning of the agitations, were to convert the mass of their fellow citizens, it was neces-sary for them to get control of the schools, and that meant a struggle with the clergy for predominance in intellectual life. Democracy also came into collision with the Church over the appointment of its officials and the distribution of Church spoils, thus continuing an ancient contest between the princes and the Church (see Vol. I, pp. 228 ff.).

It was easy to say that the Church should limit itself to faith and morals and abstain from politics entirely, but where was the dividing line to be drawn and by whom? While it was possible for the government to announce that it was indifferent to matters of faith, no government could ever declare that it was without morals and without interest in morals. On the contrary, all governments were continually making laws in-volving morals—laws respecting marriage, divorce, blasphemy, the treatment of children, crimes and misdemeanors, such as bigamy and adultery, and the licensing of theaters and plays. As a matter of fact no church could or would take the position that it had no interest in rules of right and wrong laid down by the government for all citizens, including its members. When, for example, in 1868, the government of Austria, which was loyal to the Roman Catholic Church, transferred by law ques-tions growing out of marriage from ecclesiastical to civil courts, took over the management of secular schools, and established complete equality between Catholics and all other religionists, the Pope in an allocution declared that these "damnable and abominable laws" were contrary to "the laws of the Church and the principle of Christianity," were "null and void," and were not to be obeyed. But Austria enforced them.

Religious Freedom in England

As in the development of parliamentary government, so in the promotion of religious equality before the law and the separation of religion and politics, England, by the end of the seventeenth century, began to set examples for the countries on the Continent, except Holland, where religious freedom got an even earlier start. But it took an agitation lasting more than two hundred years to remove the civil disabilities imposed on English Dissenters and Catholics in the sixteenth and seventeenth centuries, and to establish the right of anyone to hold government offices regardless of his opinions on baptism, the Trinity, or the Mass. The famous Toleration Act of 1689, which granted a certain liberty of worship to Dissenters, had not freed them from the disabilities which rested on all persons who did not belong to the State Church—namely, exclusion from municipal offices and from all places of trust, civil and military, in the State, as well as from certain educational advantages. It was therefore only by connivance, or by special "indemnity" from Parliament, that Dissenters could take any office or place in the government, although, curiously enough, they were not prohibited from sitting in Parliament.

At the close of the eighteenth century, however, dissenting sects were rapidly increasing in wealth, numbers, and influence, especially after the appearance of the Methodists. An able argument presenting their grievances was laid before Parliament in 1787; it pointed out that the successful merchant whose activities had helped to enrich the city might be punished for accepting an office in its government. It was forcibly argued that it was absurd to allow a Dissenter to enter Parliament and assist in the making of laws which he could not help to enforce by occupying the meanest office.

This plea was disregarded, and Lord North declared that the Test Act passed under Charles II, which had imposed these disabilities, was "the bulwark of the constitution to which we owe those inestimable blessings of freedom which we now happily enjoy." Dissenters had to wait forty years longer for the granting of their claims to civil rights. It was not until 1828 that Parliament was finally induced to pass an act repealing the old laws against Dissenters and admitting them freely to public offices on condition that they took an oath "upon the true faith of a Christian" not to use their influence to injure or weaken the Established Church.

During this period Catholics were not only excluded from municipal and state offices but from Parliament as well, and their religious worship was subject to serious limitations. By a harsh law of 1700 all adherents of the Catholic faith were compelled to abjure the doctrine of the Mass before reaching the age of eighteen years, under penalty of forfeiture of property for failure to comply, and Catholic priests were forbidden to exercise their functions under pain of perpetual imprisonment.

If strictly enforced, this law would have exterminated the Catholic faith in England, but in practice it was disregarded, since there was, at the close of the eighteenth century, no longer any religious or political danger from Catholics. Finally, in 1778 an act was passed removing these penalties on condition that priests and Catholic heirs of estates should abjure belief in the temporal power of the Pope, as well as in the right which he claimed of deposing princes.

Though this law gave them certain rights of worship, Catholics were still excluded from public offices until 1828, when the Test Act was repealed. The next year the Catholic Emancipation Act was finally passed. This explicitly admitted Roman Catholics to both houses of Parliament and to municipal and state offices with three exceptions. They were, however, still required to take an oath renouncing the temporal supremacy of the Pope and disclaiming any intention of injuring the Protestant religion or Protestant government established in the United Kingdom.

Though Dissenters and Catholics thus obtained their political rights in 1828-1829, the Established Church did not entirely surrender the monopoly of religion for which it had fought since the time of Elizabeth. For instance, Dissenters and Catholics could be lawfully married only by the ceremony provided in the official Book of Common Prayer, and the legal registration of their children's births depended, strictly speaking, upon baptism by an Anglican clergyman. Furthermore, since acceptance of the Thirty-nine Articles of the Anglican faith was necessary to matriculation at the University of Oxford, Catholics and Dissenters were excluded from the privileges of that institution, and though admitted to the University of Cambridge, they could not receive degrees there. Finally, they were compelled to pay tithes for the support of the State Church.

The removal of these grievances was at last begun by the reformed Parliament in 1836, when provision was made for the civil registration of births, marriages, and deaths. After prolonged agitation, repeated debates in Parliament, and widespread refusal to pay the church tithes, these were abolished in 1868. The religious test at the universities was removed in 1870, making degrees and academic offices "freely accessible to the nation." Thus by no declaration of rights or general acts, but by numerous partial measures, religious disabilities were removed and all inhabitants of the United Kingdom secured, legally at least, practical equality before the law and in the government of the country.

THE ROMAN CATHOLIC CHURCH AND PAPAL INFALLIBILITY

While the Roman Catholic Church could well rejoice in the toleration granted to its members in Protestant England, it was naturally very much perplexed about the general movement on the Continent toward complete separation of Church and State and the establishment of equality for all religions before the law.[1] Its historic position was contrary to the "novelties" of the age. It claimed to possess the only true faith and looked upon other religious beliefs as false and dangerous. What attitude should it take toward the tendencies of the waning century? Should it accept the liberal creed? Should it stand fast by its ancient privileges? Should it remain silent? Should it compromise? Could a church which professed to have the only true religion tolerate the toleration which put all religions, and by implication atheism, on an equal footing before the law and in civil society?

Confronted with this dilemma, the Pope, Pius IX, decided to fight all along the line; so he issued in 1864 a document known as the Syllabus of Errors, a collection of eighty propositions which he regarded as false. The Syllabus was an excellent summary of the leading democratic and scientific tendencies of the age and a straightforward condemnation of them all. For example, it classed as errors the following ideas and practices:

Every man is free to embrace and profess the religion he believes true.

Protestantism is nothing more than another form of the same true Christian religion, in which it is possible to be equally pleasing to God as in the Catholic Church.

In case of conflicting laws between the two powers [temporal and religious] the civil law ought to prevail.

The Church ought to be separated from the State and the State from the Church.

The Roman Pontiff can and ought to reconcile himself to, and make terms with, progress, liberalism, and civilization as lately conceived.

All these doctrines, and many more, the Pope declared anathema.

Not content with the promulgation of the Syllabus of Errors, Pius IX took a still more momentous step five years later

[1] For earlier controversies, see Vol. I, pp. 228 ff.

in calling at the Vatican a general council of Church dignitaries to consider the question of papal infallibility. The issue, it is true, was not new. The old contest in the Church as to whether final authority resided in the Pope or in the general council had been decided in practice in favor of the former, but the official declaration of the fact had been left in abeyance. Now the question was revived, and in 1870 the Vatican council, after long and grave debate, formulated and approved the doctrine of papal infallibility in the following language: "We teach and define as a divinely revealed dogma that the Roman pontiff, when he speaks ex cathedra—that is, when in his character as Pastor and Teacher of all Christians and in virtue of his supreme apostolic authority he lays down that a certain doctrine concerning faith or morals is binding upon the universal church—possesses, by the divine assistance which was promised to him in the person of the blessed Saint Peter, that same infallibility with which the divine Redeemer thought fit to invest His Church in defining its doctrine with regard to faith and morals." It must be noted that the Pope's infallibility extends *only* to definitions of faith and morals pronounced ex cathedra, and not to all he may say on these subjects on other occasions.

As may be imagined, the Syllabus of Errors and the declaration of papal infallibility aroused a great discussion not only among liberals of various schools but also among Catholics themselves. Indeed, a number of Catholic dignitaries, including several German bishops, declined to vote for the doctrine of infallibility at the council. In Germany the declaration was quickly followed by a conflict between Church and State known as the *Kulturkampf*.

THE RELIGIOUS CONFLICT IN GERMANY

At the first imperial election in 1871, Catholic voters in Germany returned sixty-three members to parliament, and Bismarck saw, or pretended to see, a conspiracy of clerical forces against the State. Jesuits were charged with having stirred up France to attack Prussia, and although there was little or no evidence to support this theory, the chancellor professed to believe in it. It was also alleged that the Pope and the Catholic bishops in eastern and southern Germany had sought to prevent the establishment of the empire under the leadership of a Protestant king.

It was undoubtedly true that some Catholics held opinions which conflicted with the chancellor's views on the supremacy of the civil government. The decrees of the Vatican Council issued in 1870 definitely asserted that the secular government might not interfere with the Pope in his relations with the clergy or with lay Catholics. German bishops received with favor a work by a Jesuit author in which he affirmed the right of the Pope to suspend and alter the civil law, and even went so far as to say that "Peace and national unity are an unqualified good only for a people in possession of the true faith. If they have not the true faith, then national division is incomparably less an evil than persistence in religious error."

Accordingly there was a clear conflict, in theory at least, between the doctrines maintained by Catholics and the views of the chancellor on the supremacy of the civil government. The open contest, however, was precipitated by divisions among the Catholics themselves. The doctrine of papal infallibility ratified by the Vatican Council in 1870 was rejected by some of the former adherents of the Roman faith, who now assumed the name of "Old Catholics" to distinguish themselves from the majority who accepted the Vatican decree. The chief exponent of the views of the Old Catholics was the distinguished historian Döllinger, who wrote a short but very learned and impressive history of the issue, entitled *Janus*. Thereupon the bishops who remained faithful to the Pope demanded that Old Catholic teachers should be removed from their places in the universities and schools, on the ground that they had refused to obey the dictates of the Church. To this demand the Prussian government declined to accede, alleging as a reason the fact that the decree in question had never been ratified by the State.

By their denunciations of its policy, Catholics now antagonized the government, and in 1872 a law was passed expelling the Jesuits and their affiliated orders from the German Empire. The following year the Redemptorists, the Lazarists, the Congregation of Priests of the Holy Ghost, and the Society of the Sacred Heart were likewise suppressed. Civil marriage was made compulsory in 1876, and civil registration of births and burials was established. To repress criticism on the part of the clergy, it was made a punishable offense for them to utter in public or to print anything designed to discredit the government. The German ambassador was withdrawn from Rome, and Bismarck, recalling the famous controversy eight hundred years earlier between the German emperor Henry IV and the Pope, which had ended in Henry's going to Italy to seek the Pope's forgiveness, declared, "We will not go to Canossa."

In addition to his imperial anti-Catholic measures, Bismarck instituted a repressive policy in Prussia which, in spite of its Protestant ruler, had granted liberty to Catholics ever since the days of the Great Elector. In May, 1873, important measures were passed which bear the name of the "May laws." One of them provided that no priest might undertake his functions until he had gone through a German preparatory school, spent three years in a German university, and passed an examination in three other faculties besides that of theology. Hence, no priest could officiate without a government certificate of his training in the government schools, which were decidedly anti-Catholic, and a bishop who appointed a priest not properly qualified was liable to a heavy fine.

As might have been expected, these measures aroused powerful opposition. The Pope declared them contrary to the constitution of the Church, the clergy in general refused to obey them, and the Catholics, as a result of these laws, were welded into a strong political party (the so-called "Center"), which secured the election of ninety-one members to the Reichstag in 1874. Even the more conservative Protestants did not approve of the harsh policy toward the Catholics, and in spite of his proud boast that he would never come to terms with the Church, Bismarck was at length forced to yield. He was wise enough to see that the Catholics were really less dangerous adversaries of absolutism and militarism than the national liberals, who wanted a ministry responsible to the Reichstag, or the rapidly-growing socialist party, which demanded radical reforms on behalf of the working classes. Pius IX died in 1878, and Leo XIII, in notifying the Kaiser of his elevation to the Holy See, expressed his regret at the strained relations existing between Rome and Berlin. Bismarck made this an excuse for withdrawing the repressive laws, and the liberals said, "He has, after all, gone to Canossa." One after another all the measures directed against the clergy, excepting the civil-marriage law, were abolished, and at length cordial relations were again established with the Vatican.

SEPARATION OF CHURCH AND STATE IN FRANCE

Successful in forcing the Protestant Bismarck to abandon his open opposition to the Catholic Church, the Pope, it seems, might have looked forward to a more peaceful adjustment of relations with Catholic France, but his difficulties there proved more troublesome than in Germany. The Catholic clergy had from the first been hostile to the Third French Republic, for they had every reason to fear that the new government, with its confidence in popular sovereignty, freedom of the press, and public schools, would sooner or later undermine their authority. The republicans were pledged to just those things which Pius IX had condemned; indeed, some of the most prominent among them regarded the Church as a serious impediment in the path of progress and, like Voltaire a hundred years before, would gladly have seen France abandon the Christian religion itself, since they believed it opposed to reason and modern science. It was inevitable, therefore, that the clerical party should do all in its power to discredit the republic and bring about a restoration of the monarchy. The Jesuits and other religious orders who maintained schools roused in the children's minds a distrust of the government, and the clergy actively engaged in electioneering whenever there was hope of electing deputies who would favor their cause. Religious newspapers represented the republic as an unfortunate accident which had put ungodly men in power, but which would doubtless speedily give way to a more "legitimate" form of government.

This attitude on the part of the clergy naturally made the republicans more strongly anticlerical than ever. They came to hate the clergy and all they stood for. Gambetta declared that clericalism was "*the* enemy." In a letter to Pope Leo XIII in 1883 President Grévy told His Holiness quite frankly that the denunciation of religion so common in France was due chiefly to the bitter hostility of the clergy toward the republic, which they had opposed from its advent, invariably siding with its enemies in all the struggles which it had faced in order to maintain itself. This letter seems to have had some effect at the Vatican, for the following year the Pope instructed the French clergy to moderate their opposition to the government. It was not until 1892, however, that Leo XIII admonished French bishops and priests to "accept the republic, that is to say, the established power which exists among you; respect it and submit to it as representing the power which comes from God."

In spite of this peaceful advice on the part of the head of the Church, there was no peace; for during the next twenty years there was an extraordinary struggle between Church and State, in which the republic proved the victor and succeeded in depriving the Church of a great part of those sources of political influence which remained to it after the losses it suf-

T

fered during the French Revolution (see Vol. I, pp. 308 ff.).
In this contest opponents of the Church had two main objects
in view: (1) to free the schools from the influence of the clergy
and thus prevent the children of France from being brought
up as monarchists and (2) to bring about the complete separation of Church and State and relieve the government from the
burden of paying the salaries of the clergy.

The first step was to increase the number of public schools
which might serve to attract pupils away from the convent and
other Church schools. By laws passed in 1881–1886 instruction was made absolutely free in the primary public schools,
children were required to attend them from the age of six to
thirteen, and no clergyman was to be employed as a teacher
in them. The private schools were also placed under strict
government supervision.

Then came an attack on monastic orders and various other
religious associations which had either been reëstablished since
the first revolution or newly created. Most of them were at
least nominally devoted to charity or to education. The Jesuits
were accused of working, as always, in the interests of the
Pope, and the Dominicans of preaching openly against the
republic, while the innumerable schools in the convents and
elsewhere were reproached with instilling monarchical and reactionary ideas into the tender minds of the children committed to their charge.

From time to time anticlerical deputies proposed the abolition of all the religious associations, and finally, in 1900,
Waldeck-Rousseau, then prime minister, committed himself
and his cabinet to a measure for greatly reducing their number.
"There are too many monks in politics," he said, "and too
many monks in business."[1] The following year the Associa-

---

[1] Sometimes the orders carried on a little industry in the interests of their
convent. For example, the monks of the great Carthusian monastery above
Grenoble manufactured the famous liqueur known as Chartreuse. The labor
parties denounced the monks for thus going into business and competing with
other manufacturers.

tions Law, aimed at monasticism, was passed. This provided that no religious order could continue to exist in France without a specific authorization from the parliament, and that no one belonging to a nonauthorized association should be permitted to teach or to conduct a school. At the time of the passage of the law there were about 160,000 members (mainly women) in the various religious associations, which maintained about 20,000 establishments. The parliament refused to grant most of the applications made by the many unauthorized associations, and as a result numerous teaching, preaching, and commercial societies which had been organized under the auspices of the Catholic Church were broken up, and within two years 10,000 religious schools were closed. In the year 1904–1905 there were over 5,000,000 French children in the public and other secular schools, and only about 500,000 enrolled in those connected with religious associations. In 1904 the Associations Law was supplemented by a measure providing that within ten years all teaching by religious associations must cease.

This attack on religious orders was only the prelude to the complete separation of Church and State which had been advocated for a century by the opponents of the Church. It will be remembered that the French Convention proclaimed this separation in 1795 and refused longer to pay the salaries of the clergy, or in any way to recognize the existence of the Church except as a voluntary association to be supported by those who wished to belong to it. Bonaparte, however, partially restored the old system in the Concordat which he arranged with the Pope in 1801. This, with a supplementary act, remained the basis of the relations between Church and State in France down to 1906.[1] Bonaparte did not give back

[1] The policy of the leaders of the French Revolution and of Bonaparte in regard to the clergy and the religious associations has already been described with a view of preparing the way for an understanding of the recent important legislation in France affecting the Church (see Vol. I, pp. 308 ff. and 378 ff.).

to the Church the property of which it had been deprived by the first French Assembly in 1789, but he agreed that the government should pay the salaries of the bishops and priests whose appointment it controlled. Although the Catholic religion was recognized as that of the majority of Frenchmen, the State also helped support the Reformed and Lutheran churches and the Jewish religious community.

From the standpoint of the government this was in many ways an excellent arrangement, for it was thus enabled profoundly to influence public opinion through its control over the clergy. Consequently, amid all the later political changes, the settlement reached by Bonaparte was retained essentially unaltered. Louis XVIII, Charles X, Louis Philippe, and Napoleon III had no desire to do away with the Concordat which increased their political power, and under their rule the anticlericals were an ineffectual minority.

With the establishment of the republic all this was changed, owing to the strong monarchical sympathies of the clergy. There were, moreover, large numbers of Frenchmen who, if not actively opposed to the Church, had no interest in religion. To this class it seemed absurd that the government should be paying forty million francs a year to clergymen for teaching the people what seemed to them nonsense and for stirring up hostility to the government. Nevertheless, it was no easy task to put asunder Church and State, which had been closely associated with one another from the times of Constantine and Theodosius the Great. It was not until 1904 that Premier Combes boldly announced his intention to undertake this separation. His plans were defeated, but his successor, Rouvier, continued the work he had begun, and after almost a year of heated debate the Separation Law was promulgated, December 9, 1905.

The main provisions of the new law were relatively simple. It suppressed all government appropriations for religious purposes but pensioned clergymen of long service and provided for the gradual extinction of the salaries of others. It declared that cathedrals, churches, the residences of bishops, and other ecclesiastical buildings belonged to the government, but should be placed at the disposal of congregations and their pastors free of charge. The management of these edifices and the control of other property of the Church were vested in Associations for Public Worship[1] (*Associations cultuelles*) composed of from seven to twenty-five persons according to the size of the commune. The Concordat concluded in 1801 was, of course, expressly abolished.

A period of twelve months was allowed for the various churches to form these associations and prepare for the full execution of the law; but it soon became evident that the Pope and a large Catholic party were determined not to accept its provisions. Crowds collided with the soldiers sent to guard the churches while inventories were being made of the property to be handed over to the Associations for Public Worship. In February, 1906, the Pope condemned the entire law in a long encyclical letter to the archbishops and bishops of France, in which he protested especially against the religious associations for which it provided. As they were really associations of private persons in whom was vested the management of Church property and finances, the Pope regarded them as not assuring the "divine constitution of the Church, the immutable rights of the Roman pontiff and of the bishops, and their authority over the necessary property of the Church, particularly over the sacred edifices." Moreover, he considered the repeal of the Concordat without consulting him as a violation of international law and a breach of faith. Unfortunately, he did not advise the French clergy just how to get out of the predicament in which they found themselves.

[1] These closely resemble the various church associations, both Catholic and Protestant, in the United States, which are, from the standpoint of the law, merely religious societies on the same footing as social, literary, or scientific associations.

The clergy, obedient to the commands of the head of the Church, refused to countenance the formation of associations, and many of them declined the proffered pensions. The nation at large, however, evidently supported the government in its plans, for the elections held in May, 1906, returned a large majority of radicals, socialists, and progressives committed to the full execution of the law.

When the year allowed for the formation of the religious associations expired in December, 1906, the Church property which had no legal claimants passed into the hands of the government. However, the minister of public worship, M. Briand, a socialist, unwilling to stop religious services, took steps to allow the churches to remain open in spite of the failure to comply with the law. At his instigation the French parliament passed a very important supplementary measure, which provided that buildings for public worship and their entire furniture should remain at the disposal of priests and their congregations even if the associations required by the original law were not formed.

In January, 1907, the Pope again denounced the government, which, he declared, was confiscating Church property and attempting to destroy Christianity in France. But it was quite clear that the republic meant to render permanent the separation of Church and State. Subsidies to the clergy were no longer provided, although the promised pensions were paid to such clergymen as applied for them. The government left the Church to choose its own bishops and priests and hold conventions when and where it wished. It converted the palaces of the bishops, the parsonages, and the seminaries into schools, hospitals, or other public institutions, although it still permitted the churches to be used for public worship. As time passed, the feelings aroused by the action of the government subsided, the clergy were given more freedom in practice than the strict letter of the law allowed, and finally in 1921 diplomatic relations with the Pope were resumed.

Difficult as were his relations with France, the Pope was on less friendly terms with the government of Italy—rather, on no terms at all. For some sixty years after the king of Italy wrested from him his temporal domains, the Pope refused to accept the loss of his temporal power as final. The Italian law of May, 1871, offered him freedom in spiritual functions, made his person sacred and inviolable like that of the king, permitted him to enjoy the honors of a sovereign prince,—including the right to send and receive ambassadors,—allowed him to live as an independent ruler in the Vatican and the other buildings and grounds left in his possession, and tendered him a large sum of money each year as an indemnity for the loss of his former property. But the Pope steadily refused to recognize the Italian government or to accept the money placed at his disposal, and continued to regard himself as a prisoner of a usurping power.[1]

[1] See pages 495 f. for the settlement in 1929 between the Pope and Mussolini, the dictator of Italy.

CHAPTER IV

THE GROWTH OF STATE ECONOMIC CONTROL

Rise of Marxian Socialism in Germany and France

Liberal thinkers who once imagined that an increase in the number of voters would bring social peace became more and more inclined to preserve monarchies and houses of lords as they watched the working classes of the Old World forming separate political parties for the purpose of using the government to promote their own aims and to modify the distribution of wealth in their own interest. On the Continent the labor movement took a radical turn, while the middle classes were struggling for power themselves. And before the century had drawn to a close even England had to face a rising labor party which was destined within a few years to force a realignment in politics.

Beginnings of a continuous socialist party may be traced back to 1863, when a General Workingmen's Association was formed in Germany at a labor congress held in Leipzig under the leadership of a brilliant thinker and orator, Ferdinand Lassalle. The prime purpose of this organization was to work for universal suffrage, in order that through their votes workingmen might force the government to furnish capital for the foundation of workshops like those which Louis Blanc had sought to establish during the French Revolution of 1848 (see Vol. I, pp. 468 ff.). After more than a year's vigorous agitation Lassalle had, however, mustered less than five thousand members for his association, and he was thoroughly discouraged before he met his death in 1864.

Notwithstanding the death of Lassalle, the campaign which

he had begun was prosecuted by his followers with greater vigor than before, although by no means all of them believed thoroughly in his program. In fact, some of the more radical among them, under the influence of the teachings of Marx, founded at Eisenach, in 1869, a new association, which bore the name of the Social Democratic Labor Party of Germany. The two groups worked side by side until 1875, when, at a general congress held at Gotha, they combined and issued an important statement of the views and purposes of the party, which long served as a kind of program for socialists everywhere. In the elections of that year for the Reichstag the socialists polled three hundred and forty thousand votes and began to arouse the apprehension of the government, which was naturally suspicious of them. At the opening of the twentieth century, their voting strength had risen to more than three million.

From Germany theories of Marxian socialism spread into France. There had long been in that country, as we have pointed out, many socialists of the Utopian variety (see pages 21 ff.). They had figured in the first French revolution, again in the uprising of 1848, and once more in the Paris Commune of 1871; but in the repression that followed this last revolt they had been killed or driven under cover. Not until 1879 did they appear in the form of a national organization, created at a labor congress held in Marseille. The next year the government granted a general amnesty to all who had taken part in the Commune, and immediately the socialists convened a great labor assembly in Paris to consolidate their forces. At that conference the doctrines of Karl Marx, expounded by Jules Guesde, were accepted as the fundamental principles of French socialism.

This congress declared in favor of secession from all other parties and the organization of a workingman's party designed to secure by the ballot the public ownership of all the means of production. As a practical program, they proposed freedom of the press, of public meetings, and of labor associations, reduction of the hours of labor, one holiday a week, free instruction, state aid for the old and infirm, employers' liability for injuries to their workmen, and the transformation of indirect taxes into an income tax.

Notwithstanding their general agreement, the French socialists were from the very first divided over the question of the best methods of attaining their aims. Broadly speaking, two groups contended for mastery, each with varying shades of opinion. In the first place, there were Marxians,—in general strongly opposed to voting for candidates of other parties, though willing to wring concessions from them in the Chamber of Deputies,—who expected socialism to be ushered in by a crisis in which the workingmen would seize the supreme power and use it for their own benefit, as the middle class had done in the previous revolutions. In the second place, there was the larger and more numerous socialist group called the "possibilists," who did not believe that socialistic ideas could be carried into effect as the result of a violent revolution, but hoped to see them realized by a gradual process in which the government would assume control and ownership of one industry after another.

Various socialistic factions, numbering six or seven at times, united at the general election in 1893 and by remarkable energy succeeded in returning about fifty members to the Chamber of Deputies, thus inaugurating a new era in French politics. The socialist vote steadily increased until in 1899 the prime minister, Waldeck-Rousseau, was forced to accept a socialist, Alexandre Millerand, as minister of commerce in order to control enough votes in the chamber to carry on the government. After that venture the possibilists were from time to time represented in the cabinet, and worked for their ends by combining with other parties, in spite of those among their socialist brethren who scorned all fusion and compromise. In reality, however, they accomplished little by this method.

Socialism in Great Britain

Although further advanced on the road to industrialism than either Germany or France, and according to Marxian theory a more fruitful soil for socialist agitation, England nevertheless remained far more conservative than the Continent in this respect. The Social Democratic Federation, formed in 1883 to promote Marxian doctrines, never succeeded in enrolling more than a handful of followers.

Convinced that the time was not ripe for the creation of a powerful party, a number of socialists organized the next year a kind of intellectual circle, known as the Fabian Society, for the purpose of spreading socialist ideas by means of pamphlets, books, and lectures. Their methods were indicated by their name, taken from the famous Roman general, Fabius, who warred against Hannibal by delays, maneuvers, and slow marches, which wore down the enemy. Embracing in their organization several distinguished thinkers, such as Sidney Webb, Beatrice Webb, G. B. Shaw, Graham Wallas, and H. G. Wells, the Fabians undertook the task of "permeating all classes with socialist ideals."

A third group, the Independent Labor party, established in 1893 under the leadership of Keir Hardie, a miner, appealed to the voters to elect socialists to Parliament but attracted no considerable attention for some years. It was not until 1903, when a high court gave verdicts to employers against two powerful trade unions for damages alleged to have been due to strikes, that organized labor on a large scale joined hands with socialists in a campaign to elect members to the House of Commons. At the general election three years later, this new combination, now known as the Labor party, succeeded in capturing twenty-nine seats in the House of Commons and winning many allies on the right wing. The number of labor members was increased to forty in the election of 1910, and to forty-two in the election of the following year.

INTERNATIONAL SOCIALISM

In response to the call of the *Communist Manifesto* bidding "the workers of the world to unite," socialistic groups of several nations early tried to form international ties. Their efforts bore fruit in 1864 in the creation of the International Workingmen's Association with a program drawn up by Karl Marx. This was the "First International," and it lasted for twelve stormy years. It adopted a definite socialist policy in 1869, and some of its members took an active part in the Paris Commune of 1871. The disaster which overwhelmed the commune and a conflict between the socialistic and the anarchistic elements produced a bitter internal strife in 1872, ending in the expulsion of Bakunin, the anarchist agitator. Clinging to a sinking ship, the socialist wing now transferred its headquarters to New York, and after a final convention in 1876 gave up the ghost. The First International was dead.

More than ten years passed. Socialism advanced. As an outgrowth of two significant labor conferences held in Paris, the Second International was established in 1891. It admitted to membership two different classes of persons. In the first category were "all associations which adhere to the essential principles of socialism:—socialization of the means of production and exchange, international union and action of the workers, conquest of public powers by the proletariat, organized as a class party." In the second category were "all labor organizations which accept the principles of the class struggle and recognize the necessity of political action (legislative and parliamentary) but do not participate directly in the political movement."

Every three or four years the Second International held a world conference. Moreover, it maintained a permanent organization consisting of two delegates from each nation represented. At its conventions socialist principles and tactics were discussed, and attempts were made to draw the socialist groups of all nations into an ever closer unity. Many and bitter were the debates at these assemblies, but by the use of clever compromises and rhetorical devices the Second International held together and seemed to grow stronger with the passage of time, until suddenly it went to pieces temporarily in the shock of the World War.[1]

SOCIAL LEGISLATION IN ENGLAND

Running parallel with this socialistic agitation was a continual stream of legislation providing government aid in improving labor conditions. This was in flat contradiction, of course, to the theories of the classical economists, sketched in the first chapter, which held that the State should not interfere in any way with hours of labor, wages, and the distribution of wealth.

But the theories did not work out well in practice. As a matter of fact, the new industrial system brought untold misery to the working classes of England. Great factory buildings were hastily erected by men ignorant of the most elementary principles of sanitary science and often too avaricious to care for anything but space enough to operate the machines and light enough to enable the laborers to do their work. Around the factories sprang up long, dreary rows of grimy brick cottages, where the workmen and their families were crowded together. To these industrial centers flocked thousands of landless and homeless men and women dependent upon the factory-owners for the opportunity to earn their daily bread. Fluctuations in trade caused long periods of enforced idleness, which resulted in great uncertainty in the life of the workman.

The introduction of steam-driven machinery had made possible the use of child labor on a large scale, and it was the condition of the children which at first attracted the attention

[1] For an account of the origin and development of the Third International, see pages 398 and 495.

of philanthropists and reformers. Thousands of little paupers were taken from the poorhouses and nominally apprenticed, but practically sold, to the proprietors of the mills. According to John Fielden, an enlightened manufacturer, the most heart-rending cruelties were often inflicted on these hapless children; they were "flogged, fettered, and tortured," and sometimes "starved to the bone while flogged to their work."[1] Nor were pauper children the only ones to suffer. Necessity or greed on the part of parents and the demand for "cheap labor" on the part of manufacturers brought many other children into industrial life. Parliamentary reports tell us of children under five years of age working in the mines, of coal-drawers but little older crawling on hands and knees through narrow subterranean passages dragging heavy carts of coal, and of mere lads laboring in pin mills at high tension for twelve hours a day. Such practices were even justified by a committee of mine-owners on the ground that, owing to the cramped conditions in the mines, children should begin work early while their backbones were flexible.

The conditions of adult labor, save in the most skilled classes, were almost as wretched as those of child labor. Women and girls were employed in great numbers in mills and even in the dark and dangerous recesses of the mines, which were badly ventilated and perilous to work in; dangerous machinery was not properly safeguarded, and the working time was excessively prolonged. Indisputable evidence of this distressing state of affairs is to be found in the bulky volumes of various parliamentary reports on factory conditions, in the memoirs of many enlightened men who investigated the life of the new industrial centers, and also in the dry pages of the statutes which reveal the wrongs that Parliament sought to

---

[1] In Robert Blencoe's memoirs of factory life we read that girls suspected of intending to escape "had irons riveted on their ankles, reaching by long links and rings up to their hips, and in these they were compelled to walk to and from the mill, to work, and to sleep."

remedy. The misery of the poor is reflected in Mrs. Browning's poem, "The Cry of the Children," in the bitter scorn which Carlyle poured out on the heads of the factory-owners, in the impassioned pages of Kingsley's *Alton Locke,* and in the vivid word pictures of Dickens.

The working classes were excluded from representation in Parliament, they were denied opportunities for education, and the statesmen of the time refused to take action in their behalf until after long and violent agitation. In this refusal Parliament was supported by the economic theorists—Malthus, Ricardo, and others—who defended the rights of mill-owners as Bossuet had defended the divine right of kings. Acting on this theory, a select committee of the House of Commons reported in 1811 that "no interference of the legislature with freedom of trade or with the perfect liberty of every individual to dispose of his time and his labor in the way and on the terms which he may judge conducive to his interest can take place without violating general principles of the first importance to the prosperity and happiness of the country, without establishing the most pernicious precedent, or even without aggravating, after a very short time, the pressure of the general distress, and imposing obstacles against that distress ever being removed." Five years later, when some starving workmen tried to destroy the new machinery to which they attributed their woes, Parliament did not hesitate to impose the death sentence on those who "riotously broke mining machinery."

Ardent reformers disregarding the advice of the theorists and discontented workmen filling the country with riot at last forced Parliament to undertake to improve conditions. Indeed, the bad ventilation, scanty food, long hours, and lack of sanitation led to the spread of epidemics in the factory districts, and action could not longer be delayed without endangering the health of the rich. Parliament, however, at first refused to do more than assume some responsibility for the pauper apprentices, by passing an act (1802) reducing the hours of labor for such children to seventy-two per week, and by making some other regulations on their behalf, such as compelling employers to furnish at least one suit of clothes a year.

An unselfish champion of the working class now appeared in the person of Robert Owen, a successful manufacturer, referred to in Chapter I, who had shown by experiments the advantages of treating employees with consideration. Beginning in 1815, he labored for four years to secure the passage of an effective measure in the interests of children. He declared to his brother cotton-manufacturers, "Deeply as I am interested in the cotton manufacture, highly as I value the extended political power of my country, yet, knowing as I do from long experience, both here in Scotland and in England, the miseries which this trade, as it is now conducted, inflicts on those to whom it gives employment, I do not hesitate to say, 'Perish the cotton trade!'" His appeal to the manufacturers to support his factory legislation was, however, unavailing, and the outcome of his efforts was the mutilation of his original bill in an act of 1819, which merely forbade the employment in the cotton mills of children under nine, and limited the hours for those between nine and sixteen to twelve per day.

New advocates of factory reform continued to urge additional measures on Parliament. Among these were Richard Oastler, Thomas Sadler, John Fielden, and Lord Ashley, to whose unselfish and untiring labors were largely due the pressure of public opinion which induced Parliament in 1832 to appoint a select commission for the purpose of investigating the whole question of factory legislation. The following year it made an unqualified report in favor of interference on behalf of children employed in factories, which resulted in a new bill still further reducing the working hours for children and providing for the first time for regular factory inspectors. In 1842 Lord Ashley carried through Parliament a mining law which forbade the employment of women and children in underground occupations.

Not satisfied with this legislation, reformers now began to work for a radical measure restricting the labor of women and children in mills to ten hours per day exclusive of meal times. This proposition gave rise to a wordy contest in the House of Commons between manufacturers and landed proprietors. In vain did a distinguished economist defend the factory-owners by declaring that their profit was made during the last hour and that its curtailment would ruin British industries; in vain did John Bright (champion of the abolition of slavery in the United States) denounce the proposition as "most injurious and destructive to the best interests of the country," "a delusion practiced upon the working classes," and "one of the worst measures ever passed." Smarting under the action of the manufacturers in forcing free trade upon them, the landed proprietors rejoiced in this opportunity to retaliate, and in 1847 the ten-hour bill for women and children became a law. In practice it applied to all adults as well, for the mills could not run after the women and children had stopped working.

With this great victory for the reformers the general resistance to state interference was broken down, and year after year new measures were carried through Parliament, revising and supplementing earlier laws, until all branches of industry were included within the scope of factory legislation. In the language of John Morley, England at last had "a complete, minute, voluminous code for the protection of labor; buildings must be kept clear of effluvia; dangerous machinery must be fenced; children and young persons must not clean it while in motion; their hours are not only limited but fixed; continuous employment must not exceed a given number of hours, varying with the trade, but prescribed by law in given cases; a statutable number of holidays is imposed; the children must go to school, and the employer must every week have a certificate to that effect; if an accident happens, notice must be sent to the proper authorities; special provisions are made for bake houses, for lace-making, for collieries, and for a whole schedule

T

of other special callings; for the due enforcement and vigilant supervision of this code of minute prescriptions, there is an immense host of inspectors, certifying surgeons, and other authorities, whose business it is to 'speed and post o'er land and ocean' in restless guardianship of every kind of labor, from that of the woman who plaits straw at her cottage door to the miner who descends into the bowels of the earth, and the seaman who conveys the fruits and materials of universal industry to and fro between the remotest parts of the globe."

LATER PHASES OF SOCIAL REFORM IN GREAT BRITAIN

Beneficent as much of this legislation proved to be, it left untouched a vast mass of poverty due to low wages, illness, unemployment, and causes other than those which may be ascribed to individual faults. Undoubtedly poverty on a large scale was one of the inevitable accompaniments of the Industrial Revolution, and in England the amount of depressing poverty was only too apparent. Mr. Charles Booth, a wealthy shipowner, feeling that there was no accurate information available in regard to the condition of the working people of London, undertook a house-to-house canvass at his own expense. With a large corps of helpers he set about ascertaining the "numerical relations which poverty, misery, and depravity bear to regular earnings and comparative comfort" and published, as the result of his survey, *Life and Labor of the People in London*, in sixteen volumes (1891–1903). In the district of East London, embracing a population of nearly a million, he found that more than one third of the people belonged to families with incomes of a guinea (about $5.15) or less a week; that 42 per cent of the families earned from about $5.50 to $7.50 a week; and that only about 13 per cent had more than $7.50 a week to live on. His studies further revealed terrible overcrowding in squalid tenements which were badly lighted, poorly equipped with water and sanitary arrange-

ments, and infested by disease. He reached the startling conclusion that throughout the vast city of London nearly one
third of the people were in poverty; that is, lived on wages
too low to provide the necessaries for a decent physical existence, to say nothing of comforts or luxuries.

It might at first sight seem that the poverty of London was
exceptionally great, but Mr. Rowntree, a manufacturer, in an
equally careful survey, proved that in the city of York, with
its population of less than eighty thousand inhabitants, toward
one third of the people were also, as in London, in dire poverty.
He showed too that the physical development of the children,
the prevalence of disease, and the death rate corresponded with
the rate of wages; in short, that health, happiness and well-
being increased as wages increased. There was reason to believe that conditions were essentially the same in many other
modern industrial cities, not only in England but throughout
the world, although this had not been demonstrated by scientific investigations.

In the course of time conditions such as those portrayed by
Booth and Rowntree, emphasized by labor and socialist agitations, attracted the attention of British statesmen who had
hitherto been busy with affairs which they deemed more important. Even the Liberals, who contained in their ranks most
of the rich manufacturers and in theory adhered to the *laissez
faire* creed of Cobden and Bright, came to the conclusion that
the government must take still more decided steps to remove
the blight of poverty from the land. Speaking as a Liberal,
Winston Churchill declared in 1909 that economic rather than
political issues were the questions of the time. "The main aspirations of the British people," he said, "are at the present
time social rather than political. They see around them on
every side, and almost every day, spectacles of confusion and
misery which they cannot reconcile with any conception of
humanity or justice. They see that there are in the modern
state a score of misfortunes that can happen to a man without

his being at fault in any way. They see, on the other hand, the mighty power of science, backed by wealth and power, to introduce order, to provide safeguards, to prevent accidents, or at least mitigate their consequences. They know that this country is the richest in the world; and in my sincere judgment the British democracy will not give their hearts to any party that is not able and willing to set up that larger, fuller, more elaborate, more thorough social organization without which our country and its people will inevitably sink through sorrow to disaster and our name and fame fade upon the pages of history."

In this spirit the Liberal government advocated, shortly after its accession to power in 1906, a series of laws designed to diminish, at least, if not to abolish, the evils of poverty, "sweating," unemployment, and industrial accidents. The provisions of the Workmen's Compensation Act of 1897 were extended to agricultural laborers and domestic servants. Under this law employers in the industries included are required to pay compensation to workmen injured in their employ, except when the accident is due to the "serious and willful misconduct of the injured workman himself." At the same time (1906) a law was passed exempting the funds of trade unions from the liability of being attached for damages caused by their officials in strikes and industrial conflicts generally. Two years later (1908) Parliament passed an act providing that "a workman shall not be below ground in a mine, for the purpose of his work and of going to and from his work, for more than eight hours during any consecutive twenty-four hours."

Going beyond specific legislation, the Liberals included a general "war on poverty" in their official program. As an installment of reform they passed in 1908 an old-age-pension law which granted a small weekly pension to all persons over seventy years of age who had an annual income of less than $150. In vain did Conservatives like Lord Robert Cecil warn the country that war might be ahead and that the fiber of the people might be weakened by such government aid to the poor. In vain did imperialists, like W. M. Fullerton, argue that the money should be spent on more armaments. With the support of the new labor members, the Liberals carried the bill through Parliament.

To help in reducing the large amount of unemployment, Parliament passed an act in 1909 authorizing the establishment of labor exchanges throughout the country charged with the duty of collecting information as to employers requiring working people and as to laborers seeking employment. Provisions were also made authorizing the government to advance loans to laborers to pay their traveling expenses to the places where employment might be found for them by the labor exchanges.

Parliament also sought during the same year to raise the level of wages in some industries which did not pay employees enough to maintain a fairly decent standard of life. A law was enacted providing for the establishment of trade boards in certain of the "sweated" trades, such as tailoring, machine lace-making, and box-making industries, or any other trade which fell below certain standards with respect to wages or conditions of labor. These trade boards consisted of representatives of the working people and of employers and also persons appointed by the government, and were empowered to fix minimum rates of wages for time-work and general minimum rates for piece-work in their respective trades. Agreements for wages lower than those fixed by the board were forbidden, and employers paying less than the minimum were liable to heavy fines.

Meanwhile opposition to these sweeping reforms was becoming intense among the Conservatives. As they were in a minority in the House of Commons, however, they were unable to do more than to protest that the country was going to ruin and that the upper and middle classes would be submerged by the rising power of democracy. In spite of their reduced numbers in the Commons the Conservatives were firmly intrenched in the House of Lords, where they had a large majority, and there they began to take up arms against measures which were, in their opinion, nothing short of revolutionary. In December, 1906, the Lords mutilated a bill which the Commons had passed for the support of a system of national, free, nonreligious schools—similar to those in the United States—and a few days later they threw out a bill abolishing the ancient practice of allowing a man to vote in all counties in which he had the requisite property to entitle him to the ballot.

These adverse actions were followed in 1909 by a clash between the Lords and the Commons over the budget; that is, over the taxes which the Liberals proposed to lay and the expenses they proposed to incur. In April of that year Lloyd George, chancellor of the exchequer in Asquith's government, laid before the House of Commons a scheme of taxation which stirred up a veritable hornets' nest. In this "revolutionary budget" he proposed a high tax on automobiles, a heavy income tax with a special additional tax on incomes over £5000 —heavier on unearned than on earned incomes—and an inheritance tax on a new scale, varying according to the amount of the inheritance up to 15 per cent of estates over £1,000,000. He likewise proposed a new land tax, distinguishing sharply between landowners who actually worked their lands and the owners of mineral lands and city lots who exacted royalties and made large profits from growth in land values. The budget also included a 20 per cent tax on unearned values in land, payable on its sale or transfer, so that anyone who sold property at a profit would have to pay a good share of the gain to the public treasury. The chancellor further suggested a special tax on undeveloped and mineral lands.

These special taxes, in addition to the other taxes, made a heavy budget; but the chancellor defended it on the ground that it was a budget for "waging implacable war against poverty." He concluded his opening speech in defense of his policy by expressing the hope that "great advance will be

made during this generation toward the time when poverty
with its wretchedness and squalor will be as remote from
the people of this country as the wolves which once infested
the forests."

At once the budget was hotly attacked by Conservatives as
socialistic and revolutionary. They claimed that the distinction between "earned" and "unearned" incomes was an un-
warranted and invidious attack on the rights of property. "If
a man," asked one objector, "is to be more heavily taxed on
an income that he has not earned than on an earned income,
on the ground that he does not have the same absolute right
to both incomes, why may not the government advance step
by step until it takes away all unearned incomes on the theory
that their possessors have no right to them at all?" Some of
the more moderate defenders of the budget shrank from an-
swering this question and contented themselves by replying
that it was a matter of degree, not of fundamental principles.
Other supporters of the budget frankly declared that a man's
right to his property depended upon the way in which he got it.

Speaking on this point, Winston Churchill said:

Formerly the question of the taxgatherer was, "How much have
you got?" . . . Now a new question has arisen. We do not only
ask today, "How much have you got?" We also ask, "How did you
get it? Did you earn it by yourself, or has it been left to you by
others? Was it gained by processes which are in themselves beneficial to the community in general, or was it gained by processes
which have done no good to anyone, but only harm? Was it gained
by the enterprise and capacity necessary to found a business or
merely by squeezing and bleeding the owner and founder of the business? Was it gained by supplying the capital which industry needs,
or by denying, except at extortionate price, the land which industry
requires? Was it derived by active reproductive processes, or merely
by squatting on some piece of necessary land till enterprise and
labor, national interests and municipal interests, had to buy you out
at fifty times the agricultural value? Was it gained by opening new
minerals to the service of man, or by drawing a mining royalty from

the toil and adventure of others? . . . How did you get it?" That
is the new question which has been postulated and which is vibrating
in penetrating repetition through the land.

Such arguments prevailed. The budget was passed in 1910
in spite of the opposition of the Lords, but the struggle led a
year later to the enactment of the Lords' Veto Bill, which has
been previously described (p. 69).

As another installment of its "war on poverty," Parliament
enacted in 1911 the National Insurance Act, which went into
effect the next year. One part of this law required the compulsory insurance of nearly all employees (except those not
engaged in manual labor and enjoying an income of more than
£160 a year) against ill health of every kind. Insured persons
themselves, employers, and the government were to make contributions to the fund. Among the benefits for the insured
were medical treatment and attendance, sanatorium treatment
for tuberculosis, payments during sickness, disablement allowances, and the payment of 30 s. to each mother on the birth
of a child.

State Socialism in Germany

Many features of the British program of social legislation
were borrowed from experiments already made by Germany.
As we have pointed out in the first chapter, German economists
did not accept the *laissez faire* doctrines of the English classical economists. On the contrary, as we have seen, many of
the outstanding thinkers in that country were state socialists.
To Schmoller, one of the leaders of this school of thought, state
socialism meant "the establishment of a friendly relationship
among the different social classes, the removal or reduction of
injustice, a nearer approach to fairness in the distribution of
wealth, and social legislation promoting progress and the moral
and material elevation of the lower and middle classes." His
fellow economist, Wagner, held that it was not only unchristian

but inhuman to regard labor merely as a commodity to be bought and sold in the market, and wages as its price.

The practical proposals of the state socialists were exceedingly numerous. They advocated providing steady employment for the working classes, reduction of the hours of labor, improvement of the sanitary and moral conditions in factories, restriction of the labor of women and children, and adequate precautions against accidents and sickness. They proposed to equalize the distribution of wealth by taxing those whose incomes were derived from rents, interest, or speculation, and favored government ownership of railways, canals, and all means of communication and transport, water and gas works, markets, and the business of banking and insurance.

Bismarck himself took a deep interest in the theories of the state socialists, and from 1878 to the close of his administration, he advocated a number of reforms for the benefit of the working people and carried out a few of them. In undertaking these measures he frankly admitted that he was only renewing the old Brandenburg policy of paternal interest in the welfare of the people and in increasing the power and prosperity of the State. He accepted the capitalist system of industry and the division of society into rich and poor as a natural and permanent arrangement, but considered it the duty of the State to better the condition of the working people by special laws, as well as to encourage industry by protective tariffs.

Furthermore, he looked upon certain reforms in favor of the working classes as the best means of undermining the influence of the socialists. His views on this subject are summed up as follows in a speech he delivered in 1884: "Give the working-man the right to work as long as he is healthy, assure him care when he is sick, and maintenance when he is old. Do not fear the sacrifice involved, or cry out at state socialism as soon as the words 'provision for old age' are uttered;—if the State will show a little more Christian solicitude for the working-man, then the socialists will sing their siren song in vain, and the workingmen will cease to throng to their banner as soon as they see that the government and the legislative bodies are earnestly concerned for their welfare."

In 1882 the government introduced two bills providing for accident and sickness insurance, which were given their final form after two years of deliberation and went into effect in 1885. According to the provisions of the first law, employers were obliged to provide a fund to insure their employees against accidents. From this fund the workmen were compensated when partially or totally disabled, and in case of death provision was made for the family of the deceased. The sickness-insurance law compelled workingmen and women to insure themselves against sickness, but helped them to bear the burden by requiring the employer to pay a portion of the premium and to be responsible for carrying out the administrative details of the law.

These measures were supplemented in 1889, after the accession of William II, by an old-age-insurance law which compelled every workman with an income under $500 a year to pay a certain proportion into a state fund which provided an annual pension for him after he had reached the age of seventy years. In case he was incapacitated earlier in life he might begin to draw the pension before he reached that age. As in other forms of workingmen's insurance, the employers paid a portion of the premium, and the State also made a regular contribution to every annuity.

These three measures constituted the main results of Bismarck's policy of aiding the workingman, for notwithstanding an early promise of the emperor, William II, no substantial addition was made to imperial labor legislation after 1889. Moreover, these measures failed, as we have seen, to accomplish the purpose which Bismarck particularly had at heart— that of checking the growth of socialist influence (pp. 107 ff.).

General Progress of Social Legislation
on the Continent

France and Italy lagged behind Germany and England in their social legislation. It was not until 1910 that the former country adopted a system of old-age pensions, based on contributions by employers, employees, and the government, but within two years more than seven million people were registered under the scheme. Italy remained content with a system of voluntary insurance against sickness and old age created under laws passed in 1898 and 1901, guaranteeing state aid and supervision. Although industrial workers, agricultural laborers, clerks, and even small property-owners could take advantage of such mutual-insurance benefits, only a small proportion of them actually did. In spite of their reputation for "radicalism," both countries were far less socialistic than England, Germany, or Austria. "Factory acts and state care of the aged and helpless," says J. H. Clapham, speaking of the year 1914, "were developed further in the United Kingdom than in France; the subordination of individual interests to the collective life of the municipality, further in Germany; urban coöperation further in England, and rural coöperation much further in Denmark. The British death duties and income tax of the twentieth century were more 'socialistic' than any French taxes. With her endless array of small holdings, her little workshops, and her thrifty peasantry and *bourgeoisie*, France was a difficult field for the pure socialist to till. So she became the home of compromise parties—radical socialists, liberal socialists, and the like, who accommodated their doctrines to facts." Indeed it may be said that with respect to factory legislation, even Tsarist Russia was in many ways ahead of both of these Latin countries, partly, no doubt, on account of the necessity of conciliating revolutionary elements in that great despotism.

The movement for state interference on behalf of the working classes was the product of many forces. To a certain extent, perhaps very largely, it resulted from the fear of the middle classes that resistance to it would create a greater danger in the form of powerful socialistic parties bent on still more radical measures. In some cases the landed aristocracy lent its support to get revenge on the mill-owners for legislation adverse to the agricultural interest. To illustrate, the leading exponent of shorter hours for factory workers in England was Lord Ashley, a great landed proprietor, who was taunted by his opponents with being more willing to reduce hours in factories than on farms. No doubt many a landowner saw in the ten-hour bill of 1847 a just retribution for the abolition of the tariff on grain which the industrial classes had brought about the year before. Likewise in Germany the landed classes generally rallied to the support of projects of social legislation.

Among the other forces driving in the same direction must be reckoned the social Catholic movement. It so happened that the factory system got its first start in a Protestant country and revealed certain evil aspects before it spread far in Catholic regions such as South Germany, France, and Italy. Moreover, the Roman Catholic Church had been historically associated with agriculture, and many of its ancient endowments were in land. Naturally it was easier for those whose incomes were not adversely affected by social legislation to support the parties that favored it. Besides this, the Roman Catholic Church continued to cling to the scholastic economy of the Middle Ages, which was essentially ethical in its teachings. In the spirit of that economy, Pope Leo XIII rejected the classical doctrines which saw "in a man nothing but a machine, more or less precious as it is more or less productive."

Shortly after he ascended the papal throne in 1878, Leo issued an encyclical condemning socialism, communism, and nihilism in strong language. Moved by appeals from many Roman Catholics for guidance on questions of capital and labor, Leo in 1891 addressed to the world a general letter on the condition of the working classes. At the very outset he declared "there can be no question whatever that some remedy must be found, and must be found quickly, for the misery and wretchedness pressing so heavily and so unjustly at this moment on the vast majority of the working classes. . . . A small number of very rich men have been able to lay upon the masses of the poor a yoke little better than slavery itself." While condemning socialism and the socialists, the Pope warned the rich not to oppress the poor and recommended charity, mercy, and virtue. He also urged the state to "provide for the welfare and comfort of the working people." Then he added a list of reforms which embraced trade unionism, minimum wages, social insurance against accidents, sickness, and old age, safety and sanitation for industries, arbitration and conciliation in industrial disputes, limitation on hours of labor, prohibition of child labor, and the promotion of small holdings in land to make workingmen independent.

Thus encouraged by papal blessing, Catholics in various countries worked out programs of social reform and induced Catholic political parties to indorse many of their projects. Indeed, this was "good politics," for it attracted votes among working people and weaned some of them away from socialism. The socialists, however, denounced it as "a clerical trick" designed to help the Roman Catholic Church hold its power over the masses.

GROWTH OF PROTECTIVE TARIFFS

While these radical departures were being made from the pure doctrine of *laissez faire* in domestic politics, another aspect of that doctrine, free trade among nations, received also a severe check. Economists of the classical school in England had combined with their demand for the abolition of state interference with hours and conditions of labor a call for the repeal of protective tariffs on grain and other imports. To carry this policy into effect, English manufacturers founded in

1838 the Anti-Corn Law League, and for almost ten years this organization, under the brilliant direction of Cobden and Bright, carried on a thoroughgoing campaign of popular education, expending in one year over a million dollars in publications and meetings. The attack was concentrated on the Corn[1] Laws because it was easier to rouse feeling against the landlords than in favor of any abstract theories of political economy. It was a war on the landed aristocracy; in Cobden's words, "Was there ever an aristocracy so richly endowed? They have the colonies, the army, the navy, and the Church, and yet they condescend to contend for a slice from the poor man's loaf." On the other hand, a member of the aristocracy, Lord Essex, described the free traders as "the most cunning, unscrupulous, knavish, pestilent body of men that have ever plagued this country or any other."

The agitation was brought to a crisis in 1845 by a failure of crops in England and a potato famine in Ireland, which raised the price of foodstuffs enormously and brought thousands to the verge of starvation, especially in Ireland. In the midst of such distress it appeared to thinking men nothing short of criminal to maintain high prices of grain by law. Consequently Sir Robert Peel, then prime minister, determined that the Corn Laws must go, in spite of the fact that he had hitherto defended them, and in 1846 he succeeded in carrying through Parliament a law which led to their practical repeal. Though compelled to resign immediately after the passage of this bill, Peel had given the whole protective system in England its death blow, since it was chiefly the tariff on grain that could claim any really active defenders.

Within ten years all the old navigation laws were abolished and English ports opened freely to the ships of other nations. Gladstone, as chancellor of the exchequer in 1852, removed the duties on one hundred and twenty-three articles entirely, and reduced them on one hundred and thirty-three more. On

---

[1] In England "corn" means grain, especially wheat.

his return to office, some fifteen years later, he made a clean sweep of all *protective* duties, retaining, for revenue purposes, those on tea, wines, tobacco, cocoa, and a few other articles.

From England the agitation in favor of free trade among nations spread to other countries. In the United States the Democratic party declared in favor of tariff for revenue only, —that is, the abandonment of protection for infant industries —and in its revenue revision of 1857 the party went far toward applying the principle in practice. Napoleon III was, with some reservations, a free trader, and tried to put some of his beliefs into effect. By decree he materially reduced the duties on coal, iron, steel, certain raw materials, and foodstuffs, and in 1860 he secretly negotiated a treaty with England providing for a lowering of French tariffs in return for concessions on the part of the English. A similar treaty was made with the German *Zollverein* (see Vol. I, pp. 512, 541), and the French tariff was revised in a free-trade direction. During the early years as chancellor of the German Empire, Bismarck drifted with the new economic current. In 1873 Germany swept away the tariff on iron, shipbuilding materials, and several other articles, and announced that on January 1, 1877, the duties on iron manufactures would be entirely abolished. The world seemed to be on the high road to a realization of Cobden's dream of universal free trade.

But appearances were deceptive. Four years after the Democrats in the United States made their savage slash into protective duties, the Republican party, under Abraham Lincoln, came to power, and during the Civil War that followed it applied a protectionist policy by raising the tariff not once but many times. In the meantime American wheat, corn, and bacon pouring into Europe from the farms of the Great West threatened French and German agriculturists with utter ruin. Although France renewed her low-tariff treaties with England and Germany after the overthrow of Napoleon III, she reverted to a moderate protectionist policy in 1881. Eleven years later France went over completely to high protection, ranking next to Russia and the United States in the level of her rates.

Meanwhile Germany reversed her low-tariff policy and set out on a protectionist course. The successful war with France, the establishment of the empire, and, above all, the payment of the French indemnity created a great "boom" in Germany. New enterprises multiplied; in Prussia alone the number of joint-stock companies increased from 410 in 1870 to 2267 in 1874; wages rose rapidly, and times were "good" until the inevitable reaction due to overspeculation set in. Prices and wages began to fall, companies failed, and factories closed. Manufacturers then commenced to demand that they be protected from foreign competition, and farmers insisted that a duty be placed upon the grain that was being shipped into the country from the United States and Russia. It was urged in Germany that "infant industries" (of which so much was heard in the United States) could not maintain themselves without aid against rival nations, especially England, which were so much better equipped with machinery, experience, and natural resources.

Moved by such arguments, Bismarck, who had formerly seemed to favor free trade, declared in the Reichstag that he was convinced that it could never be universally adopted by the nations of the earth, as some economists hoped. Even England, he argued, could not continue her free-trade policy. "Both France and America have completely forsaken free trade; Austria, instead of reducing her protective duties, has increased them; Russia has done the same. . . . Therefore no one can expect Germany to remain permanently the victim of its sincere belief in the theory of free trade. Hitherto we have thrown our doors wide open to foreign goods and so have made our country the dumping ground for all the overproduction of other countries. . . . Let us close the door and erect the somewhat higher barriers that are proposed, and let us see to it that we secure at any rate the German market for the

German manufacturers." Bismarck had another motive in advocating higher customs duties. He would thereby greatly increase the revenue of the empire, which had hitherto been largely dependent upon the contributions to the imperial treasury made by the individual states.[1]

It was under these circumstances that the imperial chancellor presented to the Reichstag in 1878 a program of tariff revision embodying two main points: (1) protective duties designed to give German industries the advantage over foreign producers; (2) a reduction of duties on raw materials not produced within the empire. In the following year the Reichstag adopted the new tariff laws by a large majority and thus initiated a system under which Germany became one of the greatest manufacturing countries in the world.

This radical change in the economic conditions in the continental countries of Europe and in the United States convinced many Englishmen that some alteration would have to be made in England's free-trade policy. In the election of 1906 Joseph Chamberlain sought to make the establishment of some form of protective tariff the leading campaign issue, and although the free traders carried the day, the arguments of the protectionists were urged with ever greater insistence. Their views were clearly summed up in a political speech made by Lord Salisbury:

We see now, after many years' experience, how foreign nations are raising one after another a wall, a brazen wall, of protection around their shores which excludes us from their markets, and, so far as they are concerned, do their best to kill our trade. And this state of things does not get better. On the contrary, it constantly seems to be worse. . . . We live in an age of a war of tariffs. Every nation is trying how it can, by agreement with its neighbors, get the

---

[1] The wisdom of his policy was amply demonstrated, for the empire thirty years later enjoyed an independent income from customs duties alone amounting to some $300,000,000, while it called on the states for contributions of $70,000,000.

T

greatest possible protection for its own industries and at the same time the greatest possible access to the markets of its neighbors. . . . I want to point out to you that what I observe is that while A is anxious to get a favor of B and B is anxious to get a favor from C, nobody cares two straws about getting the commercial favor of Great Britain.

What is the reason of that? It is that in this great battle Great Britain has deliberately stripped herself of the armor and the weapons by which the battle has to be fought. . . . The weapon with which they all fight is admission to their own markets; that is to say, A says to B, "If you will make your duties such that I can sell in your market, I will make my duties such that you can sell in my market." But we begin by saying, "We will levy no duties on anybody," and we declare that it would be contrary and disloyal to the glorious and sacred doctrine of free trade to levy duty on anybody for the sake of what we can get by it. It may be noble, but it is not business.

In spite of the fact that the issue thus raised continued to be agitated in Parliament and at general elections, the English people clung to the general policy of free trade. Customs duties continued to be laid primarily for revenue purposes and mainly on articles such as sugar, wines, and tobacco, the taxation of which yielded no material protection to British industry. Not until after the World War did Parliament veer slightly from this course by granting certain tariff "preferences" to British overseas possessions and a moderate protection for a limited number of manufactures, known as "key industries," useful in national defense. But England's loyalty to free trade formed the striking exception to the growth of state interference with "the free action" of labor and industry throughout Western civilization. Indeed, by 1914 the phrase "imperial socialism" had come into use to represent the idea of state protection for labor and state assistance for national industry in its quest for world markets. Certainly the "pure principles" of classical economy seemed far from realization as mankind moved into the shadow of the World War.

CHAPTER V

PROGRESS OF IMPERIALISM

New Phases of European Expansion

One of the most astounding characteristics of the world to-day is the control by various European governments of regions and peoples lying far distant from the nations' boundaries and often separated from them by thousands of miles. One well qualified to speak on this point says: "More than half of the world's land surface, and more than a billion human beings, are included in the colonies and 'backward countries' dominated by a few imperialistic nations. Every man, woman, and child in Great Britain has ten colonial subjects, black, brown, and yellow. For every acre in France there are twenty in the French colonies and protectorates. Italy is one sixth as large as her colonies; Portugal, one twenty-third; Belgium, one eightieth. The nations of western Europe are dwarfs beside their colonial possessions."[1]

Imperialism, the name now usually given to over-sea expansion, is a new name for an old thing. It came into general use during the closing years of the nineteenth century, about the time of the war between the United States and Spain. In the English-speaking world it seems to go back to Disraeli, for a London newspaper refers in 1898 to "that odious system of bluster and swagger and might against right on which Lord Beaconsfield and his colleagues bestowed the tawdry nickname of Imperialism." A year later in the same *Daily News* Lord Rosebery defined the word in a different mood. "I mean the greater pride in Empire which is called Imperialism. . . .

[1] Parker T. Moon, *Imperialism and World Politics*, p. 1.

Sane Imperialism, as distinguished from what I may call wild-cat Imperialism, is nothing but this—a larger patriotism." In this volume the words "empire," imperial," "imperialist," and "imperialistic" will be employed in explaining the over-sea expansion of European nations, of the United States and Japan, with no invidious implications. It is a convenient word, and more apt than "colonial," which is not broad enough to fit the case.

Imperialism is, then, the policy of claiming and governing distant regions for the purpose of controlling their products, monopolizing the trade with the natives, and investing surplus capital in the development of natural resources—mines, oil wells, railroads, sugar, rubber, and coffee plantations, and other enterprises. Sometimes this imperialism takes the form of out-right annexation, such as the acquisition of the Philippines by the United States or of Cape Colony by Great Britain. Again it assumes the form of a "protectorate," which is a declaration on the part of a nation to the effect that "this is our particular piece of land; we are not intending to take all the responsibility of governing it just now; but we want other nations to keep out, for we may annex it sooner or later." Sometimes imperialism goes no further than the securing of concessions in undeveloped countries, such as foreigners have obtained in China or citizens of the United States in Mexico; but such concessions are a fruitful source of annexations, espe-cially when the interests of investors are not thoroughly pro-tected by the government that grants them franchises. So one is enabled, by understanding clearly the needs and methods of modern business, to follow intelligently the process by which European powers helped to revolutionize the ancient civiliza-tions of India, China, and Japan, and took possession of the continent of Africa.

The expansion of Europe from the fifteenth to the end of the eighteenth century has been reviewed in the previous volume. We have seen how the Portuguese, Dutch, Spanish,

French, and British extended their possessions beyond the seas and engaged in many conflicts over foreign lands, which resulted in France's practical expulsion from India and America and in Spain's loss of holdings in the Western Hemisphere. Great Britain too had to surrender her thirteen colonies which were to grow into the United States, but retained the vast stretches of Canada. All these changes occurred under what may be called bygone auspices. Ships were small and slow, and on land no means of communication and transportation existed except messengers and pack animals. Not until the end of the eighteenth century did steam-driven machinery suggest the possibility of mass production and huge accumulations of capital which play so decisive a rôle in present imperialistic calculations. It is obvious that, with the ever-increasing mass production and ever-improving means of transportation that went on in the nineteenth century and early twentieth, imperialistic powers could cherish new dreams of conquest. The temptations were greater than ever; the facilities were enhanced beyond belief.

The progress of democracy in no way checked the advance of imperialism; it rather encouraged it. The increasing power of the bourgeoisie at the expense of the landed class in western and central Europe (described in Chapter I) enabled them to influence their respective governments more effectively than ever before in promoting trade and acquiring territory for commercial reasons. By the close of the nineteenth century the various agencies of State—armies, navies, diplomacy, and consular services—were everywhere in the Old World directed openly and belligerently to the promotion of national economic interests on the high seas, in Asia and Africa, and, indeed, all parts of the globe where goods could be bought and sold advantageously. As the middle classes improved their system of production and trade the mass of the people raised their standard of living and developed new wants. The demand for sugar, coffee, cocoa, cotton, rubber, and other commodities which could only, or best, be produced in non-European regions increased from year to year. Spinning machines in Manchester or Mulhouse worked the faster because half-naked savages in tropical countries could be induced to buy cotton loin cloth by the million yards.[1] Sugar and cocoa were made available for the breakfast tables of the multitude because empire-builders were subduing black and yellow men to the routine of furnishing these delicacies from well-regulated plantations. If socialists often assailed imperialists for cruelties practiced on the natives of Africa or Asia, they could not overlook the fact that many commodities which had come to be deemed daily necessities by the masses could be had only as the result of the organization and exploitation of native labor in distant climes.

New Means of Transportation and Intercommunication

Among the forces serving to transform the slow and intermittent processes of imperialism in the eighteenth century into a rapid movement to Europeanize the whole globe was, of course, the invention of previously unheard-of devices for moving men and goods swiftly across sea and land and of establishing throughout a great part of the world well-nigh instantaneous means of communication. It is difficult to credit

[1] In a speech delivered before the Manchester Chamber of Commerce in 1884, H. M. Stanley claimed that if the missionaries could teach the Congo negroes to wear decent cotton clothes, even on Sundays, it would mean 320,000,000 yards of Manchester cotton cloth (cheers from the audience, mainly cotton merchants). When the savages had come to wear clothes on week days, it would mean twenty-six million pounds sterling a year for Manchester business men. The speaker closed his address as follows: "There are forty millions of people beyond the gateway of the Congo, and the cotton-spinners of Manchester are waiting to clothe them. Birmingham foundries are glowing with the red metal that will presently be made into ironwork for them and the trinkets that shall adorn those dusky bosoms, and the ministers of Christ are zealous to bring them, the poor benighted heathen, into the Christian fold."—Quoted by Parker T. Moon, *Imperialism and World Politics*, p. 66

the reports which reach us of the condition of the roads in England even in the eighteenth century. In 1640 it took Queen Henrietta four days to get from Dover to London (78 miles) on the best road in the country. About this period stage wagons were running between London and Liverpool twice a week, taking ten to twelve days—a trip now less than five hours by express train. Stagecoaches were also coming in, and by 1698 promised to run regularly ("if God permits") on three principal roads, making two or three miles an hour. These conveyances were denounced to Parliament as the greatest evil that had happened in the kingdom in late years. "Those who travel in these coaches," it was asserted, "contracted an idle habit of body; became weary and listless when they rode a few miles, and were then unable or unwilling to travel on horseback, and not able to endure frost, snow, or rain, or to lodge in the field." In 1754 a company started a *Flying Coach*, so-called because it was supposed to travel four or five miles an hour. Just as the American Revolution came to an end, John Palmer, a wealthy enthusiast, with the aid of Pitt and against the hot protests of the post-office authorities, managed in 1784 to establish a line of rapid mail coaches leaving London at eight o'clock in the morning and reaching Bristol, a distance of 118 miles, by eleven o'clock in the evening (the journey is now made in less than three hours). This proved the beginning of a great improvement in the transportation of passengers and the mails, which lasted down to the building of railroads.

The discovery that steam engines could be used to propel both ships and carts (cars) made possible the rapid transportation of goods on sea and land. Manufacturers could widen their markets indefinitely, until they compassed the whole globe.

The problem of applying steam to navigation had occupied inventors long before Fulton made his celebrated experiment on the Hudson River in 1807. Toward the close of the seventeenth century it was suggested that a piston engine could be used to drive wheels for the propulsion of vessels, and in 1707 steam was actually applied to propel a small model boat on the Fulda River in Germany. During the eighteenth century a number of inventors in England and America turned their attention to the development of this idea. In 1736 Jonathan Hull took out a patent in England for the application of steam in propelling ships, and some years later two Americans, Fitch and Stevens, made several demonstrations of the practicability of steam navigation.

The honor of making the steamship a success commercially belongs, however, to Robert Fulton. In the spring of 1807 he launched his *Clermont* at New York, and in the summer of that year the "new water monster" made its famous trip to Albany. Transoceanic navigation began in 1819 with the voyage of the steamer *Savannah* from Savannah to St. Petersburg via Great Britain. The trip to Liverpool was made in twenty-five days, sails being used to help the engine.

Within a quarter of a century steamships began to replace the old and uncertain sailing vessels, and at the opening of the twentieth century they composed two thirds of the net tonnage of the world's merchant marine. In 1840 the great Cunard Line inaugurated its transatlantic service, and after that time there was steady development in the number of navigation companies, as well as of steam vessels and their capacity for speed and for carrying freight. The *Great Western*, which startled the world in 1838 by steaming from Bristol to New York in fifteen days and ten hours, was a ship of 1378 tons, 212 feet long, and had an indicated horse power of 1260, with a daily consumption of 36 tons of coal. By the time the World War opened, the *Vaterland* (now the *Leviathan*, and under the American flag) overtopped all predecessors with its tonnage of nearly 60,000 and its great length of 950 feet.

So highly developed were the marine engines at the end of the nineteenth century that "a small cake of coal which would pass through a ring the size of a shilling, when burned in the compound engine of a modern steamboat, would drive a ton of food and its proportion of the ship two miles on its way from a foreign port." According to another calculation, half a sheet of note paper will develop sufficient power, when burned in connection with a triple-expansion engine, to carry a ton a mile in an Atlantic steamer. So it came about that the cost of carrying a year's supply of breadstuff for an English workingman's family from Minneapolis to Liverpool was less than his average wage for one day. The turbine engine, in which the power of the steam is more advantageously applied than in the older piston engine, was introduced in the newer ships, such as the huge *Mauretania*. This was soon followed by the wide use of the Diesel internal-combustion engine for navigation, on account of its marvelous economy in space and in cost of operation.

Thus it became possible to make the journey from Southampton to New York, 3000 miles, in six days or less, with almost the regularity of an express train. Japan could be reached from Seattle in ten days and from San Francisco, via Honolulu, a distance of 5500 miles, in less than seventeen days. A commercial map of the world shows that the globe is now crossed in every direction by definite lanes which are followed by innumerable freight and passenger steamers plying regularly from one port to another.

The East and the West were brought much nearer together by the piercing of the Isthmus of Suez, which formerly barred the way from the Mediterranean Sea to the Indian Ocean. In ancient times a canal connected the easternmost mouth of the Nile with the Red Sea; but it had been permitted to fill up with sand, so that when General Bonaparte was ordered by the French Directory to consider its reconstruction his engineers found few traces of it. The advantages of a canal had long been fully realized before the great French engineer, Ferdinand de Lesseps, gained permission from the ruler of Egypt to organize a company to undertake the work. The line of the ancient canal was abandoned, and a great trench was dug connecting the lakes between Port Said, on the Mediterranean, and Suez, a hundred miles to the south, on the Red Sea. After ten years' work the canal was opened to traffic in November, 1869.

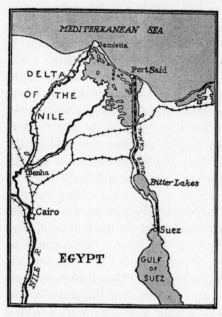

THE SUEZ CANAL

In 1884 a new international commission of engineers was appointed, which decided to enlarge the canal so as to enable steamers of greater size to pass through it. As a result it was soon used by an ever-increasing number of vessels; in 1913 over five thousand availed themselves of it, thus avoiding the detour of thousands of miles involved in rounding the Cape of Good Hope. An agreement among all the leading European powers provided that the canal was to be open at all times for warships as well as merchantmen, but that no act of war was to be permitted in its neighborhood.[1]

The Isthmus of Panama next suggested the possibility of greatly reducing the journey from the Atlantic to the Pacific Ocean. This was for years the object of discussion and negotiations. In 1872 President Grant appointed a commission to consider the construction of a canal; but nothing was done

[1] For financial complications which led the British to assume control of Egypt, see pages 171 ff.

until 1881, when De Lesseps, encouraged by the flattering success of his first venture, succeeded in organizing the Panama Canal Company in France, and work was actually begun. But the efforts to obtain the necessary funds for completing the costly enterprise led to widespread bribery of members of the French parliament, which was disclosed in 1892. This scandal was followed by the dissolution of the French company. In 1902 the Congress of the United States authorized the President to purchase for $40,000,000 the property in which the French investors had sunk so much money. Arrangements with the republic of Colombia for the construction of the canal by the United States having come to naught, the state of Panama, through which the line of the proposed canal passed, seceded from Colombia in 1903, and its independence was immediately recognized by President Roosevelt. A treaty in regard to the canal zone was then duly concluded with the new republic, and after some delays the work of the French company was resumed by the United States. In the summer of 1914 the canal was opened to the commerce of the world (see page 236).

While on the sea the steamship was taking the place of the schooner and clipper for the rapid trade, on land merchandise which used to be dragged by horses or oxen or carried in slow canal boats was being transported in long trains of capacious cars, each holding as much as twenty or thirty large wagonloads. The story of the locomotive, like that of the spinning machine or the steam engine, is the history of many experiments and of their final combination by a successful inventor. Wooden tracks had been extensively used in the eighteenth century for horse-car lines, and in 1801 Parliament authorized the construction of such a railway from Wandsworth to Croydon, a distance of nine miles. Many years before, a French inventor had demonstrated the possibility of using steam for locomotion by constructing a road wagon driven by a small engine. Other inventors were at work on the problem and thus smoothed the way for the triumph of George Stephenson (1781–1848), who reaped most of the honors.

This distinguished inventor, the son of a poor English miner, although deprived through poverty of a school education, taught himself how to read and write. He began work at the mines early in life; and being impressed with the difficulties of hauling the heavy wagons of coal and iron ore, he determined to apply to this purpose the steam engine which Watt had brought to such a degree of perfection. In 1814 he built a small locomotive, called *My Lord*, which was used at the mines; and in 1825, with the authorization of Parliament, he opened between Stockton and Darlington, in the northern part of England, a line for the conveyance of passengers and freight. About this time a road was being projected between Liverpool and Manchester, and in a competition, in which five locomotives were entered, Stephenson's *Rocket* was chosen for the new railroad, which was formally opened in 1830. This famous engine weighed about seven tons and ran at an average speed of thirteen miles an hour—a small affair when compared with the giant locomotive of our day weighing a hundred tons and running fifty miles an hour.[1] Within fifteen years trains were running regularly between Liverpool, Manchester, Birmingham, and London, and at the close of the century the United Kingdom had nearly twenty-two thousand miles of railway, carrying over a billion passengers annually.

The first railway in Germany was opened in 1835, but the development of the system was greatly hindered by the territorial divisions which then existed. It was in the great state of Prussia that construction went on most rapidly, largely under government ownership and control. Some of the lines were built directly by the government, and others were later purchased by it. This policy was continued, and in 1913 by

---

[1] It will be noted that this is the *average* speed on regular runs. For short distances the *Rocket* made thirty-five miles an hour, while the modern locomotive, as is well known, sometimes runs over a hundred miles an hour.

far the greater part of the German railways was owned by the imperial government or by state governments, only about three thousand miles out of thirty-eight thousand being in private hands. In Austria-Hungary also the majority of the lines were owned or operated by the government.

The first railway in France was built in 1828, but, owing to the timidity of investors, the development was slow. Five years later the government took up the project of connecting Paris and the principal cities by railway lines, and after prolonged debates it guaranteed in 1840 the interest on the investment required in the construction of a line from the capital to Orleans. Two years later the government agreed to furnish about one half of the capital necessary to build a vast railway system throughout France, leaving the work of construction and operation largely in the hands of private companies. As a result of this intervention on the part of the state, three types of railways grew up in France: those largely financed by the government but operated by private companies; those entirely private; and those owned and operated by the state. When Louis Philippe ascended the throne of France in 1830, there were only thirty miles of railway in the country; in 1860 there were four thousand miles; and when the World War came, over twenty-five thousand miles. Of the total mileage only about one twelfth belonged to the government, but according to the terms of the franchises the other French railways will eventually revert to the state (1950–1960).

By the opening of the twentieth century all Europe was bound together by a network of over two hundred thousand miles of railways, the United States was welded into a nation by more than two hundred thousand miles of track, and railway construction was rapidly advancing in Africa and Asia, furnishing cheap transportation for the products of Western mills and mines. By 1900 the Trans-Siberian road connected Europe overland with the Pacific (see page 161), and Russia had pushed lines southward to Persia and Afghanistan. Be-

fore the World War opened, British India had approximately
thirty-five thousand miles, and China about six thousand miles
of railways. Even Africa had fifteen thousand miles, most of
which was in Egypt, Algeria, Tunis, and the British possessions. Construction had already begun on a line from Cairo
to the Cape, and enthusiasts promised that trains would soon
be running through jungle lands which were first penetrated
by the white man in Queen Victoria's reign.[1]

Quite as essential to the world market as steamship and railway lines were the easy and inexpensive means of communication afforded by the post, telephone, telegraph, and cable. The
"penny post" is now so commonplace as no longer to excite
wonder, but to men of Frederick the Great's time it would have
seemed impossible. Until 1839 in England the postage on an
ordinary letter was a shilling for a short distance. In that year
a reform measure long advocated by Rowland Hill was carried,
establishing a uniform penny post throughout Great Britain.

The result of reducing the rate of postage for letters to this
nominal sum exceeded all expectations in vastly increasing the
frequency with which people wrote to one another. Other
European countries followed the example of Great Britain in
reducing postage, and international postal agreements made it
possible to send mail at a nominal cost for thousands of miles,
across the boundaries of many countries. At the opening of
the twentieth century a letter could be carried from Basuto-
land in South Africa to Montreal, Canada, for two cents, in
less time than it took news to cross the Atlantic when Queen
Victoria came to the throne.

No less wonderful was the development of the telegraph—
partly the work of an American inventor, Samuel Morse, who
made his first important test in 1844. Within little more than
fifty years Great Britain had over fifty thousand miles of line
owned and operated by the government, transmitting nearly
ninety million messages annually; France had about one hun-

[1] This railroad has not yet been completed.

dred thousand miles of line, over which fifty million messages annually passed; and Russia had twice the French mileage of wire, carrying twice the annual number of messages. Moreover, distant and obscure places in Africa and Asia were being brought into touch with one another and with Europe. China had fifteen thousand miles, connecting all the important cities of the empire and affording direct overland communication between Peking and Paris. The network was spreading into Africa—the French, German, and British possessions being already well equipped. After a preliminary experiment, regular cable communication between England and America was opened in 1866, and this achievement was quickly followed by the construction of a system of cables putting the whole world into instant communication. In October, 1907, Marconi established regular communication across the Atlantic by means of the wireless system of telegraphy discovered some years before.

The enterprises made possible by these bewildering inventions yielded enormous profits, thus accumulating capital for which, as in the case of commodities, markets were sought abroad. Loans were made to countries economically backward. Joint-stock companies were formed to develop railways and mines in regions remote from Europe. At the opening of the twentieth century Great Britain was said to have had approximately ten billion dollars invested in over-sea undertakings; one fifth of the industrial enterprises in Russia were financed by foreigners, especially French investors; and most of the railways in China were built by European capitalists. The German financiers supplied money for great banking houses in Brazil, Argentina, and Chile, which, in turn, stimulated the construction of factories and railways.

Even political events which seemed to have a purely local bearing often contributed to the drive which carried European enterprise and dominion beyond the seas. Defeats and checks at home might be offset by "compensations" abroad. Thus, for example, France, beaten by Germany in 1870 and stripped of two valuable provinces, turned to Africa and Asia for outlets for economic and military activities, and was encouraged in this by Bismarck, who hoped in this way to aid the French to forget their disaster. Very soon the forces created in Germany by unification and industrialization transformed that country into an imperial power seeking markets and territories abroad. Likewise the unification of Italy was followed by Italian colonizing undertakings in Africa and the eastern Mediterranean. Evidently, therefore, imperialism was not a minor and incidental phase of European development, but a fundamental part of it, growing out of the internal necessities of Europe, together with national ambitions.

If we look carefully into the history of imperialism we find, therefore, that it has passed through several stages. In the beginning it was essentially commercial, or "mercantile" (Vol. I, p. 269), growing out of efforts to discover gold, silver, and spices, to capture slaves, and later to purchase the commodities of distant lands and to exchange European goods for them. With the great upswing of European machine industries, imperialism became industrial in character; that is, it was primarily connected with finding new outlets for enormous production and procuring raw materials for expanding factories. Vast accumulations of capital from these industries then produced another phase of imperialism: to the older struggle for commerce and markets was added a rivalry for opportunities to invest surplus profits in backward places of the earth. By the side of merchants and mill-owners were now found bankers pooling huge sums of money and making loans to governments and corporations, native and foreign, operating in undeveloped countries. As the demand for oil, rubber, and other materials mounted, imperialism took on a decided "raw-material" aspect —the quest for substances essential to manufacturing.

Finally, it should be noted that there is a political phase of imperialism. It is true that governments were often forced to engage in imperialistic undertakings by the demands of their respective citizens interested in such enterprises. It often happened, however, that statesmen and diplomats, eager to add to their power and laurels, anxious to increase what they called the "prestige" of their countries on the world stage, frequently urged business men to go into foreign trade and investments and offered them political backing for their undertakings. Thus powerful economic and political forces were enlisted on the side of European expansion.

MISSIONARY ACTIVITIES AND IMPERIALISM

In enumerating the forces which made for European expansion, the enterprise of Christian missionaries must be included. Indeed, the way for imperialism was often explored and made smooth by preachers of the Word ardently following the command "Go ye into all the world and preach the Gospel to every creature" (Mark xvi, 15). As soon as America was discovered and the sea route opened to the Far East, friars braved every danger to carry the Christian religion to them that sat in darkness. The Franciscans and Dominicans, active in such work, were reënforced about 1540 by the powerful Jesuit order. Francis Xavier began his famous missionary career in 1542, first visiting India and then Japan, and dying within sight of the shores of China, yearning to penetrate that mysterious land. The activities of his fellow Jesuits in Canada and the Mississippi Valley and in South America have been mentioned earlier.[1]

In 1622 the great missionary board of the Roman Catholic Church was given its final organization and the name it still retains, *Congregatio de Propaganda Fide*, with its headquarters in Rome. In its colleges and schools missionaries are trained for their work and taught the requisite languages. Its

[1] See Vol. I, pp. 193, 199. For the activities of the Jesuits in China and Japan, see pages 257 ff.

T

printing office issues the necessary books and tracts. Of the various Catholic associations which have been created to assist in its work, the most important is the Society for the Propagation of the Faith, which, since its formation at Lyon in 1822, has contributed millions of dollars to the cause. The Roman Catholic Church now reckons several million adherents in Turkey, Persia, Arabia, India, Siam, Indo-China, Malaysia, China, Korea (Chosen), Japan, Africa, and Polynesia.

For a long time after the Protestant revolt the reformed churches showed little ardor in foreign missions, although as early as 1556 Calvin's city of Geneva sent men to preach the Gospel in Brazil. The Dutch undertook to Christianize the East Indies in 1602, and their rivals, the English, also did something to promote missions. Among the earliest Protestant missionary associations was the Society for the Promotion of Christian Knowledge, founded in 1695 and conducted under the auspices of the Church of England. In the eighteenth century the Moravians and Methodists took up the work of converting the heathen, and in 1792 William Carey, a cobbler and Baptist minister, formed the Baptist Missionary Union.

The United States entered the field in 1814, when the American Board of Foreign Missions was organized. As time went on, practically all the Protestant denominations established each its board of foreign missions; and the United States rivaled Europe in the enthusiasm and energy of the missionaries it sent out, and in the generous support its people gave them. About the middle of the nineteenth century the various boards began to hold conferences with the object of rendering their work more efficient by coöperation and by dividing up the fields among themselves. Bible societies engaged in translating the Scriptures into every known language and scattering copies of it broadcast. It was estimated that in 1905 Protestants contributed about twenty million dollars a year to foreign missions. This sum served to support some fourteen or fifteen thousand missionaries.

Missionaries were usually the first to bring regions remote from Europe into contact with Western civilization. They not only spread a knowledge of the Christian religion and its standards of morality but also carried with them modern scientific ideas and modern inventions. They reduced to writing the languages of peoples previously ignorant of the existence of an alphabet. They conquered cruel superstitions, discouraged human sacrifices and cannibalism, and did much to make the lot of woman more tolerable. Their physicians introduced Western methods of treating the sick, and their schools gave an education to millions who without them would have been left in complete barbarism. Finally, they encouraged thousands of Japanese, Chinese, and representatives of other peoples to visit Europe and America, and thus prepare themselves to become apostles of Western ideas among their fellows. The explorations and investigations carried on by the missionaries served vastly to increase European knowledge of the world and its inhabitants. Their maps and their scientific reports on languages and customs in many instances proved of the highest value. They also created a demand for Western commodities and opened the way for trade.

In some instances the missionaries doubtless showed too little appreciation of the ancient culture of India, China, and Japan (see page 258). They often rudely denounced the cherished traditions and the rooted prejudices of the peoples to whom they came. Even the most prudent and sagacious among them could hardly avoid arousing the hostility of those whose most reverenced institutions they felt it their duty to attack.[1] So it came about that the missionaries were often badly treated, underwent great hardships, and were occasionally murdered by infuriated mobs. This sometimes led to armed interference on

[1] Some anthropologists discover what they believe to be evils in the interference of the missionaries with native habits, especially in the insistence on clothes in hot climates and the introduction of European notions of marriage. See, for example, Pitt Rivers's *Clash of Culture*.

the part of their respective governments, and more than once, as we shall see, served as an excuse for annexations and the formation of protectorates and spheres of influence.

We have now recalled some of the chief incentives and methods of the new imperialism. We must next describe its progress, at least in outline. It is a difficult problem for historical writers to arrange the varied history of the European countries themselves in a coherent and effective form. The task grows even more perplexing when it comes to dealing with the ever more complicated relations of European governments to the rest of the world. As has been said, Western civilization, chiefly through imperialistic ambitions, has reached the uttermost parts of the earth, and tends to alter the conditions of its peoples and bring them within the sphere of a single all-pervading cosmopolitan civilization, such as has never before been known in the story of mankind. The New World was largely peopled from Europe, and the ancient modes of life of its inhabitants profoundly modified. Into such crowded countries as India, Japan, and China, each with its special culture, came the Europeans to upset customs and beliefs of long standing and arouse new types of conflict and new emulations. As for Africa, only its outskirts were known to Europeans until the end of the nineteenth century. Its interior was inaccessible and inhabited by scattered tribes of savages or barbarians.

From this point onward the development of Europe will become the development of the world, for such has been the course of history. It is impossible to disentangle imperialism from the spread of European inventions, business and military methods, political ideals, and scientific knowledge and research. To this dissemination the European countries have made their contributions commonly by violence, sometimes by peaceful penetration, each according to special circumstances. The order of presentation here adopted after careful reflection sets aside a special chapter (the following) to trace the growth of the greatest of all imperial enterprises—the British Empire. The relations of the Old World to the New, of which something was said in the first volume, will be reviewed. Finally, before moving on to the World War, the transformation of the Far Eastern countries under the impact of aggressive Western nations will be briefly considered. The remainder of this chapter will be devoted to the expansion of France, Germany, Italy, and Russia and to the opening up of Africa.

EXPANSION OF FRANCE

Leadership in the newer imperialism on the continent of Europe fell to France, which for three hundred years had been engaged in rivalry with Great Britain. While solving grave problems at home, the Third Republic pushed forward its commercial, exploring, and military enterprises until it built up a colonial dominion vaster than that lost during the eighteenth century in the conflicts with England, though less valuable and less inviting to French emigrants. When the Third Republic was established, French colonial possessions consisted of Algeria in northern Africa, the Senegal region on the west coast of Africa, some minor posts scattered along the Gulf of Guinea down to the Congo River, a foothold in Cochin China, and a number of small islands in various parts of the world. The basis of territorial expansion had thus been laid; and after the quick recovery which followed the reverses of the Franco-Prussian War, the French government frankly committed itself to a policy of imperialism.

While the National Assembly was deliberating on the form of government at home (pp. 40 ff.), a revolt in Algeria forced France to formulate a colonial policy. That province had been seized in 1830 on account of the refusal of the native ruler to give satisfaction for having slapped the French consul-general in the face at a public reception. After the defeat of France by Germany in 1870, the Algerians rose in a serious insurrection that was not put down until more than two hundred battles and skirmishes had been fought. The last of the important rebellious chieftains was subdued in 1874.

The great province of Algeria thus acquired is only slightly smaller than France itself and has a population of over six million, of whom only about eight hundred thousand are of European origin.[1] It is divided into three departments, each sending one senator and two deputies to Paris. It has a railway system of nearly three thousand miles, and a large number of institutions for primary, secondary, and higher education; and it carries on a lively traffic, especially in grain, wine, olives, and metals. Nevertheless, the receipts derived from taxes and other sources of revenue do not meet the cost of maintaining the civil and military government.

To the east of Algeria lies the province of Tunis, equaling in area the state of New York and having a population akin to that of Algeria in race and religion. For a long time after the conquest of Algeria, France maintained friendly relations with the ruling bey of Tunis and secured from him important concessions for building railways, telegraph lines, and other public works. A pretext for a further advance was finally found: Tunisian tribes were accused of disturbing the peace of the Algerian border, and it was rumored that Italy was contemplating the annexation of the region. In 1881, therefore, France dispatched troops into Tunis, and after some serious fighting occupied the province. The bey was forced to sign a treaty binding himself to conduct his government according to the wishes of the French, and thus he virtually surrendered the administration of his possessions to French officials.

While these enterprises were bringing northern Africa under French dominion, a series of daring explorations and conquests in western and central Africa were adding vast regions and millions of African natives to the French colonial domain.

[1] The French also mapped out and occupied a huge desert region to the south, which is now united with Algeria.

France had taken formal possession of the province of Senegal, on the west coast, as early as 1637, but no serious efforts to extend her control inland were made until the annexation of Algeria called attention to the possibility of joining the two provinces. The Senegal River afforded special opportunities for advancing inland, and by 1865 one of the most distinguished of the French governors and explorers was able to announce that all the upper Senegal region had been occupied. The steady pressure inland still continued, however, and Timbuktu was conquered in 1894.

Four years later Marchand, a French explorer, pressed eastward across the desert and reached the Nile region, where he raised the French flag at Fashoda, over lands claimed by the English. An English force, however, compelled Marchand to lower the flag, and for a time it looked as if the two countries might come to blows. After some parleying, however, the French withdrew, and the two nations arranged the disputed boundaries between them, thus closing the "Fashoda incident," as it was called.

A post on the equator at the mouth of the Gabon River, bought in 1839, became the base for celebrated expeditions headed by Du Chaillu and De Brazza, which added a vast region north of the Congo River more than twice the size of France, and now known as French Congo.[1]

While the French explorers were pushing their way through the jungles of the Senegal and Congo regions or braving the sand storms of the Sahara,[2] French missionaries and commercial agents were preparing the way for the annexation of the

[1] In addition to their larger African dependencies the French in 1914 controlled Guinea, the south of Senegal, the Ivory Coast, and the native kingdom of Dahomey. For mandated territories acquired from Germany, see page 505.

[2] In the contest for the east coast of Africa the French took little part. In 1862 they purchased from a native chief the post of Obok, but it was not actually occupied until 1884. After that time, however, slight additions of land were made, and the post grew into French Somaliland, a province of about twelve thousand square miles.

island of Madagascar. That island, larger in area than all France and rich in agricultural, textile, and mineral products, had been the object of attention on the part of France since the age of Louis XIV. Using as a pretext the murder of some French citizens by the natives, the French waged war on the ruler of Madagascar (1883–1885), and succeeded in establishing a protectorate over the entire island. Later they accused Queen Ranavalona III of bad faith and of inability to suppress brigandage. A second war, which broke out in 1895, ended in the deposition and expulsion of the queen.

In addition, the Third Republic held extensive colonial dominions in Asia, where French missionaries and traders had been attracted under Colbert's administration in the age of Louis XIV. Though still retaining the five towns which remained to them in India after the close of the disastrous Seven Years' War, France was precluded from further gains in the peninsula of Hindustan by the success of the English. As the Dutch remained powerful in the islands to the east, the most promising field for the French lay in the crumbling empire of China. The vast peninsula washed on the west by the Gulf of Siam and on the east by the China Sea was occupied in part by kingdoms and provinces over which the emperor of China exercised a vague sort of suzerainty. On the eve of the Revolution, French missionaries had found an excellent opportunity to extend their influence in Anam by persuading Louis XVI to intervene in a dispute over the succession to the throne, and certain lands were received as a reward from the successful contestant for the crown.

Interest in the province of Anam was renewed about 1850, when some French missionaries were murdered there. Napoleon III waged war on the king in 1857, forcing from him the payment of an indemnity and the cession of a small portion of his territory. The foothold thus obtained formed the basis for rapid expansion in every direction; a protectorate was extended over the kingdom of Cambodia in 1864; and in 1867

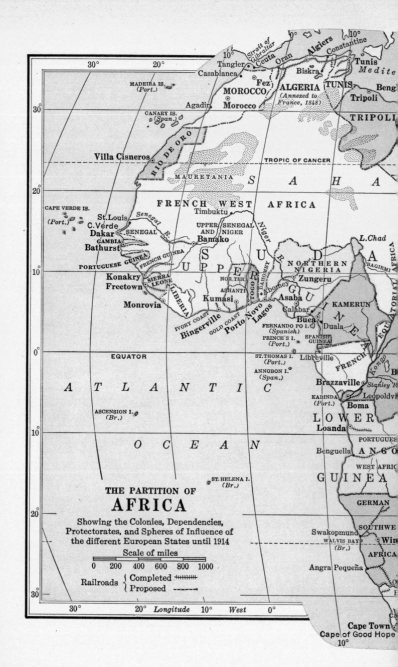

THE PARTITION OF
AFRICA

Showing the Colonies, Dependencies,
Protectorates, and Spheres of Influence of
the different European States until 1914
Scale of miles

0   200   400   600   800   1000

Railroads { Completed ┼┼┼┼┼┼
Proposed --------

30°   20° *Longitude*   10°   *West*   0°

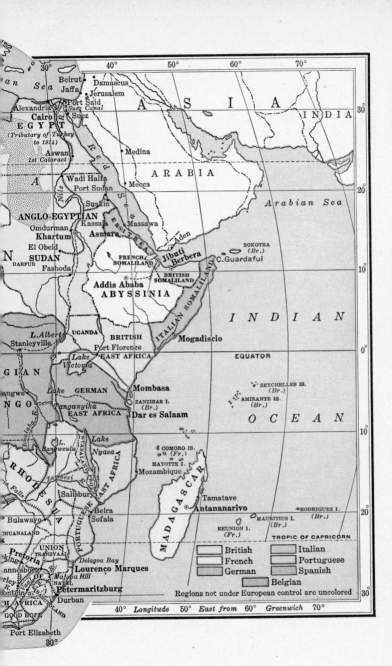

Cochin China was entirely annexed. An attempt in 1873 to force the opening of the Red River in Tongking to navigation led to a war with the ruler of that province and resulted in the extension of a protectorate over all of Anam, of which Tongking was a district. This defiance of the Chinese emperor's claims at length stirred him to resistance; but the war of 1884, which ensued, cost him all his rights over Tongking and the remainder of Anam. In 1893 France extended her authority over the territory of Laos, to the south.

French possessions were thus brought into close contact with the provinces of southern China, into which French influence penetrated in the form of railways and mining concessions. France therefore became deeply involved in the rivalry of the powers of the world in the Far East, among which the United States had to be reckoned after its annexation of the Philippine Islands, lying just eastward from the coast of French Indo-China.

Expansion of Germany and Italy

If unification contributed to the rise of an imperialist movement in Germany, this was no part of Bismarck's original design. An agriculturist in his sympathies, he lent little countenance at first to projects for acquiring foreign dominions. His motto was not "More land" but "More safety" for Germany. When an African question was once raised with him, he replied: "The risk is too great for me. Your map of Africa is a very fine one, but my map of Africa lies in Europe. There is Russia; on the other side is France; we are in the middle. That is my map of Africa." Furthermore, Bismarck was fearful of producing a dangerous rivalry with England; in fact, he sought an alliance, not competition, with that great colonizing and imperial power.

But the "iron chancellor," although he could direct armies, was not a master of the economic forces that were revolutionizing Germany under his very nose. German citizens were not content to sit idly by and watch other manufacturers and traders, aided by their governments, snatch the distant territories which had so far escaped European control. So in 1878 an African Society was established for the purpose of carrying on explorations and educating public opinion in favor of colonial expansion. Numerous trading posts were built, especially along the western coast of Africa, and the agents at these centers began to urge the government not only to protect them but also to secure a firmer control over the natives and their trade by the seizure of territory. In spite of many misgivings about the ultimate value of distant colonies peopled by barbarous races, Bismarck was induced to take steps toward the acquisition of territory in Africa.

He sent out Dr. Gustav Nachtigal in 1884 for the purpose of establishing German control at certain points along the western coast of Africa. The English Foreign Office was notified that this enterprise was designed merely to gather information for the German government on the state of commerce. Before the English government was aware of the real character of the expedition, the German agent had induced native chiefs to acknowledge a German protectorate over two large provinces, Togoland, in Upper Guinea, a region about the size of the state of Indiana, and Cameroons, adjoining the French Congo—in all an area of over two hundred thousand square miles.

In the same year F. A. Lüderitz, a Bremen merchant, acting under orders from Bismarck, raised the German flag at Angra Pequena (a point on the west coast a short distance above the English possessions at the Cape), where German merchants and traders had been active for some time. This region had long been coveted by the Cape colonists, but the delay of the English government in taking action allowed it to fall into the hands of the Germans. By subsequent agreements with Portugal and England, who controlled the adjacent regions, the German government carved out a block of territory estimated at over three hundred and twenty thousand square miles, an area far greater than all the rest of the German Empire put together. This colony bore the name of "German Southwest Africa," but its entire European population in 1910 was only about twelve thousand, approximately five sixths German.

Even larger territories were secured by Germany in East Africa. In 1884 the Society for German Colonization sent Dr. Karl Peters to discover what could be done in that region. The sultan of Zanzibar was induced in 1888 to lease a narrow strip of territory over six hundred miles long to the Germans, and in two years transferred all his rights to the German Empire for a million dollars. A few German settlers then established plantations of coco palms, coffee, vanilla, tobacco, rubber, sugar, tea, etc., and the government founded several experiment stations for determining the possibilities of profitable agriculture. Railways were begun, and telegraphic communication established.

At the same period German agents found their way into the Pacific and occupied a region in New Guinea, to which the name of "Kaiser Wilhelm's Land" was given. The Caroline Islands (except Guam, which belongs to the United States) and a part of the Solomon group were also acquired. In the partition of the Samoa Islands in 1899 Germany received the major part.

Like united Germany, united Italy was not long in conceiving imperial ambitions. Recalling the days when their Roman ancestors had conquered Carthage, the Italians attempted to obtain control in Tunis by winning special concessions from the bey; but their efforts were frustrated by the French, who had, as we have seen, occupied the province and established a protectorate over it. Fortified in 1882 by the Triple Alliance with Germany and Austria-Hungary, the Italians continued their imperial policy, turning their attention now to Abyssinia, near the outlet of the Red Sea. An army of occupation was dispatched thither in 1887, and after some fifteen years of intermittent warfare, treaties, negotiations, and massacres of their troops by the natives, the Italians were able to make themselves masters of an area about twice the size of the state of Pennsylvania, inhabited by half a million of nomad peoples. The new colony received the name of "Eritrea." The coast region south from Cape Guardafui to British East Africa and the equator was also made an Italian protectorate, known as Italian Somaliland. This has now an area of about two hundred thousand square miles and a population, almost entirely native, of nine hundred thousand, including approximately one thousand Italians. Neither of these colonial enterprises proved profitable to Italy. It cost much to secure them, and, owing to the tropical climate, only a few thousand Italians, including the army of occupation, settled there.

Reinsured by the third renewal of the Triple Alliance, made in 1902, in which Germany was compelled to promise support for Italian ambitions in northern Africa even at the expense of a war with France, Italy finally succeeded in getting possession of Libya, containing the two districts of Tripolitania and Cyrenaica. The occasion of this achievement was a quarrel with Turkey, which led to a war in 1911. Since the early part of the eighteenth century Tripoli had been under Turkish dominion, although the Arab population managed to maintain a large measure of actual independence. Without much difficulty the Bank of Rome, which handled the funds of the Holy See, and the Bank of Italy, with government support, entered into connections with local chiefs for the purpose of developing industries in Tripoli; but for various reasons, including interference on the part of Turkish officials, the enterprises lost money.

This was the state of affairs in 1911, when the Italian government took advantage of the dispute with Turkey to combine an imperial undertaking with the rescue of the two banks. At the end of the war with Turkey (see pages 306 f.) in 1912,

Italy annexed the whole region lying between Algeria and Tunisia on the west and Egypt on the east. The Bank of Rome recouped some of its earlier losses by a contract to finance the expeditionary forces, and the Bank of Italy recovered ground in other directions. By this same operation against Turkey, Italy got possession of several islands in the eastern Mediterranean, including the Dodecanese group, with the understanding that all except Rhodes were to be handed over to Greece.

In striking contrast to the other powers of western and central Europe—Great Britain, France, Germany, and Italy—stands Spain, who could once boast that the sun never set on her empire. After losing her colonies on the American continents, she made no compensating gains in other parts of the world, and at the close of the nineteenth century received the final blow in a war with the United States.

The cause of this war was the chronic disturbance which existed in Cuba under Spanish government and which led the United States to decide upon the expulsion of Spain from the Western Hemisphere. In 1895 the last of many Cuban insurrections against Spanish authority broke out, and sympathy was immediately manifested in the United States. Both political parties during the presidential campaign of 1896 declared in favor of the Cubans, and after the inauguration of McKinley a policy of intervention was adopted. The American government demanded the recall of General Weyler—whose cruelty had become notorious—and a reform in the treatment of prisoners of war. In February, 1898, the battleship *Maine* was mysteriously blown up in the harbor of Havana, where it had been sent to protect American interests. Although the cause of this disaster could not be discovered, the United States, maintaining that the conditions in Cuba were intolerable, declared war on Spain in April.

The war was brief, for the American forces were everywhere victorious. Cuba and Porto Rico were lost to Spain, and by the capture of the city of Manila in May the Philippine

Islands also fell to the United States. Peace was reëstablished in August, and representatives were shortly sent to Paris to arrange the final terms. Cuba was declared independent; Porto Rico, with the adjoining islands of Vieques and Culebra, and the Philippines were ceded to the United States. The following year the Caroline and Pelew islands were transferred to Germany, and thus the territory of Spain was reduced to the Spanish peninsula, the Balearic and Canary islands, and her small holdings in Africa.

RUSSIAN EXPANSION

During these years of imperial operations on the part of Western powers, Russia was pushing out to the east and south, offering as one of her excuses the necessity for an outlet to an ice-free port. In the second half of the nineteenth century the expansion of Russia in a southerly direction was very rapid. In 1846 her southern boundary ran along the lower edge of the Aral Sea. In 1863 Russia, asserting that the Turkestan tribesmen pillaged caravans and harried her frontiers, sent forces which captured the cities of Turkestan, Chimkent, and Tashkent, and two years later organized the region into the new province of Russian Turkestan. Shortly afterward the ameer of Bokhara declared war on the Tsar, only to have the Russians occupy the ancient city of Samarkand (where Alexander the Great had halted on his eastward march) and later establish a protectorate over Bokhara, which brought them to the borders of Afghanistan. In 1872 the khan of Khiva was reduced to vassalage. During the following years (1873–1886) the regions to the south, about Merv, down to the borders of Persia and Afghanistan, were gradually annexed. In 1876 the province of Khokand, on the boundary of the Chinese Empire, was seized and transformed into the province of Ferghana. By securing railway concessions and making loans to the Shah, the Russians became powerful in Persia, and thus all along their southeastern frontiers they were struggling for predominance against British influence—at least until 1907, when the two countries, by treaty, delimited their respective "spheres."

Closely connected with this rapid expansion was the construction of great railway lines built largely by the government with money borrowed from capitalists in western Europe. Some of the railroads were constructed chiefly for political and military purposes, others were designed to connect the great industrial centers, and still others to support the expanding frontiers. Railway-building was first seriously undertaken in Russia after the disaster of the Crimean War, when the soldiers suffered cruel hardships in consequence of the difficulty of obtaining supplies. By 1878 upward of eight thousand miles had been built, connecting the capital with the frontiers of European Russia. In 1885 the railway advance toward the frontiers of India was begun; within a short time Afghanistan was reached, and communication was opened to the borders of China. Important lines were also built in the region between the Black Sea and the Caspian.

The greatest of all Russian railway undertakings was the Trans-Siberian Railway, which was rendered necessary for the transportation of soldiers and military supplies to the eastern boundary of the empire. Those interested in its construction urged also that it would serve to develop the trade and industry of Siberia. The chief difficulty lay in raising the necessary capital; and a very large amount was necessary, since the corruption and dishonesty among the Russian officials and contractors was so great that the sum demanded was four or five times larger than would have been required had the work been efficiently done.[1] The money was, however, obtained by heavy loans secured mainly from French capitalists, and the first sod was turned at Vladivostok in May, 1891.

---

[1] The Manchurian railroad cost the Russian people $115,000 per mile, while the average cost of an American track across the western plains was originally $13,000 to $15,000 a mile.

Communication was established between St. Petersburg and the Pacific in 1900, and a branch line southward to Port Arthur was soon finished (see accompanying map). One could then travel in comfort, with few changes of cars, from Havre to Vladivostok, via Paris, Cologne, Berlin, Warsaw, Moscow, Irkutsk (on Lake Baikal), and Harbin, a distance of seventy-three hundred miles. A first-class ticket from London to Nagasaki, Japan, cost less than two hundred dollars, a little more than half the cost by the Suez Canal. The Russian peasant could travel, in less comfortable cars, from St. Petersburg to Irkutsk, a distance of nearly four thousand miles, for fifteen dollars. By this operation Russia thrust herself down into China and even carried her enterprises into Korea, thus awakening alarm in Japan and coming into collision with the outposts of that empire. The Russo-Japanese War which resulted will be described in Chapter VIII.

THE EXPLORATION OF AFRICA

Not until the latter part of the nineteenth century did the interior of the vast continent of Africa begin to become known to Europeans. We have seen in the preceding sections how France, Germany, and Italy had appropriated large areas of it, but Europeans had not made their influence felt beyond the periphery. In order to understand the fate of this new ground of European competition, it is necessary to say something of its character, its past, and its exploration by Western adventurers.

The northern shores of Africa belong to the Mediterranean world, and the lower valley of the Nile was, so far as we now know, the seat of the first highly developed civilization. Carthage was an African city and a redoubtable rival of Rome, which succeeded it. The upper reaches of the Nile, however, remained a mystery. The main body of the continent appears to have been unknown to the Greeks and Romans, and no one

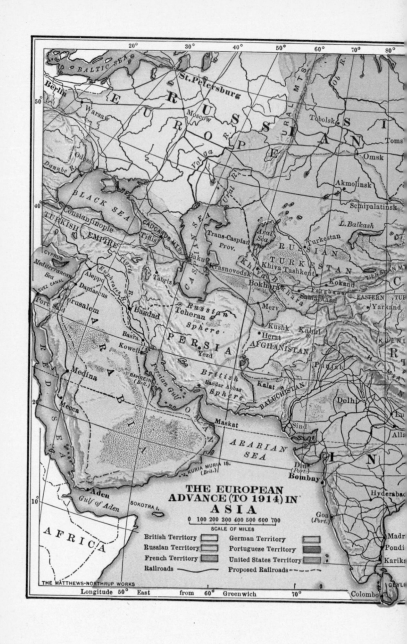

THE EUROPEAN
ADVANCE (TO 1914) IN
ASIA

SCALE OF MILES
0 100 200 300 400 500 600 700

British Territory
Russian Territory
French Territory
Railroads

German Territory
Portuguese Territory
United States Territory
Proposed Railroads

THE MATTHEWS-NORTHRUP WORKS

Longitude 50° East from 60° Greenwich 70°

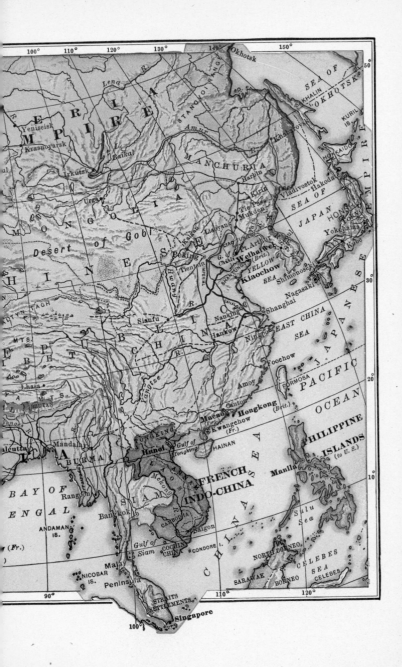

suspected that it extended five thousand miles to the south of
the Mediterranean. It seems to have been inhabited from ancient times by the same kinds of savage or barbarous tribes
which the modern Europeans discovered as they advanced into
its interior.

Shortly after the death of Mohammed in 632, his followers
began the conquest of Egypt and northern Africa, and in less
than a hundred years they subdued all the region which had
formerly been ruled from Rome. From Cape Guardafui, on the
extreme east, to Cape Verde, lying on the Atlantic nearly five
thousand miles to the west, they introduced their civilization
and religion, so that today in the towns of Tunis and Morocco
one sees many things to remind him of the conditions in Palestine or Arabia. The Mohammedans built up a flourishing trade
with the interior; they traversed the deserts and opened cara-
van routes through the sandy wastes; they pushed their trading settlements down the east coast as far as a point opposite
Madagascar; they made maps of that portion of the continent
with which they had become familiar and described its climate
and appearance. The knowledge which the Mohammedans
had acquired naturally spread into Spain, which long formed
a part of their dominions; and it appears probable that the
Portuguese also, who began to explore the west coast of Africa
in the fifteenth century, received such information as they
possessed from the Moors.

So things stood when the Portuguese discovered the mouth
of the mighty Congo River in 1482, and Diaz rounded the
Cape of Good Hope in 1486. Twelve years later Vasco da
Gama, as we know, succeeded in sailing around the southern
point of the continent and up nearly to the equator on the eastern coast, where he came in contact with the Mohammedan
merchants, who had long been trafficking with the ports of
India. He was therefore encouraged to strike boldly across
the Indian Ocean, and reached Calicut in safety. Although the
Portuguese became chiefly interested in the trade with India

T

and the Spice Islands, far to the east, they established trading posts in Africa at the mouths of the Senegal and Gambia rivers and to the south of the Congo, besides colonizing Madeira and the Cape Verde Islands. Moreover, Vasco da Gama had taken possession, in the name of the king of Portugal, of the island of Mozambique.

In spite of such auspicious beginnings, Africa remained the "Dark Continent" for more than three centuries after these first settlements, partly owing to its singular physical characteristics. No other large division of the earth's surface is so rounded and so little indented as Africa. It has very few good harbors, and there is a long series of lofty mountain ranges, extending almost completely around the outer edge of the continent, which effectively separate the coast from the high table-lands of the whole interior. The great South African plateau averages three thousand feet in altitude. There are few navigable rivers, for most of the streams are broken by cataracts as they flow down from the plateau into the sea. The interior is also protected from invasion by deserts—the vast Sahara on the north, a well-nigh rainless and riverless region, while to the south, above the Cape of Good Hope, there is another great tract which is nearly rainless. Except on the northern margin there were no large towns, and the torrid regions which form so great a part of Africa were occupied mainly by savage tribes.

The very abundance of native labor early suggested to the Europeans that the uncivilized African people could be utilized to supply the slave market. Lisbon became the first center of a form of trade which seems inhuman and horrible to us now, but which in the fifteenth century was sanctioned by a papal bull. Christians of that day argued that the slave-trader gave the heathen black man an opportunity to save his soul, even though his body became the property of those who brought him the light of the Gospel.

Some London merchants as early as 1553 dispatched ships to trade along the coast of Guinea. The Portuguese did what they could to resist the newcomers, but one of the English adventurers brought back a cargo of 400 pounds of gold, 36 hundredweight of pepper, and 250 ivory tusks, thereby demonstrating to his countrymen the importance of the trade with Africa. During Elizabeth's reign the English came to recognize that the chief value of Africa lay in the supply of slaves which it afforded. In 1562 the famous Captain Hawkins captured three hundred negroes on the Guinea coast and, with the aid of the Lord, he firmly believed, was able to reach the West Indies and dispose of his living cargo in Hispaniola. This opened the traffic with America, which, in addition to all the cruelty and misery that it involved, gave rise in the nineteenth century to the horrors of the American Civil War and transmitted to the United States of today the serious race problems which still remain unsolved. It is estimated that in the latter part of the eighteenth century English ships carried away from Africa over fifty thousand slaves a year. The wealth of Liverpool so largely flowed from this business that a celebrated actor, when hissed by an audience in that city, taunted its citizens with dwelling in a town the very stones of which were cemented by the blood of African slaves.

The Dutch naturally entered into competition with the English and Portuguese in Africa, as they had in the trade of the Indies. They expelled the Portuguese from their most important strongholds on the west and east coasts, and established their control on the Gold Coast by building forts in close proximity to the English settlements. As a halfway station on the route to India the Dutch established a post at the Cape of Good Hope in 1652. The colony did not grow rapidly, however, and its population scarcely reached ten thousand at the opening of the nineteenth century.

Just before the accession of Louis XIV the French founded a station, St. Louis, at the mouth of the Senegal River, which, as we have just seen, was destined to become in later times an important basis for the extension of their power in northwest

Africa. They were able to work their way inland and open up relations with the natives—naturally with the main aim of securing their share of the slave trade.

Notwithstanding these various enterprises, no serious attempts had been made by any of the European powers to colonize any portion of Africa before the close of the Napoleonic wars, in 1815. Indeed, the suppression of the slave trade had discouraged further activities for a time; for this traffic had been more profitable than the combined trade in gold, ivory, gum, and other African commodities.

The situation in 1815 may be summed up as follows: In northern Africa the Sultan of Turkey was the nominal suzerain of Egypt and of the so-called Barbary States, that is, Tripoli, Tunis, and Algeria. Morocco was, however, an independent state, as it still is, under the sultan of Morocco. France maintained her station at the mouth of the Senegal River; the most important Portuguese possessions were in Lower Guinea and on the east coast opposite the island of Madagascar; the British held some minor posts along the west coast and had wrested Cape Colony from the Dutch during the Napoleonic wars. The heart of Africa was still unknown; no European power contemplated laying claim to the arid waste of the Sahara Desert, and the more attractive regions of the upper Nile were ruled by semicivilized Mohammedan chiefs.

For fifty years after the Congress of Vienna the advance of European powers in Africa was very slow indeed. England and France were, it is true, gradually extending their sphere of influence, and explorers were tracing the rivers and mountain chains of the interior. France, as has been explained, conquered Algiers during this period, and formally annexed it. The Dutch Boers, disgusted with English rule, had migrated to the north, and laid the foundations of the Transvaal and Orange River colonies (see following chapter).

The latter half of the nineteenth century was, however, a time of active exploration in Africa. It is impossible here even to name all those who braved the torrid heat, the swamps and fevers, and the danger from savages and wild beasts. Under the auspices of the Royal Geographical Society of England a search was begun for the mysterious sources of the Nile, and a lake lying just south of the equator was discovered in 1858 and named Victoria Nyanza. In 1864 Sir Samuel Baker discovered another lake, Albert Nyanza, to the northwest and explored its connections with the Nile River. David Livingstone had visited Bechuanaland twenty years before and pushed up the valley of the Zambezi River, tracing it nearly to its source. In 1866 he explored the regions about the lakes of Nyassa and Tanganyika and reached a point on the upper Congo. This expedition attracted general attention throughout the civilized world. Livingstone's long absence roused the fear that he was, perhaps, the prisoner of some savage tribe; and on his return to Lake Tanganyika he was met by Henry Stanley, another explorer, destined to rival him in fame, who had been sent out by the *New York Herald* to search for him. Livingstone, who was both missionary and explorer, continued his work until his death in 1873.

Two years later Lieutenant Cameron, at the head of an English expedition which had also been organized with the hope of finding Livingstone, on learning of his death, started from Zanzibar, on the Indian Ocean, and struggled through the heart of Africa until he caught sight of the Atlantic Ocean at Benguella, south of the Congo River. The same year Stanley set out upon an expedition which is regarded as the most important in the annals of African exploration. After visiting lakes Victoria Nyanza and Tanganyika, he journeyed across the country to the river Lualaba, and followed its course until he proved that it was only the headwaters of the Congo, down which he found his way to the Atlantic. Meanwhile other explorers, French and German, as well as English, were constantly adding to the knowledge of a hitherto unknown continent.

Stanley's famous journey through the heart of "Darkest Africa" naturally aroused the intense interest of all the European powers; and within ten years after his triumphant return to Marseille in 1878, the entire surface of Africa had been divided up among the powers, or marked out into "spheres of influence." Two generations ago a map of Africa was for the most part indefinite and conjectural, except along the coast. By 1900 its natural features had been largely determined, and it was traversed by boundary lines almost as carefully drawn as those which separate the various European countries. The manner in which the British, French, Germans, and Italians established their claims in Africa has been mentioned already, but something must be said of the Belgian Congo, Morocco, and Egypt.[1]

BELGIAN CONGO

The history of the vast Congo Free State may be said to begin with a conference held in Brussels in 1876 under the auspices of the king of Belgium. Representatives of most of the European countries were invited to attend, with a view to considering the best methods of opening up the region and of stopping the slave trade which was carried on by the Mohammedans in the interior. The result was the organization of an international African Association, with its center at Brussels. The enterprise was, however, in reality the personal affair of King Leopold, who supplied from his own purse a large portion of the funds which were used by Stanley in exploring the Congo basin, establishing posts, and negotiating hundreds of treaties with the petty native chiefs.[2]

[1] England's African policy is described on pages 171 ff. and 196 ff.

[2] Sir Harry Johnson, a celebrated British explorer and student of native African languages, tells in a vivid way the manner in which treaties were concluded with negro chieftains: In a long canoe with forty natives he was paddled through the jungle up the Cross River in Nigeria until he came to a large village. He was carried to a hut where a hundred human skulls grinned

Very soon the activity of the African Association aroused the apprehensions of the European powers interested in Africa, especially England and Portugal, and a congress was called at Berlin to consider the situation. This met in November, 1884, and every European state except Switzerland sent delegates, as did the United States. The congress recognized the right of the African Association to the vast expanse drained by the Congo River, and declared the new territory a neutral and international state, open to the trade of all nations.

The following year King Leopold announced to the world that he had assumed sovereignty over the Congo Free State, and that he proposed to unite it in a personal union with Belgium. He gradually filled the government offices with Belgians and established customs lines with a view to raising revenue.

The Belgians had not gone very far in their development of the Congo when they were charged with practicing atrocious cruelties on the natives. There is reason to think that the hideous reports published in the newspapers were much exaggerated, but there is little doubt that the natives, as commonly happens in such cases, suffered seriously at the hands of the European invader. King Leopold claimed ownership over the vacant land, and in this way roused the hatred of peoples who had been used to roam freely in every direction. By a system of "apprenticeship" many of the blacks were reduced to the condition of slaves. Labor was hard to secure, for the natives

at him while he explained through an interpreter that he was the representative of "a great white queen, who was the ruler of the White People." He desired to make a treaty to take home to his queen. Being well drunk with palm wine, the leaders of the tribe "splodged" their crosses on the form which he produced from his dispatch box. He then got under way as speedily as possible, lest the villagers might eat his servants. He gave them some beads and cloth, and they returned the compliment with a hundred yams, two sheep, and a necklace of human knuckle bones. This diplomacy of the jungle was, of course, a joke to the negroes; but it was taken seriously enough by the Europeans, for it represented an advance in civilized penetration. (The facts of this episode are taken from Professor Moon's *Imperialism and World Politics*, p. 101.)

were accustomed to a free life in the jungle and did not relish driving spikes on railways or draining swamps for Belgian capitalists. The government therefore ordered native chiefs to supply a certain number of workmen, and on their failure to meet the requirements it was customary to burn their villages. The government also compelled the natives to furnish a certain quantity of rubber each year; failure to comply with these demands also brought summary punishment upon them.

The British government took care to report the conduct of the Belgian officials to the world, and it aroused loud protests in Europe and America; but those who knew most about African conditions suspected that the English had a selfish interest in exaggerating the horrors of the situation, with the hope of ultimately extending their own control over the Congo regions. At all events, King Leopold and his agents stoutly maintained that they had been misrepresented, and claimed that their rubber business did not kill as many natives as the whisky which was such an important source of revenue to other nations, especially Great Britain. Whatever truth there may have been in these alleged exposures, they led the Belgian ministry to take up the question of the Congo. As a result of the controversy, the government of Belgium assumed complete ownership of the Free State in 1908 and put it under the minister for the colonies.[1]

Morocco

Far more agitating to European powers than the Belgian Congo was Morocco, which was nominally independent, under a sultan of its own, at the opening of the twentieth century. Its population, a curious mixture of Berbers, Tuaregs, Arabs, and Negroes, had not materially changed its civilization during the previous thousand years. The fierce tribesmen often defied the

---

[1] The Portuguese still control remnants of the possessions to which they laid claim when South Africa was first brought to the attention of Europe, namely, Guinea, Angola, and Portuguese East Africa.

rule of their sultan at Fez. A bandit leader, Raisuli, for instance, made a regular practice of seizing Christians and holding them for ransom. This was one of many instances which illustrated the inability of the sultan of Morocco to control his subjects and protect foreigners.

Europeans, especially the French, in spite of many difficulties, gradually developed relations with Morocco. They carried on a trade in almonds, gum, and the famous Moroccan goatskin, and also lent money to the sultan. The necessity of coming to an agreement in regard to their dealings with Morocco led to a conference of the powers—discussed below— held at Algeciras, Spain (just across the bay from Gibraltar), in 1906. Their representatives agreed on the formation of a police force under French and Spanish officers, and the organization of a state bank, to be controlled by the powers.

In the summer of 1907 a number of foreigners were killed by the fanatical natives at Casablanca. The French brought up their warships, which proceeded to bombard the town, and several encounters took place between their troops and the Moroccans. This proved a decisive step toward the occupation of Morocco by France. Her control of the neighboring Algeria made the annexation of Morocco particularly tempting to her; and after a lively tilt with Germany, French supremacy in Morocco was recognized in 1911, while Germany got "compensation" for her Moroccan interests in the form of a small slice of France's territory in the Congo district.

THE BRITISH IN EGYPT

In order to complete our survey of Africa, it is necessary to consider the singular circumstances which served to bring Egypt under the control of the British. This ancient center of civilization had, as we have seen, been conquered by the Arabs in the seventh century. Eight hundred years later it was overrun by the Ottoman Turks, and in 1517 was organized as a province of the Turkish Empire. With the decline of the Sultan's power the country fell under the domination of the Beys, the leaders of a curious military band known as the Mamelukes; and it was against these that General Bonaparte fought in 1798. Shortly after Nelson and the English had frustrated his attempt to bring Egypt under French rule, a military adventurer from Albania, Mehemet Ali, compelled the Sultan to recognize him as governor of Egypt in 1805. A few years later he brought about a massacre of the Mamelukes and began a series of reforms. He created an army and a fleet, and not only brought all Egypt under his sway but established himself at Khartum, where he could control the Sudan,[1] or region of the upper Nile. Before his death in 1849, he had induced the Sultan to recognize his heirs as rightful rulers of Egypt.

The importance of Egypt for the Western powers was greatly increased by the construction of the Suez Canal, begun in 1859; for both Port Said, on the Mediterranean, and Suez, on the Red Sea, are Egyptian ports. The Egyptian ruler, Ismail I, who came to the throne in 1863, had his head turned by the vast wealth which he believed that the canal would bring him, and by the extraordinary prosperity which Egypt was enjoying during the Civil War in America. This she owed to the enhanced price of Egyptian cotton in the European markets as a result of the cutting off of the American supply. With the consent of the Sultan, he assumed the title of "Khedive," and began a career of reckless extravagance and dissipation. European money-lenders encouraged his high living, until, by 1876, he had involved his country in debt to the amount of nearly four hundred and fifty million dollars. In order to meet his financial embarrassments, he sold a great block of his Suez Canal stock to the British government for some twenty million dollars.

[1] The term "Sudan" (see map on page 154) was applied by the Mohammedans to the whole region south of the Sahara Desert, but as now used it commonly means the Anglo-Egyptian Sudan only.

This sacrifice brought no appreciable relief, and the Khedive's creditors in England and France began to grow nervous. Those who held Egyptian securities thereupon entered into negotiations with the British and French governments. To secure control of the Egyptian finances, agents were sent to Egypt who induced the Khedive to establish a new department of the government to deal with the public debt; this was put in charge of two comptrollers-general appointed, respectively, by England and France. All sources of income devoted to the payment of the debt were turned over to these commissioners; indeed, from 1879 to 1882 the whole financial system of the country was practically in their hands.

This foreign intervention naturally aroused discontent. The country was overtaxed; appropriations for public improvements were reduced; and the old hatred of Moslem for Christian was again awakened. Some discontented army officials, headed by a certain Arabi, took advantage of this dissatisfaction to organize a mutiny. They forced the Khedive to summon a national assembly, with the hope that they could in this way get control of the government. When Great Britain and France protested against this interference with existing arrangements, the cry of "Egypt for the Egyptians!" rang through the country. Christians were attacked in the streets, and Arabi's party began to fortify Alexandria as an act of defiance to the powers.

A British fleet was, however, lying in the harbor, and its commander ordered the work of fortification to be stopped. Finding that his commands were not obeyed, he bombarded the city, silenced the forts, and drove out Arabi. Additional British forces were immediately sent to Egypt; they landed at Port Said, and after a great victory at Tel el Kebir, a point lying between Port Said and Cairo, they captured the city of Cairo and forced Arabi to surrender, thus putting an end to the revolt.

England was now in a peculiar position. France had declined to join in suppressing the rebellion, and England's actions were viewed with suspicion by the other powers, who felt that she planned to annex Egypt. The English government announced, however, that the occupation of Egypt was temporary, and would continue only until a stable government should be established and the finances put upon a proper basis.

France now withdrew from the joint control over the Khedive's treasury, and an English financial adviser was substituted for the former comptrollers-general. In September, 1882, the Khedive disbanded his whole army and intrusted the organization of a new army to a British officer, who was given the title of "Sirdar." The army had a full strength of some sixteen thousand men and included over a hundred British officers. After the rebellion of 1882 a British army of occupation of about five thousand men remained in Egypt, for whose maintenance the British government contributed half a million dollars annually.

Trouble, however, soon arose in the Sudan, where a revolt against the Khedive's government was organized under the leadership of Mohammed Ahmed, who claimed to be the Messiah, and found great numbers of fanatical followers who called him El Mahdi ("the leader"). General Gordon—the same officer who had helped Li Hung Chang put down the Taiping rebellion in China (see page 255)—was in charge of the British garrison at Khartum. Here he was besieged by the followers of the Mahdi in 1885, and after a memorable defense fell a victim to their fury. This disaster was avenged twelve years later, when, in 1897–1898, the Sudan was reconquered, and the city of Khartum taken by the British under General Kitchener. Until 1914 Egypt remained nominally under Turkey, but actually was controlled by Great Britain. In December of that year Egypt was declared a British protectorate and continued in that state until 1922, when it became an independent kingdom—subject to certain reservations touching British interests.

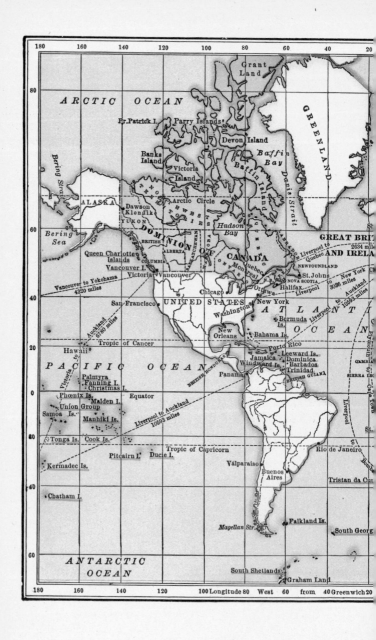

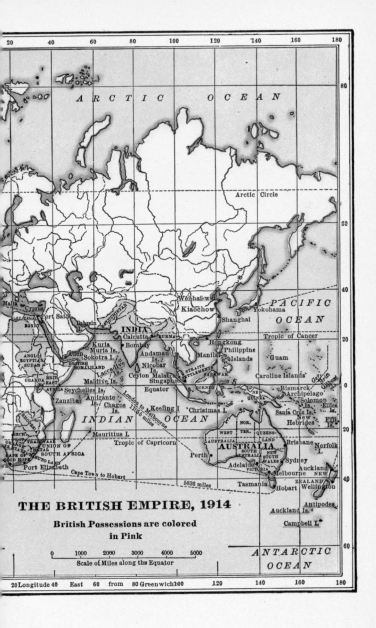

THE BRITISH EMPIRE, 1914

British Possessions are colored
in Pink

CHAPTER VI

THE BRITISH EMPIRE BEFORE THE WORLD WAR

ADVANTAGES OF GREAT BRITAIN IN EMPIRE-BUILDING

Of all the empire-building powers of the Old World, Great Britain enjoyed the most continuous expansion. Except for the temporary setback caused by the loss of her thirteen colonies in America, her arms and commerce, each promoting the other, advanced steadily in all quarters of the globe from the age of Elizabeth onward. By the development of her sea power, and favorable combinations and alliances on the Continent, Great Britain was able to get the better of the other acquisitive nations—the Spaniards, Dutch, and French—in a long succession of wars, and finally, in the twentieth century, of the Germans when they grasped at the trident. The British were aided by the French against the Dutch, by the Dutch against the French, by the Germans against Louis XV and Napoleon, and latterly by the French against the Germans.

Economic circumstances, as well as arms and diplomacy, promoted British expansion overseas. During the first half of the nineteenth century Great Britain stood easily at the head of all the nations of the world in the output of her mines and factories and the vast extent of her commerce. She had laid the foundations for this supremacy during the eighteenth century, when she gained the control of India and Canada and certain important islands, and in the early part of the nineteenth century, when she secured her interests in southern Africa, Australia, and New Zealand. This expansion enabled her to reap the full advantage of her new machinery, which had so marvelously increased her power of production. No invading armies had harried her fields, burned her shipping, or sacked her towns. Indeed, the wars from which the Continent suffered usually served to increase rather than lessen England's prosperity, owing to the demand they caused for the products of her looms and foundries.

Under these circumstances the annual trade of Great Britain, including exports and imports, rose from about one hundred and thirty-five million dollars in 1798 to over five hundred millions in 1850. She was already supreme on the seas in Napoleon's time, and her mercantile marine steadily increased in order to distribute the goods which she produced to all parts of the earth.

The other nations were far behind her in all these sources of commercial strength. Napoleon's efforts to render the Continent independent of England and her colonies had failed (Vol. I, pp. 391 ff.); there was not a single steam engine in France in 1812, and it was not until after Napoleon's fall that France set herself seriously to compete with England by the introduction of machinery. Germany was less favorably situated than France, since it had for years been the main theater of long and devastating wars. It was not a united nation but a collection of practically independent states which were divided, previous to the development of the *Zollverein*, by high tariff duties and embarrassed by a great variety of coinage. Italy and Austria suffered from similar disadvantages.

The United States of America, now so formidable in every market of the world, had in 1815 a small and scattered population. Its interests were almost exclusively agricultural; and although its ships enjoyed a considerable carrying trade on the high seas, its people lacked the capital necessary to develop the immense natural resources of the country and thereby become a serious menace to the manufacturers of the Old World.

While Great Britain, through its inventors and manufacturers, was leading all other countries in the output of goods for sale, British soldiers far away on the frontiers of the British dominions were fighting Rajputs in India, Zulus in Africa, and Maoris in New Zealand, and widening the borders of the empire whose foundations had been laid in the eighteenth century. The story of the early contest for dominion—the rivalry with the Dutch in the Spice Islands, the wars for Spanish trade, the struggle with France in India and North America—we have brought down to the settlement at Vienna, which left England foremost among the commercial and colonial powers of all time. The task of developing the resources acquired in India, Africa, Canada, and Australasia was one of the important problems which the eighteenth century bequeathed to the nineteenth.

BRITISH INDIA

Turning first to India, the British rule, in the opening years of the nineteenth century (Vol. I, pp. 183 ff.), extended over the Bengal region and far up the Ganges valley beyond Delhi. A narrow strip along the eastern coast, the southern point of the peninsula, and the island of Ceylon had also been brought under England's control, and in the west she held Bombay and a considerable area north of Surat. In addition to these regions which the English administered directly, there were a number of princes, such as the Nizam of Hyderabad, over whom they exercised the right of "protection." They had secured a foothold which made it evident that the Mogul emperor, who retained but the shadow of power at Delhi, could never recover the shattered dominions of the great Aurangzeb. The French and Portuguese possessions had declined into mere trading posts, and in the heart of India only one power disputed the advance of the English toward the complete conquest of the peninsula.

This one power was a union of native princes known as the Mahratta Confederacy (see map, p. 190, Vol. I). The country occupied by this confederation extended inward from the

Bombay coast and was inclosed on the western border by mountain ranges. When the Mohammedan invaders under Baber swept down into the peninsula, they easily conquered the plains to the eastward, which were occupied by peaceful peasants; but to the westward the boldest of the native Mahrattas fled to the mountains, and from their strongholds there they frequently dashed down into the plains and harassed the Mohammedan rulers. These terrible warriors rode horses famed for their fleetness, and when attacked they easily took refuge in their inaccessible mountain fastnesses or in the wild jungles of the valleys. In the time of Louis XIV these occasional ravages grew into a war of conquest and occupation under a powerful leader by the name of Sivaji, who carved out of the Mogul's dominions a realm for himself which was called Kokan.

The kingdom thus founded grew in time into a vast realm, but its ruling family sank into "do-nothing kings," and the real power fell into the hands of a mayor of the palace called the Peshwa, who had his seat of government at Poona. At the opening of the nineteenth century the kingdom had fallen apart, and beside the domains of the Peshwa there were four other great districts, ruled by viceroys bearing the titles of "Gaekwar of Baroda," "Sindhia of Gwalior," "Holkar of Indore," and "Bhonsla of Nagpur." The Mahratta kingdom was therefore only a loose confederation, and the ruling princes were usually warring with one another except when pressure from without compelled them to unite. The prevailing disorder was increased by the fact that scattered among their territories there were innumerable petty rulers who might be compared to the imperial knights of the Holy Roman Empire.

If it had not been for the jealousy that existed among the Mahrattas, they might have checked the growing power of the English and seized India for themselves as it fell from the relaxing grasp of the great Mogul. As it was, they constituted a powerful barrier in the way of the extension of British

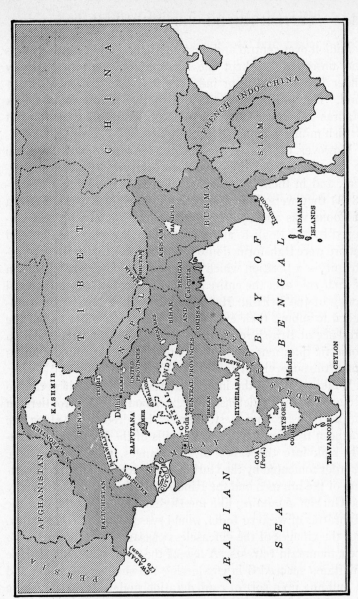

INDIA AND FARTHER INDIA IN 1914

dominion over central and western India, and by their restless and unsettled life kept the surrounding territories already under British control or influence in a constant state of turmoil. They encouraged the wild native horsemen to attack Madras and ravage the Bengal frontier, and repeatedly put British military genius to a severe test.

However, the lawless Mahrattas were unable in the long run to resist the steady and disciplined pressure of European warfare, and in their last great conflict with the British (1816–1818) they were finally conquered. The office of the Peshwa of Poona was abolished, a large part of his territory was annexed by the English, and the rulers of Baroda, Gwalior, and Indore were transformed into feudal princes under British sovereignty—a position which they retain today. The extension of their rule over the entire peninsula now became the avowed policy of the British. Henceforward native states were compelled to submit their external disputes to them, to accept the presence of British residents at their courts to advise them on domestic questions, and, finally, to place their military forces under the supervision of British officers.

While pacifying the interior of India the British were also occupied with the defense and extension of their frontiers on the north, east, and west. For six hundred miles along the northern frontier, where the foothills of the Himalayas gradually sink into the valley of the Ganges, there was chronic disorder fomented by the Gurkhas—a race composed of a mixture of the hill men and the Hindu plain dwellers. Periodically the Gurkha chieftains, like the Highlanders of Scotland or the Mahrattas of western India, would sweep down into the valley, loot the villages of the defenseless peasants, and then retire to their mountain retreats. A few of the most powerful of these chieftains succeeded in conquering the smaller hill tribes and in building up a sort of confederation under a rajah in whose name they governed Nepal, as their kingdom was called. They then sought to extend their sway at the expense of the British

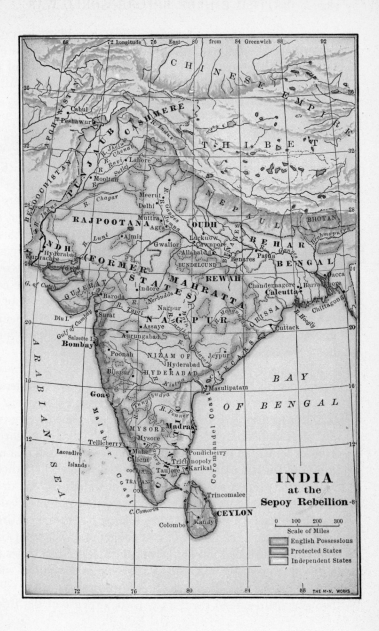

INDIA
at the
Sepoy Rebellion

0   100   200   300
Scale of Miles

English Possessions
Protected States
Independent States

THE M·N. WORKS

in the Ganges valley, but were badly beaten in a two years' war (1814-1816) and compelled to cede to the British Empire a vast western region, which brought the Anglo-Indian boundary at that point to the borders of Tibet, high up into the Himalaya Mountains.

While the British were busy with the Mahrattas and Nepalese, the Burmese were pressing into the Bengal districts from the east; and as they had never met the disciplined Europeans in armed conflict, they were confident that they would be able to expand westward indefinitely. Their ambitions were, however, checked by the British (1824-1826), and they were compelled to cede to the victors a considerable strip of territory along the east coast of the Bay of Bengal. Having thus made their first definite advance beyond the confines of India proper, the British, after twenty-five years of peace with the Burmese, engaged in a second war against them in 1852 and made themselves masters of the Irawadi valley and a long, narrow strip of coast below Rangoon.[1]

After the gains made at the expense of the Burmese, the northwestern frontier next attracted the attention of the conquering British. In the valley of the Indus, where the soldiers of Alexander the Great had faltered on their eastward march, there was a fertile region known as the Sind, ruled over by an ameer, who seems to have shown an irritating independence in his dealings with the British. On the ground that the ameer's government was inefficient and corrupt, the British invaded his territory in 1843, and after some brilliant campaigning they wrested his domain from him and added it to their Indian empire, thus winning a strong western frontier. This enterprise, which has been severely condemned by many British writers, was scarcely concluded when a war broke out with the Sikhs in the northwest, which resulted in the addition of the great Punjab region farther up the valley of the Indus, northeast of

[1] Additional annexations were made after another Burmese war waged in 1884-1885.

Sind, and the extension of the boundary of the Anglo-Indian Empire to the borders of Afghanistan.[1]

In addition to this policy of annexation through war with the natives, a process of "peaceful assimilation" was adopted under the governorship of Lord Dalhousie (1848–1856), who quietly transformed "protected" states into British provinces whenever the direct line of the ruling houses became extinct. Through the application of this "doctrine of lapse," as it was called, the territories of the rajah of Nagpur and other princes came under the direct control of the British government. In 1856 Lord Dalhousie deposed the nawab of Oudh and annexed his fertile domains, on the ground that "the British government would be guilty in the sight of God and man if it were any longer to aid in sustaining, by its countenance, an administration fraught with the suffering of millions."

Inevitably the conquest and annexation of so many native Indian states stirred up intense hatred against the British aggressors. In the provinces which were under the direct administration of the British, ruling families and the official classes attached to them had been set aside, and in those which were merely under the suzerainty of the conquerors as feudal states, the rulers chafed at their vassalage. The Mohammedans cherished a religious abhorrence for the Christian intruders, in addition to their bitterness at the loss of their former power. The native Mahrattas had good reason to feel that only the advent of the British had prevented them from transforming the peninsula into a Mahratta empire. Finally, the sudden and violent "pacification" of a country which for centuries had been

[1] The province of Baluchistan, on the northwest, was brought under British dominion by gradual annexations beginning in 1876 and extending down to 1903. Several of the districts were formally organized as British Baluchistan in 1887. In attempting to extend their authority over the neighboring Afghanistan, the British waged two wars with the ruler of that country, one in 1837–1843 and another in 1878–1880. The problem how to maintain control over Afghanistan and use it as a protecting state against Russia's southeasterly advance still constitutes one of the fundamental issues of Anglo-Indian politics—no matter who rules at Moscow.

the prey of ambitious military adventurers left no further scope or outlet for their troublesome energies, especially as the British monopolized, for the most part, all the highest and most lucrative positions.

For the repression of all these elements of discontent the British depended largely upon the aid of native soldiers. Indeed, from the days of Plassey (1757) down to the war in the Punjab, sepoys had formed the bulk of the English armies, even in the process of conquering the peninsula. Though outnumbering the British five to one, they had been, on the whole, heroic and faithful soldiers, sharing both glories and defeats with their white companions in arms. It is true there had been occasional mutinies among them, but these had been speedily suppressed and had never spread to any alarming extent.

Nevertheless, the embers of discontent remained, and they were fanned into a consuming flame in 1857 by several military reforms undertaken by the English government. The year before, the British had become impressed with the advantages of a new rifle invented by a Frenchman. This was loaded with a paper cartridge containing powder and ball, which was slipped into the barrel and then rammed down into place. In order to slide more easily into the gun the paper was greased, and the soldier had to tear off one end of it with his teeth so that the powder would take fire when the cap was exploded.

The introduction of this new rifle seemed innocent enough, but the government had not taken into account certain religious scruples of the sepoys. The Hindu regarded touching the fat of a cow as sacrilege, and to Mohammedans touching the fat of swine was contamination. The government soon heard of this grievance and, promising not to use the objectionable grease, offered to allow the soldiers to substitute some other kind of lubricant. Peace was thus maintained for a time; but in May, 1857, some soldiers at Meerut, in the broad plain between the Jumna and the Ganges, refused to receive the cartridges served out to them and were thereupon sentenced to prison for ten years. Their native companions rallied to their support and rose in rebellion; the next day, May 11, the soldiers mutinied at Delhi, massacred the English inhabitants of the city, and besieged the garrison; in a few days the entire northwest was in full revolt. Lucknow, with its population of seven hundred thousand natives, rose against the British and besieged them in their fortifications. At Cawnpore, about forty miles to the south, a thousand British men, women, and children were cruelly massacred after they had surrendered, and by the middle of July all Oudh and the northwest seemed lost.

Immediately after the insurrection at Meerut the governor-general telegraphed to Bombay, Madras, and Ceylon for instant help. Though there were as yet no railroads in the rebellious provinces, the telegraph helped to save the empire. Aid was at once sent to Lucknow under the command of General Colin Campell, a hero of the Napoleonic and Crimean wars, and in November he succeeded in relieving the brave garrison, which had held out for nearly six months. Many of the sepoys remained loyal, and with aid from the coast provinces city after city was wrested from the mutineers, until, by the end of November, British India was saved, but at a frightful cost.

The English in India were terrified by the revolt, for they fully realized how few they were compared with the millions of natives about them. Reports indicate that as the British gradually suppressed the rebellion they took harsh revenge by wholesale executions accompanied by cruelties not agreeable to recall. But more conciliatory measures prevailed as the excitement died down.

After the suppression of the sepoy rebellion, the Parliament of Great Britain revolutionized the government of India. The administration of the peninsula was finally taken entirely out of the hands of the East India Company, which had directed it for more than two hundred and fifty years (see Volume I, pp. 171 ff.) and vested in the British sovereign, to be exercised under parliamentary control. In November, 1858, a royal proclamation announced to the inhabitants of British India that all treaties made under the authority of the East India Company would be maintained, the rights of feudatory princes upheld, and religious toleration granted. The governor-general of the company in India was supplanted by a viceroy, and the company's directors in London surrendered their power into the hands of the Secretary of State for India. The Mogul of Delhi, successor of the great Aurangzeb, was expelled from his capital; but when, nearly twenty years later (on January 1, 1877), Queen Victoria was proclaimed "Empress of India" amid an illustrious gathering of Indian princes and British officials, the pomp and magnificence of the ancient Moguls were invoked to bind their former subjects more closely to their English conquerors.

After the great mutiny the British government in India was concerned chiefly with problems of internal reform and administration and with the defense of the frontiers, especially on the northwest. The proportion of natives to white men in the army was greatly reduced, and the artillery placed almost entirely in charge of the latter. Codes of law and of criminal procedure were introduced in 1860 and 1861. The construction of railway lines was pushed forward with great rapidity for military and economic purposes, so that the vast interior might be quickly reached by troops and an outlet opened for its crops of cotton, rice, wheat, indigo, and tobacco.

About thirty-five thousand miles of railway were in operation before the World War. Calcutta and the frontier of Afghanistan were linked by a line touching Lucknow and Delhi, the ancient Mogul capital, and connected with Bombay by two branches, one of which was continued in a southeasterly direction entirely across the peninsula to Madras, and thence to the coast opposite Ceylon. Cotton mills rose by the tombs of ancient kings, cities increased rapidly in population, and the foreign trade by sea expanded steadily until the outbreak of the World War. Over fourteen hundred newspapers, printed in twenty-two languages, including Burmese, Sanskrit, and Persian were published in 1914; educational institutions were provided for seven and a half million students.[1] In short, an industrial and educational revolution took place in India, and Governor Clive would scarcely recognize his office were he called to the post of viceroy today, with all its responsibilities of military, railway, and educational administration, and the extraordinary obligations that come with the terrible famines produced by the periodic failure of the crops.

As a result of the methods by which British dominion was extended in the peninsula, British India became, at the opening of the twentieth century, a collection of provinces, varying in size, language, population, and customs. To these must be added a number of states ruled by native princes under British protection. The total area which was under British authority was 1,766,642 square miles, and the population reached the astounding number of over two hundred and eighty-seven millions, of whom less than one million were European in origin. The government of this immense empire was vested in the hands of a viceroy, appointed by the crown, and a local council composed of the heads of the finance, military, commerce, and other departments of the government, likewise chosen by the crown. Subject to the acts of the Parliament of Great Britain, the viceroy and this council legislated for British India and enforced their laws through the governors of the nine great provinces into which it was divided. This local government, however, was subject to the Secretary for India in England, —a member of the British cabinet, assisted by a council of ten men, nine of whom must have had experience in India.

[1] Yet in 1914 scarcely a third of the boys attended school in British India, and about 6 per cent of the girls. The proportion able to read and write was still very small. Not two million knew English. (These data are taken from the Statesman's Year-Book, 1916.)

As time went on, Western ideas of national independence and self-rule began to influence leaders in India. A demand made itself felt that the peoples of India should be granted a share in their government or even complete independence. During the World War this spirit became so strong that Great Britain was compelled to establish an Indian parliament and make other concessions in the direction of self-government (pp. 526 ff.).

THE DOMINION OF CANADA

When the English government was established in Canada, after the capture of Montreal in 1760, only about two hundred of the sixty-five thousand inhabitants were of English origin; the rest were French. Barriers of race, language, laws, and religion separated the conquerors from the conquered. For a few years the English administration, not unnaturally, was badly adapted to the needs of its new subjects; but in 1774, on the eve of the war with the American colonies, the British Parliament, in order to insure the allegiance of the Canadians, passed the famous Quebec Act—one of the most remarkable enactments in the history of English law. In an age of intolerance it recognized the Catholic faith, allowed the clergy to collect their tithes, perpetuated the French civil law, and left French customs and traditions undisturbed.

Under this act the new colony stood patriotically by England during the American Revolution, and though France was herself allied with the revolting colonies, the Canadians repulsed their advances and received fugitive Loyalists in great numbers. The latter, known as the United Empire Loyalists, settled in what are now the Maritime Provinces and also in Upper Canada—the region lying along the Great Lakes, which was to become the province of Ontario. It is estimated that by 1806 about eighty thousand Loyalist immigrants had crossed the frontier from the United States, the British government offering lands and subsidies to encourage their coming.

The influx of an English population necessitated a change in the government, which had been designed especially for the French. Consequently, in 1791 representative government was established in Canada by a new act of Parliament. The country was divided into two provinces: an upper one, Ontario, inhabited by the English; and a lower one, Quebec, which had long been the home of the French. Each province was given a governor, a lieutenant governor, and a legislature composed of a council appointed by the governor and an assembly elected by popular vote. To prevent disputes over taxation such as had led to the American Revolution, it was provided that no British taxes should be imposed on Canada except for the regulation of commerce, and in such instances only by the colonial legislatures. Thus Canada was freed from contributions to the military and naval forces of the mother country.

Under this new government the English and French inhabitants once more showed their loyalty to England when the armies of the United States prepared to invade Canada during the War of 1812, for the old Loyalists in Ontario still remembered with bitterness their expulsion during the American Revolution. The French Canadians likewise flocked to the support of the English cause, and the result of the conflict was merely to increase the ill will already felt for the neighboring republic, whose designs of annexation were regarded with distrust and aversion.

Amicably as the Canadians in the two provinces coöperated against the United States, they were constantly troubled by domestic dissensions. In Quebec the quarrel was between the great mass of the French citizens and a small group of English who controlled the government. In Ontario, although there was no question of nationality, there was some bitterness between the newcomers in the province and the officials, who were nearly all from the old Loyalist stock. In 1837 this ill feeling developed into open rebellion. The uprising in Ontario was headed by William MacKenzie, a Scotchman and a radical, who hated the "Tories" and became an impassioned advocate of independence. In the French province of Quebec the malcontents found a leader in Louis Papineau, who dreamed of establishing a French republic on the banks of the St. Lawrence. The rebels, however, did not manage their enterprise very skillfully, and were easily dispersed with little loss of life.

The pacification of the revolted colonies was committed to the care of Lord Durham, a liberal statesman, who was given full power to restore order and introduce reforms. The result of his mission was a new act of Parliament, the Act of Union of 1840, which united the two provinces into one, with a single legislature of two houses and a ministry responsible to it. Within ten years Nova Scotia, New Brunswick, and Prince Edward Island were likewise enjoying self-government through responsible ministries.

This was an important step in the direction of the Canadian federation which was organized a few years later. By the British North America Act of 1867, Ontario, Quebec, New Brunswick, and Nova Scotia were united into the Dominion of Canada, with the provision that the remaining provinces and territories might be admitted later. This federation was given a constitution providing for a governor-general representing the sovereign of England; a Senate, the members of which were appointed for life by the governor-general; and a House of Commons elected by popular vote. In methods and spirit this government is remarkably like that of Great Britain, for the real administration is in the hands of a cabinet selected by the governor-general from the party having a majority in the lower house. The new plan of federation went into effect on July 1, 1867—a day which is celebrated as the Canadian national holiday, like the Fourth of July in the United States.

After the formation of the federation the history of the dominion was characterized by rapid material development and the growth of a national spirit among the Canadian people. The great western regions were divided into territories and provinces, just as the western part of the United States was organized into territories and then into states. In 1869 the extensive rights which the Hudson's Bay Company had possessed for more than two hundred years over vast regions encircling the Hudson Bay were purchased. The province of Manitoba was laid out in 1870; in 1871 British Columbia, which had been occupied after the settlement of the Oregon controversy with the United States, was admitted to the federation; Prince Edward Island followed two years later; and in 1905 the great provinces of Alberta and Saskatchewan came into the union, leaving only Newfoundland outside. The tide of immigration steadily rose, so that the population, which was a little over half a million in 1820, was more than five millions at the close of the century.

To bind these distant provinces together a network of railways, including great trunk lines, was constructed. The Canadian Pacific connects Montreal with Vancouver, almost three thousand miles away; and as there is a magnificent line of steamers running from that point to Japan, the valley of the St. Lawrence is only fourteen days' journey from Yokohama, the gate of the Orient. There is also steamer service to Australia, so that European travelers bound for the southern Pacific often prefer the Canadian route to the trip through the Suez Canal or around South Africa. Though still principally an agricultural and timber-growing country, Canada is now undertaking manufacturing on a large scale, and the output of her coal, iron, copper, and lead mines steadily increases, owing to the investment of capital derived from Great Britain and the United States.

This development of Canadian industries under the encouragement of protective tariffs and government bounties is closely connected with the growth of a feeling that Canada constitutes a nation by herself, in spite of her position as a member of the British Empire. The close trading relations which were once fostered between Canada and the United States by reciprocity treaties guaranteeing mutual interests were hampered by the protective policy which the government at Washington followed after the close of the Civil War. As a result Canada was driven to look more and more to Great Britain as her industrial ally rather than to the neighboring republic. In the seventies Sir John Macdonald made the idea of a "national policy," or protection for Canadian interests, a current political issue; and after that time both the Conservative and Liberal parties labored to make Canada an independent manufacturing nation. In the fostering of this "colonial nationalism," as it was aptly called, there was found no more ardent advocate than the distinguished premier Sir Wilfred Laurier.

This incipient nationalism, as we shall see (pp. 468 f.), in connection with the defense of the empire, raised grave questions in regard to the relations between Canada and the mother country, which called from time to time for adjustment.

Canada is inevitably brought into close relations with the United States, although the probability of their ever uniting seems very slight at present. Along the western portion of the border, laborers cross back and forth, and thousands of French and British Canadians have settled in New England. Millions of dollars from the United States aid in the development of Canadian resources. The same system of coinage—dollars and cents—is used on both sides of the frontier, and no additional postage is required when letters are sent across the line. The same books are read by both peoples, whether written by Canadian, English, or American authors.

THE AUSTRALASIAN COLONIES

The Australasian colonies of Great Britain—Australia, Tasmania, New Zealand, and some of the minor islands—were practically unoccupied when the English colonists began to flock there in the nineteenth century. The aborigines of Australia and Tasmania were never very numerous or warlike.

They belonged to a very low grade of civilization and never seriously opposed the invaders. It is true that the English found a much higher degree of intelligence, as well as a more warlike spirit, among the Maoris of New Zealand. These from time to time offered the same kind of resistance that the North American Indians opposed to the early settlers. Although they managed to retain possession of extensive areas of land, their number, which is slightly above sixty thousand, is so small that their presence can hardly produce a race problem.

The English were therefore free, in these vast regions, to work out in their own way a democratic government suited to the conditions in which they found themselves. They were neither forced into conflict with other European peoples, as in Canada, nor compelled to control alien races, as in India.

The continent of Australia, with the neighboring island of Tasmania, somewhat exceeds in extent the area of the United States, while New Zealand alone is somewhat larger than the island of Great Britain. Although a great part of Australia lies in the temperate zone, the northern region nearest the equator is parched in summer, and the whole central portion suffers from a scarcity of water, which makes vast areas of the interior permanently uninhabitable unless some means of irrigation on a large scale can be introduced. The eastern and southern coasts have always been the chief centers of colonization. Melbourne, in the extreme south, lies in a latitude corresponding to that of Washington, St. Louis, and San Francisco in the Northern Hemisphere. The country affords gold, silver, coal, tin, copper, and iron. Tasmania and New Zealand are more fortunate than Australia in the diversity of their scenery and the general fertility of their soil, while their climate is said to possess all the advantages of the mother country without her fog.

The English occupation of Australasia belongs to the nineteenth century. The Portuguese, in their eager hunt for the Spice Islands, may perhaps have come upon Australia, but it long remained an unknown portion of the globe, as shown by the rude outline of *Terra Australis* (or "Southern Land") which appears on the maps of the Elizabethan Age. In 1642 a Dutch seaman, Tasman, discovered the island which now bears his name (originally called Van Diemen's Land). He also sighted in the same year the islands to the east, which, in spite of their almost Alpine character, were named New Zealand, after the low-lying meadows at the mouth of the Rhine. The Dutch did not, however, occupy these lands. Later they were brought to the attention of the English by the famous voyages of Captain Cook. He skirted around the entire coast of New Zealand in 1769–1770, and then sailed westward to Australia, reaching land at a point which, owing to its luxuriant foliage, he called Botany Bay. He took possession of the land in the name of the English sovereign, and it was given the name of "New South Wales," on account of its fancied resemblance to the Welsh shore line.

In 1787 England decided to establish a convict colony at Botany Bay, as deportation was a punishment very commonly inflicted in those days for what would now seem to us petty offenses. Just north of Botany Bay lies a marvelous harbor, Port Jackson, around which the town of Sydney grew up and became the chief city of New South Wales, the first of the six sister states which now form the Australian federation.

By 1840 so many colonists had settled in New South Wales that the British government ceased sending offenders there. Live stock was imported, and sheep-raising, now the chief industry, was introduced about the same period.

The discovery of gold in 1851 produced an influx of prospectors similar to that which had peopled California two years earlier. In 1855 the colony, which had been granted more and more freedom by the mother country, was given a parliament composed of two houses, an upper chamber of members appointed by the king for life, and a lower one elected by popular vote. From that time on, the colonists were left practically free to manage their own affairs.

Tasmania, with its town of Hobart established in 1804, had also been used by the English as a place of exile for political offenders as well as for criminals. The beauties of the island, however, attracted free settlers in increasing numbers, and Tasmania was separated from New South Wales in 1825. Thirty years later, after the transportation of criminals had ceased, the island received a government similar to that of New South Wales.

The settlements which had grown up around the town of Melbourne were in 1851 united into the colony of Victoria. In 1859 the region far to the north of Sydney was organized into the colony of Queensland and given a government similar to that of the other states. Its development, however, was not so rapid as that of Victoria or New South Wales, since a great portion of the interior was a desert that could be utilized only after extensive irrigation. A penal settlement established on the west coast, some two thousand miles from Sydney, grew very slowly into the colony of Western Australia. Lastly, South Australia, with its town of Adelaide, should be mentioned. This colony, lying between Victoria and Western Australia, never had the misfortune of being used as a criminal station.

It was natural that in time the people of these colonies, speaking the same language and having the same institutions, should seek a closer union. The question of a federation was long discussed, and at last, in 1899, a federal constitution, which had been drafted by a general convention composed of delegates from all the states, was accepted by the people. In 1900 the British Parliament passed an act constituting the Commonwealth of Australia on the basis of this draft. The six states—New South Wales, Tasmania, Victoria, Queensland, South Australia, and Western Australia—were formed into a union similar to that of the United States. The British crown is represented by a governor-general; the federal parliament is formed of two houses, a Senate, consisting of six senators from

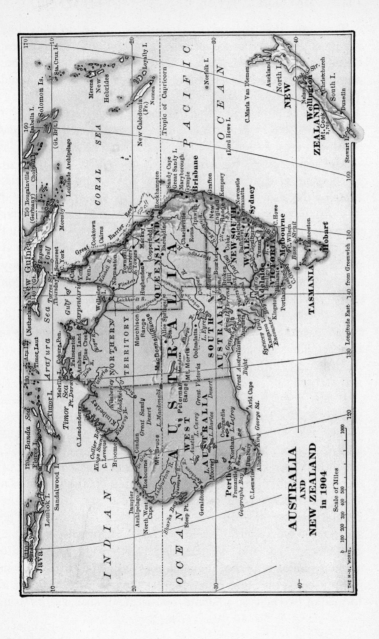

AUSTRALIA
AND
NEW ZEALAND
in 1904

Scale of Miles
0 100 200 300 400 500

each state, and a House of Representatives chosen in the same way as in the United States. This body has extensive power over commerce, railways, currency, banking, postal and telegraph service, marriage and divorce, and industrial arbitration. Women as well as men have the right to vote.

To the southeast of Australia, twelve hundred miles away, lie the islands of New Zealand, to which English pioneers began to go in the early part of the nineteenth century. In 1840 the English concluded a treaty with the native Maoris, by which the latter were assigned a definite reservation of lands on condition that they would recognize Queen Victoria as their sovereign. English settlers established the city of Auckland on North Island; and twenty-five years later New Zealand became a separate colony, with the seat of government at Wellington. Under the auspices of the New Zealand Company, colonization was actively carried on, and before long the whites began to press in upon the reservations of the Maoris. This led to two revolts on the part of the natives (1860 and 1871), which were, however, speedily repressed and were not repeated.

As industries increased New Zealand began to make noteworthy experiments in social reform. During the last decade of the nineteenth century workingmen became very influential and were soon able to carry through a large number of measures which they thought to their advantage. Special courts were established to settle disputes between employers and their workmen; an old-age pension law was enacted; and various measures were adopted for checking the creation of large estates, especially by taxing them more heavily than small farms. The right to vote was extended to women.

The colony of Victoria vied with New Zealand in social reforms. Its government attempted to stop "sweating" in the poorly paid industries; and public boards composed of employers and workmen were established for the purpose of fixing the minimum wages and standards of work, so that these matters could no longer be arranged by private bargaining

T

between individuals. The system of secret voting which originated in Australia—the so-called "Australian ballot"—is one of the reforms which spread beyond Australasia, and is in use both in England and in the United States.

GROWTH OF THE BRITISH EMPIRE IN AFRICA

The chief centers of British advance in Africa were two— the Cape of Good Hope, at the extreme south, and Egypt,[1] in the north. Cape Colony was permanently acquired, as we have seen, at the Congress of Vienna in 1814, some eight years after its actual seizure from the Dutch during the war with Napoleon. When this colony passed into the hands of the British, it contained slightly over twenty-five thousand people of European descent, mainly Dutch; and it is from this original Dutch stock that the majority of the present white inhabitants are derived, although immigration from England set in after the fall of Napoleon. These Dutch settlers were a sturdy, resolute people, strongly attached to their customs, including their slave system, and, though of peaceable spirit, unwilling to submit to interference. It was just these characteristics which the new rulers overlooked. Shortly after their occupation the British reconstructed the system of local government and the courts; they insisted on the use of the English language; and finally, in 1833, they abolished slavery, setting aside a considerable sum of money as compensation to the slave-owners, a great deal of which, however, was appropriated by shrewd financiers because it was made payable in London.

Owing to these grievances, about ten thousand of the Boers[2] left the Cape during the years 1836 to 1838, and, pushing northeastward beyond the Orange River into the interior,

---

[1] For the circumstances which led England to interfere in Egyptian affairs, see pages 171 ff.

[2] *Boer* is the Dutch word for "farmer" and has come to be especially applied to the Dutch population of South Africa.

partly inhabited by warlike savages, set up a new colony. During the succeeding years large numbers of the Boers moved farther eastward and northward into the regions now known as Natal and the Transvaal. For a time they had their own way in these unpromising wildernesses; for the English at the

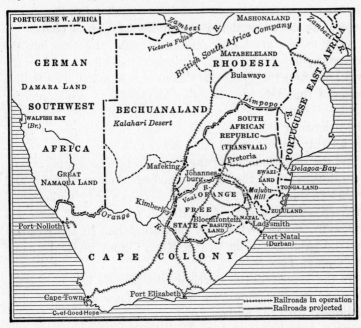

SOUTH AFRICA JUST BEFORE THE BOER WAR

Cape were too few in number, and the home government too little interested in the distant land, to follow them up and claim sovereignty over them.

Natal, however, was on the seacoast, and the British had no desire to see a strong unfriendly state established there. Consequently they sent troops over to occupy Durban (then called Port Natal), which had formerly been the seat of some English settlers. These troops came into conflict with the Dutch there in 1842 and drove them out—adding more bitterness to the ill will which the Boers already felt for the English. The conquerors cared little, however, for Dutch opinion, and six years later (in 1848) they seized the Orange River Colony, which the Boers had founded between the Orange and Vaal rivers. They justified this act of aggression by claiming that the anarchic conditions there and the troubles with the natives constantly endangered the tranquillity of Cape Colony.

Once more a great Boer migration began, this time into the region beyond the Vaal, where pioneers had already shown the way; and here the Transvaal Colony was founded. The British believed that the vast inland wilderness was good only for cattle-raising and rude agriculture and was therefore not worth the trouble of annexation and defense. Accordingly, in 1852, by a treaty known as the Sand River Convention, they recognized the independence of the Boers in the Transvaal region, guaranteeing them the right "to manage their own affairs and to govern themselves according to their own laws, without any interference on the part of the British government." This was followed, two years later, by the recognition of the freedom and independence of the Orange River Colony under the name of "Orange Free State."

In the Transvaal the Dutch lived a pioneer life, having little government and desiring but little. They were constantly embroiled with the natives; and as time went on, the British began to complain, as they had previously of the Orange River Colony, that the disorders constituted a standing menace to the peace of the neighboring colonies. Whether or no there was much justification for this claim, Great Britain in 1877 annexed the Transvaal Republic, whose independence it had recognized twenty-five years before, and insisted on retaining it in spite of a great memorial from the Dutch inhabitants petitioning for the restoration of their freedom. The government thus imposed upon the Boers was extremely galling, and in 1880 they organized an insurrection and destroyed at Majuba Hill (1881) a small detachment of English troops.

At that time Gladstone was in office; and, turning a deaf ear to the demands of the imperialists for vengeance, he determined to recognize that independence for which the Dutch had fought. Consequently he concluded a convention with the Transvaal provisional government by which autonomy under the suzerainty of the queen of England was granted to the Boers, except that their foreign affairs were to be under British control. Regarding this measure not as an act of magnanimity on the part of the British government but as a concession wrung from it by force of arms, the Boers resolved to secure complete independence, and succeeded in 1884 in obtaining a new convention recognizing the Transvaal as free and independent in all respects except the conclusion of treaties with foreign powers. They thus regained, for all practical purposes, the freedom which they had enjoyed before the annexation of 1877.

The very next year (1885) gold was discovered in the southern part of the Transvaal, and wild lands which the negroes had despised and from which the Boers could scarcely wring a scanty living now became exceedingly valuable. Thousands of miners, prospectors, and speculators, and the customary rabble of the mining camp, began to flow into the Transvaal, and within a short time the population had trebled. The Boers were now outnumbered in many places by the *Uitlanders*, or "foreigners," as they were called. The Dutch recoiled from handing over their country to a group of foreign miners and speculators. In order to retain their supremacy they put all sorts of obstacles in the way of the newcomers, who wished to acquire citizenship and the right to vote, hoping by this policy to keep the government in their own hands.

It was now the turn of the Uitlanders (who were largely British) to protest. They declared that their energy and enterprise had transformed a poor and sparsely settled country into a relatively populous and prosperous one; that they had enriched the treasury of an almost bankrupt government; and that since they also had a stake in the country, they should be allowed a voice in making the laws and in the administration of justice. They maintained, moreover, that the Boer government was old-fashioned and corrupt, and that the Uitlanders were forced to pay taxes for being badly governed. They tried to effect a change in the Transvaal constitution, and, failing in that, planned in 1895 an insurrection against the Boer authorities.

The conspiracy was encouraged by Cecil Rhodes, prime minister of Cape Colony and head of the British South Africa Company.[1] It is alleged that he was supported in this by ministers then in control of the British government. Dr. Jameson, an agent of the company who was much interested in promoting some of Rhodes's great schemes, started for the interior of the Transvaal at the head of an armed band of the company's forces with the intention of coöperating with leaders who were preparing for an uprising at Johannesburg. The enterprise miscarried, however, and the insurgents were captured by the Boers.

This "Jameson raid," as it is called, only served further to embitter the Boers and afforded them a pretext for collecting large military supplies in self-defense. The president of the Transvaal Republic, Paul Kruger, was firmly opposed to all compromise with the Uitlanders. He had been associated with Boer history since the Great Trek, or migration of 1836, when, as a boy of ten, he had first learned to distrust and hate the British. He was practically master of the little oligarchy that controlled the republic, and he secured the adoption of measures against freedom of the press and of assemblage, to stop the agitation of political questions; he steadily disregarded the petitions of the Uitlanders, who were demanding equal

[1] The British South Africa Company was formed in 1889 under the direction of Cecil Rhodes and was granted extensive powers in the region north of the Transvaal Republic, comparable to those enjoyed earlier in India by the East India Company.

rights with the Boers, and entered into an offensive and defensive alliance with the Orange Free State to the south.

The British now maintained that the Boers were aiming at the extinction of their dominion in South Africa; the Boers, on the other hand, asserted that the British were planning the overthrow of the two Dutch republics. Claims and counterclaims on both sides served to create a complicated situation. Negotiations failed to bring a settlement, and in October, 1899, the Transvaal Republic issued a declaration of war against England, following it up by an invasion of Natal and Cape Colony, in which the burghers of the Orange Free State joined. At first victorious, the Boers were finally defeated, and the two republics were annexed to the British Empire as the Orange River Colony and the Transvaal Colony.

During the struggle between Boer and Briton in the interior, the two peoples lived amicably enough and prospered side by side in Cape Colony and Natal. The boundaries of Cape Colony were extended by many annexations to the north until it had an area about five times that of the state of New York. Its population before the World War exceeded two million and a half, of which over two thirds were colored. The European element, however, was increasing by immigration from Great Britain. Cabinet government was established in 1872, and the legislative power was vested in two houses, both elected by popular vote. The principal towns are Cape Town, the capital, and Kimberley, the center of the great diamond fields.

The self-governing colony of Natal originated with the expulsion of the Boers in 1842 and the annexation of the region to Cape Colony. Some years later it was again made a separate colony, and in 1893 it was given a cabinet government of its own. Here, as at the Cape, the negro population predominated, being in 1911 over four times that of the European and Asiatic residents combined.

Shortly after the conquest of the two Boer republics, the British government took up the task of organizing its South

African colonies. Representative government was established in the Transvaal in 1906 and in the Orange Free State the following year. The next highly important step was taken in 1910, when the Union of South Africa was formed by an act of Parliament. This created a federation including four states —the Cape of Good Hope, Natal, the Transvaal, and the Orange Free State. A legislature of two houses was established. The upper chamber, or Senate, was composed of four members appointed by the governor-general, to speak especially for the colored races, and thirty-two members representing the four provinces, eight from each.

The lower chamber, or House of Assembly, was to consist of representatives apportioned among the provinces roughly according to their European population and elected by the qualified voters in the respective provinces. The executive powers were vested in a governor-general appointed by the British crown, working with the federal prime minister and cabinet.

In this new Union of South Africa the Boers outnumbered the British, and the first four ministries were headed by military leaders who had fought to maintain the independence of the Dutch settlers—Generals Botha, Smuts, and Hertzog. The British by their conciliatory policy won the allegiance of the Boer population to the Union, and enjoyed their hearty support when the World War came.

In addition to these colonies, Great Britain had acquired before 1914 three enormous provinces in southern Africa occupied almost entirely by negroes. North of Cape Colony, between German Southwest Africa and the former Boer republics, lay the Bechuanaland protectorate, inhabited by peaceful native tribes engaged in agriculture and cattle-raising. Beyond Bechuanaland and the Transvaal was Rhodesia, which was acquired through the British South Africa Company by two annexations in 1888 and 1898 and brought under the protection of the British government. A railway from Cape Town was

completed through Bulawayo and across the Victoria Falls by
1906, and then rapidly pushed northward through British Central Africa, the third great native province, which was organized under British authority in 1891. The acquisition of this
region brought the British inland possessions to the junction of
German East Africa and the Congo Free State, which blocked,
for the time being, further annexations to the north. At the
close of the World War certain German dominions were placed
under the control of Great Britain, and her sway was thus
extended from Cape Town to the Nile valley.[1]

BRITISH IMPERIAL FEDERATION

After their foundation the various English-speaking colonies
went their several ways, making laws for themselves, managing their own affairs, and levying duties on goods coming from
the mother country itself as well as from foreign nations. They
enjoyed the protection of the British army and navy, without
any corresponding burden of taxation beyond voluntary subsidies and the occasional equipment of regiments. So complete
was their exemption from any real interference on the part of
the Parliament at Westminster that many statesmen of Gladstone's generation believed that in the fullness of time they
were destined to form independent nations—"to fall from the
tree like ripe fruit."

[1] In addition to its colonies in southern and central Africa and its control in
Egypt (pp. 171 ff.), Great Britain owned British East Africa, acquired by the
extension of a protectorate over the sultanate of Zanzibar in 1891 and by subsequent treaties with France, Germany, Italy, and the Congo Free State, which
delimited the provinces of Uganda and the East African protectorate. The
special importance of British East Africa lay in the fact that it enabled Great
Britain to control the headwaters of the Nile and afforded a protection for the
Sudan and Egypt, to the north. British Somaliland, on the Strait of Bab-el-
Mandeb, was secured in 1884 in connection with the establishment of the English
power in Egypt. Along the west coast Great Britain had five centers,—Gambia,
Sierra Leone, the Gold Coast, Lagos, and Nigeria,—the beginnings of which
date back to the days of Drake and Hawkins, when the British were ravaging
the coast for slaves to carry to the New World.

However, during the last quarter of the nineteenth century a movement in the direction of a firmer union began to take shape. The extension of telegraph, cable, railway, and steamship lines had made possible a much closer connection between the mother country and her most distant colonies than existed between Oregon and the capital of the United States before our great transcontinental railroads were built.

Moreover, there appeared a school of British thinkers and statesmen who set to work by propaganda and practical measures to consolidate the British Empire, strengthen its defenses, and promote friendly relations with the United States. About the middle of the nineteenth century the British Foreign Office ceased to oppose the expansion of the United States in the Western Hemisphere. Disraeli became an outspoken imperialist in his later days, as we have seen (p. 133). In 1866 an English publicist, Charles W. Dilke, made a trip around the world, visiting the various English-speaking countries, and two years later published a book called *Greater Britain*, in which he boasted of the vast territory in possession of "Anglo-Saxons." Their lands taken together constitute an empire "five times as great as the empire of Darius and four and a half as large as the Roman Empire at its greatest extent."

Dilke argued that "in power the English countries would be more than a match for the remaining nations of the world, whom in the intelligence of their people and the extent and wealth of their dominions they already considerably surpass. . . . Italy, Spain, France, and Russia become pygmies by the side of such a people." The dominion of the world by "our race" he thought "essential to the freedom of mankind." In a later work, entitled *Imperial Defense*, he denied that war was wicked, and asserted that it was "imposed upon states by an irreconcilable opposition of purposes." This "vigorous doctrine" appealed to many Englishmen and soon became popular in Germany too, where it was developed by enthusiasts.

Dilke's *Greater Britain* was followed by a flood of "imperialistic" literature. In 1883 John R. Seeley, a professor at Cambridge, issued his book *The Expansion of England*, which recalled the colonial and commercial features of the long duel between Great Britain and France from 1688 to 1814. Imperial interests were exalted by Professor Seeley, and the idea was denounced that the colonies might in time drop off like ripe fruit. Joseph Chamberlain became a spokesman for imperialism and declared that all parts of the "English democracy would stand shoulder to shoulder to maintain the honor and integrity of the Empire."

In the same vein Tennyson wrote:

> Britain's myriad voices call:
> "Sons be welded each and all
> Into one imperial whole.
> One with Britain, heart and soul!
> One life, one flag, one fleet, one Throne!"

Imperialism seemed "aggressive altruism" to Rudyard Kipling, and so in 1899 he wrote his famous poem "The White Man's Burden":

> Take up the White Man's burden—
>   Send forth the best ye breed—
> Go bind your sons to exile
>   To serve your captives' need;
> To wait in heavy harness,
>   On fluttered folk and wild—
> Your new-caught, sullen peoples,
>   Half-devil and half-child.
>
>   . . . .

On the other hand, there were those who felt that no good could come from the fighting in foreign lands. The poet Housman devotes many of his verses to mourning the fate of the brave lads sent "to Afric and to Ind":

The Queen she sent to look for me,
    The sergeant he did say,
"Young man, a soldier will you be
    For thirteen pence a day."

. . . .

My mouth is dry, my shirt is wet,
    My blood runs all away.

. . . .

Tomorrow after new young men
    The sergeant he must see,
For things will all be over then
    Between the Queen and me.

And I shall have to bate my price,
    For in the grave, they say,
Is neither knowledge nor device
    Nor thirteen pence a day.

Such as Housman were easily disposed of as "mollycoddles," who knew neither honor nor glory, and the propaganda went merrily on. The Royal Colonial Institute founded in 1868 denounced the proposed break-up of the empire and protested "against doctrines so injurious to our interests and so derogatory to our honor." The Imperial Federation League (1884) was succeeded by the British Empire League, established in 1895. Federationists in all parts of the empire sought by conferences, pamphlets, books, and newspapers to arouse an imperial patriotism, which might in time lead Englishmen to merge their colonial loyalty into a loyalty to the great empire, just as the pride of the citizen of the United States in his particular state gives way before national patriotism.

The practical program of the federationists included three general proposals. (1) They advocated strengthening the political bonds between the colonies and the mother country by giving the colonies representation in Parliament or by creating an imperial committee consisting of representatives from the colonies working in conjunction with the government of Great Britain. (2) They proposed to establish a commercial union for the empire by introducing a general system of tariffs favoring British goods everywhere. (3) They advocated, and partially carried into effect, a general scheme of defense for the whole empire.

To further the realization of some form of federation, periodical conferences of the premiers of the self-governing colonies were held in London, beginning with the inaugural meeting in 1887, on the fiftieth anniversary of Queen Victoria's accession. The discussions were prolonged, but the practical results meager. The conference of 1887 expressly excluded the question of imperial federation and considered principally naval defense. The conference of 1897, under the presidency of the colonial secretary, denounced any treaties that might hamper the commercial relations between Great Britain and the colonies; that of 1902 approved giving preference to British goods, but it did not accept Joseph Chamberlain's proposition to establish an imperial council. The conference of 1907, composed of representatives of Canada, Transvaal, Cape Colony, Natal, Australia, New Zealand, and Newfoundland, made a quadrennial imperial conference a permanent institution.

As time went on, this agitation, reënforced by the growing menace of German competition, began to produce concrete results. In 1898 Canada enacted a preferential tariff giving Great Britain a material reduction on all dutiable goods. This policy, inaugurated by Canada, of making special arrangements between the mother country and her colonies was gradually extended, so that, by the opening of the World War, Great Britain and nearly forty of her possessions were united into a tariff union. The necessity of being prepared to defend the commerce of the empire led Australia to introduce in 1911 a new military system based upon the compulsory training of its citizens, and to develop the royal Australian navy in connection with the British marine in the Pacific. In Canada the

Conservatives, on coming into power, voted a large appropriation in 1911 to build battleships "as Canada's contribution to the British Grand Fleet."

Germany's commercial expansion and her development of a mighty navy must have exercised a powerful influence on these preparations. As early as 1897 the London *Saturday Review* expressed the consternation in England and the probability of a great conflict: "A million petty disputes build up the greatest cause of war the world has ever seen. If Germany were extinguished tomorrow there is not an Englishman in the world who would not be richer. Nations have fought for years over a city or right of succession; must they not fight for two hundred and fifty million pounds of commerce? . . . England has awakened to what is alike inevitable and her best hope of prosperity. *Germaniam esse delendam!*" The writer believed that Russia and France would be Great Britain's allies in the coming conflict; and he saw the German fleet sent to the bottom of the sea, and Germany itself partitioned among its enemies. So the British as well as the Germans had been looking for the great day of reckoning years before it came.

The Irish Question

Of all the vast and varied dominions included in the British Empire, "John Bull's other island," about half the size of Great Britain, has been the most constant and poignant source of trouble to the British government, and for the longest time. The grievances of the Irish—who differ from the English in race and sentiments—have caused insurrections, incited to murder and riot, induced military oppression, overthrown ministries, blocked the business of Parliament for days, and contributed to the ancient ill will between England and the United States; and, in spite of volumes of statutes designed to establish peace and amity, the ancient evils continued to plague successive Parliaments until after the close of the World War.

The original source of Irish discontent is to be found in the repeated invasions of their island by the English, who long treated them as a subject race. For centuries after the earliest conquests under Henry II (1154–1189), the authority of the English sovereigns extended only to certain eastern districts known as "the Pale." To the north and west the wild Irish chieftains and their people dwelt in practical independence under Irish law and custom, constantly fighting among themselves and against the invaders. Within the Pale and on its borders the English barons built great castles and reduced the peasants to serfdom (see map, p. 212).

Henry VII (1485–1509) determined to get a firmer grip on Ireland than his predecessors had secured, and sent over an able administrator, Sir Edward Poynings, who forced the Irish parliament established within the Pale to accept certain measures which bore the name of their author, and which remained in vigor for four centuries. These provided that English statutes should have the same force in Ireland as in England, that no Irish parliament could be called without the English king's consent, and that no acts could be passed until first approved by king and council. While this new system did not work any great hardship so long as the authority of the Irish parliament was confined to the English Pale, it completely destroyed the independence of the Irish when it was later extended to the entire island.

Henry VIII (1509–1547) took the title of "King," instead of that of "Lord," of Ireland, which his predecessors had borne, and ordered the Irish to adopt the English language, English dress, and even the English fashion of cutting the hair. This, however, was unimportant when compared with his attempt to force them to accept him instead of the Pope as head of the Church. Though the Irish people clung steadfastly to the Pope and their ancient faith, all government officials were compelled to take the oath acknowledging Henry as supreme head of the Church; monasteries were suppressed, the monks were driven out, and their lands were seized and handed over to Henry's supporters.

This interference in Irish religious matters was continued under Edward VI, when the Catholic clergy were expelled from their parishes and Protestant priests installed in their places. These were to be supported by tithes collected from a people still loyal to the old faith. When the form of the English Church was finally fixed under Queen Elizabeth, it was forced in its entirety upon the Irish. They were compelled to accept Elizabeth as supreme governor in things spiritual as well as temporal and to attend Protestant services under pain of severe penalties.

Although this religious settlement could be made really effective only within the Pale, it was the source of great friction, and toward the close of Elizabeth's reign nearly all of Celtic Ireland made a united and desperate attempt under O'Neill to throw off English rule. This uprising was, however, cruelly suppressed, and such havoc wrought in the island that a contemporary declared that "nothing was more frequent in the ditches of the towns, and especially in wasted countries, than to see multitudes of these poor people dead, with their mouths all colored green by eating nettles, docks, and all things which they could rend up above ground." Extensive areas, especially in the north, were declared forfeited and were handed over to English and Scotch settlers, thus adding to the bitterness which already existed between the natives and the foreign colonists.

This bitterness took the form of sullen resentment until the quarrel between Charles I and Parliament gave the Irish another excellent opportunity to revolt (1641). Hoping to regain the lands which had been taken from them, as well as to shake off the hated English yoke, they savagely attacked the English and Scottish colonists, especially in the northern part of the island, and committed atrocities which repaid with interest the outrages of which the English had been guilty in the preceding century. After Cromwell and the Puritans executed

Charles I in 1649, the Irish declared in favor of his son, Charles II, and Cromwell immediately crossed over into Ireland to put down resistance to his newly established Commonwealth. With fire and sword he scourged the country. At Drogheda he put two thousand to death after the garrison had surrendered, saying, "I am persuaded that this is a righteous judgment of God upon those barbarous wretches who have embrued their hands in so much innocent blood; and that it will tend to prevent the effusion of blood for the future— which are the satisfactory grounds to such actions which otherwise cannot but work remorse and regret." Within six months the whole island was reconquered.

This conquest was the occasion of a new and more extensive confiscation of Irish lands. Thousands of Irish landlords and peasants were driven from the soil to make room for large colonies of the English conquerors. Great estates were apportioned out among the soldiers. It is estimated that before the uprising of 1641 the Protestants held only one third of the arable land in Ireland, while forty years later they owned about two thirds of it.

But the woes of Ireland were not yet at an end; for that unhappy land became involved in the English revolution of 1688, which resulted in the expulsion of the Catholic king, James II, who naturally found many supporters among his Irish subjects. They refused to recognize the Protestant king, William III, who thereupon undertook a new subjugation of Ireland. In this war the native Irish had again to bear the brunt of the conflict; for they alone were loyal to the Catholic James, while the colonists favored William. Two years of fighting brought Ireland once more under the English yoke.

This renewed victory was followed by measures designed to stamp out Catholicism altogether and to make Irish industry and commerce subservient to the interests of English manufacturers and farmers. Both public and private teaching by Catholics was prohibited, nor might children be sent out

T

of the island to be educated. Parish priests were allowed to
remain only under onerous conditions, while bishops, monks,
and friars were ordered to leave the country. Catholics were

IRELAND, SHOWING THE BOUNDARIES OF THE PALE UNDER HENRY VIII

forbidden to carry firearms; they could not buy land, or lease
it for more than thirty-one years; and by turning Protestant
the son of a Catholic could secure possession of his father's
property.

To prevent farmers in Ireland from competing with those in England, the English Parliament prohibited the importation of cattle, sheep, swine, beef, pork, mutton, butter, and cheese from Ireland. To crush the Irish woolen industry it prohibited the sending of woolen goods to any other country than England, from which they were practically excluded by high protective duties. Moreover, the landlords, many of whom lived in England and never even visited their estates, charged the peasants high rents and evicted them when they failed to pay.

Quite naturally Ireland was filled with discontent from Cork to Sligo and from Dublin to Galway; local disorders were chronic during the eighteenth century; and by constant agitation the Irish finally managed to secure the reform of some of the old laws. Fearing that the Irish might break away during the American Revolution, England conceded to Catholics the right to buy land and relieved them of the necessity of stating under oath where they had last heard Mass. Again, in 1793, when the French Revolution was in progress, and England was going to war with the new republic, the English government freed the Irish Catholics from the restrictions which had been imposed upon their religion, gave them the right to vote for members of their Parliament, and opened important civil and military offices to them.

These concessions did not, however, satisfy the Irish, and, hoping for assistance from the French, they planned another desperate uprising. The rebellion of 1798, like all previous attempts, was put down with great loss of life, and the English government decided to destroy entirely the appearance of legislative independence by abolishing the Irish parliament altogether. This body, which had been under the complete control of the English crown since the passage of Poynings's Act, was in no way representative of the Irish people. The House of Lords was composed of Anglican prelates and nobles, and the House of Commons, which was assumed to represent the people, was closed to Catholics, who made up nine tenths of the population. Moreover, the Irish parliament had every vice of the English system of rotten boroughs. Almost one half of the three hundred members were chosen by twenty-five landlords.

Nevertheless, it was not because the Irish parliament was corrupt and undemocratic that the English government determined to abolish it, but because it enjoyed a larger measure of independence than was deemed compatible with the security of the English rule. The Act of Union was accordingly passed, in 1800, suppressing it altogether and providing for the representation of Ireland in the Parliament of Great Britain. Ireland was assigned one hundred members in the British House of Commons, and twenty-eight temporal peers, chosen for life by the Irish baronage, were admitted to the House of Lords. This measure, by which the Irish representatives at Westminster were swallowed up in an overwhelming majority of English and Scotch, was stoutly opposed by Irish patriots; but by flagrant bribery, which Lord Cornwallis, who was charged with a portion of the negotiations, called "dirty business," the Irish parliament was induced to accept the proposed change and to put an end to its own existence.

The agitation of the Irish question was now transferred to the Parliament of the United Kingdom of Great Britain and Ireland, and the first great contest took place over the provisions which excluded Irish, as well as all other Catholics, from that Parliament. Again and again the measure for admitting Catholics was introduced, debated, and defeated. Finally, in 1821, it was passed by the House of Commons, only to be rejected by the Lords. In 1828 Daniel O'Connell, although he well knew that he would not be admitted to Parliament, stood for the district of Clare and was triumphantly elected in the midst of great excitement. Convinced that civil war could be averted only by yielding, the Duke of Wellington, then prime minister, consented to the introduction of a bill for relief. It was under these circumstances that the Catholic Emancipation

Act (which we have described on page 92) was passed, and the Irish Catholics were admitted to Parliament and to practically all civil and military offices, on condition that they would abjure the temporal power of the Pope and disclaim any intention of injuring the authority of the English Church.

The admission of Catholics to Parliament, however, did nothing to allay the state of chronic poverty and distress among the peasants of Ireland. The report of a government commission in 1836 showed that while English agricultural laborers received an average wage of eight to ten shillings a week ($2 to $2.50), those of Ireland got scarcely one fourth that small amount. Nearly one third of the entire population, which was nevertheless increasing rapidly, subsisted chiefly on potatoes—commonly on an inferior, coarse variety which had once been cultivated for swine alone. The census of 1841 revealed the startling fact that in the case of 46 per cent of the population the entire family lived in a single-roomed cottage, and that seven tenths of these rooms were unfit for human habitation.

In spite of this desperate and well-nigh universal wretchedness, Ireland was drained of millions yearly to pay landlords whose ancestors had secured estates after the wars and confiscations of Cromwell and William III—landlords, moreover, who rarely set foot in Ireland and took little or no interest in their tenants beyond the collection of their rent. Money that should have gone to improve, stock, and fertilize Irish land was spent in London or in traveling on the Continent. The annual rent had to be wrested from the people by the landlord's agent at any cost; and if it was not paid, the tenant was speedily evicted from his cottage and lands, often without any compensation for such improvements as he had made with his own hands and at his own expense.[1]

---

[1] In 1847 the rent paid to absentee landlords was estimated at four million pounds, or about a third of the entire rental of Ireland. From 1839 to 1843, according to O'Connell, a hundred and fifty thousand peasants had been evicted.

.The height of Irish misery seems to have been reached in the "Black Year of Forty-seven." In 1846 the potato crop, upon which one third to one half of the population depended for food, failed almost entirely, and the government was compelled to open temporary relief works (building roads, etc.), in which toward a million persons sought employment. At one time a third of the entire population was in receipt of charity; yet thousands died of starvation.

According to the report of the census commissioners in 1851, "No pen has recorded the numbers of the forlorn and starving who perished by the wayside or in the ditches, or of the mournful groups, sometimes of whole families, who lay down and died, one after another on the floor of their cabins, and so remained uncoffined and unburied until chance revealed the appalling scene."

It was in the midst of this terrible famine that the stream of emigration began to flow toward America, and a steady decrease in the Irish population set in. Within half a century four million emigrants left the shores of Ireland for foreign countries, principally the United States, but they did not leave behind them in the "old country" their bitter resentment against England, which they believed had wronged them so deeply.

Through all these years of distress and famine the Anglican Church, which had been established in Ireland under the Tudors, continued to draw ample revenues from the tithes and endowments. Though its members numbered but one tenth of the population, it was in possession of the ancient churches of the island; its fourteen hundred benefices had a revenue of three million dollars a year; its twenty-two bishops and archbishops enjoyed together an income of seven hundred and fifty thousand dollars a year; and, not content with this, an extra *cess*, or tax, for general purposes, yielding about three hundred thousand dollars, filled the cup of bitterness against the Established Church to overflowing. The tithes were collected from the peasants only with the utmost difficulty, and pitched battles were often fought between them and the police when the latter undertook to drive off cattle to pay the tithe. The opposition grew into an organized movement; a favorite amusement was to make the tithe proctor eat the paper authorizing him to seize property for the debt; and in one case a company of lancers and two companies of the Ninety-second Highlanders, with two pieces of artillery, were detailed to keep order at the sale of one cow for a peasant's tithe. In 1833 only about twelve thousand pounds out of the hundred and four thousand due could be secured by the government, which had assumed the burden of collecting the money.

For years this contest over the tithes continued, and, with other grievances, it led in 1858 to the formation of a powerful society known as the Fenians, from *Fianna Eirinn*, or "national militia." This society was especially strong in the United States, where enormous sums of money were collected to further the agitation carried on by the organization. A great convention was held in Chicago in 1863 to plan a special campaign in Ireland, and at the same time Stephens, a leader in the movement, founded a paper in Dublin called *The Irish People*, which openly advocated rebellion against British rule. Stephens was soon arrested for conspiracy; but he escaped to America, though many of his supporters were condemned to penal servitude. An attempt of the Fenians to blow up the Clerkenwell jail in London, where a conspirator was imprisoned, resulted in the death of twelve and the injury of more than a hundred persons. The English government, thoroughly alarmed, put down Fenianism by military force, but at the same time decided to remove some of the abuses which had given rise to the movement.

Disestablishment and disendowment of the Anglican Church in Ireland were made the great issues in the general election of 1868, and the Liberal party, which favored these measures, was carried into power by a huge majority. The Methodists and Baptists, who supported Gladstone, Bright, and the other Liberals, were heartily opposed to the Anglican Church in England itself, and therefore all the more desirous to see its destruction in Ireland; and the workingmen, newly enfranchised by the Reform Bill of 1867, had no marked sympathy for Irish landlords. Under these influences Parliament in 1869 disestablished the English Church in Ireland and abolished its hated tithes, but allowed it to keep the beautiful buildings which had been seized in the period of the Reformation, and created a fund for the support of the Anglican clergy in Ireland.

The land question, which had always been a fundamental one, remained unsolved. The tithe collector had gone, but the equally hated agent of the absentee landlord remained. Even in an age of manufacturing, three and one half out of the four and one half millions of the Irish people were still dependent upon the cultivation of the soil. An investigation by a land commission showed that between the landlord and the tenant there were often three middlemen who made their living from the necessities of the peasant, whom they had entirely at their mercy. The emigration to America had not relieved the intense competition for land; and as tenants generally held it at the will of the landlord, they could be driven from their holdings with little difficulty. And it was a terribly serious matter for the peasant to be evicted, for even a dirt floor and a smoky peat fire were preferable to the open moor.

In 1879 a great Land League, with Charles Stewart Parnell, a member of Parliament, at its head, was established with the aim of securing three things for the Irish peasant—fair rent, fixed holding, and fair sale. That is, they asked for legislation providing that the rent should not be fixed by the landlord at any amount he thought he could get, but by a court taking into consideration the fair value of the land; that the tenant should hold as long as he paid the rent so fixed; and finally, that, should he surrender his holding, he should be allowed to sell his improvements to the tenant who succeeded him.

Parnell, with the support of the Irish members in Parliament, resorted to "filibustering" until that body was forced in 1881 to pass a land act granting these three demands. This measure was later supplemented by land-purchase acts, by which the government put at the disposal of the tenants money to buy their holdings, with the privilege of repayment on the installment plan. The last of these acts, passed in 1903, during the administration of Arthur Balfour, appropriated a practically unlimited amount for this purpose and offered a considerable inducement to landlords to sell, so that the land question seemed in a fair way to be settled to the satisfaction of the peasantry.[1]

All these concessions made by the English government did not, however, settle the Irish question; for the demand for "Home Rule," or complete legislative independence of Ireland, was still extensively advocated and frequently debated in the House of Commons. As we have seen, the union of 1801 was really forced upon the Irish by bribing those who could in no way be regarded as representing that nation. The repeal of the Act of Union was warmly urged by Daniel O'Connell after the emancipation of 1829, and at the general election of 1834 forty members of Parliament favored Home Rule. In 1842 *The Nation* was founded to champion the cause, and a staff of brilliant writers were engaged to voice it. A Repeal Association was organized, monster meetings—said to have been attended by half a million people—were arranged by O'Connell, and the examples of Belgium and Greece in winning independence were cited as indications of what the Irish might do. All Ireland seemed on the verge of rebellion, and Irish Americans planned an invasion of Canada. The British government met this agitation by stationing thirty-five

[1] The Land Purchase Act of 1885, passed by Lord Salisbury's government, set apart twenty-five million dollars; that of 1888, a second sum of the same amount; that of 1891 devoted one hundred and seventy million dollars to the purchase of lands; and that of 1903, an almost unlimited sum.

thousand troops in the island, and O'Connell, in spite of his violent and inflammatory speeches, shrank from the test of civil war.

O'Connell died in 1847; but the cause of Home Rule did not perish with him, for it was taken up by the Fenians and the Land League and thus kept steadily before the people. In 1882 a decided impetus to the movement was given by the shocking murder of Lord Frederick Cavendish and Thomas Burke, the Undersecretary for Ireland, in Phœnix Park, Dublin. This deed aroused the horror of the civilized world and convinced Gladstone that nothing short of Home Rule could solve the perennial Irish problem. After the parliamentary election of 1886, which gave him a small majority in the Commons and made him dependent upon the Irish members for their support, he undertook to secure the repeal of the Act of Union. Many of his followers, however, who did not believe in the policy of Home Rule, broke away from his leadership and formed the party of the Liberal Unionists, thus defeating the bill by about thirty votes. Seven years later, when Gladstone was again in power, he brought forward a new Home Rule bill providing that the Irish should have a parliament of their own at Dublin and also retain representation in that of the United Kingdom. This bill, though passed by the Commons, was rejected by the House of Lords. For some years thereafter the issue almost dropped out of English politics; but the majority of the Irish members of Parliament continued to agitate the question, and the great Liberal victory in the elections of 1906 again raised hopes for Irish independence.

Many of the victorious Liberals favored self-government for Ireland on principle; others, for policy's sake. Herbert Asquith and Lloyd George had to cast about for votes to push through their startling social reforms (pp. 118 ff.), which were hotly opposed in both houses. So they found a compromise advisable, according to which the Irish Nationalists agreed to support the Liberal reforms, and the Liberals to bring up a new bill for Irish Home Rule. Twice this bill was passed by the Commons,—in 1913 and 1914,—and it was in a fair way to become a law under the Lords' Veto Act (p. 69). Then came the World War, and it was laid aside. This may have been due in part to the loud outcries of the Protestant inhabitants of Ulster, the northern province of Ireland, who violently and relentlessly opposed the bill on the ground that it would subject them to a government controlled by a Catholic majority. Some of the more daring of the Ulsterites even threatened to oppose by arms any attempt to separate them from the United Kingdom.

So great was the tension in Great Britain in the summer of 1914 that Germany was encouraged to think that these difficulties might keep the British out of the war. This hope proved to be an illusion; but during the great conflict Irish extremists, angered by the failure to pass the Home Rule bill, did their best to hamper the British military operations. In 1916 there was an insurrection in Dublin, which was quickly suppressed. The ancient animosities only smoldered, however, and, as we shall see, something like a civil war followed the conclusion of a general European peace and ended in the creation of the Irish Free State (pp. 465 ff.).

CHAPTER VII

THE NEW WORLD AND THE OLD

Relation of American Civilization to European

It is usually taken for granted that the history of the Western Hemisphere is essentially a branch or continuation of European development in a new setting. The countries of the New World were originally European colonies, and the languages, literatures, sciences, and political institutions of Europe were inevitably carried across the sea by the settlers. However secure the present political independence of the nations of North and South America, it may be argued that they did not originate their civilization but borrowed it. Even in those portions of Latin America where the ancient Indian population predominates, European culture has vastly modified the old ways. Viewed from this standpoint, the history of North and South America is indeed a phase of European history. The two continents not only have their rich heritage from the Old World but also continue to be deeply affected by the course of affairs across the Atlantic.

On the other hand, the two Americas, especially the United States, have exercised a far more profound and varied influence upon Europe than has been recognized—until recently, at least. Most European writers have failed to perceive this, and even American historians have not emphasized it sufficiently. Since the World War, however, the United States has come to loom so large in world affairs that it seems appropriate here to review the chief ways in which the New World has long been deeply affecting the Old. The story may prove somewhat prosaic, but it is none the less significant. Not until the World

War were masses of American troops fighting in Europe. No Cortes or Pizarro ever sailed from American shores to conquer and despoil a European people. While American artists and writers and philosophers have not infrequently gained some recognition in Europe, they have played no such part as American inventors and business men in altering European habits. It is in the realm of economic, political, diplomatic, and military affairs that the interaction of the Old and the New World is most clear and unmistakable.

Economic Influences of the Americas on Europe

It is common enough for Europeans to tax the people of the United States with an excessive striving for money. But this would seem to be one of the most obvious elements in America's European heritage. The Spanish conquerors were, in any case, urged on by an insatiable thirst for gold which was shared by their pious rulers. The streams of gold and silver which flowed into Europe from Peru, Mexico, and other sources in the New World greatly altered the conditions which Europe had inherited from the Middle Ages. The influx of money enriched kings, financed wars and gave them a new character, augmented the resources of capitalists (thus stimulating commerce and manufacture), altered price levels, and, in general, forwarded the dissolution of the old feudal order and hastened the transformation of western Europe from an agricultural into an urban civilization. No historian has as yet fully analyzed the effects of the increase of gold and silver. We do not even know very accurately how much was transported across the Atlantic. The most reliable estimates, it is true, seem to indicate a rather insignificant amount as compared with present standards; but one must remember that a constant process of inflation has been going on in modern times, so that the value of the precious metals in relation to commodities has steadily decreased. In the days of the

Spanish galleons, gold went much further than now. From the first voyage of Columbus to 1521, the annual importations would seem to have been, at the old valuation, some $250,000; during the following quarter of a century the amount rose to $3,000,000 yearly, and then dropped to $1,400,000 toward the end of the century. Even if most of this treasure flowed into Spain in the first instance, it quickly found its way into other countries in payment for manufactured goods.

England, for example, began to be affected as early as the reign of Henry VIII. The well-known economic historian Cunningham says: "After 1521 silver found its way into England in large quantities, and the rise of prices, which had already begun, went on with unexampled rapidity. In 1549 the price of wheat suddenly shot upwards; only in exceptional years did it fall back to anything like the previous level, and during the century preceding the Great [Puritan] Rebellion, the ordinary prices of commodities were quadrupled." Thus, not only were kings and princes enriched, but the general level of prices was raised, affecting wages, standards of living, rents, accumulation of capital, and, in short, the whole social order of western Europe. The movement from feudalism to capitalism, with its manifold influences on ideas and life, was assuredly hastened; indeed whole areas of Europe, now highly industrialized, might have remained agricultural had it not been for the precious metals from the New World and for the commerce set in motion by them.

Even more important was the influx of wheat, corn, pork, cotton, tobacco, and other raw materials from the New World. Before the end of the eighteenth century, English farmers were complaining that grain from the English colonies in America was affecting domestic prices and cutting into their Continental market. Perhaps an Austrian economist was right when he attributed to American wheat a deeper influence on European history than that wrought by gold and silver. Besides helping to depress European agriculture and accelerating the movement of the peasants from the land to industrial cities, it supplied bread for countless millions of factory workers in England, France, Germany, and Italy. It was cotton from Southern plantations that kept spinning machines of Europe whirling from the days of Arkwright and Crompton down to our own time, when Egyptian and Indian cotton have begun to augment the supply.

On the other side of the ledger must be set the account of American imports from the Old World. If American gold and silver stimulated the rise of European capitalism, the two Americas later furnished enormous markets for the investment of European capital. The early canals, roads, railways, and infant industries of the United States were extensively financed by English and Dutch capital. During the Civil War in the United States, both contestants borrowed heavily in the Old World, German financiers buying large blocks of Northern bonds.

By 1913 Great Britain had five billion dollars, and Germany two billions, invested in Latin-American countries; and they were steadily increasing their holdings. Indeed, it has been roughly estimated that, apart from the possible demand for goods caused by the destruction wrought by wars, South America alone, in the development of her rich natural resources, might absorb the capital accumulations of the world during the rest of the twentieth century. It was by the sale of her American securities that England was able to make enormous purchases of munitions in the United States during the first stages of the World War. What would happen to Europe if the capital outlets in the New World, particularly South America, were closed?

If the two Americas furnished bread and meat for millions of Europe's industrial workers, they also took in exchange the products of loom, forge, and kiln. In 1772 England's exports to her American colonies almost equaled in value her entire export business in all parts of the world seventy years before.

By the end of the eighteenth century the annual trade of Latin America with the world had risen to more than a hundred million dollars—a sum about equivalent to the official value of all the exports and imports of Great Britain at the time. In 1910 Great Britain's exports to the United States and Latin America exceeded in value her exports to France, Germany, and Italy combined; while the Latin-American trade of Germany was growing far more rapidly than her commerce with the world at large. The standards of living, indeed the very living, of millions in Europe hung upon the demands of American markets.

In addition to providing a market for European manufactures, the two Americas served as a huge reservoir into which could be poured the surplus populations of the Old World— Irish fleeing from British rule and from poverty, Germans searching for political liberty and economic opportunity in the New World, Jews hunting for religious freedom, the starving and discontented peasantry of southern and southeastern Europe in quest of a livelihood. Between 1820 and 1909 more than twenty-seven million immigrants found their way into the United States alone. Until about 1890 there was enough unoccupied fertile land in that country to furnish a farm for every immigrant who cared to go to the frontier; vast areas of the West were brought under cultivation by Irish, German, and Scandinavian immigrants.

While sending their sons and daughters by the million to the United States, Germany and Italy supplied a rising stream of migration to South America. Nearly three million Europeans—mainly Italians, Portuguese, Germans, and Spaniards —went to Brazil between 1829 and 1910. More than one fourth of the Argentine population in 1909 was European in birth—Italians, Spaniards, French, English, Swiss, Germans, and Austrians. On the eve of the World War there were more than half a million Germans in Latin America. Whole sections of Brazil were colonized by them, and some German econo-

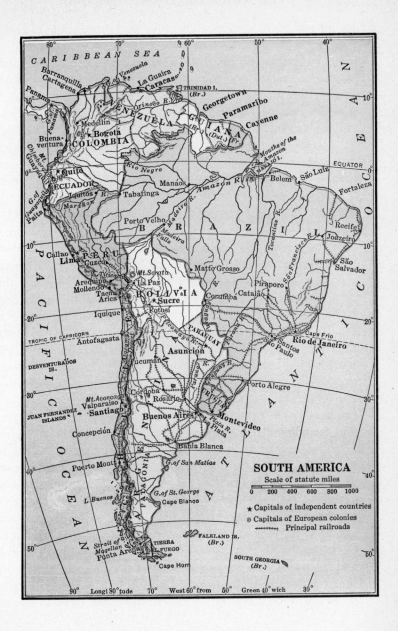

SOUTH AMERICA

Scale of statute miles

0   200   400   600   800   1000

★ Capitals of independent countries
⊙ Capitals of European colonies
++++++++ Principal railroads

mists thought the rise of independent German states in South America was not beyond the realm of possibility. Whenever there was an industrial depression or a great crop failure in Europe, poverty-stricken thousands fled from their native lands, relieving the pressure at home and finding a livelihood in the Americas.

Once safely in the New World, immigrants wrote letters back to their countrymen, urging them to cross the water, giving them extravagant notions of prosperity, and filling them with discontent. How far was the fermenting democracy of Europe due to the letters written by immigrants to their relatives and friends? What revolutions did Europe escape by having this outlet for her increasing millions? What will be the effect of the new restrictive policy, adopted by the United States, limiting immigration, especially from southern and eastern Europe?

The impacts of the United States on the Old World also extended toward the setting sun,—across the Pacific Ocean and through the Far East. Independence had scarcely been declared, in 1776, when American sea captains began to sail from Boston, New York, and Philadelphia for the Orient, carrying American goods to be exchanged for tea, spices, and other Eastern products. From year to year this traffic grew, and with it went warships from the United States navy to protect and advance the commerce thus developed. When Great Britain broke open the ports of China in the Opium War, the United States quickly insisted on similar rights, and in 1844 established formal relations with the Celestial Empire. It was Commodore Perry, in command of American warships, who forced Japan to unlock her barred gates and to enter into close relations with Western civilization (pp. 258 ff.).

Long before the middle of the nineteenth century, the United States had vital interests in the Hawaiian Islands and served notice on Europe that these islands were within the American sphere of influence. In 1867 the United States

T

bought Alaska from Russia and raised its flag on its distant islands almost at the very portals of Japan. A few years later an American navy officer acquired for his country a naval station in the Samoa Islands, making it apparent to England and Germany that they would have to reckon with a newcomer in the islands of the Pacific. In 1898 Hawaii, the Philippines, and other islands of the Pacific came under the Stars and Stripes, and in 1900 the United States coöperated with European powers in suppressing the Boxer rebellion and attempting to settle the troubled estate of China.

In the contest for concessions—such as the right to construct railways, and other material advantages—the government at Washington had to be considered by European cabinets at every turn. In the economic and educational development of China and Japan, American missionaries and business men played a rôle of increasing importance. Thus no small part of the European civilization transferred to the Orient went by the way of America.

As the nineteenth century merged into the twentieth, capitalists from the United States entered into competition with European bankers in international finance. In 1899 Morgan and Company in New York floated the first significant foreign loan issued in the United States—the bonds of the Mexican Republic. This was followed soon by a loan to Great Britain to help her finance her war with the Boer republics. Not long afterward a huge block of Japanese bonds was sold in New York to aid the "Empire of the Rising Sun" in paying the expenses of defeating Russia in eastern Asia. Thus American capital contributed to the extension of English supremacy in Africa and of Japanese supremacy in Manchuria. A little later China, on a gentle hint from President Roosevelt, allowed American bankers to share with England, France, and Germany in a loan of $50,000,000. Once dependent on Europe for capital to develop its resources, the United States was now becoming a competitor with Old World bankers for business in all quarters.

In no part of the world was the pressure of United States business enterprise on European competitors stronger than in Latin America, where the rivalry of England, France, and Germany for markets in which to sell goods and for investment opportunities grew sharper as their industries multiplied. "There is no need," said Napoleon III in 1861, at the launching of the French expedition to Mexico in support of Maximilian (Vol. I, p. 549, note), "for me to enlarge upon the common interest which we in Europe have in seeing Mexico pacified and endowed with a stable government. Not only has that country . . . attracted much of our capital and many of our fellow countrymen . . . but if it were regenerated it would form an impassable barrier to the encroachments of North America; it would form an important opening for English, Spanish, and French trade while exploiting its own wealth; and lastly, it would render great services to our manufactories by extending the cultivation of cotton."

Still more deeply interested was Great Britain. For many years the British Foreign Office opposed, by diplomatic suggestion, the sale of Mexican territory to the United States, and at one time it tried to get the United States to join with England and France in guaranteeing the possession of Cuba to Spain. By a steady extension of her activities in Central America, with a view to controlling the canal zone, Great Britain early came into collision with the United States. But through the Clayton-Bulwer Treaty, signed in 1850, England and the United States arrived at a compromise by agreeing to neutralize the canal, if it should be built, and assuring equal privileges to the shipping of all countries. Though regarded by many citizens of the United States as a victory for British diplomacy, this agreement was followed by a more cordial feeling between the two countries. Six years later Disraeli publicly stated in the House of Commons that it would be unwise for Great Britain to look upon the further extension of the territory of the United States with the extreme jealousy hitherto cherished, and suggested that England might get more trade than hitherto if the regions were reduced to orderly government by the arms of the United States. Yet in surrendering territorial ambitions Great Britain increased her efforts to multiply trade and investment opportunities, as we have seen; and Germany, not far behind, added rapidly to the proportion of her share.

Into this Latin-American sphere of economic activity, business enterprise from the United States pressed with increasing eagerness. The annexation of Porto Rico and the establishment of a protectorate over Cuba in 1898, the revision of the Clayton-Bulwer Treaty in the Hay-Pauncefote Treaty of 1901,—which permitted the United States to construct the Panama Canal,—the purchase of the Virgin Islands from Denmark in 1917, the extension of authority over Haiti, Santo Domingo, Nicaragua, and other regions, by various operations, between 1907 and 1924, were merely signs of the intensifying competition of the United States. Indeed, these signal political events were quickly followed by a multiplication of American investments and a growth of American trade. For example, between 1899, the date of the first intervention in Nicaragua by the landing of United States marines, and 1910, American trade with that country rose from three to nine million dollars a year. Between 1899 and 1925 United States investments in Mexico rose from $185,000,000 to about $1,318,900,000, while trade increased surprisingly. In the opening years of the twentieth century the trade and investments of the United States in Colombia, Ecuador, Peru, and Bolivia had reached a point that made the economic predominance of the United States seem only a question of time.

Although England and Germany, particularly after 1900, were officially maneuvering for the support of the United States in their coming war, the business men and imperialists of the two countries certainly resented "Yankee intrusion" into their spheres of influence. Some of the German editors were quite outspoken. "It is not true," said a Hamburg news-paper in 1896, "that the world is divided up. It never is. The whole of Central and South America is at present to be had for the right nation. German emigrants can, if they are so minded, create a German empire there." About the same time another German publicist remarked significantly: "We need a fleet capable not only of coping with the miserable forces of South American states, but powerful enough, if need should arise, to cause America [that is, the United States] to think twice before making any attempt to apply the Monroe Doctrine in South America." From France too came voices warning the South American states to maintain order, keep peace among themselves, and look to Europe for protection against the United States.

In a circuitous manner the "Yankee imperialism" brought about a marked change in the cultural relations of Latin America with Europe, especially with Spain. For a long time after the Spanish-American republics declared their independ-ence, there existed among them a decided hostility to the mother country—a hostility akin to that felt for England in the United States after 1776. It was not until 1836 that Madrid formally recognized the independence of Mexico, and it was near the end of the century before treaties of amity were made with the last of the rebellious children. But this accord, particularly after the Spanish-American War, was followed by a "Pan-Hispanic movement," intended, among other things, to unite all Latin-American nations, under the leadership of editors, historians, artists, and men of letters, against the Anglo-Saxon advance. Histories were written attacking the United States for aggression and urging a Latin-American confederation under the presidency of Spain; His-panic congresses were held periodically; and societies and institutions were founded to promote cultural unity.

After pointing out the advance of the United States into the Caribbean, a Madrid editor suggested a barrier: "It is still possible to avoid the danger. The Spanish-Americans must, in union with the mother country, fight for their land, their religion, and for their race." In Latin America itself the Pan-Hispanic movement gathered momentum during the early years of the twentieth century, expressing itself in multiplying books and articles calling for unity against the "Yankee Colossus." Although it made no changes in the policy of the Washington government, and did not check the flow of capital from the United States into Latin America, it represented a real sentiment to be reckoned with in the League of Nations and in negotiations among the European powers.

AMERICAN DIPLOMATIC RELATIONS

Into the diplomatic as well as the economic calculations of the Old World, the Western Hemisphere entered with increasing prominence, particularly after the Civil War, when the United States became a great industrial power. In the endless negotiations and alliances of the European nations growing out of efforts to obtain national advantages or to maintain the balance of power, considerations respecting America had long been present. At no time did the colonial nations—Spain, Portugal, France, Holland, England, and, later, Germany— lose sight of commercial and territorial issues beyond the Atlantic, even when they apparently dealt with local questions. For example, it was to uphold her Continental position and to penalize her imperial rival, Great Britain, that France made an alliance with the rebellious American colonies in 1778 and aided in the creation of the American republic.

If the weakness of the United States during its early years prevented it from exerting a decisive influence on the rivalries of the Napoleonic period, its enunciation of the Monroe Doctrine in 1823 gave it a new status in European diplomacy. Judging from their operations in Asia and Africa, the imperial powers of the Old World would have seized large sections of

South America had it not been for the possibility of conflict with the United States. Indeed, it looked occasionally as if one or more of them were willing to take that risk. At all events, controversies involving the Monroe Doctrine, directly or remotely, furnished materials for many a wordy exchange in diplomacy.

For many years after Napoleon III's disastrous attempt to found an empire in Mexico under his tutelage, no European government saw fit to raise any vital issues touching Monroe's famous principles; but in 1895, during the presidency of Grover Cleveland, a serious dispute with Great Britain occurred under that head. This argument grew out of a quarrel between England and Venezuela over the western boundary of British Guiana. Claiming that Great Britain was trying to take away some of her territory, Venezuela appealed to President Cleveland for aid, and in 1895 he instructed his Secretary of State, Richard T. Olney, to invite the British government to submit the issue to arbitration. Olney's message to London, besides being in the nature of a demand, included a blunt declaration that "the United States is practically sovereign on this continent, and its fiat is law upon the subjects to which it confines its interposition."

To this defiant note Great Britain made a stiff reply, asserting that the Monroe Doctrine was not binding in international law and refusing to submit the dispute to arbitration. Thereupon President Cleveland asked Congress to create a commission to look into the boundary question and announced to the world that it would be the duty of the United States to resist "by every means in its power" the attempt of Great Britain to take any land determined of right to belong to Venezuela. At once the belligerent newspapers in both countries began to talk of war, but in the end the British government agreed to arbitrate the case. The tribunal set up under this arrangement decided that the British claims were, on the whole, justified.

The Venezuela issue had scarcely been settled when European diplomacy was set agog by a far more serious disturbance in Latin America—the intervention of the United States in Cuba, and the Spanish-American War. When President McKinley began to spar with the government of Spain in 1897, the German emperor tried to work up a European combination to save "the monarchical principle." Austrian sympathies were enlisted. The Pope was approached. But England was cold to these endeavors, although the British ambassador did join in the collective appeal made by diplomats to McKinley on behalf of peace. After Dewey's victory at Manila Bay, the German Foreign Office, informed by the American ambassador that the United States had no territorial ambitions, began to hope that Germany might share in the coming division of the "fat spoils." With this in view, it sounded the British government. Unable to secure any help in that quarter, the Kaiser still remained optimistic. As late as July, 1898, the German ambassador in Washington was instructed that "His Majesty, the Emperor, regards it a principal object of German policy to leave unused no opportunity which may arise from the Spanish-American War to obtain maritime fulcra in eastern Asia." When the government of the United States, having learned that England preferred that it keep the Philippines, decided to annex the whole archipelago, Spain turned to Germany for aid and comfort; but the Berlin Foreign Office had by this time reached the conclusion that the Anglo-Saxon combination was too strong to be swayed by any kind of Continental negotiations.

Within a short time Venezuela again came to the fore, when European powers became nervous about the debts she owed their citizens. For several years that country had been ruled in a high-handed manner by a military dictator, Cipriano Castro, who showed small respect for the claims of foreigners to rights previously granted by local politicians. After making more than one diplomatic protest, England, Germany, and

Italy decided to bring the dictator to terms by force. In December, 1902, they sent ships of war to Venezuelan waters. A blockade was established, four Venezuelan gunboats were sunk, and two forts at Puerto Cabello were bombarded. Immediately public feeling in Europe and the United States was aroused to a high pitch of excitement, and the diplomats of the countries involved were thrown into a fever of negotiation. In the end a proposal from Venezuela to arbitrate, transmitted by the United States government, was accepted by the blockading powers, and the tempest blew over.

According to stories made current by the biographer of John Hay, Secretary of State, and by ex-President Roosevelt, Germany was the originator of this armed intervention and was coerced into arbitrating the claims only by a threat from Roosevelt to use the American fleet against the invaders of the Western Hemisphere. As a matter of fact, it now appears to be well established that England proposed the enterprise, that the Kaiser was chary about taking part in it for fear of awakening hostility in the United States, and that Germany had decided on arbitration in principle before the proposal arrived from Washington. In any case, it was the state of public opinion in the United States and the firm stand of President Roosevelt, rather than any tenderness for Venezuela, that produced the pacific outcome. There were many people in England and Germany who resented what was called "North American insolence," but the governments of the two countries, already engaged in the bitter economic and naval rivalry that was to eventuate in the World War, had to be careful about raising up enemies in the United States.[1]

Nevertheless, the Mexican revolution of 1911, vitally affecting important economic interests in the Old World, might well have led to serious complications if England and Ger-

[1] Perhaps a similar anxiety not to alienate the United States was a factor in inducing Great Britain to agree to the Hay-Pauncefote Treaty of 1901, which gave the United States the sole right to build the Panama Canal.

many had been in a position to exert pressure without regard to the Monroe Doctrine. As things turned out, Great Britain acquiesced in President Wilson's Mexican projects in exchange for the abolition of the Panama tolls, which discriminated in favor of American vessels and thus ran counter to the equality provided for in the Hay-Pauncefote Treaty. Other difficulties in Latin America sank into the background when the World War engrossed the attention of all the great European powers interested in the Western Hemisphere.

Those fearful of entangling alliances have sometimes declared that the Monroe Doctrine meant not only no European interference in America but also no American interference in Europe. We have seen that the United States was successful in extending its territory, in preventing the establishment of French domination in Mexico, in frustrating European coercion of Venezuela, in freeing Cuba from Spanish rule, and in constructing the Panama Canal under its own auspices. When it came, however, to the principle that the United States should abstain from all participation in European affairs and in those of the Far East, this proved impracticable. The government at Washington had repeatedly taken an active part in the diplomatic negotiations of the world before its spectacular intervention with armed forces in 1917. Representatives of the United States attended a conference as early as 1880 to consider the situation in Morocco. Four years later it participated in the congress at Berlin to help decide questions that had arisen in regard to the Belgian Congo, and it was the first country to recognize its flag.

When the Russo-Japanese War came (see pages 269 ff.), President Roosevelt thought the interests of the United States demanded that its government should take a hand in adjusting the balance of power in the Orient. He remembered that Germany, France, and Russia had intervened in 1895 to neutralize the victory of Japan over China, and he believed that Japan should be strengthened to offset the influence of Russia in the East. "As soon as the war broke out," he wrote to the English ambassador in Washington, "I notified Germany and France in the most polite and discreet fashion that in event of a combination against Japan to try to do what Russia, Germany, and France did to her [in 1895], I should promptly side with Japan and proceed to whatever length was necessary on her behalf. I, of course, knew that your government would act in the same way, and I thought it best that I should have no consultation with your people before announcing my own purpose." This was strong language and meant that if the advice went unheeded President Roosevelt was committed to active intervention on the side of Japan.

The Kaiser and the Tsar, who were engaged at the time in trying to form an alliance, feared that if the news of their doings leaked out, there would be trouble with the United States. In case the negotiations became public, as William II wrote to Nicholas II, "America would immediately join England—which on no account must be allowed. . . . It will be the main task of Russian and German diplomatists to stop America joining England." Although the compact between the two sovereigns came to nothing, on account of the opposition of the Russian bureaucracy, it was clear that the United States was already deeply involved in the world's balance of power.

President Roosevelt finally induced Russia and Japan to send representatives to Portsmouth, New Hampshire, where a treaty was signed, September, 1905, ending the war. He then entered into a secret understanding with England and Japan for maintaining the status quo in the Orient. He personally favored a general alliance, but said that the Senate would never approve it and that he "might as well strive for the moon." So he sent to Tokyo a secret agent, who made a simple agreement with the premier of Japan, which was recorded in a highly confidential memorandum. According to this understanding, Japan undertook to respect American

dominion in the Philippines, and the United States promised
to accept Japanese dominion in Korea as established by force
of arms.

At the same time Roosevelt's emissary in Tokyo assured
the Japanese premier that the people of the United States
were "so fully in accord with the people of Japan and Great
Britain in the maintenance of peace in the Far East that,
whatever occasion arose, appropriate action of the government of the United States in conjunction with Japan and
Great Britain, for such a purpose, could be counted upon by
them quite as confidently as if the United States were under
treaty obligations." On hearing of the affair, a well-known
Tokyo editor blurted out, "In fact, it is a Japanese-Anglo-
American alliance." For practical purposes it was, although
the people of the United States knew nothing about it until
1924, when Tyler Dennett found the document among the
Roosevelt papers and made it public.

When Germany and France in 1905 seemed on the verge
of war over the division of spoils in Morocco, the German
chancellor, Von Bülow, knowing the American attitude toward
"the open door," sounded President Roosevelt, and the President, through his personal relations with the French and German ambassadors in Washington, skillfully won the consent
of France to an adjustment of the dispute at a conference
to be held at Algeciras. "It is a diplomatic secret," wrote
Roosevelt's biographer Bishop, "that President Roosevelt is
entitled to the credit of arranging the important Algeciras
Conference of 1906, and dictating the terms on which war between France and Germany, with the possible involvement of
England as an ally of France, was averted." Although this
claim is excessive, President Roosevelt was doubtless influential in the negotiations that staved off a conflict at that time.

Recognizing the fact that the United States was definitely
an important weight in the world's balance of power, King
Edward VII approached President Roosevelt on his own ini-

tiative in 1905, saying, "You, Mr. President, and I have been called upon to superintend the destinies of the two great branches of the Anglo-Saxon race, and this trust should, in my opinion, alone suffice to bring us together." In the same spirit Roosevelt sent Senator Lodge to King Edward with instructions to inform His Majesty that "we intend to have the United States and England work together [in Europe] just as we are now working together in the Far East." Indeed, communications had gone so far that in 1913 an American historian of undoubted competence, Roland G. Usher, declared that a secret agreement had been reached, binding the United States to come to the aid of England and France in case of war against Pan-Germanism.

Although this allegation was officially denied, there was some truth behind it. Two years before, Roosevelt, then in private life, had declared: "As long as England succeeds in keeping up the balance of power in Europe, not only on principle, but in reality, well and good; should she, however, for some reason or other fail in doing so, the United States would be obliged to step in, at least temporarily, in order to reestablish the balance of power in Europe, never mind against which country or group of countries our efforts may have to be directed. In fact, we ourselves are becoming, owing to our strength and geographical situation, more and more the balance of power for the whole globe." And so fate willed it, for the United States helped to prevent Germany from establishing her hegemony on the Continent.

From the first the government of the United States has given official sanction to peaceful methods of settling international disputes. Not long after the establishment of American independence, the United States and Great Britain set an example to the world by submitting, under the Jay Treaty of 1794, three highly important controversies to mixed commissions for adjudication; and, except for the dispute which culminated in the War of 1812, all quarrels that arose between the two countries were disposed of by arbitration or some kindred pacific process. Among these issues were the *Alabama* claims, settled by a tribunal set up at Geneva in 1872, and the question which arose in the administration of President Cleveland over the boundary between Venezuela and British Guiana, involving the Monroe Doctrine. An Alaskan-Canadian boundary dispute was also adjusted in 1903 by a special tribunal, in which one of the British members took the side of the United States against Canada. From time to time, controversies with France, Spain, Portugal, and Denmark were likewise adjusted by arbitration or conciliation. Indeed, conciliatory and judicial processes for keeping peace among nations were so frequently successful that many enthusiasts hoped to apply them universally, and thus put an end to war for all time.

The peace movement, now so powerful, may be said to have originated in the early days of the American republic (see pages 299 ff.). It is true that plans for universal peace had been suggested long before, but none of them struck a deep root in popular sentiment. Certainly the first association to promote that cause by public agitation was the American Peace Society, founded in New York in 1828. "Although the independence of the United States was won by the sword," said John Bassett Moore, "the founders of the American Republic were accustomed to look upon war as a measure that could be justified only as a choice of evils. Standing armies and elaborate preparations for war they deprecated as a menace to liberty. Having proclaimed the basis of their political system the consent of the governed, they cherished as their ideal a peaceful nation, always guided by reason and justice." As far back as 1832 the senate of Massachusetts resolved that "some mode should be established for the amicable and final adjustment of all international disputes instead of resort to war."

In 1890 both houses of Congress by concurrent resolution requested the President on proper occasions to negotiate with foreign countries treaties of arbitration for the adjustment of differences which could not be settled by ordinary diplomatic methods. Representatives of the United States attended both of the Hague conferences, to consider the reduction of armaments and measures to avoid new wars. By a series of compacts with twenty-five different countries, negotiated in 1908 by Elihu Root as Secretary of State, the United States bound itself to arbitrate all issues of legal nature not involving "national honor" or "vital interests." Carrying this idea a step forward, William Jennings Bryan, Secretary of State under President Wilson, made "cooling off" treaties with twenty-four nations. These agreements bound the contracting countries to submit all disputes "of every nature whatsoever" to a commission of inquiry and not to declare war during the investigation, allowing at least a year for the inquiry.

INFLUENCE ON EUROPE OF AMERICAN POLITICAL EVENTS AND IDEAS

If we turn from direct connections with the Old World to the purely domestic history of the United States, we find that not a single significant phase of American political development has been without influence on European policy and opinion. The reverberations of the American Revolution reached the far corners of the Old World. The great formulation of human rights contained in the Declaration of Independence and the first state constitutions strengthened the hopes of French philosophers, like Condorcet, whose writings helped to forward the French Revolution. The French publicist the Comte de Saint-Simon, who founded a school of French socialism and was the teacher of August Comte, one of the outstanding figures in the history of social thought, was a soldier under Washington, and drew from the American experiment in republicanism faith in the possibilities of an ideal order. The successful launching of the new American government under the presidency of Washington seemed to realize what had been merely an aspiration.

Again, the struggles between Hamilton and Jefferson, between the Federalists and Republicans, had their effect on the course of Anglo-French rivalry in the Old World. Leaning toward England rather than France, Washington and Hamilton were able to keep the United States from heeding the French call for help under the treaty of alliance made in 1778, when France came to the aid of the American Revolutionists. Instead of supporting France, the United States remained neutral, and its citizens supplied England with the wheat, bacon, and corn so useful in her struggle against the Revolutionary armies and Napoleon. Throughout the long-drawn contest over the embargo and similar measures of commercial regulation, the fate of the Napoleonic empire was to some extent determined by American domestic decisions. Had the United States really been prepared for the War of 1812 and dealt effective blows at Great Britain, Napoleon might have died in Paris instead of St. Helena.

No less interesting to European observers, if less important in fact, was the Jacksonian upheaval, which really brought "the people" into power for the first time in the history of Western civilization. Starting in 1828, it synchronized with the French revolution of 1830 and the English parliamentary reform of 1832. It was in this period that white manhood suffrage was established in the United States after years of agitation. The American republic had been founded on property. Until the advent of Jackson the country had been governed by "an aristocracy of wealth and talents." Now the "common man" prevailed. And the radical experiment attracted a new school of European thinkers. While Jackson was in the White House, Alexis de Tocqueville visited this country and from his notes wrote a remarkable work, *Democracy in America*—addressed to Europeans then wrestling with the problems of democracy themselves. In the same period

Harriet Martineau traveled in the United States and wrote another remarkable book on the American experiment—addressed to the rising liberal party in England.

In the ferment of English opinion the American experiment was an active factor. "Of the various French republics that have been tried," wrote Carlyle, "or that are still on trial—of these it is not needful to say a word. But there is one modern instance of democracy, nearly perfect, the Republic of the United States, which has actually subsisted for threescore years or more, with immense success as is affirmed; to which many still appeal, as to a sign of hope for all nations, and a 'Model Republic.' Is not America an instance in point? Why should not all nations subsist and flourish on democracy, as America does?" Yet he did not relish the idea. "Cease to brag to me of America," he added, "and its model institutions and constitutions. To men in their sleep nothing is granted in this world: nothing, or as good as nothing, to men that sit idly caucusing and ballot-boxing on the graves of their heroic ancestors, saying, 'It is well, it is well!' . . . America's battle is yet to fight."

As the rivalry of political parties—Democrats and Whigs —grew sharper over the annexation of Texas, the Mexican War, slavery, and the tariff question, Europe still remained interested. Great Britain, France, and other powers recognized Texas, on its revolt from Mexico, in 1836, as an independent nation, and no doubt Great Britain looked with favor on the continued independence of that republic. Soon after the Mexican War closed, with large annexations on the part of the United States, ambitions of Great Britain on the Pacific coast were surrendered. Then Napoleon III, just transformed from a president into an emperor, began to dream of checking "Yankee advance" into Latin America. "If a stable government is set up by means of French arms," he argued, "we shall have opposed an impenetrable dike to the overflow of the United States." When spokesmen of the slave

T

interests in the United States demanded the annexation of Cuba, as an offset to the growing North, and even the seizure of the island by violence, naturally Spain was in trepidation. Fear of the United States helped to drive that country into coöperation with Napoleon in the Mexican expedition, soon to be undertaken. The victory of the Democrats over the Republicans in 1856, followed by a reduction of the tariff in a free-trade direction, was gratifying to English and French manufacturers interested in enlarging their American markets.

Throughout the Civil War in the United States, the fate of liberal parties in the Old World trembled in the balance. Everywhere the governing classes hoped that the conflict would end in the disruption of the American republic, demonstrating on a large scale the failure of democratic institutions. Napoleon III watched the course of the war like a hawk, and from the outset worked hard to effect a combination with England to intervene on behalf of the South.

The English ruling classes were equally antagonistic to the North. After the first battle of Bull Run, in which the Unionists suffered a terrible disaster, English conservatives exulted. "We may hope at last," exclaimed the *Saturday Review*, "that the delusive confusion between freedom and democracy is finally banished from the minds of Englishmen." *Blackwood's Magazine* was more caustic. "We are glad that the end of the Union seems more likely to be ridiculous than terrible. . . . The venerable Lincoln, the respectable Seward, the raving editors, the gibbering mob, the swift-footed warriors of Bull's Run are no malicious tricks of fortune played off on an unwary nation, but all of them are the legitimate offspring of the great Republic. . . . In the hope that this contest may end in the extinction of mob rule, we become reconciled to the much slighter amount of suffering that war inflicts on America." In this spirit the English government sympathized with and lent assistance to the Confederacy. Had it not been for the Union victories at Vicksburg and Gettysburg, England

and France would doubtless have recognized the independence of the Southern states and tried to break the blockade of the Southern ports.

On the other hand, liberals in the Old World, especially England, took the opposite tack. The French republican journal *Le Siècle* kept up a running fire on Napoleon's policy, and sustained a lively faith in Northern victory until the end. In England liberal opinion, led by John Bright, was marshaled resolutely on the side of the North and acted as a restraining force on the government in its tendencies to lend comfort to the South. Engaged in a struggle for the extension of the suffrage at home, English liberals made common cause with the party of Abraham Lincoln. "You wish the freedom of your country," said Bright, at a great meeting in London. "You wish it for yourselves. . . . Do not then give the hand of fellowship to the worst foes of freedom that the world has ever seen." The defeat of the North, he insisted, meant a defeat for democracy in England. Labor leaders shared that view. Karl Marx, then in exile in London, helped to organize a huge mass demonstration of working people to voice their sympathy with the government at Washington in its life-and-death struggle with slavery. And the victory of the North was followed by new democratic advances in the Old World. Two years after Appomattox, England gave the ballot to working-men—"shot Niagara," as Carlyle put it. In three more years the empire of Napoleon III was in the dust, and a republic erected on its ruins.

For a long time after the Civil War, Europe was less affected by the domestic issues of American politics. The people of the United States, busy with reconstruction and with the rounding out of the Far West, were not engaged in making any new world-shaking experiments. No doubt England, France, and Germany would have welcomed a reduction of the American tariff on their manufactures, but they had to reconcile themselves to the inevitable. Beyond question the McKinley

Tariff Bill of 1890 had serious consequences in Europe and was disastrous to some of England's industries. The Russian Tsar and the German Kaiser seriously discussed "the combination of Europe in a struggle against McKinley and America through a common protective tariff union, with or without England." The Tsar took it up with the French government on the occasion of a visit to Paris, but nothing came of the project.

By this time, as Henry Adams said, "Germany as the grizzly terror had frightened England into America's arms," and the tariff sank to a minor position. In exchange for British sympathy during the war with Spain the McKinley administration expressed American sympathy for England during her war with the Boer republics. The advent of "the grizzly terror" and the adoption of what seemed to the British a program of imperialism by the United States tended, as we have seen, to draw the two countries together.

If European liberals welcomed the progress of the United States as demonstrating the virtues of democracy, conservatives never ceased to fear "the American invasion." In many articles and lectures Matthew Arnold, although professing some democratic sympathies himself, inveighed against what he called the "Americanization" of English civilization. By that he meant the leveling-down process, the conquest of quality by quantity, the vulgarization of learning and the arts. He feared, he said, that "the dangers of America will be ours; the dangers which come from the multitude being in power, with no adequate ideal to elevate or guide the multitude." A similar antithesis was also discovered by Latin-American writers between "Yankee civilization" and "Hispanic culture." Speaking of the United States, a Uruguayan poet expressed the Latin judgment in the following words: "The apex of its ethics is the ethics of Franklin, a philosophy of conduct which ends in the mediocrity of honesty, the utility of prudence; in whose bosom never surges holiness nor heroism. . . . It is a weak, dull creature when it endeavors to climb the dizzy heights."

In short, when the French writer André Siegfried, in 1926, declared that the debate between the United States and Europe "becomes a dialogue, as it were, between Ford and Gandhi," he merely phrased in another form the antagonism between the two civilizations as it had been conceived by other critics for half a century or more. The "American peril," political, economic, and cultural, had already become widely recognized in Europe before the World War; and as time went on, it appeared to European critics increasingly clear that Ford seemed to be getting the better of Gandhi.

CHAPTER VIII

THE AWAKENING OF THE FAR EAST

Peculiar Position of China and Japan

Peculiar circumstances saved eastern Asia and the adjoining islands from the fate that befell Africa and India as European commerce and arms spread to the four corners of the earth. Although five fundamental races made up the population of China—Chinese, Manchus, Mongols, Turks, and Tibetans—they were, unlike their Indian neighbors, held together by the powerful Manchu dynasty, which ruled at Peking from 1644 down to 1912. Until its authority began to wane near the end of the nineteenth century, it was able to keep invading Europeans fairly at bay, and by that time the very jealousy of these conquering foreigners prevented any one nation from getting possession of China, as Great Britain had of India, or any arrangement for the partition of the huge Celestial Empire, as in the case of Africa.

A similar and even more effective unity existed in Japan under the nominal sway of the emperor at Kyoto and his vicegerent, or *shogun*, at Tokyo. Furthermore, the Japanese proved themselves exceedingly ingenious in adopting Western ideas—in building battleships, creating disciplined armies, using high explosives, and constructing railways and factories. This made the conquering imperial nations of the West think twice before attempting to overrun and annex Japanese territory. That was not all. Learning well the lesson from her Western teachers, Japan adopted an imperialistic policy herself and thus disturbed the ancient game played by Great Britain, Holland, France, Germany, and Russia, which was joined by the United States in its later stages. For these reasons, among others, the Far East deserves a separate chapter in the history of modern Europe.

EARLY RELATIONS OF EUROPE WITH CHINA

The first expeditions of the Portuguese around the Cape of Good Hope, the rivalry between them and the Dutch and English for the trade with India and the Spice Islands, and the final victory of the English over their French competitors in Hindustan have all been described in Volume I. It was inevitable that the vast and highly civilized Chinese Empire should attract the attention of the adventurous traders, and a Chinese report informs us that "during the reign of Ching-tih (1506) foreigners from the West called Falanki,[1] who said that they brought tribute, suddenly entered the Canton River and by their tremendously loud guns shook the place far and near. This was reported at court; and an order was returned to drive them away and stop their trade. About this time the Hollanders, who in ancient times inhabited a wild territory and had no relations with China, came to Macao in two or three large ships. Their clothes and their hair were red, their bodies tall, their eyes were blue and were sunk deep into their

[1] Probably the Chinese got from the Mohammedans the idea of calling the Western peoples Franks, the old name given them during the Crusades. Previous to the opening of the nineteenth century, the Chinese knew little or nothing of Europe, and Europe very little of them. The Romans called China Serica ("Silk Land"), and two or three of the emperors, including Marcus Aurelius, sent embassies thither with presents to the ruling monarch. Missionaries from Persia made an early attempt to introduce Christianity into China in the eighth century. These attempts were renewed by the Franciscans and Dominicans in the thirteenth century. The noted Venetian traveler Marco Polo became the trusted official of the Mongol emperor of China, Kublai Khan (1259–1294), who made him governor of Yangchow, near Nanking, on the Yangtze River. For half a century the Florentines and Genoese were able to carry on some trade with China, but the fall of the Mongol dynasty (which Genghis Khan had established in 1213) and the accession of the Chinese Ming line of rulers (1368) brought relations with Europe practically to an end until the arrival of the Portuguese early in the sixteenth century.

heads. Their feet were one cubit and two tenths long, and their strange appearance frightened the people."

All the early attempts to establish business relations with China encountered serious obstacles. The haughty demeanor of the officials, who regarded the merchants as representatives of barbarous races, the widespread corruption among the governing class, and the humiliating demands of Chinese ceremonial were enough to discourage the most enterprising. When in 1655 the Dutch sent two envoys to the Chinese emperor, they were only received on condition that they would prostrate themselves before his throne and strike their heads nine times on the earth as evidence of their inferiority. In the eyes of the Chinese they were only tribute-bearers to the "Son of Heaven." Foreigners were frankly told that China did not need their goods, since she produced all that was necessary, that foreign merchants must comply with regulations established by officials, and that threats and entreaties would be alike unavailing.

In the eighteenth century Canton remained the only port in which foreign commerce was regularly permitted. Here all communications between the foreign merchants or their governments, on the one hand, and the Chinese government or local merchants, on the other, were made through the *hong*, a small band of Chinese traders who received all goods from abroad and arranged the prices of both imports and exports. The foreign settlement at Canton is still confined to the so-called "Compound," a district set apart from the great Chinese city.

Meanwhile the Portuguese doggedly clung to their factories at Macao, where as early as 1537 they had rented a trifling bit of land from the Chinese. English and Dutch traders would now and then take refuge there when troubles occurred at Canton. The English made repeated attempts to get into direct communication with the government at Peking, but the emperor insisted that the "barbarians" should keep away

THE FAR EAST
IN 1914

from his capital in the north and confine their operations to Canton. After the close of the Napoleonic wars England sent Lord Amherst, in 1816, to visit Peking and if possible secure from the emperor himself the removal of the grievances which English merchants suffered under the viceroy and other local Chinese officials with whom they had been forced to deal in Canton. But Lord Amherst refused to perform the *kotow*, or obeisance, required of "foreign devils," and was hustled south to Canton. When Lord Napier was appointed Superintendent of Trade in China in 1833, the Canton authorities refused to recognize him, and denounced him as "a lawless foreign slave" and "a dog barbarian of a foreign nation" for venturing to violate the law by arriving at Canton at night. The English must, they declared, continue to deal with the hong, and not attempt to negotiate with the central government.

Although Chinese traders of Canton and the local mandarins[1] profited by the commerce with the Europeans, the Chinese government steadily refused to treat foreign nations as equals. China seemed to its own people infinitely superior in its extent and in its ancient civilization to the lands of the West, of which they knew very little, and whose customs they detested and were in no way tempted to imitate. And there was much to encourage this complacent attitude. China proper (excluding its vast dependencies of Mongolia, Manchuria, Eastern Turkmenistan, and Tibet) is nearly three times as large as the combined area of Great Britain, France, and Germany; it would cover the whole of the United States east of the Rocky Mountains without Texas. A distance of twelve hundred miles separates Canton and Peking, and it is nearly as far from Shanghai to the borders of Tibet. China reckons its population as more than four hundred millions,[2] and can

---

[1] "Mandarin" was the name given by Europeans to Chinese officials; it is not a Chinese word.

[2] The population is really unknown. Perhaps it is between three and four hundred millions.

trace back its uninterrupted civilization to a period long ante-dating the development of Greek culture.[1]

The commercial relations which the English had repeatedly sought to secure peacefully were finally established as the result of a conflict known as the Opium War. Opium is said to have been introduced into China by the Arabs in the thirteenth century. It is derived from the seed capsule of a certain species of poppy which is extensively raised in India. England had, by the opening of the nineteenth century, prac-tically monopolized the business. The Chinese had long re-garded the trade in that dangerous commodity with disfavor. An edict of 1796 asserted that it caused the greatest injury to both the minds and manners of men, and prohibited its im-portation. Moreover, its purchase by the Chinese tended to drain the country of its supply of silver. In spite of the laws Chinese officials and British merchants kept up a lively trade in the forbidden drug at an enormous profit, and the imports amounted in 1837 to about seventeen million dollars.

Against this nefarious traffic the Chinese government finally resolved to take a determined stand, and an imperial commis-sioner was sent to Canton for the purpose of suppressing the traffic. He seized and burned twenty thousand chests of opium which the dealers had on hand, and practically expelled the foreign merchants from Canton. These measures and the com-missioner's attempt to force the British merchants to give up the opium traffic led to violence, and the Chinese fleet sent out to execute his orders was fired upon by British battleships.

While the British government did not formally declare war, Canton was blockaded in 1840 by British forces. Amoy,

---

[1] There are a large number of interesting books on China: Giles's *China and the Chinese* forms a good introduction. The recent political history, so far as Europeans are concerned, is clearly explained by Douglas in his *Europe and the Far East*, and by Vinacke in his *History of the Far East in Modern Times* (1928). See also Thomas Francis Carter's *The Invention of Printing in China and its Spread Westward* (Columbia University Press, 1925), which shows the high de-velopment of Chinese civilization during the Dark Ages in Europe.

Ningpo, Shanghai, and even Nanking were taken by the British, and the Chinese were easily overwhelmed by the men-of-war from the West. In August, 1842, the Chinese, who had been driven to sue for peace, agreed, in the Treaty of Nanking, to pay a heavy indemnity, to treat British officials thenceforward as the equals of Chinese mandarins of the same rank, to cede to the British the island of Hong Kong (which lies at the mouth of the Canton River), and to open to foreign commerce the ports of Amoy, Foochow, Ningpo, and Shanghai (along the coast between Canton and the mouth of the Yangtze River) on the same terms as Canton. The opium question was left unsettled.

This triumph of the British was the signal for other powers to open relations with China. It was clear that the Chinese were now likely to be in a different frame of mind in regard to foreigners than formerly. American merchants had a warehouse in Canton as early as 1801, and after the Opium War, in 1844, Caleb Cushing, an American commissioner, negotiated a commercial treaty with the Chinese emperor, which extended certain trading privileges to the United States. In the same year France also secured similar concessions.

Five Chinese ports were now open to foreign trade, and Belgium, Prussia, the Netherlands, and Portugal also participated in the new commercial advantages. Chinese hostility to foreigners remained, however, as strong as before; frequent riots occurred, foreigners were maltreated, and the emperor, Hsien Fêng, continued to believe it his patriotic duty to prevent all foreign advance. The same year in which the Crimean War came to an end Napoleon III united with England in a joint embassy to the Chinese emperor, which was backed up by an armed force. Negotiations proving fruitless, the allies took possession of Canton and established a provisional government there. A request of England, France, Russia, and the United States that the emperor appoint a Chinese minister to negotiate in regard to international questions was refused;

whereupon French and English ships proceeded northward along the coast, battered down the forts which guarded the mouth of the river on which Tientsin lies, and in 1858 reached that city. Thus foreign operations were transferred to a region dangerously near the imperial city of Peking.

The emperor, whose beautiful summer palace had been looted and destroyed by the allies, and who was now threatened in his capital, offered to negotiate; but hostilities broke out again, and not till 1860 were matters adjusted. Under compulsion the emperor agreed to pay an indemnity to the British and French for the expense to which they had been put in invading his empire, and Tientsin was declared an open port. After that time other ports were opened to European trade, and by 1900 there were over forty points where foreign merchants could conduct operations, although Canton and Shanghai were still the most important. Some towns inland were also opened and offered advantages for extending commerce far beyond the seacoast, to which foreign merchants had been confined for three centuries and a half.[1]

China's troubles did not come entirely from without, for a terrible rebellion raged during the fifties. Ever since the year when Louis XIV began his reign, China had been governed by a foreign race, the Tartar Manchus, who had succeeded in putting one of their leaders on the throne in 1644. Some of the Manchu sovereigns showed themselves very enlightened, especially K'ang Hsi, whose reign of sixty years roughly corresponds in time and character with that of Louis XIV. He received the affable Jesuit missionaries who visited his court, and studied astronomy, physics, mathematics, and medicine with them. Under his auspices an encyclopedia of no less than five thousand and twenty volumes was prepared, embracing all the lore of the Chinese. He permitted the Christians to build a church in Peking and even

---

[1] The occupation of China's former dependency of Anam, including Cochin China and Tongking, has been described on pages 154 f.

contributed to the expenses. During the reign of Emperor Ch'ien Lung (1736–1795), who emulated the enlightened policy of K'ang Hsi, the dynasty reached its height.

Under his successors the prestige of the Manchu emperors waned, and the reverses of the first war with England and the humiliating Treaty of Nanking suggested to a certain Hung the possibility of a successful revolution. The Taipings, as Hung's followers called themselves, took the great city of Nanking in 1853, and put many thousands of the hated Tartars, to which race the Manchus belong, to death—man, woman, and child—in order that "not a root should be left to sprout from." The Manchu government made little progress in suppressing the rebellion so long as the weak and dissolute Emperor Hsien Fêng lived. But he became "a guest in Heaven" in 1861, and the real power in China passed into the hands of Tzu Hsi, his favorite concubine, the famous "Dowager Empress," who was one of the foremost rulers of the world until the time of her death in 1908.[1]

Her minister, Li Hung Chang, set to work to put down the rebellion. He arranged with an American named Ward to raise a foreign corps to aid the Chinese government. Ward captured several towns held by the Taipings, but was killed while leading an attack. He was succeeded by Major Charles Gordon, an Englishman destined to become famous in Africa (see page 174). With Gordon's help Li Hung Chang recovered the towns, including Nanking, which had fallen into the hands of the rebels, and brought to an end a civil war which had lasted twelve years and cost millions of lives. But in the process the government was materially weakened and hence less able to resist foreign encroachments.

[1] The ambitious Tzu Hsi arranged that her little son, T'ung Chih, should succeed to the throne, and in this way became practically regent for many years. On his death in 1875 she secured the succession of his cousin Kuang Hsü, as he was renamed, that is, "Succession to Glory." His mother was a sister of the powerful dowager empress, who, as aunt of the little emperor (born in 1872), continued to reign in his name.

How Japan became a World Power

‚To the northeast of China lies a long group of islands which if they lay off the eastern coast of North America would extend from Maine to Georgia. This archipelago, comprising four main islands and many smaller ones, constitutes the Empire of Japan. In the middle of the nineteenth century Japan was still almost completely isolated from the rest of the world, but through a series of extraordinary events she became one of the most conspicuous members of the family of nations. American newspapers deal as fully with her foreign policy as with that of France or Germany; we are familiar with the portraits of her statesmen and warriors, and her exquisite art has many admirers in Europe and America. Her people, who are somewhat more numerous than the inhabitants of the British Isles, slightly resemble the Chinese in appearance and owe to China the beginnings of their culture and their art, for it was Buddhist missionaries from Korea who in the sixth century first aroused Japan from its previous barbarism.[1]

Little is known of the early Mikados (emperors) of Japan, but from the twelfth century to 1867, sovereign powers were exercised by one great feudal lord after another, known as the *shogun,* or commander in chief of the empire (somewhat as the mayor of the palace had ruled in the Frankish kingdom), while the emperor lived in retirement in his capital of Kyoto. In 1600, by a great victory over his rivals, the last of the shogunates was founded by Tokugawa Iyeyasu, who for talents in war and administration deserves to rank with Napoleon and Bismarck. Japan was really ruled by the Tokugawa family until the restoration of the emperor in 1867.

---

[1] The Japanese language has nothing in common with the Chinese. It is built up much like a European language and can be written by means of signs representing syllables. Nevertheless, the Japanese are accustomed to use the Chinese characters in their books and even in their newspapers, the less familiar characters being sometimes accompanied by a translation into Japanese.

During this period conditions in Japan resembled those in western Europe in the Middle Ages. Scattered about the country were the castles of powerful feudal lords (*daimios*), who continued until the nineteenth century to enjoy powers similar to those of the vassals of medieval European kings.

Rumors of the existence of Japan reached Europe through the Venetian traveler, Marco Polo, at the end of the thirteenth century. Both Columbus and John Cabot imagined that they had reached the famed island of Cipango when they sighted land, but the Portuguese navigator Pinto appears to have been the first European to reach Japan, in the year 1542. Some years later the great Jesuit missionary, Francis Xavier, accompanied by some Japanese who had been converted to Christianity at Goa, made the first attempt to preach the Christian faith in the island. Spanish missionaries from Manila carried on the work, and it is reported that 300,000 converts had been made by the year 1595.

In the main, the Japanese were a tolerant people, and their local rulers were anxious for trade with the Portuguese; so some of the feudal lords compelled their subjects to become Christians and occasionally accepted the new religion themselves. Owing, however, to the arrogance of the Portuguese Jesuits and, later, of the Spanish Franciscans and Dominicans, who refused to obey the edicts of the shoguns, successive attempts were made to rid the country of them. When a Spanish ship arrived about 1595 its pilot was asked how Spain had acquired such vast territories. He replied: "Our kings begin by sending into countries they wish to conquer missionaries, who induce the people to embrace our religion, and when they have made considerable progress, troops are sent who combine with the new Christians, and then our kings have not much trouble in accomplishing the rest." This infuriated the shogun, and twenty-six Christians, including six Franciscans, were executed. Edicts ordering the Jesuits to leave the country were repeatedly issued but not obeyed, since the mis-

sionaries courted martyrdom. Emissaries sent to Europe returned with reports that priests kept Christian countries in
a constant turmoil. The Japanese rulers thus formed a most
unhappy notion of Christianity. Besides, they had many illustrations of the intolerance of its representatives in the destruction of Buddhist temples and images and the persecution
of Buddhist priests in regions where the missionaries succeeded in converting the local lords.

After the death of Iyeyasu in 1616, the policy of the government became increasingly harsh. In 1638 a large number
of Christians, mainly converts, assembled on a peninsula near
Nagasaki and were defeated and massacred. The government
expelled the Portuguese and ordered that no Japanese should
under any circumstances leave the country. A trading station
was conceded the Dutch, who carried on business under humiliating regulations. There seems to be no doubt that had the
missionaries, who were few in number, conducted themselves
with more discretion, Japan might have been deeply affected
by contact with European countries. As it was, for over two
hundred years, Japan remained a nation apart, having practically no intercourse with foreigners.

In 1853 Commodore Perry visited Yokohama with a message from the United States government to the "Sovereign of
Japan," asking that arrangements be made to protect the
property and persons of Americans wrecked on the coasts,
and that the right be extended to Americans to dispose of their
cargoes at one or more ports. Supposing that the shogun was
the ruler of Japan, it was he to whom Commodore Perry
presented his demands. These led to a long and earnest discussion in the shogun's council, as to whether foreigners
should be admitted or not, but their demands were finally
conceded, and a few years later extensive commercial privileges were granted to them.

At last the Mikado awoke from his long lethargy to declare
that the shogun had no right to conclude a treaty or to admit

foreigners to the sacred soil of Japan. Nevertheless, the foreigners went on negotiating with the shogun, and within the next few years several of the European powers had arranged to trade at the ports of Hakodate, Yokohama, Nagasaki, and a little later at Kobe. Attacks, however, were made upon foreigners in the name of the emperor. An Englishman by the name of Richardson was killed in 1862 on the great high road between Yedo (Tokyo) and Kyoto, by the retainers of the powerful daimio of Satsuma, whereupon the English bombarded Kagoshima, the stronghold of the Satsuma clan.

This produced an extraordinary change of heart in the leading clan, one of the most important in Japan, for its leaders saw that the foreigners were much more powerful than the Japanese, and that Japan would suffer as China had done unless she acquainted herself with Western science and inventions. The next year English ships bombarded Shimonoseki, on account of the refusal of its feudal ruler, the lord of another powerful clan, the Chosu, to permit them to pass freely through the Inland Sea. About the same time an American war vessel also bombarded Shimonoseki in retaliation for hostile acts committed by the Chosu daimio. These demonstrations of force produced an effect similar to the bombardment of Kagoshima, and public opinion in Japan gradually changed in favor of the admission of foreigners.

Not long afterward, in January, 1867, the Mikado Mutsuhito, then fifteen years of age, ascended the throne. He named the era which opened with his advent *Meiji* (that is, "enlightened rule"), and his reign well justified the name. In March, 1868, he invited Sir Harry Parkes, representative of Great Britain, as well as the representatives of France and the Netherlands, to Kyoto. He was deeply chagrined by an attack made upon the retinue of Sir Harry Parkes and publicly declared that anyone who molested foreigners would be acting in opposition to His Majesty's express orders, for he would be guilty of the "heinous offense of causing the

T

national dignity and good faith to suffer in the eyes of the treaty powers, to whom His Majesty feels that he is bound by relations of friendship." With this episode official resistance to the foreigners, their trade, and their religion may be said to have closed.

Meanwhile a great revolution was taking place in Japan; the power of the shogun was rapidly declining, and in October, 1867, he was forced to resign his office. This left the Mikado not only the nominal but also the real ruler of Japan. He emerged from the ancient seclusion in the sacred city of Kyoto and moved the capital to Yedo, which was given the new name Tokyo, or "eastern capital." The "period of the Restoration" now began. The feudal princes who had, in general, sided with the Mikado against the shogun, agreed peacefully to surrender their titles and prerogatives in the interests of their country, and in July, 1871, feudalism was formally abolished throughout the empire. Serfdom was also done away with (with compensation to the landlords), and the army and navy reformed in accordance with Western models.

After this date the modernizing of Japan progressed with incredible rapidity. Although many Japanese continued to carry on their ancient industries, kneeling on their straw mats, with a few simple implements and no machinery, Western industries were introduced side by side with the older arts. Students were sent abroad to investigate the most recent achievements in science; imperial universities were established in Tokyo and in other important cities, and the system of education completely revolutionized. There was not a steam mill in the islands when Commodore Perry cast anchor there; within fifty years there were over eighty great cotton factories, with a hundred thousand employees. Since the railroad between Tokyo and the neighboring port of Yokohama was opened in 1872, over eight thousand miles of railways have been constructed, and the Japanese, who are very fond of travel, can go readily from one end to the other of their archipelago. Great towns sprang up. At the opening of the twentieth century the urban district of Tokyo had nearly two million inhabitants, and the manufacturing city of Osaka toward a million. The total population of the island is now about sixty millions, one half that of the United States, but crowded into an area of less than one hundred and fifty thousand square miles.

With this industrial progress came inevitably a demand for representative government, and as early as 1877 petitions for a constitution were laid before the emperor. Four years later he announced that a parliament would be established in 1890, and a commission was sent to Europe to study constitutional government there. In 1889 a constitution was completed which vested the powers of government in the Mikado and a parliament of two houses—a chamber of peers, and an assembly elected by popular vote restricted by property qualifications.

Japan's chief danger lay in the aggressions of the European powers, who might at any time treat her as they were treating China. But by the sudden and thoroughgoing revolution just described she was able to protect herself. Guided by a liberal-minded monarch and by a group of statesmen of extraordinary ability and unsurpassed probity and patriotism, she reformed her whole system of government, and, arming herself with every means of defense suggested by modern science, she was able to hold her own in two serious conflicts with other powers seemingly greatly her superiors in strength.

War between Japan and China and its Results

After carrying out the various reforms mentioned above, Japan found herself confronted, like the Western nations, with the necessity of extending her trade and securing foreign markets. Her merchants and shippers became the rivals of the Europeans in the neighboring seas, where her commerce has increased far more rapidly than that of the Western nations. Japan was becoming a naval power.

On the opposite side of the Sea of Japan lies Korea, a kingdom which has become well known throughout the world on account of the two bloody wars to which the question of its possession has given rise. In the sixteenth century the Japanese had invaded the peninsula, which had not then been claimed by China. Japan was able to hold it for a time, but later the Koreans, with the aid of the Chinese, reëstablished their independence, and thereafter both China and Japan regarded themselves as rival suzerains of the Korean kingdom. As Japanese trade developed, the question of control over the disputed kingdom reached a serious stage, and in 1894 it led to war between Japan and China. But the Chinese, with their ancient weapons and organization, were no match for the Japanese, who had eagerly adopted every device of Western warfare. In a short time the Chinese armies had been driven from Korea, and the campaign was transferred to the neighboring Manchuria, where the Japanese took Port Arthur. China then called upon the Western powers for assistance, but they did not take action until Japan, in the Treaty of Shimonoseki, had forced China's representative, Li Hung Chang, to recognize the complete independence of Korea (which practically meant opening it up to the Japanese) and to cede to Japan Port Arthur, the Liaotung peninsula on which it lies, and the island of Formosa.

Having watched the course of events with jealous eyes, Russia, France, and Germany now intervened to prevent Japan from securing a foothold on the mainland. Russia was the real leader in this intervention, for she coveted just the region which had been ceded to Japan. Japan was exhausted by the war with China and at that time had no adequate navy. Therefore the Mikado withdrew from Manchuria, on the ground that Their Majesties, the emperors of Russia and Germany, and the republic of France had united in a recommendation to his government not to occupy the newly acquired territory, for the reason that this "would be detrimental to the lasting peace of the Orient."

The result of this compromise was to throw China into the arms of Russia, who proceeded to take every advantage of the situation. China had been forced to pay a heavy indemnity to Japan in lieu of the cession of the Liaotung peninsula; and when the Chinese government attempted to borrow a large sum from England to meet this obligation, Russia interfered and herself loaned China eighty million dollars without security. In this way China became dependent upon her as a creditor. A Russo-Chinese bank was established late in the same year (1895), which proved to be an efficient agent of the Russian government. On the pretext of providing for the great debt, the bank was to receive taxes, coin money, pay interest on public bonds, and construct railway and telegraph lines. The Russians were permitted by the Chinese emperor to build a railroad across his territory—the Chinese Eastern —which would enable them to reach Vladivostok by a direct line from Irkutsk. Moreover, in order to guard the railway line, Russian soldiers were to be introduced freely into Manchuria. These arrangements gave Russia a great advantage over the other European powers, since she controlled the Chinese government through its debt and occupied Manchuria with her soldiers.

Meanwhile the Germans found an excuse for strengthening themselves in the same region. A German missionary having been murdered in the province of Shantung, which lies opposite Korea, a German squadron appeared in Kiaochow Bay in November, 1897, landed a force of marines, and raised the German flag. As a compensation for the murder of the missionary, Germany demanded a long lease of Kiaochow, with the right to build railways in the region and work mines.

The treaty which made this settlement also provided that "if at any time the Chinese should form plans for the development of Shantung, for the execution of which foreign capital is necessary, the Chinese government, or such Chinese as may be interested in the scheme, shall, in the first instance, apply to German capitalists." This is an excellent example of the anxiety, already alluded to, of the European nations to find outlets for their surplus capital. After acquiring Kiaochow the Germans built harbors, constructed forts, military barracks, machine shops, etc. In short, a model German town was constructed on the Chinese coast, which, with its defenses, constituted a fine base for further extension of Germany's sphere of influence.

At first the Tsar hoped to balk the plans of Germany, but decided later to secure additional advantages for himself. Accordingly, Port Arthur and the waters adjacent to the Liaotung peninsula upon which it lies were leased to Russia in March, 1898, for a period of twenty-five years, subject to renewal by mutual consent. Port Arthur was to be open only to Chinese and Russian vessels, and Russia immediately began to build fortifications which were believed to render the town impregnable. A railway was constructed to Harbin, connecting Port Arthur with the Trans-Siberian Railway and with Vladivostok. This at last gave Russia a port on the Pacific which, unlike Vladivostok, was free from ice the year round.

Learning of these negotiations, Great Britain sent a fleet northward from Hong Kong to the Gulf of Chihli, and induced China to lease to her Weihaiwei, which lay just between the recent acquisitions of Germany and Russia. Great Britain, moreover, believed it to be for her interest to be on good terms with Japan, and in 1902 an offensive and defensive alliance was concluded between the two powers, binding each to assist the other in case a third party joined in a conflict in which either was involved.

The Boxer Rising

The foreigners were by no means content with establishing trading posts in China; they longed to develop the neglected natural resources of the empire, to open up communication by railroads and steamships, and to "Westernize" the Orientals, in order that business might be carried on more easily with them, and new opportunities be found for profitable investment.

The first railroad in China was built by British promoters in 1876, from Shanghai to Wu Sung, a point some fifteen miles to the north of that city. The Chinese, however, were horrified by this innovation, which they felt to be a desecration of the graves of their ancestors. Yielding to popular prejudice, the government purchased the railroad, destroyed it, and threw the locomotives into the river. Nevertheless, five years later, the Chinese themselves, with the aid of British capital, began the construction of an imperial railroad system. In 1895 other foreigners besides the Russians were once more permitted to undertake the construction of railway lines, and within a few years some three thousand miles of road were open for traffic. The capital, Peking, was connected with Hankow on the Yangtze River by a line running southward, and this line is being continued to Canton. From Peking a line was built northeast to Mukden, where it connects with the Trans-Siberian Railway. The French and Germans were also interested in opening up the regions within their spheres of influence, and the British planned to push into the interior of China a line running northward from Rangoon through Mandalay.

In 1898 the internal waterways of China were opened to foreign ships. Several lines of well-equipped steamships began to ply on the Canton River and follow the waters of the Yangtze River for a thousand miles inland. Over fourteen thousand miles of telegraph lines were put in operation, affording overland connection with Europe. The imperial post, organized in 1897, soon had branches throughout the empire.

Inevitably intercourse with European nations affected the historic policy and ideals of the Chinese government. In 1889 a decree was issued establishing an annual audience in which the emperor might show his "desire to treat with honor all the foreign ministers resident in Peking." A few years later the cumbersome ancient ceremonial was abolished, and foreigners were received in a manner which indicated the recognition of their equality with Chinese of the same rank. In 1898, when Prince Henry of Prussia visited Peking, he was cordially greeted by the emperor, who shook hands with him in Western fashion and conversed with him on a familiar footing.

In the same year a series of decrees was issued with the object of reforming the army on models offered by those nations that had given so many proofs of their military superiority. New schools and colleges were planned with a view to starting the country on the road to progress. Chinese students were sent to Europe to study foreign methods of government, agricultural schools were built, patent and copyright laws were introduced, and a department of mines and railroads was established, so that China might no longer be obliged to leave these matters entirely in the hands of foreigners. Journalists were even encouraged to write on political questions.

These abrupt changes aroused the superstitious horror of the conservative party. And they found a sympathetic leader in the dowager empress, who succeeded in putting an end, for the time being, to the distasteful reforms. But Europeans, both missionaries and business men, continued their activities. Thereupon the conservatives became convinced that it was necessary to organize a great movement to drive out the "foreign devils," who had been, in their eyes, steadily undermining the ancient traditions of China.

Among those hostile to the foreigner, there were none more conspicuous than the members of the secret society of the

"Boxers," or, as they appear to have called themselves, the Order of the Patriotic Harmonious Fists. They were quite willing to coöperate with the dowager empress in carrying out her designs against foreign influence. Claiming to be invulnerable and to exercise certain magical powers, they easily won over a large part of the population in northern China, and roused them against the Christian invaders. They insisted that the Western nations were "lacerating China like tigers"; that railways were built through the graveyards, and that the misfortunes of the times were due to the displeasure of their ancestors, whose memory was desecrated by locomotives. They alleged, moreover, that the new machinery was throwing workmen out of employment, and they summoned every patriotic Chinaman to rise in defense of his country.

The party in favor of meeting the "Christian peril" by violence rapidly increased. The Boxers, who were arming and drilling, knew very well that neither the Chinese officials nor the imperial troops would interfere with them. With impunity they murdered missionaries and traders in the provinces; and although the government at Peking always declared that it was doing all it could to suppress disorder, the representatives of foreign nations in the capital became thoroughly alarmed. On June 20, 1900, the Boxers, supported by native troops, killed the German ambassador, Baron von Ketteler, while on his way to the palace to expostulate with the government. The Europeans were then besieged in the several legations and in the Catholic cathedral; but, for some reason which is not clear, the Chinese did not murder them all, as they might easily have done.

Immediately the powers determined to intervene by armed force; and in August a relief expedition, made up of Japanese, Russian, British, American, French, and German troops, fought its way from Tientsin to Peking, and brought relief to the imprisoned foreigners. The Chinese court left Peking, and the royal palace was pillaged by the foreign troops, whose scandalous conduct disgraced the Western world. Diplomatic exchanges were now opened, and the aged Li Hung Chang rendered his last services by negotiating an agreement in which China made certain reparations, including the payment of an indemnity of three hundred and twenty millions and a promise to repress all antiforeign societies.

Although the dowager empress still retained her power, the work of reform was again undertaken. The modernization of the army was resumed, and students were sent abroad in considerable numbers to investigate Western methods of industry and government. By one of the most momentous decrees in the intellectual history of China, the ancient classical system of education, which had for centuries been deemed an essential preparation for public office, was abolished in 1905. Students preparing for the government service were no longer examined upon Confucius and asked to write essays on such subjects as "How the moonlight sleeps on the lake." The new examination questions dealt with the history of the West, with Metternich and Bismarck, and with such grave questions as the relation of capital to labor and the methods of stimulating machine industry. Even the dowager empress was obliged to yield to the progressive party, and in October, 1907, she went so far as to announce that China should prepare herself for the introduction of representative government and of a parliament.

Russo-Japanese War (1904–1905)

Scarcely had the troubles due to the Boxer rising been adjusted when a new war cloud appeared in the East. The interest of Japan in finding markets has already been mentioned. The occupation of Manchuria and Port Arthur by the Russians seriously threatened Japanese extension in that direction; and when Russia secured from Korea a lumber cession in the Yalu valley and sent Cossacks to build forts in that region, Japan, who regarded Korea as lying within her sphere of influence, made a vigorous protest. Russia had agreed repeatedly to withdraw from the district, but had always failed to keep her promises when the time came. She had, moreover, guaranteed the integrity of Korea, upon whose territory she was now encroaching. Accordingly, in the summer of 1903 Japan opened negotiations with the Tsar's government with the object of inducing it to explain its purposes in Manchuria and Korea. Russia delayed and refused to commit herself. Losing patience, the Japanese broke off diplomatic relations on February 5, 1904, and opened hostilities.

Japan was well prepared for war and was, moreover, within easy reach of the field of conflict. The Russian government, on the contrary, was rotten to the core, and it was already engaged in a terrible struggle with the Russian people (see pages 78 ff.). The eastern boundary of European Russia lay three thousand miles from Port Arthur and the Yalu River, and the only means of communication was the single line of badly constructed railroad that stretched across Siberia to the Pacific.

Three days after the war opened, the Japanese fleet surprised the Russian battleships lying off Port Arthur, sank four of them, and drove the rest into the harbor, where it succeeded, in the main, in keeping them "bottled up." A second fleet, which had been stationed at Vladivostok, was defeated early in May, thus giving Japan control of the seas. At the same time the Russians were driven back from the Yalu, and the Japanese under General Oku landed on the Liaotung peninsula, cut off Port Arthur from communication with Russia, and captured the town of Dalny (now called Dairen), which they made their naval headquarters. General Oku then began pushing the Russians northward toward Mukden, while General Nogi was left to besiege Port Arthur. For months the world watched in suspense the heroic attacks which the Japanese, at deadly cost to themselves, made upon the Russian fortress. Meanwhile fighting continued to the north along the line of the railroad. In October the Japanese were victorious in a fearful battle which raged south of Mukden for days, thus putting an end to General Kuropatkin's designs for relieving Port Arthur. As winter came on, the Japanese redoubled their efforts, and the fortress at last surrendered on January 1, 1905, after a siege of seven months.

During the winter the Russians naturally suffered far more than the Japanese, whose whole conduct of the war afforded one of the most extraordinary examples on record of military organization and efficiency. By means of an ingenious system of telephones they kept every division of the army in direct communication with the war office in Tokyo; and by the strictest discipline they saved their troops from disease, and the wounded from contagion in the hospitals. Late in February fighting again began, and for three weeks the Russians struggled against the combined Japanese armies; but on March 9 they deserted Mukden and moved northward, after forty thousand of them had been killed and over a hundred thousand wounded.

On learning of the destruction of its fleets in the Pacific, the Russian government decided to dispatch its Baltic squadron to the Orient. After some strange adventures, which aroused both the amusement and the disgust of those who were following the war,[1] the fleet arrived in May in the Korea Strait, where Admiral Togo was waiting for it. In a few hours he sank twenty-two of the Russian vessels and captured six. The Tsar's fleet was practically annihilated, with terrible loss of life, while the Japanese came out of the conflict almost unscathed.

Desirous, as he said, of keeping Japan and Russia strong enough to balance each other (see page 236), President Roose-

[1] As the squadron was passing through the North Sea the Russians fired upon a fishing fleet off Dogger Bank, and later they alleged that they had mistaken the poor fishermen for Japanese. This is but one of numerous examples of the incompetence which was shown by the Russians during the course of the war.

velt, acting under the provisions of the Hague Convention (see page 302), took measures which brought about peace. After consulting the representatives of Japan and Russia at Washington and ascertaining the attitude of the neutral powers, he dispatched notes to the Tsar and the Mikado, urging them to open negotiations. This invitation was accepted, and on August 9, 1905, the first session of the conference was held at Portsmouth, New Hampshire. On September 5 the Treaty of Portsmouth was signed. This recognized the Japanese influence as paramount in Korea, which, however, was to remain "independent."[1] Both the Japanese and the Russians were to evacuate Manchuria; the Japanese were, however, given the rights in the Liaotung peninsula, Port Arthur, and the South Manchurian Railway which Russia had formerly enjoyed. Lastly, the southern part of the Russian island of Sakhalin was ceded to Japan.

REVOLUTION IN CHINA

From every point of view the Russo-Japanese War was humiliating to China. It was fought on her soil; and, at its close, territory belonging to her was (in fact, if not in theory) handed over to Japan as if it had been the outright property of Russia. And no small part of the humiliation was attributed by the Chinese people to the incompetence of the Manchu dynasty at Peking. In spite of its efforts, mentioned above, to modernize China, it had been unable to create an army strong enough to protect the country against foreign invaders. The last of the dynasty, a little boy who came to the throne in 1908 at the age of two, was surrounded by a ring of councilors more interested in their personal fortunes than in the fate of the empire. Weakened by divisions among themselves,

[1] Notwithstanding this pledge Korea was definitely annexed to Japan in 1910, and the Korean emperor deprived of his authority. In 1919 it was formally incorporated into the Japanese Empire, and its name changed to "Chosen."

they could not agree on heroic measures to save the monarchy from ruin. Meanwhile the demand for reforms, eloquently voiced by Dr. Sun Yat-sen in the south, grew more imperative. Students returning from the West took up the cry that old-fashioned ways must be abandoned and democratic institutions established. After a long struggle the agitators were able in 1912 to force the abdication of the boy emperor and the proclamation of a republic.

It would be a mistake, however, to attribute this event to a widespread longing for democratic government among the three or four hundred million people of China. Perhaps 90 per cent of them were unable to read and write; the great majority knew little or nothing about popular government and had enjoyed no experience in the art. Poverty and taxes were important motivating forces among the rank and file, and the ambitions of the politicians and military men in the several provinces contributed to the antagonism against Peking. China was overpopulated, at least in large areas, and facilities were wanting for the transportation of people from the overcrowded regions to the more sparsely settled districts. From time to time large sections of country were visited by terribles famines; according to estimates, nine million people perished in the famine of 1878. In 1910–1911 a similar disaster, accompanied by pestilence, ran through many provinces, bringing starvation and death to millions. In addition to the poverty came heavier taxes to meet the war indemnity imposed by Japan after her victory in the Chino-Japanese War; and on top of the Japanese indemnity came the still larger indemnity imposed by the powers after the Boxer rebellion. It was not difficult to convince a peasantry ground to earth by taxes and afflicted by famines that a change in government might bring relief; at all events, it appeared that things could be no worse.

But the proclamation of a republic and attempts to make constitutions did not automatically solve China's problems.

In a compromise between the more democratic leaders of the south and the old statesmen of the north, Yüan Shih-k'ai, a military man associated with the imperial régime, was made president. Almost immediately a contest opened between the chief executive and the national assembly, which was convened at Peking in the spring of 1912; and as the dispute wore on, the power of the president steadily increased. As an outcome the parliament was dissolved, and in the autumn of 1914 Yüan announced that he would himself assume the title "Emperor of China." This proclamation was greeted by riots among the populace and protests from the powers, especially Japan; a strong government in China meant that the foreigners could no longer do as they pleased in that helpless country. Frightened by this resistance, the president declared that he would never accept the title of "Emperor" and that his action had been a mistake based on the assumption that the people really wanted him to occupy the "Dragon Throne."

Two years later, death removed him from the scene. The national assembly was reconvened, a new president elected, and work on a constitution resumed. By this time the central authority at Peking had been fatally weakened, and military governors in several provinces, often little more than bandits in thin disguise, had virtually declared their independence. After China was drawn into the World War, largely under pressure from American and English diplomats, the strength of the military men was increased, and the "politics" of China became little more than a scramble among them for the spoils of office, accompanied by periodical civil wars. Chinese affairs ran in this course until, and even after, the triumph of the Nationalist party in 1927 (see pages 532 ff.).

CHAPTER IX

ORIGINS OF THE WORLD WAR

SOURCES OF INFORMATION

In August, 1914, Germany and Austria-Hungary were at war with Russia, France, Great Britain, Belgium, Serbia, and Montenegro, and soon with Japan. Before the struggle came to a close, it had spread around the world, gathering within its fatal sweep Turkey and Bulgaria on the side of the Central Powers, and Italy, Portugal, Rumania, the United States, China, Cuba, Panama, Brazil, Greece, Siam, and Liberia on the side of the "Entente." In life and property the cost of the conflict was so terrible, in glory and profit the outcome was so dubious, that no government was willing to assume responsibility for starting the incredible disaster.

During the war each side accused the other of being primarily "guilty" of the outrage upon humanity and employed this accusation as propaganda to arouse its peoples to more and more strenuous efforts; and after peace was restored the subject continued to be debated by historians, editors, politicians, and street-corner philosophers. When the fighting came to an end, the question was given a highly practical significance, owing to the fact that the huge bill for damages submitted to Germany was framed on the theory that the Central Powers should and must bear the whole burden of responsibility.

Certain primary facts must be considered before one can begin to do any intelligent thinking about "war guilt" (see the close of this chapter). At the outset we should be on our guard against the popular habit of speaking of nations as if they were persons. When we say that "England did this" or

"Germany did that," we really mean that the government of the moment did it. The habit is convenient but misleading. At best, in more or less democratic countries the government is a party affair; it is elected by a majority or a plurality of the voters; and it is usually manipulated by a small group of "insiders." In autocratic countries it is the monarch, and the clique around him, who decide when war is to begin and who the enemy is to be.

Governments, not the people, carry on the negotiations which end in war. In a speech delivered before the Harvard Alumni in June, 1927, Alanson B. Houghton, the American ambassador to Great Britain, described the process with precision:

War does not originate from time to time simply in a sudden and uncontrollable impulse on the part of one great national mass to go out and slaughter another. War is possible, no doubt, because these masses are willing, under conditions, to fight, but these conditions are themselves an integral part of the problem. Before a war is conceivable there must be an issue. And that issue, broadly speaking, is the outcome of a series of maneuvers by which the masses concerned are brought into positions of opposition. Obviously this maneuvering is not done by the masses themselves. . . . The maneuvering is done by little groups of men called governments. These little groups seek constantly and naturally to gain supposed advantages of one sort or another for their own nations. Out of their efforts to enlarge or to strengthen or to maintain the interests entrusted to their charge, the masses they represent are gradually maneuvered into positions which, to say the least, cannot be easily surrendered. If the process continues, sooner or later a situation arises in which an agreement between these small groups becomes impossible. Then, on the ground that their lives and families and property are somehow involved and endangered, these great masses of men and women, roused by every power of organized appeal and propaganda, are ordered under arms, and war follows. The entire process is in control of the smaller groups. They make the issue. They declare the war. . . . And the very men through whose in-

T

strumentality, consciously or unconsciously, this dreadful catastrophe has been brought about, explain it on the ground that, human nature being what it is, any other determination was impossible.

Mr. Houghton's thesis is amply illustrated by the secret documents bearing upon the outbreak of the World War which were made public during and after that conflict. Ordinarily a generation that fights a war is permitted to know just so much about its origin as the governments concerned see fit to disclose. Usually fifty or a hundred years are allowed to pass before the secret archives are opened and scholars are given access to the authentic documents bearing on the war. But, owing to the accidents of the late war, this rule was violated. During their occupation of Belgium the Germans searched the archives and issued volumes of Belgian papers on pre-war diplomacy. On overthrowing the Tsar's government the Bolsheviki opened the Foreign Office in Petrograd and exposed, to an astonished world, secret treaties and secret relations between Russia, France, and England. After the November revolution of 1918 the German Social Democrats broke the seal on the British archives, and since that time more than fifty imposing volumes of secret documents on European diplomacy between 1870 and 1914 have been issued. Likewise the downfall of the Austro-Hungarian monarchy was followed by the publication of important papers taken from the Foreign Office in Vienna. In view of such circumstances Great Britain allowed two British scholars to select from her archives and print a number of significant documents bearing on the origins of the war, having due regard for the susceptibilities of her people and her former allies. Thus, by one process or another, a glare of light has been thrown upon the governmental maneuvers which ended in the great cataclysm of August, 1914. Moreover, these diplomatic papers have been supplemented by memoirs, letters, explanations, and other materials from the pens of many statesmen who took part in the momentous operations.

ANCIENT CONTINENTAL GRUDGES

In getting at the origins of the conflict, it is not enough to study the doings of the men who had a hand in precipitating it. As President Wilson once remarked, the war was "the result of many causes, some of long origin." Some of them lay deep in rivalries that began centuries before any of the statesmen of 1914 were born. Others sprang from the changing social and economic life of contemporary Europe, especially the growth of population, the rise of machine industries, the increasing struggle for new markets in which to sell goods and invest money. As a result of ancient grudges and modern competitions the governments, or "small groups of men," who did the maneuvering in the summer of 1914 were by no means free to consider the immediate dispute on its merits. Any account of war origins which does not take these long-standing grudges and competitions into consideration is bound to be superficial.

At the very outset we must remember that the various peoples of Europe had been fighting for centuries about one thing or another. Cæsar's *Commentaries* tell us about the wars between the Romans and the Germans on the Rhine in the first century before the birth of Christ. All through the Middle Ages the Continent was in the turmoil of war—the Hundred Years' War between England and France illustrating the chief business and glory of kings and princes. After the discovery of America new colonial and trade ambitions gave new causes for fighting, in which all the sea powers took an active part. During his long reign Louis XIV invaded the Rhine regions from time to time, plundered the people, burned their houses, and seized their territories. In the eighteenth century Prussia, under the Hohenzollerns, became a powerful rival of France, preyed upon her Polish and German neighbors, and played an important rôle in the general conflicts of that age. Not long afterward Napoleon, at the head of triumphant French armies, overran all western and central Europe, defeated the Germans in many battles, carved up their territories, and ordered them about like vassals. In this welter of bloodshed England had thrown her weight first on one side and then on another in an effort to maintain a balance of power—that is, to prevent any one nation from becoming a menace to her security, real or supposed.

Out of these ancient rivalries sprang a number of special grievances and situations which were sources of national irritation and served as grounds of patriotic appeal for statesmen engaged in diplomacy.

ALSACE AND LORRAINE

First among the historic grievances may be placed the annexation of Alsace and Lorraine by Germany in 1871, producing a desire for revenge which made it possible for republican France to ally herself with despotic Russia. The importance of this problem can scarcely be overestimated, and a review of its origin is necessary. A great deal of ingenuity has been expended in efforts to show that Alsace-Lorraine "belonged of right" to France or to Germany; stout books bristling with learning have been written on both sides of the case. But the historian with no nationalist bias to uphold will speak with caution on this issue. Indeed, he will be inclined to render no verdict at all; for he knows full well how difficult it is at times to establish the rightful ownership of private property in ordinary courts of law, to say nothing of tracing the ownership of two provinces composed of many fragments whose history reaches back two thousand years through a maze of anarchy, rivalries, intrigues, and wars.

The territory included in Alsace was once a part of the Roman Empire, and on the break-up of that dominion it came under Frankish conquerors. Through many centuries it was passed back and forth from one warlike ruler to another, until finally this congeries of medieval towns and feudal holdings went to the House of Austria, which acquired the imperial title in 1273. There it remained for centuries. At length, on the close of the Thirty Years' War in 1648, certain parts of it were transferred to France. Not long afterwards the ambitious Louis XIV began to seize other fragments, including the city of Strasbourg, and almost completed its annexation before his death. Bits of Alsace that were left were added to France in the course of the revolutionary wars which followed the upheaval of 1789. During all the centuries from the disruption of the Roman Empire onward, the major portion of the people of Alsace were Teutonic in race and spoke a German dialect. But their long affiliation with France, with its more liberal traditions after 1789, turned their affections to that country rather than to any of the German states to the east.

Lorraine stood on a somewhat different footing. Like Alsace, it was tossed back and forth among princely families through the centuries, varying in size as fragments were added to it or taken away according to the trading standards of the old game. At one time it enjoyed a precarious independence between France on the one side and the Holy Roman Empire on the other; but it was always an object of special interest to the former and was at length incorporated in France in 1766 as a result of an arrangement with the last duke, Stanislaus, father-in-law of Louis XV, and deposed king of Poland (Vol. I, p. 144). It remained in French hands until the Franco-Prussian War of 1870. Far more than Alsace it was French in population and sympathies.

When Alsace and "German Lorraine" were annexed by Germany, the two provinces, through their deputies in the French National Assembly, heartily protested against the transfer. Nevertheless, the victor was relentless, and immediately began a process of Germanization. Inhabitants who insisted on retaining their French nationality had to transfer their domiciles to France; compulsory German education was introduced; and the provinces, instead of being erected into German states, were treated as a *Reichsland*, or territory directly subject to the German Empire. Not until 1911 were the provinces granted a constitution and a certain measure of self-government. From the beginning there was friction between the government and the people—just as there was after the retransfer of the provinces to France in 1918. The process of assimilation was continued in spite of opposition on the part of autonomists and of the advocates of restoration to France. By 1910, it was officially reported, at least 85 per cent of the people used the German language as their daily tongue.

Whatever the merits of the claims—French and German—to these provinces, it is certain the French government and many French patriots absolutely refused to be reconciled to the loss of Alsace-Lorraine. Again and again after 1871, the German government sounded France with a view to establishing friendly relations on the basis of the status quo, but every attempt in this line failed. Books and articles flowed from French presses, deploring the loss of the provinces and insisting that France would never be satisfied until they were returned. Her alliance with Russia in 1891 was viewed in wide circles as a pledge that a war of revenge (*revanche*) was coming. Indeed, the Tsar on a visit to France hinted that something of the kind might come out of their secret understandings. French historians and statesmen cherished and nourished the hope. Raymond Poincaré, for example, publicly declared that there was no use for his generation to go on living if Alsace and Lorraine were not to be recovered. Marshal Foch confessed that "from the age of seventeen, I dreamed of revenge, after having seen the Germans at Metz."

With unwavering consistency the French government contended that annexation was not final, and conducted its diplomacy with a view to recovering the "lost territory" in the next war, if and when it came. Only socialists and extreme radicals

—and a few historians—were inclined to acquiesce in the loss of the provinces; and they took this position largely because they could see no solution except in a war that might cost France the lives of as many soldiers as there were people in the two territories. And so it turned out in the end—leaving German nationalists as determined to recover the provinces in the next war as the French nationalists had been between 1871 and 1918.

PROBLEMS OF SOUTHEASTERN EUROPE

If Russia might be of use to France in recovering Alsace and Lorraine, France could reciprocate by helping Russia in her efforts to gain certain long-sought ends in southeastern Europe. Prime among these was the ambition to supplant Turkey in the possession of Constantinople and the control of the Dardanelles. For a long time Russia had striven to get an outlet to an ice-free port through which her bulky grain and timber could pass to foreign markets. To break through to the Mediterranean was her great goal in the Crimean War, but England and France joined Turkey in balking this project (Vol. I, pp. 606 ff.). Again, in 1878, after defeating the Turks in a successful war, Russia was forced to postpone her design by a combination of powers led by Great Britain (Vol. I, pp. 608 ff.). Zealous in protecting the route to India and her property in Egypt, England preferred to bolster up Turkey rather than to admit a powerful rival to her Mediterranean sphere. Beaten in her southward drive, Russia turned to the Far East and wrested a coveted outlet from China at Dalny (Dairen) and Port Arthur, only to come into collision with Japan and lose it in the costly war of 1904–1905. Baffled in the East, Russia, under the direction of two restless spirits, Sazonov, the foreign minister, and Izvolsky, ambassador to Paris, once more shifted her diplomacy to the south. This time Russia found England, already fearful of Germany, more willing to come to terms with respect to Turkey. A decided impetus to the Russian project was given in the spring of 1912, when the Turks closed the Dardanelles temporarily, blocking the Russian grain trade and causing huge losses to England, Rumania, Bulgaria, and Greece as well.

Interwoven with the question of the Dardenelles were far more perplexing problems in the Balkans—problems connected with driving the Turks from their remaining European holdings and organizing the territories gained from them. The situation was bewildering on account of the number of peoples and races involved and the extent to which the ambitions of European nations were engaged. Quite correctly the Balkan Peninsula has been called an ethnological museum; for it contains Bulgars, Greeks, Albanians, Germans, South Slavs (Serbs and Croats), Turks, Rumanians, and Italians, to say nothing of various minor groups. Moreover, these peoples are not sharply separated by high mountain ranges and rivers into definite geographical unities, but are more or less intermingled, especially at troublesome frontiers. Religion as well as race divides them: some are Roman Catholics, others are Greek Orthodox, still others are Moslems,—leaving out of account all minor sects. Among the most active of these peoples were the South Slavs, scattered from southern Austria almost to the Ægean Sea; and of this race one group—the Serbs—took the leadership in throwing off Turkish rule early in the nineteenth century and in struggling for the unity of all South Slavs (Yugoslavs) under one flag.

In the agitations of southeastern Europe (see the last chapter of Volume I), the great powers were deeply interested. Russia, as we have seen, had decided reasons for winning the Straits, and, besides, she looked upon herself as a kind of protector of the Eastern Orthodox Christians in the Balkans. Austria and Hungary also had claims and designs. Not without, reason did they declare that they had saved Europe from the Turks by standing fast on many a battlefield. As the Turkish invaders had been forced back, Hungarians and Austrians had advanced their borders to include new territories and peoples, and at the opening of the twentieth century they had under their government a majority of the South Slavs that had been freed from Turkish rule.

Owing to her affiliations with Austria-Hungary and her trade expansion in the southeast, Germany was likewise interested in the constant disturbances in the Balkans. Equally alert on the west was Italy; for many Italians lived under the Austrian flag on the Dalmatian coast, and Italian imperialists longed to make the Adriatic an Italian sea. Though far away, England had even more at stake—in Egypt, in the Suez Canal, and in holding back the Teutonic advance down the Danube. Closely knit with Russia in a political and military alliance and having designs of her own in Turkey, France could not be indifferent to any readjustment in the Balkans.

Apart from these historic rivalries, which helped to keep the region in turmoil, the chief disturbing factor, perhaps, was the agitation among the South Slavs for unity,—or at least autonomy,—and naturally Serbia, as an independent nation, formed the center of this movement. In June, 1914, the Yugoslavs were distributed under three flags: Serbian, Austrian, and Hungarian. Poets and dreamers among them foretold a great day when they would all be united. To these prophecies the South Slav peasants under Austria-Hungary listened more cheerfully because they were governed by alien races and most of them were tenants on the estates of great landlords—Hungarian and Austrian. In southern Hungary, in Croatia-Slavonia, and in Bosnia-Herzegovina landlordism was widespread, and the tillers of the soil labored under burdensome rents and services.

Inasmuch as the assassination of the archduke Francis Ferdinand, heir to the Austro-Hungarian throne,—the deed which precipitated the World War,—occurred in Sarajevo, the capital of Bosnia-Herzegovina, certain conditions must be recalled that made for discontent among the people of those provinces. In this inquiry we must note at the outset that in 1878 more than half the peasants in Bosnia and Herzegovina were *kmets*—that is, for practical purposes, serfs bound to the soil by tenures akin to those long prevailing in western Europe under feudalism. A large proportion of both free and servile peasants held plots of land scarcely big enough to afford them more than a scanty living. It was the wrath of these half-starved peasants that flamed up in the revolution of 1875 and that led to the transfer of the provinces to Christian Austria-Hungary. During their fifty years of occupation the new rulers did little to improve the condition of these "land toilers," most of them Serbs and Croats. Projects of agrarian reform were voted, no doubt, and many kmets were "freed"; but they were still subject to heavy economic burdens, so that their status was little improved by the change. In 1910 there were 111,033 families working entirely or partly under servile tenures, and 136,854 families enjoying complete "freedom." In practice, the Austro-Hungarian administration did less to ease the burdens of the peasants than to uphold the rights of Moslem landlords in Bosnia and Herzegovina. The administration was closely affiliated with that oppressive and oppressing class—not unnaturally, for Hungary was practically governed by great landlords, and Austria was partly subjected to that class. On the other hand, Serbia was a peasant democracy, and after the collapse of the Central Powers, in 1918, abolished servile tenures in Bosnia and Herzegovina by one stroke.

Such were the general conditions in the Balkans, which served to give the events there during the early twentieth century a world-wide importance (see pages 304 ff.).

IMPERIALISTIC RIVALRIES

Besides these sources of discontent and disorder on the continent of Europe, there were, as we have seen, new rivalries growing out of the efforts of France, Italy, and Germany to acquire trade and colonies in Asia, Africa, and other parts of the world (see Chapter V). This was, it is true, an old policy which Spain, Holland, France, and Great Britain had been carrying on for more than three hundred years, but it gained in intensity and entered new phases as the nineteenth century drew to a close. We recall that France, deprived of most of her colonial possessions in her successive wars with Great Britain, renewed her imperial ambitions under Napoleon III, and after the disaster of 1870 sought compensations in Asia and Africa. Behind this expansion now stood an ever-growing group of French capitalists and manufacturers, whose increasing wealth gave force to the movement. Italy, having achieved her unity about the time the Third French Republic was established, likewise entered the race, especially in Africa.

Still more significant was the industrialization of Germany, which followed swiftly the victory over France. Possessing greater coal and iron resources than either France or Italy, the Germans advanced rapidly in mechanical inventions, improved manufacturing methods, and shipbuilding. From an agricultural country, continental in outlook, Germany was swiftly transformed into an industrial country somewhat after the fashion of England, with a world outlook and world trading ambitions. Whereas she had formerly been fairly content with selling foodstuffs to England and taking manufactures in return, Germany now became a formidable competitor of England in every corner of the earth. The pace at which the Germans developed their foreign trade may be inferred from the fact that within ten years it increased in value from about $1,700,000,000 (in 1894) to approximately $3,500,000,000. This meant that German bankers, traveling men, and "business-boosters" were active everywhere, trying to sell German goods to other nations, like the same classes in other countries. It also meant that the German government was eager to get all the territories and trade privileges—not yet secured by France, England, Holland, Russia, and the United States—that it could buy or seize in various places.

To promote the growth of industry at home and trade abroad the German government did everything it could to aid business men. It granted money to steamship companies so that they could operate in all the waters of the world in competition with steamship companies of other countries. For the purpose of protecting this commerce, the German government steadily increased its navy, so that it could have battleships and gunboats to send anywhere on a moment's notice whenever business men or missionaries got into trouble. With a view to keeping domestic trade in German hands it put high protective tariffs on foreign goods coming into Germany. In other words, the German government backed business men, and business men backed the government. It was impossible to determine clearly where the work of the one began and that of the other ended.

Instead of being satisfied with this peaceful progress and growing business, a great many German leaders thought they had more grounds for discontent than ever. Until about 1890 the Germans had been deeply engrossed in domestic affairs, trying to establish unity and "adjust their frontiers." After that time, as their foreign trade grew they took an increasing interest in what was going on in all parts of the world. But when they began to seek trade and territories abroad, they found that England, France, and other rivals had got ahead of them and taken about everything available. The Germans studied history and read how England had by her naval power wrested India and Canada from France and deprived the Dutch of various colonies, and how the French had seized territory in Asia and Africa at will.

So German imperialists complained that they had been cheated out of their "place in the sun." They lamented the fact that millions of Germans had been compelled to migrate to the United States and South America instead of to German colonies, where they would increase the power of the fatherland. "We must see to it," exclaimed the historian Treitschke, a spokesman of this party, "that the outcome of our next successful war is the acquisition, by whatever means, of *colonies*." With such ideas in mind the German Navy League (an organization modeled after one in England) and other patriotic societies began to clamor for steady increases in the army and navy to defend the country and to advance its interests abroad. While it is true that not many German people joined these societies, they had an influence greater than their numbers seemed to warrant; for they had money, and could keep paid agitators working among the masses.

The views of the German military and naval party were well stated by the Prussian crown prince when he said, in 1913: "Our country is obliged more than any other country to place all its confidence in its good weapons. Set in the center of Europe, it is badly protected by its unfavorable geographic frontiers and is regarded by many nations without affection. Upon the German Empire, therefore, is imposed more emphatically than upon any other people of the earth the sacred duty of watching carefully that its army and its navy be always prepared to meet any attack from the outside. It is only by reliance upon our doughty sword that we shall be able to maintain that place in the sun which belongs to us and which the world does not seem to be very willing to accord to us."

How many German people believed that the army and the navy were merely for "defense," and how many expected to use them in the next war to get more territory at the expense of their neighbors, no one can tell. But one thing is clear— namely, that there was a large party in Germany bent on following the example of other imperialist powers and snatching more land in the next great brawl. This made the German military party a real menace to the same party in England, Russia, and France in particular, for these three countries owned most of the earth that did not belong to other independent nations. In short, German industry, trade, army, and navy could not increase indefinitely without coming into collision with the other great powers of the world.

Whenever there was trouble in any part of the world involving German interests, the German government took a hand in the affair. In 1898, during the war between Spain and the United States, as we have seen (p. 234), the Kaiser "sounded" Great Britain with the view of getting her to join in dividing any territory that might be annexed at the end of the conflict. Only when he was bluntly informed that Great Britain would not help, and that the United States intended to keep what had been won by the sword, did William II desist from interference. He managed, however, to induce Spain to sell to Germany, at a good price, the Carolines and some other small islands in the Pacific. The next year (1900) Germany joined the other powers in suppressing the Boxer rebellion in China, the first over-sea military expedition of the German Empire. Not long afterwards, when France and England were negotiating over Morocco, Germany intervened to assert the claims of her business men to a share in the good things. In these cases and in other ways the German government made it known that it also intended to use its army and navy in advancing and protecting its trade whenever opportunity offered.

While trying to hold the scales fairly between agriculture and manufacturing, the French government and French bankers worked hard to extend their colonial possessions and make loans abroad. As we have seen, the Third Republic acquired great territories in Africa and southeastern Asia, and some important islands, such as Madagascar. Significant, also, for French business men were the great loans which the French made to other governments and to other business men in various parts of the world. Especially heavy were the loans to Russia to pay for building railways, electric-light plants, and factories, for opening mines, and, above all, for military purposes. Wherever opportunity offered, therefore, French business men were on the ground with goods to sell and money to lend, just like the business men of Germany and England. Wherever a quarrel arose, such as the dispute over the Boxer rebellion, French armies were used to protect French interests. In Morocco especially the French were busy at the opening of the twentieth century in increasing their military control and their trade. It was there that the French came into the sharpest collision with the Germans. In short, France, like Germany and Great Britain, was a world power.

PERIODICAL "CRISES"

As the competition for trade and empire increased in intensity, wars in different parts of the world, and incidents but little short of war, revealed the inner nature of the economic rivalry and kept European countries in alarm. We may profitably recall these as antecedents of the World War. After Japan defeated China in 1896, France, Germany, and Russia intervened to deprive Japan of her spoils of war in Manchuria. In 1898 the United States destroyed the last remnants of the Spanish empire and directly entered the European game as a "world power." The next year England was at war with the Boers in South Africa and closed this military season with the annexation of the two republics. In the meantime France and England had a collision in northern Africa known as the "Fashoda incident," which brought the two countries to the verge of trial by battle. In 1900 the Boxer uprising in China against all foreigners led to a temporary coöperation among Western powers, followed by a hot dispute over the division of "rights" in China. In 1904 Russia and Japan were locked in deadly grapple, which closed with a settlement that gave Japan what she had won once before, in her war with China. This contest was scarcely brought to an end when Germany, finding that her growing economic interests in Morocco were threatened by France (backed by Great Britain), displayed a menacing mood which was temporarily allayed at the international conference at Algeciras in 1906. Two years later Austria-Hungary almost set Europe aflame by annexing outright Bosnia and Herzegovina, which had been under her management since 1878. Indeed, it seems probable that if Russia had not been sorely crippled by the recent war with Japan, she might have let loose a general European conflict in 1908. When Germany discovered that in spite of the Algeciras settlement, promising "the independence of Morocco," France was steadily extending her power over that country, the German government sent a small gunboat, *The Panther*, to Agadir, on the coast of Morocco, as a notice that it would not stand idly by if France appropriated the dominion of the sultan of Morocco. Talk of war surged through the Old World; but once more peace was preserved by a settlement in which France made some compensations to Germany in the Congo region for her losses in Morocco.

Although sending about gunboats and battleships to protect national interests was not new, the intrusion of Germany was generally viewed in England and France as "saber-rattling." At all events, there was constant pushing and shoving among the various powers in their efforts to sell more goods and get more territory. Each push and shove created new alarms and greater friction, especially as the patriotic newspapers of every country generally insisted on treating their government as an innocent lamb, and its opponents as ravening wolves. In this way the mass of the people, who probably did not know where Sarajevo or Agadir was, were stirred to a nationalist frenzy by distorted news and by bitter editorials. For

example, the jingo newspapers in both Germany and France
assailed their respective governments for a "dishonorable surrender" when the two countries came to terms after the Agadir
incident in 1911. The wars from 1911–1914, immediately
preceding the World War, are described below (pages 304 ff.).

THE SYSTEM OF SECRET ALLIANCES

During these troubled years of the opening twentieth century, the great powers of the Old World were gradually forming into two armed camps, as we now know from the secret
papers revealing their treaties, notes, and conversations. On
the one side were aligned Germany, Austria-Hungary, and
Italy. This union was an extension of the alliance made between Germany and Austria-Hungary in 1879, "for strictly
defensive purposes," to use the language of the statesmen who
formed it. Three years later this dual contract was changed
into the Triple Alliance by including Italy within its scope.
Like the first, this new arrangement was also "defensive."

When it was renewed in 1887, however, a change was made
in its spirit. Austria-Hungary and Italy then agreed that in
case of trouble in the Balkans they would coöperate in the division of any territory acquired, on the basis of reciprocal compensation. At the same time two special articles were put into
the treaty between Germany and Italy. Germany undertook
to come to the aid of Italy if the latter should find it necessary to take action in northern Africa leading to a war with
France. If in such a war Italy sought to guarantee the "security of the frontiers of the Kingdom" by annexing part of
France, Germany was to impose no obstacles and was, in fact,
to aid in this project "if need be, and in a measure compatible
with circumstances." At later renewals in 1891, 1902, and 1912
the Central Powers were forced to make concessions to Italy's
imperial ambitions in order to keep her in the partnership.
Although this alliance was defensive on its face, the military

T

men of the three countries, especially Germany and Austria-Hungary, were in constant secret communication, making preparations for what is known in diplomacy as "eventualities"; and warlike statesmen in the three countries felt that they could count upon holding the union together in case of a war promising spoils of fair proportions.

On the other side of the widening chasm was the Triple *Entente*, composed of Russia, France, and England. This too rested on secret treaties, notes, and conversations. For practical purposes its origins may be traced to an agreement between Russia and France formally concluded in 1891. The text of the document is short. The object of the accord, it states, is the maintenance of the general peace. Whenever any question arises to threaten that peace, the two governments are to act in concert. They are, nevertheless, to discuss at once the military and other measures necessary for simultaneous coöperation in case of war. This secret document was supplemented, three years later, by a secret military convention providing for combined and instant operations in case either party was attacked by any member of the Triple Alliance, for immediate mobilization without preliminary notice, and for instant forward movements to the frontiers. The number of men to be employed against Germany was fixed, and strict secrecy was pledged. In 1899 a revision of the text added a new purpose to that of preserving the general peace—namely, the task of maintaining "the equilibrium of the European powers." Besides strengthening this understanding by means of numerous military conversations, Russia and France concluded in 1912 an understanding for naval coöperation in case of war. In accordance with the diplomatic arrangements, military officers of the two countries agreed upon the number of men and guns and the strategy to be employed against Germany, in case war came. On the basis of plans for joint military action, the foreign offices of Russia and France carried on communications respecting every crisis that arose in Europe, working in the closest harmony and counting on mutual support.

All these agreements, conversations, and exchanges were, of course, veiled in the deepest secrecy. Nevertheless, news leaked out that certain understandings had been reached. From time to time members of the French Chamber of Deputies asked the foreign minister questions respecting the exact nature of the obligations and benefits involved. More than once the issue was raised: Must France resign herself to the *fait accompli*—the loss of Alsace-Lorraine? But every time the minister's answer was vague and evasive—and satisfactory to the majority of the Chamber, for they too believed that secrecy was best. Hence not until the Russian archives were broken open by the Bolsheviki did the people of France know the nature of the commitments made in their name by the government of the Republic.

The third member of the Triple Entente, England, came into the combination long after France and Russia formed their first alliance in 1891. For many years England stuck to a policy of "splendid isolation," fearing entangling alliances and hoping to make a free choice in case the balance of power on the Continent was threatened by war. Until near the close of the last century the British government was often in conflict with Russia in Asia and with France in Africa, and was, on the whole, more hostile to them than to Germany. Indeed, it made more than one approach to Germany with a view to an understanding; but in each case the German government drew back, fearing that by an arrangement with England it might, among other things, incur deeper enmity on the part of France and Russia.

Unable to come to terms with Germany and alarmed by the rapid growth of the German navy, the British government began to look around for useful friends. Long a rival of Russia in China and on the Indian frontiers, it first sought help against danger there by making a treaty of alliance with

Japan in 1902. Three years later these two powers reached a secret understanding with the United States, in which the three undertook to uphold the existing arrangements of things in the Far East against all possible disturbers, meaning of course Russia, France, and Germany (see page 237).

Thus fortified by makeweights against Russia, Great Britain then sought a settlement of troublesome issues with the Tsar. By a formal treaty signed in 1907 the two powers arranged a bargain, dividing their spheres of control in Asia and adjusting all irritating questions. This was followed by many conversations and the close coöperation of the two governments in dealing with diplomatic problems as they arose in Europe. To seal the friendship great Russian loans were floated in England, and huge sums were sent to Russia to aid in building factories and railways and in equipping the Tsar's army and navy. Finally, in the spring and summer of 1914 a program of coöperation on the sea, in case of a war with Germany, was worked out by secret conversations among naval officers with the full approval of the two governments. There was no formal alliance; but for practical purposes— as Sir Edward Grey, the English foreign minister, said—they were on about the same footing as allies.

In spite of all precautions, news of this naval understanding escaped the official ban. Naturally, the German government was frightened, and was calmed only when Sir Edward Grey assured the German ambassador in London that the alarm was false. This seemed to be confirmed by a flat denial from Russia. In the House of Commons, Grey was asked point-blank whether "any naval agreement has recently been entered into between Great Britain and Russia." To this inquiry Grey responded cleverly that there were no unpublished agreements "which would restrict or hamper the freedom of the Government or Parliament to decide whether or not Great Britain should participate in a war." Thus English public opinion was soothed, and the people were convinced that there was nothing in the rumor.

While the secret Anglo-Russian understanding was developing to the point of perfection, Great Britain and France were drawing together for coöperation in the event of war. Indeed, the Anglo-French entente had begun to take form somewhat earlier than the combination with Russia, and served to promote the formation of the latter; for France, already allied with Russia and preparing with her for war, was eager to bring Great Britain into the circle that was being drawn around Germany. Although England and France had been on the point of war over empire in Africa in 1898, the quarrel was smoothed out, and six years later they came to terms over Egypt and Morocco in an open treaty—supplemented by secret articles which practically gave France a free hand in Morocco after publicly vowing that there was no intention to alter the political status of that country. In the Morocco crisis of 1905 England supported France; then by a series of conversations, especially in 1912, the two governments arranged for closer coöperation in diplomacy and strategy if war should come. In accordance with these interchanges, provisions were made for joint naval and military action. Arrangements were perfected for deploying the British, French, and Russian fleets and for landing British troops on the Continent, should the contingency arise. After holding these conversations, France concentrated her fleet in the Mediterranean and left her Atlantic coast undefended, on the theory that she could count on British assistance.

Yet these negotiations between Great Britain and France did not constitute a treaty of alliance. Indeed, it was specifically understood that none of these arrangements were to "restrict the freedom of either government to decide at any future time whether or not to assist the other by armed force." When questioned in Parliament concerning the nature of these secret understandings, responsible British ministers could always answer, as in the case of the Russian ties, that there were no agreements that would restrain or hamper

Parliament in deciding whether or not to take part in a war, should it come. When, early in August, 1914, Sir Edward Grey revealed for the first time the nature of these secret plans, he reassured Parliament that it was free to choose its own course. As a matter of fact, the cabinet had already authorized the use of the British fleet against Germany in the Channel; and Grey, the chief author of these conversations, "which left Great Britain free to decide," declared that he himself felt bound by obligations of honor incurred under them to join France and Russia in the war with Germany. In other words, the minister who made the arrangements which left Great Britain free believed that they bound her with obligations of honor.

Rivalry in Armaments

Running parallel with the alignment of the powers into two hostile camps were stupendous preparations for war on land and sea and in the air. A new turn had been given to the practice of "preparedness" during the wars of the French Revolution, when "nations" were armed. In 1798 a law was passed in France making every young man liable to serve in the army from his twentieth to his twenty-fifth year. The idea that every able-bodied man might be called upon for national defense was not new; but conscription, or forced military service, had hitherto been looked upon as a last resort in time of extreme danger. Although passed as an emergency measure, the French law of 1798 marked the beginning of a permanent system under Napoleon and, as an eminent English military expert said in 1910, "ultimately compelled all Europe to adopt similar legislation."

The first country to adopt the new French system was Prussia. After suffering a terrible defeat at the hands of Napoleon at Jena, Prussia began to build up an army by adopting conscription. By a general law then enacted, every able-bodied male subject in Prussia was made liable to military service. Thus Prussia became "a nation in arms." As we know, it was this new army that took an important part in driving Napoleon from German soil and in defeating him finally at Waterloo.

Although the Napoleonic peril was thus ended, Prussia, contending that the French peril remained, did not repeal the conscription law. When, fifty years later, William I and Bismarck were preparing to Prussianize all Germany and foresaw a war with Austria, the annual levy of recruits was increased, and the period of active service was lengthened from two to three years, and the term of service in the reserve to four years. In this way Prussia secured an effective army of four hundred thousand troops. With these soldiers she defeated Austria in 1866, overthrew the second Napoleonic empire in 1870, and gained her end of consolidating Germany into the German Empire, with the king of Prussia at its head.

Stung by the defeat of 1870, France adopted two years later a "system of universal and obligatory military service without exemptions and exceptions." In a short time all the European powers except England were at work building up greater and greater armies by conscription; that is, they required all the able-bodied men to enter the army for two or three years and then to hold themselves in reserve to be summoned in case of war. The number which each country had under arms at any one time depended upon the amount of money the government could secure and the length of the service—one, two, or three years, as the case might be. To conduct the training of the soldiers and form a permanent body to lead in war, a large body of regular officers was continuously maintained. To furnish supplies—rifles, cannons, powder, clothing, and the like—huge factories were built, which afforded great profits to the owners and made them all ardent supporters of bigger and better armies.

The result of this system was a steady increase in military competition among the powers of Europe. If one added a few thousand soldiers to the army, all its neighbors felt compelled to do likewise. So, like a rolling snowball, militarism grew as the years passed. Figures are usually dull, but anyone who studies the following table for a minute will gain a valuable education in militarism. This table[1] gives the number of men in the standing armies of Europe at three dates:

	1895	1910	1914
Germany	585,000	634,000	812,000
Austria-Hungary	349,000	327,000	424,000
Italy	238,000	288,000	318,000
Russia	910,000	1,200,000	1,300,000
France	572,000	634,000	846,000

As we have noted, the only European power that did not adopt conscription was Great Britain; but she relied upon her navy, which she kept at a strength equal to that of any two other powers. For this practice Englishmen offered two reasons. The first was that England had a larger population than could be fed from her own farms, and therefore she had to depend upon food sent from overseas. In the second place, it was urged that England, being primarily a manufacturing nation dependent upon trade in all parts of the world, simply had to command the "sea lanes." In other words, England defended her navy on the same ground as the other powers defended their armies—self-protection.

It would be a mistake, however, to imagine that the rivalry of the Continental nations was confined entirely to the building up of land armies. On the contrary, these powers, as well as England, claimed that they needed navies also. Russia urged that it was necessary for her to have ships to defend her interests in the Baltic, in the Black Sea, and in the Far East, where Siberia faced the Pacific Ocean. France had

[1] Moon, *Syllabus on International Relations*, p. 75.

colonies and trade in all parts of the earth which called for protection. Germany likewise, as we have seen, began to build a navy as her over-sea business increased. Early in his reign Kaiser William II declared that Germany's future lay upon the sea, and he was deeply stirred on reading a book by an American writer, Captain Alfred Mahan, showing that England's safety lay in keeping her supremacy on the ocean. Beginning about 1895, Germany undertook an extensive ship-building program, adding more and more battleships as time passed. Although the German government insisted that its idea was to keep up with France and Russia in this game, England regarded the German navy program as a serious menace to her supremacy on the sea. So the race kept up. In the ten years between 1904 and 1914 France and Russia spent, in round numbers, $1,500,000,000 on their combined navies; Germany and Austria-Hungary, $1,200,000,000; and England, $1,600,000,000.

FAILURE OF THE PEACE MOVEMENT

The mounting costs of military preparations and the perils of a war involving such masses of men and munitions led many people to advocate a reduction in armaments and the establishment of machinery for the pacific settlement of international disputes.[1] In 1898 the Tsar of Russia was moved to call a conference of the great powers at the Hague to consider methods for maintaining peace and for the curtailing of military expenditures. The proposal originated in the Russian war department, apparently with General Kuropatkin, who had become greatly alarmed by a survey of the new artillery equipment which Germany had just completed with a view to overcoming by sheer weight of metal the superiority of Russia and France in man power. Aware that Austria-Hungary would soon follow the German example, General Kuropatkin faced

[1] For the part played by the United States, see pages 239 ff.

a real dilemma: a common reduction of armaments or an enormous expenditure to bring Russia up to the new level of military efficiency. With the peasants bowed to earth under oppressive taxation, which took away almost half their income, an additional drain might renew revolutionary troubles, even though France would help with generous loans. Under such circumstances a reduction of armaments seemed the better hope, especially since Russia could count on outnumbering Germany and was backward in industries for the production of engines of war.

At all events, the Tsar issued a call to the powers, inviting them to take part in a convention held in the interest of peace. The summons cited "the longings for general pacification . . . especially pronounced in the consciences of civilized nations," and drew attention to the fact that "the preservation of peace has been put forward as the object of international policy." It then referred to the staggering burden of armaments and to the economic crises induced by such wasteful expenditures. Hence the necessity and desirability of a peace conference— "by the help of God, a happy presage of the century which is about to open."

When the Tsar's call reached Germany, covered by a mantle note from the German ambassador in St. Petersburg, the Kaiser became excited. He wrote on the margins of the papers dealing with the project that the idea of reducing armament expenditures was "Utopian," that the Tsar had put weapons of agitation into the hands of German democrats and socialists, that the English ministers would have "a colossal laugh" over it, that the idea was simply naïve, that the English, having no army, would be glad to see reductions in that sphere, and that, generally speaking, the whole business was sheer nonsense. When His Majesty read in one of the later documents that Germany ought to be careful not to strain relations with the United States by warlike talk, and that the American people were praying every Sunday in their churches for a successful outcome of the peace conference, he exclaimed, "May Heaven forgive these hypocritical pharisees," referring perhaps to the recent Spanish-American War and the conflict with the Filipinos then raging.

While the Kaiser was pouring his scorn on the American and English "hypocrites," he contrived a bit of hypocrisy on his own account. Although he saw in the Tsar's proposal, besides dangerous nonsense, a sneaking plan for weakening Germany, William wrote sweetly to "dear Nicky." He told the Tsar that the peace suggestion "once more places in a vivid light the pure and lofty motives by which your counsels are ruled." He said there would be difficulties in the way of accomplishment, but "the main point is the love of mankind which fills your warm heart. . . . Honor will henceforth be lavished upon you by the whole world. My government shall give the matter its most serious attention." After writing this letter, the Kaiser threw his whole weight against the accomplishment of anything important at the conference, even mild arbitration projects excluding questions of national honor.

Although the archives of France and England, unlike those of Russia and Germany, were not violated by revolutionists, there is evidence to show that the governments of those countries were not optimistic about the Tsar's scheme. English statesmen privately ridiculed the "frivolity," "deceit," and "nonsense" displayed in the Russian proposal. Delcassé, the clever French diplomat, then engaged in forwarding the maneuvers which were to make the World War inevitable, quietly told the German ambassador that France and Germany had the same interest in frustrating the peace conference; that neither of them had any intention of weakening her armed forces or discussing any such proposition; that they could not approve any limitations on the complete independence of nations; but that they might possibly make some slight concessions respecting arbitration, just to save Nicholas II's face. Then the cynical French diplomat added, "Besides the Tsar, we must be careful about public opinion in Europe, for it has been stirred up by this thoughtless step of the Russians."

Under such circumstances it is not surprising that the Hague Conference, when it assembled in 1899, instead of trying to diminish armaments, contented itself with expressing a pious opinion that a limitation of the present military burden was extremely desirable and with recommending the nations to "examine the possibility of an agreement as to the limitation of armed forces by land and sea." The powers, however, agreed to recognize the right of any nation to offer its services to warring countries for the purpose of mediation. They further recommended parties unable to come to agreement by negotiation to submit matters "involving neither honor nor vital interests" to the investigation of an impartial International Commission of Inquiry, to be constituted by an arrangement between the parties to the controversy.

Finally, the powers agreed upon the establishment of a Permanent Court of Arbitration, to which disputants might submit issues on which they were at variance. This court consists of persons (not more than four from each country) selected by the respective nations from among their citizens "of recognized competence in international law, enjoying the highest moral reputation, and disposed to accept the duties of arbitrators." From this long list of eminent personages any powers engaged in a controversy may choose a number to form a tribunal for their special case. The close of the First Hague Conference was shortly followed by a large number of treaties between the powers of the world, agreeing to submit to arbitration all questions "which affect neither national independence nor honor"; but it was generally admitted that the conference had done little toward providing a way to settle those vital issues which actually give rise to great wars.

Nevertheless, the outcome of the experiment encouraged the friends of international peace to believe that more practical agreements might be reached which would mitigate, if not prevent, the evils of war. Accordingly, President Roosevelt in 1904 suggested a second conference, but yielded the honor of issuing the call to Nicholas II, who the following year again sent invitations to over fifty nations, asking them to participate in the consideration of certain important questions, including the peaceful settlement of international disputes and the regulation of warfare on land and sea. The conference opened at the Hague on June 15, 1907, with the representatives of forty-seven nations in attendance, and adjourned on October 18. The proposal of the United States for a permanent international court to which certain matters *must* be referred was defeated. The pressing question of disarmament was dismissed by a resolution declaring, "It is highly desirable that the governments should resume the serious study of the question of limiting armaments." In fact, the conference confined its attention mainly to drawing up treaties regulating the actual conduct of war, the laying of submarine mines, the treatment of prisoners, the bombardment of towns, and the rights of neutrals in time of war. In other words, no steps were taken to reduce military and naval expenses or to advance compulsory arbitration, but a serious effort was made to obtain more agreements on the rules of "civilized warfare" —agreements that were generally broken in the World War, which soon followed.

Thus the Hague Conferences failed to take effective measures for preventing war. Instead of reducing armaments and developing permanent machinery for dealing with international disputes, the European powers persisted recklessly in their old ways. Military preparedness on land and sea rapidly increased, and the historic methods of diplomacy continued to be used to soften the recurrent collisions already described.

We have now recalled those general conditions which made Europe a sort of gigantic bomb which could at any moment be set off in one of hundreds of ways. In order to see how a little detonation in the Bosnian city of Sarajevo came to produce the general explosion, we turn now to the occurrences in the Balkan Peninsula during the few years before the outbreak of the war.

Although war between Germany and the Entente Powers was narrowly averted in 1911, the fatal conflict was only postponed. Conditions in the Balkan region, in which Austria-Hungary and Russia were vitally interested, were destined to lead to the final catastrophe, in which the ancient dynasties of the Hohenzollerns, the Hapsburgs, and the Romanovs, with all their ambitions and pretensions, came to a tragic end.

THE BALKAN WARS

In a former chapter (Vol. I, chap. xv), we traced the gradual disruption of Turkey during the nineteenth century and the emergence of the Balkan states of Serbia, Greece, Rumania, and Bulgaria. When the Serbian and Bulgarian people, driven to desperation by the atrocities of the Turks, had revolted in 1876, Russia had come to their aid and defeated the armies of the Sultan. Then Austria-Hungary and England had intervened and induced the Tsar to submit the whole Balkan matter to the Congress of Berlin. Here it was decided by the powers that Serbia, Rumania, and little Montenegro should be free and independent of Turkish rule, and that Bulgaria should also be independent except for the payment of tribute to the Sultan. The province of Bosnia and the small territory to the southwest, called Herzegovina, were taken from the Turkish government and were turned over to Austria-Hungary to administer.

No one was satisfied with the compromises made at Berlin. A few years later (1885) Bulgaria quietly annexed the district south of her (Eastern Rumelia) and so considerably increased her territory. In 1897—to recall what was said at the close of Volume I—Greece risked a war with Turkey, with the hope of increasing her realms, but was defeated. Turkey was anxious at all costs to hold on to the remnant of her once large dominion in Europe left her by the Congress of Berlin, including Macedonia and Albania. The European powers were well aware of the massacres, assassinations, and robberies going on in Macedonia under Turkish rule; but they dreaded the general war which might develop if any attempt were made to take the region from Turkey and divide it among Serbia, Bulgaria, and Greece, all of which laid claim to it as rightfully theirs. Nevertheless, in 1908, thirty years after the unsatisfactory settlement at Berlin, a series of events began which in six years led to the World War.

During the opening years of the twentieth century there had developed in Turkey a small party of reformers, known as Young Turks, who were especially strong in the army, where as officers they had to study the ideas and methods of Western nations. In 1908 a so-called "Committee of Union and Progress" was formed in the Turkish port of Salonika. In July this committee declared that Turkey must have a constitution and that the reformers would march on Constantinople if the Sultan did not yield. The aged Sultan, Abdul-Hamid, did not feel that he was in a position to oppose the movement; so at last even Turkey got something that passed for a constitution. The election of representatives to the Turkish parliament took place, and the assembly was opened by the Sultan with great pomp in December, 1908.

This "bloodless revolution" attracted the attention of Europe, and everyone wondered whether the Young Turks, who were few in number and impractical in their notions of government, would really succeed in reforming such a thoroughly corrupt government as that of Abdul-Hamid, who had hated and cruelly suppressed every tendency toward betterment during his long reign.

Taking advantage of the crisis in Constantinople, Bulgaria immediately seized the opportunity to declare itself entirely

independent of Turkey. Next Austria-Hungary proclaimed
the annexation of Bosnia and Herzegovina, the two Slavic
provinces of Turkey which it had been managing since the
settlement at the Congress of Berlin. It set to work to assimilate the provinces as completely as possible and to suppress
the inclination of their inhabitants to join their Slavic relatives
in Serbia. A glance at the map (p. 352) will show how important these provinces were for Austria-Hungary, since they
connected the main body of its possessions with Dalmatia and
the ports of the Adriatic.

Meanwhile the Young Turks encountered ever-increasing
difficulties. They naturally thought that it would be a wise
thing to deprive the unruly populations of Albania and Macedonia of their arms. This led to a vast amount of trouble.
The Albanians had always been willing to fight for the Turks,
but on their own terms, and they had no inclination to join
the regular army or to pay taxes, as the new government
wished. So there were successive revolts in Albania and Macedonia, and the disorder under the new constitution was worse
than under the former despotism. Then the officials and politicians who liked the old ways of doing things organized an
uprising in Constantinople which had to be put down.

In September, 1911, the troubles of the new Turkish government in Constantinople were multiplied; for Italy declared
war on Turkey, alleging that Italian subjects in Tripoli were
not properly treated. All Europe protested against this action
by Italy as "high-handed"; but Italy replied that she was
merely following the example set by other countries—protecting the lives and property of her citizens by annexing a
country beset by chronic disorders. Turkey was no match for
Italy. There was not a great deal of fighting; but Italy took
possession of such portions of Tripoli as she could hold with
her troops, and also captured certain islands in the eastern
Mediterranean. The Young Turks did not feel that they
could face the unpopularity of surrendering the regions oc-

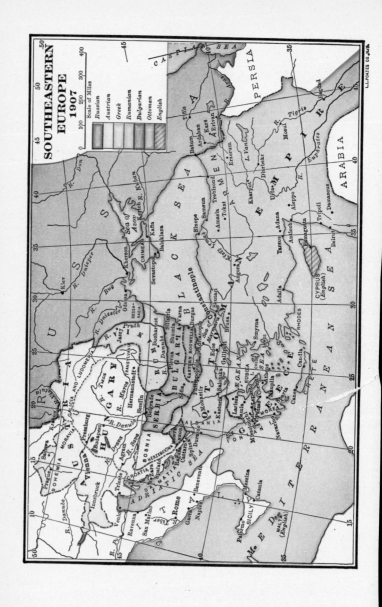

SOUTHEASTERN
EUROPE
1907

Scale of Miles
0 100 200 300 400

Russian
Austrian
Greek
Rumanian
Bulgarian
Ottoman
English

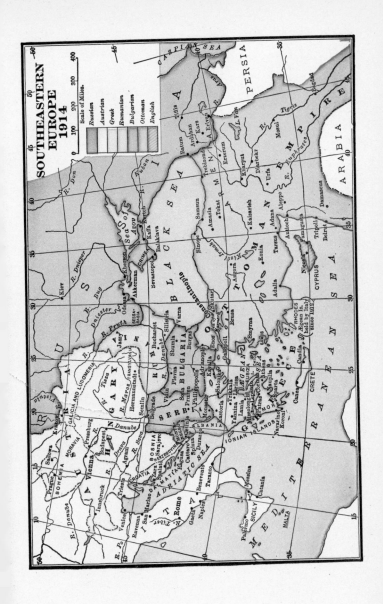

SOUTHEASTERN
EUROPE
1914

Scale of Miles.

Russian
Austrian
Greek
Rumanian
Bulgarian
Ottoman
English

0 100 200 300 400

cupied by Italy; but after the war had dragged on for a year they were forced, in October, 1912, by the oncoming of a new Balkan War, to cede Tripoli, reserving only a vague Turkish suzerainty. Italy also continued to hold the island of Rhodes.

Seeing the Turkish government beset by difficulties, Venizelos, the statesman who had been reorganizing Greece with the ability of a Cavour, secretly arranged an alliance with Bulgaria, Serbia, and Montenegro for a war with Turkey, which began in October, 1912. The Turkish army proved feeble, and the Bulgarians were able in a few days to defeat it, invest the important fortress of Adrianople, and drive the Turkish forces back close to Constantinople. At the same time the Greeks advanced into Macedonia and Thrace, while the Montenegrin and Serbian army defeated the Turkish army sent against them and attacked Albania.

At this stage Austria began to grow very nervous lest the Serbians should establish themselves on the Adriatic, and she flatly forbade Serbia to hold the Albanian port of Durazzo. Had Russia been inclined to support Serbia at that moment, the World War would probably have broken out at the end of 1912 instead of two years later. Serbia, however, backed down. A truce was arranged, and representatives of the Balkan states and of Turkey met in London to see if a peace could be established. The powers advised Turkey to give up everything in Europe except Constantinople and the region immediately to the west. The Young Turks decided, however, to fight a little longer, and the war was resumed in January. Everything went against them; and in May preliminaries of peace were signed in London in which Turkey turned over Macedonia and Crete to the Balkan allies.

But Serbia, Bulgaria, and Greece were all jealous of one another, and the division of the booty immediately led Bulgaria to turn round and wage war on Greece and Serbia. There was a month of frightful carnage (July, 1913); and then the Bulgarians, defeated on all sides (for the Turks even

T

recovered Adrianople, and the Rumanians invaded Bulgaria from the east), agreed to consider peace, and delegates met in Bucharest, the capital of Rumania.

The treaties concluded at Bucharest between the Balkan kingdoms disposed of practically all of Turkey's possessions in Europe. The Sultan was left with Constantinople and a small area to the west, including the important fortress of Adrianople. The great powers, particularly Austria, insisted that Albania should be made an independent state, so as to prevent Serbia from getting a port on the Adriatic. The rest of the former Turkish possessions were divided among Greece, Serbia, Bulgaria, and Montenegro. Greece received the important port of Salonika and the island of Crete, as well as a considerable area in Macedonia. Bulgaria was given an outlet to the Ægean Sea on the south, but lost considerable strips of territory to Rumania and Serbia. Serbia was nearly doubled in area, and so was Montenegro.

The Balkan wars revived all the old bitter rivalry between Austria-Hungary and Russia, and within a year led to a general European conflict unprecedented in the annals of history. In order to understand the situation the reader should carefully review the pages on the structure of Austria-Hungary and study the map of the curiously constructed Dual Monarchy (Vol. I, pp. 556–557). The government at Vienna was largely controlled by the German element in the mixed population of Austria, and did all it could to keep the Slavic population in Bohemia and Moravia, the Ruthenians of Galicia, and the Slovenes of the south in a condition of political subordination. In Hungary the Magyar nobility asserted their supremacy as against the Slovaks and Rumanians within the Hungarian boundary on the north and east, and the Slavonians and Croats to the south. Both the Slavs to the north (Czechoslavs) and those to the south (Yugoslavs) bitterly resented the arrangements which deprived them of their proportionate influence in both Austria and Hungary.

With the outright annexation by Austria-Hungary of Bosnia, in 1908, the situation had become worse than ever. The neighboring Balkan state, Serbia, was alarmed and indignant, as the annexed provinces were mainly peopled with South Slavs, especially Serbs and Croats, and the Serbians had long cherished the ambition of uniting with them and the Montenegrins in a new South Slavonic state which should reach from the Danube to the Adriatic. Russia also was angered. But she had not yet recovered from the war with Japan and her own revolutions; and when Germany declared that she would support Austria, —with arms if need be,—Russia was obliged to submit to the humiliation, as she viewed it, of being unable to protect those of her own race in the Balkans.

For the government at Belgrade the annexation of Bosnia by Austria was indeed a serious setback. Serbia was now apparently shut in from the sea for all time to come, and so would be dependent for a market for its farm products upon its enemy across the Danube—Austria-Hungary. This would keep it in the condition of a weak and somewhat dependent state, which was what Austria wanted.

In the wars of 1912–1913, however, Serbia had burst its boundaries on the south and all but reached the Adriatic through Albania. Again Austria interfered, and had an independent prince set up in Albania in order once more to shut off Serbia from the sea. The Serbians felt that the natural rewards of their victories had been denied them by their powerful but jealous neighbor, and bitter feelings resulted.

The situation at the end of the Second Balkan War augured ill for the peace of Europe. Although Austria had managed to frustrate Serbia's hope of getting a port on the Adriatic and had succeeded in having Albania made an independent principality under a German prince, Serbia had, as we have seen, nearly doubled her territory, and there was every probability that the Serbs would continue to cherish their plan of uniting the discontented South Slavs in the neighboring provinces of Austria-Hungary—Slovenia, Bosnia, Croatia, and Slavonia; hence the Dual Monarchy's animosity.

Against the union of the Slavs—*Pan-Slavism*, as it was called—Germany was prepared to put forth all her energies. If Russia dominated the Balkans and took Constantinople, it would put an end to Germany's plans for extending her trade and control in southeastern Europe; above all, it would block the German scheme for a railroad from Berlin to Bagdad and the Persian Gulf. Germany had already arranged for a "concession" from Turkey to construct this road, and it was being rapidly built. Since the trains were to run through Serbian territory, the Serbs themselves began to fear German power more than ever.

In this clash of interests in southeastern Europe, many Germans, on their side, drew together in a movement known as *Pan-Germanism*. Their idea was to unite all Germans in Germany and in Austria-Hungary for the purpose of promoting their trade and defending their countries. In patriotic circles, therefore, it became the fashion to speak of Pan-Germanism as challenging the threatening hosts of Pan-Slavism.

The year 1913, following the collision between Austria and Serbia over Albania, brought forth, it will be recalled, renewed activity in military "preparedness" (pp. 296 ff.). About the same time both Germany and France made great increases in their armies. Which began first is not certain. Probably they both began about the same time. At all events, Germany added to her standing army in that year, and the Reichstag voted approximately a billion marks for unusual military expenses. France enlarged her army by extending the period of active service from two to three years. In complete understanding with France, the Russian government made heavy appropriations; and the French commander, General Joffre, was summoned to help in reorganizing the Russian army and perfecting plans for a joint war against Germany, should it come. Austria-Hungary gave special attention to strengthening her artillery. England devoted still larger sums to her navy. Even Belgium introduced universal military service on the assumption, which was generally made, that if war came the Germans would try to pass through her territory on the way to France.

FATAL FLOUNDERING OF DIPLOMATS IN JULY, 1914

Such was the state of European alliances, international jealousies, and warlike preparations in 1914. Only an incident of one kind or another was necessary to start a European war; for it is difficult to believe that such intense rivalry, intrigue, and arming could have gone on much longer without producing a widespread conflict. At last the pretext came. On June 28, 1914, the archduke Francis Ferdinand, heir to the Austro-Hungarian throne, and his wife were assassinated in Sarajevo by a young Bosnian student, Gavrilo Princip, who, in collusion with a number of discontented Serbo-Croats, had hatched the plot in Belgrade. Undoubtedly the deed was the outcome of the long agitation among the South Slavs designed to throw off the Austro-Hungarian yoke. Undoubtedly it was prepared with the connivance of some high officials in Serbia, but whether with the full knowledge of the Serbian government remains a disputed point.

This murder enraged the Austrians and the Hungarians. As Harry Elmer Barnes has said, somewhat the same temper existed in Vienna and Budapest after the assassination as would be created in the United States if the president and his wife were shot at El Paso, Texas, by a Mexican assassin believed to be secretly supported by the government of Mexico. At all events, the Austro-Hungarian government on July 23 sent a harsh ultimatum to Serbia containing a long list of peremptory demands. It gave Serbia forty-eight hours in which to promise the suppression of anti-Austrian propaganda in newspapers, schools, and secret societies; to dismiss from the army or government office anyone who was objectionable to Vienna; and to give permission to Austrian officials to sit in Serbian courts with a view to enforcing these demands and bringing accused persons to justice. In reply, Serbia agreed to all these humiliating conditions except the last, and offered to refer that to the Hague Tribunal. Although even the German emperor thought that the humble Serbian reply met the requirements of Austro-Hungarian honor, the Foreign Office in Vienna took no such view of the answer from Belgrade. It was bent on punishing the Serbs and putting an end to Yugoslav propaganda for independence and national unity. And in spite of Germany's efforts to "localize" the conflict and confine the issue to Serbia and Austria, the controversy soon involved all parties to the Triple Alliance and the Triple Entente; for whatever the merits of the Serbian case, neither Russia nor England could look with satisfaction on an extension of Austrian and German power in the direction of Turkey and the Straits.

So seven foreign offices—London, Paris, Berlin, St. Petersburg, Vienna, Rome, and Belgrade—and a small army of ministers and ambassadors scattered over Europe became involved in feverish negotiations. For days the telegraph and telephone wires hummed. Reams of dispatches were written. Innumerable local conferences were held—all in an apparent effort to find a peaceful solution, saving the pride and honor of all parties. Various schemes to preserve peace were suggested. Germany wanted to "localize" the quarrel on the understanding that Vienna would make pledges assuring Serbian territorial integrity; but neither Russia nor France would accept this proposal. Italy advanced a scheme by which Serbia was to yield to Austria's demands on the advice and under the protection of the powers; but none of the other countries took this seriously, in spite of its good features. On July 24 Sir Edward Grey proposed that Germany, France, Italy, and England should endeavor to relieve the dangerous tension between Vienna and St. Petersburg; Germany agreed to this if "localization" should fail. But Russia and France would not consent. Then Grey suggested a conference of the ambassadors of the four powers in London. Germany rejected the scheme because it looked like summoning Austria before a European court of justice; France accepted it on condition that Germany first exert pressure on Vienna; Italy was favorable to it; Russia opposed it and offered as an alternative "a direct conversation" between Vienna and St. Petersburg. Blocked in this movement, Sir Edward Grey then agreed that direct conversations would be the best method of all.

But the direct exchange of views between Vienna and St. Petersburg came to naught. The imperial government of Austria-Hungary, directed by Count Berchtold, constantly spurred to harsh and immediate action against Serbia by the military party headed by Conrad von Hötzendorf, went rapidly forward with military preparations, sure of the German support promised immediately after the assassination of the archduke. Rejecting the reply from Belgrade as unsatisfactory, Austria-Hungary declared war on Serbia on July 28. Now thoroughly alarmed by this turn in affairs, the German chancellor, Theobald von Bethmann-Hollweg, began on July 30 to bring serious pressure on Austria in the interest of moderation and peace. But this tardy demand from Berlin was treated cynically in Vienna. Besides, it was too late; for on the evening of that day the Tsar, hoping for peace and yet besieged by his military staff, consented to a general mobilization of the Russian army—an action directed against Germany as well as Austria. This meant war, according to the creed of military men. When the diplomatic negotiations reached an impasse at the end of July, 1914, it was they who took the helm, on the practical ground that, war being inevitable, everything must turn on its real and supposed "necessities."

Russia, Great Britain, and France had 141 regular divisions of troops, 61 reserve divisions, and 37 cavalry divisions.

Austria-Hungary and Germany had only 82 regular divisions, 48½ reserve divisions, and 22 cavalry divisions. Moreover, owing to the great number of Poles, Czechs, and South Slavs in the Austrian army, its fighting zeal was known to be low. It was clear that the main brunt of the conflict must fall on Germany, overwhelmingly outnumbered. On the other hand, it was notorious that the Russian forces were slow in getting into action. Under these circumstances Germany's prospects for victory hung on speed, while the Entente allies were freer to bide their time, counting on their numbers, their economic superiority, and a blockade by sea, to win the war in the end.

Learning of Russia's general mobilization, Germany called upon the Tsar to stop it, pending a continuance of diplomatic negotiations. Receiving no favorable reply, Germany declared war on Russia on August 1. The next day, the British foreign minister, Sir Edward Grey, informed France that in case of war the British fleet would defend the Channel coasts against the Germans. After repeatedly sounding the British government with a view to discovering the terms on which it would stay out of the war, including a suggestion that Belgian neutrality might be respected, Germany on August 2 demanded of Belgium a free passage for her troops on their way to France—a demand indignantly rejected. Turning to France, the German government asked her what was to be her course in view of the war just declared between Germany and Russia. When France replied that she proposed to protect her own interests, Germany countered by declaring war on France, August 3.

All eyes were now turned on Great Britain. The British government, having rejected all of Germany's suggestions relative to the neutrality of Belgium, now issued an ultimatum calling on Germany to respect that neutrality on pain of war. But German armies had already plunged across the Belgian frontier; and accordingly, on August 4, Great Britain found herself siding with the enemies of the Central Powers. As for

Italy, it held back for the time being, maintaining neutrality on the ground that the terms of the Triple Alliance did not apply to the situation.

SO-CALLED "WAR GUILT"

No sooner had the war started than each side accused the other of being responsible for the outbreak. After it was over, Germany was compelled by force and against her vigorous protests to sign a treaty which placed the responsibility upon the Central Powers. Since then literally thousands of books, articles, and pamphlets have been written to prove one alliance or the other "guilty." The most careful historians have been chary about rendering verdicts in the case. It is easy to show that if Germany had, before it was too late, put pressure on her ally, Austria-Hungary, in the interest of peace, the war might not have come to pass—then. On the other hand, it is equally easy to show that if France had put similar pressure on Russia, her ally, to preserve peace, war might not have happened—then. Or if England had early warned Germany about the danger of a general war, or told Russia and France that it was not to be tolerated, war might not have come— then. So, at least, it seems. But in the storm of conversations, dispatches, and telegrams, with all parties seeking to protect their respective national interests, and all in mortal fear of one another, who could be sure of anything? Unless it can be shown that one of the contending statesmen deliberately omitted to do something which he knew would have preserved peace, how, then, can responsibility be placed exactly? And if the Sarajevo crisis had been passed safely, would it have been possible to maintain peace long against the growing pressure of rivalries and armaments?

When in after years some of the leaders on the side of the Entente looked back calmly on the events of 1914, especially in the light of the diplomatic revelations, they were inclined to be less certain that the sole responsibility for the conflict rested on the Central Powers. In his memoirs published in 1925 Sir Edward Grey gave his deliberate judgment in the following verdict:

More than one true thing may be said about the causes of the war, but the statement that comprises the most truth is that militarism and the armaments inseparable from it made war inevitable. After 1870 Germany had no reason to be afraid, but she fortified herself with armaments and the Triple Alliance in order that she might never have reason to be afraid in the future. France naturally was afraid after 1870, and she made her military preparations and the Dual Alliance [with Russia]. Britain, with a very small army and a very large empire, became first uncomfortable and then (particularly when Germany began a big-fleet program) afraid of isolation. She made the Anglo-Japanese Alliance, made up her quarrels with France and Russia, and entered the Entente. Finally, Germany became afraid that she would presently be afraid and struck the blow while she believed her power to be invincible. Heaven knows the whole truth about human affairs, but I believe the above sketch to be as near to a true statement of the causes of the war as an ordinary intelligence can get in a few sentences.

In this statement, Grey disposes of the idea that Germany alone was responsible for inflicting the war upon innocent and unsuspecting parties, although he still wishes to put, in a vague way, some special onus on that country.

Poincaré, Grey's French associate in the understandings preceding the war, confessed in 1925 that he did not believe that Germany and Austria desired more than a localization of the conflict with Serbia at the outset. "I do not claim that Austria and Germany," he said, "in this first phase, had a conscious, thought-out intention of provoking a general war. No existing document gives us the right to suppose that at that time they had planned anything so systematic." This admission, like that of Grey's, rejects the theory that the war was produced by a deliberate conspiracy on the part of the Central

Powers. Indeed, on a fair view of the tangled story, it seems that Lloyd George was somewhere near the truth when he exclaimed that the statesmen of Europe just stumbled into the war.

In coming to any kind of conclusion on this vexatious subject, it is well to recall once more that the heritage with which the statesmen of Europe had to deal in the summer of 1914 was, in a large part, fixed by a destiny over which they could have exercised little influence. Europe was a vast complex of nations, many of them hoary with age and incrusted with traditions as hard as steel and not so pliable. The great pressures of the time—Russia's drive on the Straits, France's longing for revenge, Irredentism in all directions, and the rivalry for markets—were as natural as the rising and setting of the sun. The division into "races" and languages, the arrangements of classes, the schemes of inherited government, the mental colorations of the various orders of society—these things seem to have been beyond the reach of individual wills.

The practice of, the belief in, and the traditions of war were deeply embedded in European civilization. Likewise inescapable were the nationalistic and democratic stirrings, which made historic monarchies and aristocracies appear as anomalies—and hence, to superficial thinkers, "wicked." Then there were the accepted policies of insulted patriotism that justified, indeed demanded, conduct which in private life would have been spurned as dishonorable and criminal. All these things were very real; no premier, diplomat, Tsar, or Kaiser invented them or could with impunity ignore their reality. Evidently, therefore, a large part of the drama was "determined" in advance by the heritage—the posture of affairs which lay beyond the reach of statesmen.

There are other points to be added. None of the governments that were parties to the quarrel believed in the peaceful solution of all such disputes. They believed, rather, in the emergent inevitability of war. All were preparing for it, straining every nerve in the process. All looked upon war as a possible instrument of national advantage, to be used for that advantage on due occasion. All found the acceptance of war an easier way out of their pressing dilemma than a prolonged, arduous, and hazardous effort to remove social grievances and international rivalries by legislation, negotiation, adjustments, and understandings. None of them had an ardent and sacrificial faith in peace as the source of the good life. All of them, or nearly all, looked upon the iron ration of war as a tonic for national debility. All of them, or most of them, laughed at efforts to work out machinery for the establishment of permanent international concord. In all the countries concerned there were military or naval castes, or both, eager as children to try out their new toys in the great game of war.

All the leaders, or nearly all, were Christian gentlemen, intelligent, honorable, and pacific; yet all were preparing for war, and pursuing policies that led directly into an abyss. All thought it proper in national interest to resort to espionage and bribery in the advancement of their ends; at least the statesmen of Russia, Austria, Germany, Serbia, and France made use of such practices. Of England's methods we know less; for England has published only selected papers, and even the choice of those printed is sometimes disingenuous, if not worse. All governments suppressed passages in official documents for the purpose of deceiving their countrymen and issued statements which were false in both intention and results. All were prepared to take territory and property belonging to some other country or people. All were willing in the name of patriotism to violate nearly every principle of the moral code.

Indeed, as was pointed out by Professor Albrecht Mendelssohn-Bartholdy in his Williamstown lectures for 1926, the governments of Europe had drifted into such a condition that no responsible statesman believed in the sincerity of the opponent who undertook negotiations with him. In many cases the men on the one side of the table knew that the men on the other side were lying, while the prevaricators themselves knew that the listeners knew that they were lying. More intricate involutions of duplicity seem impossible. For example, the military plans made by the general staffs of Germany and Italy under the renewal of the Triple Alliance in 1901 were soon filched by the French secret service, and the filching was quickly discovered by the Germans, who thereby learned how innocent the French were when they looked innocent. To cap the climax the German General Staff kept the news of the robbery from the other ally, Austria, because they believed the plans worthless anyway!

Again, we have high authority for the statement that at least by 1913 the German secret service discovered the nature of the Anglo-French agreement of 1912 and the fateful Anglo-Russian conversations of the same period. Hence, when the German officials read Grey's statements in Parliament declaring that no serious commitments had been made, they suspected that the statements carried a false meaning, at the very least; and thus they knew more than most of Grey's colleagues in the cabinet, to say nothing of members of Parliament and British citizens. There is reason for believing that the British secret service was equally efficient; in fact, British writers boast of it.

After devoting many years to the study of the origins of the war, an American historian, Sidney B. Fay, sums up his conclusions in the following manner: None of the powers wanted a European war, although each of them was quick to imagine the possibility of great advantages in a fortunate outcome. Why did the war break out? "Because in each country political and military leaders did certain things which led to mobilizations and declarations of war or failed to do certain things which might have prevented them. In this sense, all the European countries, in a greater or less degree, were re-

sponsible." But the effort to arrange the powers in the order
of their responsibility is to be deprecated, for it is impossible
to separate remote from immediate causes and fix the deed
which turned the balance in favor of the armed conflict.

The movement for Serbian unity sprang from a perfectly
natural impulse; so did Austria's action in self-defense against
a tendency threatening her territorial integrity. Germany did
not plot a European war, did not want one, and made genuine,
though too belated, efforts to avert it. Germany's inferiority
in numbers made the invasion of Belgium a strategic necessity
—at least in the eyes of her military men. It was the hasty
Russian general mobilization, set in motion while Germany
was still trying to bring Austria to accept mediation proposals,
which finally rendered the European war inevitable. President
Poincaré made efforts for peace, but devoted himself rather
to minimizing French and Russian preparatory measures and
emphasizing those of Germany, for the purpose of winning
British support in a struggle which he regarded as inevitable.

Sir Edward Grey offered "many sincere proposals" looking
to peace; but they all failed, only partly on account of Germany's attitude. It is not impossible that he might have prevented war if he had warned Germany that England would
enter it or had urged France and Russia to take a moderate
position; but there were hazards in both lines of procedure—
political and military. He could not be sure of English popular support until Germany had decided to go through Belgium.

From the foregoing considerations, Professor S. B. Fay
argues that "the verdict of the Versailles treaty that Germany
and her allies were responsible for the war . . . is historically
unsound."

CHAPTER X

THE WORLD WAR. PART I

Novel Features of the War

It would be idle to pretend that the military events of the World War can be recorded even in the barest outline within the compass of this book. Already hundreds of volumes have been written about them. And there is not a single important campaign or maneuver which is not the subject of lively controversy with respect to what actually happened. French writers give one view, English another, and German a third. To go into the claims, allegations, charges, countercharges, and recriminations which have collected about a single great battle of the World War, such as that of the Somme in 1916, for instance, would consume all the pages of this manual. Owing to the semi-technical character of the questions involved, only military men can discuss them with authority, and they differ violently among themselves on vital points. Therefore it seems the better part of discretion to limit our discussion to the outstanding phases of the conflict and to the novel features of combat introduced during this great cataclysm—the first real world war in the age of science, machinery, and democracy.

The story of previous wars can be told mainly in terms of armies, commanders, campaigns, and victories. In them man power, equipment, and strategy were the chief determining factors. To be sure, the size of cannons had been greatly increased since the Middle Ages, and breech-loading rifles had taken the place of old-fashioned muzzle-loaders. But previous to 1914 only a relatively small part of the energies of nations had been employed in their respective wars. In the World

War, on the other hand, whole nations were embattled; "business as usual" became impossible; nearly all the available men were mobilized for battle duty; the remainder of the adult population was enrolled so far as necessary to provide the sinews of war; vast loans, domestic and foreign, were floated; peaceful industries were transformed into munitions plants; all sciences and arts were enlisted to devise more effective methods for dealing death and destruction. Spiritual and intellectual energies were likewise mobilized. Prayers, sermons, poems drawings, pictures, editorials, newspaper stories, were employed to forward the work at the Front, upholding patriotic convictions and seeking to demoralize the enemy. The World War was a war of finance, science, machinery, democracy, civilization. In fact, the new conditions of Western social and economic life, which had been developing during the preceding fifty years, had revolutionized warfare—so deeply that even military men were dumfounded by the strange unforeseen factors which threw out their old calculations.

If the World War opened true to form with grand marches of mobilized armies commanded by distinguished generals, it was scarcely a month old when surprises began; and as it unfolded, the ingenuity of science supplied revolutionary devices in swift succession. In accordance with the plans of the German general staff, its armies swept through Belgium, leaving death and ruin in their train. Imposing fortresses proved old-fashioned, and crumbled before the new artillery. Ahead of schedule the armies burst into France; by September 1 the vanguard was within twenty-five miles of Paris. It seemed as if the German project to deal a paralyzing blow to France, to force another Sedan, and then to destroy Russia leisurely was to be realized with almost mechanical precision. The English and French armies were driven back with terrible losses; the French attempt to strike at Germany through Alsace-Lorraine utterly failed in attaining its objectives. But in making their amazing advance, the German armies, instead of extending their right wing to the sea and carrying all before them, according to the original plan formulated by General Schlieffen, swerved to the southeast, leaving the right flank exposed to an enveloping attack by British and French forces to the west. Taking advantage of this situation, the French commander, General Joffre, made a stand near the Marne River early in September and counterattacked, while French and British forces threatened to turn the German wing to the west. Then to save themselves, the two German armies under Von Kluck and Von Bülow decided, on September 9, to retreat to the Aisne River. The grand German scheme for a quick conquest collapsed.

Why did this happen? No simple answer is forthcoming. On the German side, General Ludendorff attributed the outcome to mistakes on the part of the German high command, to the withdrawal of men from the west for the purpose of stopping Russians in the east, and above all to the failure of the German government in time of peace to prepare for such a contingency by increasing its available man power. On the side of the Entente, the victory at the Marne is ascribed to the strategy worked out by the French and British before the war —strategy designed to mislead the Germans by continuous retreat, drawing out their lines of communication, filling them with delusive hopes, and then striking them by concentrated reserves at the proper moment. No small share of the responsibility for the German failure is laid by critics on the chief of staff, General von Moltke, the bearer of a historic name, who made innumerable miscalculations and remained far away from his advancing armies (partly on account of feeble health) instead of keeping in close touch with hourly events.

On the Eastern Front as well, the armies of the Central Powers met with surprises. The unexpected rapidity with which the Russians mobilized enabled them to make an initial advance into East Prussia and to drive southward into Austria with extraordinary success. Moreover, instead of overwhelming little Serbia at once, the Austrian armies sent against her

T

were at first defeated and driven back across the Danube. So difficulties in the east forced the Germans to transfer troops from France and to lend aid to their hard-pressed Austrian allies. Under General Hindenburg they quickly drove the Russians over the border, invaded Poland, and helped the Austrians to check the Russian "steam roller." Before many weeks had passed the great designs of military men had come to naught. There had been no Waterloo, no Sedan. Both sides now settled down to a long war of attrition, summoning to their aid man power, economic resources, science, machinery, art, propaganda, and diplomacy. One novel feature after another entered into the conflict.

Among the first was prolonged trench warfare on a vast scale. On September 13 the Germans stopped their retreat from the Marne and took their stand along the Aisne, where they "dug in" and defeated all efforts of the French and English to dislodge them. Then also began a race for the Channel ports, in which the Germans overran all of Belgium except a small corner in the southwest and came into a deadlock with the British, Belgians, and French. Before winter the embattled forces had burrowed into lines of trenches extending from the North Sea to the Swiss frontier. For four years this subterranean front remained substantially unchanged; dents were made here and there, but the position of the front was not radically altered (see maps, pp. 348–349). Although for various reasons there was more mobility on the eastern battle lines, trench warfare was also employed there whenever possible and became an important factor in the conflict.

Of course trench warfare was not altogether novel, but it was given new aspects in the World War. Trenches were longer, deeper, and better defended by steel, concrete, and barbed wire than ever before. They were far stronger and more effective than chains of forts, for they formed a continuous network, sometimes with four or five parallel lines linked by interlacings. They were dug far below the surface of the earth out of reach of the heaviest artillery. A single fort or a series of forts could be taken by siege, but no such operation was possible against hundreds of miles of trenches. Grand battles with the old maneuvers were out of the question. Only by bombardment, sapping, and assault could the enemy be shaken, and such operations had to be conducted on an immense scale to produce appreciable results. Indeed, it is questionable whether the German lines in France could ever have been broken if the Germans had not wasted their resources in unsuccessful assaults, and the blockade by sea had not gradually cut off their supplies. In such warfare no single general could strike a blow that would make him immortal; the "glory of fighting" sank down into the dirt and mire of trenches and dugouts.

Confronted by the trench deadlock, the combatants cast about more feverishly than ever for scientific devices to gain some advantages over the enemy. Among the new forms of combat gas warfare assumed a place of increasing importance. It is true that the Hague conference of 1907 adopted a convention forbidding "poison or poisoned arms," and that in August, 1914, none of the powers were equipped to use gas on the battle front. But as early as October of that year the Germans were charged by the English with starting gas war by firing shrapnel containing poison fumes. At all events, in April, 1915, the Germans made a gas attack along four or five miles and were able to make a deep breech in the Anglo-French front. From that time forward gas was used with deadly effect by all parties. From month to month new and more powerful chemicals were employed, producing a decided change in military methods.

A persistent gas, like "mustard," would stay for days and even weeks in the same area, if weather conditions were favorable, and make it utterly untenable. Heavy gas sank down into the deepest dugouts and trenches. When used in shells for bombardment it could be spread over a wide belt, hampering the movement of troops and supplies. Dropped by bombing planes on towns behind the enemy lines, it demoralized the civilian population. According to careful estimates, poison gas was responsible for 16 per cent of the casualties in the British armies and 33 per cent in the American armies. At the close of the war all parties were rapidly developing this form of combat, and had the struggle lasted a year or two longer, vast regions on both sides would have been smothered with even more terrible poisons.

Counter measures were, of course, speedily taken, especially in the form of masks to be worn by soldiers, but such devices did not eliminate the terrors of gas. Often it stole upon the men without any odor to betray its coming and struck them down before they could adjust their protectors. The mask increased the heavy equipment which infantry had to carry and hampered its movements. The constant peril of gas put an added strain on soldiers at the Front. In districts flooded with gas there could be no eating and drinking, for the removal of the mask for an instant might be fatal. Far behind the line gas bombs might disorganize communications and cut off supplies at crucial moments. Indeed, gas was found to be such a deadly weapon that after the close of the World War all the great powers, except Germany, which was forbidden to manufacture it for military purposes, went in vigorously for the development of "chemical preparedness," and boasts were made that secret inventions had rendered it possible to wipe out whole cities by a single successful bombing attack.

The use of gas in the war went along with the perfection of a second new device, the airplane. Previous to the conflict flying had been mainly in the experimental stage. It had not been adapted to commercial requirements, and its military advantages were as yet uncertain. Nevertheless, at the outset both sides had airplanes, and the Germans had giant dirigible Zeppelins which they hoped, in vain, would be extensively employed against the enemy. Flying machines in small numbers did reconnaisance work along the front, discovering and reporting enemy movements. Their effectiveness for such purposes soon demonstrated that another revolution in warfare was at hand. Immediately the belligerents set themselves the task of developing faster and more powerful planes with a larger cruising radius. Before the war came to an end machines were flying at a speed of one hundred and fifty miles an hour or more, and serving as military weapons for bombing and gassing.

Late in 1914 German planes succeeded in dropping projectiles on English soil. From that time forward there were repeated raids and counter, or so-called "retaliatory," attacks, in which great damage was done far behind the battle lines, bringing home the idea that the old separation between civilians and active combatants could no longer be maintained. Thus it was made perfectly clear, said a British expert, that "direct attack on the morale of enemy civilian populations must be an inevitable accompaniment of any future war, and that nations must prepare accordingly for this eventuality."

On actual warfare at the Front the airplane, of course, had a profound influence. It facilitated observations for artillery firing preparatory to infantry advances, and the radio permitted instant communication of news from a plane to gunners and officers. By dropping bombs it destroyed railway stations, munition dumps, railway lines, roads, and other means of communication for bringing men and materials to the Front. Aërial photography made possible minute surveys of enemy positions and the rapid distribution of information to attacking forces. Successful attacks with gas bombs and explosives could demoralize, or at least hamper, great movements of troops. A few men with high-powered planes could destroy more lives and property in an hour than a whole army in Napoleon's day. Military success now depended not only on numerical superiority but also on technical equipment. This had become so well recognized by the opening of 1918 that Great Britain created an Air Ministry by amalgamating all the aviation branches of the navy and war offices. In spite of the devices for warding off airplanes, their offensive power could not be destroyed.

Another mechanical contrivance brought into warfare was the "tank," or armored motor car, introduced by the British and employed first in September, 1916. With its caterpillar tread, the tank could move forward over the roughest ground, climb steep grades, lunge across trenches, crawl out of shell holes, crash through ordinary buildings, and crush breastworks into the earth. Its heavy steel armor made it invulnerable to rifle and machine-gun fire. Its machine-gun equipment made it a terrible weapon of offense. Hence it could plow its way through barbed-wire entanglements and networks of trenches amid a hail of bullets which no infantry could survive, spreading death and destruction in its path. When first used in the Somme drive, tanks proved a great surprise to the Germans and were highly effective over a small area. But the British made the same kind of mistake the Germans made in introducing poison gas—they did not wait until they had enough tanks to operate over a front sufficiently wide to permit a complete break through the enemy lines. Yet pleased with the first experiment, the British and French devoted great skill and labor to the perfection and manufacture of tanks; the Germans followed their example; and near the close of the war tanks had become, like airplanes, a primary branch of military equipment. The final turn in the tide in 1918 was attributed in a large measure to the extensive use of tanks along the Western Front. Although the Germans had invented various counter weapons, they found nothing efficient enough to stay the march of these steel cars.

While these new death-dealing devices were being introduced, along with many minor machines such as flame-throwers, the older weapons of war, especially artillery, were made more effective and powerful. In the early days of the war the Germans gave a terrifying demonstration that long-range guns and high explosives were to give new aspects to the conflict. They made devastating use of a great Krupp gun, which could hurl fifteen miles a huge shell weighing about a ton and filled with explosives. Before the struggle closed they had manufactured a gun capable of throwing a shell about seventy-five miles. With the makers of guns, chemists kept pace in devising destructive compounds. In their attack on Verdun in 1916 the Germans massed together hundreds of seventeen-inch guns hurling huge shells, each of which exploded with a force that spread ruin and death over a circle about one hundred feet in diameter.

On the sea as well as on the land technology changed the nature of warfare; in fact, wrought a revolution in it. The flying machine was transformed into a hydroplane with a wide cruising radius for scouting purposes. The submarine made obsolete old-fashioned duels by battleships, such as Nelson had waged at Trafalgar in the days of Napoleon. Under-sea boats had been used in the Civil War in the United States; the Confederates made a small submarine, propelled by hand, which discharged torpedoes, and they employed it with deadly effect against a Union vessel, the *Housatonic*. In 1863 France built a submarine one hundred and forty-six feet long and twelve feet in diameter, driven by compressed air; from that time forward this new fighting device was enlarged and perfected. The gas engine and electric motor made possible an immense increase in size, cruising radius, and effectiveness, while high explosives multiplied the destructiveness of torpedoes. When the World War opened the belligerents were equipped with submarines—Great Britain had about fifty and Germany twenty-eight; but their potentialities and revolutionary character were as yet unknown. Within a few months battleships were driven to cover, and the Germans began to use submarines in a war on the commerce that was bringing their foes the necessary supplies. Had they possessed enough of these U-boats in the beginning they might have brought Great Britain to her knees, in spite of her boasted sea power. As things turned out, the

Entente allies were able to offset these attacks with mines, nets, and depth bombs. Moreover, the British hit upon the clever scheme of fitting out merchant ships with concealed guns,— "Q-ships," they were called,—which lured submarines to the surface and then destroyed them by rapid gun fire.

The efficiency of all these engines of destruction was increased by the use of wireless telegraphy as a means of coördination. At the outbreak of the war all the combatants were equipped with wireless apparatus, and great attention was devoted to improving it. Its uses were innumerable. It was employed on airplanes to signal to gunners and to report to headquarters on the movements and disposition of troops. Cables and telegraph wires could be cut, but the wireless was immune to all such interruptions. With perfect ease France and Russia could communicate in code through the air across the German Empire. The radio linked army divisions in a single network, kept submarines in touch with their bases, and spread propaganda to friend and foe. Mountains, armies, forts, trenches, and national boundaries could impose no barriers to its range. It brought French in the Argonne and Russians in the Carpathians closer together, so far as communication was concerned, than the right and left wings of great armies in the old days, when messengers on horseback carried dispatches.

Besides having a revolutionary effect on actual fighting, these mechanical and chemical contributions to warfare brought about a revolutionary relation between the military forces and the civilian population. A chemist in a distant laboratory experimenting with more terrible explosives might render obsolete in a few days many of the rules and maneuvers to which soldiers had been trained. By making the conditions of the Front radically different from month to month, chemicals and machines forced commanders to revise continuously their methods and tactics. Once military authorities told civilians what supplies they must have; now civilians told soldiers what new and deadly devices could be used.

The World War had not raged many days before army men, accustomed to laying great stress on old discipline and past experience, found themselves in a bewildering world. "I cannot help wondering," exclaimed Sir John French, commander of the English expeditionary forces, "why none of us realized what the modern rifle, the machine gun, motor traction, the airplane, and wireless telegraphy would bring about!" It is not surprising. Military men relied mainly on tradition; the new warfare was scientific; and the advancement of science depends on the freest use of the experimental method. Evidently, the determination of the nature and methods of warfare was passing from professional warriors to technicians working with test tube and machine tools.

Coupled with universal service, which mobilized man power for the Front, mechanical and chemical warfare reënforced the national character of the conflict. The enormous demand for war materials—machine guns, artillery, explosives, shells, planes, trucks, tanks, poison gases, and other supplies—meant that all hopes of victory must hang upon the mobilization of factories, industrial workers, and food-producers behind the lines. There was scarcely an industry, from machine-tool factories to photographic-film laboratories, that could not be utilized somewhere in the production of goods for "winning the war." Thus, those too old and those too young to fight could be enrolled in war industries, and women could take the place of men at the lathe and the chemical vat.

Long accustomed to many branches of machine industry, women now extended the area of their economic opportunities. Besides carrying on their activities as nurses and Red Cross workers, they entered naval and war offices in various capacities ranging from clerks to boiler-cleaners, magneto-repairers, and photographers. In 1915 the London Society for Women's Suffrage opened a training school for women in munitions-making and metal-welding. It is said that practically all the work on gas masks in Great Britain was done by women. With all the people enlisted, negligence, opposition, and strikes in the industrial world became as serious as laxity and mutiny at the Front. In short, each belligerent nation was fused into a compact, mobilized whole, straining every nerve, employing every science and art, summoning all powers of ingenuity in one common effort—the defeat and destruction of the enemy.

DIPLOMACY AND SECRET TREATIES

While mobilizing their forces for combat, the belligerent governments resorted to diplomacy and propaganda, with a view to winning friends and disconcerting their foes. The first accession to the side of the Entente allies came within less than a month after the outbreak of the war, when Japan took up arms against Germany on August 23. About a week before this action the Japanese government delivered an ultimatum demanding the withdrawal of German warships from Chinese and Japanese waters and the surrender of the leased Kiao-chow territory, "with a view to the eventual restoration of the same to China." Failing to receive a satisfactory reply, Japan proclaimed war, landed troops in Shantung, and invested Tsingtao, with a certain degree of British coöperation. In November the Japanese had possession of the peninsula. After that achievement Japan aided the Allies by furnishing supplies, patrolling the Pacific Ocean, keeping warships in and near Indian waters, and exercising a mollifying influence on Indian revolutionists.

Indeed, the war produced a great industrial boom in Japan. Shipyards expanded, industries multiplied, and war profits enlarged the middle class, thus helping to submerge still deeper the feudal heritage that had come down from ancient times. Moreover, participation in the war gave Japan an important place at the European council table. Yet it should be noted that the decision to join the Entente was not made without a struggle. There was a strong party in Japan which favored

uniting with the Central Powers, annexing more of the mainland, and crushing the British Empire in the East. Fortunately
for the Entente allies, that party did not prevail. If her positive contributions to their victory were not great, Japan's
refusal to join the Central Powers was certainly important in
its consequences.

The addition of Japan to the Allied forces was somewhat
offset in November, 1914, when Turkey made common cause
with the Central Powers by declaring war against their enemies.
For a long time Berlin and Vienna had been preparing for this
event. German army officers had modernized the Turkish
army; German capitalists had furnished money and talent for
developing Turkish trade and industries; and the Berlin-
Bagdad Railway promised Turkey the advantages of swift
communication with western Europe. On the other hand, Turkey could expect few favors from the Entente. British and
French soldiers had once fought with Turkish troops against
Russia, but now they were united in helping the Tsar. Russia
was bent on pushing out through the Straits and annexing Constantinople. Great Britain was eager to expand her sphere of
control between the Suez Canal and India. France had interests in Syria and other parts of Turkish territory. For these
reasons the Turks reckoned they had more to hope for from a
combination with Germany and Austria. But although they
fought bravely they contributed little to the strength of the
Central Powers. Indeed, their action led Great Britain to annex Cyprus and to put an end to Turkish suzerainty in Egypt.
It also encouraged the Italians, with their ambitions in the
Mediterranean, to join the other side.

Within a month after Turkey's declaration of war, a decided
change occurred in Italian policy. When Italy announced in
August, 1914, that, under the circumstances, she was not bound
by the terms of the Triple Alliance to join the Central Powers,
she assumed a position of neutrality. But in December of that
year the Italian government informed Austria that the attack

on Serbia had changed the status of things in the Balkans, and that Italy was entitled to "compensation" under the conditions contained in the last renewal of the Triple Alliance. Such compensation was to include the cession to Italy of Austrian territory along the Adriatic. A tug of war now opened between German and Austrian diplomacy, on the one side, and French and British, on the other, for the purpose of inducing Italy to enter the war. Naturally, Germany urged Austria to make satisfactory offers of her territory, and naturally, also, Austria shrank from handing over Germans as well as Italians and Croats to Italy. Since Great Britain and France were offering to Italy the territory of enemies, they could afford to be more liberal, and in the end they won.

By a secret treaty signed in London early in 1915, the Entente allies promised Italy the Trentino and the Tyrol up to the Brenner Pass, Trieste, Istria, northern Dalmatia, and adjoining islands. Italy was also to get Valona, to conduct the foreign affairs of Albania, and to retain the Dodecanese islands already occupied by her (see page 306). Should Turkey be divided, Italy was to have a share. If France and Great Britain took German colonies in Africa, then Italy was to have compensations. On May 24, 1915, Italy opened war on Austria-Hungary; a little more than a year later she was at war with Germany too.

In the seesaw of diplomacy the Central Powers scored next by bringing Bulgaria into the war on their side. Smarting from the humiliations of the Second Balkan War, of 1913, in which it was stripped of important possessions by Greece, Serbia, and Rumania, the Bulgarian government cast about in the storm for the best chance to recover territory it claimed—especially Serbian Macedonia. The Entente Powers, however, had little to offer. They did try to induce Serbia to make concessions, but failed to accomplish that design. On the other hand, in this case the Central Powers were in a better position to make large promises at the expense of an enemy—Serbia. Besides, King Ferdinand of Bulgaria was a German prince, and his sympathies were with Vienna and Berlin rather than Rome and London. After much parleying and many threats on both sides, Bulgaria declared war on Serbia in October, 1915, and with the aid of Austro-German armies completed the conquest of that country, compelling the Serbian government to take refuge on the island of Corfu, and the scattered remnants of its troops to seek shelter at Corfu and Salonika.

A great diplomatic drive was now concentrated on Rumania, an associate of the Triple Alliance at the outbreak of the war. Although the king, Ferdinand, was a Hohenzollern, his government, like the others, had to consider all the possibilities of the situation. In return for its assistance the Central Powers could grant to Rumania coveted portions of Russian territory in Bessarabia, when and if won. On the other hand, the Entente could make a more attractive tender—Bukowina, Transylvania, and the Banat of Temesvár—at the expense of Austria-Hungary. In return for this promise, coupled with a pledge of active military assistance from Russia, France, and Great Britain, Rumania declared war on Austria-Hungary August 27, 1916. At first this action merely brought disaster to Rumania, for the combined forces of the Central Powers and their allies quickly overcame the Rumanian armies, occupied the country, and exploited it for their purposes. In the end, however, the Allied victory gave Rumania all the territory offered in the treaty and more besides, including a large section of southern Russia, at whose expense the Allies were willing to be generous after the Bolshevist revolution eliminated that country from the war.

Amid the swirling events in the Balkans, Greece occupied a ticklish position. Its Mediterranean front was controlled by the naval forces of the Entente; on the landward side lay the peril of invasion by the armies of the Central Powers, vividly illustrated by the fate of Serbia. Moreover, Greece was sharply divided into parties, one pro-Ally in its sympathies and another pro-German, with a middle faction interested primarily in preserving neutrality. The king, Constantine, was accused of leaning to the side of the Central Powers, and color was given to this charge by the fact that his wife was a sister of the Kaiser; but he indignantly denied the allegation and maintained that he was merely trying to conserve the interests of Greece. However that may be, his premier, Venizelos, was undoubtedly pro-Ally and, on the strength of promises of territory from the Entente, would have carried his country into war in 1915 if the king had not dismissed him. For a time the Greek government adhered to a policy of armed neutrality which was supposed to involve a certain benevolence toward the Entente Powers. At all events, Anglo-French forces were landed on Greek soil at Salonika for the purpose of aiding Serbia, whose borders lay not far to the north. A great outcry was made in certain quarters against this "breach of neutrality," but the Entente gave no heed to it.

While the Greek army, commanded by the king, stood mobilized at their backs, the French, British, and Serbs on the Salonika front were in a precarious position. If Greece should swing over to the Teutonic cause, the forces of the Entente might easily be crushed between two millstones. Feeling constrained by a necessity akin to that claimed by the Germans in Belgium, the Allies, late in 1916, seized the Greek postal and telegraph system, commandeered the Greek navy, expelled from Greece the diplomatic representatives of the Central Powers and their allies, censored the newspapers of Athens, and blockaded the Greek coast. In vain did the Greek government protest against this violation of its neutrality and its soil; the Entente Powers cited old treaties and other documents to show that it was "legal." To make matters worse for the king and his ministers, popular revolts, many of them engineered by a committee of national defense formed at Salonika under Allied protection, broke out in various parts of the country. Early in the following year these uprisings merged into a revolution headed by Venizelos, who was supported by the

Entente, and a French high commissioner virtually took charge of the country. The king was forced to abdicate, pro-German leaders and advocates of peace were expelled, the premier was ousted, and Venizelos installed at Athens. In the summer of 1917 Greece formally joined the Entente in its war on the Central Powers. When he drove out the king the French high commissioner explained that Constantine had "manifestly on his own initiative violated the Constitution of which England, France, and Russia are the trustees," and had besides lost the confidence of "the protecting powers." At all events, Greece was now coöperating with the Entente.

With the accession of Greece to the Entente cause, all Europe, except Spain, Switzerland, Holland, and the Scandinavian countries, was now drawn into the great conflict. Little Portugal, long allied with Great Britain, had been invited by the British government in 1916 to seize all German merchant ships in her harbors, and compliance with this request shortly afterward brought a declaration of war from Germany and Austria-Hungary. Diplomacy could go no further in the way of gathering recruits in Europe. In spite of great difficulties and perplexities the remaining neutrals managed to cling to precarious peace until the end. Their trade was rigidly controlled by the belligerents, and their losses in shipping were enormous; but their merchants reaped huge profits from the business of war. On the whole, however, the condition of the masses in the neutral countries was far from prosperous. They suffered from what amounted in practice almost to a fuel-and-food blockade, and the disorganization of industries brought about by the curtailment of raw materials from overseas. In fact, things became so bad in the Netherlands in 1917 that whole cities were on starvation rations, and alarming food riots broke out. Troops were called in, and bloodshed accompanied the restoration of order.

While the diplomats of the belligerent countries were laboring hard to win the support of neutrals, they were also busy with calculations respecting the divisions of spoils among themselves to be made at the end of the war. Many of these calculations on the Entente side were incorporated in notes and conventions, later given to the public by the Bolsheviki and made famous throughout the world as the "secret treaties." The war was only a few months old when Russia, France, and Great Britain reached a secret understanding about partitioning the Near East. Russia was to get Constantinople and the Straits, the city itself becoming "a free port." Persia was divided between Russia and Great Britain in the form of "spheres of influence," thus making the agreement of 1907 more definite. Russia in return agreed to recognize the special interests of France and Great Britain in Turkey. Later understandings provided for larger cessions of Turkish territory to Russia,—especially on the Black Sea,—recognized generous British claims in Mesopotamia, confirmed French pretensions in Syria, and gave Italy a share of southwestern Turkey in the neighborhood of Adalia and Smyrna. When Greece came into the war, certain concessions in the form of Turkish territory were made to meet her expectations, at least in part. When all this distribution was completed, there was little left of Turkey—on paper. It was agreed that "the Holy Places should remain under Moslem rule," and the Arabs were to be "independent."

In February, 1917, Russia and France, after much negotiation, reached a secret agreement for slicing off large parts of Germany and Austria-Hungary. Russia was to have an absolutely free hand in determining her western frontiers, and France was to have similar liberty on her side—a liberty which included, besides Alsace-Lorraine, the Saar Region and other extensive districts west of the Rhine inhabited entirely by Germans. Indeed, Clemenceau long afterward declared on his visit to the United States that if it had not been for the treaty signed by President Wilson (but rejected by the Senate) promising American aid to France in the future, he would have demanded the Rhine at the peace table in 1919.

While this distribution of territory was going on, Japan insisted on having her share. By secret arrangements Great Britain, Russia, France, and Italy assured Japan that she might have Shantung and the German islands in the Pacific north of the equator. Knowing that the European powers were busy, Japan forced the Chinese government to accede to a number of "demands"—at first twenty-one, but later reduced to fifteen—which virtually established a Japanese protectorate over China. And to fortify their position in the Far East, Russia and Japan in 1916 made a secret offensive and defensive alliance, directed in fact against the United States, although nominally against any third power that attempted to become dominant in China. Such were the "secret treaties" dividing the fruits of victory among the Entente Powers and their allies in anticipation of success.

Closely knit in one compact unity, the Central Powers did not have to carry on such extensive diplomacy between themselves or to divide the fruits of victory in advance with such meticulous care as did the widely scattered and less harmonious Entente allies. Although many imperialists in Germany drew up and urged large programs of annexations to be made east and west and overseas, the German government was careful about committing itself officially to any of these schemes. Undoubtedly the annexationist temper ran high in Germany, so high in fact that the government did not dare to state that it would even restore Belgium to its full rights after the war was over. Not until defeat stared it in the face did it look with favor on a peace with "no annexations and no indemnities."

What Germany and Austria-Hungary would have done had they won the war is indicated in the terms imposed on beaten Russia at Brest-Litovsk in 1918 (see page 370), and on Rumania about the same time by the treaty of Bucharest. Both Russia and Rumania were stripped of valuable territories and laid under heavy economic burdens. When the distinguished English journalist J. L. Garvin called the conditions of Brest-

T

Litovsk "the most shameful and merciless terms" imposed on
any nation in modern times, he prudently added "up to then,"
thus making allowances for what was done at Versailles. It is
generally agreed among liberal Germans that the Treaty of
Brest-Litovsk was one of the three or four major blunders
committed by the governing class between 1914 and 1918—a
blunder that helped to nerve the Allies for supreme efforts to
escape such a doom.

PROPAGANDA

Among the novel features of the World War must be placed
highly organized propaganda on a large scale. The practice,
of course, was old. It is said that during the American Revolution patriots distributed handbills among British soldiers offering them a bonus and free land if they would desert King
George's cause. A few years later both the British and French
carried on lively propaganda in the United States with a view
to enlisting aid in their wars on land and sea. But peculiar conditions favored the extensive use of propaganda during the
World War. The first was the existence of democracy and
great literate publics. In the old days the king declared wars
and enrolled soldiers; the king's will was law. But now millions of common people had to be conciliated and convinced.
Whole nations were at war, and each government faced the
task of keeping its own masses in line and breaking down and
demoralizing enemy masses. To sustain the will to war among
its own people and to destroy the will to war among enemy
peoples was second only in importance to the work of getting
men and materials to the battle front. While democracy made
propaganda more necessary, modern devices made it more
efficient than ever. Swift printing presses, rapid photography,
the penny post, the radio, moving pictures, and the airplane for
dropping leaflets put unlimited resources at the command of
astute manipulators of words, phrases, and pictures.

All warring countries were quick to perceive the importance

of propaganda and speedily set up special agencies to carry on the business. In August, 1914, Great Britain established a small bureau which in the main operated as if it were a private organization engaged in sending out pamphlets. Later other divisions were created in the Home Office, the Foreign Office, and the War Department. Near the end of the war some of these agencies were coördinated under a "Minister of Information," with Lord Northcliffe as "director of propaganda in enemy countries." In Germany several departments of government gave attention to propaganda, and the Great Headquarters of the Army, dissatisfied with the civilian work, organized a "press service" of its own and even censored materials issued by the civilian branches. France employed her customary diplomatic, military, and naval agencies, maintained a "Press House," and sent special missions abroad. Although the Germans were credited with being the most assiduous of all propagandists, a careful study made by Professor Harold D. Lasswell (*Propaganda Technique in the World War*) shows that they were outnumbered and outrivaled in the somewhat unscrupulous business of spreading abroad "information" useful in winning the war.

By the comparative method Professor Lasswell discovered that the propaganda agencies of all the belligerents had similar "objectives" and employed similar "techniques." Hence a synthetic view of the art is possible. Each government undertook to mobilize the fighting spirit of its own people by creating in them a hatred and loathing for the enemy. This was one of the prime objectives. The second great end sought was to demoralize the enemies by stirring up a revolutionary spirit among their people and in their armies—a dangerous game likely to produce unexpected results. The third objective was to win allies by frightening, cajoling, or tempting neutrals and getting them to enter the war against the enemy. The fourth was to keep neutrals from joining the enemy, if it was not possible to win them over. These were the chief ends pursued by war propagandists of all belligerents; and the work of governments was supplemented by the labors of individuals and private societies.

As all the warring countries employed similar agencies and had similar objectives, so all of them resorted to similar devices. The first design was naturally to paint the enemy in the blackest colors, to ascribe to him what Professor Lasswell calls "Satanism," making him the fiend incarnate. Under this head the enemy was accused of willfully planning the war, exceeding all others in armaments, starting the war, mobilizing first, springing it on unprepared and peace-loving peoples, violating international "right and law," and committing the first acts of violence.

Under this head also came long lists of "authentic" atrocities committed in connection with the normal violence of war. The official German thesis claimed that Germany had been "encircled" by relentless enemies under the leadership of England, that Russia mobilized first, that the Russians and the French had been guilty of terrible offenses against German soldiers and civilians, and that Germany had striven for peace with all her might. The war was only a few days old when the Kaiser formally protested to President Wilson against the atrocities of his foes. On the other side, the Entente had a similar catalogue: Germany had willed the war, started it, assailed the "sacred rights of small nations" by violating Belgian neutrality, and done horrible deeds out of sheer wantonness and inborn cruelty.[1]

In general, the "Satanizing" theory took the form of stories from the battle front, which the newspapers eagerly seized and spread among the masses. Since army officers in charge and civil governments at home both censored and drafted dispatches, it was easy to imagine atrocities and to exaggerate

[1] For the Entente indictment of Germany, see Lasswell, p. 85; for Germany's bill of indictment against her foes, see page 86. Here the misdeeds of the respective belligerents as described by their opponents are catalogued.

the inevitable horrors of fighting. To question any of these tales was to incur the charge of treason or at least of favoring the enemy. In vain did a number of American war correspondents sign a statement declaring that the Entente reports of German atrocities in Belgium in 1914 were false; as time went on the tales were enlarged and circulated over the names of distinguished men. Equally futile were efforts in Germany to counteract reports of Russian atrocities in the east; for example, when a supposed victim, who had started one of the false stories, repented, and offered a denial, the German authorities refused to allow the disclaimer to pass the censor. Undoubtedly, there were horrors enough on both sides, and wanton acts were committed by sadistic soldiers; but a large part of the atrocity news was childish credulity elaborated with an intense impulse to blacken the enemy and rouse the fighting passions of the multitude.

As the war wore on propaganda widened from atrocity news to include a great range of ideas and mental "stereotypes." Both sides made an appeal to God and enlisted the help of the clergy. "Go to church and kneel before God and pray for his help and for our gallant army." Such was the advice of the Kaiser to his people at the opening of the conflict. "I believe in the power of right, in the crusade for civilization, and in France, the eternal, the imperishable, the essential. . . . I believe in ourselves; I believe in God." Thus the French creed was formulated by a propagandist. A French religious paper made the struggle "a war of Catholic France against Protestant Germany." This, of course, was resented by Catholics in Germany and perhaps by Protestants in England, but it served its purpose very well for domestic consumption. When Turkey joined the Central Powers a great deal was made by the Entente of the war between Christianity and Mohammedanism, in spite of the fact that Great Britain was enrolling Mohammedans in India and Arabia, and France was importing Mohammedans from Africa. To religion was added race. "The race war appears," exclaimed a French paper, *La Croix*—a war between Latins and Slavs on one side and Teutons on the other. Germans replied in kind; it was a war of Germanic *Kultur* against Slavic barbarism. There were difficulties here also, for the Entente included the English, who were supposed to be Teutonic, and the Central Powers had in their armies Magyars and Slavs; but the excited public was not always alert in discovering ethnological discrepancies.

On the Entente side, or rather in England and France,— scarcely in Russia,—the conflict was represented as "a war for democracy and for the liberation of peoples." It was a case of popular government against class government—a struggle for the emancipation of subject races from the dominion of the Teuton. Liberty was to be given to Frenchmen in Alsace-Lorraine, to Italians and Slavs under the Hapsburg yoke. To this type of propaganda the Germans replied by assailing the autocratic government of the Tsar, which certainly had little savor of democracy, and by offering liberty to Ireland and India. It was, of course, a bit difficult to make a clean-cut case for "democracy against autocracy," liberty against imperialism, out of the alignment of powers; but each side conveniently overlooked facts contrary to its pretensions. Indeed, calling attention to such inconsistencies could easily be ascribed to "enemy propaganda."

From religion, race, and politics it was but a step to civilization. Each side discovered that it was fighting to save everything in life worth saving—true religion, art, science, morality, music, and business. The Germans continually harped on their *Kultur* and its superior virtues. The Slavs were told by their propagandists that they were fighting to preserve Slavic civilization from contamination with the decadent West. Italians and French were dying to save Latin civilization. "Civilization at Issue!" exclaimed the *London Evening Standard* when the storm broke. Although there was some difference of opinion as to the meaning of the term "civilization," all parties to the war made persistent use of it for the purpose of stimulating enthusiasm among the masses.

While "atrocities" were played up constantly in the newspapers, other issues were expounded in pamphlets and books by distinguished professors, journalists, and men of letters. One of the favorite devices was to convict the enemy "out of their own mouths," by publishing anthologies of their "wicked and foolish sayings." Many volumes of extracts from the writings of German militarists and imperialists were issued by the Entente to show that the German nation loved war and was bent on pillage. *Gems of German Thought*, compiled by William Archer, had an immense vogue. *Hurrah and Hallelujah*, a collection of extravagances from German clergymen made by Professor Bang, a Dane, was calculated to convince the foes of Germany that her preachers were almost blasphemous in defending their country.

On the other hand, an eminent German sociologist issued for the benefit of his countrymen a book entitled *Warlike England as Seen by Herself*, containing extracts from British writings showing to what lengths Great Britain was willing to go in conquering other races and seizing their territory for the purpose of making profits out of trade. Besides these more or less private undertakings, each belligerent government prepared a collection of official documents designed to show how the enemy really started the war, while *it* worked for peace. In every case, as we know now, these "official" publications were characterized by omissions, distortions, modifications, additions, and falsifications, deliberately intended to mislead the reader; but all of them had the appearance of good faith and plausibility.

The importance of the United States for the European belligerents made it a special battle ground for propagandists, for the large numbers of its foreign elements—British, Canadians, Germans, Russians, Czechs, Yugoslavs, Italians, and Hungarians—espoused the cause of one side or the other. As soon as the war began representatives of the German cause, official and private, formed societies for the advancement of their interests and started varied activities designed to convince the Americans that Germany was right, that they should stay out of the war, and that they should lend no financial and material assistance to the Entente. A campaign to raise money to buy milk for German babies was begun mainly to show "the cruelties of the British blockade." Editorial writers on the Hearst papers were enlisted. Two societies were formed to lend local color to such activities: the "Organization of American Women for Strict Neutrality" and the "American Truth Society," the latter giving particular attention to stirring up the Irish against Great Britain. Another special group was formed to protest against the British cotton blockade and enlist sympathy for the Teutonic cause in the cotton-growing states. With a view to stopping the export of horses to the Entente, a moving picture was prepared showing the terrible fate of a noble fire horse killed on the Flanders front. Some of this work was done so quietly and so secretly that it had the appearance of validity. It was difficult to tell where German interests ended and American interests began.

In influencing America the Entente Powers were more active, more ingenious, and more successful than their rivals. British and Canadians, whose names were the same as those common among Americans of the old stock, could work under cover with more facility, and they had the unlimited assistance of the British government. As Great Britain controlled the sea and the cables and censored the news from Europe, most of the daily reports had the Entente rather than the Teutonic color. With respect to "regular British propaganda" in the United States, the methods have been described by Sir Gilbert Parker, who took charge of that enterprise shortly after the outbreak of the war. Sir Gilbert's office maintained a continuous study of American opinion and reported weekly to the British cabinet. He himself kept in constant touch with American newspaper men in England and arranged for them to have access to distinguished British political leaders for interviewing purposes. He supplied more than three hundred American newspapers with an English paper giving Entente accounts of the war.

"We established," explained Sir Gilbert, "connection with the man in the street [in the United States] through cinema pictures of the Army and Navy, as well as through interviews, pamphlets, etc.; and by letters in reply to individual American critics, which were printed in the chief newspaper of the state in which they lived and were copied in newspapers of other and neighboring states. We advertised and stimulated many people to write articles. We utilized the friendly services and assistance of confidential friends; we had reports from important Americans constantly, and established associations by personal correspondence with influential and eminent people of every profession in the United States, beginning with university and college presidents, professors, and scientific men, and running down through all ranges of the population." Thus were the minds of Americans prepared for participation in the war on the side of the Entente.

CHAPTER XI

THE WORLD WAR. PART II

First Phase of the War on Land (1914–1916)

None of the plans of the military leaders for a short and glorious war were realized. The German general staff had hoped to deal France a knock-out blow and then dispose of Russia at its leisure. This scheme failed. The Anglo-French-Russian project was equally simple in its broad outlines. The Germans were to be lured deeper and deeper into Belgium and France, while the Russian "steam roller" crashed into Germany and Austria in the east; then at the proper moment a counterattack was to be launched on the west, catching the Germans at a fatal distance from their base of supplies. But the Russian steam roller broke down when the Germans sent Hindenburg against it in August, 1914, and the Germans in the west, instead of collapsing under the recoil, managed to dig in and stand fast in northern France.

After the Germans were defeated in their project for capturing Paris, they proceeded to overrun Belgium. They took Antwerp on October 10 and occupied the whole country except a tiny corner southwest of Ostend. They had hoped to push on to Calais and utilize this port nearest to England as a base of attack against the British Isles, but they were checked at the Yser River. They treated the Belgians as a conquered people, exacting huge tributes, partly burned the city of Louvain, executed many citizens, deported thousands of Belgians to Germany to work in war industries, and seized any machinery or supplies that they desired. Their treatment of their neighbor, whose safety from invasion they themselves had

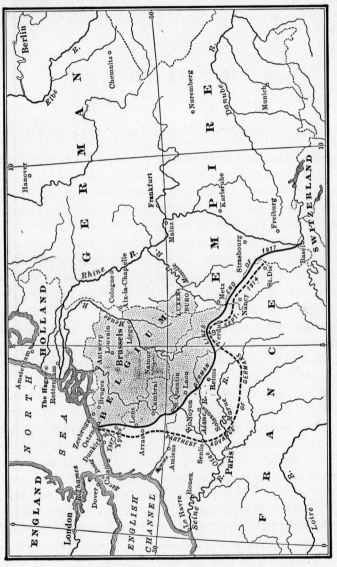

THE WESTERN FRONT, 1914–1917

Germany, Austria-Hungary, and their Allies
Countries at War with Teutonic Allies

THE EASTERN FRONT, 1914–1917

solemnly guaranteed, did more to rouse anger in the rest of the world than any other act of the German government.

The southernmost of the German armies, and the only one which had ventured to advance directly on France without passing through neutral territory, was at first unable to make much headway. Nevertheless, before long it succeeded in establishing its trenches within French territory just east of the Meuse on a line running east of Verdun and St. Dié (see map). The French, however, invaded southern Alsace and managed to occupy a little German territory in that region. Thus the first three months of the war saw the Germans in practically complete possession of Belgium and Luxemburg, together with a broad strip of northeastern France filled with prosperous manufacturing towns, farms and vineyards, and invaluable coal and iron mines.

For four long years the lines established after the battle of the Marne and the check on the Yser did not change greatly in spite of the constant fighting, occasional titanic "drives," and the sacrifice of hundreds of thousands of men on both sides. The Germans were not able to push very much farther into France, and the Allied forces were equally unsuccessful in their repeated attempts, at terrible sacrifice of life, to smash the German front. Both sides "dug themselves in," and trench warfare went on almost incessantly, with the aid of machine guns, shells, and huge cannon. Airplanes flew hither and thither, observing the enemy's positions and operations and dropping bombs on his trenches and supply depots. Poisonous gases and liquid fire, used on both sides, added their horrors to the conflict.

On the Eastern Front no such deadlock occurred. There the battle line swayed forward and back over an immense stretch of territory, but neither side had been able to deliver a paralyzing blow when Russia collapsed in 1917 as a result of an internal revolution. At first the Russians advanced far more rapidly than had been expected, and then failed to hold their gains.

Early in August, 1914, they swept into East Prussia, only to be defeated and driven out by Hindenburg within a month. In greater force the Russians drove to the southwest into Austrian Galicia, inflicting serious defeats on the Austro-Hungarian armies and capturing the city of Lemberg early in September. Appreciating at once the gravity of the situation, the Germans combined with the Austrians, checked the Russian drive, baffled the Tsar's troops in their efforts to pass the Carpathians, and finally, in the summer of 1915, rolled back the Slavic host. In a united assault along the whole front, two German commanders, Hindenburg and Mackensen, attempted to overwhelm Russia and put her out of the war. They captured Warsaw in August, cleared the Russians out of Poland and most of Galicia, and at the close of 1915 had occupied Kurland, Livonia, and Estonia. But the Russians stood fast along a line running in a southerly direction from Riga to the border of Rumania. So the German hopes for a crushing victory that would make Russia sue for peace were disappointed.

On the Balkan front as well military events at first ran in favor of the Central Powers. It is true that Austria-Hungary, hard pressed by the Russians in the north, was at the outset defeated by the seasoned veterans of Serbia and Montenegro, but diplomacy and arms changed the scene in time. In November, 1914, as we have seen, the Teutonic allies were reënforced by the Sultan, who issued a call to all faithful Mohammedans to wage a "Holy War" on the enemies of Islam. In October of the following year Bulgaria joined the Teutonic combination. By a series of lightning strokes Serbia was now overcome. While Austro-German forces under General Mackensen drove southward across the Danube, the Bulgarian army invaded Serbia from the east. At the end of November the conquest of Serbia was announced by Mackensen, as scattered bands of Serbs and Montenegrins fled over the mountains into Albania to find refuge at last on the Greek island of Corfu. When the year 1915 closed, the Central Powers and their allies occupied a solid block of territory reaching from the Baltic to the Adriatic, and from northern France to Asia Minor. Direct rail communication between Berlin and Constantinople was opened with much ceremony. A number of high German officers now believed that great efforts should be concentrated on Russia, with the aid of Turkish and Bulgarian allies. "This," said General Ludendorff, "would presumably have so weakened Russia as to arouse in her a desire for peace and would also have put an end to the economic distress of the Quadruple Alliance." Yet the German high command set aside this project in favor of a massed assault on the western line at Verdun.

Against the combination of powers in the southeast, the Entente allies could at first make little headway, owing to a division of councils and a conflict of interests. Although Italy joined them in the spring of 1915, her activities were mainly confined to attacks on Austria in the mountain regions of the northeast. She lent no aid to Serbia; in fact, having won from the Entente allies a promise of the Dalmatian coast inhabited largely by Croats and Serbs, Italy's ambitions came into sharp collision with those of Greater Serbia. Yugoslav nationalism also demanded the Dalmatian coast.

In the Near East the outlook was equally discouraging for the Allies. The English and French made a desperate effort to force the Straits and capture Constantinople early in 1915, but their expedition resulted in failure. They made a combined attack from the sea on the outpost forts at the Dardanelles, only to be repulsed with heavy losses in battleships. Frustrated in this effort, they then effected a landing on the peninsula of Gallipoli, aided in this enterprise by contingents from Australia and New Zealand, which had come to the Mediterranean by the Red Sea. After sacrificing about a hundred thousand men, killed and wounded, in this land campaign, the Allied forces found themselves unable to advance against the Turkish troops ably officered and well munitioned by the Germans. In the end they were forced to admit that the attempt had been badly managed and was a tragic mistake. In January, 1916, the last of the trenches at the tip of the peninsula were abandoned. In southeastern Turkey the British were successful; they invaded Mesopotamia and Syria, captured Bagdad in March, 1917, and occupied Jerusalem near the close of that year. Thus the British project for gaining a solid block of land stretching from Egypt to India seemed on the point of realization, in spite of the urgent demand for the concentration of energies on the Western Front, where the fate of the war hung in the balance.

While the Teutonic powers were beating back the armies of Russia and driving their great wedge to the southeast through the Balkans, the French and British on the Western Front were trying to relieve their allies in the east by keeping German forces busy in northern France. Besides numerous local attacks, they made two huge offensives in 1915. In the first, which occurred in March, the British took the lead by launching a terrific assault on the Germans in the neighborhood of Lille with a view to taking that important industrial city, but by the most heroic efforts they only managed to advance their line for a mile or two along a short front.

Before they had recovered from the exhaustion of this enterprise, the Allied forces near Ypres were subjected to a mass attack by the Germans, aided by their new weapon, poison gas. For a time it looked as if the Germans might break through, but all they could do was to make a little gain along a narrow front. Fighting now flamed up in the region of Arras, where the French, hoping to aid the hard-pressed Russians in the east, advanced on the German trenches, while the British operated to the westward. Here too a month's fighting produced no marked gains in territory.

The second great offensive against the Germans, made in September, 1915, was concentrated principally in the sector between Reims and Verdun. By this time the Allies had 3,250,000 men on the Western Front pitted against fewer than 2,000,000 Germans, and they counted on their superiority to

THE MATTHEWS-NORTHRUP WORKS

AUSTRIA-HUNGARY

1867–1918

SCALE OF MILES

0 10 20 30 40 50   100   150

effect a complete break through the entrenchments of the enemy. After a terrific bombardment, accompanied by the use of poison gas, the French and British hurled themselves into the breaches blasted by the artillery, only to be stopped within a few thousand feet.

At the close of 1915 it looked as if a stalemate had been reached in the west. Neither side could attack without a preliminary bombardment, and this could not take place without bringing up huge masses of munitions—a movement which the enemy could not fail to observe. Hence there could be no surprise; the foe always had time to bring up reserves in anticipation of an assault. Moreover, bombardment so cut up the ground that the infantry had to advance over barriers and through shell holes in disorderly masses. The use of cavalry was practically impossible, and artillery had to be dragged forward over mounds and ridges so slowly that a continuous covering of the charging troops was out of the question. War had reached a new stage of evolution.

Yet it seemed that the war, if won at all, would have to be won in the west. Having driven the Russians back and withstood successfully terrible hammering by the Allies in France, the Germans decided to attack the ancient fortress of Verdun. The loss of this outpost would greatly discourage the French, for it was popularly regarded as one of the country's chief strongholds. Moreover, the fact that Metz, a very important center of German supplies, lay not far east of Verdun served to increase the German chances for breaking through the French lines at this point. Under the general command of no less a personage than the German crown prince, great masses of troops were brought together, and the assault began on February 21, 1916.

For a time the French lines gave way, and friends of the Allies throughout the world held their breath, for it seemed as if the Germans were about to crush French defenses and again threaten Paris. But the French recovered and held their own

T

once more. The English troops were now numerous enough to take over more of the Front to the north. A series of costly encounters followed, but the French were able during May and June to push the Germans back from the positions occupied in the first onrush. By July all danger of a German victory at that point seemed to be over.

Educated by such dreadful experiences, Great Britain nerved herself for mightier efforts. At the opening of the war that country had an available force of about one hundred thousand men—which, according to the standards of the time, was grotesquely inadequate in numbers. On the other hand, Germany, Russia, and France had their millions of trained men, owing to their long-established system of universal military service. For a time England tried to increase her army by voluntary enlistments, and on the whole succeeded very well. But after much discussion and opposition, she introduced (May, 1916) a system of universal compulsory military service, which included all able-bodied men between the ages of eighteen and forty-one (limits which were extended later to include men from eighteen to fifty years of age, with restricted service also for those between fifty and fifty-five).

Shortly after this momentous step was taken, the British and French began, east and north of Amiens, their long-talked-of drive, the battle of the Somme, which lasted for four months— from July to November, 1916. Here the new military invention, the so-called "tank," made its first appearance and did effective work in breaking barbed-wire entanglements and crushing German entrenchments. The English had also fifteen-inch mortars for hurling shells. In huge masses the Allied troops surged against the German front, but they could not force their way through it at any point. The Germans retreated only a few miles, and the cost to both sides in killed and wounded was terrible.

While the battle of Verdun was raging, the Italians, who had made but little progress against the strong Austrian fortifications, were suddenly pushed back by a great Austrian drive in May, 1916. By the middle of June they had not only lost the little they had gained but had been forced to evacuate some of their own territory. At this point the Russians, in spite of the loss of Poland, attacked Austria once more and again threatened to press into Hungary. So Austria had to give way in Italy in order to defend her Galician boundary, and the Italians were able not only to regain what they had lost but also to advance somewhat on their way, as they hoped, to Trieste.

The momentary success of the Allies, especially the gains of Russia in the southeast, encouraged Rumania to join in the war on the side of the Entente in August, 1916. With a great rush Rumanian troops invaded Transylvania, which Rumania had long claimed as properly hers. Notwithstanding the pressure on the Somme, the Germans immediately sent two of their best generals and, with the help of the Bulgarians, attacked Rumania from the west and south and captured Bucharest, the capital, in December, 1916. About two thirds of Rumania was soon in possession of her enemies, and the Germans could supplement their supplies from her rich stores of grain and abundant oil wells.

Convinced that General Falkenhayn was responsible for the failure on the west, the Kaiser dismissed him and put at the head of the General Staff Field Marshal Hindenburg, assisted by General Ludendorff as quartermaster-general. So the year 1916 closed with a deadlock and with both belligerents profoundly discouraged about the prospects for final victory on any battle front.

Only in her distant colonies, which her navy could not defend, had Germany suffered material losses in territory by the close of 1915. Japan quickly captured the German port of Kiaochow and took possession of the German stations in the northern Pacific, while the Australians and New Zealanders captured those in the southern Pacific. Troops from the South African Union, with the hearty coöperation of the Boers—

Britain's late enemies—occupied German Southwest Africa. The remainder of Germany's colonies, Togoland, Cameroons, and German East Africa, gradually fell into the hands of the English or French. The question as to whether she should have them back or receive any indemnity for them was one of the serious problems developed by the war.

War On and Under the Sea

Had the war been confined to the continent of Europe and Asia Minor, the stalemate reached by the close of 1916 might have continued indefinitely, but the conflict on the day of its outbreak involved the network of commerce stretching from the ports of Europe to the uttermost parts of the earth, especially the enormous trade between the United States and all countries of the Old World. Possessing an overwhelming naval power, Great Britain destroyed or drove to cover the few German warships on the ocean and forced German merchant ships to take shelter in neutral or home ports. In this way German commerce in the ocean lanes was entirely cut off, and a blockade was declared against the whole German coast. Hence Germany's trade with over-sea countries had to be carried on through neutrals.

Theoretically, the blockade was governed by certain rules of "international law." In the first place, neutral ships carrying goods not useful for military purposes—that is, "non-contraband of war"— were free to sail where they would, subject to any blockade established. In the second place, ships carrying contraband goods to a belligerent could be seized if caught on the high seas, and any vessels suspected of being engaged in this business could be overhauled and searched. In the third place, a blockade by sea, to be lawful, had to be "effective." Finally, a peaceful merchant ship, whether belonging to a belligerent or neutral, could not be destroyed or sunk without providing for the safety of crew and passengers.

These general principles left two important questions unanswered. "What is an effective blockade?" "What is contraband of war?" As mistress of the seas Great Britain soon furnished the answers. It had long been understood that a blockade to be effective must be maintained by a continuous patrol of the waters near the enemy's ports. But the German submarines made it impossible for Great Britain to keep up any such patrol. Nevertheless, she declared a blockade and managed to force all parties concerned to give heed. With respect to "contraband of war," Great Britain put a broad interpretation on the term, which embraced nearly every important article of commerce, including cargoes of grain and flour.

Not only was trade with Germany thus intercepted, but neutral commerce was likewise limited. Great Britain took the position that materials useful in war, such as oil, cotton, and gasoline, even though destined for neutrals such as Holland or Sweden, might find their way into Germany or, at all events, release goods for sale to that country. Hence she materially restricted the trade of nations not engaged in the war. Alleging that the Germans were sowing mines in the North Sea, Great Britain instructed ships bound for Scandinavian countries to come by British waters for inspection and sailing directions. In effect, Americans were now licensed by Great Britain to trade in certain commodities and certain amounts with neutral countries; their ships were held up, searched, and kept in British ports until judicial decisions could be reached respecting their rights. Against these extraordinary measures the American government protested vigorously, declaring that they were "not justified by rules of international law or required under the principles of self-preservation."

Against these alleged violations of international law Germany likewise protested, and some of her naval officers urged that her navy, though far inferior in strength, should make a supreme effort to break the iron ring drawn by Great Britain. Indeed, it was supposed in some circles that at the very outset there would be a decisive engagement between the two opposing navies, but nothing of the kind ever occurred. The only significant sea engagement that took place during the entire war was the battle of Jutland between a portion of the German high-seas fleet and a stronger detachment of British warships in May, 1916. For several hours the conflict raged, until mist, smoke, and darkness put an end to it without a decision. In the struggle the British lost three battle cruisers, three armored cruisers, and eight destroyers, and 6097 men and officers killed; while the Germans lost one battleship, four light destroyers, five other vessels, and 2545 men and officers killed. Forty-five British ships were engaged against twenty-seven German ships. After the battle was over, both sides claimed the victory and accused the other of not daring to come out and try it again. The Germans said that they afterwards hunted for the British in vain, and the British retorted that they had hunted the Germans in vain.[1] At all events, no second such general naval encounter occurred. The British kept their battleships well protected at their bases and made no grand effort to attack the German seaports; and the Germans likewise kept their battleships under safeguard and ventured no great assault on the British coast. Thus the question was raised as to whether the airplane and submarine had not made obsolete the great hulks which had once dominated the seas.

Finding it impossible to break the British blockade or to compel Great Britain to modify her "illegal" control over commerce, Germany announced that in retaliation, on and after February 18, 1915, the whole of the English Channel and the waters around Great Britain would be deemed a war zone, and every enemy ship found therein would be destroyed. The German decree added that since the British admiralty had ordered the use of neutral flags by English ships in time of

[1] Anybody interested in this verbal battle can read accounts by the commanding officers printed in *These Eventful Years*, Vol. I, pp. 327 ff.

distress, neutral vessels would be in danger of destruction if found in the forbidden area. It was clear that Germany intended to employ submarines to destroy shipping. A new factor was thus introduced into naval warfare, one not provided for in the accepted laws of war. A regular warship when overhauling and sinking a merchant vessel could easily take its crew and passengers on board for safe-keeping as prescribed by international law; but a submarine ordinarily could do nothing of the sort. Of necessity the lives and the ships of neutrals, as well as of belligerents, were put in mortal peril. Germany defended this conduct on the ground that it was made imperative by British violations of international law ruinous to German trade in the necessities of life.

The response of the United States to the ominous German order was swift and direct. On February 10, 1915, President Wilson warned Germany that if her commanders destroyed American lives and ships as threatened by that decree, the action would "be very hard indeed to reconcile with the friendly relations happily subsisting between the two governments." The American note added that the German imperial government would be held to "strict accountability," and that all necessary steps would be taken to safeguard American lives and American rights. This was firm and clear language, but the only response received from Germany was a suggestion that, if Great Britain would allow food supplies to pass through the blockade, the submarine campaign would end.

Meanwhile Germany continued to ravage shipping on the high seas. On January 28 a German raider sank the American ship *William P. Frye* in the south Atlantic; on March 28 a British ship, the *Falaba*, was sunk by a submarine, and many on board, including an American citizen, perished; and on April 28 a German airplane dropped bombs on the American steamer *Cushing*. On the morning of May 1, 1915, Americans were astounded to see in the newspapers an advertisement, signed by the German Imperial Embassy, warning travelers of the dangers in the war zone and notifying them that anyone who ventured on British ships into that area did so at his own risk. That day, the *Lusitania*, a British steamer, sailed from New York to Liverpool. On May 7, without warning, the ship was struck by two torpedoes and in a few minutes went down by the bow, carrying to death 1153 persons, including 114 American men, women, and children. A cry of horror ran through the country. German papers in the United States and a few American people argued that the passengers on the ill-fated steamer had been duly apprised of the danger and had deliberately taken their lives into their hands; but the general public was deeply shocked.

On May 14 the Department of State at Washington made public a note to Germany on the *Lusitania* case. It said bluntly to the German government: "No warning that an unlawful and inhumane act will be committed can possibly be accepted as an excuse or palliation for that act or as an abatement of the responsibility for its commission." It called upon that government to disavow the act, make reparation as far as possible, and take steps to prevent "the recurrence of anything so obviously subversive of the principles of warfare." The note closed with a caution to Germany that the government of the United States would not "omit any word or any act necessary to the performance of its sacred duty of maintaining the rights of the United States and its citizens and of safeguarding their free exercise and enjoyment." Germany in reply merely temporized.

In a second note, made public on June 11, the position of the United States was again affirmed. William Jennings Bryan, the Secretary of State, had resigned because the drift of President Wilson's policy was not toward mediation but the strict maintenance of American rights by force of arms, if need be. The German reply was still evasive, and German naval commanders continued to sink merchant ships. In a third note of July 21, 1915, Wilson made it clear to Germany that he meant what he said when he wrote that he would maintain the rights of American citizens. Finally, after much discussion and shifting about, the German ambassador on September 1, 1915, sent a brief note to the Secretary of State: "Liners will not be sunk by our submarines without warning and without safety of the lives of noncombatants, provided the liners do not try to escape or offer resistance." Editorially, the *New York Times* declared, "It is a triumph not only of diplomacy but of reason, of humanity, of justice, and of truth."

POSITION OF THE UNITED STATES DURING THE EARLY PHASES OF THE WORLD WAR

Meanwhile public opinion in the United States respecting the war was profoundly stirred. When the conflict began in 1914, President Wilson declared that the government would observe strict neutrality, and a few days later he urged American citizens to avoid taking sides in a war which did not directly concern them. But it was impossible for the American people to remain indifferent when such tremendous events were being reported every day, and it was becoming increasingly evident that the outcome, whatever it might be, would have a deep effect on the affairs of the United States. Moreover, propagandists were persistently adding to the natural excitement. German-language newspapers in the United States eagerly defended the Central Powers and laid the responsibility for the war at England's door. On the other hand, many British subjects in America from England and Canada did all they could to convince the people that Germany was the real offender and guilty of all kinds of crimes besides. No doubt a great body of Americans were sorely grieved by the German invasion of Belgium, the burning of Belgian towns, the deportation of Belgians, and the sinking of merchant ships by submarines. Those of English descent naturally felt themselves drawn to England in her struggle for existence. Those of democratic sympathies disliked the arrogant talk of the Kaiser about God and himself, and hoped that the military party which ruled Germany would be overthrown in the war.

The bitter feelings already roused by the war were increased by the activities of foreign spies and agents of one kind or another. Germany had a number of representatives in the United States denouncing England and the Entente allies and doing all they could to stir up enmity toward them. Very early in the war the minister of Austria-Hungary had to be sent home for concocting a scheme for damaging the great steel mills which were supplying England and France with arms and munitions. At the same time England also had her full quota of agents working up sentiment on the other side. Thus many Americans were utterly bewildered by the clamor of conflicting propaganda.[1]

Disputes about the merits of the belligerents were sharpened as President Wilson dispatched note after note to Germany expostulating against the indiscriminate manner in which the submarines sent vessels to the bottom—not only British ships, like the *Lusitania*, carrying American passengers, but also American ships and those of other neutral nations. On all sides the President was urged to break off diplomatic relations with the German imperial government, even though in September, 1916, it promised to reform its submarine policy. Wilson, however, refused to be driven from his position. He informed Germany, it is true, that he would omit no word or act in resisting her submarine activities, but he steadfastly sought ways of peace; and for a time it appeared to some as if peace might come, as he said, "without victory."

[1] There was a very bitter difference of feeling between the pro-Germans and the friends of the Allies in regard to the exportation of arms and munitions. Since Germany had no way of getting supplies from the United States, owing to British control of the Atlantic, she maintained that it was *unneutral* for the manufacturers in the United States to sell arms to the Allies. Yet it had always been considered the right of neutrals to sell to any belligerent any supplies they are in a position to furnish. When the Germans succeeded in getting a freight submarine, the *Deutschland*, over to New London, Connecticut, the captain found people willing enough to sell war supplies to Germans.

In December, 1916, after the Central Powers had occupied Poland, Serbia, and Rumania, and Germany seemed to be victorious on all hands, she made what she called a peace offer. She proposed that the belligerents send representatives to some point in a neutral country to consider the terms of settlement. In any case, the Central Powers would thus find their position strengthened. A lull in the war would enable them to recuperate. If the proposition to attend such a meeting should be rejected by the Allies,—as it was,—it would seem, in German eyes, to throw the burden for continuing the fearful conflict upon the Allies. Whoever might have been responsible for beginning the war, Germany now said that she had been the first to propose to end it. The Kaiser proclaimed exultantly that the Allies had at last cast off the mask of hypocrisy and plainly revealed their "lust of conquest." The refusal of his adversaries to consider peace also furnished an excuse for a resort to the unrestricted submarine warfare which Germany was contemplating. She argued that if Germany's enemies really proposed to "crush" her, no means of self-defense on her part could be too ruthless.

Before the Allies had replied to the German peace suggestion, President Wilson intervened (December 18) with a circular note sent to the belligerents, calling attention to the fact that both sides seemed to agree that there should be a league for maintaining peace and that small states should be protected, but saying that neither side had stated the "concrete objects" for which it was fighting. He accordingly suggested a conference on the essential conditions of peace. Germany expressed herself as ready for a meeting of delegates to consider peace terms. The Allies, however, declined to negotiate, but went so far in replying to President Wilson (January 10, 1917) as to give a definition of the oft-used terms "restoration," "restitution," and "guarantees," and to lay down conditions of peace which the Germans rejected as "intolerable."

Not discouraged by the failure to bring the belligerents together, President Wilson in an address on January 22, 1917, stated his view of the essentials of peace. He said that peace must, among other things, provide for equality of right for both great and small nations, security for "subject peoples," direct outlet to the sea for every great people, "freedom of the seas,"[1] and limitation of armaments. He declared:

No peace can last, or ought to last, which does not recognize and accept the principle that governments derive all their just powers from the consent of the governed, and that no right anywhere exists to hand peoples about from sovereignty to sovereignty as if they were property.

There can be no sense of safety and equality among the nations if great preponderating armaments are henceforth to continue here and there to be built up and maintained. The statesmen of the world must plan for peace, and nations must adjust and accommodate their policy to it as they have planned for war and made ready for pitiless contest and rivalry.

But all these peace negotiations came to naught; the war went on, and the United States was speedily drawn into the awful conflict.

Entrance of the United States into the War

At the very moment when the German government was exhibiting an apparent interest in President Wilson's efforts to bring about peace, the German military leaders were planning a still more rigorous use of their submarines than they had hitherto made.

In January, 1917, Great Britain, in order completely to cut off supplies from Germany, extended the area which she

[1] In time of peace the high seas—that is, the ocean outside of the three-mile limit drawn along the coast—are free to all and are not supposed to be under the control of any particular government. It is in time of war that the question of "the freedom of the seas" arises. England was in a position at the opening of the war to cut off Germany's maritime commerce. By way of reprisal Ger-

declared to be in a state of blockade. Germany then proclaimed to the world that in order to make head against "British tyranny" and Britain's plan for starving Germany, she proposed to establish a vast barred zone extending far to the west of Great Britain, in which sea traffic with England would be prevented by every available means. In this way, she flattered herself, the British, who drew much of their food from distant regions, would soon be reduced to starvation and the war brought to a speedy end. One of the most irritating features of Germany's plan was a project for leaving a narrow lane through which the United States was permitted to send one ship a week, provided it was painted with bright stripes of color and carried no contraband.

On February 1, 1917, the Germans opened their unrestricted submarine warfare in this great barred zone. President Wilson immediately responded by breaking off diplomatic relations with the German government on February 3 and sending Count von Bernstorff home, to the great relief of those who had criticized the President for being too patient. Although Wilson expressed the hope that Germany's deeds would not measure up to her words, the sinking of American ships went on, and popular opinion was more and more aroused against Germany. Hostility was intensified by the publication of a letter from the German minister of foreign affairs to the Mexican government, which proposed that, if war broke out between the United States and Germany, Mexico should attack the United States and should receive Texas, New Mexico, and Arizona as its reward.

It was finally evident that war was unavoidable unless the

---

many established vast barred zones, in which she sank not only her enemies' vessels but also those of neutrals which ventured to neglect her warnings. So the ocean was anything but free during the conflict. Another element in the freedom of the seas is the control of such narrow passages as the Dardanelles, the Strait of Gibraltar, the Suez and Panama canals, and the entrances to the Baltic. It is hard to imagine any arrangement that will keep the seas open and safe so long as wars continue to take place among maritime powers.

United States was to surrender its rights on the sea and acquiesce accordingly in Germany's policy. President Wilson
summoned a special session of Congress, and on April 2, 1917,

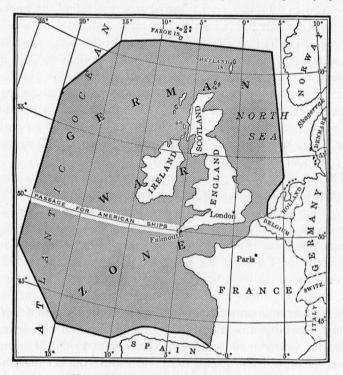

GERMAN WAR ZONE OF FEBRUARY 1, 1917

Late in the year 1917 and early in 1918 the German government extended the
barred zone so as to include the islands off the coast of Africa, Madeira, the
Cape Verde Islands, and the Azores, in order to cut the routes between Europe
and South America

read a memorable address to its members in which he said
that Germany had to all intents and purposes declared war
on the United States. "Our object," he maintained, "is to vin-
dicate the principles of peace and justice in the life of the
world, as against selfish and autocratic power." The free and

self-governed peoples of the world must combine, he urged, "to make the world safe for democracy," for otherwise no permanent peace was possible. He proposed that the United States should fight side by side with Germany's enemies and aid them with liberal loans.

Both Houses of Congress approved by large majorities the proposed resolution that the United States had been forced into war. Provisions were made for borrowing vast sums; old forms of taxation were greatly increased, and many new ones were added. In May, 1917, conscription was introduced, and all able-bodied men between the ages of twenty-one and thirty-one were declared liable to military service. Preparations were made for training great bodies of troops to be sent across the Atlantic to aid the cause of the Allies, and measures were taken for building ships to replace those destroyed by German submarines. The people of the United States showed themselves eager to do their part in the war on "autocracy and militarism."[1]

The Russian Revolution; the Bolsheviki

By a strange coincidence, just as the United States was preparing to enter the World War, one of the chief belligerents, Russia, started upon a revolutionary course which led to great modifications in the problems of war and peace. We must now consider the astonishing upheaval leading to the overthrow of the old Russian despotism, the retirement of Russia from the war, and the proclamation of revolutionary war aims.[2]

---

[1] When the unrestricted submarine sinkings began (February 1, 1917), the German newspapers informed their readers that England would speedily be brought to her knees. But while hundreds of ships were sunk, thousands came and went from English ports, managing in various ways to escape the U-boats. Then by economy, raising more food, and building more ships, England, with America's help, successfully offset the losses caused by the continual sinking of their merchant ships by the Germans.

[2] For the revolutionary events which had been taking place in Russia immediately preceding the war, see page 78 ff.

The world conflict had hardly opened in 1914 when it revealed the corruption, the weakness, the inefficiency, indeed, in some cases the treason, of the Tsar's court and his imperial officials. The millions of Russians who perished in the trenches on the Eastern Front in vain endeavors to advance into Germany and Austria-Hungary or to stem the tide of German invasion were ill supported by their government. Alarmed by blunders in the administration, the Duma became unmanageable, and in December, 1916, it passed a resolution declaring that "dark forces" were paralyzing the government and betraying the nation's interests. This referred especially to the German wife of the Tsar, and the influence exercised over her and the court by a monk named Rasputin, who opposed every modern reform. When, in response to popular wrath, Rasputin was murdered, the angry Tsar proceeded to dismiss the liberals from the government and to replace them by the most unpopular bureaucrats he could find. He seemed to be declaring war on the whole liberal movement and reverting to the methods of Nicholas I. Meantime the country was becoming more and more disorganized. There was a distressing scarcity of food in the cities and a growing repugnance to the war.

Early in March, 1917, affairs reached such a pass that bread riots broke out in Petrograd, troops refused to fire on the people, and the Tsar's government found itself helpless. When ordered to adjourn, the Duma defied the Tsar and called for the establishment of a provisional government. Hastening back to Petrograd from the Front, the Tsar was stopped by representatives of the new provisional government on March 15, 1917, and induced to sign on behalf of himself and his son an abdication in favor of his brother, the Grand Duke Michael. But Michael refused the honor, unless it was authorized by a constitutional assembly, thus removing from the scene the Romanovs, who had ruled Russia for more than three centuries. There was no longer any such thing in the world as "the Autocrat of all the Russias." The Tsar's relatives renounced their rights, his high officials were imprisoned in the very fortress of Peter and Paul where they had sent so many revolutionists, and political prisoners in Russia and Siberia received the joyous tidings that they were free. Later the Tsar and members of his family were shot by the Bolsheviki. The world viewed with astonishment this abrupt and complete collapse of an ancient system of tyranny.

For the purpose of carrying on the work of government, a revolutionary cabinet was formed, composed, on the whole, of men of moderate views, with Alexander Kerensky, a socialist, as minister of justice. The new cabinet declared itself in favor of many reforms, such as liberty of speech and of the press, the right to strike, the substitution of militia for the old police, universal suffrage—including women. But the socialists were not content, and through their council of workingmen's and soldiers' delegates began to exercise great power. By July, 1917, all the more conservative members of the provisional government had been forced out to make room for socialists. A desperate attempt to lead the flagging Russian troops forward to victory against the enemy utterly failed, and as time went on the demand for an immediate peace "without annexations and indemnities" became louder and bolder.

At length the storm which had long been gathering broke. Early in the revolution the council of workmen's and soldiers' deputies, or "soviet," set up in Petrograd, had begun to dispute the authority of the Duma. All over Russia similar soviets, or councils of workmen, soldiers, and peasants, were instituted, and finally in November, under two leaders, Lenin and Trotzky, supported by soldiers, the soviets overturned the Kerensky government, founding instead "a dictatorship of the proletariat." The faction which engineered this enterprise was known as the Bolsheviki, or "majority men," a term earlier given to them because they constituted a majority at a certain conference of the Russian socialists.

With their power once fairly established, the Bolsheviki pro-

T

ceeded to abolish private property in land and capital and to institute a "communist system." They bitterly denounced the war as an "imperialist struggle for trade and territory," and they called upon the warring powers to join them in a peace conference. Receiving no replies, they opened the Russian archives and published the secret treaties drawn up by the Allies against Germany. Then, late in December, they instituted peace negotiations with the Central Powers at Brest-Litovsk, near Russia's western boundary.

At the peace conference the Russian delegates submitted their program of "no annexations and no indemnities," and complained of the extortion practiced by the Teutonic allies. But the Bolsheviki were helpless in the face of the German demands. Finland and the Ukraine (which comprises a great part of southern Russia) declared themselves independent and (under German influence, it was supposed) established governments of their own. So on March 3, 1918, the representatives of the Bolsheviki concluded a peace with the Central Powers in which they agree to "evacuate" the Ukraine and Finland and to surrender Poland, Lithuania, Kurland, Livonia, and certain districts in the Caucasus, all of which were to exercise the right of establishing such governments as they pleased. It is estimated that Russia lost about a third of her population, a third of her railways, nearly three fourths of her iron mines, about 90 per cent of her coal mines, and her chief industrial towns and richest fields. Thus Russia was dismembered, and all the western and southern regions came under the strong influence of the Germans. Shortly after, the capital of Russia was transferred from Petrograd to Moscow (see pages 396 ff., 421 ff., 470 ff.).

ISSUES OF THE WAR

The entrance of the United States into the war and the revolutionary withdrawal of Russia raised grave questions respecting the war aims of both belligerents. Was the conflict merely an imperialist quarrel over trade and colonies, as the Bolsheviki alleged? Or did it involve nobler ends affecting the rights and liberties of mankind?

Naturally, the war rendered acute every chronic disease which Europe had failed to remedy in the long period of general peace. France had never given up hopes of regaining Alsace-Lorraine. The Poles continued to aspire to appear on the map as an independent nation. Both the northern Slavs of Bohemia and the southern Slavs in Slovenia, Croatia, Slavonia, Bosnia, and Dalmatia were discontented with their relations to Austria-Hungary, of which they formed a part. The Irredentists of Italy had long laid claim to important coast lands belonging to Austria. Serbia and Bulgaria were bitterly at odds over the arrangements made at the close of the Second Balkan War, especially in regard to Macedonia. Rumania longed for Transylvania and Bukowina. Then there were the old questions as to what was to be done with the remaining vestiges of the Turkish Empire in Europe, and who was to control Syria and Mesopotamia. In the Far East, Japan's interests in China offered an unsolved problem. The Germans emphasized the necessity of doing something about the discontent with British rule in India and Ireland.

To these older grievances the progress of the war had added new territorial perplexities. At the close of 1917 the Central Powers were in military possession of Belgium, Luxemburg, northeastern France, Poland, Lithuania, Kurland, Serbia, Montenegro, and Rumania. Great Britain had captured Bagdad and Jerusalem. In Africa all the German colonies were in the hands of her enemies, and in the Pacific her possessions had been taken over by Japan and Australia. Were all these regions, conquered by one or the other of the belligerent groups, to be given back or not? Then what about Belgium, mulcted and abused and pillaged by its conquerors? And what of northeastern France, so terribly devastated? Was not reparation due to these unhappy victims of the war?

To many humane people, however, these questions seemed of minor importance compared with the overwhelming world problem of how mankind should conspire to put an end to war forever. The world of today—compared with that of Napoleon's time, when the last great international struggle took place—is so compact, and the nations have been brought so close together and are so dependent on one another, that it seemed as if the time had come to join in a last, victorious *war on war*. In 1815 it required a month or more to cross the Atlantic; in 1915 less than six days were necessary; and above its waves airplanes were soon to be soaring, far swifter than any steamer. Formerly the oceans were great barriers separating America from Europe and the Orient from America; but, like the ancient bulwarks round medieval cities, they have now become highways on which people of all nations hasten to and fro. Before the war express trains were regularly traversing Europe from end to end at a speed of from forty to fifty miles an hour, and the automobile vied with the locomotive in speed, whereas at the time of the Congress of Vienna, no one could get about faster than a horse could travel. The telegraph, telephone, and radio made it possible to flash news to the most distant parts of the earth more quickly than Louis XVIII could send a message from one part of Paris to another. The wireless apparatus kept vessels, no matter how far out at sea, in constant touch with the land.

Largely on account of these inventions and the myriad commercial ties, nations had come to depend on one another for food, clothes, and every sort of necessity and refinement. Britain hoped to end the war by cutting off Germany from her usual communication with other countries, and Germany flattered herself she could starve England by sinking the thousands of vessels which supply her tables with bread and meat. Even the rumor of war upsets the stock exchanges throughout the world. Nations read one another's books, profit by one another's scientific discoveries and inventions, and go to one another's plays. Germans, Italians, French, and Russians contribute to musical programs listened to in New York, Valparaiso, or Sydney. We continue to talk of *independent* nations, but only a few isolated, squalid, savage tribes can be said any longer to be independent of other peoples. In an ever-increasing degree America is a part of Europe, and Europe is a part of America, and their histories tend to merge into the history of the whole world.

In many startling ways the war served merely to emphasize all these things, which were being recognized in the previous quarter of a century. The Hague conferences, the establishment of the international Hague Tribunal, and the various arbitration treaties had all been directed, at least in some measure, toward the suppression of the plague of war. International arrangements in regard to coinage, postal service, commerce, and transportation had encouraged good understanding and coöperation. Innumerable international societies, congresses, and expositions had brought foreign peoples together and illustrated their manifold common interests.

The old problem of armaments—the possibility of getting rid of the crushing burden and constant peril of vast standing armies and the competition in dreadnaughts and cruisers—was made a burning question by the war, because the European nations involved were bound to emerge from the conflict either bankrupt or with unparalleled financial obligations. At the same time the progress in the deadly art of killing one's fellow men advanced so rapidly with the aid of scientific discovery and the stress of war that what was considered adequate military preparedness before the war would seem absurdly inadequate after its close. Giant guns, aircraft, tanks, and poisonous gases, among other things, had been added to the older devices of destruction, and the submarine suggested a complete revolution in naval strategy.

To idealists the great issue of the war was really "militarism," which included two closely associated problems. First, should diplomats be permitted any longer to carry on secret negotiations and pledge their respective nations to secret agreements which might involve war? Secondly, should a government be permitted to declare war without the approval of the great mass of its citizens? Those opposed to Germany were all in hearty agreement in regarding her as representing the most dangerous form of militarism, which had plunged the whole world into a horrible war and would, unless destroyed, remain a constant menace to future peace. And the Germans defended their armaments on the ground that they were in constant peril from ancient foes, Russia and France, equally given to militarism.

To the countries enrolled in the war against the Central Powers, especially England and the United States, it seemed that the German system of government and the ideals of the German ruling class were dangerous to the peace and safety of the world. At the head of Germany stood the Kaiser, king of Prussia and German emperor, claiming to rule by God's will. Under him were the chancellor—his personal appointee—and the cabinet, all chosen by the emperor. The Bundesrat, or upper house of the parliament, consisted of representatives of the various German principalities and kingdoms and the three free cities. The lower house, the Reichstag, composed of delegates elected by German voters, could talk as much as it liked, but it had, as we have seen (p. 48), little control over the cabinet and practically no control over the use of the army. It is true that an offensive war could not be declared without the consent of the Bundesrat or supported without grants of money from the parliament, but all that the Kaiser and the war party had to do to escape this check was to proclaim a war "defensive."

As if to emphasize the monarchical character of the German system, the Kaiser continually gave offense to people in England and the United States who believed in democracy by repeatedly speaking of himself as the "anointed of the Lord."

Again and again he talked about making his own will supreme, no matter what the German people wanted. Never did he weary in praising his mighty army and warning all the world against its strength and prowess. If Germany was in fact no worse an offender than other European countries, it was certain that the Kaiser gave the appearance of being the greatest "saber-rattler" on the globe. Germans who laughed at him too openly or who even boldly criticized his views and conduct were likely to be quickly imprisoned for lese majesty—the crime of insulting "the All-Highest."

Practically independent of the Reichstag was the German army. First of all, it was directed by professional officers appointed by the Kaiser. Its high commanders formed a small, secret circle that looked upon the German house of representatives with slight respect. During the negotiations preceding the outbreak of the World War, they had a secret wire connecting them with the high command of the Austrian army, and while the German chancellor was urging peace, they were advising the Austrians to stand firm. The subordinate officers of the army were recruited largely from the upper classes, especially the feudal lords of Prussia (Junkers), now enriched not only by their lands but also by investments in German industries. As a general thing, the army officers regarded the mass of the people as useful to do hard work and to serve as "cannon fodder" for the army.

However, it was a serious mistake to suppose that this system was without general support in Germany. On the contrary, the ruling classes and a large portion of the people defended it on a clearly reasoned-out theory. The Germans, they said, were surrounded by enemies and were forced to maintain an invincible army for self-defense; therefore its primary purpose was not offensive, but to protect the fatherland against unscrupulous neighbors, who in previous centuries had kept Germany disunited and helpless and made her lands their battle ground. That army, ran the argument, had freed Germany of Napoleon I and had prevented Napoleon III from overrunning the country. Moreover, it was said, if the Reichstag interfered too much with the army, its secrets would become known, and in time of danger it might be prevented from striking soon enough to win a war. Finally, the upper classes thought the army might be very useful if the socialists should attempt to organize an uprising at home, as they often threatened to do. Consequently many Germans who did not like the army's methods accepted them as a necessary evil.

If the German military party, as it claimed, did not actually want war, there was doubt about its methods and plans after the war was started. Operating on the theory that severity and terror were useful in gaining ends quickly, it invaded the neutral country of Belgium and carried off Belgian citizens to work in German factories and mines. In any case, whatever defense was offered, its conduct was shocking to a great body of English and American people, who had never had any experience with a large professional army.

More than this. After the war began the German military party supported the demands of the imperialists, who proposed that in the hour of victory new colonies and territories should be annexed and the conquered nations be forced to pay heavy indemnities. It even resisted the idea of restoring and freeing Belgium after that helpless country had been overrun in the haste to get into France. There was no doubt about what the German military party would have done if it had come out triumphant. All its ideas of right were made plain in the severe terms imposed on the Russians by the Treaty of Brest-Litovsk in 1918, when Russia surrendered. It was widely believed that if Germany had won the war she would have despoiled France and England as well, and then challenged America on land and sea. It was this state of affairs which led many American people who did not think England, France, and Russia guiltless in the war to fear Germany and hope for her defeat.

On the other hand, as has been said, the mass of German people, whatever their opinion of the Kaiser and *Junkertum*, believed that they were fighting for national existence against warlike and imperialist powers. German critics pointed out the rigors of Tsarist despotism, made light of British pretentions to democracy, and declared that France and England, in spite of their parliaments, had carried on secret diplomacy, ignored the people's representatives, and maneuvered Germany into a war which she could not avoid. Nor would the Germans allow any distinction between the "imperialism" with which they were charged and that practiced by their opponents in various parts of the earth. In possession of many secret papers secured by their agents from Entente sources, the German government was convinced that it was the victim of an "encirclement" designed to destroy Germany as a great commercial and military state. When in December, 1917, the Bolsheviki threw open the Russian archives and published the secret treaties by which the Entente allies divided the spoils of victory in advance and provided for the dismemberment of Germany and Austria in the east and west, the German government gave wide currency to these revelations in order to reënforce its previous contentions and excite the people anew for a defense of the fatherland to the last ditch.

Thus, in the bitter discussion of war aims the belligerents in Europe were unable to arrive at a clear definition of issues with right all on one side and wrong on the other. President Wilson attempted to meet this difficulty after the United States entered the war by formulating a set of principles to control a "peace of justice." When, for example, Pope Benedict XV on August 1 sent forth a peace message in which he urged Christendom to cease from its fratricidal carnage, lay down its arms, and revert in general to the status quo ante, President Wilson answered that no peace was possible with the existing irresponsible government of Germany.

This power is not the German people. It is the ruthless master of the German people. . . . We cannot take the word of the present rulers of Germany as a guarantee of anything that is to endure, unless explicitly supported by such conclusive evidence of the will and purpose of the German people themselves as the other peoples of the world will be justified in accepting. Without such guarantees for disarmament, covenants to set up arbitration in the place of war, territorial adjustments, reconstitution of small nations, if made with the German government, no man, no nation could now depend on.

In his message on the opening of Congress on December 4, 1917, President Wilson was still more emphatic:

The people of Germany are being told by the men whom they now permit to deceive them and to act as their masters that they are fighting for the very life and existence of their Empire, a war of desperate self-defense against deliberate aggression. Nothing could be more grossly or wantonly false, and we must seek by the utmost openness and candor as to our real aims to convince them of its falseness. We are in fact fighting for their emancipation from fear, . . . of unjust attack by neighbors, or rivals or schemers after world empire. No one is threatening the existence or independence or the peaceful enterprise of the German Empire. . . . We intend no wrong against the German Empire, no interference with her internal affairs.

Lloyd George reiterated this last sentiment in a speech before the House of Commons.

Again, on January 8, 1918, President Wilson summarized his program of world peace, in fourteen points. The chief of these were: No secret international understandings or treaties; absolute freedom of navigation in peace and war, except when portions of the sea might be closed by international understanding; removal of economic barriers and reduction of armaments; impartial adjustment of all colonial claims; restoration of Belgium and evacuation of territories occupied by the Teutonic allies during the war; righting of the wrong done to France when Alsace-Lorraine was seized by Germany; freeing of Asiatic dependencies of Turkey; and the formation of a general association of nations for the purpose of insuring the independence of great and small states alike. This program was heartily and unreservedly approved by the representatives of the English workingmen and made clearer than any previous declaration the war aims of the United States.

The World at War

One result of the entrance of the United States into the war was a great increase in the number of Germany's enemies during the year 1917. Cuba and Panama immediately followed the example set by the North American republic; Greece, after much internal turmoil and dissension, finally, under the leadership of Venizelos, joined the Allies (see pages 335 ff.); in the latter half of the year Siam, Liberia, China, and Brazil proclaimed war on Germany. Thus the war became literally a world conflict. The governments of nearly a billion and a half of the earth's population were involved in the amazing struggle. Thirteen hundred and forty millions of people were committed by their rulers to the side of the Allies, and the countries included in the Central European alliance had a total population of about one hundred and sixty millions. Thus nearly seven eighths of the population of the globe were nominally at war, and nine tenths of these were arrayed against one tenth, led by Prussia. Of course the vast populations of India and China bulk large in these figures, but they had little or no part in the active prosecution of the war. And after the Russian revolution had destroyed the old government, Russia, with its millions of inhabitants, could by the end of 1917 no longer be reckoned an active factor.

As for the countries which remained neutral, they included a population of perhaps one hundred and ninety millions. Holland, Switzerland, Denmark, Norway, and Sweden were far too close to Germany to risk breaking with her, even if they had wanted to do so. Spain and a number of Latin-American states, including Mexico and Chile, held aloof. But no country could escape the burdens and afflictions of a war of such magnitude. Real neutrality was almost impossible. Everywhere taxes and prices rose, essential supplies were cut off, and business was greatly dislocated.

In addition to the increase in Germany's enemies, the chief military events of 1917 were the following: In March the Germans decided to shorten their lines on the Western Front from Noyon on the south to Arras on the north. They withdrew, devastating the land as they went, and the French and English were able to reoccupy about one eighth of the French territory that the enemy had held so long. The Germans were disturbed by fierce attacks while establishing their new line of defense, but in spite of great sacrifices on the part of the French and British, this "Hindenburg" line was so well fortified that it held, and with slight exceptions continued to hold, during the year. The English made some progress in forcing back the enemy on the Belgian coast with the hope of gaining Zeebrugge, the base from which German submarines made their departure to prey on English commerce. Attempts to take St. Quentin, the important mining town of Lens, and the city of Cambrai were not successful for another year; but the terrible slaughter went on, and tens of thousands were killed or wounded every week.

Realizing that they were fighting against growing odds, the Germans on March 21, 1918, began a great drive on the Western Front with the hope of gaining a decisive victory and forcing the Allies to sue for peace. Germany was now in a desperate hurry, for she knew that her U-boat warfare was not reducing England to starvation, that the United States troops were beginning to arrive in ever-increasing numbers, and that the German plans for getting supplies from Russia were meeting with little success. Moreover, the German people were undergoing all sorts of bitter hardships and might at any time begin to complain that the final victory which the Kaiser had been promising from the first was all too long in coming.

When this great spring drive began, the southern and eastern portions of the Western Front were held by French armies, and the northern line by the British. Hindenburg and his generals decided to strike at the southernmost of the British armies, in the region of the Somme. If they could defeat it, they would thereby separate the French and British and so prevent them from helping one another. For several days the Germans were victorious and were able to push the British back almost to Amiens. But the French rushed to the aid of their allies; the drive was checked, and Amiens, with its important railroad connections, was saved. No previous conflict of the war had been so terrible as this. It is estimated that over four hundred thousand men were killed, wounded, or captured. Moreover, the Germans only regained the devastated territory from which they had retired a year before, and their fierce efforts to advance beyond it came to naught.

The grave danger in which the Allies found themselves finally convinced them that their safety lay in putting their forces— French, British, Italian, and the newly arriving troops from the United States—under a single commander in chief. All agreed that the French general, Ferdinand Foch (appointed March 28, 1918) was the most likely to lead them to victory. Their confidence was justified.

Everyone knew that the Germans would soon make a second drive somewhere on the long front of one hundred and fifty miles, but at what point the Allies could only conjecture. The new blow came on April 9, when the Kaiser's armies attempted to break through the British defenses between Arras and Ypres, with the intention of reaching Calais and the English Channel. The suspense was taut for a time; but after retreating a few miles, the British made a stand and were ordered by their commander to die, if necessary, at their posts. This checked the second effort of the Germans to break through. In the latter part of May the German armies made a third great attack, this time in the direction of Paris. They took Soissons and Château-Thierry, which brought them within about forty miles of the French capital. In June they made a feebler effort to extend toward the south gains they had succeeded in making in the first drive. Here they were also opposed by American troops, who fought with fresh bravery and ardor beside the French. And here the German successes came to an end.

The first contingent of United States soldiers had arrived in France in June, 1917, under the command of General Pershing, who had a long and honorable record as a military commander. By the first of July, 1918, about a million American troops had reached France and were either participating actively in the fierce fighting or being rapidly and efficiently trained. They had taken their first town by the end of May, 1918, and gained great distinction for themselves by coöperating with the French in frustrating the German attempt to break through at Château-Thierry. Northwest of that town they forced back, early in June, the German troops sent against them. In these conflicts the American marines were especially conspicuous.

During the following weeks the Germans lost tens of thousands of men in minor engagements. Finally, on July 15, 1918, they made a last great effort to take Reims and force their way to Paris, but this drive was speedily turned into a retreat. During the following month the combined efforts of the French and Americans drove the Germans far back from the Marne and put an end to their hopes of advancing on Paris. The French general Mangin warmly praised the valor of the Americans during these "splendid days" when it was his privilege to fight with them "for the deliverance of the world." Then the British began an offensive on the Somme east and south of Amiens. By the end of September the Germans had been pressed back to the old Hindenburg line; even this was pierced at some points, and the Allied troops were within a few miles of the Lorraine boundary.

The American troops in France, numbering slightly over two million men before the armistice was signed, November 11, 1918, were scattered along the Western Front; it is estimated that nearly one million four hundred thousand actually took part in the final struggle against the Germans.[1] It is impossible to mention here all the battles in which the forces of the United States fought side by side with the French or the British as the hosts of the enemy were rapidly pushed back. In the middle of September the Americans took the St. Mihiel salient, bringing their lines within range of the guns of the German fortress of Metz. Reënforcing the British, they showed great courage in capturing the St. Quentin canal tunnel, where thousands of lives were sacrificed. In the Argonne forest, and especially in the capture of Sedan on November 7, the United States troops were prominent. In the months from June to November, 1918, the battle casualties of the American Expeditionary Force—killed, wounded, missing, and prisoners —amounted to about three hundred thousand.

On the other fronts the fortunes of war were turning in favor of the Allies. Germany, instead of being able to get supplies from demoralized Russia, met resistance at every point. The people of the Ukraine resented her domination and began to look to the Allies to assist them in forming their new republic. In Finland civil war raged between the "White Guard" (Nationalist) and the "Red Guard" (Bolshevik), while British and American troops on the Murmansk coast to the north coöperated with Russian forces opposed to the Bolsheviki. At Vladivostok—far away across Siberia—British, Japanese, and American forces landed intending to work westward through Siberia and, President Wilson said, "to steady any efforts at self-government or self-defense in which the Russians themselves may be willing to accept assistance."

[1] The United States proposed to have at least four million men in France by June 30, 1919. The limits of the draft were extended so as to include able-bodied men between the ages of eighteen and forty-five.

As a part of the great forward movement organized by General Foch, the combined Serbian, Greek, British, and French forces in the Balkans once more became active in Serbia and rapidly pushed back the Bulgarians, who, with the help of the Germans and Austrians, had overrun the country three years before. Since neither Germany nor Austria could now send aid, the Bulgarians threw up their hands on September 29, 1918, and asked for an armistice. This was granted on condition of absolute surrender. The defection of Bulgaria proved decisive, for Turkey could not keep up the fight when cut off from her western allies, and Austria-Hungary, open to invasion from the south, was in no position to maintain another front.

Turkey's collapse quickly followed the downfall of Bulgaria. In Palestine, General Allenby followed up the capture of Jerusalem (December, 1917) by the relentless pursuit of the Turkish armies. Combined British and French forces speedily conquered Syria, taking the great towns of Damascus and Beirut, and calling on the Syrians to celebrate their final deliverance from century-long subjugation to the Turks. The Turkish army in Mesopotamia was also captured by the British. So Turkey was forced to follow Bulgaria's example. On October 31 she accepted the terms of surrender imposed by the Allies.

Fall of the Hohenzollern and Hapsburg Dynasties; Close of the War

Thus the eastern allies of the Central Powers were dropping away as their great drive in the west was being turned into retreat. The oncoming troops from the United States, steadily streaming across the Atlantic, brought new hope to the Allies; for the Americans were fresh and were backed by the wellnigh inexhaustible resources of the United States.

The German people now began to feel that they had been grossly deceived by the military authorities. The ruthless use of the U-boats had not forced England to plead for peace, but had aroused a new and mighty enemy across the Atlantic, whose armies were transported across the ocean in spite of the submarines. The victory over Russia, so wildly celebrated in Berlin at the opening of 1918, and the hard terms imposed by the Treaty of Brest-Litovsk had not yielded food supplies for the German armies and the suffering population in accordance with promises held out at the time. With her commerce ruined, her debt enormously increased, and all prospects of forcing her foes to pay her bills blighted, the condition of Germany was hopeless. Deserted by her eastern allies and supported only by feeble Austria-Hungary, Germany had to face almost alone a coalition of the whole world.

Austria was now at the end of her tether. Torn by internal dissensions, threatened by a revolt of her subject nationalities, disheartened by scarcity of food and by the reverses on the Western Front, she sent a note to President Wilson on October 7 requesting that an armistice be considered. By the end of the month her armies were giving way before the Italians, who in a second battle of the Piave not only swept the Austrians out of northern Italy but quickly occupied Trent and the great seaport of Trieste. On November 3 Austria-Hungary unconditionally surrendered, accepting the severe terms that the Allies imposed on her.

But by this time, however, Austria-Hungary had disappeared from the map of Europe. The Czechoslovak republic had been proclaimed, and the Yugoslavs of the Dual Monarchy had severed their former connections. Hungary itself was in revolt and was proclaimed a republic. Amid these circumstances, Charles, the Hapsburg emperor of Austria and king of Hungary, abdicated (November 11).

While her eastern bulwarks were crumbling, Germany's condition on the Western Front became steadily worse. About the middle of August General Ludendorff declared at a crown council that all hope of a military victory had vanished, and

T

the high command decided that diplomatic measures must be taken to reach an understanding with the enemy at the proper moment. On September 10 General Hindenburg suggested an appeal without delay to the belligerents through the mediation of a neutral power. A few days later Ludendorff grew badly frightened and exclaimed that a breakdown might happen at any time. In this emergency the military authorities came to the conclusion that an appeal must be made directly to President Wilson, asking for peace on the basis of the Fourteen Points. It does not seem that the German government counted with much confidence on the power of Wilson to compel the Allies to accept his program at the peace table, but in the hour of distress it tried to make the best haven in sight.

Recalling the bitter hostility which President Wilson had expressed toward the old rulers of Germany, the military and civil authorities realized that some changes would have to be made in the government before he would listen to any peace proposals. Hence on the evening of October 1 Prince Max of Baden, a man of moderate views, was summoned to take up the chancellorship, while representatives of the socialists, progressives, and liberals were given office under him. With this new civilian front formed, Ludendorff drafted the note to be sent to President Wilson during the night of October 3–4, accepting his peace program and requesting an armistice. For a month President Wilson carried on negotiations designed to "smoke out" the military and imperial rulers of Germany, compel a reconstruction of the constitution in a democratic direction, and, in effect, force the abdication of the Kaiser. Besides insisting on internal changes in Germany, President Wilson made it plain that the Allies would not stop their advance unless Germany surrendered on such terms as to render it impossible for her to renew the war. "For," the President added, in his third note, "the nations of the world do not and cannot trust the word of those who have hitherto been the masters of German policy."

Once more the German war council, including the Kaiser and the crown prince, made a vain effort to save the old system. General Ludendorff was dismissed, and the Allies were informed that far-reaching constitutional changes had been effected, assuring the people complete control not only over the government but over the military powers as well (October 27).

Meanwhile the Allied forces were closing in on the Germans all along the line from the North Sea to the Swiss boundary, compelling them to retreat with enormous losses of men and supplies. On November 9 it was announced, to the astonishment of the world, that His Majesty, Emperor William II, had abdicated. He soon fled to Holland. The crown prince gave up his claims to the throne, and the House of Hohenzollern was a thing of the past. The king of Bavaria had been forced out the day before, and all the former monarchies which composed the German Empire were speedily turned into republics. On November 10 a revolution took place in Berlin, and a socialist leader, Friedrich Ebert, assumed the duties of chancellor with the consent of the previous chancellor and all the secretaries of state. Even Prussia had become a republic overnight. The old German Empire was no more.

In order to understand, partially at least, the abrupt abdication of the Kaiser one must consider the following circumstances: The war had of course been conducted by the military command with which the emperor was closely identified. The people at large had been taught that the army was invincible, and that the victory of the Germans was assured beyond a peradventure. Not only was the idea of defeat and surrender unthinkable, but the extreme nationalists conjured up visions of great territorial extensions and huge war indemnities to be collected from the conquered. The military authorities controlled the propaganda and told the people what they wished them to believe. In order to enhearten the masses, they reported only victories, not defeats; only advances, not forced retreats. After four years of assurance, or at least lively hopes, of victory, suddenly, in the autumn of 1918, the military party was unable longer to hide the truth. The German people were awakened to the fact that the military command had been consistently deluding them, and that the invincible German army was on the verge of surrender. With this terrible humiliation, they could hardly fail to identify the Kaiser.

During the war the governing classes of Germany—the ruling princes, landed families, and great capitalists—while calling upon the people to bend to the load had made not a single gesture in the direction of democracy until they were powerless to make gestures at all. In the midst of the World War, the empress, who was a high Tory in her own style, said to the chancellor, "Herr Bethmann, when we win the war, you must take good care that the Social Democrats lose the right to vote." The tenacious efforts of the ruling classes to hold fast to all their old powers and to yield nothing to popular majorities prevented any concessions to democracy. "In July, 1917," Max of Baden says in his *Memoirs*, "the Kaiser, by right of constitution and custom, had the power to call to the head of the government the man he considered best qualified. Had his choice fallen on a convinced advocate of franchise reform and of no annexations, the Reichstag majority would have accepted the lead of such a chancellor without harassing him with a system of suspicious supervision." The Kaiser either would or could not make even this concession at that time. Every surrender was too late, for events moved swiftly.

When the leading generals decided to start peace negotiations with President Wilson before they met complete defeat, they were unwilling to confess that they had brought the country to ruin. So they requested the chancellor to sign the note of October 4 (p. 386). When he demurred, the Kaiser said impatiently, "The supreme military command considers it necessary; you have not been brought here to make difficulties for it." The notes which passed between the German government and President Wilson have been summarized above. One of the chancellor's chief advisers warned him that no change in the German government short of a republic would satisfy President Wilson. No such suggestion was formally made, but the chancellor was convinced that the retirement of the Kaiser was implied as a preliminary to an armistice. He said, "The demand for abdication would not have been brought up for discussion in my cabinet if Wilson had not deliberately forced the problem of the Kaiser on the German people." So it was partly as an obstacle to a favorable peace that the Kaiser was forced to retire. But he delayed too long, and the peace, as we shall see, was harsh beyond the worst fears of the Germans.

Meanwhile negotiations in regard to an armistice were in progress. Representatives of the German government met General Foch on November 8, 1918, and learned the conditions which the Allies had drawn up for their acceptance.

By the terms of the armistice the Germans were required to evacuate within two weeks all the territory they occupied— Belgium, northeastern France, Luxemburg, as well as Alsace-Lorraine. Moreover, the German troops were to retire beyond the right bank of the Rhine, and that portion of Germany which lies west of the river was to be occupied by troops of the Allies. All German troops in territories formerly belonging to Austria-Hungary, Rumania, Turkey, and Russia were to be immediately withdrawn. Germany was to hand over her war vessels, surrender all her submarines and vast supplies of war material, and put her railroads at the disposal of the Allies.[1] These provisions were designed to make any renewal of the war on Germany's part absolutely impossible. Hard as were the terms, the Germans accepted them promptly, and on November 11 the armistice went into effect. The World War was at an end.

[1] In the armistice, signed on November 11, 1918, Germany was required to surrender 25,000 machine guns, 2500 heavy guns, 2500 field guns, 1700 airplanes, 5000 locomotives, 150,000 railroad cars, 5000 motor trucks, 6 battle cruisers, 10 battleships, 50 destroyers, all her submarines, and much other equipment of military character.

CHAPTER XII

A PERTURBING PEACE

THE PEACE CONFERENCE OF 1919

On January 18, 1919, the anniversary of the day in 1871 when the German Empire had been proclaimed, and in the very hall at Versailles where that ceremony had taken place with much pomp, representatives of the Allied and Associated Powers assembled to formulate the terms of peace and remake the map of Europe. It was a marvelous spectacle. Seventy delegates spoke for thirty-two states. The United States, Great Britain, France, Italy, and Japan had five representatives each. Belgium, Brazil, and Serbia were each assigned three. To Canada, Australia, South Africa, India, China, Greece, Hejaz, Poland, Portugal, Rumania, Siam, and Czechoslovakia, there were allotted two apiece, and the remaining states—New Zealand, Bolivia, Cuba, Ecuador, Guatemala, Haiti, Honduras, Liberia, Nicaragua, Panama, Peru, and Uruguay—each had one delegate.

President Woodrow Wilson, who, contrary to the opinions of his political advisers, insisted on attending the Conference in person, acted for the United States. The spokesman for England was David Lloyd George, once a suspected radical reformer, now the idol of a victorious nation; for France, the grim-visaged premier, Clemenceau, the "Tiger," whose resolute will had aroused all Frenchmen for the last supreme effort; for Italy, the prime minister, Vittorio Orlando, soon to be driven out of his own country by the Fascists for not demanding enough at the peace table. What historic memories did the scene recall to the imagination! It carried the minds of informed spectators back through the long years of Europe's painful travail—back through the wars for Italian and German unity, the Napoleonic struggle, the French Revolution, the partition of Poland, even to the very days when the empire of Rome stretched from the heather of Scotland to the sands of Arabia. What distant and strange lands did it conjure up! The ends of the earth were brought together. The dusky Siamese from the realm of Rama VI and the black spokesman from Liberia sat in conference with the yellow marquis from Japan and the white premier from Australia.

This magnificent assemblage was, however, mainly ceremonial. It seldom met, and then only for the purpose of approving decisions already made. The real work of settling the affairs of the world was first committed to a supreme council of ten members, representing the United States, Great Britain, France, Italy, and Japan. This was later reduced to five. Then Japan dropped out, and finally Italy, leaving only President Wilson and Premiers Lloyd George and Clemenceau—the "Big Three"—who assumed the burden of all the great decisions. On May 6, 1919, their work was completed, and in a secret session of the full conference, at which a digest was read to the assembled delegates, the whole treaty was approved—a few of the powers making reservations or objections. The next day the treaty was presented to the Germans, who, after strenuous and indignant protests, finally signed on the last day of grace, June 28. The German treaty, by far the most important, was followed by agreements with Austria, Hungary, Bulgaria, and Turkey, supplemented by special treaties guaranteeing the rights of minorities in several countries. Collectively, these elaborate documents formed the legal basis of the general European settlement.

The combined treaties make a huge volume. The German treaty alone embraces about eighty thousand words. As a whole, they cover an immense range of subjects—a range so great that only the broadest outlines can be given here. For the purposes of simplicity and clearness, the principal features may be grouped under five main heads: (1) the territorial settlement in Europe; (2) the destruction of German military power; (3) reparations for damages done by the Central Powers (pp. 540 ff.); (4) the disposition of German colonies and protectorates; (5) the League of Nations (pp. 564 ff.). We turn first to the alterations of European boundaries.

THE NEW MAP OF EUROPE

By the terms of the Treaty of Versailles, Germany gave up Alsace-Lorraine to France, and the three towns of Moresnet, Eupen, and Malmédy to Belgium without any referendum to the people. She also ceded a great part of her province of Posen and West Prussia to the restored Polish nation, and she agreed that some of her Silesian possessions should join Poland if the people, by a popular vote called a *plebiscite*, decided in favor of it.[1] She made a similar agreement with regard to Schleswig to determine whether its people preferred to join Denmark, and in 1920 parts of that territory went to Denmark by popular vote. Danzig was made a free city under the control of the League of Nations but within the Polish customs frontiers. To assure to the Poles an outlet to the sea, a "corridor" was cut through German territory, separating Prussia into two parts—an action destined to be a source of great friction. Besides giving up this land in Europe, Germany surrendered all her over-sea colonies, to be turned over later to the British Empire, France, Portugal, Belgium, and Japan under "mandates" of the League of Nations.

By a separate treaty signed at Saint Germain-en-Laye near Paris on September 10, 1919, Austria recognized the fact that the war had broken up the old Austro-Hungarian Empire. In

---

[1] The popular vote took place, amid some violence, in 1920. On the basis of this the League of Nations in 1921 divided upper Silesia between Poland and Germany.

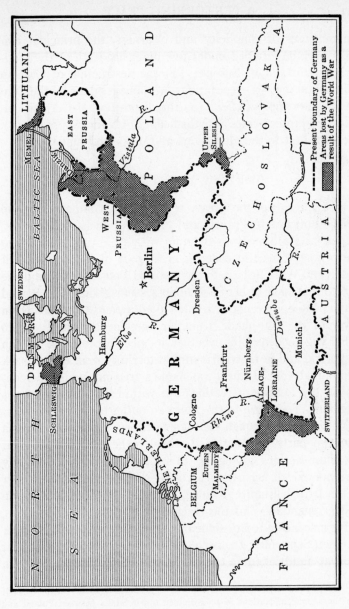

GERMANY SHOWING LOSSES AFTER THE WORLD WAR

Present boundary of Germany
Areas lost by Germany as a
result of the World War

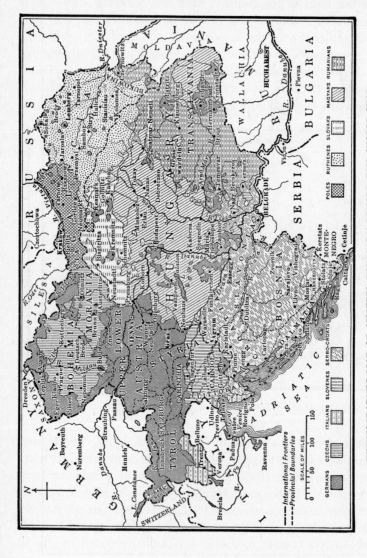

ETHNOGRAPHIC MAP OF AUSTRIA-HUNGARY BEFORE THE WORLD WAR

the last days of the conflict, while the Austrian armies were
crumbling, several of the various nationalities that had long
been united under the government at Vienna declared their
independence. To the north, a large section acquired long ago
in the partitions of Poland was handed over to the new Polish
republic. Between Austria-Hungary and Poland a new Slavic
state, Czechoslovakia, was formed, and Austria recognized its

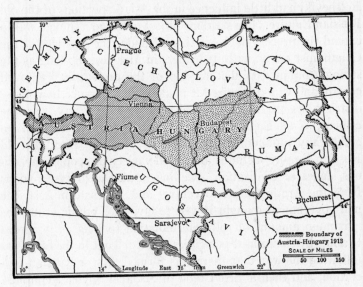

THE AUSTRIAN REPUBLIC AND THE HUNGARIAN MONARCHY

independence. To the south, Trent, South Tyrol, Trieste, and
Istria were ceded to Italy, and several provinces and districts
were united with the enlarged kingdom of Serbia, to form
Yugoslavia. To the east, Hungary was declared independent,
but large cessions were made to Rumania and Yugoslavia. By
this process the once proud Austrian Empire was dissolved,
and Austria transformed into a republic, reduced in size to
an area less than that of Ireland.

Although Russia was not represented at the Paris Peace

Conference, her boundaries were readjusted in the general settlement. We have spoken of the break-up of Russia just before the close of the war (p. 370). The new Bolshevik government, by the treaty of Brest-Litovsk (March, 1918), "withdrew" from Finland, the Baltic states, Poland, and the Ukraine, and from portions of the Caucasian region. White Russia declared its independence, and for the time being the Bolsheviki had little influence in the Asiatic portions of the old Russian Empire. The supreme object of the government was to extend the process of "sovietizing" under the auspices of the Communist party, with its leaders in Moscow. So long as the strongly organized "dictatorship of the proletariat" enjoyed control and was recognized it made little difference how many districts set up republics. The Communist party was the cement, as an English writer has said, which could bind together any number of "autonomous" states. Since the old Russian Empire included an untold variety of peoples in various stages of civilization, dwelling in all the diverse regions from the Arctic Ocean to central and far-eastern Asia, the new government thought it wise to give each ethnic group the maximum amount of self-determination so long as it agreed to abide by communist principles. So it fell out in the ten years following the war that there was formed, first a Russian federation, and then a vast Union of Socialist Soviet Republics, which included practically all the former Russian Empire except Finland, the Baltic states, and Poland.

The former dominions of the Tsar now fall into two classes. First, there is what we may call Russia proper, namely the Russian Socialist Federal Soviet Republic. This comprises the provinces of Old Russia and Siberia. It was called a federation because it included eleven autonomous republics, which had sprung up in Russia itself and in eastern Siberia, and a number of "areas," some of them described as "autonomous."

Second, there is the Union of Socialist Soviet Republics, which has been formed by the adhesion of six other soviet

WESTERN PORTION OF UNION OF SOCIALIST SOVIET REPUBLICS

states that have joined Russia proper but are at liberty to withdraw from the federation. These six soviet republics are White Russia, the Ukraine, the Transcaucasian Socialist Federal Soviet Republic (composed of three republics—Armenia, Azerbaijan, and Georgia), the Turkmen Republic, the Uzbek Republic, and the Tadjik Republic, the last three having been established after the war, in the regions of central Asia conquered by the Tsar's forces in the latter part of the nineteenth century (pp. 160 ff.).

It will be noted that the word "Russian" does not appear in the title of the Union. The Bolsheviki, unlike rulers of the old régime, are—in theory at least—indifferent to nationality and language. They are intent on spreading their doctrines, which they believe are essential to all peoples, regardless of race or speech. The Russian Communist party is practically dominant in the Third International, whose object is to unite the workers of the world, wherever they may live. There is no call to "Russify," only to "sovietize," converts. The constitution of the Russian Socialist Federal Soviet Republic and of the larger Union will be considered later, as well as the policy of the Bolsheviki after the revolution of 1917 (see pages 470 ff.).

Out of three great fragments taken from Russia, Germany, and Austria, the republic of Poland was formed by revolutionary Polish leaders in 1918, and its independence was recognized by the Treaty of Versailles. Thus was restored the unity that had been destroyed by the three partitions which had taken place in the eighteenth century, nearly a hundred and fifty years before (Vol. I, pp. 155–161). In this way was realized the long-cherished dream of the Poles—the ideal for which Kosciusko had fought so valiantly after serving under Washington in the war of American independence, and for which so many Poles had given their lives in the years that followed the destruction of their state.

For other branches of the Slavic race, the defeat of the Central Powers in the World War brought the "great day" of re-

joicing. Among the peoples that cheered President Wilson's
ideal of self-government for each nationality, there was none
more enthusiastic than the Czechs, of whom there were many in
the United States. Indeed, their most popular leader, Thomas
Masaryk, came to America during the war and helped to carry

YUGOSLAVIA, THE KINGDOM OF SERBS, CROATS, AND SLOVENES,
SHOWING THE VARIOUS COMPONENTS

on the agitation against Austria-Hungary. At the close of the
struggle the old territories of Bohemia, Moravia, Silesia, and
Slovakia united in forming the republic of Czechoslovakia,
with Masaryk as president. Beaten in battle, Austria had to
accept the new nation as an equal.

By a curious turn of fate the little kingdom of Serbia, on
which the mighty Austria-Hungary had declared war so lightly
in the summer of 1914, came out of the conflict considerably

larger and more powerful than Austria herself. In the general
settlement at the close of the war, Carniola and the southern
portions of Styria[1] (combined under the name Slovenia),
Croatia, Slavonia, Voyvodina, Bosnia, Herzegovina, Dalmatia, and Montenegro were united with Serbia to form the
kingdom of the Serbs, Croats, and Slovenes—Yugoslavia.

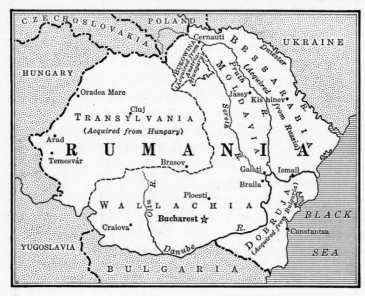

GREATER RUMANIA

Rumania likewise profited from the ruin of Austria-Hungary
and the collapse of Russia. She had joined the Allies in the
war on the Central Powers, after making terms as to what
she should receive when the spoils were distributed at the end.
When at last the Allies were victorious, Rumania was rewarded. She annexed Bessarabia (which had belonged to
Russia since 1812), Bukowina (which was a part of Austria),
Transylvania, and other portions of Hungary. In October,
1922, King Ferdinand and Queen Marie, who had succeeded

[1] For these old provinces of Austria see accompanying colored map.

to the throne in 1914, were crowned with great splendor as rulers of the enlarged kingdom. In vain did the Russians protest that Bessarabia had been stolen from them, and that they would never surrender it. In vain did Hungarians declare that they would never accept their fate—"No, never!" Thus was Greater Rumania launched upon its uncertain course.

For centuries the Christian powers had cried that "the Turk must be driven from Europe." Indeed, since the opening of the nineteenth century the territory ruled by Turkey in Europe had been diminished step by step, and it seemed in 1919 that at last the Turks would be driven back across the Straits. They had joined the Central Powers in the war and had shared their defeat. It looked as if their doom was at hand. In fact, in August, 1920, the Turkish representatives at the Peace Conference were forced to sign the Treaty of Sèvres, which reduced their country to a petty state and imposed upon it a heavy burden of damages.

In the meantime a powerful party of Turkish patriots, calling themselves Nationalists, had been organized under the leadership of Mustafa Kemal. Determined to save their country at all costs, they refused to abide by the Treaty of Sèvres, overthrew the Sultan, proclaimed a republic, and announced that they were ready to fight. When the Greeks declared war on Turkey to secure some of the territory awarded to them in the treaty, the Nationalists badly defeated the invaders. As the Allies were now in no mood for another war, they came to terms in July, 1923, and signed the Treaty of Lausanne, which in effect marked a victory for Turkey.

By the provisions of this treaty the Allied forces were to evacuate Constantinople and turn that city over to the Turkish government. The Dardanelles were to be open for the passage of ships of all nations, but it was agreed that the Straits belonged to Turkey. Although Turkey lost Syria, Mesopotamia, Palestine, and Arabia (p. 384 and pp. 514 ff.), she regained Smyrna and she won back Eastern Thrace, thus keeping a

T

foothold in Europe. Besides winning these territorial advantages, she got rid of the hated "Capitulations," or right of foreigners in Turkey to be tried by their own courts according to their own laws (see pages 514 ff. and map).

As an ally of the Central Powers, Bulgaria also was punished by a loss of territory. On the west a portion of Macedonia was turned over to Yugoslavia; on the south a small section was ceded to Greece; on the north a rich region on the Black Sea, the Dobruja, was transferred to Rumania. In this way Bulgaria was cut off entirely from the Ægean Sea and merely allowed a right of passage to and from it for commercial purposes.

The disposition of the German colonies and portions of the old Ottoman Empire also presented knotty problems. After much discussion an ingenious solution was adopted. It was agreed that the German colonies and some of the former Turkish provinces, which were in a backward stage, should be placed under the control of certain powers which were to act as "mandatories" for the League of Nations and administer these territories as "a sacred trust of civilization." In accordance with this arrangement, all the German colonies were turned over to the Allied and Associated Powers and later assigned to their respective mandatories. German East Africa went mainly to Great Britain, and German Southwest Africa to the Union of South Africa (pp. 202 and 505). Togoland and Cameroons were divided between Great Britain and France. German holdings in the southern Pacific were assigned to New Zealand and Australia, and those north of the equator, to Japan. The mandatory principle applied to backward races was not adopted in the case of German rights in Shantung, all of which were transferred to Japan. It was this action, which China deemed a violation of her rights, that led the Chinese delegation to withhold their signatures from the treaty.

This brief review of the territorial changes in Europe forms a prelude to further developments, which will be dealt with in

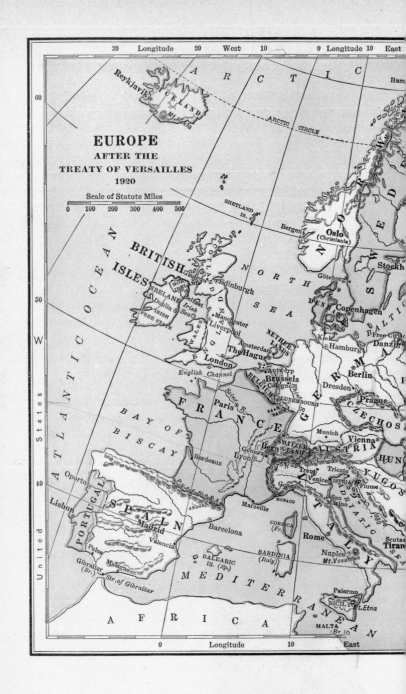

EUROPE

AFTER THE
TREATY OF VERSAILLES
1920

Scale of Statute Miles

0   100   200   300   400   500

very lowfrom 30 Greenwich 40 50 NOVAYA ZEMLYA 60 70

OCEAN

NORTH CAPE

FINLAND

White Sea
Archangel

Dvina R.

RUSSIAN

SOCIALIST FEDERAL SOVIET REPUBLIC

SIBERIA

URAL MTS.

Lake Ladoga
Leningrad (Petrograd)
Helsingfors
G. of Finland
Revel
ESTONIA
Riga
LATVIA
LITHUANIA
Kovno
Vilna
WHITE RUSSIA
Warsaw
POLAND
Lemberg
GALICIA
Budapest
HUNGARY
RUMANIA
Bucharest
Danube R.
Belgrade
BULGARIA
Sofia
Balkan Mts.
Salonika
GREECE
Athens
CRETE

Volga R.
Nizhni Novgorod
Moscow
Samara
Ufa
Ural R.

UNION OF SOCIALIST SOVIET REPUBLICS

Kiev
UKRAINE
Dnieper R.
Odessa
Sea of Azov
Astrakhan
CASPIAN SEA
Baku
Tiflis
CAUCASUS MTS. Mt.Elbrus
TRANSCAUCASIA
Batum

BLACK SEA

Constantinople
TURKEY
Angora
ANATOLIA

Japan

from 30 Greenwich 40

COMPARATIVE AREA
400 MILES
250 MILES
PENNSYLVANIA
45,000 SQ. MILES
THIS RECTANGLE CONTAINS
100,000 SQ. MILES

succeeding pages. The most essential thing for one desirous of understanding the course of affairs is to study carefully the accompanying general map of Europe and the more detailed maps of particular regions. The actual outlines of the old and new states and a comparison of them with the European boundaries before the war (see map, p. 40) are more illuminating than many pages of text.

The Punishment and Crippling of Germany

In the formulation of the terms of peace at Versailles everything proceeded upon the assumption that the Central Powers had been guilty of bringing on the war and that the Allies were innocent. It mattered not whether it was a question of territorial changes, of damages to be paid, or of punitive restrictions on German commerce—the principle of German guilt controlled all decisions. Early in the transactions at Versailles the Allied and Associated Governments appointed a special committee to report on the "responsibility of the authors of the war." And this committee rendered a categorical judgment, as follows: "The war was deliberately planned by the Central Powers and by their allies, Turkey and Bulgaria, and is the result of actions which were committed with premeditation and intentionally in order to make it inevitable." No verdict could be more sweeping or definite. Wronged and innocent statesmen, ran the argument, had assembled at Paris to decide the fate of guilty offenders.

The representatives of the various nations which had lately been in arms against Germany felt that their fellow countrymen were in a mood of wrath that demanded vindictive measures. Lloyd George, for example, agreed to the punishment inflicted on Germany, with the idea that his constituents would be satisfied with nothing less and that he could not return home with the hope of a cordial reception unless the old enemy was bled white.

The commission on reparations and economic matters, appointed by the Peace Conference to draw up the bill of damages to be collected from the Central Powers, likewise operated on the theory of "sole guilt." In various messages President Wilson had taken the position that there should be no punitive annexations and indemnities, and that reparations should be limited in general to the cost of restoring the invaded areas; but before accepting the armistice terms, the Allies interpreted "restoration" to mean "that compensation will be made by Germany for all damage done to the civilian population of the Allies, and their property, by the aggression of Germany, by land, by sea, and from the air."

On this assumption the majority of the commission on reparations took the ground, to use the language of Bernard Baruch, an American member, that "the war being a wrongful act by Germany, Germany was responsible for all the loss and damage, direct and indirect, which resulted therefrom." "One of the Allies," Mr. Baruch continues, "went even further and made claim for loss and damage resulting from the fact that the armistice was concluded so unexpectedly that the termination of hostilities involved it in financial loss. . . . Both Mr. Hughes [premier of Australia] and Lord Sumner [another British representative on the commission] also likened the situation of Great Britain to that of Belgium, on the ground that Great Britain's war costs had resulted from Germany's breach of the treaty establishing the neutrality of Belgium, to which Great Britain was a party." Premier Hughes declared that "every Australian who had placed a mortgage on his house to buy a war bond was as definitely entitled to reparation as was every Frenchman whose house had been burned by the Germans." In the mind of some of the Allied agents the main issue was whether to destroy Germany utterly as "a guilty criminal" or let her live in order to permit the victors to squeeze money out of her, like juice out of a lemon, "until you can hear the pips squeak," as Sir Eric Geddes put it.

Thus, on the confident assumption of German guilt, the Peace Conference drew up the clauses dealing with Germany's bill of damages—"reparations," to use the more euphonious term. What should be the nature of the bill and what should be included in it? On this question there was great diversity of opinion. The American members of the committee on reparations consistently urged that a definite sum be fixed, and that the armistice terms should be strictly interpreted to mean only "damage done to the civilian population of the Allied and Associated Powers." But on both points the Americans surrendered on instructions from President Wilson. Allied estimates of damages exceeded the American estimates by billions of dollars and went far beyond Germany's ability to pay. No agreement on a fixed sum could be reached. So, after weeks of acrid discussion, it was decided to leave the amount of reparations indefinite—to be determined later by a Reparations Commission.

The Allied representatives at the conference also insisted that there should be included in the bill for damages the cost of pensions and "separation allowances," or payments granted by the Allied governments to the families and dependents of men in military service. To this contention the American members on the commission replied that these were war costs, not damages done to civilian populations. The deadlock was again broken by President Wilson, who in this case sided against his advisers; pensions and separation allowances were included, thus doubling at one stroke the amount to be collected from Germany—in all about $33,000,000,000, as later reckoned by the Reparations Commission in 1921.

Besides imposing on Germany a huge and indefinite bill for damages, the Peace Conference laid upon her commerce and business enterprise many onerous restrictions. For a period of five years—which could be extended by the Council of the League of Nations—the right of Germany to regulate her own commerce and fix her customs dues was limited in the interest of Allied trade and industry. All the property, rights, and interests in Germany belonging to persons, associations, and corporations of the Allied countries were to be restored immediately in full; on the other hand, subject to certain exceptions, the "Allied and Associated Powers" reserved the right to liquidate all property belonging to Germans within their respective territories and to apply the proceeds to the bills drawn up against the German government, leaving the former German owners to collect as best they could from their own government.

Under these provisions Germans owning property in former enemy countries lost millions invested in land and business enterprises, and had a hard struggle to get anything back; at the end of ten years many of their patents had been confiscated, and large sums of money due them were still unpaid. By way of a supplement, the Allies, in taking away from Germany her over-sea possessions, seized the railways and other government property there and left Germany responsible for the payment of debts incurred in creating this property. The Elbe, Oder, Niemen, and Danube rivers were internationalized from certain points to their respective outlets and placed under the control of international commissions on which Germany had a minority representation. The ports of Hamburg and Stettin were forced to lease to Czechoslovakia for a period of ninety-nine years free zones for the direct transit of goods coming from or going to that country.

German railways were laid under the obligation to provide certain through services in the interest of the Allied countries. The vessels of all nations were given the same rights on the Rhine as the German vessels enjoyed; the best German vessels and tugs were to be transferred to France; France was authorized to use the river for power and irrigation; and the entire stream was placed under an international commission. To complete the disruption of Germany's network of world trade, her great submarine cable lines were handed over to the victors, for their advantage, and privately owned lines, less depreciation, were credited to the reparations account.

Although France gave up her long-cherished demand for the whole west bank of the Rhine, she forced Germany to cede to her "in full and absolute possession, with exclusive rights of exploitation, unencumbered and free from all debts and charges of any kind, the coal mines situated in the Saar Basin" —a rich mineral district, purely German in population. Germany was compelled to renounce the government of this territory in favor of the League of Nations, as trustee. At the end of fifteen years the inhabitants of the region were to be called upon to "indicate the sovereignty under which they desire to be placed." Taking advantage of this provision, a number of French imperialists laid plans for detaching the Saar Basin from Germany when the day of the referendum arrived, if not sooner. As a part of the Rhine policy, Germany was forbidden to maintain or construct any fortification on either bank to the west of a line drawn fifty miles east of that river, thus leaving the whole district open to invasion from the west.

In connection with reparations the entire economic life of Germany was subjected to the control and inspection of the Reparations Commission. This commission and its agents, maintained at the expense of Germany, were given in Germany the rights and immunities enjoyed by duly accredited diplomatic representatives of friendly powers. Furthermore, the German government was pledged to supply "all information which the commission may require relative to the financial situation and operations and to the property, productive capacity, and stocks and current production of raw materials and manufactured articles of Germany and her nationals, and, further, any information relative to military operations which in the judgment of the commission may be necessary for the assessment of Germany's liability for reparation." Germany agreed to make the laws and issue the orders required to give full effect to this control over her industries and finances.

Among the miscellaneous provisions of the Treaty of Versailles was an article providing for the trial of the Kaiser. The Allied and Associated Powers publicly arraigned "William II, of Hohenzollern, formerly German emperor, for a supreme offense against international morality and the sanctity of treaties," and proposed that he should be tried by a tribunal of five judges chosen by the United States, Great Britain, France, Italy, and Japan. This court was to be "guided by the highest motives of international policy, with a view to vindicating the solemn obligations of international undertakings and the validity of international morality." A request was to be directed to the government of the Netherlands for the surrender of William in order that he might be put on trial.

As a guarantee ("sanction") for the execution of the terms imposed by the treaty, it was stipulated that German territory west of the Rhine was to be occupied by Allied and Associated troops for a period of fifteen years, subject to arrangements for a gradual withdrawal if the conditions of the treaty were faithfully carried out. But "if at that date the guarantees against unprovoked aggression by Germany are not considered sufficient by the Allied and Associated Governments, the evacuation of the occupying troops may be delayed to the extent regarded as necessary for the purpose of obtaining the required guarantees." Moreover, if the Reparation Commission found that Germany was refusing to fulfill all or any part of her treaty obligations with regard to reparation, either during or after the expiration of the fifteen-year period, then all or part of the region west of the Rhine was to be reoccupied by Allied and Associated forces. Germany agreed in advance to accept any arrangements made for such occupation in the future and to pay all costs.[1]

[1] The troops of the United States were withdrawn in 1922, and arrangements were made, in 1929, at the Hague Conference on the Young plan (pp. 542 ff.) for retiring all foreign troops from Germany (except the Saar) by June, 1930.

To complete the supremacy of the victors, Germany's military power was destroyed. The entire navy, with minor exceptions, was turned over to the Allied and Associated Powers, and the total equipment for the future was limited to six battleships, six light cruisers, and certain small vessels, but no submarines. The total number of enlisted men and officers for the army was fixed at not more than one hundred thousand, the former General Staff was dissolved, and the manufacture of munitions was restricted.

Against the severe terms of this treaty, the German delegation at Paris indignantly protested. It insisted that the transfer of millions of German citizens to surrounding countries was contrary to President Wilson's principle of self-determination. While admitting that according to present conceptions of right an injustice had been done in 1871, when Alsace-Lorraine was annexed by Germany without consulting the people, the delegation argued that an injustice was now being done by returning the provinces with their large German element, without a referendum allowing the inhabitants to decide their fate. While accepting in full the obligation to pay Belgium and France for damages done to the civilian population, Germany objected to the size of the bill and to the inclusion of pensions and separation allowances, to making payments to Serbia, Italy, and other countries, and to the dictatorial powers over her economic life vested in the Reparations Commission. She contended that there was an incompatibility between the attempt to collect such an immense bill and the action of the Allies in taking away her colonies, shipping, cables, and other means for producing wealth with which to meet her obligations.

"No limit is fixed," ran the German counter proposals, "save the capacity of the German people to pay, determined not by their standard of life, but solely by their ability to meet the demands of their enemies by their labor. The German people would thus be condemned to perpetual slave labor." In accepting the League of Nations, Germany objected to being excluded from it at the outset and to being thus treated as an outlaw among the countries of the world. But in filing objections the German delegation made definite offers to make payments up to a maximum sum far in excess of the amount the Allies were finally compelled by economic necessity to accept at the hands of the Young Commission in 1929 (pp. 542 ff.).

In response to these German proposals the Allies made a sarcastic reply. They recited once more the horrors of the war, listed German misdeeds committed during the conflict, and laid the entire responsibility for planning and starting the war on the Central Powers. With respect to President Wilson's promise of a peace of justice, they argued that to compel Germany to pay for damages done "to the very uttermost of her power . . . is of the essence of justice." The German delegation had referred to President Wilson's statement that war was not being waged on the German people but on their imperial masters and had called attention to the fact that now the Germans had effected a revolution, overthrowing their old government. In their reply the Allies declared that the revolution had been postponed until the German armies were defeated, that the German people had subscribed to war loans, obeyed the government, supported the war. "They shared the responsibility for the policy of their government, for at any moment, had they willed it, they could have reversed it." Although some concessions were made, the Allies insisted that the main principles of the treaty should stand unchanged, and prepared to invade Germany in case the government failed to sign the document as finally drawn. Under these circumstances the German delegation, as we have seen, signed the treaty at Versailles on June 28, 1919, thus accepting a verdict imposed on them by force.

On the day after the peace treaty was finally signed, Colonel E. M. House, the intimate adviser of President Wilson, entered in his diary a record of misgivings. "To those who are saying that the Treaty is bad," he noted, "and should never have been made and that it will involve Europe in infinite difficulties in its enforcement, I feel like admitting it." Still, the difficulties were great, and he doubted whether anything else was possible under the circumstances. "And yet," he went on to say, "I wish we had taken the other road, even if it were less smooth, both now and afterward, than the one we took. We would at least have gone in the right direction, and if those who follow us had made it impossible to go the full length of the journey planned, the responsibility would have rested with them and not with us."

As a matter of fact, President Wilson did at one time threaten to break off negotiations and sail for home, but the responsibilities for such an action were immense, in view of the Republican victory in the congressional elections of November, 1918, and the certainty that his political foes would make the utmost capital out of the charge that he had been "tender to the Germans." So he stayed to the end, counting on the slow working of time and the League of Nations to undo what seemed to him the impossible and vengeful features incorporated in the treaty of peace.

PLIGHT OF EUROPE AFTER THE WAR

Under the terms of the Paris settlement Europe went about the bewildering task of putting her house in order. The condition of affairs at the close of the war in 1918 was quite different from that at the end of the Franco-German war in 1871, when a moderate bill of damages could be collected from the conquered, and the soldiers marched home. The whole continent of Europe, except the Scandinavian countries and Holland, Switzerland, and Spain, had been directly involved in the war. Entire nations, not merely armies, had been embattled. Nearly all able-bodied men of fighting age had been sent to the front, while the men, women, and children left behind had been mobilized to furnish food and materials for the nations at war.

All available factories had been turned from peaceful industries to the manufacture of war materials. Foreign trade had
been demoralized—in the case of Germany, almost destroyed.
The map of Europe had been remade. Emperors, kings, and
princes had been overthrown. And to crown the disorder, there
had been a communistic revolution in Russia that threatened
to spread to other countries and upset all that had been left
of the old régime.

It is now estimated that from first to last nearly sixty million men were mobilized by the belligerents on both sides—
taken away from pursuits of peace to those of slaughter and
destruction. Of the staggering total about eight or nine million, mainly boys and young men, were killed or died of wounds
and disease. Of those who returned home from the front approximately eighteen million carried wounds—ranging from
minor hurts to terrible injuries from bullets, shrapnel, gas,
and shell shock that forever disabled them for useful labor
of any kind.

When the soldiers returned from the front and proposed to
resume their regular work, they found awaiting them often
unemployment and always greatly increased living expenses.
The total cost of the war in money paid out for fighting and in
damage done to property could hardly be determined accurately, but the best estimate places it at more than three hundred billion dollars; that is, a sum at least equal in amount to
the value of all the farms, houses, factories, railways, office
buildings, furniture, telephones, telegraphs, mines, and other
property in the United States from the Atlantic to the Pacific.
The national debt of Italy was raised from three billion to
eleven billion, that of France from seven billion to twenty-
seven, that of Germany from one billion to forty (leaving out
of account her bill for damages), and that of Great Britain from
three and one-half billion to thirty-four. In the case of Italy
the debt was almost equal to the total national wealth, and the
government of France owed a sum equal to half the amount

that the French people possessed. Since heavy taxes had to be laid to pay these debts, there were good grounds for disputes among the voters of the various nations as to who should pay the most.

Afraid to tax the people heavily, all the war governments on the Continent began to issue paper money in vast quantities —that is, inflated the currency and raised the cost of living with every new flood of paper notes. Gold and silver practically went out of circulation. Day after day carloads of printed money were spread abroad among the people, until the state of affairs became simply absurd. The French franc, once worth about twenty cents, gradually fell until it reached about two cents in specie value. The German mark, worth about twenty-four cents when the war broke out, stood at seven cents in 1918, and then fell with lightning rapidity. By November 30, 1923, Germany had four hundred quintillion marks in circulation. In the summer of that year an American traveler paid a billion and a half marks for a dinner in a German restaurant and gave the waiter a tip of four hundred million marks—in all about three dollars in United States currency. In Russia, as someone said, only astronomers accustomed to deal in billions and trillions could keep a grocery store.

Naturally, it was very difficult for anybody to do any regular business while this abuse of paper money lasted, and the people who depended on wages and salaries for a living were driven almost to desperation. For example, a German mechanic who agreed to work a week for two billion marks might find on pay day at the end of the week that the money in his envelope would buy only about half as much as on Monday, when he began. Evidently nothing could be done to reëstablish industry on sound principles until a new monetary system was put into effect.

The state of European industries after the war added to the general distress. All northern France had been overrun by armies and lay in ruins. Russia was racked by revolution, and manufacturing was almost at a standstill. Germany was shaken from center to circumference. Nearly all her banks, industries, investments, and commercial enterprises in various parts of the world had been seized by the victorious Allies. Her colonies and all the German property in them had been taken over by the conquerors. In their endeavor to ruin Germany's over-sea business, the Allies had confiscated all her merchant ships of 1600 tons burden and over, and half her ships between that tonnage and 1000 tons. Austria, once the manufacturing center for a large and prosperous empire, was now reduced to a petty state with banks, factories, and business concerns enough for a country five or six times as large. And as all the new states that rose after the war wanted to be independent manufacturing countries, they put high tariffs on goods imported, thus injuring their neighbor's business. In addition to all this, there was the legacy of hatred bequeathed by the war, which made the peoples of the various countries unwilling to buy from their former enemies or do business with them on fair terms. To crown it all, plagues, fevers, and famines ravaged eastern and southeastern Europe, spreading misery, starvation, and death in their wake.

CHAPTER XIII

CHIEF FACTORS IN RECONSTRUCTION

THE NEW CONSTITUTIONS OF EUROPE

As a result of the war, there were necessarily new forms of government to be devised to meet the novel conditions. The old states of Germany, Austria, and Russia had to frame republican constitutions to take the place of their former monarchical organization. New states had appeared (Poland, Finland, Latvia, Lithuania, Estonia, Czechoslovakia, and Yugoslavia) whose territories had, with slight exceptions, been subject to foreign rule and whose new independence demanded the creation of appropriate institutions. Many serious difficulties faced those who had to draw up the new constitutions and attempt to launch them successfully. It will be recalled that there was a time of great uncertainty in the United States after independence was established, although it had excellent political traditions compared with the new states of Europe. Several years were required to agree on a constitution and several years more to get the government into smooth working order. Anyone who knows the history of the United States between the years of 1783 and 1795 can easily imagine the problems which the new countries in Europe had to meet after their independence was proclaimed.

When these new plans of government are reviewed together, it is seen that they present certain similarities among themselves, and also certain contrasts with the older constitutions, such as those of France and the United States. All the states which rose on the ruins of the three great empires—Germany, Russia, and Austria-Hungary—were republics, with the ex-

ception of Hungary, which fell under a provisional dictatorship and kept the crown of Saint Stephen ready for a day of
restoration. None of them declared openly in favor of a
monarchy and called in a prince to rule over them. Everywhere chambers of peers speaking for great landlords were
swept away; everywhere supreme power was declared to be
vested in the people. "Privileges or discriminations due to
birth or rank and recognized by law are abolished," run the
words of the new German constitution. While Russia restricted the right to vote to citizens "who earn their livelihood
by productive labor and soldiers and sailors in the Red army
and navy," this rule, in theory at least, excluded from voting
only a small part of the adult population—about 1 per cent
of the people over eighteen years of age in rural regions and
perhaps as high as 6 per cent in the cities. In other words, the
general tendency of the new European constitutions was in the
direction of republican and democratic principles rather than
of monarchical and upper-class rule.

The World War, which was supposed to be a supreme test
of masculine valor, hastened the establishment of woman suffrage. It is true that the woman-suffrage movement was well
under way before the war broke out, but the conflict quickened
rather than retarded it. Nearly all the new constitutions
granted women the right to vote, and several of the old constitutions were amended in the same direction. Within less than
a decade after the war began, the ballot had been given to
women in Austria, Czechoslovakia, Denmark, Great Britain,
Estonia, Finland, Germany, Latvia, Lithuania, the Netherlands, Norway, Poland, Russia, Sweden, and the United
States. Of the great Western powers that took part in the
"war for democracy," only France and Italy refused to
admit women to the suffrage. In addition to proclaiming the
political equality of the sexes, the German constitution declared that "men and women have fundamentally the same
civil rights."

By a remarkable series of laws Great Britain applied many of the principles implicit in the German provision. In 1919 Parliament passed a general act abolishing a long list of disqualifications imposed on women, and opened to them nearly all public offices and the civil vocations and callings, including the practice of law. In 1924 a mother was made legally competent to act as the guardian of her own children on the death of the father—a right previously withheld from her. A revision of the British property law in 1926 made drastic changes in favor of women, granting them substantial equality with respect to both personal and real property. In other countries similar legislation enlarged the legal rights of women and liberalized divorce laws. Thus more than a hundred years after Mary Wollstonecraft (Vol. I, p. 347) issued her famous call for liberty, "the emancipation of women" seemed at last in sight. "Feminism" had become respectable.

Turning now to the machinery of government, we find that on the eve of the World War there were, broadly speaking, two kinds of popular rule. One was the English parliamentary system, already described (pp. 54 ff.), in which the majority in the parliament selected the cabinet officers and directed the whole government; the other was the American "presidential system," in which the legislative and executive departments were kept separate—the legislature making the laws, and the president appointing his own cabinet and enforcing the laws.

When the constitution-makers set to work in Europe after the war, they generally adopted the English plan rather than the American. They provided, it is true, for a president, but they gave him few powers. To the legislature they assigned the right of controlling the cabinet and supervising the enforcement of the laws. In Poland, for example, the president was given, in constitutional theory, a position akin to that enjoyed by the president of France: he was made a figurehead, without even the right to veto laws, and the cabinet was made responsible to the parliament. In Czechoslovakia, on

T

the other hand, the president was given a veto; he was authorized to dissolve the parliament and call a new election, and he was empowered to appoint cabinet officers, but only men approved by the parliament.

When the Germans were making their constitution in 1919, they considered the American system very carefully. Conservatives wanted to copy it, to some extent at least, arguing that a strong and independent president was necessary to hold the country together and keep order. Radical socialists, fearing the rise of a Bonaparte, opposed the presidential system strenuously, advocating in its place an executive council responsible to the parliament. Between the extremes lay the final compromise. The German president, unlike his neighbor west of the Rhine, is not elected by the legislative chambers in joint session but directly by the voters at large. In contrast with the American president he does not have the veto power, but he may place a check on laws by referring any bill passed by parliament to the people for decision at the polls. He cannot appoint his cabinet officers at his own pleasure, as the American president does, but must take men who are acceptable to the majority in the parliament. In case of a controversy between the parliament and the president, the former may propose the recall of the latter. In that case an election is held. If the president is defeated, he goes out of office; if the balloting is in his favor, the parliament is dissolved.

Almost all the new constitutions provided schemes for giving each political party a number of representatives in parliament corresponding closely to the number of its votes cast in the elections. Such a scheme is called "proportional representation." Under the old system of straight election (which obtains generally in the United States except in a few cities—for example, Cleveland), whenever a party gets a majority or, as a rule, a plurality of the votes in a district, all its candidates are declared elected, and the minority has no representative at all. Thus it may happen in a city election, for instance, that the Republicans have twelve thousand votes and win all the aldermen, and that the Democrats have eleven thousand votes and do not win a single seat. Under proportional representation each party is assigned a number of seats, "proportioned" roughly to the number of votes it can muster. The method for reaching this result is complicated and need not detain us, but it is important to remember that a large number of the European countries have adopted the principle in one form or another.

From the Declaration of the Rights of Man, issued during the French Revolution, down to 1918, a great deal was heard about "rights"—about property rights and freedom of speech, of the press, and of religion. Little was said about the "duties" of citizens toward the government—apart from paying taxes and bearing arms—and not much about the duty of the government toward the people. In other words, the emphasis was on individual rights. The new constitutions of Europe, except that of Russia, also proclaim the rights of man, but they add important sections on the duties of citizens and governments. The German constitution, for example, announces that property rights carry with them "property duties," to be exercised in a way to serve "the general welfare." It also states that "the regulation of economic life must conform to the principles of justice, with the object of assuring humane conditions to all. Within these limits the economic liberty of the individual shall be protected."

Russia departed frankly from all precedents. Instead of guaranteeing the rights of property, the Russian constitution abolishes them. It proclaims not the rights of man but "the rights of laboring and exploited peoples." Instead of giving the right to vote to property-owners, as was the old custom generally in Europe, it takes it away from them and confers it only upon "productive laborers." A great deal was said in other countries also about establishing "workers' councils," and the German constitution actually provided for these as well as for a regular parliament; but the experiment did not prove to be of any special significance. In short, the new constitutions of Europe were compromises of some kind between individualism and socialism, some leaning in one direction and some in the other.

So much for the more striking characteristics of the new European constitutions. Owing to their size, their importance in European affairs, and the radical character of their revolutions, the new constitutions of Germany and Russia invite special attention.

When the German government appealed for peace in the autumn of 1918, President Wilson replied that he could not take the word of the present rulers in Germany and asked to hear from the German people. Not long afterwards the old autocratic class system was completely overthrown. The Kaiser abdicated, and the princely rulers of the several German states followed his example. Thereupon a republican form of government was established for each of the states and for the federation as a whole.

The new federal constitution, adopted in 1919, conferred on all men and women over twenty-one years of age the right to vote. It provided that the president of the republic should be elected by popular vote for a term of seven years. In place of the old Federal Council (*Bundesrat*) it set up a National Council (*Reichsrat*), or upper house of the parliament, consisting of one representative each from the small states and certain additional members from the larger states, on the basis of population. This corresponds to our Senate so far as it is made up of representatives of the various states (*Länder*) in the German Federation. The *Reichstag*, or lower chamber, is elected by the voters on principles of proportional representation.

It should be noted that those who drew up the new German constitution retained the old name of *Deutsches Reich*, in spite of the fact that there was no longer an emperor. This is to be explained by the fact that *Reich* means "dominion" or "realm" as well as "empire" in the historic sense of the word.

In the general overturn Prussia was declared a republic. The old three-class system of voting (p. 50) was abolished, and a democratic constitution was adopted for that ancient kingdom over which the Hohenzollerns had so long ruled "by the grace of God." Equal suffrage was given to all men and women. The diet, or lower house of the Prussian legislature, was authorized to choose the premier, and he was empowered to select the other members of the cabinet. The Prussian house of lords was abolished, and in its place was put a state council composed of members elected by local district assemblies. In a word, where the Hohenzollerns and the Junkers had once run things to suit themselves, there was founded a republic, governed by a parliament elected by the people without any distinction between rich and poor, men and women. It looked as if the impossible had come to pass.

Going beyond these reforms in the old system, the Germans adopted a number of new devices in their government. They introduced proportional representation, as we have seen; and while they refused the president the veto power over laws passed by the parliament, they allowed him, if he wished, to refer such laws to the voters for approval or rejection at the polls. They also adopted the principle of the initiative and referendum so extensively used in Switzerland and in the western part of the United States. The new German constitution contains an article which permits one tenth of the qualified voters, by petition, to propose a law—that is, "initiate" it— and require the government to submit it to the people for their verdict at an election. If one twentieth of the voters dislike a law passed by the parliament, they may compel the government to refer it to the people for their judgment, on a referendum.

The new Russian constitution, adopted in 1918 and later amended in several details, presented a sharp contrast, as we have already said, to the other constitutions of the world. In the first place, it abolished private ownership of land, declaring all land to be common property for the use of the people.

It likewise "nationalized" banks, forests, mines, waterfalls, and factories; that is, added them to the railways and other property already owned by the government. In short, it declared that the means of production and distribution were national property and put the management of this property in the hands of commissions representing the all-Russian Congress of Soviets. It even attempted to close private stores and shops and to transfer all their business to government officers.

Under the new constitution Russia proper and Siberia were formed into the Russian Socialist Federal Soviet Republic. Instead of giving the vote to all men and women alike, it expressly excluded from the suffrage merchants, employers, capitalists, and those living upon rent, interest, or profits. By a later decree, however, it was provided that such persons might be allowed to vote if they could show that they were in fact living on an income from their own labor.

All governmental power in Soviet Russia was declared to be in the All-Russian Congress of Soviets, not elected directly, like the members of the House of Representatives in the United States, but indirectly, by local councils or soviets of working people and peasants. In the village the peasants elect the members of the local soviet, and in the factories, offices, and educational institutions of the cities the workers elect the members of their local soviet. In turn these local soviets elect delegates to the soviet of the canton (or county); the canton soviet chooses delegates to a district soviet; the district soviet elects delegates to a provincial soviet; and so on up to the All-Union Congress.[1] This, it will be noted, is a system of election similar in principle to that formerly applied to United States senators when they were chosen by the state legislatures—a system which the American people declared to be undemocratic, and abandoned in favor of direct election by the voters.

[1] Only housewives vote on a residential basis. For an admirable account of the whole system by a competent American scholar, see S. N. Harper's *Civic Training in Soviet Russia* (1929), especially pages 109 ff.

The executive department of Russia under this arrangement consists of (1) a Central Executive Committee elected by the All-Russian Congress and (2) a Council of People's Commissaries which is in effect a cabinet with a president and with great departments of administration. In theory the government grants freedom of opinion and conscience to all citizens, but in reality it is a dictatorship, representing the few hundred thousand communists who control the army and the elections, and who hold the chief offices.

The Union of Socialist Soviet Republics has been mentioned above (p. 396). It is made up of seven members—the Russian federation and the soviet republics of the Ukraine, White Russia, Transcaucasia, Turkmenistan, Uzbekistan,[1] and Tadjikistan—and is the promise, in the eyes of the communists, of a world-wide federation. Five branches of administration are reserved for the government of the Union, foreign affairs, defense, foreign trade, transport, and posts and telegraph. In other branches of government the Union either leaves the initiative or complete authority to the several states. The departments are under the charge of "commissariats," resembling Western government departments.

A general assembly (the Union Congress of Soviets) convenes at Moscow, usually once a year. Its fifteen hundred delegates are elected by the city soviets and the provincial soviet congresses. The members of the latter are sifted out by the various county and rural congresses from representatives originally elected by the village soviets. The assembly ordinarily sits for about ten days, and elects what is essentially a federal parliament (the Union Central Executive Committee) of two houses: (1) the Union Council, a kind of house of representatives, composed of members proportionally representing the seven constituent republics; (2) the Council of Nationalities, a

---

[1] Uzbekistan, formed in 1924, lies east of the Turkoman Republic and does not appear on the map on page 397. It includes portions of Bokhara and the Samarkand region (see map, p. 518).

sort of senate, containing representatives of every republic and autonomous territory little or big.

The federal parliament is convened three times a year. It elects a ministry, or cabinet, made up of the heads of departments. This is called the Union Council of People's Commissaries and supervises the several departments over which the Union has jurisdictions.

When neither the Union Congress of Soviets nor the Union Central Executive Committee is in session the sovereign authority rests in the Presidium, a standing committee elected by the two houses of the Central Executive Committee by a complicated process. The Presidium has among other rights authority to carry on diplomatic negotiations, to conclude political treaties with other powers, to change the frontiers of the Union, to declare war and conclude peace, to ratify international treaties, and it may revise decisions of the ministry.

It will be seen that this system of government gives the right of suffrage to over 95 per cent of the people, and permits a large number of delegates from the most remote districts to gather once a year at Moscow, knowing that under the constitution their "congress" is the supreme authority of the Union. At the same time this assembly does little beyond accepting the reports of parliament, and the actual governmental operations are very largely in the hands of the powerful Presidium, or board, of the Central Executive Committee, which is easily controlled by the Communist party. In fact, the whole federation is more or less of a shadow: Soviet Russia is the dominant partner, and Russian communists are the ruling power.

The history of Germany and Russia after the war will be sketched in the following chapters, as well as that of Italy, which took an unexpected turn.

PROGRESS OF SOCIALISM AND COMMUNISM

At the close of the war the socialistic parties of Europe found themselves stronger than ever in numbers, as the elections from 1918 to 1920 showed, and face to face with novel conditions. Hitherto, they had been agitating minorities concerned almost entirely with theories and doctrines. True, socialists had frequently been elected to parliaments and occasionally, particularly in France, socialists had held portfolios in coalition ministries, but they had never had an opportunity to test their theories in the fire of practice. Whenever an ardent socialist had tried to draw an exact picture of the new order of things to be built on the ruins of capitalism, he was certain to be dismissed by his colleagues as a dreamer and a Utopian; the general policy was to let the future take care of itself and to confine operations principally to theorizing and propaganda. But after the war the face of things was changed. In Russia communists, backed by a Red army, had possession of the government and the power to enforce their decrees. The first president of the German republic was a socialist, and in 1924 the Labor party in Great Britain was called upon to form a ministry, which was composed mainly of socialists. Everywhere in Europe there was a swing of voters to the left. To be sure, the left itself was broken into many factions, but it was more numerous than ever.

This transformation of socialists from agitators into powerful factors in politics was the result of many causes. The war itself had increased the authority of governments everywhere; conscription, nationalization, heavy taxation of the rich, and the regulation of economic life were state measures. Not without warrant did the socialists contend that a large installment of socialism had proved essential to the conduct of the war. The disillusionment of four years of fighting ran in favor of the socialists. They had been the only party that had consistently condemned war and opposed the imperialism that had been largely responsible for the world conflict. Misery, hunger, and suffering brought a deepening discontent in all sections of all countries.

The struggle had not been raging many weeks before tens of thousands who had come to cheer remained to curse. Even the peasants, the bulwark of conservatism, grew restless as governments regulated the prices of their produce while the prices of manufactured goods rose rapidly. If peasants did not go over wholesale to the socialists, they made a shift to the left in their old parties, forcing their leaders into radical activities. With the increase in the demand for munitions, factories multiplied, the number of industrial workers directly susceptible to socialist agitations grew in size, trade unions added millions to their membership, and the area of discontent widened. Indeed, in 1917 the mutterings of unrest became so ominous in England, France, and Italy that it was necessary to send over a delegation of more conservative American trade unionists to exert a mollifying influence on their labor brethren in the Allied countries.

The international situation during and after the war likewise contributed to the strength of the socialistic parties. If out of patriotism most of them supported their respective governments, they did so on the definite understanding that they were fighting in defense of their country, not for imperialism, forcible indemnities, and territorial aggrandizement. Accordingly, they had something to say about "war aims" that could not be ignored by rulers, and their hand was strengthened by President Wilson's announcement of democratic aims on the part of the United States. No one condemned imperialism, conquest, and autocracy more vigorously than he, and his speeches, broadcast throughout the world, were fuel to the socialist fires. Socialists had continually assailed war as a menace to civilization and a curse to labor, and as the conflict proceeded in Europe millions who had no knowledge of socialism were driven by facts to a similar position. To them it seemed that war was more dangerous than socialism; and as no other parties came out so boldly on this serious issue, socialists gathered recruits among advocates of peace in no way sympathetic with their economic views. To many also it appeared that socialism was a powerful support for a "clean peace"—one that would do justice to nations and leave behind no bitter roots of new wars.

After the World War was over, and the harsh terms of the Treaty of Versailles were made known, socialists took the lead in criticizing that settlement and in advocating a revision in the interest of international concord. Accordingly, all those who wished to spread healing among the nations, whatever their economic theories, found themselves ranged with the socialists. In every country the inflamed nationalism that made for rivalry and discord was vigorously attacked by socialists, who thereby won over many former opponents.

Among the forces that helped to enlarge the socialistic contingents were the agitations caused by the revelations of secret diplomacy discussed above (p. 337), particularly in England. When the Russians published the secret treaties and documents showing that the truth about the alliances and ententes had been concealed from the people, and that the Allied powers were also fighting for imperialistic ends, popular indignation rose to a high point everywhere. English Liberals were especially shocked and disgusted. Their leaders, Asquith and Grey, became hopelessly discredited in wide circles of their own party.

This trend in English political thought is illustrated in a book, *From Liberalism to Labor*, by Sir Charles Trevelyan, a prominent Liberal who led a regiment of his party over to the Labor camp. While assuming that Asquith and Grey were honest, he declared that their state of mind was "almost more hopeless and deplorable than if they had followed the policy [of secrecy] with a Machiavellian intention of deceiving the House of Commons." Concerning the feeling after the publication of the secret treaties, Trevelyan says, "For the first time the conviction became widespread that the war was, after all, an imperialistic war." In his eyes the Treaty of Versailles was the sour fruit of this old tree, and the treatment of Germany after the peace was more atrocious than many horrors perpetrated during the passions and excitement of the conflict itself.

Besides all this, the majority of the Liberals in the British government had joined with the Tories in suppressing freedom of speech and press—ancient rights and liberties—and thus arrayed themselves on the side of the enemies of democracy. Hence, reasoned Trevelyan, there was nothing to do but to go over to the Labor party, which had doggedly striven for peace, opposed wars of imperialism, and stood stanchly for a material reduction of armaments. Undoubtedly, it was in this spirit that millions of British voters cast their ballots for Labor candidates.

Peculiar circumstances, no less than the spread of discontent among the people, were responsible for the rise of socialists to power in Russia and Germany. In the former country the extreme socialists were merely a handful in 1917, but they formed the only political organization willing to grant the two demands made by the peasants, who formed more than nine tenths of the population; namely, an immediate stoppage of the war and the distribution of land among the people without compensation to landlords. Russian liberals wanted the worn-out country to keep on fighting; Milyoukov, one of their leaders, was as eager to get the Straits away from Turkey as any officer of the Tsar had ever been. Timid socialists offered land to the peasants, but with payment to the former owners.

When Lenin and Trotzky cried out, "End the war and give land to the people," they rallied to their side myriads of peasant soldiers who did not know the difference between socialism and astronomy. Such were the conditions that made it possible for the Bolsheviki to rise to power. As one of their representatives put it, "We saw a wild horse flying across the plains of Russia; we grabbed him by the mane, swung ourselves onto his back, and rode him without saddle and bridle, unable to do much guiding ourselves." In this honest confession there is more truth about the Communist Revolution in Russia than in a thousand formal accounts.

Likewise in Germany the spectacular rise of the socialists to the head of the government in 1918 was in large part the result of changes in no way due to socialist agitation. The war itself decimated the Prussian landed aristocracy, which had so long been dominant in Germany; the flower of its youth sank down in blood on the battlefields of France and Russia. When the iron hand of this party was relaxed, an opportunity was afforded for the party which stood next to it in organization and unity, and that was the Social Democratic Labor party of Germany. The other important groups—Liberals and Catholics—had neither the numbers nor the discipline of the socialists. So when the Western Front crumbled in 1918, and Ludendorff was forced to add a "democratic façade" to the German government for the purpose of placating President Wilson, the Social Democrats had to be taken into the reckoning, especially as communist riots and uprisings on the left were threatening something more revolutionary still. All attempts to get a working government composed of the other factions failed, and the chancellor, Prince Max of Baden, was compelled to surrender his office to "Comrade" Ebert. With the Prussian landed gentry downed and the bourgeoisie too timid to risk revolution, the Social Democrats, though not in a majority, took over the German government. This was one more illustration of the truth that determined minorities may work revolutions when unwittingly provided with easy opportunities by their political foes.

Despite their growth in numbers, however, the socialists were unable to carry out to any great extent their fundamental ideal; namely, nationalization of the means of production. Only in Russia was a general nationalization of industries actually attempted by a government possessing efficient military power. The outcome of that experiment in providing prosperity for labor was not such as to encourage socialists in other states to emulate the example of Moscow.

Austrian and German socialists found additional reasons for refraining from radical measures of nationalization in the hour of their early triumph. They were, as we have seen, in a minority and, unwilling to risk a military dictatorship, they were lacking in power to carry their program into effect. If the government should take over more property, they argued, then it could be forced by the victorious Allies to pay larger reparations. Moreover, industry was disorganized by the war and threatened with general bankruptcy. "For socialization generally, no time could be more unfortunate than the present," wrote a German leader in December, 1918. "Germany is starving, raw materials are lacking, machinery has deteriorated. Any upheaval may discredit socialism for years." In vain did the communists taunt them with "cowardice," with failure to demonstrate the courage of their convictions; the Social Democrats left capitalism intact. And as Russia embarked on her new economic policy, the capitalist régime of production recovered its former confidence generally throughout Europe.

Yet the socialist vote, with fluctuations, showed a general tendency to increase: socialist cabinets were formed in Germany, Finland, Denmark, Sweden, and Great Britain from time to time; and social legislation, attacking the evils of poverty, unemployment, sickness, and old age, was extended even by conservative governments. Great socialistic housing schemes were carried out in Great Britain, Vienna, and Germany. If, as some said, Marxism was dead, the retort could be made that the doctrine of laissez faire also was dead.

All these epoch-making events, in which socialists played such an important rôle, in turn had a deep influence on their own doctrines and tactics. Hitherto socialists had been talking; usually differences of opinion could be smoothed over by general phrases. But when socialists came face to face with revolution, with the possibility of getting into power, with the necessity of making decisions respecting action, then they were in another world and could not possibly settle their disputes by coining compromises in words. An action was either to be taken or not, and party members were either for it or against it. Hence all the old differences among socialists were accentuated, and the solid ranks they had formed while in the opposition were shattered by violent differences as to goal, methods, tactics, and the actual management of government business. Accordingly, it is necessary to review changes in the socialist doctrines formulated by Marx and his immediate successors in theoretical economics. Of course, it may be said that these changes had roots in older views, but in the course of the decade that followed the war they were brought into sharper relief. Broadly speaking, socialists of the post-war period were divided into four schools.

1. First of all was the left-wing group, generally known as "communists," but neither the name nor the views held by them were new. Marx and Engels called their celebrated proclamation of 1847 *The Communist Manifesto*, and the Russian Bolsheviki, who perhaps had the best claim to the title, used it as practically synonymous with "socialist." In fact, they named their new federal state the "Union of Socialist Soviet Republics" and employed the term "socialism" in their official documents. Yet the political party which governed Russia after the revolution of 1917—the only party tolerated by law—was the Communist party. Therefore, in spite of the confusion that exists in the actual use of the terms, it is convenient to reserve "communism" to cover that form of socialism attempted in Russia.

In general, communism is characterized by its emphasis on certain tactics and ideas. Like Fascism, it rejects the notion that radical reformers can attain real power in government by winning a majority of the voters and then carry out a program of complete nationalization by peaceful processes. It is possible enough, communists contend, for socialists to get into office by way of elections, but they would find the permanent civil servants (the bureaucracy), the army, the police, the capitalists, and the professional classes solidly arrayed against them and hence would be unable to accomplish anything important. Therefore, runs the communist creed, the upper classes must be conquered by armed working classes and subjected to severe military and police rule until extinguished or thoroughly subdued to the communist order of things. Under the Tsar the upper classes in Russia excluded the workingmen and peasants from the right to vote; under communism the former ruling classes were excluded from all share in the government. The communist leaders disguised their own power under the term "the dictatorship of the proletariat." As their ultimate goal radical communists advocate an equal distribution of the annual product among all working members of society.

2. From both the tactics and the equalitarian creed of communism, the German Social Democrats and the British Labor party officially dissent, sometimes quite as vigorously as middle-class economists themselves. They adhere to the democratic idea of winning the voters by "appeals to reason" and gradually extending government ownership and control by peaceful methods. They cite statistics to show that if the higher incomes of the upper classes were equally distributed among the people, the additional amount received by families of the working classes would be almost trivial—assuming that the annual production of wealth would continue to be the same under socialism as under capitalism.[1] They also call attention

[1] A great deal of nonsense has been written on "dividing up" income. In reality little is known about the subject. It is not easy to define the "income" of a nation (A. L. Bowley, *The Measurement of Social Phenomena*, pp. 196–225), and the statistics dealing with the matter are far from adequate. Dr. Morris A. Copeland, of Cornell University, on the basis of the best attainable data, esti-

to the fact that the communists in Russia do not pay equal wages and salaries to all government employees, but differentiate among them according to skill and competence. Nor do the German Social Democrats and British Laborites propose to nationalize all "property"; their program embraces public ownership of only the great industrial undertakings that are already highly organized in trusts and cartels, such as railways, mines, and cardinal industries in general. Moreover, some of their leaders now speak of coöperation between capital and labor under "socialist state supervision."[1] Hence it is well to reserve the word "socialist" to characterize the school that would proceed to power by the democratic method, and would materially limit the area of "nationalization."

3. The recognition of obvious difficulties in the management of great industries by governments and politicians led to the formation of a third type of socialism known as Guild Socialism. Its creed can be best stated in the language of one of its former British advocates, G. D. H. Cole:

Under it the management of each industry would be in the hands of a National Guild, including all workers in the industry. All the Guilds would be linked up in a Guild Congress representing the whole body of producers. Each Guild would administer its own internal affairs, and matters of common interest would be discussed and settled by the Guild Congress. . . . The Guilds would be in possession of the *management* of industry, the state would be the *owner* of the means of production. . . . The Guilds must come through industrial unionism out of the trade unions of today.

Although the ideas of this system run back into the guild organization of olden times (Vol. I, pp. 218 ff.), it did not become the subject of a general agitation until the foundation of

mates the total "realizable income" of the United States at $745 per capita, or on the average $3725 per family of five (*Current History*, August, 1929, p. 816); but to assume that there would be that much to distribute under socialism is to assume something that cannot be proved.

[1] For this latest phase of socialist thought, see G. D. H. Cole's *The Next Ten Years of British Social Economic Policy* (1929).

T

the National Guilds League in Great Britain in 1915. It was brought forcibly to public attention two years later by the publication of a government report (The Whitley Report on Joint Standing Industrial Councils) which proposed the formation of labor councils in all "organized industries" to preserve industrial peace and to give workers a "greater share in the control of their industry." Regarding this as an installment of Guild Socialism, advocates of the scheme took advantage of the opportunity to make a widespread agitation in Great Britain; but they made little headway, and after a season of debate popular interest in their scheme seemed to decline. Mr. Cole himself publicly renounced it in the book cited above.

4. A similar fate overtook the fourth type of socialism generally known as "syndicalism," represented in the United States by the I. W. W. movement (Industrial Workers of the World). The term itself comes from the Latin word *syndicus*, meaning the agent or spokesman of an organized group, and derivative names had long been applied, especially in France, Spain, and Italy (p. 491), to clubs, companies, trade unions, and corporations of various kinds. As used in the labor movement, a "syndicate" was "an association of workingmen of the same or of similar trades, held together by bonds of common interest," but in the hands of French radicals, such as Fernand Pelloutier and Georges Sorel, syndicalism became the philosophy of a revolutionary socialism, tinged with anarchism. With respect to tactics it invoked "direct action" by organized labor—general strikes to enforce demands and sabotage or the stoppage of industry by crippling machinery. Ultimately the syndicalists proposed to seize the industries in which they worked, abolish governments, and manage economic affairs through federations of syndicates. For a time syndicalism had a great vogue, particularly in Latin countries, but as the revolutionary furor of 1917 died away it also lost ground everywhere.

In combating the growth of socialism in its various forms, the business men of Europe gave increasing attention to

American industrial methods, which produced such remarkable "prosperity" for manufacturers and high wages for working people. They attributed a large part of Europe's distress to socialism and "government meddling with private enterprise." They demanded more freedom to manage their affairs in their own way, assuring "labor" that thereby the output would be increased, and that the workmen would automatically share in the enlarged income. Some of the great corporations in the United States have adopted the policy of selling stock in their respective companies to employees at reduced rates and on the installment plan. Making the workmen stockholders serves to identify them with their company and blunts the sharp distinction between capital and labor.

These "capitalistic" arguments and policies the socialists tried to meet by asserting that American prosperity was due not to business methods but rather to the abundance of rich natural resources in the United States, to mass production for the huge domestic market protected by a high tariff, and to the exploitation of the farmer. They insisted that European industries were being consolidated by great national and international trusts and cartels and that socialism offered the only alternative to government by "a financial oligarchy." Unmoved, therefore, by the American example, European socialists continued to attack industrialism according to their various theories.

In addition to attempting to decide momentous domestic questions, the socialists tried to weave anew the threads of internationalism snapped by the war. When the conflict broke out the secretary of the Second International (pp. 110 f.) moved the office of the society to the Hague and proposed a general congress of socialists to discuss the condition of Europe. Finding that this was out of the question, he invited the socialists of neutral countries to send delegates to a convention at Copenhagen in 1915. From this conference went forth an appeal to the socialists of the warring countries to stop the bloody conflict, but the answer was negative. Two years later the Second International summoned a conference at Stockholm, moved to this action by demands from extremists in Switzerland, led by Lenin, who had called for revolution against war. Delegates from Austria, Germany, Russia, Holland, and the Scandinavian countries appeared at Stockholm, but the governments of England and France refused to issue passports to representatives of labor organizations selected to attend the conference. Though the convention never met formally, fruitless discussions showed that the Second International was powerless to bring any pressure to bear on the belligerent governments.

Failure at Stockholm gave a signal to radical socialists. Denouncing all "social patriots," as they called their comrades who remained loyal to their respective governments, they invited revolutionists who "meant business" to join in forming a Third International. The call went out from Moscow by wireless in January, 1919, and in March radicals arrived from the four corners of the world to create a new world federation of communists. At a second congress, held the following year, twenty-one theses, or conditions of membership, were drawn up, and "socialists" everywhere were ordered to accept these terms or be cast into outer darkness. The Third International declared war on "the whole capitalist system and the old yellow Social Democratic parties," on imperialism, on the Second International, and on militarism as a system. Parliamentary action was tolerated merely as a form of propaganda. Only revolutionary communists were to be admitted to the new association; no weaklings, doubters, or reformers were to be accepted. Instead of the loose federal organization which formed the Second International, the Moscow fraternity established a highly centralized system, dominated by a small committee at Moscow. Subject to decisions of periodical congresses, this committee could lay down rules, admit and expel members, and issue orders to its agitators everywhere. Composed in large part of Bolsheviki affiliated with the All-Russian soviets, it was in fact an agency of that government, in spite of its nominal independence.

Meanwhile the Second International began to show signs of renewed vitality. In February, 1919, it held at Bern a general conference, which was attended by representatives of nearly all the old affiliated organizations. In opposition to Moscow, the conference condemned dictatorship by a section of the working class and favored the use of democratic methods in establishing the socialist order. The following year a second convention worked out a new program along the lines sketched by the British Labor party. At later assemblies there was discussion of a possible compromise with Moscow, but nothing came of it; so the two Internationals continued as separate, and often hostile, organizations.

Running somewhat parallel to these events in the socialist world were activities among trade unionists. They had formed an International Federation of Trade Unions at Copenhagen in 1901, which was disrupted, like the Second International, by the war. In 1919 this organization was restored to working order, with a program of social legislation which went far beyond trade unionism pure and simple. As a result, Samuel Gompers, head of the American Federation of Labor, seceded, denouncing the International Federation in round terms. On the other hand, Russian labor, dominated by communists, condemned it as too conservative and proceeded to form an association of Red International Labor Unions, which attracted a small following. To these trade-union groups were added two other international labor organizations: the International Workingmen's Association, with syndicalist or anarchist tendencies, and the International Federation of Christian Trade Unions, affiliated in various countries with Catholic political parties. Of them all the International Federation of Trade Unions showed the greatest strength, not only in membership but also in arranging international coöperation in time of strikes. But every effort to form a "united front" was hampered by internal divisions over policy and by nationalistic interests which often transcended the claims of the "international brotherhood of labor."

The Agrarian Revolutions

Since most of the books, newspapers, and magazines are published in cities, and since the cities are the centers of education and discussion, the problems of urban finance, industry, manufacture, and capital and labor occupy the foreground of modern thought. For every book on agriculture there are a score on manufacturing, railways, and socialism. And yet in 1918 Europe was still primarily agricultural from Russia to Spain. In England alone did the industrial population outnumber the farming population, and for all countries agriculture, of course, furnished food supplies, raw materials, and markets. Cities may fall into decay and nations live, but if agriculture perished cities would disappear and grass grow in their streets. Melancholy ancient ruins bear witness to this fact in many places of the earth.

Moreover, the way in which the land of any country is held, bought, sold, and divided among the heirs of deceased persons helps materially in shaping the political and economic character of the people. If it is held in large estates by a few landlords and tilled by serfs or tenants, we have one type of society; if it is divided into numerous small farms tilled by the owners and their families, we have another type. This has been a commonplace of history from the days of Aristotle to our own. And many of the great movements of history, especially its revolutions, have been connected with conflicts over the distribution and tenure of land. By many philosophers a large freehold farming, or peasant, class has been held to be the very foundation of order, morality, and good government; it was in the name of the people that Lloyd George, before the World

War, proposed to break up the great estates of England into small farms by taxation and other measures of legislation (p. 120).

Thus, into any balanced picture of modern civilization agriculture must enter. It has in the past been the basis of a feudal aristocracy, with all that implied for war and politics. It can serve, on the other hand, as the basis of a thrifty peasant democracy. As a complement to industry, it may be developed to provide home markets and create a "closed-economic state," self-sufficient and nationalistic in economy. Involved in the system of tenure also is the question of efficiency in production. Which produces more wheat and meat per acre—the large estate or the petty holding of the peasant? Beyond question the inhabitants of rural districts are more religious, more attached to their churches, more respectful toward priest and parson, than the vast, migratory, socialistic masses of the cities. For this reason changes in agrarian economy are closely related to politics, war, and culture.

As we have pointed out above, serfdom in the medieval sense had legally disappeared throughout Europe by the end of the nineteenth century except in some parts of the Balkans, where marked traces had remained, largely as a result of Turkish rule. But the abolition of serfdom did not mean that every peasant got a holding of his own large enough to support himself and his family. Far from it. In England the peasants were turned into tenants rather than freeholders; most of the land was still kept in great estates owned by lords and tilled by renters and laborers; and in spite of the Lloyd George measures just mentioned, legal barriers still stood in the way of buying land in small plots. Across the Channel in France the great revolution begun in 1789 transferred about one half the superficial area of the country to peasant proprietors, leaving a large class of landlords intact.

In Prussia a still larger proportion of the land was left in the hands of great owners after the reforms by Stein and

Hardenberg in 1807. The abolition of serfdom in Russia in 1861 did not create a free and prosperous peasantry (Vol. I, pp. 595 ff.). On the contrary, the people who received land by the decree had to pay for it; the state compensated the landlords; the peasants had to shoulder heavy taxes to reimburse the state. Moreover, vast estates held by landlords and the imperial family were left untouched and were cultivated by laborers and renters. In 1914 Hungary, as an English traveler reported, "was a medieval state varnished over with an appearance of modernity. Real power was in the hands of the great nobles and the smaller landowners, and the great landlord ruled on his estate with almost unfettered authority, having his own court of justice where his own peasants would be tried and condemned for acts offensive to his rule." In Rumania the condition of the peasants was worse, if anything, than in Hungary. The depth of their discontent had been revealed in 1907, when they revolted so dangerously that eleven thousand of them were killed by troops in restoring "law and order."

To the southwest, in Croatia and Slavonia, under Hungarian administration, great landlordism was the rule, and the mass of tenants were Slavic in race; while across the borders in Bosnia and Herzegovina, under Austro-Hungarian authority, both serfdom and landlordism remained intrenched in spite of some efforts at reform. In short, in 1914 millions of Germans, Russians, Czechs, Hungarians, Rumanians, Croats, Serbs, and Italians lived as tenants on great estates in a condition of economic bondage far removed from the liberty of the farmer or peasant proprietor. Here, no less than in the turbulent industrial cities, were the materials for a revolutionary outburst.

For a wide-reaching peasant uprising, no less than an uprising of the proletariat, Russia gave the signal in 1917. According to Leon Trotzky, "owing to the war the army played a decisive rôle in the events of the Russian revolution, and the army was peasant." It was the determination of the peasants to have the soil of the great landlords that made possible the Bolshevik triumph; the Bolsheviki alone among the politicians in Petrograd had the will to give the peasants the land immediately and without any compensation to its historic owners. It is true that the decrees affecting this change did not divide the land into small farms among private persons, but transferred it to the state—the peasantry at large. However, the peasant did not care much about "juridical theory" so long as he received his share of soil from which to gain a living.

Though producing elsewhere no such drastic transformation, agrarian unrest spread from Russia to Poland, Bohemia, Prussia, all parts of the Austro-Hungarian Empire, and even to the mountain fastnesses of Bosnia. The green banner of the peasants was raised beside the red banner of the proletariat. In Croatia, Slavonia, and the Banat revolutionary peasants sacked and burned the castles of their landlords, as the peasants of France had done in the momentous days of August, 1789. For a time it looked as if all of eastern Europe would go "Bolshevik," in the sense that the landlord as well as the capitalist would be utterly destroyed, and the land given outright to laborers bent on founding soviet republics. These agrarians were not communists by any means; but, blandly ignorant of Marxian dialectic, they were quite prepared to make common cause with anyone who would help them attain their ends.

For a few years,—that is, as long as the Bolshevik menace loomed on the eastern horizon,—efforts were made in various countries to destroy great landlordism and to transform tenants and laborers into landowners. By a proclamation of December 24, 1918, Alexander, prince regent of the new kingdom of the Serbs, Croats, and Slovenes, announced that steps would be taken to abolish all vestiges of serfdom, divide large holdings, and make every subject the "master of his own land." Within two months preliminary decrees initiated this reform, while assuring compensation to most of the dispossessed landlords.

In the wake of the revolution that spread through Rumania, Hungary, Czechoslovakia, and Poland went laws and ordinances declaring that estates were to be broken up, that land was to be given to the landless, and that free peasant democracies were to be created. In a more moderate tone the German constitution of 1919 provided that "the distribution and use of the land are to be supervised in such a way as to prevent its misuse and to promote the object of insuring to every German a healthful dwelling and to all German families, especially those with numerous children, homesteads corresponding to their needs." Supplementing this declaration, the government of Prussia served notice on great landlords that compulsory expropriation would follow if they did not voluntarily cut up and sell a certain proportion of their great estates.

Along the lines marked out by these ordinances the various states undertook land division, some going far in that direction and others stopping early in the process. It was easy, of course, for the "succession states," such as Poland, Czechoslovakia, Rumania, and Yugoslavia, to confiscate the property of the former Hapsburg princely families; and this was quickly done. But the readjustment as a whole was beset with obstacles. While Yugoslavia could sweep away by decree serfdom in Bosnia, Herzegovina, and Macedonia, the business of parceling out land and settling starving laborers on it was infinitely difficult. A socialistic government in Berlin could order Prussian landlords to make provision for selling land to peasants, but as long as the peasants were not fired by revolutionary zeal, the landlords did not need to worry about parchment and seals. Though Hungary seemed for a few months on the verge of an agrarian revolution, reaction restored the former landlords to their ancient supremacy.

In other countries reaction likewise halted the agrarian movement, at least temporarily. A conservative government in Rumania, for instance, delayed and dallied for about ten years, until in 1928 a threatened peasant uprising drove it from power and installed as premier Julius Maniu, a leader committed to a more thoroughgoing program.

Yet, after a decade positive results could be recorded: the agrarian revolution in Russia seemed to be firmly established; about a half a million *kmets* (practically, serfs) in Yugoslavia had been emancipated; and millions of tenants from the Baltic to the Adriatic had been changed into small owners. Outside of Russia great landlordism had nowhere been destroyed, but the area tilled by peasants had been enlarged. Moreover, landed aristocracies had been materially reduced in political power as compared with capitalists, peasants, and industrial workers.

In the disorders and uncertainties that accompanied the process agricultural production rapidly declined; for in an age of machinery, farming on plots of five to ten acres was wasteful and crude. Indeed, in 1929 it was possible to deliver American wheat in Belgrade at a lower price than the petty farmers in the neighborhood could afford to grow it. Thus doubts were raised as to whether the traditional scheme of confiscating and dividing estates was indeed a sound solution of the agricultural problem. At all events, after ten years of agrarian reform, with the competition of American farmers growing constantly keener, agriculture in central and eastern Europe was demanding relief as vigorously as the representatives of agricultural regions of the West and South in the Congress of the United States. Feudal landlordism was certainly dying, but the future of the land and agricultural economy was by no means determined. It is one of the most fundamental and complicated of all the problems that mankind now faces.

New Phases of the Old Conflict between Church and State

Accompanied by the dissolution of empires and political revolutions, the crisis of the World War could not fail to give new aspects to the ancient relations of governments and churches. As we have already indicated (pp. 93 ff.), the countries of Europe had halted at different points along the road to the complete separation attained in the United States and marked out as the goal of liberals everywhere. Only two general principles were almost universally accepted in this connection. The first of these, religious toleration,—that is the right to worship or not according to conscience,—was established in all countries in theory and, to a large extent, in practice. Even Spain provided in her constitution that no one should be molested on account of his religious opinions, "provided he show the respect due to Christian morality." "Frozen" Russia of the Tsarist age likewise proclaimed that "all religions may be freely professed," although certain very decided restrictions were imposed on Jews. The second general principle widely established in Europe by 1914 was that no one should suffer civil or political disabilities on account of his religious views. But everywhere churches enjoyed privileges of one kind or another. In most countries,—England, Russia, Prussia, and Serbia, for example,—a particular church, Protestant, Catholic, or Greek Orthodox, was established by law and usually supported, in part at least, by taxation or grants from the public treasury. During the war the Pope naturally sought to conserve Catholic interests, but his path as servant of the Prince of Peace was strewn with thorns. All his efforts to bring about peace were without avail. And in the end he had to witness the collapse of a great Catholic power—Austria-Hungary.

But, in keeping with its historic traditions, the Catholic Church made the best of the circumstances and before many years could report gains highly gratifying to its defenders. Wherever possible the Catholic clergy sought to win greater control over the schools and was highly successful in Italy, Spain, and Bavaria. By a treaty with the Italian dictator, Mussolini, in 1929, the Pope attained an independent position as a sovereign prince within a small but autonomous territory, and the Catholic religion was declared to be the sole religion of the Italian state (p. 495). The escape of Russian Poland from Tsarist domination gave the Catholic Church in that region a new lease of life, with a larger freedom. "Everywhere," wrote a distinguished French publicist, André Geraud, in 1929, "people turn to the Apostolic power. . . . England herself decides to make her legation at the Vatican permanent. States that have annexed territory ask the Holy Father to help them in the task of absorbing their new Catholic subjects [Rumania, Yugoslavia, and Greece]. The newly created nations [Rumania, Czechoslovakia, Latvia, Lithuania, Albania] remember that religion is one of the time-honored forces of civic consolidation. . . . In the year 1928, something unheard-of in modern times, three prelates of the Church were functioning as prime ministers of secular states—Seipel in Austria, Shrámek in Czechoslovakia, Koroshetz in Yugoslavia. . . . The national movements . . . turn to her on bended knees: concordats with Latvia in 1922, with Bavaria in 1924, with Poland in 1925, with Lithuania in 1927 [and with Italy and Prussia in 1929] . . . bring the Church advantages which a Holy Alliance proper would never have yielded."[1]

On the other side of the ledger, however, had to be set some losses to organized religion. In Russia the state church was disestablished, disavowed, and abolished in a Bolshevik war on religion as the "opiate of the people." The new German constitution allowed citizens to free themselves from paying taxes to support churches by merely renouncing their membership, and declared that there was to be no "state religion" in Germany. The collapse of Austria-Hungary deprived the papacy of its most powerful supporter in Europe. Although France renewed diplomatic relations with Rome, she made no effort to disturb the fundamental settlement of 1906 (pp. 98 ff.). In England, after virulent debates, Parliament twice rejected, in 1927 and 1928, amendments of the Prayer Book proposed

[1] *Foreign Affairs*, July, 1929, pp. 571 ff.

by the high authorities of the Established Church and raised anew propositions to deprive that institution of its privileged position as a state church.

For every Catholic prime minister in a small country could be cited a socialist prime minister in a large country,—Russia, Germany, and England,—and it was well known that socialists were fairly agreed on the proposition that churches and religion should be retired from the public to the private sphere. Hence it seemed probable that the ancient controversy over the relations of Church and State, which had played such a conspicuous part in the history of medieval Europe, would long continue to occupy the attention of priests and politicians in the Europe of the future.

CHAPTER XIV

DEMOCRACY IN CENTRAL AND WESTERN EUROPE

GERMANY AND AUSTRIA AS REPUBLICS

In striking contrast to eastern and southern Europe (see Chapter XV), the countries of the north and west managed to keep democratic institutions on a fairly even keel. Though badly shaken by the war and radical agitations, Switzerland, Holland, and the three Scandinavian nations extended rather than restricted the application of the democratic principles which had been gaining ground everywhere during the opening years of the twentieth century. Switzerland retained her federal constitution of 1874 intact, with the initiative and referendum; and by an amendment carried in 1921 the Swiss provided that all international treaties concluded for an indefinite period or a term of more than fifteen years could be referred to the voters on proper petition, in this way subjecting foreign affairs to the control of the people through the ballot box.

By acts passed during and just after the war the Netherlands introduced woman suffrage and proportional representation for the lower house of the parliament. Norway, having given women the vote in 1913, made them eligible to cabinet offices in 1915 and added proportional representation four years later. In the very midst of the war Denmark had adopted a new constitution which established universal suffrage for men and women, and in 1920 a general application of proportional representation was made. Restored and enlarged after the peace, Belgium revised her historic constitution in 1921; the practice of giving additional votes to men with certain educational and

447

property qualifications was abolished, straight manhood suffrage was introduced, and the parliamentary vote was conferred upon certain war widows, mothers, and other women who had borne special burdens during the war. In all these countries popular suffrage and parliamentary government continued to function during the troubled years that followed the World War.

In Germany the tendency of affairs was in the direction of stability and the orderly solution of economic questions, but the task of reconstruction was beset with difficulties. Soon after coming into power during the crisis of November, 1918, the socialist government had to agree to a humiliating peace, which imposed immense burdens on an impoverished people. In this connection it also had to assume responsibility for transferring to the former enemies a large amount of movable property, such as locomotives, cars, cattle, coal, and timber, and for laying heavy taxes to meet the reparation bills. While administering these bitter doses to the people, it had to dispel the illusions of victory which had been nourished by the military command until the very end. Surrounded by a ring of foes bent on dismembering Germany and collecting every mark that could be wrung from her, President Ebert's administration had to establish a new government to take the place of the bureaucratic empire that had fallen into ruins.

Nor was this all. For years socialist leaders had preached the overthrow of capitalism and the nationalization of the means of production; behind them stood restive millions demanding a fulfillment of the revolutionary pledges. What was to be done? If, as has been pointed out earlier, the German government assumed the ownership of vast industrial property in the name of socialism, then the Allied and Associated Powers could all the more readily collect its huge bill for damages. If, like Russia, Germany should attempt to nationalize capital and repudiate her debts, an iron ring of Allied armies could bring her revolutionary government to a speedy end. Unless such a revolution could spread to France, England, and the United States, it could scarcely be carried out in Germany. Since the socialists were in reality in a minority, they could only hope to realize their ideas immediately by setting up a soldiers' and workers' soviet on the Russian model.

The difficulties of the socialist government were increased by cleavages in its own ranks. It was divided against itself into a right wing of Social Democrats and a left wing of Independent Socialists. It was threatened not only by the old imperialists, bent on a monarchical reaction, but by the communists, under the leadership of Karl Liebknecht and Rosa Luxemburg, trying to engineer a revolt in the Russian style. Even after these uncompromising radicals had been arrested and shot,—murdered, it is said, in cold blood,—there remained a communist group of serious proportions determined to take advantage of every opportunity to embarrass the socialist government and transform it into a soviet system. The communists alleged that the moderate socialist by their failure to take drastic action had "betrayed the working class," and were to be more savagely condemned than the monarchists, who, after all, by their military policy had unwittingly delivered the country into the hands of the people.

During the winter of 1918–1919 the new republic had to cope with disorders in many districts. There were bloody collisions with the communists, or Spartacists, as they called themselves after the leader of the great slave revolt in Roman times. In February, 1919, after reactionaries had murdered the socialist premier in Bavaria, Kurt Eisner, communists took advantage of the confusion to proclaim a soviet republic in Munich and were frustrated only by vigorous action on the part of the national government. Meanwhile the elections for the convention to draft the new constitution (see pages 420 ff.) showed that all the radical parties combined had only fourteen million votes against sixteen million cast by the capitalistic and conservative parties. Thus the power to determine the form of government for Germany was wrested from the hands

T

of the socialists at the ballot box. Following this defeat came the disastrous Versailles treaty in the summer of 1919, involving immediate demands on Germany and putting a huge mortgage on the economic future of the country.

Emboldened by the outcome of the constitutional conflict, the parties of the right drew together with a view to ousting the socialist administration. In March, 1920, a body of monarchist troops, led by Kapp and Lüttwitz, marched into Berlin demanding the overthrow of the Ebert régime. Taken by surprise, the government fled to Stuttgart and seemed to be on the high road to ruin, when it was saved by a general strike called by its supporters. Trains were stopped, water was cut off, electric lights were put out, food supplies curtailed, and the whole life of Berlin suddenly paralyzed. Baffled by this amazing situation and unable to overcome it by the bayonet, Kapp and Lüttwitz gave up their project, and the revolt, or *Putsch*, as it was called, collapsed. Thereupon Ebert's government returned to the capital.

The conservatives, however, were not even yet ready to accept the situation. Extremists among them planned and executed a series of political murders designed to frighten and drive from power moderates as well as socialists. In 1921 they shot Matthias Erzberger, a leader of the Catholic Center party, who had taken part in the Versailles settlement and coöperated with the Ebert administration. The next year they killed Walter Rathenau, a brilliant economist with capitalist affiliations, who had stood loyally by the new republic and worked for a "rationalization of industry" in a socialistic direction. They prepared a long list of victims and actually attempted to murder Philipp Scheidemann, the parliamentary leader of the majority socialists. Not until the government took extraordinary police measures and enacted a special law against political murders did this terrorism of the right wing come to an end.

Unable to win a majority of the members of the Reichstag in the election, the socialists formed a coalition in 1923 under the

direction of Dr. Gustav Stresemann, a leader of the Nationalists. By that time it had become evident that as a minority
they could not cope with the problems pressing upon the country. The inflation of the currency had plunged the nation into
financial chaos. Technical defaults in the payment of reparations had given France and Belgium an excuse to invade the
Ruhr, demoralizing this rich industrial region and leading to
the deadlock of passive resistance on the part of the people.
In this dark hour the Stresemann cabinet set to work. Within
a few weeks it came to terms with France over the Ruhr,
withdrew official support from passive resistance, and devised
measures to get the industries in working order. It then took
up the question of inflation, and by a heroic measure, based on
confidence in the soundness of German economy, it stabilized
the mark by substituting a *Rentenmark* for the old paper, thus
restoring this unit of coinage to its former purchasing power.
By the Dawes plan for the discharge of reparations, which
went into effect the following year, additional solidity was
given to the financial structure of Germany. Internal security
was further strengthened by the Locarno treaties and other
negotiations mitigating the rigors of the Versailles settlement
(see pages 553 ff.).

It is noteworthy that at none of the elections held after the
establishment of the Weimar Constitution did the socialists
poll a majority of the votes. As the result of the first campaign
held in 1920 the two wings won about two fifths of the ballots.
The two elections held in 1924 showed violent fluctuations. At
the first, communists and monarchists made great inroads on
the moderate parties; at the second, these extremists suffered a severe setback. When it became necessary, the following year, to elect a new president on the death of Ebert, the
issue of the republic against a monarchy seemed to emerge
clearly. At the first balloting no candidate received a majority,
but the Nationalists of the right wing came out at the head of
the list. At the second election, which had to be held because

no one obtained a majority at the first, General Hindenburg entered the lists—at the request of the former Kaiser, it was alleged—against Dr. Wilhelm Marx, of the Catholic Center, who sought to rally the whole republican strength. From a hard-fought contest Hindenburg emerged victorious by a narrow margin, and his triumph was hailed as a violent swing toward the royal and conservative order of things.

However, to the surprise of his friends and foes, the new president adhered loyally to the republican constitution and made no effort to transform his office into a dictatorship preliminary to the restoration of the Hohenzollerns. With great dignity and circumspection, he pursued a moderate course. Moreover, the next election to the Reichstag, held in May, 1928, showed a decided slump in the nationalistic and conservative forces and brought marked gains to the parties of the left, especially the socialists and communists. The Social Democrats won 152 seats, the German Nationalists 73, the Center party 62, Communists 54, People's party 45, Democrats 25, with the remaining seats scattered among five or six other factions. Necessarily, the cabinet, as before, had to be a coalition, with the inevitable weakness of that type of parliamentary government.

Austria's case was worse than Germany's. Stripped of more than three fourths of her former territory and population by the Paris treaties, Austria was but a ghost of the ancient Hapsburg empire. Separation from Hungary and the loss of rich provinces to Yugoslavia deprived her of her granaries, while the establishment of Czechoslovakia took away some of her most flourishing industrial regions. Vienna, long the banking and commercial clearing house for a great empire, was suddenly reduced to the position of the capital of a petty state surrounded by hostile countries engaged in tariff wars against Austrian goods.

While the old economic structure was falling about their ears, revolutionaries, with the socialists at their head, proclaimed Austria a republic in November, 1918. They likewise declared Austria to be a part of the German Reich, for they were firmly convinced that their little country could not stand alone. To their surprise this union with Germany was forbidden by the triumphant Allies, and Austria was forced to sign the Treaty of St. Germain, which forever prohibited federation with Germany, except with the consent of the Council of the League of Nations, in which France could always block the proposal. As advocates of union prophesied, a period of deep distress now opened for Austria—a period of currency inflation, misery, and starvation. At last the League of Nations, disturbed by the terrible conditions, worked out a scheme of financial reconstruction for Austria. This included a large loan, and from 1922 to 1926 the League coöperated with the Austrian government, stabilizing the currency, balancing the budget, and helping to get business enterprise on its feet again.

It was with the greatest difficulty that Austria managed to avoid a dictatorship of the right or left. Vienna, possessing nearly one third of the population, was in socialist hands, with the red flag flying over the city hall. In the rural districts the Catholic party, known as the Christian Socialists, dominated the situation. In the national parliament no party had a majority. The elections of 1927 returned 73 Christian Socialists, 71 Social Democrats, 12 Pan-Germans, and 9 of the Peasants' party. By a coalition of parties on the right, Dr. Ignaz Seipel, a Christian Socialist, was able to keep himself in power as chancellor most of the time from 1922 to 1929, and only by a similar combination was his successor elected. Meanwhile there was continual friction between the Vienna municipality and the national government. The socialists organized a kind of private Red Guard and the conservatives, besides intrenching themselves in the regular national guard, formed Fascist bands for the avowed purpose of establishing a White dictatorship. From time to time there were collisions, ending in bloodshed. Only the most skillful maneuvering on the part of the political leaders prevented a fight to the finish. If, as a great many people hoped, Austria was ultimately to be united with Germany, in spite of the prohibition imposed by the Allies, it was understood that neither a Red nor a White dictatorship would be welcome to the government in power at Berlin.[1]

THE WESTERN SLAVIC STATES

In no part of Europe was the attempt to launch democratic government made under more unfavorable circumstances than in Poland, which had, even in the eighteenth century, been the standing example of inefficient government (Vol. I, pp. 155–156). Composed of three great sections long separated and ruled by alien governments, the people were lacking in political experience and unity of spirit. Devastated by war throughout great regions and with a poverty-stricken peasantry, the country was wanting in the first essentials of orderly government. And at the very outset of their career the Polish patriots who undertook to direct affairs came into conflict with their neighbors over boundary questions. Rejecting the proposals of the Paris Peace Conference, the Poles seized Eastern Galicia, in which Ruthenians formed a majority of the population and absolutely refused to give it up. They likewise refused to accept the eastern boundary recommended by the treaty conferences, and by making war on Russia enlarged their possessions in that direction. Although the League of Nations assigned Vilna to Lithuania, a Polish military adventurer, with a small body of troops, boldly seized that city in 1920, and Poland held fast to the booty in spite of vigorous protests. In fact, Poland and Lithuania were theoretically in a state of war from 1920 until 1927, when through the mediation of the League of Nations a kind of truce was patched up, leaving Poland in possession of Vilna.

[1] For the situation in Hungary, see the following chapter.

Poland had equally grave difficulties with Germany. The transformation of Danzig, with its German population, into a "free city," the separation of Prussia into two parts by the narrow strip known as the Polish Corridor (giving Poland access to the sea), the dispute over Upper Silesia (pp. 569 f.), and problems connected with the treatment of minorities in both countries kept their relations at a high tension. Germans could not go from one part of their country to the other without passing through Polish territory and, except on special trains, suffered the irritations of customs and passport inspections.

With its foreign affairs complicated, the Polish government was also distracted in dealing with domestic questions. They alone were sufficient to consume its energies—the subdivision of estates and the settlement of poverty-stricken millions on the land, the creation of a currency and banking system, rehabilitation of industry, and adjustment of quarrels among minorities composing nearly a third of the population. At the outset of its career Poland was really governed by its president, General Josef Pilsudski, of peasant origin, a former socialist military officer and leader in the struggle for Polish liberation. Although a provisional parliament was selected in 1919, Pilsudski appointed and dismissed ministers without consulting its wishes. When a new president, duly chosen under the constitution, was assassinated in 1922, Pilsudski came to the rescue as the chief of the military staff and acted as a virtual military dictator. But his position was insecure, and he was in constant conflict with the parliament. After four years of bickering he decided to put an end to uncertainty. So in 1926, surrounded by a band of faithful followers, he seized Warsaw, took charge of the government, filled the public offices with his military adherents and, without formally abolishing the parliament, set up a military régime.

His administration was strengthened by a reorganization of Polish finances under American auspices and by the floating of a huge loan in the United States, accompanied by the installation of an American financial adviser in charge of important branches of taxation, expenditures, and banking. From year to year Pilsudski increased his power. When, in 1929, the premier resigned because he objected to being an "office boy," Pilsudski made one of his officers prime minister and appointed more of his "colonels" to civil posts. However, the continuance of parliament gave a semblance of regularity to the military dictatorship.

Poland's Baltic neighbors to the north—Lithuania, Latvia, Estonia, and Finland[1]—found the way of independence and self-government no less beset by difficulties. Small in area, mainly agricultural in occupation, forced by radical movements to redistribute the land of great estates, and subjected to lively Bolshevik influences on their eastern borders, they moved forward from one crisis to another, perhaps gaining experience and stability in the process.

After suffering the terrors of a desperate struggle between communists and monarchists, Finland managed to settle down to popular government under a democratic constitution, with an active coalition of agrarians and socialists on the left. When once a fair start was made in the division of the old landed estates, the Finnish people, mainly peasants, with a high degree of literacy, gave less attention to revolution and more to the development of their extensive coöperative societies. As a rule the government was controlled by agrarians and socialists, but they were agreed in suppressing revolutionary communist agitations. Difficulties with Sweden over the Aaland Islands were adjusted by the League of Nations in favor of Finland; and boundary disputes with Russia were settled by negotiation, but not in a manner to dispel all fears of aggression.

Estonia, Latvia, and Lithuania were likewise forced to allay agricultural unrest by dividing great estates and, in spite of

---

[1] The Finns and Estonians are not Slavs, it must be remembered. They belong to the Ural-Altaic family, and are proud of their special languages (see Vol. I, pp. 563 ff.).

their resistance, were constantly disturbed, especially Latvia, by Bolshevik agitations. In Lithuania radical riots occurred in 1929, followed by an attempt to assassinate the premier. While in general the trend among these three little Baltic states was in the direction of social order, their position between Poland and Russia was precarious, and it was with difficulty that they managed to avoid being drawn into the Russian sphere of influence.

Czechoslovakia made her way through the first decade of independence without resorting to a dictatorship. Formed out of the three Austrian provinces of Bohemia, Moravia, and Silesia, and two sections from Hungary (Slovakia and Ruthenia), the new republic had within its borders a large number of Germans, Hungarians, and Ruthenians who were far from pleased with their position. Composing about three sevenths of the population, they resented the supremacy of the Czechs and complained that their rights were infringed by the government at Prague. Moreover, the Slovaks themselves added to the friction by protesting against the amount of influence allotted to them in the republic.

Besides making adjustments among quarreling citizens, the Czechoslovak government had to deal with agrarian questions involving the division of great estates and the establishment of thousands of petty proprietors on the soil. It also confronted the problem of helping to secure outlets for the important industries of the country that once served the Austro-Hungarian Empire but now found their market limited to the area of a minor state. Yet, notwithstanding the division of parliament into numerous parties, always at loggerheads, the Czechoslovak leaders succeeded in consolidating the new state and keeping it out of economic and political bankruptcy. No doubt this achievement was largely due to the tact and skill of its president, Thomas Masaryk, and its foreign minister, Edward Benes, both of whom were students, philosophers, and moderate socialists.

France after the War

France, the traditional home of revolutions, moved forward along conservative lines after the close of the war. Undoubtedly there were some grounds for unrest in the country. Everywhere industry and business had been dislocated. Two million people had been rendered homeless by war; one tenth of the land laid waste; farms, forests, railways, industries, and roads destroyed; nearly two million men killed; and the national debt raised to a staggering total. Communism revived, especially after French working people learned from Bolshevik revelations of the secret diplomacy, from which they got the impression that the French government had coöperated with Tsarist Russia in helping to bring on the world conflict. Large bodies of French socialists went over completely to communism and advocated a proletarian dictatorship for France. Frightened by such manifestations of discontent, the conservative parties united in a Nationalist bloc, and in a campaign of "higher patriotism" in 1919 won a comfortable majority in the Chamber of Deputies. For five years this bloc governed the country, borrowing money to pay for reconstruction in northern France and to meet current expenses, on the theory that Germany could finally be made to reimburse the treasury.

Although there was a swing to the left after the elections of 1924, and Edward Herriot, head of the Radical Socialist party, was installed as premier, his term was brief. Reckoning with a timid middle class of the second rank, the Herriot ministry did not dare to lay the taxes necessary to stabilize finances and restore the depreciated franc. One finance minister after another was tried as the franc continued its downward course, reaching at last a value of about two cents. On all sides there was talk of a "strong man," or dictator, to save the day. But a more prosaic method was chosen. In 1926 Raymond Poincaré was again called to head the cabinet to prevent a ruinous financial crash. Within a few months he increased taxes materially, introduced economy in administration by cutting off many useless jobs, set to work consolidating the confused floating debts, balanced the budget, and "pegged" the franc at about four cents. Thus "the franc was saved" without making any changes in the form of government created after the establishment of the Third Republic. When, in 1928, an appeal was made to the voters in a general election, the policies of Poincaré received popular approval, indicating general contentment with the course of events.

Apart from foreign affairs, the most serious problem now confronting the French government was the adjustment of relations with Alsace-Lorraine, which had given Germany so much trouble for nearly fifty years. Germany had granted the provinces a local legislature in 1911; France had a highly centralized administration admitting of no such self-government. The majority of the people in the provinces were Catholic in religion—at once loyal to the Pope and devoted to the principle of clerical direction in the lower schools. France, though Catholic in faith, had recently broken with the Church and the papacy, and had introduced secular control over education. Most of the people in the provinces spoke a German vernacular, and the French government insisted that during the first two years of elementary schooling French should be used exclusively.

Here were grounds for conflict, and local autonomists, organized in a *Heimatbund*, were quick to formulate their demands: the fullest autonomy within the framework of France, legislative and administrative independence with a local legislature elected by the voters, maintenance of existing relations between State and Church, autonomy for the local railways, development of progressive social legislation, a recognized place in public life for the German language to which it seemed entitled, since it is spoken by a majority of the people of these provinces and is one of the great languages of the world. To offset this strenuous opposition, the French government made some concessions, suppressed the most outspoken German-language papers, and tried and condemned to prison or exile certain of the prominent autonomists. Agitators were made to understand that Alsace and Lorraine were to be assimilated to the historic administrative system of France.

With considerable difficulty the religious question in the provinces was adjusted, at least temporarily, in connection with a general settlement with the papacy by the French government. In spite of an anticlerical flare-up under Herriot, the drift of policy was in the direction of a friendly relation with the Pope. In connection with her imperial policy in Africa and the Near East, France found it expedient to arrive at a working agreement with missionaries and was inclined to modify, on political grounds, the violent anticlericalism of former days. In 1921 diplomatic relations were renewed with the Vatican by the appointment of an ambassador. On his part, the Pope agreed to pay France "liturgical honors" on certain holy days in churches of the Near East. In connection with reciprocity he repudiated the French Catholic party that was still openly and actively working for the overthrow of the republic and a restoration of a monarchy. A decree of 1926 put its chief journal, *L'Action Française*, on the *Index* of prohibited publications, and condemned the works of two prominent ultramontane leaders, Charles Maurras and Léon Daudet. On the whole, a consolidation of conservative forces marked the course of the French government in the troubled years that followed the war, and agitators of communist tendencies were subjected to rigorous police surveillance. Nevertheless, the former trend toward collectivism was continued, for in 1928 the Parliament enacted a comprehensive social insurance law.

GREAT BRITAIN AND HER SELF-GOVERNING EMPIRE

Great Britain, the traditional home of free speech, freedom of the press, and free agitation did not escape altogether the shock of revolution that disturbed so many countries on the Continent. For several years there had existed in England a socialistic Labor party, which advocated a peaceful change from capitalism to socialism (p. 109), and in the election of 1906 it had captured a number of seats in Parliament. During the World War there was a kind of truce between the English parties. Indeed, in 1915 the Liberals and Conservatives formed a coalition which remained in force until the armistice. At a general election held in 1918, while the war fever was still high, the coalition secured 467 seats, over two thirds of them belonging to the Conservatives. Yet in spite of the general reaction the Labor party increased its votes and its membership in the House of Commons.

But Lloyd George, who remained prime minister, had done his work, and the coalition fell apart. His cabinet resigned, and he was replaced by a Conservative leader. Then the Conservatives, hoping to increase their numbers, decided to "go to the country," by having a new election in November, 1922. They came off very well. Owing to the creation of the parliament of the Irish Free State (see below), the number of members in the House of Commons had been reduced from 707 to 615. Of this total the Conservatives won an overwhelming majority. The Labor party secured 142 members; the Liberals only 114.

Being second in strength, the Labor party became for the first time the recognized "opposition" in Parliament. A year later (December, 1923), the prime minister, Stanley Baldwin, called a general election, setting as the issue the proposition that some form of protective tariff should be introduced to remedy the depression in business and the consequent widespread unemployment. This challenge to free trade, the historic doctrine of the Liberal party, moved the Liberals to array themselves against the Conservatives along with the Labor party. As a result the Conservatives were reduced to 258 seats, while Labor, rising to 192 members, retained its second place, with the Liberals holding the balance of power. Mr. Baldwin saw that he could not count on the support of a majority in the House and recommended to the king that the opposition be asked to form a ministry.

Accordingly, in January, 1924, George V requested Ramsay MacDonald, the most influential member of the Labor party, to organize a cabinet, and thus a Labor government was installed in England. Knowing that it commanded only a minority in the House of Commons and could live only with the support of the Liberals, the MacDonald government had to move cautiously. In no direction did it make any radical innovations. Its scheme of taxation was no more extreme than that of Lloyd George, adopted years before. Its foreign policy, in general, was based on sympathy for distracted Europe, and MacDonald, as his own foreign minister, did his best to restore friendship among the war-worn countries across the Channel. Especially did he attempt to establish cordial relations with Russia by recognizing the Soviet government, and to bring France and Germany together by encouraging the formation and adoption of the Dawes plan (p. 541).

But MacDonald's Russian policy aroused great opposition among the Conservatives and Liberals, particularly his scheme for making a loan to Russia to help her toward restoring her industries. Realizing that the Liberals were unlikely to support him, MacDonald chose a less important issue as a test of his power—the so-called Campbell case. The editor of a communist weekly had been arrested for the publication of an article deemed seditious, but the attorney-general decided to withdraw the case. The Conservatives viewed this action as an interference with the course of justice and as due to pressure from the extreme element in the Labor party. A demand for an investigation into the matter was regarded by Mr. Mac-

Donald as the equivalent of a vote of "lack of confidence" in his government, and he recommended that the king dissolve Parliament. The issue of the campaign turned on the hazards of socialistic government versus "security," and the Conservatives won a large majority in the House of Commons.

For five years Premier Baldwin's party ruled Great Britain in the name of conservatism, and yet, as a London correspondent of the *New York Herald-Tribune* cabled, such a government in the United States would be deemed radical, if not socialistic. It did not repeal any of the important labor laws enacted by its predecessors. On the contrary, by an act passed in 1925, it extended the system of unemployment insurance established five years previously, and at the same time it made more thoroughgoing provisions for pensioning widows, orphans, and the aged. Its commission, appointed to inquire into the depressed state of the coal-mining industry, reported in favor of nationalizing the mines and operating them by private agencies under government lease and supervision—a scheme too drastic in nature for the Conservatives. In 1927 the Baldwin ministry even proposed a reorganization of the House of Lords, which would have shocked its Tory predecessors; but it could not carry the scheme through Parliament because it was too mild for the Liberals and Laborites and too much of an innovation for the extreme right. Unable to reform the House of Lords, it reformed the Commons by revising the act of 1918 —which gave the vote to women over thirty years old—by cutting the age limit down to twenty-one, thus introducing the so-called "flapper vote." In foreign affairs the Baldwin ministry continued the imperialist tradition of the Conservative party, embarking with a light heart on a program of rivalry with the United States in naval construction.

Nevertheless, the Baldwin ministry, heavily supported as it was by the business interests, was unable to restore the economic prosperity which had been enjoyed by Great Britain before the war. In spite of their best efforts, with government assistance in many lines, British industrialists could not raise their exports to a figure above 75 per cent of the pre-war total. The coal, textile, iron, and machinery industries in particular suffered from depression. In 1920 the export of coal had fallen to less than half the amount in 1913, and no relief appeared to be in sight. Mine-owners threatened a cut in wages and a curtailment of production "to save the industry," and the government, frightened by the idea of an increase in unemployment, voted a subsidy in 1925 to keep the crippled industry going.

When, early in 1926, the coal operators announced a change in the wage scale, the miners' unions appealed to their labor colleagues for help, and as a result in May there was a general strike of miners and transport workers, tying up mines, railways, and shipping. For nine days business was paralyzed throughout Great Britain, and timid conservatives imagined that the country was on the edge of a Bolshevik revolution. But their fears were groundless. The strikers did not force a decision of any kind. On the contrary, the managers called off the general strike on a vague promise from the government that the question of wages in the coal industry would be made the subject of immediate negotiation. With what result? After continuing their struggle for months, the miners had to surrender, accepting defeat, a reduction in wages, and an increase in unemployment. Instead of continuing its aid to the coal industry, the government withdrew its subsidies, and passed, in 1927, the Trade Disputes Act, forbidding general strikes and making it illegal for trade unions to take from members a percentage of their wages for the benefit of the Labor party without their express approval. Thus the relations of capital and labor were further embittered, while more than a million continued to be unemployed and business remained in a state of stagnation.

When, after a tenure of nearly five years, the Baldwin ministry appealed to the country in a new election, in the spring of 1929, it was confronted by a long bill of indictment for its failures. Especially was it charged with having done nothing to relieve unemployment. Making this a prominent issue, the veteran Welsh statesman, David Lloyd George, tried to stage a return of the Liberal party to power by promising to solve the problem with no material expense to the taxpayers. Combining a discussion of this question with an attack on the Trade Disputes Law, MacDonald made a powerful appeal to the Labor constituencies, pledging himself to adopt immediate measures for relieving unemployment, and to repeal the act so objectionable to the trade unions. During the campaign the Baldwin party was taken severely to task for the breakdown of various disarmament conferences and, above all, for permitting naval rivalry with the United States to reach a serious stage. Both Lloyd George and MacDonald declared in favor of peace as a national policy, and promised to advance it by constructive action.

In the elections which ensued the Conservatives, owing to three-cornered contests, were defeated[1] and Labor made heavy gains, while the Liberals came in far behind, though materially strengthened. Although the Labor members formed the most numerous party in the Commons, they still did not command a majority of the House; they could only govern with help from Liberals or Conservatives, as in 1924. Under these circumstances MacDonald formed his second Labor cabinet in June, 1929. Among his first public statements was an announcement that he intended soon to visit President Hoover for the purpose of discussing an agreement respecting the reduction of naval armaments—a promise which he fulfilled in the autumn. He was received with great enthusiasm.

Scarcely less disturbing to the conservative guardians of British traditions was the movement for Irish independence that flamed up during the World War. A temporary truce in the long struggle between England and Ireland, effected by the passage of the Home Rule law in 1914 (p. 221), was broken

---

[1] The popular vote in contested constituencies was as follows: Conservative, 8,658,918; Labor, 8,384,461; Liberal, 5,305,123.

T

by the suspension of that law for the period of the war. Just as, a hundred years before, many Irish leaders had hoped that Napoleon would destroy the hated power of England, so now many of them looked to Germany to accomplish this. Certainly some of them entered into relations with German agents. At the same time a revolutionary movement broke out in southern Ireland under the direction of the Republican, or Sinn Fein, party. The aim of this revolt was nothing short of complete independence and the establishment of an Irish republic. For five years, from 1916 to 1921, Ireland was in a state of insurrection. In January, 1919, the Republicans proclaimed the independence of Ireland, and an Irish legislative body, the Dail Eireann, was created. It chose as president of the new republic, Eamonn de Valera, a college professor. The new government was not recognized by Great Britain; and there followed two years of assassinations, imprisonments, executions, and savage fighting between the Irish troops and the so-called "Black and Tans" sent over by the British "to maintain order." For a time all attempts to reëstablish peace seemed fruitless.

At length a truce with the more moderate Irish Republicans was arranged by Lloyd George, and at a conference in London, a form of Irish freedom was worked out. Article I of the treaty, concluded in December, 1921, reads:

Ireland shall have the same constitutional status in the community of nations known as the British Empire as the Dominion of Canada, the Commonwealth of Australia, the Dominion of New Zealand, and the Union of South Africa, with a Parliament having powers to make laws for the peace, order, and good government of Ireland, and an executive responsible to that Parliament, and shall be styled and known as the Irish Free State.

The new government was set up at Dublin, the Irish Free State was admitted to the League of Nations, and Irish diplomatic representatives were sent abroad.

Ulster refused to join with the south and was permitted to have its own "Government of Northern Ireland," with a local parliament and the right to send thirteen members to the

THE IRISH FREE STATE AND NORTHERN IRELAND

British House of Commons. The more extreme Republicans continued to fight for the complete independence of Ireland, but it was hard to convince the British that it would be safe to have an entirely independent power to the west which might make common cause with their enemies should war come. Ireland at last had Home Rule,—a larger measure than most of the earlier advocates had demanded,—but she was neither entirely unified nor completely emancipated from British control.

Signs of an independent spirit, such as filled Ireland with unrest, appeared in mild forms in the five self-governing dominions of the British Empire (Canada, Newfoundland, South Africa, Australia, and New Zealand), to say nothing of India, where special problems existed (p. 526). The dominions coöperated loyally with the mother country during the war; but they indicated that they were helping as equals and of their own accord, and not because they were bound as provinces of the British Empire to render aid. Recognizing the changed temper in the colonies, the British prime minister, Lloyd George, invited the premiers of the self-governing dominions to meet in London in 1917 as a kind of "Imperial War Cabinet."

When they assembled the representative of Canada said bluntly, "We meet here as equals. Ministers from six *nations* sit around the council board, all of them responsible to their respective parliaments." Four of the dominions were represented at the peace table in Paris and were admitted to the League of Nations as if they were independent countries; in fact, Canada, Australia, South Africa, New Zealand, together with India and the Irish Free State, became full-fledged members of the League, sharing power in its Assembly with Great Britain.

At imperial conferences held in 1921, 1923, and 1926 the idea of equality among the self-governing dominions was given a still more definite form. Indeed, on November 20, 1926, a kind of new constitution for the British Empire was issued by the conference of that year. The report declared that the title of the king should be changed so as to recognize Ireland and the British dominions beyond the seas as enjoying equality with Great Britain. It added that the governor-general sent out from London to each of these dominions should not be regarded as the agent of the British ministry, but should stand in the same relation to the local parliament as the king himself to the Parliament in England. The general principle was adopted that the dominion legislatures were on an equal footing with the Parliament of Great Britain. It was also agreed that in some cases it might be desirable for self-governing dominions to send diplomatic representatives to foreign countries, and in keeping with that principle Canada appointed a minister to the United States. Carrying independence in foreign relations a step farther, a rule was drawn up to the effect that "neither Great Britain nor the Dominions could be committed to the acceptance of active obligations [by treaties with other nations] except with the definite assent of their own governments."

The British Empire is but one of the striking experiments in the federation of states which forms a highly significant feature of modern times. The United States was the first grandiose attempt of the kind. Then came the former German Empire, which departed widely from the American model. Canada and Australia and South Africa all adopted a federal form of government. The Union of Socialist Soviet Republics was formed on unprecedented principles. Then there is the League of Nations, which repudiates the idea that it is a superstate in any sense and yet takes action on international issues among its members and may exercise an important influence without being in a position to give the sanction of armed force to its decisions. The adherents of the World Court and of the international bank to be established under the Young plan of reparations suggest a sort of highly specialized federation. All are devices for a harmonious combination of independence, self-government, and autonomy on the part of individual states with the growing exigencies of international understanding.

CHAPTER XV

STARTLING EXPERIMENTS IN GOVERNMENT

THE BOLSHEVIK RÉGIME

To all outward signs the revolutions which followed the World War hurried forward the democratic process which had been such a striking characteristic of the nineteenth century (chap. ii). Monarchies had disappeared on every hand; nowhere in Europe was there left a king who could in truth call himself the State. Where a monarchy survived the storm, it was subjected to parliamentary control. With the downfall of monarchs on the Continent went the collapse of aristocracies and the disappearance of houses of lords as checks on popular government. The world conflict itself had been called a "war for democracy," to make the world "safe for democracy." At last it seemed that the remaining vestiges of opposition to the "prevailing of the people" had been destroyed and that government by the masses, according to the Liberal program, was to spread throughout Europe.

Yet it was evident that this extension of democracy, such as it was, had fallen on evil times—a period of international hatreds, social disorder, financial bankruptcy, industrial paralysis, starvation, and disease. Its success would, under the circumstances, be little short of a miracle; and at the very moment of its general recognition, democracy was attacked from four sides: by a proletarian dictatorship in Russia, by a middle-class dictatorship in Italy, by national parties rallying around dethroned monarchs, and by revolutionaries bent on substituting economic for political parliaments. We turn first to Russia.

No item in the Bolshevik creed was more emphatic than the rejection of parliamentary democracy in the historic sense. Lenin declared that "the most democratic bourgeois republic is nothing more than a machine for the suppression of the working class by the bourgeoisie, for the subjugation of the mass of the toilers by a handful of capitalists." As for democratic equality, it was, in his opinion, simply a farce. "To secure actual equality and actual democracy for the toilers, for workmen and peasants, one must first take from capitalists the possibility of hiring writers, of buying up publishing houses, of controlling newspapers, and, to this end, one must throw off the yoke of capital." To Lenin what had been called democratic freedom was likewise a delusion. "Capitalists have always called 'freedom' the freedom to make money for the rich, the freedom of the workers to die of hunger. Capitalists call 'freedom' the freedom of the rich, freedom to buy the press, freedom to use wealth to manufacture and support so-called public opinion."

Soviet government, he then went on to argue, would give to the toiling masses that real liberty and equality which they had been promised by political democracies, would put the laboring classes in power, and would bring about "true democracy," that is, equality and liberty. Thus government would not be by and for the rich but by and for the poor. "The dictatorship of the proletariat is the forcible overcoming of the resistance of the exploiters, that is, of an insignificant minority of the population—landlords and capitalists." Working people and poor peasants in Russia were to govern, to be sure, though, for the time being, not by majority vote but as permitted and directed by a small minority of the population—the communist dictators and their party officeholders and supporters.

Yet, as in all other human affairs, there was development in the communist experiment in Russia. It did not move in a straight line to a goal. As we have seen, the Bolsheviki were not commissioned by the Russian people in 1917 to apply communist doctrines to the economy of the country. Far from it. They came to power because they had an armed force at their command and were willing to give the masses what they wanted—namely, peace and land. Once in power, the communists did not proceed immediately to "nationalize" all industries, but evinced caution in that respect. Indeed, they did not make peace with Germany until after they had appealed to President Wilson, asking what military aid would be forthcoming in case of a renewal of hostilities, and had failed to receive any reply to their appeal. In short, they were driven by those outside their ranks to take more hasty and radical measures than they might otherwise have done.

In the first place, thousands of middle-class employees in private establishments and in government offices struck soon after the Bolsheviki seized the government—quit work and "sabotaged" the new order, turned the tables on the working class. Frightened capitalists shut their factories. Private banks closed their doors. To prevent a complete collapse the Soviet government quickly nationalized these enterprises. During the six months that followed the November revolution of 1917, about 230 establishments were seized, many of them by local authorities, and at least one half of them for refusal to coöperate with the government or for "sabotaging" it. To the rapid communistic development brought about by internal troubles was added the "war communism," ascribed to the necessity of defense—first against the Germans, then against the Allies and the United States, and finally against the various counter-revolutionary attacks of former Tsarist officers with the aid and encouragment of the Allies. Undoubtedly, the Bolsheviki were committed to communism and intended to apply it in some form; but the method and the speed of the revolution were largely determined by events beyond their control.

Besides nationalizing land and great industries, the Soviet government abolished the state religious establishment—the Greek Orthodox Church—and confiscated its property. Its precious objects of art were gathered together with the crown jewels and plate and similar property taken from private persons; experts were employed to classify this booty; the finest art objects were placed in the national museum; many jewels were sold abroad; and a great deal of gold and silver was melted down for coins. After disestablishing the church and taking its property, the Soviet government sought to stamp out all religion, denouncing it as "an opiate for the people," and to substitute for it the dogmas, philosophy, and ideals of communism, viewed as a secular religion. Those who had been persecuting Jews were now persecuted themselves. Naturally, the Greek Orthodox Church encountered the most intolerance, for it had been intimately associated with the hated government of the Tsar (Vol. I, pp. 111, 117, 574 ff.).

But after a season of turmoil religious worship was again permitted under strict limitations. The situation in 1929 is thus described by an informed and careful American scholar, S. N. Harper:

Any group of citizens may petition to be allowed to form a religious society for the purposes of worship. The society is registered if the application is approved by the local Soviet authority. A church building will be turned over to the society, which is held responsible for its maintenance; the church remains the property of the people, and the society is liable for any destruction or damage. Regular and fixed assessments on members are forbidden; the subscriptions must be absolutely voluntary. The society must confine itself strictly to the field of religion; it cannot carry on any educational work, except seminaries to train its clergy.

Religious societies were forbidden to engage in any civic or business activities. Since all other organizations were, for practical purposes, under governmental authority, the churches naturally attracted people who refused to accept the communist order of things—shopkeepers, the richer peasants, technicians, and the "new bourgeoisie" generally. Hence they were under constant suspicion as the centers of counter-revolutionary activities, and such liberty as they enjoyed was strictly guarded. In this respect the Jewish faith was quite as much under the Soviet ban as Christianity; if there was more toleration for Mohammedanism, it was for strategic reasons, not on account of any tenderness toward it on the part of the communists.

It was one thing for the Bolsheviki to overturn the Tsar's government, to issue proclamations declaring land and factories to be public property, and to disestablish the state church; it was something entirely different for them to run railways, manufacture shoes, coats, and other goods, raise wheat, and produce all the other things required for general prosperity. Moreover, after the first excitement was past, the leaders of the Bolsheviki saw that there was not to be an immediate uprising of the working classes all over the world, as they had hoped. Indeed, the conservative newspapers in other countries continually reported that the Bolsheviki were about to be overthrown themselves. Nothing of the sort occurred, however. On the contrary, the Red Army put down, one after another, White military officers (Kolchak, Denikin, Yudenitch, and Wrangel), who attempted to restore the old order in Russia. By 1923, after the Bolsheviki had been in power for five years, it looked as if their tenure were fairly secure.

However, they now had before them more difficult tasks than those of fighting. They had to run the factories, mines, ships, electric-light plants, banks, stores, and railways which they had seized—"nationalized," as they called it. This required engineering skill and ability in management; it could not be done by making speeches before cheering soviets. Besides being difficult in itself, the task was made doubly hard because Russian factories and railways had run down badly during the war and the revolution, and, as the new Russian government had repudiated old Russia's debts, it could not easily borrow money abroad to repair damages and buy new machinery. Something had to be done; for five sixths of the people were peasants in desperate need of clothing, shoes, plows, and other manufactured commodities. They demanded supplies at the hand of the Soviet government, and the government stores and factories were unable to meet their needs.

Thus the Bolsheviki had to surrender some of their communistic ideas. In fact, they adopted what they called a New Economic Policy—"Nep," for short. They allowed private persons to open stores and shops, under government regulation; they cut down the power of the workers' councils in government factories and sought to increase production by introducing stricter central management; they invited foreign capitalists to come into the country to develop the mines, oil wells, and other industries, promising to respect their property rights and allow them to earn good profits; they stopped paper-money inflation and put their currency on a specie basis. Instead of defying other countries as "capitalistic," the Soviet government began to cultivate friendly relations and succeeded in winning recognition from Germany, Italy, France, England, Japan, and nearly all the other nations of the world except the United States. While the government of Russia thus remained in the hands of communists, and the Bolsheviki still talked of working-class uprisings in other lands, Russia was gradually drifting back, not toward the old feudal autocracy of the Tsar but in the direction of private enterprise coupled with state socialism. As a matter of fact, nearly all the people were peasants, who owned the land they tilled and were not much concerned about the government so long as they could live with a fair degree of comfort.

As a result of this new economic policy, the simple communist system, as conceived by the faithful, developed into a very complex social order. The railways and most of the great industries remained in the hands of the government and were administered by state trusts and combines, each operating on its own basis under government supervision. Merchandising was carried on by state stores, coöperative stores, and small private traders, while foreign business was retained as a government monopoly. Under the new economic policy, grain production was increased, and the thrifty and more prosperous peasants enlarged their supply of cattle and implements, thus separating themselves more sharply from the poorer peasants. In the great state industries three or four million working people were employed and furnished members for the Communist party, which formed the bulwark of the "proletarian dictatorship" and governed the country. Although there was not supposed to be any middle class, as a matter of fact the industrial workers were outnumbered perhaps two to one by government employees, private traders, employers in small industries, technicians, educators, and professional people. Thus, in spite of revolutionary decrees the fixed level of communist equality was broken at many points, furnishing grounds for differences of opinion.

This new economic policy was only a few years old when a formidable opposition developed against the Soviet government, under the leadership of Trotzky and other Bolsheviki of the November revolution of 1917. These critics declared that they were fighting for "the life interests of the 'lower classes,' the rank and file of industrial workers, the farm hands, and the poorer peasants; for forms of organization which will permit those interests to dominate politically over the others; and for honest scientific thinking about the problem of fulfilling those interests." This great object, they averred, was to defend "the proletariat against the indubitable encroachment of three anti-proletarian elements—the *nepmen*, or new capitalists; the *kulaks*, or rich peasants; and the gradually crystallizing class of political, industrial, and trade-union bureaucrats, who inevitably fall more and more under the influence of the nepmen and kulaks."

Besides this conflict in ideas there were differences of opinion about the future of the communist experiment in Russia. One party, perhaps the more nationalist in sentiment, laid stress upon coming to terms with capitalistic countries, borrowing money from them, and proceeding as rapidly as possible with the industrialization of Russia along communistic or, at all events, state-socialistic lines. The other entertained doubts about the possibility of realizing the communist ideal in Russia alone and looked forward to new wars among the capitalistic powers to usher in the world revolution so ardently prophesied. After weeks of acrimonious debate the Soviet government exiled Trotzky and many of his partisans in 1928; but instead of easing its pressure on the rich peasants, it announced at once a program for diminishing their rights, increasing their taxes, and promoting communism in agriculture.

Although old Russian bonds rose on the foreign exchanges when Trotzky was exiled, they soon declined when the government announced its determination to make no concessions to conservatism and private enterprise. Indeed, the expulsion of Trotzky and of other opposition leaders brought no relaxation in the communist policy of the government in any direction. The Soviet authorities went forward as rapidly as possible with a "five-year industrialization program," with the aid of an internal "industrialization loan" and of credits advanced by American, British, and German capitalists. New factories were built, hydroelectric plants constructed, and old enterprises operated at a higher speed. When the Soviet government celebrated its tenth anniversary in November, 1928, it boasted that the industrial production of Russia, as valued in pre-war rubles, was greater than in 1913, and pointed to this as a victory for communism. Its critics, however, replied that in reality this was no achievement worthy of note, because in the Tsarist days Russian production had doubled every ten years. They contended also that, in the process, many of the industrial plants inherited from the former régime had been worn out, that new capital to repair them was not in evidence, that the prices of goods were two or three times as high as in 1913, and that the country as a whole was suffering from a "goods famine." Thus, while the communists were celebrating their economic gains, their opponents in Russia and abroad were asserting that "what is claimed by the communists as a meritorious accomplishment proves in reality to be a ten-year setback." But such arguments had no effect upon Soviet industrial policy.

Furthermore, the Soviet government made special efforts to apply communistic principles to agriculture—a branch of economy that had been highly individualistic. After a period of oppression it attempted to assist the coöperative societies formed by peasants for the purchase and sale of goods, thus helping to make war on private village merchants. It raised money for its rural program by floating a domestic "agricultural-development loan," and secured credits for farm machinery in foreign countries. On public lands (embracing millions of acres) it established or enlarged "model farms," tilled on a coöperative principle by the latest appliances, including Fordson tractors. It sought expert advice from Thomas Campbell, an American capitalist who farms thousands of acres by machinery, and laid out a program for the socialization of agriculture on a large scale. Its fundamental purposes were to increase the output of agricultural produce and to prove to peasants that coöperative farming was better for all parties than old-fashioned individualism. Yet all these Soviet undertakings comprised only a small part of Russian agriculture,—less than 3 per cent of the acreage in 1929,—and the lack of capital prevented their rapid expansion.

Hence the recovery of Russian agriculture continued to depend upon the 24,000,000 farms in the hands of the peasants themselves. The key to the situation was held by the great mass of middle peasants, each with a holding of medium size and a small supply of stock and tools. While taxing the rich peasant heavily, and otherwise making life uncomfortable for him, the Soviet government dealt gently with the middle peasant, hoping to win him over gradually to communist methods.

On one thing, however, all peasants—rich, middle, and poor—agreed: they did not want their former landlords back again, and they did not want to pay for the land the Bolsheviki had nationalized for them. Doubtless this fact, more than Bolshevik advances in agriculture, gave the Soviet government great strength among the rural masses.

No small part of its popular support was due also to the amazing educational activities of the Soviet authorities. Finding the great body of the people wholly illiterate and the former beginnings of a school system in ruins, the Soviet government set to work teaching the masses to read and write, partly with a view to making "good Communists" out of them. Little headway was made with the elementary schools at first, owing to the lack of teachers and facilities; but by 1926 there were relatively as many children in the primary classes as in 1914, and factory and village schools for adults had been set up in many parts of the country. After that date, advance in reducing illiteracy was fairly rapid, and in 1928 the government announced that at the existing rate of expansion it would have in effect by 1934 a system of universal and compulsory education for all children up to the age of twelve.

In the scheme of instruction for the so-called labor schools, great emphasis is laid on the adaptation of the child to his environment—nature, the community, economic life, and Soviet citizenship. "For the first year," says S. N. Harper, "the child studies the seasons of the year, the daily work of the family, and the relation of the family to the school. In the second year, nature study covers air, water, the sun, plants, and domestic animals; the everyday work of the village or the part of the city in which the child lives is taken up; and the administrative institutions of the village or city are studied. For the third year [the studies] bring in the economic activity, the administrative institutions, and the history of the region in which the city or village is located. In the fourth and last year . . . the national economy of the Soviet Union and of other countries, and the governmental organization of the Soviet Union as compared with that of other countries, with pictures of the past life of the human race," are included in the program. On this basis pupils advance to the study of modern society, revolutionary movements, and communist principles.

The fundamental purpose of Soviet education from the bottom to the top is to teach all the children that the communist system is the best scheme of government and economy in the world, that the Marxian dogmas constitute the truth, and that all others are false. "The future Soviet citizen whom we are training," writes a communist educator, "must be a stalwart and healthy proletarian, a class and revolutionary fighter, a scientifically conscious and organized builder of the new socialist state. He must be a dialectic materialist, armed to the teeth with the necessary knowledge and ability to oppose exploitation and mysticism in all its forms. He must be a collectivist in all economic and social activities, in order to oppose steadfastly private property and individualistic aims, on which the class of exploiters has built up its power. . . . The future citizen must be a revolutionary activist with habits of self-organization and of organization in common with others."

To this educational-propaganda program are added the theater, the museums, the moving picture, and the radio, likewise controlled by government officers. By these powerful agencies the cruelties of the Tsarist régime are recalled continually in striking form, and the work of the Soviet authorities for laborers and peasants is represented in the most favorable light. In the same cause the press is enlisted. The publishing of books, newspapers, and periodicals is controlled by Soviet officers, central or local, or by committees of the Communist party. Over everything printed there is a strict censorship. No press can be set up except under government scrutiny; no book can be published until approved by the censor. "Helpful criticism" designed to point out minor shortcomings in the Soviet order is permitted; indeed, the columns of the newspapers are opened for this purpose. But no attacks on Soviet institutions as such, demanding their overthrow, are allowed. During the controversy between the Trotzky faction and leaders of the Soviet Communist party, the opposition complained bitterly that they were not given a fair hearing in the papers, even though they professed great attachment to Soviet institutions. One of the charges against the Trotzky group was that it maintained a secret, or "underground," press. In short, the censorship rules of the Tsarist days continued in force; only the tables were turned.

Yet propaganda alone did not sustain the Soviet order. Besides the Red Army, drilled and disciplined in communist doctrines as well as arms, the Soviet government had under its close supervision the Russian trade unions. Although membership in them was made voluntary in 1922, they grew so rapidly (after a brief period of decline) that seven years later official reports placed the total number of trade unionists at ten millions. At that time the unions were theoretically regarded as nonpolitical organs and enjoyed freedom to conduct collective bargaining respecting wages, hours, and shop conditions, and even to carry on strikes. But since the unions were all organized in government works or in private establishments under strict government control the theory amounted to little. In practice about one third of the unionists were communists; certainly the most active elements belonged to that party, and all the leaders of high rank were equally "orthodox" in their economic views. Strikes seldom occurred in private industries and were practically outlawed in government enterprises.

In theory the government, being a dictatorship of the working classes, was controlled by them and bowed to their will. In reality there were frequent differences of opinion between the unions and the managers of state undertakings, so that communist members had to play the rôle of mediators. The latter represent the government in the unions, and the unions in the government. Although it was once thought that the

T

trade unionists in each plant could take it over and run it themselves, a little experience demonstrated that a nation-wide (even an international) organization of markets and technical skill in management were as necessary as labor. For this reason a national trust was formed in each important branch of industry, and technicians were engaged as directors of plants. Since the government controlled the trusts and appointed the managers, it really stood in the position of a large-scale employer and called upon the trade unions for coöperation. The government enhanced its influence over trade unions in this relation by granting their members many special privileges, such as lower prices at the government stores and advantages for their children at the public schools.

Although the Soviet government maintained these friendly relations with the trade unions, it encountered difficulties in securing engineers and experts willing to coöperate sympathetically with it in its efforts to promote industry and trade. In all branches of technology old Russia was backward in 1917, and most of the technicians were strongly opposed to the communist régime. Many of them fled the country, especially the foreign engineers previously employed by Russian business enterprises, and perhaps a majority of those who remained behind had no desire to see the Soviet system succeed. Yet without these competent experts industry and commerce simply could not be carried on and expanded to meet the needs of a rapidly growing population. So the Soviet government had to make terms with them and employ them at relatively high salaries. But it distrusted them, surrounded them with espionage, and hampered their work by subjecting them to the control of political committees and officers who knew little or nothing about technical processes. To train up a new generation of engineers and managers imbued with communistic principles required time, if it could be done at all, and the fate of the Soviet experiment seemed to hang more on expert intelligence than on "vigorous propaganda of the communist truth."

Mussolini and the Fascisti

Of all the Western countries that came out of the war victorious, Italy was the most disturbed by radical agitations. In that kingdom the old Socialist party adopted communistic principles, and in the election of 1919 carried six times as many cities and towns as in the previous election of 1913. Thus encouraged, Italian communists in several industrial centers believed the time ripe to follow the Russian example. They seized factories, expelled the proprietors, and proclaimed the dictatorship of the proletariat here and there in the manufacturing districts. In the agricultural regions there was an epidemic of strikes accompanied by considerable violence. The premier of Italy at the time, Giolitti, decided to shed no blood. He let the communists keep possession of the factories for several days, until they learned that it took special talent to operate them and market their output.

But the middle classes of Italy were not so calm as the government. They were dismayed by the threats of the communists and the disorders that had accompanied the recent progress of radicalism. Among the Italian citizens who watched the course of events was a young journalist, Benito Mussolini, a stormy petrel of radical politics. Born in 1883, the son of an Italian blacksmith, Mussolini started life as a schoolmaster in Switzerland, where he went as a youth after receiving an education and a teacher's diploma in the land of his birth. In his new home he took up the study of socialism, adopted Marxian doctrines, and became a fiery agitator. For his dangerous teachings he was expelled from Switzerland. Shortly after his return to Italy he became the editor of the leading socialist paper, *Avanti!* and he was busily engaged in socialist propaganda when the World War began.

Almost immediately Mussolini declared himself in favor of the Entente Allies. Breaking with the Socialist party, which finally expelled him, he threw himself into the movement designed to force Italy into the war, and when that event occurred the hot young radical rushed into the army. Receiving a slight wound from the explosion of a trench mortar he returned to Milan, where he edited his patriotic journal, *Il Popolo d'Italia*, and attacked socialists with all the fervor he had once employed against the bourgeoisie.

Seeing the communists organizing in bands to seize factories and get possession of the government and committing a good deal of violence and many murders in the operation, Mussolini decided to organize a countermovement. Hence in the spring of 1919 he began to form, in opposition to the radicals, what he called Fascist Fighting Groups.[1] Before many months had passed, Italy was covered with a network of such societies dedicated to the self-chosen task of exterminating the followers of Lenin and the advocates of all forms of communism, socialism, and political democracy. They fell upon their foes, driving communist mayors and councilors out of office, beating and killing, until they practically silenced the radicals in the name of Italian patriotism.

Yet it would be a mistake to assume that *Fascism* sprang up full-armed overnight and had before it from the outset a definite goal. In the beginning the term *fasci*, or "groups," had no special meaning; it was as common as the word "society" in the United States and was used by many Italian associations formed for various purposes, particularly those that were nationalistic, or Irredentist, in their aspirations. Previous to the war there were several societies of this character in Italy, with the Nationalist Association founded in 1910 in the lead. Like the Pan-German Society in Germany, the Navy League in Great Britain, and kindred fellowships in other countries, they favored expansion through the acquisition of new territories and the development of an empire. They took

---

[1] The Italian word *fasci* (pronounced "fä'shē") is derived from the Latin *fasces*, the name for the bundles of rods which were the Roman symbols of strength in unity. It was not used first by Mussolini's local societies.

the position that Italy, poor in natural resources and growing rapidly in population, must "expand or explode"—a form of the German theory of "world dominion or downfall." These nationalistic groups favored the war on Turkey in 1911, with its promise of territory in Tripoli, and they received a great impetus from the excitement caused in Italy by the outbreak of the World War. Many of them favored taking advantage of the quarrels among neighbors to get the largest possible price for Italian assistance—compensation in territories at somebody else's expense. And, indeed, the Italian government, by a secret treaty, the Pact of London, concluded just before it declared war on Austria, received definite promises of large territorial gains (p. 334).

At the close of the struggle, when President Wilson opposed Italian claims along the Dalmatian coast on the ground that they violated the principle of Yugoslav nationality, Italian imperialists were bitterly disappointed. Italy did receive, it is true, material additions of territory to the northeast,—some of it inhabited by Germans,—but her allies, France and England, made off with the lion's share of the colonial spoils in Africa and Turkey. Accordingly, strong indignation was aroused throughout the country, and the blame for the failure was laid on the politicians of the old school, especially Orlando, Italy's spokesman at Paris. This disappointment was deepened by the industrial depression, the rise in the cost of living, the heavy debt and taxes, and the general disillusionment which came fast upon the peace.

Following the custom of people in all countries, discontented Italians laid the blame on the government. It was accused of surrendering Italian rights, of incompetence and decrepitude, of being deceived by modern democratic ideas not appropriate to Italian life. Hundreds of professors, philosophers, and journalists began to celebrate the ancient grandeur of the Italian people. "Everything," ran a Nationalist manifesto in 1918, "calls Italy to the resumption of her imperial mission:

the tradition of Rome, of Venice, and of Genoa; the political genius of the race, which has always made it a master in the art of governing peoples; her geographical position, which links her by land to continental Europe and at the same time bids her dominate the whole Mediterranean basin, where today the heart of three continents beats." To writers of such exaltation, this Italian policy did not spring from economic selfishness, but was "the very essence of idealism; a demonstration that God, the immanent spirit, had moved from Germany and is now manifesting himself in Italy, his new abode in the creative process of history." To Italian patriots of this class, democracy, peace, and internationalism were merely hypocrisies with which "the industrial and colonial empire of the British" and "the money and banking empire of the Americans" covered their operations.[1]

However, Mussolini did not arrive immediately at this definite form of assurance nor any other positive conviction. At one time he laid emphasis on the republican tendencies of Fascism; at another, on its loyalty to the royal house. At one time he spoke favorably of democracy and the League of Nations; at another, he condemned both without mercy. In 1919 he had a program that included universal suffrage for men and women, proportional representation, abolition of the Senate, an eight-hour day, a heavy levy on capital, a high inheritance tax, an almost complete confiscation of war profits, and a serious curtailment of clerical privileges.

Within two or three years he had abandoned this program and was declaring that Fascism "is not a museum of dogmas and principles." The aim of Fascism, he said, was "the general good," and he steered to the right or the left according to circumstances. In fact, he took a wholly "relative" position, which would be called in French politics "opportunism," but in his view of statecraft appeared to be "higher wisdom." In 1921 he maintained that "Fascism is the strongest of all here-

[1] H. W. Schneider, *Making the Fascist State*, p. 24.

sies that strike at the doors of the churches. Tell the priests, who are more or less whimpering old maids: 'Away with these temples that are doomed to destruction; for our triumphal heresy is destined to illuminate all brains and hearts.'" Not long afterward he was extolling religion, making terms with the Catholic party in Parliament, praising the Catholic Church as a great cultural institution, and settling the ancient dispute between Italy and the papacy by making decided concessions to the latter (1929).

In spite of the facility with which Mussolini could veer to the left and the right, he and his followers at first made no great political headway. In the election of 1921 they managed to secure only thirty-five seats in a parliament of five hundred and eight members. Meanwhile the socialists and communists were declining in strength; strikes were decreasing; the danger from Bolshevism had passed; and it looked as if Italian politics might resume a normal course. But owing to party divisions among the voters, no group had a majority in the Chamber of Deputies; the great classes in Italian society—middle classes, industrial workers, and Catholic agrarians—were so balanced that a cabinet could be formed only by a coalition. For days in the autumn of 1922 the government was deadlocked, the distracted king negotiating first with one politician and then with another in a vain effort to effect a combination. Public business drifted. Public patience was exhausted.

At this juncture a great Fascist congress was held in Naples, and revolution was broached as a solution for the problem presented at the capital. A few days later thousands of black-shirted[1] Fascists gathered near Rome and at a signal began to march into the city. Thoroughly frightened, the acting head of the government tried to induce the king to proclaim martial law; but in vain, for the king was afraid that the army would not support him. In his desperation the king at last invited Mussolini to form a ministry, and the offer was accepted with

[1] The red shirts of Garibaldi's republican followers had fallen into disrepute.

alacrity. By compromises with the Liberals and the Catholic Popular party, he managed to organize a government, but Fascists, including himself, held only four out of the fifteen posts. Dismissing the Fascist squads in Rome, he set to work governing with the aid of the parliament which he had so often derided. Had a revolution taken place? Not yet; for the forms of parliamentary government remained intact, and Mussolini proposed no extreme measures, economic or political.

Before a year had passed, the new premier was at loggerheads with the Popular party and enraged over continued opposition in the Chamber of Deputies. Determined to secure a majority with which he could govern, he forced through the parliament a "reform bill," which provided that any party receiving a plurality in an election should have two thirds of the seats in the Chamber. In the first campaign held under this law, in 1924, the Fascisti won in a "landslide." Mussolini had his majority, but there were still minorities to raise questions and to accuse his government of terrorizing the voters in the recent balloting. When it was rumored that an able Socialist deputy, Matteotti, was about to make a telling speech exposing Fascist methods, including some corruption, he was cruelly murdered by Fascist patriots.

For a time it looked as if Mussolini could not survive this outrage, but he did. He reorganized his cabinet and declared war on the Socialist minority, which had seceded from the parliament and refused to coöperate with men whom it called "murderers." He established a strict censorship of the press, discharged anti-Fascists from the government, abolished the Socialist party, crushed the trade unions, and imprisoned or exiled to the desolate Lipari Islands, north of Sicily, hundreds of intelligent persons objectionable to him. With the aid of the "rump" parliament, supplemented by "unofficial" violence on the part of local Fascist groups, opposition was silenced, and the Italian government was rapidly converted from a constitutional monarchy into a despotism.

Finding that the courts were holding up, on legal grounds, many of the decrees which he was profusely issuing, Mussolini reconstructed the judicial branch of the government, simplifying and consolidating the laws in the process. This was accompanied by a political "house-cleaning," by the abolition of duplicate and unnecessary offices, a reduction in the number of state employees, and the establishment of Fascists in power in all branches of the administration. By decree the prime minister was made responsible to the king, instead of to the parliament,—that is, in fact responsible to nobody but Mussolini, —and he was given authority to make decrees having the force of law. In 1925 elective mayors and municipal councils were abolished, and authorities appointed by the central government were substituted. The next year subprefectures were swept away, and the kingdom was laid out into provinces, all governed by officers selected in Rome.

In this way Mussolini freed himself from interference by elected officials and representatives; he selected his own cabinet members without having to go through the usual tedious negotiations with parliamentary groups; he made laws by decree whenever the parliament delayed or refused to act; and he selected all the important officials of the kingdom from the top to the bottom. In the meantime he reorganized the Fascist party, vesting supreme authority in the hands of a Grand Council composed mainly of party officials, and putting the actual management of party affairs in the hands of a Directorate elected by this Council. In effect, things were so arranged that a small body of men, who had power to choose their own successors, could dominate the party, with very little control by the rank and file. In other words, a sort of "college of Fascist cardinals" was established, the survivors electing new members as old members dropped out. Fascism was thus incorporated to endure forever.

While Mussolini was making all these political changes,— which, after all, had little effect on the life of the people,—his minister of finance, De Stefani, carrying on an economic policy that conformed in the main to historic English Liberalism, insisted that the State should not interfere with business. Inheritance taxes were abolished; and war legislation regulating and controlling industries was repealed, to the great satisfaction of the manufacturers. Economy was preached with a zeal and in a style that must have pleased his contemporary, President Coolidge, in the United States. War was made on everything that savored of "state socialism."

All over the kingdom business men rallied to the administration, seeing in it a hope of final freedom from control by the government and by trade unions. "There have always existed two opposed conceptions of history," explained De Stefani, "the individualistic and heroic conception of our Latin race and the socialistic, gregarian conception which is Teutonic, and characteristic of current socialism. So-called 'scientific socialism' is a foreign product—a product exported by a German Jew. Solidly opposed to socialism stands the individualistic conception we have inherited from Liberals, from our own forefathers." The solution of the problem of overpopulation he found in cutting down consumption, increasing the savings to be used in production, and, if need be, in imperial expansion by war. "A financial policy based on the persecution of capital," he said, "is a mad policy."

Among the capitalists only the bankers were discontented with this régime; they believed that Italy needed more foreign loans (which brought commissions and business to them) to stabilize the lira and furnish resources for Italian industry. But it was among the working classes and petty bourgeoisie that the chief opposition to the economic measures of Fascism arose.

Although organized communism and socialism had been practically stamped out by police measures and Fascist lynching parties, the working classes were asking themselves just how they were to benefit by the new order of things. Black-shirted agitators began forming "syndicates" among laborers. One of these organizers, Edmondo Rossoni, utilized the experience he had gained in the I. W. W. propaganda among Italians in the United States. In French and Italian usage the word "syndicalism" (see page 434) is employed in several senses. At one extreme it means the organization of all laborers into unions federated on a national scale for the purpose of enforcing demands on employers and ultimately "conquering" capitalism. At the other extreme it implies merely the formation of pacific industrial associations, sometimes including both employers and employees, and a collaboration of industrial classes, rather than war between them. In the latter form it is sometimes turned to account by Catholic writers in advocating a return to the guild system of the Middle Ages.

At all events, on old foundations an elaborate network of organizations was built up in Fascist Italy, divided horizontally into employers and employees, and vertically into special groups such as agriculture, industry, banking, and transportation. In these syndicates some Fascist writers discovered "the cells of a new and greater social organism," which was to take the place of "the modern and decadent parliamentary state." Employers, organized into a National Confederation of Industry, saw in their union a source of strength against labor encroachment. Labor leaders struggling for more power against employers had various purposes in mind: some of them hoped merely for a recognition of trade unions and for more bargaining power, while the radicals aimed at the practical supremacy of labor in national affairs. Finally, the friction between capital and labor became so great that Mussolini was forced to take it into account and bring about some kind of settlement. This was done with a fine flourish.

In 1925 the *laissez faire* minister of finance was dismissed, largely as a result of the hostility of the banks to his fiscal policy, and with great rejoicing on the part of the labor leaders. Later in the same year the general secretary of the Fascist party summoned the directors of the rival industrial and labor confederations to a conference and forced them to come to a compromise. This took the form of a royal decree legalizing what is known in the United States as "collective bargaining." All labor contracts were to be made henceforward by official representatives of capital on the one side and of labor on the other. Thus the labor syndicates were given a kind of monopoly of labor organization, and employers were required to deal with them. On its side, labor drafted a great "Charter of Labor," which was published widely as a momentous document, but was, in fact, merely a statement of hopes,—not a description of legal or economic realities.

By a general law enacted in 1926, dealing with "collective labor relations," the status of syndicates and economic organizations of various kinds before the law was generally defined. Syndicates could be composed of employers alone, employees alone, or both, the latter type of organization being of little or no significance. Collective bargaining was again recognized. Strikes and lockouts were forbidden. Labor tribunals were instituted to hear disputes relative to labor contracts and other matters. Especially severe punishment was provided for public employees who struck against the government. In this way labor secured in Italy the legal recognition which had long been accorded in England, France, and Germany. In exchange it surrendered the right to strike. The government was placed in the position of an arbiter, holding the balance between two powerful classes fully organized. All depended upon its ability to weather every crisis by effecting a compromise which both sides would accept. In the main the employers' unions had slight grounds for complaint.

With various economic groups well organized and legally recognized, it was only a step to the substitution of an economic parliament for the political parliament. Mussolini had long wanted to "bury universal suffrage" and had condemned "politics" in vigorous language. To meet his wishes the Fascist Grand Council in 1928 drew up a new law reorganizing the government, and it was forced through the parliament, in spite of objections based on the ground that it violated the constitutional charter of the kingdom. In creating the "corporate state" the law recognized thirteen national economic confederations—six composed of employers and six of employees in industry, agriculture, merchandising, maritime and aërial transportation, land transportation and inland water transportation, and banks, with an additional one made up of Fascist syndicates of "intellectuals." Each of these confederations was empowered to nominate a certain number of candidates for the new "corporate parliament" of the kingdom; from the total of these nominees the Fascist Grand Council was to select the official list of candidates for the parliament and to submit the list to the syndicate members for their approval or rejection en bloc. In case of rejection the syndicates could make new nominations and submit their lists directly to the electors registered on the electoral lists.

When the first election was held under strict Fascist supervision, in March, 1929, the Fascist "slate" prepared by the Grand Council was approved by an overwhelming vote. The new chamber which met soon afterward was not permitted to discuss any subject or vote on any bill not on the agenda, except with the approval of the premier; and all "opposition" was eliminated, though members were allowed to make "objective criticisms." Since among the syndicates, especially of employers, the registered members had a certain voice in controlling their affairs, an element of popular representation was reintroduced, and talk about "democracy" was revived. Indeed, Mussolini himself exclaimed on one occasion that a new state had been created in Italy,—a state "expressed in an accentuated, organized, authoritarian democracy, in which democracy the people circulate freely." For the time being, however, he was himself the state in fact, and arrangements had been made to insure permanent Fascist control by the organization of the self-perpetuating Grand Council of the party which has been described above.

But as President William Howard Taft once remarked of the initiative and referendum in the United States, votes did not produce bread or shoes. The economic life of Italy flowed steadily forward underneath these political changes. The *laissez faire* minister of finance was, as has been noted, forced out of office. The government was compelled by circumstances to abandon its policy of "noninterference" with business and to resort again to the policy of regulation and control. To employers eager to conduct their business in their own way, interference by labor syndicates recognized by the government was nevertheless interference, although it bore a new name. The government still had to deal with land problems presented by great estates, with unemployment, public works, railways, and other economic issues. Capital and labor, bankers and industrialists, were still at loggerheads, even if legally compelled to follow certain procedures and to avoid extremes. The problem of finding work and increasing capital remained, and the urge to seek an outlet by imperialist expansion was as powerful as ever. Amid many theories and much verbiage the Fascist state felt its way forward.

At the end of eight years it could claim as achievements the stabilization of the lira, improvement in the efficiency of the railways, a balanced budget, the attainment of "law and order," and a better condition of public finances—the last due in part to the fact that the United States canceled nearly all the Italian war debt on the theory that Italy was unable to pay in full. How much these results were due to Fascism could not be determined; in England, Germany, and France similar adjustments were effected without destroying democracy. Indeed, as a French critic remarked, France did not deem it worth while to abolish liberty in order to get the trains to run on time. Nor was it possible for impartial students to discover how real these Italian achievements were in fact; for all criticism was silenced at home, and foreign journalists were forbidden to write anything displeasing to the dictatorial régime. For example, nothing could be found out about the financial state of Italy except from government reports, which were Fascist political documents subjected to no informed and critical scrutiny at home or abroad. Fascists were under the impression that Italy had been exalted among the nations of the earth by her imperial policy; but that was a matter of opinion, and, in fact, imperialism was nothing new in Italy or the world at large.

To Mussolini must be ascribed, however, the "solution," or at least a settlement, of one of the great questions which had baffled all previous Italian governments—namely, the problem of the relation of the papacy and the State created by Italian unity in 1871. As we have seen, that issue remained open after the papal estates had been seized and the Pope driven into retirement in the Vatican. All attempts to bring about an adjustment failed, especially as the government was often anticlerical and unwilling to make terms with the Church. Although he had been once violently anticlerical himself, Mussolini changed his views or saw the necessity of securing Catholic support in politics. So in February of 1929 Mussolini and the Pope reached an agreement. The Italian government ceded to the papacy a small area in the neighborhood of the Vatican, to be held outright as an independent state,—Vatican City,—where the Pope was henceforward to enjoy all the independence of a sovereign prince. A large indemnity was paid to the Pope, part in cash and part in Italian bonds—thus, as had been pointed out, giving the papacy a "considerable stake in the Italian government." Furthermore, certain concessions were made to the Catholic clergy in Italy. In return the Pope laid aside his old hostility to the Italian government. If, as critics maintained, Mussolini solved the problem by giving the Pope all that was demanded, he at least removed one source of powerful opposition to Fascism. Still, the rejoicing was found to be somewhat premature; for the terms of the pact were general, and a few weeks after it was signed a lively controversy arose over the meaning of some of its clauses, especially those dealing with the rights of the Catholic clergy in Italy.

In international relations Mussolini maintained from the start what is known in diplomacy as a "vigorous foreign policy." In an eloquent address in 1927 he declared:

> We must be ready at a given moment to mobilize five million men and be able to arm them; we must strengthen our navy and also our aviation, in which I believe more and more, and which must be so powerful that the roar of its motors can drown out every other sound on the peninsula, and the surface of its wings hide the sun from our land. Then, on the morrow, when, between 1935 and 1940, we shall be at a point which I would call crucial for European history, we shall be able to make our voice heard and to see our rights finally recognized.

For advocates of peace he repeatedly expressed utmost contempt. When Italian members of a boundary commission were murdered in Greece, he promptly bombarded Corfu, killing a number of women and children in retaliation. He completed the annexation of the Dodecanese and Rhodes, established a virtual protectorate over Albania, countered France by entering into cordial relations with England, and cultivated Hungary and Bulgaria with a view to a combination against Yugoslavia, pending eventualities in Dalmatia. Yet he kept in working relations with the League of Nations, took part in conferences, paid occasional tributes to peace, and signed various peace documents. His followers could say that his vigorous policy meant "peace with honor." Perhaps one of his greatest problems was that of restraining the passions of nationalism and imperialism to which he had appealed while making his way to power. Certainly a large number of ardent Fascisti looked forward to the glorious war of the future which was promised to them.

About a year after Mussolini made himself dictator in Rome a similar revolution occurred in Spain, which, like Italy, had been disturbed by strikes and labor agitations inspired, to some extent at least, by the revolt in Russia. In addition to these troubles came a war in Morocco, where Spain's troops were badly defeated by the natives, and her portion of Morocco almost wrested from her. Under these circumstances some discontented officers in the army laid the blame on the cabinet, seized Barcelona, and encouraged a general uprising in various provinces. Frightened by this display of force, the cabinet resigned, and King Alfonso called in the leader of the revolt, General Primo de Rivera, and asked him to assume the position of dictator. The parliament was then dissolved, and a committee of military officers was put in charge of the country. Freedom of the press was suspended, criticism of the government was severely punished, and such democracy as Spain had enjoyed was practically suppressed. Nevertheless, a temporary national assembly of selected persons was created, and in July, 1929, a project for a constitution containing democratic features was laid before it for consideration. Though outwardly the dictatorship of General de Rivera was akin to that of Mussolini, he had behind him no such organization as that of the Fascisti, and he undertook no such extensive internal reforms. If it failed to make as great a stir throughout the world as the Italian experiment, it at least inspired military leaders in neighboring Portugal to establish in 1926 a dictatorship on a similar model.[1]

DISTURBANCES IN SOUTHEASTERN EUROPE

In southeastern Europe governments staggered along after the war from one crisis to another, with a confused alternation of dictatorships and popular elections.

[1] For the military dictatorship in Portugal see *Foreign Affairs* (New York), October, 1928, pp. 41 ff.

T

Hungary, as we have seen, started out hopefully in a democratic direction in November, 1918, as a republic under the presidency of Count Michael Karolyi, who took Wilsonian liberalism seriously, projected a division of the great feudal estates, and looked to the Allies for support. This support was not forthcoming, and the Paris Conference aroused great indignation in Hungary by stripping her of two thirds of her former territory and three fifths of her population, incidentally transferring with the territory large bodies of people belonging to the Magyar race. Shaken by starvation and Bolshevik agitations, Hungary "went Red," in 1919; Count Karolyi was expelled, and Bela Kun became dictator. Besides proclaiming communist principles at home, Kun became involved in war with the Czechs and Rumanians in an effort to save territory for Hungary. The Rumanians, with the support and sympathy of the Hungarian aristocracy, invaded and plundered the country and occupied Budapest.

This was followed in 1920 by the establishment of a White Terror in place of the Red Terror, with the usual proscription of communists and Jews. The new régime, in which Admiral Nicholas Horthy served as dictator and regent for the king to be, was frankly monarchist in spirit and policy and was sustained mainly by the old landed aristocracy which had successfully blocked the division of estates. Thinking the time favorable for a restoration, the former Hapsburg king, Charles, made an attempt in 1921 to regain the crown of St. Stephen; but his project was frustrated by the opposition of the Allies, especially the "Little Entente," composed of Czechoslovakia, Rumania, and Yugoslavia.

Nevertheless, some gestures were made in a democratic direction. A general election was held in 1920, under the police supervision of the dictatorship, and a kind of provisional parliament instituted. In 1926 a new upper chamber was created, more representative in character than the old Chamber of Magnates (Vol. I, p. 557), but still thoroughly conservative in form and spirit. At the general election held in that year the government won a large majority and continued the policy of marking time, hoping that a fortunate turn in foreign alliances would bring back the monarchy and some of the lost territory. Powerful propaganda in favor of a treaty revision was carried on in England by Lord Rothermere (Harmsworth) and the *Daily Mail*, which was under his control. In 1927 Mussolini expressed himself publicly in support of revision, perhaps with the thought that while Hungary was getting a slice of Yugoslavia in the east, Italy might make long-desired gains on the Adriatic coast.

Launched with great rejoicing on the part of the idealists who had long dreamed of South Slav unity, Hungary's neighbor to the south, Yugoslavia, was nevertheless destined to a troubled career. The new family was not very happy on the day of its union. Apart from a large number of Hungarians, Germans, Bulgarians, and other minorities included within its boundaries, its members were, in remote origin, of the same race; but for centuries they had been separated, living mainly under alien governments (Vol. I, p. 565 ff.). As a result they differed widely among themselves in social, economic, political, and religious matters. Indeed, it might be said that in many respects they were distinct peoples joined by the fortunes of war under one king, Alexander Karageorgevitch. The Slovenes and Croats, Catholic in religion and more advanced industrially than the Serbs, tended to face the West and to despise the Serbs, whom they sometimes denounced as "Balkan barbarians." The Serbs, on the other hand, adhered to the Greek Orthodox Church, were an agricultural people, and were less Westernized than the other elements in the kingdom.

However, the Serbs, though outnumbered, had decided advantages when it came to setting up a government at the close of the war: they had a strong monarchy, an army of seasoned soldiers, a treasury, a set of public officials, and considerable experience in self-government; while the Croats and Slovenes, long under Austro-Hungarian rule, were lacking in most of these things. Under such circumstances the Serb politicians naturally took the lead and after the fashion of their kind looked after their own interests in framing a highly centralized constitution in 1921. None of the racial groups could command a majority in the national parliament. From the first election, held in 1920, to that held in 1927 the voters of the kingdom were divided into five or six parties, largely along racial and sectional lines. Every cabinet—and there were twenty-three ministerial reconstructions in ten years—was a coalition representing two or more parties, likely to be pulled down in a few weeks and powerless to agree on important policies of action.

As a result the government of Yugoslavia was practically paralyzed except when it came to voting the budget and tax laws. Great issues connected with land reform, the development of industries, and the use of natural resources were pressing, but no ministry could command a majority sufficiently united, for a long enough period, to effect a solution of these questions. Meanwhile the friction between the racial sections continued almost unabated. It is true that there was a sign of reconciliation in 1925, when the leader of the Croatian Peasant party, Stephen Raditch, entered a ministry headed by the veteran Serb statesman, Nicholas Pashitch; but the truce was only temporary. Within a few months Raditch was out of the cabinet; and his party, although it did not withdraw from the parliament, kept up a fierce opposition to the government in power, especially to the Radicals, who were mainly Serb in origin.

Exasperated by constant criticism from the Croats, a Serb member of the parliament in the summer of 1928 shot three of his Croatian colleagues, killing two instantly and mortally wounding Stephen Raditch. Thereupon the entire Croatian delegation withdrew from Belgrade, leaving the Serbs and Slovenes to direct affairs in their own way. No signs of a break in the deadlock appeared, and early in the year 1929 King Alexander proclaimed a dictatorship, dissolved the legislature, and placed a Serb military officer at the head of the ministry. Though the Croats at first rejoiced to see the Serb and Slovene politicians suppressed, they were by no means pleased with the new state of affairs. They had complained that the Serbs monopolized the offices, laid unfair taxes, and were too friendly to Italy; and the grounds for their objections, such as they were, remained under the new régime.

The troubles of the Serbs, Croats, and Slovenes were slight as compared with those of their relatives on the east, the Bulgarians. To punish Bulgaria for entering the war on the side of the Central Powers, the Allies, as we have noted, transferred to Yugoslavia certain border districts and cut her off from the Ægean Sea by depriving her of Western Thrace. Moreover, they awarded to Rumania the rich farm lands of the upper Dobruja, between the Danube and the Black Sea. Saddled with a heavy debt and long oppressed by a military and monarchist party in Sofia, the capital, the peasants of Bulgaria, inspired perhaps by the Russian example, formed a peasant party and for a time got possession of the government. This produced a reaction against them, ending in the murder of their leader, Stambolisky, in a great deal of disorder, and finally, in 1923, in the establishment of a military dictatorship representing the middle classes, the bureaucracy, and the militarists. Martial law was introduced, the Communist party was dissolved, and the power of the peasantry was broken. At the end of ten years of peace Bulgaria had less democracy than on the fateful day when she decided to throw in her fortunes with the Central Powers.

Bulgaria's northern neighbor, Rumania, though overwhelmed by the Germans in the war, emerged from the struggle with a territory twice as great as the old kingdom. Besides Rumanians this "Greater Rumania" (see map, p. 400) now included Serbs, Hungarians, Russians, Bulgarians, and Turks, to say nothing of the large Jewish population long held in subjection. Frightened by the peasant revolution in Russia, the royal government promised to break up the great estates and give the land to the peasants; but as time went on, the middle classes and military men got a strong grip on things and stopped this reform. Communists and agitators were put in jail. Jews were deprived of civic equality. To add to the troubles already mentioned, there was so much contention in the new kingdom and so much poverty that American bankers declined to risk lending money to the Rumanian government, pleased as they were to meet the Rumanian queen, Marie, when she visited the United States in 1926. Not until a peasant champion, Julius Maniu, leader of the Nationalist party, got the helm as premier in 1928 was the dominance of the military and financial class broken and politics started again in a liberal direction.

In no country in the Balkans was the alternation of democracy and dictatorship more vividly illustrated than in Greece. When the young king, Alexander, died of a monkey bite in 1920, his father, Constantine, whom the Allies had ousted (see pages 336 f.), was recalled to the throne. For less than two years he wore his uncertain crown. Enraged by disasters in the war on Turkey, some army officers returned to Athens, overthrew Constantine, tried and executed several ministers and military men deemed responsible for the crash, and finally drove out King George, who had won the throne on the expulsion of his father. As a result of a popular election the old liberal minister, Venizelos, was recalled to power in 1924, only to flee from the scene after a month in office.

His departure was followed by the proclamation of a republic, which was confirmed by popular vote. Several months of uncertainty passed. In 1925 General Pangalos upset the new republic by establishing a military dictatorship. For about a year he tried to govern Greece, but was expelled, in turn, by another general, who proclaimed the restoration of the "constitutional republic." A new democratic constitution was drawn up. Popular elections held under it brought Venizelos back again in 1928, with the announcement that an era of reconciliation with her neighboring countries and of domestic economic development was to open. The first months of the new régime were marked by the fulfillment of promises,—notably a treaty of friendship with Yugoslavia,—and Greek patriots now hoped that they were to sail in smoother waters.

Albania, to the northwest of Greece, after many vicissitudes passed under a military leader, Ahmed Zogu, who proclaimed himself king in 1929. Nominally independent, the tiny realm was in fact a kind of Italian protectorate.

CHAPTER XVI

GROWING INFLUENCE OF WESTERN IDEAS IN AFRICA AND ASIA

AFRICA AFTER THE WAR

On the vast continent of Africa the World War worked many changes and raised new problems. Echoes of European revolutions in the name of democracy ran all along the coast and penetrated the huts of negro chiefs in the interior. There were uprisings against Great Britain in Egypt, against Italy in Libya, against Portugal in Mozambique. There were mutterings of discontent among the millions of natives and Hindu laborers of South Africa. "All the Senegalese democracy," exclaimed a negro candidate for the French parliament in Senegal in 1919, "whether Europeans or natives, have equal rights since they perform equal duties." Black soldiers who served by the thousands in the French armies "for the liberation of peoples" carried back with them to Africa the idea that rightly "Africa belongs to the Africans," instead of serving as a basis for exploitation by European imperialism. Native troops took part in the local wars which accompanied the capture of the German colonies and heard the Germans abused for doing what other white men had been doing in Africa for centuries.

The high cost of living and rumors of labor discontent in Europe produced unrest among native workmen on plantations and in cities. For example, a strike of municipal employees at Johannesburg in 1919, which the whites tried to put down by judicial orders, the rifle, and the lash, ended in a riot in which there were seventy-six casualties. An official investigation disclosed the fact that the natives were formulating their demands more intelligently and clearly than before the war, that "the race consciousness of the South African native is steadily growing, and the spread of education is bringing in its train a realization of the disabilities under which the native races labor."

Besides introducing revolutionary ferments, the war wrought territorial changes. The German colonies were handed over to the victors. But new formulas and gestures accompanied the transfer. The conquerors who received the colonies were called mandatories, and they were to act on behalf of the League of Nations in the discharge of "a sacred trust of civilization." Togoland and Cameroons were divided between France and Great Britain. German Southwest Africa went to the South African Union, while German East Africa was distributed among Belgium, Portugal, and Great Britain. The status of these "mandated" territories varied. German Southwest Africa was for practical purposes incorporated in the South African Union as an integral portion of its territory and subject to its laws. On the other hand, the British mandate for East Africa contained elaborate stipulations worked out by the Council of the League of Nations, providing for the protection of native rights, and for equal commercial rights for all nationals of states belonging to the League.

The humanitarian language of these documents would seem to indicate that a considerable change has taken place since the days when British and American slavers swooped down on native villages and carried off cargoes of black men and women to toil on the plantations and in the mines of the New World. Moreover, each mandatory must report annually to the Council of the League, and a permanent commission examines the reports and advises the Council with respect to the execution of the "sacred trust." When Germany was admitted to the League she had, as a member of the Council, a voice in the "supervision" of the mandated territories and, under the terms of a commercial treaty negotiated with the South African

Union in 1929, German nationals received favorable terms in the matter of trading and developmental undertakings.

After Germany was deprived of her possessions, Great Britain and France were the dominant powers in Africa. They possessed the lion's share of the territory. France held most of the huge shoulder between the Mediterranean and the Gulf of Guinea, including the Sahara, and Great Britain commanded vast stretches between the Cape of Good Hope and Egypt. Belgium retained the Congo, enlarged by acquisitions from Germany, and Portugal kept her precarious grip on Angola and Mozambique, and a few minor holdings, likewise enlarged by cessions from Germany. Libya, Eritrea, and Italian Somaliland remained under Italian sovereignty, and Spain still clung to a few fragments of her once magnificent empire.

Only two native states preserved the semblance of independence. The ancient empire of Abyssinia was able to stave off absorption by Great Britain and Italy and was admitted to the League of Nations (1923). The Free and Independent Republic of Liberia on the west coast owed its origins to the American Colonization Society formed in 1816 to promote the resettlement of American negroes in their original home. The first settlement, made in 1821, was named Monrovia in honor of the President of the United States. Although it lost a portion of its territory under the pressure of France and Great Britain, Liberia still maintained its position as "the only Negro republic in Africa," and continued to look to the United States for diplomatic assistance and for capital to develop its resources, especially its rubber plantations.

With these states Egypt may, perhaps, be properly classed as "independent." When the Turks joined the Central Powers in 1914 that ancient land escaped from the nominal rule of the Sublime Porte. A few months after the outbreak of the war, Great Britain proclaimed a protectorate over Egypt, making it a part of the British Empire; and the title of Sultan was substituted for that of Khedive. Thus the authority which Great

Britain had actually exercised since 1882 was formally established; but it did not remain long undisputed. In Egypt, as everywhere else, the spirit of nationalism was abroad, and Egyptian leaders soon demanded full rights of self-government. Responding at length to their agitations, the British government agreed in 1922 to recognize Egyptian independence; the Egyptian sultan was proclaimed king; and a new "democratic" constitution was drawn up. However, to safeguard her economic interests, Great Britain insisted on installing a high commissioner in Egypt to keep watch over the course of affairs, reserved control over Egyptian defenses, and maintained in the "kingdom" an army of occupation for emergencies.

To zealous Egyptian Nationalists this "independence" appeared more imaginary than real, and they refused to accept the new order as final. So they continued their agitation and stirred up a deep popular feeling against the British authorities, which sometimes broke out in violence. Even the Conservatives in Great Britain, in spite of misgivings, were compelled to give heed, and shortly after the Labor cabinet was formed under Premier MacDonald in 1929, the high commissioner was recalled, and a treaty was drawn up assuring a larger independence to Egypt. According to its terms, British troops were to be withdrawn except from the Suez Canal zone; British support was promised to Egypt in her application for membership in the League of Nations; and an alliance was to be made "between the high contracting parties in consecration of their friendship." When and if ratified, this document will give Egypt substantial independence, but even it falls short of the demands presented by Egyptian extremists.

In economic development Africa seems to stand at the gateway of a great future. It is rich in natural resources—fertile land, timber, tin, copper, oil, gold, and diamonds. Its soil and climate are favorable to the cultivation of cotton, coffee, rubber, cacao, sugar, bananas, and palm oil—products ardently desired by Europeans and necessary to their industries. Notwithstanding popular impressions that Africa south of the Mediterranean shore line is a vast tropical jungle, it presents great diversities of climate. Not only in South Africa but also on the high plateaus of the interior there are vast districts suitable for white settlements and still unoccupied. Moreover, with the conquest of tropical diseases and the advancement of sanitation, even the least salubrious regions are being made habitable for whites. And the deserts may be redeemed by irrigation.

In area Africa is about the size of Europe and North America combined, and yet it has a population of only 135,000,000, approximately. Apart from one network of railways along the Mediterranean shore and another in South Africa, it is deficient in means of transportation. A few railroads penetrate the interior for short distances on the east and west coasts, and a line from Cape Town to Cairo is being pushed forward; but huge areas as large as France or Germany are still without means of rapid communication. Here is work enough to occupy capital and business enterprise for years to come.

The opening of Africa has inevitably raised race questions of the first magnitude. Such crops as cotton, coffee, and sugar cannot be produced profitably by natives on small farms, even if they were inclined to adopt the ways of white farmers; on the contrary, these crops must be grown on great plantations under European supervision. Now Negroes do not naturally take to the restraints of organized agriculture. Most of them, like the North American Indians, prefer the free, primitive life to which they have been long accustomed. As a result the Europeans, in order to get an adequate labor supply, have resorted to compulsion—the rifle and the lash—to corral natives and keep them at work. In promoting their interests all the imperial nations operating in Africa have been guilty of brutality and tyranny. Amid the most favorable circumstances contacts between civilized and backward peoples have been accompanied by frightful evils, and the semislavery of forced labor invites the exhibition of the worst passions.

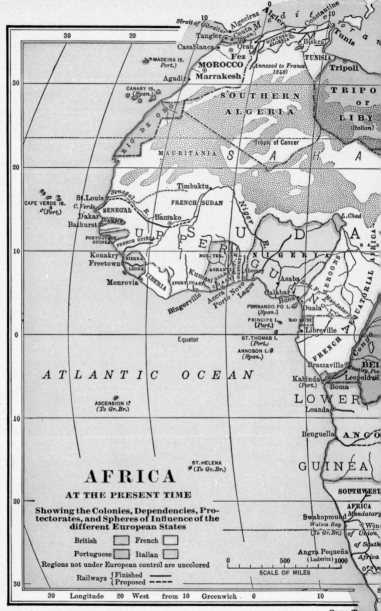

AFRICA

AT THE PRESENT TIME

Showing the Colonies, Dependencies, Protectorates, and Spheres of Influence of the different European States

British | French
Portuguese | Italian

Regions not under European control are uncolored

Railways { Finished ——— Proposed ------ }

SCALE OF MILES
0   500   1000

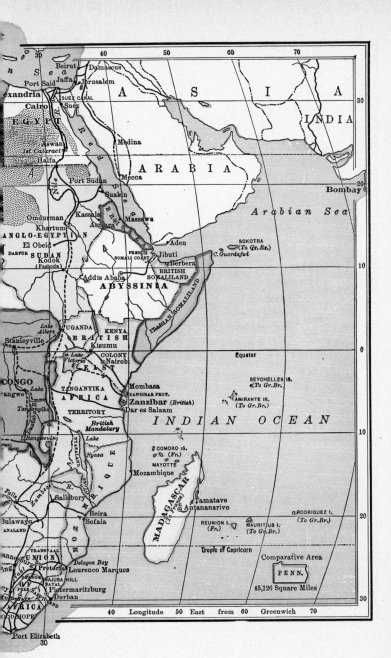

ASIA

INDIA

Beirut
Damascus
Port Said Jaffa Jerusalem
SUEZ CANAL
exandria
Cairo
Suez
EGYPT

Medina

ARABIA

Mecca

Bombay

Aswan
1st Cataract
Halfa

Port Sudan

Suakin
Omdurman
Kassala Massawa
Khartum Asmara
ANGLO-EGYPTIAN
El Obeid
DARFUR SUDAN
KODOK
(Fashoda)

Aden
SOKOTRA
(To Gr. Br.)
C. Guardafui

FRENCH
SOMALI COAST Jibuti
Berbera
BRITISH
SOMALILAND

Addis Ababa
ABYSSINIA

Arabian Sea

ITALIAN SOMALILAND

Lake
Albert
UGANDA KENYA
Stanleyville BRITISH
Kisumu
Lake COLONY
Victoria Nairobi
EAST
CONGO
TANGANYIKA
angwe AFRICA
Tanganyika TERRITORY
L.Bangweulu

Mombasa
ZANZIBAR PROT.
Zanzibar (British)
Dar es Salaam

British
Mandatary
Lake
Nyasa

Equator

SEYCHELLES IS.
(To Gr. Br.)

AMIRANTE IS.
(To Gr. Br.)

INDIAN OCEAN

Falls
Zambesi R. Salisbury
ANALAND
Bulawayo

COMORO IS.
(Fr.)
MAYOTTE
Mozambique

MADAGASCAR
(To France)
Tamatave
Antananarivo

Beira
Sofala

REUNION I.
(Fr.)

RODRIGUEZ I.
(To Gr. Br.)
MAURITIUS I.
(To Gr. Br.)

Tropic of Capricorn

TRANSVAAL
UNION
Pretoria
ORANGE Delagoa Bay
FREE Lourenco Marques
MAJUBA HILL
NATAL
Pietermaritzburg
AFRICA Durban
OD HOPE
Port Elizabeth
30

Comparative Area

PENN.

45,126 Square Miles

40   Longitude   50   East   from   60   Greenwich   70

Entirely apart from its abuses, the servile labor system has brought other problems. It has helped to break down tribal life and customs without supplying the natives with substitutes for such stability. Herded in compounds and driven to their daily tasks, they have often adopted the white man's vices and diseases without acquiring his virtues. At the same time they have come into touch with European radical ideas which have made them unwilling to accept servitude without protest. From year to year the number of intelligent Africans, educated in Europe and the United States, increases, race consciousness intensifies, and opposition to oppression stiffens. Already the Declaration of the Rights of Man issued in 1789 is quoted in inflammatory speeches in French colonies; already news of a revolution in the name of the proletariat in Russia is spread among Negro laborers in the coast towns; already there are violent racial collisions in South Africa, accompanied by conflicts over the suffrage and officeholding. Evidently white men cannot "develop" Africa entirely on their own terms.

To this development each of the two greatest imperial powers in Africa—France and England—stands in a peculiar relation. The French people have never raised against Negroes the color bar generally established among the Anglo-Saxons. As one of the able Negro spokesmen, W. E. B. DuBois,[1] has put it:

England knows Negroes chiefly as colonial "natives" or as occasional curiosities on London streets. America knows Negroes mainly as freedmen and servants. But for nearly two centuries France has known educated and well-bred persons of Negro descent; they filtered in from the French West Indies, sons and relatives of French families and recognized as such under the Code Napoleon. . . . It was not that the French loved or hated Negroes as such; they simply grew to regard them as men with the possibilities and shortcomings of men, added to an unusual natural personal appearance.

This attitude was confirmed by French colonial experience.

[1] See his article, "Worlds of Color," in *Foreign Affairs* for April, 1925.

Strictly speaking, the French "colonies" in Africa were not colonies at all but imperial possessions inhabited almost entirely by Africans. In none of them was there a large settlement of whites, comparable to that in South Africa, who came into competition with Negro laborers or were likely to be overwhelmed by an increasing Negro population. This accounted in some measure for the absence of friction between the two races. But there were also positive reasons for French deference to their colored subjects. During the World War, as we have remarked, France discovered in her African colonies an immense reservoir of man power for her struggle against her numerical superior, Germany. By various methods, "by appeal, by deceit, and by half-concealed force," she recruited 310,000 colonial laborers for service behind the lines and 535,000 colonial soldiers, four fifths from North and West Africa, for the battle front.

In combat these African troops demonstrated their valor as fighting men. Indeed DuBois contends that "but for Black Africa Germany would have overwhelmed France before American help was in sight." At all events, France appreciated the help rendered by her Negro soldiers, and the French government was careful to protect them against race discrimination on the part of their white comrades in arms. After the war was over colored troops were employed to occupy certain districts in Germany, and the German municipal authorities were required by French orders to treat the Negroes in the same way as they did other French soldiers.[1] When American visitors in Paris objected to the presence of Negroes in the restaurants they frequented, French authorities refused to permit their exclusion.

Having found her African troops able to fight well under the conditions of "civilized warfare," France, in her search for security, made preparations after the World War to maintain large forces of colonial troops for future eventualities. French

---

[1] R. L. Buell, *Europe: A History of Ten Years*, p. 43.

military officers looked forward with confidence to the colonies as a makeweight against Germany and planned to have nearly a million colored soldiers trained under the flag by 1935. Moreover, France frequently employed Negroes in high administrative posts in her colonies, assured citizenship to her African subjects, and gave representation in the French parliament to vast districts of Africa. In their battle against the British for world markets, French capitalists counted on the rapid growth of agriculture and industry in Africa.

Suppose, exclaims DuBois, that "Latin Europe should evolve political control with black men and Asiatics having a real voice in colonial government, while both at home and in the colonies democracy in industry continued to progress; what would this cost? It would mean, of course, nothing less than the giving up of the idea of an exclusive White Man's World. . . . France moving along this line would perforce carry Italy, Portugal, and Spain with it. . . . The plans of those who would build a world of white men have always assumed the ultimate acquiescence of the colored world in the face of their military power and industrial efficiency, because of the darker world's lack of unity and babel of tongues and wide cleft of religious difference. . . . Now one part of the white world bids for dark support by gifts of at least partial manhood rights."

Whatever significance this development may have for the future, it is certain that French imperialism in Africa will proceed along new lines. Naturally, France will not surrender the security afforded to her in Europe by her African troops. Nor will she be able to prevent those contingents trained on French soil from imbibing European ideas of "liberty, equality, and fraternity." This action alone will be sufficient to increase the discontent already at work in her African possessions. Coupled with industrial and missionary activities in the colonies, it can scarcely fail to bring about important changes all the way from Algiers to the Belgian Congo.

Although a great deal has been said and written about "white solidarity" in the British African possessions, it is by no means as assured as sometimes imagined. Negro soldiers were employed by the British in conquering the German colonies. In various regions of western Africa, Negroes have been given the right to vote in local elections and to hold office. Through the efforts of missionaries many Negroes have been educated in Great Britain and have taken back home "democratic notions." And their agitations have borne fruit. In 1920, for example, a congress of Negroes convened on the Gold Coast, sent a delegation to London to present grievances and an appeal to King George through the Colonial Office. Among the demands was a call for changes in the constitutions of the several British west African colonies, giving "the people an effective voice in their affairs, both in the legislative and municipal governments." Although the Colonial Office declined to receive the delegation or grant the demands, the summoning of the congress and the dispatch of the delegation were proofs of democratic stirrings in British Africa. Many citizens in Great Britain were friendly to the delegates, joined in their appeal to the government, and insisted that to block the development of self-government in Africa was to lay up perils for the future.

In the Union of South Africa, on the other hand, where there is a large white population, the maintenance of a strict color line is widely regarded as necessary to the continuance of the European civilization already established. Jan Smuts is reported to have said at a recent British imperial conference:

If there was to be equal manhood suffrage over the Union, the whites would be swamped by the blacks. A distinction could not be made between the [East] Indians and Africans. They would be impelled by the inevitable force of logic to go the whole hog, and the result would be that not only would they be swamped in Natal by the Indians, but the whites would be swamped all over South Africa by the blacks, and the whole position for which the whites have striven for two hundred years or more would be given up. So far as South Africa was concerned, therefore, it was a question of impossibility. For white South Africa it was not a question of dignity, but a question of existence.

Such advocates of white supremacy support their case by a definite line of reasoning. They insist that the whites brought civilization to South Africa, stopped the bloody wars among tribes that had been going on for centuries, reclaimed the land for high-grade agriculture, developed industries and mining, abolished famines, and overcame various native diseases. Under white protection the native population has grown rapidly. Children of former wild tribesmen are educated in white schools. They monopolize most of the unskilled labor, push into the upper trades, and enter the professions. Content with a lower standard of living, they crowd their white competitors to the wall. If permitted to vote they would take over the government, use it to their advantage, and subject the white population to their notions of interest and justice. To reasoning of this character is attributed the white solidarity in South Africa.

Still another aspect of the racial question is presented in the British dominions in eastern Africa, embracing the territories of Kenya, Uganda, Nyasaland, Northern Rhodesia, and the Tanganyika mandated territory.[1] In that region dwell about 12,000,000 natives, 50,000 East Indians, and 28,000 white settlers, and the British government has taken measures to colonize veterans of the World War in certain districts of high altitude and mild climate. Inevitably friction arose among the three elements of the population. The whites demanded self-government for themselves and the right to deal with local labor and land questions in their own way. Indians and natives resisted this movement.

In 1924 the situation became so tense that the British government appointed a parliamentary commission to inquire into the matter and make recommendations. After a three-year

[1] R. L. Buell, "Two Lessons in Colonial Rule," *Foreign Affairs*, April, 1929.

T

study the commission reported that the greater part of the region was not fit for white settlement, that eastern Africa was not to be regarded as a home for the white race but as a source of foodstuffs and raw materials, and that the British government was under obligation to protect and develop native agriculture and industry. In short, the whole region was to be retained mainly by the natives under the guardianship of the British government. It was, therefore, a case of "Africa for the Africans" under British tutelage. Should this policy be followed in practice a distinct turn would be given to the control of a vast region in central and eastern Africa.

THE TURKISH REPUBLIC—THE NEAR EAST

Turning from Africa to the Near East, we find the forces of European modernization also at work. Turkey, stripped of an immense territory and burdened with debt, made strenuous efforts to take on the Western style of civilization. As we have seen, at the close of the Balkan wars in 1913 the possessions of Turkey in Europe had been reduced to Constantinople and a little patch to the west, known as Eastern Thrace. During the World War, Egypt, the Hejaz, Mesopotamia, Syria, and Palestine escaped, in various ways, from Turkish control.

When the armistice was concluded the Allies demanded that Turkey give up her chief seaport, Smyrna, as well as Eastern Thrace, to the Greeks. This action, as we have said, aroused a Nationalist movement in Turkey under a vigorous leader, Mustafa Kemal Pasha, who made Angora, not Constantinople, the headquarters of the new government (pp. 401 ff.). As soon as they were in power the Nationalists refused to recognize the settlement which the Sultan had made with the Allies. Kemal's army repulsed the Greeks, who had marched into Asia Minor from Smyrna. Moreover, the Turks quickly discovered that they could gain support from Italy and France, whose business men hoped to gain oil and trade concessions.

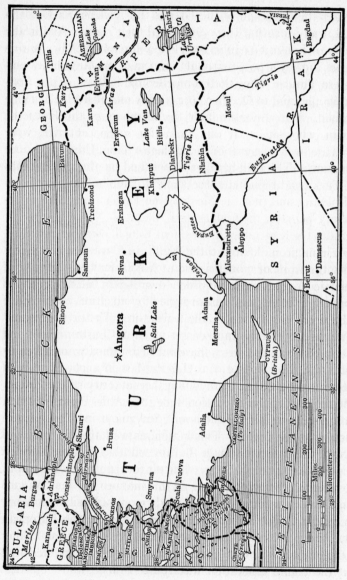

TURKEY AFTER THE TREATY OF LAUSANNE

After the expulsion of the Greeks the Turkish Nationalists stood firmly for what they considered their rights. And in the Treaty of Lausanne (July, 1923) they forced the Allies to recognize Turkey's possession of Smyrna, Constantinople, and Eastern Thrace. They then compelled the Sultan to leave Constantinople, and in October, 1923, they established a Turkish republic. A few months later the members of the House of Osman, who had ruled the Turks for seven centuries, were exiled and went the way of the Hohenzollerns, Hapsburgs, and Romanovs. The caliphate was abolished on the ground that the Turks had repudiated the ancient combination of religion and politics and that the Moslems no longer needed an intermediary between themselves and Allah.

Under the leadership of President Kemal, who was in reality, if not in name, a dictator, the Republic of Turkey set zealously about the work of modernization. A National Assembly convened in Angora declared that sovereignty belonged to the people and that it was to be exercised by an elective legislature and a president chosen by the legislature. The privileges and immunities formerly enjoyed by aliens in Turkey under the system of Capitulations were abolished. Steps were taken to reorganize the courts and revise the law in accordance with Western models, thus abandoning the authority of the Koran. Schemes for popular education were projected. Turkish women ~e allowed to take off their veils and go out in public places, m   to the horror of devout adherents of the old order of thing Efforts were made to discard the ancient Turkish script, o   ~abic alphabet, so difficult to write and read, and to substitute   ~oman alphabet; in this manner the Turkish language was to   ~implified and made more accessible to Western readers. Th ~z and turban gave way to the European hat. An agitation w   began to substitute Sunday for Friday as the day of rest. On   ~rks shook their heads and declared that the young generatio. ~s going mad.

When the Sultan's rule w   ~oken by the World War, the

various people dwelling in the immense peninsula of Arabia, extending southward from the southern boundary of Turkey to the Red Sea, the Persian Gulf, and the Indian Ocean, entered upon an uncertain and precarious political career. Syria, as we have seen, was handed over to France as a mandate under the League of Nations, but the Mohammedans in that province, constituting two thirds of the population, resented this limitation on their independence. During the war they had coöperated with British troops in destroying Turkish authority over them and had been given vague promises to the effect that an independent Arab state or confederation of states would be established at the conclusion of the conflict. Confronted by the determination of the French to have Syria as a part of their share of the spoils distributed at Versailles, leaders among the Arabs stirred up desperate revolts, and France had to pay dearly in men and money for her "trust." Even the Christians in Syria, numbering about one fifth of the inhabitants, although under the special protection of France, showed no more affection for their new ruler than did their Moslem neighbors, and leaders among them also joined in the general movement for national independence. Thus it became necessary for the French to maintain a strong military force in Syria for the purpose of keeping their mandate in working order.

The remainder of Arabia came more or less under British influence and control, at least for a time, as a result of the turn given to affairs by the World War. The British government had long laid claim to a special interest in several parts of the peninsula on various grounds. It was naturally anxious to protect the Suez Canal, as the gateway to India and the Orient, and to control Aden (with its hinterland) at the entrance of the Red Sea, for similar reasons. Rivalry with Russia, and later with Germany, in Persia led Great Britain to give particular attention to the neighboring Mesopotamia (Irak) in the northeast, and the discovery of oil there added to British concern about its future. This solicitude had been intensified when the

Germans chose the Arabian port of Al Kuwait on the Persian Gulf as the eastern terminus of their Berlin to Bagdad Railroad and helped the Turks strengthen their defenses on this frontier. If Turkey, sustained by German capital and military science,

THE NEAR EAST

could make her control over Arabia really effective, British interests of vital importance would be threatened. Thus, when the World War came, the stage was set for a revolt in Arabia.

As soon as the conflict opened in August, 1914, the British increased their military forces in the Near East and made plans for striking at the Sultan's dominion. Fortunately for their designs there were many Arab chieftains who could be induced by promises of power and payments in cash to coöperate in demolishing Turkish supremacy, already more nominal than real in many places. Powerful among these discontented leaders was Sherif Husein, Amir of Mecca, who assumed in 1916 the title "King of Hejaz." One of his ambitious sons, Amir Faisal, was induced by Colonel T. E. Lawrence to assist in the campaigns against the Turks, with signal success.[1] But not long after the war was over, Husein was overthrown by another and far superior chieftain, Ibn Saud, organizer of the Wahabis, a warlike Moslem sect bent on purifying the religion of Mohammed; and in 1926 the victor proclaimed himself King of Hejaz and Sultan of Nejd. So strongly was he intrenched that Great Britain, with some misgivings, recognized the independence of his realm the following year, although he was known to be violently anti-British and, according to rumors, was about to proclaim a Holy War against them with a view of driving them out of the peninsula.

While Ibn Saud was laying his plans and establishing his supremacy in Nejd and Hejaz, Faisal, the son of the former ruler, was consolidating his power in Irak (previously known as Mesopotamia), to the northward in the Tigris-Euphrates valley. This region, which had been the scene of strenuous rivalry from 1904 to 1914 between British, German, and Dutch capitalists striving to get possession of the old fields, was wrested from Turkey during the World War by the British with Arab assistance. At the close of the struggle Irak was assigned under a mandate to Great Britain, subject to the supervision of the League of Nations; and in 1921 Amir Faisal was proclaimed by the British high commissioner, on the basis of a popular vote, King of Irak.

Faisal, however, and many Arabs in the new kingdom were not satisfied with their status under foreign tutelage, and serious friction, leading to violence, soon arose between the natives and the British authorities. As a result Great Britain and King

---

[1] Colonel Lawrence has given a remarkable account of his experiences in his *Revolt in the Desert*, which depicts vividly the habits and moods of the Arab.

Faisal had to make new adjustments in special treaties. On her part, Great Britain undertook to recognize the independence of Irak and to use her good offices in securing its admission to the League of Nations; while King Faisal bound himself to be guided by the advice of the British high commissioner "in all important matters affecting the international and financial interests of the British government." In the meantime a constitution was adopted and a parliamentary form of government instituted. In 1927 a regular airplane service was opened between Bagdad and Beirut, to supplement the transdesert automobile traffic between the two cities. But the country was poor and the revenues from taxes were so small that the mandate over Irak proved an expensive luxury for Great Britain.

As a matter of fact, Great Britain's solicitude was largely due to the position of the Mesopotamian kingdom on the land route to India and to the fear that the kingdom, if set entirely free, might be absorbed in a large Arab state or confederation, which would seriously affect all British interests in the Near East. Another important consideration was the continued development of the oil fields already mentioned. After the war Great Britain and France took over the German oil rights in Irak and embarked on an extensive program of promotion. Later, on demands and protests from the government of the United States, American oil concerns were permitted to share in the enterprise, thus strengthening foreign interests in the kingdom. Although the whole adventure was costly to British taxpayers, the British government felt bound to maintain its authority in the face of increasing difficulties. Yet in 1929 it made new promises to Irak respecting a speeding up of the process of withdrawal.

Equally perplexing to the British government was the administration of Transjordan—a wedge of land lying between Irak and Palestine and forming a part of that mandated territory. Falling heir to this region on the dissolution of the Turkish Empire, Great Britain helped to install in authority the elder brother of King Faisal of Irak—"His Highness the Amir Abdullah Ibn Husein, K.C.M.G., G.B.E." But the amir's days were full of trouble. Ibn Saud of Nejd fell upon his land and in spite of British mediation managed to seize a valuable section of it. Then difficulties arose among his people. They resented the assignment of Palestine to the Jews as a national home. They fought among themselves; for the nomad groups of Transjordan continued to prey upon the settled farming communities as they had for centuries. Ardent "Nationalists" demanded complete independence.

In response to this agitation the British government in 1923 issued a proclamation, subject to the approval of the League of Nations, to the effect that it would recognize an independent government in Transjordan under Amir Abdullah if established on a constitutional basis, and on the further condition that the British government be placed in a position to fulfill its international obligations respecting the region. This proposition was still under discussion when in 1929 a violent conflict arose between the Arabs and Jews in adjoining Palestine.

Historic Palestine, with its holy places dear to Jews, Christians, and Mohammedans, had been for centuries a land of the deepest interest to all these peoples. The Jews had never ceased to look upon it as a homeland from which they had been driven by conquerors. Jewish leaders in the nineteenth century had founded a powerful Zionist movement to promote the return of Jews to the soil of their fathers. They held congresses, created a strong Zionist organization, raised large sums of money, and promoted the formation of Jewish colonies in Palestine. To ardent Zionists the outbreak of the World War seemed to furnish at last an opportunity to realize their dreams. Accordingly, they approached the British government with a proposition that the Turks should be driven from Palestine and that the country, at the conclusion of the war, should become a national home for Jews under British protection.

Apparently, the British government sounded the Russian government with a view to securing at least its friendly interest. But the proposition was full of difficulties. France had claims in that region, and the announcement of such a scheme might stiffen Turkey and arouse apprehensions among Arab Moslems who were aiding the British in breaking up the Sultan's dominions.

A number of circumstances, however, conspired to bring the British government around to the Zionist point of view. The British conquest of Palestine was almost in sight at the opening of 1917. In March the anti-Jewish régime of the Tsar was overthrown by revolution in Russia. In April the United States, with its immense Jewish population, entered the war. It now became apparent that a declaration in favor of Zionism would help to rally Jews throughout the world, not overlooking their powerful financial resources, to the cause of the Allies. The idea was in harmony with Allied professions respecting liberty, self-government, and democracy and offered a contribution to the settlement of the Jewish problem in various countries.

Besides, there were practical considerations to be taken into account. As a British writer put the case, "The settlement in Palestine of a Jewish population attached to Great Britain by ties of interest and sentiment might well be of value in guaranteeing the permanent security of the approaches to the Suez Canal." In other words, the Zionist program, if it could be carried out without alienating the Arabs already coöperating with British forces against Turkey, would fit into Great Britain's general Arabian policy.

At all events, the British foreign secretary, Balfour, in November, 1917, wrote to the powerful Jewish leader and banker, Lord Rothschild, stating that His Majesty's Government looked with favor on the establishment of a national home for Jews in Palestine and would endeavor to facilitate it, on the understanding that nothing should be done to prejudice the rights of non-Jewish communities in the region. This announcement, known as the Balfour Declaration, was immediately approved by France and the United States. In conformity to this promise the Supreme Council of the Allies, in 1920, placed Palestine under a British mandate and made Great Britain responsible for carrying the Balfour Declaration into effect.

In the meantime the British government explained that the Declaration did not involve imposing Jewish nationality upon all the inhabitants of Palestine, "but the further development of the existing Jewish community, in order that it may become a center in which Jewish people as a whole may take, on grounds of religion and race, an interest and pride." In 1923 the military government, which had been set up in Jerusalem after the conquest of that city by General Allenby in December, 1917, was superseded by civil authority—the British high commissioner assisted by a Legislative Council elected in part by the citizens of Palestine. At the same time the Jewish population was empowered to elect a National Committee to represent it in its relations with the British administration.

Immediately there began a small migration of Jews to the new home. Capital, raised especially in Great Britain and the United States, flowed into the development of agriculture and industry. Waste regions, neglected by the Arabs for centuries, were redeemed by irrigation and hard labor. Hospitals were erected, a university founded, electric-light plants built, and an era of prosperity, such as Palestine had never known, was opened. Even the Arabs profited from the movement. Many of them made fortunes in real estate. Better markets were established for their produce. Industries gave employment to the urban population and roads and public works to rural inhabitants.[1]

[1] Perhaps it is not too much to say, with H. M. Kallen, that "the only section of the population to whom the Balfour Declaration has been an unmixed good is the Arab."

The Arabs were nevertheless far from pleased with the course of events in Palestine. Leaders among them protested against the Balfour Declaration when it was issued, objected to the establishment of the mandate, refused to coöperate in the election of members to the Legislative Council, and carried their objections to the League of Nations. Riots marked the celebration of Easter in Jerusalem in 1920; the next year outbreaks in and around Jaffa resulted in the death of more than a hundred people and injuries to about four hundred. In 1925 a general strike greeted the opening of the Jewish University. Marauders from the interior harassed Jewish agricultural colonies on the eastern frontier, and surly feelings marked efforts to arrive at a peaceful understanding with the Arabs everywhere in Palestine. Inasmuch as the Moslems, according to the census of 1922, numbered 590,000 as against 89,000 Jews, 80,000 Christians, and a few thousand belonging to other sects, they naturally wished to maintain the political superiority to which they felt entitled by their overwhelming majority. They, too, were "Nationalists," like the other peoples of the world, and looked on the British mandate and the Jewish invasion as an interference with their designs for independence and union with neighboring Arab states. Hence the outbreaks that occurred in the summer of 1929, resulting in a great loss of life, were merely symptoms of a religious and racial antagonism that could be held in check only by powerful police and military forces. Involving as it did all of Great Britain's interests in the Arabian peninsula, this antagonism raised important issues of British imperial policy.

In the Moslem world stretching from Turkey to India history was already in the making when the war came. Russia and Great Britain, in connection with their program of union against Germany, had in 1907 divided Persia into two spheres of influence, with a kind of neutral zone as a buffer between them. But Germany in her quest for trade in the southeast had sought to break through these barriers in the name of "the open door." In 1914 German and Turkish agents tried to arouse the Persian Moslems against their "imperialist" foes. Well aware of the danger to their interests, Russia and Great Britain rushed troops to their respective spheres of influence, and a desultory guerrilla war was begun in the disputed territory. To the disorders thus created, the triumph of the Bolsheviki in Petrograd and Moscow added confusion; for they broke the Anglo-Russian truce, denounced all such "imperialist" enterprises, and called on the Persians to strike for independence against the British.[1]

Although at first this attempt failed, owing to the superior force of the British and the activities of the British oil interests, the Persians were thoroughly inoculated with nationalistic ideas. In 1925 they overthrew their feeble ruler, on the ground that he had not been able to withstand foreign aggression, and established a new dynasty under Reza Khan, a military leader who had risen from the ranks. Public finances were reorganized under the supervision of an American expert, the army was strengthened, and the government began to show more independence in dealing with "the alien invaders." Without surrendering their special interests in Persia, Great Britain and Russia had to assume a more cautious rôle. The spirit of self-determination was strong under the "Crown of Darius."

A similar spirit swept through Afghanistan, which, like Persia, had been the subject of an Anglo-Russian agreement in 1907, acknowledging British supremacy and the right of Great Britain to control foreign affairs at Kabul. As in the case of Persia, Turkish and German agents were active and tried to induce the Afghans to break with Great Britain during the World War, but without effect, largely on account of the facility with which British troops could be thrown into Afghanistan from India. However, in 1919 agitation for independence bore fruit in the

---

[1] The Bolsheviki "sovietized" the regions north of Persia and Afghanistan belonging to the old Russian Empire. The new states of Uzbekistan and Tadjikistan joined the Union of Socialist Soviet Republics (see page 423).

assassination of the amir, the installation of his son, Amanullah, a young and progressive ruler, and preparations for war on the British overlords. A serious clash was averted only by a compromise reached in 1921. Great Britain recognized the independence of Afghanistan and allowed its government to send ministers to foreign countries. The following year constitutional government was established as a part of a general movement to "modernize" Afghanistan in the Turkish style, including the "emancipation of women." Deeply offended by this introduction of "infidel" ideas and customs, Moslem priests stirred up hostility among the masses and kept the régime of "enlightenment" in constant uncertainty. In the summer of 1929, after a season of civil war, Amanullah Khan was driven out, and a "reactionary" sovereign installed in his stead. Continually anxious about Moslem troubles in neighboring India, Great Britain had to keep a watchful eye on the "independent kingdom of Afghanistan."

RESTLESS INDIA

India was seething with discontent when the thunders of the world conflict came rumbling from the West. The construction of railways opening up the interior, the rise of factories in industrial centers, and the education of Indian youth in Western ideas at home and abroad had brought revolutionary changes in the life and opinions of ancient India. In the development of the Indian National Congress, founded in 1885, the course of this evolution could be traced. At the beginning the Congress timidly advocated the gradual introduction of "constitutional government." But steadily the "young radicals" gained on their conservative sires, demanding the approval of a program for independence. In 1906 the left wing was strong enough to split the Congress. Although the moderates still refused to be driven into "dangerous thoughts" and the leader of the radicals was imprisoned for sedition, the spirit of revolt was evidently abroad. At the end of ten years—namely in

1916—the Congress went on record in favor of a thoroughgoing "home-rule program," a step short of independence. Meanwhile the All-India Moslem League, organized in 1906, after abstaining from political agitations, came out flatly in 1913 for a "system of self-government suitable for India."

Such was the state of affairs when the occupation of Great Britain with the World War and the democratic professions of the Allied belligerents emboldened Indian Nationalists to demand an extension of the reforms begun in 1909 by Lord Morley as Secretary of State for India. These admitted elective members to the legislative and executive councils of the viceroy and to the councils of the provincial governors (p. 186). To the ferment of opinion caused by the war itself were added disturbances created by the rising cost of living and the transfer of 800,000 Indian soldiers and 400,000 laborers overseas for fighting and for civilian work behind the lines.

With the Near East aflame and the fate of the war hanging in the balance, the British government announced in August, 1917, that "the policy of His Majesty's government is that of increasing the association of Indians in every branch of the administration and the gradual development of self-governing institutions, with a view to the progressive realization of responsible government in India as an integral part of the British Empire." It added, however, that progress in this policy could be achieved only through successive stages, and that the British government and the government of India must be the judges of the time and measure of each advance and must be guided by the degree of coöperation received from those upon whom "new opportunities for service" were to be conferred. Shortly afterwards the British premier appealed to the people and government of Indian to put forth greater efforts to prevent the spread of "German tyranny" to the East.

The promise of self-government announced in 1917 was followed the next year by the notorious Rowlatt Act, giving the authorities in India summary powers to arrest, try, and punish agitators guilty of "seditious acts and language." As often happens, this measure designed to allay discontent actually aggravated it. While the number of arrests for "sedition" increased, the meetings of protest multiplied, and the demands of the Nationalists became more radical. President Wilson had declared that the Allied and Associated Powers were fighting for "the liberation of peoples" everywhere, and Indian patriots now insisted on an immediate application of the creed to their particular situation. The fact that the mass of the people were not educated for democratic government did not damp the ardor of their leaders on the left wing.

At this juncture a movement headed by Mahatma Gandhi gave a new turn and more power to the Nationalist agitation. Gandhi had left his native land at the age of nineteen to study law in London and in due time had been admitted to the bar, where he soon gave evidence of a promising career. Shortly after his return to India a business engagement took him to South Africa, in 1893. While there he became interested in the attempts of Hindu immigrants to secure rights as settlers against the limitations imposed by the whites. In championing their liberties he was drawn to the doctrine of nonresistance associated with the name of Tolstoy, gave up his lucrative law practice, and organized a colony for Indians who shared his religious views. For his opinions he suffered poverty, imprisonment, and rough treatment at the hands of mobs, but nothing could shake him from his faith.

Returning to India in 1914, Gandhi threw himself into the home-rule movement, advocating resistance to British authority in the form of peaceful noncoöperation. This involved refusal to take part in elections, to hold office, to send children to the government schools, and to recognize the authority of the courts of law. Later the policy was extended to include a return to the spinning wheel and the hand loom for the manufacture of cloth, and a boycott of foreign goods.

Tolerant in matter of religion, Gandhi was able to work

with the Moslem Nationalists and bring the two great religious bodies—Moslem and Hindu—into the common cause in spite of their historic differences. Thus, in a broad sweep Gandhi appealed to all the people of India to put an end to British rule by a peaceful refusal to coöperate with British authorities. He denounced the Rowlatt Act, mentioned above, as "an insult" to every Indian. The methods employed by General Dyer in suppressing an "unlawful assembly" in Amritsar in 1919, which resulted in the death of four hundred Indians and the wounding of many more, added strength to Gandhi's movement. The very next year, the once conservative Indian National Congress voted in favor of noncoöperation. In spite of Gandhi's insistence on peaceful methods, many of his followers committed acts of violence. Indeed, disturbances became so widespread that he was arrested and imprisoned as a seditious leader.

While putting down resistance with a strong hand, the British government made concessions to Indian Nationalists by an important act of Parliament, passed in 1919. This new measure, which went into effect two years later, created a legislature for British India, consisting of the governor-general and two chambers, each containing a majority of representatives elected by popular vote. Under a system of restricted manhood suffrage the ballot was conferred upon about five million Indians. Besides laying a wider popular basis for the national government, the new law established legislatures in the provinces on similar principles and transferred many powers from the central to the local authorities, thus enlarging local autonomy. In this way the British government conciliated the more conservative Indian Nationalists and gave evidence of its intention to advance home rule for India by a gradual process.

However, the new system applied, as we have said, only to British India—a region embracing about 900,000 square miles and 250,000,000 people ruled directly by the British sovereign.

T

It did not apply to the native "states" of India, numbering about five hundred, large and small, with a territory of 700,000 square miles and a population of approximately 70,000,000. Although subjected to Great Britain in accordance with numerous treaties and agreements, these states are governed by native princes of varying rank, in harmony with monarchical traditions. They are independent of one another and of British India. It is true that Great Britain created by royal proclamation in 1921 a Chamber of Princes, composed of the most powerful rulers in person and representatives of the smaller states, but this assembly was intended to be a consultative rather than a governing body.

Naturally, these semi-independent princes do not look with favor upon a democratic movement that would put an end to their authority by absorbing their states into the greater nationalism. In fact, some of them might readily attempt to extend their sway by force of arms if British dominion were broken by independence. Unless they can preserve a certain autonomy by federation, they would prefer to keep their present "liberties" rather than to suffer extinction in a consolidated nation. At all events, the princely rulers of the larger states are no more eager than the Moslem minority to be governed by an All-Indian parliament elected by popular vote. A British committee of inquiry, after a careful study of the Indian states, reported in 1929 that "it had found no practicable method of federalization between the Indian states and British India." It added that "the existence of two Indias must be recognized," and recommended that henceforward British relations with the princes should be conducted through the viceroy as the representative of the king-emperor rather than through the government of British India. The committee did not reject the possibility of federation, but declared that "federalism must be approached with caution because of the passionate attachment of the princes as a whole to their independence and sovereignty."

From what has just been said it is clear that the reforms enumerated above by no means "solved" the Indian "problem." Moderates accepted them as installments of a program of home rule to be realized in time. Radicals continued to insist on complete independence as the true goal. Nor did the British government rest in its efforts to find a more satisfactory basis of coöperation with the people of India. It appointed another royal commission, headed by Sir John Simon, for the purpose of investigating the new régime and making recommendations respecting additional steps to be taken. This commission began its work late in 1928 and after seven months' study on the ground in India announced that its report, when drafted, would be drawn in no partisan spirit. Indian Nationalists awaited it with expectancy, as marking another stage in the development of home rule or as giving a signal for renewed agitation. Meanwhile bitter controversies raged in Great Britain over the question whether the Indians were "fit for self-government," especially in view of the enormous British interests in India that would be put at the mercy of an autonomous or independent nation.

REPUBLICAN CHINA AND THE FAR EAST

Upon the whole of the Orient, from the ice-bound regions of eastern Siberia to the tropical plantations of Dutch Java, the violent agitations and dislocations of the World War had a profound effect. It is true that the territorial changes brought about by the conflict were slight: German rights in Shantung were transferred to Japan, and German islands north of the equator were handed over to her as mandated territories. In significance these transactions in land were slight; for the islands were small, and Shantung was later surrendered to China. The fundamental influences of the war on the Far East were political and economic. Germany, though she later came back as a commercial competitor, was eliminated as a military power from the rivalry of imperial nations in that quarter of the world. At the same time the collapse of the Tsarist régime and the rise of Bolshevism changed the aspect of Russian operations in China and India. Whatever their ambitions or goal, the Russians now appeared as agitators, inviting Asiatic peoples to cast off the yoke of "European imperialism" and to revolt against their own capitalists and landlords.

Only four commercial powers—Great Britain, France, the United States, and Japan—were now operating extensively along traditional lines in the Oriental sphere; and the intellectual climate for their undertakings was not the same as in 1914. Germany was out of the game, and Russia was revolutionary. Moreover, from the standpoint of historic imperialism, the United States was revolutionary also; for, in waging war on Germany, President Wilson proclaimed to all the earth the doctrines of democracy and self-government—the rights of people to govern themselves and determine their own destiny. To subjects of imperial powers in the Far East this was a call to revolt, and to China an open invitation to "drive out the foreigners." According to rumors that were current among Korean peasants, President Wilson was to come in an airplane and bring them the coveted independence from Japanese rule!

To the disorders which started in China soon after the overthrow of the empire in 1912 (pp. 271 ff.), the World War and its aftermath only added greater and deeper unrest. The republican government—with a president and a parliament—established at the time of the revolution in 1912 never succeeded in attaining complete authority over the country. On the contrary, in various places arose numerous war lords with great armies, as in feudal Europe after the break-up of the Roman Empire, and the provinces of China became almost independent of the central administration. In the dissolution, three cities—the old capital, Peking, Mukden in the north, and Canton in the south—became the chief centers of military adventurers and political leaders. From these cities armies went out from time to time seeking to conquer the rest of the country.

In this state of affairs the government at Peking, which was supposed to speak for the nation, consisted merely of a president and a cabinet set up by the war lord temporarily in authority at the capital. It had little power within the walls of the city and less outside, although it was officially recognized by the foreign governments, including the United States. Being short of money, it was lacking in almost everything else. Its chief source of revenue, the customs duties, was controlled by a foreign agency which collected the money, paid first the interest on certain of China's foreign debts, and then turned the balance over to the Peking treasury.

With Peking powerless, the fighting among the war lords continued and, to add to the confusion, there sprang up another great antiforeign movement akin to the Boxer unrest at the opening of the century. In spirit this was a Nationalist movement also and had its strength among the masses of the people. Thus, while their own government was falling about their ears, patriotic Chinese united in declaring "the foreigners must go." They called for the abolition of the foreign law courts, in which foreign judges tried their own people for offenses committed in China, and heard lawsuits affecting aliens, even when Chinese were involved. They demanded that China should have the right to fix her own customs taxes, now regulated by foreign powers under treaties. They insisted on a return of the territory held by Great Britain, Japan, and other countries and on the cancellation of all special rights enjoyed by foreigners in the "treaty ports." Coupled with this ardent Nationalist movement were communist agitations among agricultural laborers in the country and industrial workers in the cities. In 1927 China was racked from one end to the other by civil war and class conflicts.

At last in 1928 prospects for a respite appeared in sight. Led by General Chiang K'ai-shek, the Nationalist army from the

South had swept northward beyond the Yangtze River, occupied Hankow in the west and Nanking in the east, and driven out of Peking Marshal Chang Tso-lin, the war lord of Mukden, forcing the downfall of the northern government. Under the auspices of a central committee speaking for the *Kuomintang*, or Nationalist party, a new provisional government, established at Nanking in September of the previous year, began to function with some promise of regularity. Composed largely of young Chinese who had been educated abroad or under Western influences at home, it announced a policy embracing nationalism, the emancipation of China from foreign control, democracy in politics, and state socialism in economics. These doctrines had long been preached by their revered leader, Sun Yat-sen (died, 1925), whose body was enshrined in a magnificent tomb built for him at Nanking, the new capital to which the seat of government was transferred from Peking (renamed Peiping—"Northern Peace"—in 1928). Although occasionally disturbed by communist agitations and threatened with renewed civil conflict by some of the surviving war lords, notably the "Christian General," Fêng Yü-hsiang, the Nationalist government was able by 1929 to proceed energetically with efforts to reorganize its finances, introduce stable administration, construct national defenses, promote education, deprive all foreigners of the right to exterritoriality (or their own law courts), and emancipate China from all alien interference.

With its powerful neighbor, Russia, the government of China had to make many important readjustments after the Bolshevik revolution of 1917. For a few years disorders reigned along the Russo-Chinese frontier, and it was not until Soviet authority was finally extended over all Siberia that the way was prepared for a resumption of relations between the two countries. This took place in 1924. In the settlement Russia disclaimed the imperialist pretensions of the Tsar and renounced various rights in China, including extraterritoriality and her concession in the foreign section of Tientsin. By a compromise the two governments arranged for a joint control over the Chinese Eastern Railway, which had been built under Russian direction, according to the terms of an agreement reached in 1896, for the purpose of providing a direct line across Manchuria, thus shortening the Trans-Siberian route to Vladivostok by hundreds of miles.

Despite this apparent settlement of their outstanding differences, the relations between China and Russia remained in a parlous state. Bolshevik agents took an active part in the agitations of the southern Chinese, which culminated in the triumph of the Nationalist party at Nanking in 1927. So far Russian help was acceptable. But if the Chinese Nationalists were willing to make use of Russians in expelling the military government at Peking and in forcing concessions from other foreign powers, they had no intention of taking orders from Moscow. On the contrary, when they were once safely installed at Nanking, they expelled the Russian emissaries from China, accused the Soviet government of carrying on communist agitations in spite of its pledges, and then in 1929 boldly seized the Chinese Eastern Railway, bringing the two countries to the point of war. Although, after a season of threats and counterthreats, they promised in words to make a new compromise respecting the railway question, it was evident that troubles in the Far East were not removed by the overthrow of the "imperialist" system of the Tsars. Neither Russia nor Japan was willing to surrender valuable economic advantages in China, which had been accumulated through years of diplomatic and military effort. In short, the old struggle of the powers for favorable positions in the Orient was still in evidence, and no end was in sight. Unless peaceful methods for solving such questions can be applied, Manchuria, as often contended, may provide the opening scene for the next titanic conflict over commerce and empire.

Japan, in contrast to her ancient neighbor, China, was able, under her emperor and a powerful ruling class of landlords and capitalists, to keep order at home and extend her commerce abroad. During the momentous years when the Western industrial nations were engrossed in the World War, Japan's factories, mills, and mines multiplied, and her great cities, such as Osaka, Tokyo, and Yokohama, spread out under smoky skies like Manchester in England or Essen in Germany. Amid the old-fashioned, low Japanese houses and shops, tall modern buildings, six or eight stories high, arose in the cities. As a system of universal education was successfully operated, newspapers increased their circulation until the greatest dailies could boast of a million readers. With industries came trade unions and a labor movement; with a labor movement came democratic and socialistic agitations; and in 1925 the Japanese parliament, stirred by popular demands, adopted a universal manhood-suffrage law increasing the number of voters from three million to fourteen million. Though the terrible earthquake and conflagration which shattered Tokyo and Yokohama in 1923 checked Japan's prosperity, the people set to work with great zeal to restore their ruined cities, and within a few years were almost back to the normal basis. On the death of the emperor Yoshihito in 1926 he was succeeded by his son, Hirohito, who had visited the West and was in hearty sympathy with efforts to modernize his country industrially.

In the international affairs of the Far East the revolutionary events of the epoch opening in 1914 brought significant readjustments and raised new issues. Once more the close relation of the Occident and the Orient, which we have illustrated in Chapter VII, was demonstrated by striking examples. The inauguration of President Wilson and the subsequent announcement that in due time the Philippine Islands would be granted independence were followed by a relaxation of the vigorous support which Roosevelt and Taft had given to American business enterprise in the Far East. In 1917 the government of the United States, in an understanding with Japan known as the Lansing-Ishii exchange of notes, recognized that "Japan has special interests in China, particularly in the part to which her possessions are contiguous." Indeed the indifference which the Wilson administration displayed in the matter of pushing American business in China became so great that the American minister resigned his post as a gesture of protest.

Taking advantage of the anti-imperialist policies of President Wilson and the preoccupation of the European nations with the war, the government of Japan extended its power on the mainland as rapidly as possible, following European traditions in this respect. With or without the approval of the British government—a point yet clouded by uncertainty—Japan declared war on Germany, seized all the German rights and property in Shantung, and extended the area of its military and economic activities far beyond the original German zone. The next year Japan laid before the Chinese president "twenty-one demands," enlarging Japanese control in China. Later these demands, reduced to fifteen, were incorporated in a series of treaties which China was forced to sign under a military threat. In effect these treaties extended the Japanese lease on the South Manchurian Railway to ninety-nine years, gave Japanese capitalists special advantages in China in matters of trade, investment, and industry, bound China to buy a fixed amount of munitions from Japan, and provided for the employment of Japanese military, economic, and financial advisers at Peking. Although the Chinese government later declared these treaties invalid on the ground that they had been made under duress, Japan continued to insist on their legality. At all events they were followed by a great influx of Japanese capital into China and the extension of Japanese influence in every direction in that helpless republic.

Japanese power on the mainland was also temporarily augmented by the coöperative expedition sent to Siberia in 1918 by Great Britain, the United States, and Japan. If President Wilson's idea was merely to "steady efforts at self-government" in that part of Russia, Japan certainly made use of the occasion to transport a large body of troops to the region and authorized them to penetrate far into the interior, apparently with a view to making territorial gains in the process. After American troops were withdrawn in 1920, Japanese forces continued to hold strategic places in Siberia. Moreover, a strong military party in Tokyo frankly avowed the desire to develop for Japan a kind of Monroe Doctrine in her neighborhood, such as the United States had maintained in the Western Hemisphere.

Under these circumstances the Washington Conference was called in 1921 (p. 560). The return of the Republicans to power under President Harding had meant a reversal of President Wilson's easy-going commercial policies in the Far East. Harding found American interests decidedly "menaced" in that part of the world and resolved to bring about a new dispensation. Therefore, besides making certain reductions in naval armaments, the Washington Conference gave particular attention to Oriental issues. As a result, the Anglo-Japanese alliance was disrupted, the Lansing-Ishii agreement was annulled, Japan agreed to return Shantung, and a wordy resolution about the "open door" in China was adopted. In this way the attempt of Japan to extend her hegemony on the Asiatic continent was checked by Western intervention. A policy of watchful waiting was substituted, for Japan could not lightly surrender her great economic interests on the mainland, especially since the immigration laws of Australia, Canada, and the United States closed the gates of these countries to her growing population.

In recognition of the importance of Oriental affairs for the world, there was formally organized in 1925 an Institute of Pacific Relations, composed of unofficial representatives of the countries bordering on that great ocean. At the first conference, held in Honolulu that year, prominent delegates from religious, labor, business, and educational circles discussed with amazing frankness the problems of the Pacific likely to cause controversies in the future, and sought by methods of research and conciliation ways and means of adjusting conflicts peaceably. Shortly after the first conference closed, the permanent Institute was founded, and arrangements were made to hold periodical conventions for a similar exchange of views. Although created and supported entirely by private persons, the Institute immediately awakened wide interest on both sides of the ocean and served to draw the attention of the whole world to the problems of the countries washed by the waters of the Pacific—problems as fateful to mankind as those of the Atlantic. By throwing light on these issues the sponsors of the Institute hoped to reduce friction and smooth the way for adjustments without recourse to arms.

CHAPTER XVII

QUEST FOR INTERNATIONAL PEACE AND UNDERSTANDING

The Question of German Reparations

Besides readjusting their domestic affairs, the peoples of Europe had to reëstablish their international relations on a new basis. It was soon discovered that the severe terms imposed on Germany by the Treaty of Versailles were not easy to carry out. Holland refused to surrender the Kaiser for trial, as ordered by the Allies, and practically all the charges of high crimes and misdemeanors brought against the Germans in connection with the War were allowed to drop as baseless. As a matter of fact, when the cases of "atrocities" were sifted, nearly all of them were found to be deliberate lies, mere rumors, or gross exaggerations.[1]

The most vexatious question was the amount of the damages, or "reparations," that the Germans were to pay. In the treaty of peace, as we have seen, the total sum had been left indefinite, to be determined later by a Reparations Commission representing the victors. After many conferences and much argument, the bill was fixed in 1921 at $33,000,000,000—a staggering sum, which the German government declared impossible of payment, even in installments extending over a period of forty-two years. A deadlock followed. Then the Allies proposed a reduction, but the German government insisted that it could not pay more than $12,500,000,000. Great Britain suggested a compromise. France and Belgium stood firm for

[1] An English member of Parliament, Arthur Ponsonby, has given them a searching examination in his *Falsehood in War-Time* (1928).

540

every penny. Impatient at delay and claiming that willful defaults had been made, they ordered their troops in January, 1923, to invade the industrial region of Germany beyond the Rhine, especially the cities in the Ruhr valley, with instructions to collect from Germany by force if necessary. The Germans resisted, and the operation proved a failure as a bill-collecting enterprise. Meanwhile the German currency was being inflated to the bursting point (see page 413).

During the height of this controversy Charles E. Hughes, the American Secretary of State, suggested in a public speech that quarreling and fighting would not solve the problem, and hinted that a committee of expert business men should be appointed to draw up a plan for disposing of the reparations issue. In November, 1923, after long negotiations the Reparations Commission appointed two such committees of experts, one of them headed by General Charles G. Dawes, former director of the budget of the United States and later vice president. At length a report known as the Dawes plan was drawn up, approved by the Allied governments, accepted by Germany, and put into effect in the autumn of 1924.

Involving as it did enormous sums of money, the Dawes plan was very long and very complex, but certain general principles were embodied in it. First of all, it was based on the idea of restoring the independence of Germany by the speedy withdrawal of foreign soldiers from her soil. Secondly, it provided that the inflation of the currency should stop, and a sound monetary system be installed. In the third place, it created a new German bank under the supervision of the Allied powers to manage the business of collecting the reparations. Finally, it stipulated that, beginning in 1924, the German government should pay into this bank a certain sum of money annually, rising to the normal sum of 2,500,000,000 gold marks by 1928–1929, and that the bank should in turn distribute the money so received among the Allies according to a scheme of percentages agreed upon. For the first year four fifths of the amount paid into the bank was derived from a foreign loan, a large part of which was floated in the United States.

The immediate effect of the adoption of the Dawes plan was to revive confidence in Europe and to stop temporarily the official bickering about reparations that had been going on for six years. Nobody was exactly satisfied with it, but nearly everyone agreed that it was the best and fairest scheme yet proposed. How it would work out, however, was uncertain. The real test was to come in 1929 when the larger payments began. Germans said that the bill was too great and could not be paid. Practical business men suggested waiting to see what would happen when pay day came.

Before the more onerous terms of the Dawes settlement came into effect, serious deficiencies were recognized in its provisions, and a new conference for the revision of that scheme was held in Paris in the year 1929 under the chairmanship of Owen D. Young, of the General Electric Company, acting with the approval of the United States government. Early in June this new committee of experts reached an agreement on another form of reparations adjustment which, by common consent, bears the name of the presiding officer. Like the preceding document, the Young plan was a long and complicated state paper of more than fifty pages, difficult to summarize adequately. The fundamental purpose of the committee was that of "rounding off the work of their predecessors which was advisedly left incomplete."

Into the causes of the war, the responsibility for its outbreak, and the justice of the reparations demands, the conference of experts did not go. According to its own report, it sought to "banish the atmosphere of war, obliterate animosities, its partisanships, its tendencious phrases." Tacitly, however, it accepted certain political limitations inherent in the situation. The Allied powers were victorious and determined to exact from Germany all that was economically possible, and Germany, with some of her richest territory occupied by foreign soldiers, seemed compelled to pay whatever the victors decided upon as the limit of their concessions, considering the chances of collection. War and politics had created an obligation, whether just or unjust, and business had been kept in confusion by the very uncertainty of that obligation. Under such circumstances and with such ends in view, the conference carried out its task and referred its proposals to the respective governments for ratification. The prime features of the scheme may be summarized under four heads:

1. In the first place, the exact sum which Germany was required to pay each year between 1929 and 1988 was fixed at a definite figure in gold marks; and the total represented a material reduction in the amount demanded by the Allies in the Dawes plan. Until 1966 the average payment is to be slightly over 2,000,000,000 marks, or approximately $488,000,000. After that year the payment will be materially reduced. Of this annuity a part is unconditional and must be paid at all costs, while the payment of the other part is to depend upon economic conditions and is subject to postponement. Distribution of the proceeds among the Allies is to be made on a fixed-percentage basis.[1]

2. In the second place, the money for each annual payment is to be derived from two sources: the German budget or tax levies and the German railways. With respect to this point the conference recorded its conviction that "the basis of security for the payment of annuities is a solemn undertaking of the German government to which no further guarantee can add anything whatsoever."

3. Closely coupled with this reliance upon the "solemn undertaking" of the German government is the third feature of the plan—namely, the abandonment of political supervision in the collection of the reparation annuities. The Dawes plan

---

[1] Some readjustments were made in this feature of the Young plan at a conference at the Hague in the summer of 1929, after the British chancellor, Philip Snowden, bitterly assailed it as unfair to Great Britain.

had provided for an agent-general and certain commissions resident in Germany and exercising, in the name of foreign powers, a constant scrutiny over the finances of the republic, the management of the railways, and the conduct of industries, pledged for the payment of reparations. The Young plan, in accepting Germany's official pledge to pay, makes unnecessary this interference with her internal affairs. It therefore orders the earliest possible termination of the economic surveillance —the work of the office of reparations payments and the Reparations Commission—which had been imposed on Germany after the signature of the Treaty of Versailles.

4. But, of course, the receipt of Germany's payments and the distribution of the proceeds among the claimants in accordance with the fixed-percentage scale made necessary the creation of some kind of central financial institution—the fourth feature of the Young agreement. Accordingly, the committee decided to establish a central bank to discharge these two prime functions and others considered below. This bank is to be governed by a board of directors consisting of the governor of the central bank in each of seven coöperating countries,— Great Britain, Belgium, France, Germany, Italy, Japan, and the United States,—together with certain additional members. Foreseeing that the United States government might decline to participate *officially*, the conference provided that the bankers to represent that country on the board may be selected by the other members. The additional members of the directorate mentioned above, nine in number, are to be chosen by the board from lists furnished by the governors of the banks in the several participating countries. Furthermore, each of the seven governors is empowered to appoint a special director representing finance, industry, and commerce.

As indicated above, the immediate duty of the Bank for International Settlements, though perhaps not its prime function in the distant future, is to receive Germany's payments on reparations account and to distribute these payments among the countries entitled to receive them. Considering the magnitude of the sum involved and the intricacy of the operation, this business in itself constitutes a gigantic undertaking, which is to endure, nominally at least, until 1988. But this is only one phase of the bank's work, and, as already hinted, does not in itself reveal the true significance of the new institution for international finance.

In fact, it is to be a *world superbank*, with large power for carrying on a general banking business, subject to the limitations of the central banks of the various countries. It may deal directly with the national central banks, or through them acting as its agents, and with other banks, individuals, and corporations throughout the world in all cases in which the respective central banks do not enter an objection. It may buy and sell gold and make advances to central banks on gold security. It may buy and sell, for its own account, bills of exchange and other short-term obligations of prime liquidity, including checks drawn or indorsed by central banks. It may open and maintain accounts with central banks. It may rediscount the bills of central banks and make loans to them on the security of such bills. It may buy and sell, for its own account, intermediate or long-term securities other than shares. This is not all. It is a bank of limited issue. It is empowered to issue its own obligations for long or short terms, secured or unsecured, for the purpose of relending to any central bank, in each case by the specified decision of the board of directors by a two-thirds vote. It is also a bank of deposit.

In carrying on its operations connected with German annuities and international settlements, the bank may receive deposits of a nature consistent with its functions. The directors may determine when applications to make deposit accounts come within its scope. In all cases such deposits must be in currencies which meet the requirements of the gold standard. It may receive deposits from the central banks of the respective countries, either current or investment accounts. It may

T

serve as a clearing house for general settlements among central banks, receiving deposits in that relation. Besides the annuity payments from Germany, the bank is to have a special deposit from the German government not to exceed one hundred million marks. With subscriptions to its capital stock, the annuity funds, and its other deposits, the bank would therefore start with an enormous assured business. In November, 1929, after careful consideration, it was decided, against the objection of Belgium, that the headquarters of the new international bank should be at Basel, Switzerland.

Even from this brief survey it becomes apparent that this new Bank for International Settlements has vast potentialities for stabilizing, directing, and controlling the world-wide operations of international capital, with its gigantic influence in the promotion of industrial, agricultural, and governmental enterprises in established nations and in the economically backward places of the earth, chiefly in Asia, Africa, and South America. Some of these implications are mentioned in the report of the Young committee. It calls attention to the fact that the proposed distribution of capital stock will associate with the bank all the countries interested in reparations and all the financial markets that may subscribe to its issues. It refers to the advantages which the bank will have in its exemption from the governmental and fiscal requirements of all countries and hence in its opportunities to transact business on a purely economic basis, without respect to the demands of national industrialists and politicians. It is to be, in fact, a politically emancipated fiscal institution for world business.

The Young report emphasized the fact that it would be desirable for the bank to broaden the extension of credit "in the interest of world trade" and to serve as an international settlement institution, which would eliminate the costs and risks involved in the shipping and reshipping of gold. "In the natural course of development," concluded the committee on this point, "it is to be expected that the bank will in time become an organization not simply or even predominantly concerned with the handling of reparations but also with furnishing to the world of international commerce and finance important facilities hitherto lacking. Especially is it to be hoped that it will become an increasingly close and valuable link in the coöperation of central banking institutions generally—coöperation essential to the continuing stability of the world's credit structure." Not without warrant did J. P. Morgan, in his laconic statement to reporters on his return to New York from the conference, lay emphasis on the proposed bank as a significant feature of the new resettlement.

Should the plan be ratified by the powers and fully realized, there will be a World Parliament,—the League of Nations,— a World Court, and a World Bank! American students will recall with interest that Alexander Hamilton's United States Bank was a powerful economic influence in cementing the states of the Union.

THE WORLD COURT

One of the most notable accomplishments of the League of Nations was the creation of an international court provided for by Article XIV of the Covenant—commonly known as the World Court. In February, 1920, the Council of the League appointed a committee of jurists of international reputation to draw up a plan for the proposed court.[1] This committee drafted a statute which, with some amendments, was approved by the Assembly of the League in December of the same year. The statute was then embodied in a protocol, or treaty, which was to be signed by nations wishing to become members of the Court immediately, and was then to be left open for the signature of those countries which might later

---

[1] Among the members of this committee was Elihu Root, former Secretary of State, who acted in a *personal* capacity and not as the *official* representative of the United States.

decide to join. When the Assembly met the following year (December, 1921), twenty-eight countries had ratified the treaty, which then went into effect. The Court held its first session at the Hague on January 30, 1922. By the end of 1928 forty-seven members were enrolled in the Court.

It must be noted that this Permanent Court of International Justice is not to be confused with the Court of Arbitration, which was created at the Hague Conference of 1899 (pp. 302 ff.). The Permanent Court, or World Court, consists of fifteen judges, who are elected by the Assembly and the Council of the League of Nations. They are to serve for nine years and may be reëlected. The seat of the Court is at the Hague, and sessions are to be held each year, continuing until all cases in hand are settled.

In general, the nations which have joined the Court are not bound to submit *all* cases in dispute to the Court, but they may do so *voluntarily* when they see fit. However, they may, by signing a special agreement, bind themselves to accept the jurisdiction of the Court as *obligatory* in all disputes concerning (1) the interpretation of a treaty, (2) any question of international law, (3) the existence of any fact which, if established, would be considered a breach of international law, (4) the nature and extent of the damages to be paid, or reparation made, for such a breach of international obligation. Of the states that have joined the World Court, a large majority have accepted the obligatory jurisdiction of the Court.

The first serious consideration of an international court took place, as we have seen, at the Hague conferences. The nations, however, wished to retain their complete independence and to submit only such questions as they saw fit. So they refused to consider seriously *compulsory* arbitration and trial. The result was the founding of a limited Court of Arbitration, which consisted of a list of judges chosen by the nations participating in the conferences, from which a tribunal was to be selected for each case that came up. The Court was established at the

Hague, and was presented with a handsome building called the Peace Palace, the gift of Andrew Carnegie. The Hague Court of Arbitration differs from the World Court (also established at the Hague) in a number of fundamental points. The Hague Court is a court of *arbitration* which seeks to adjust disputes through compromise; the World Court, on the other hand, is a court of law whose decisions and advisory opinions are based on legal rules. The Hague Court lacks continuity in its work, since its judges change from time to time; the World Court, composed of judges who devote all their attention to the work of the tribunal, promises by its continued practice to build up a new body of international law.[1]

Having many close connections with Europe, in spite of its refusal to join the League of Nations, and professing always to desire a peaceful settlement of international disputes, the United States had to consider the question of joining the World Court established by the League. A large number of American citizens urged this action on the government. On February 24, 1923, President Harding proposed the acceptance of the Protocol by the United States, but with the following reservations formulated by Secretary Hughes: That the United States should not become involved in any legal relation with the League of Nations, or assume any obligation under its Covenant; that the United States should participate in the election of judges; that the United States should pay a fair proportion of the expenses of the Court; that the statute of the Court should not be amended without the consent of the United States.

Late in 1925 President Coolidge indorsed the Court, and then the question of the entry of the United States was warmly debated in the Senate. Finally, on January 27, 1926, the Senate

---

[1] Among the judges who were chosen for the World Court in September, 1921, was Professor John Bassett Moore, a distinguished American authority on international law. On his resignation in 1928 he was succeeded by Charles E. Hughes.

ratified the proposal with practically the same reservations as those made by Secretary Hughes. An additional reservation, however, stated that the Court was not to render an advisory opinion "touching any dispute or question in which the United States has or claims an interest" without the consent of the United States. Furthermore, the United States would not join the Court unless all the other members of the Court accepted the reservations made by the Senate and agreed to abide by them. After examining the American proposals, the leading countries concerned declared that they were unable to accept the conditions presented. The issue seemed to be closed.

Nevertheless, to the surprise of the general public, near the end of his administration in 1929 President Coolidge took up the subject again. He sent the former Secretary of State, Elihu Root, abroad to confer with a committee of jurists created by the League of Nations for the revision of the statute of the Court. As the result of a semiofficial discussion of differences, a compromise was reached with respect to the reservations proposed by the United States and the objections advanced by the signatory powers. This compromise was embodied in a series of articles to be submitted to the Assembly of the League of Nations, the government of the United States, and the signatory powers, for approval or ratification. Before many months elapsed the League Assembly and all but three countries involved had accepted the "Root plan" for the admission of the United States to the World Court. In November, 1929, the signature of the United States was about all that was needed to complete the transaction.

PROJECTS FOR PEACE AND SECURITY

The most difficult problem which the League of Nations has had to face is the question of disarmament. Any attempt to persuade a nation to reduce the military forces on which it has been wont to depend for protection arouses all the old-time fears and suspicions and is met with strong opposition. This is not due to perversity but to a feeling that it is not safe to rely on any defense but force. The third Assembly of the League recognized the principle that the two problems of *disarmament* and *security* were inseparable; it is not possible to expect a nation which is in danger of attack to reduce its armaments without falling back upon some guaranty of security, such as the promise, in the Covenant, of help if attacked (Article XVI). The Hague conferences called to consider disarmament— among other things—failed, and the Washington Conference of 1921, although it established a set ratio of strength for battleships, did not regulate auxiliary war vessels, such as cruisers and submarines, or land armaments, and failed to do more than denounce the most effective method of destruction— chemical warfare.

These obvious difficulties led to the search for other solutions, such as compulsory arbitration and the *outlawing* of war. A number of plans were brought before the League. In 1924 a Draft Treaty of Mutual Assistance was accepted by some members of the League, but rejected by others. Its main feature was that *it declared aggressive war a crime*. The signatories were to assist the victims of "aggressive" war and were also to reduce their armaments in proportion to the security offered by the treaty. But "aggressive" was not defined.

An alternative scheme, known as the "American plan," was drawn up by an unofficial committee of Americans and became an official document of the League. The great contribution of this plan was its *definition of an aggressor* as one who goes to war without obeying a summons to an appropriate international tribunal or without accepting the unanimous decision of the Council. The plan also called for international inspection of armaments and for recurring conferences on disarmament in which outsiders (for instance, the United States) could join.

These two plans became the basis for the Geneva Protocol adopted by the Assembly of the League in 1924, which outlawed aggressive war and plainly stated that a nation is an aggressor when it refuses the alternatives for war. Aggressive war is for the first time in history officially declared to be a crime; and although defense is regarded as legitimate, it is not to be based on the individual judgment of one party to a controversy. The Protocol calls upon the members of the League to come to the assistance of a nation that is attacked. The states decide individually in what ways they will assist, each having due regard to its geographical position and peculiar situation.

At a meeting of the Council in March, 1925, the British government announced that it sympathized with the objects in view, but said that it could not accept the Protocol, because a *general* obligation to assist the victim of aggression put too heavy a burden upon a world empire, so long as the United States was not included in the League. It urged that a more satisfactory solution would be to supplement the Covenant of the League of Nations by making special arrangements to meet special needs; those nations whose differences might lead to war should be brought together by means of treaties framed with the sole object of maintaining between them an unbroken peace.[1]

In spite of the establishment of the League of Nations, none of the recently warring countries felt altogether certain about the future. Though triumphant over Germany for the moment, France knew that her population was smaller than Germany's, and that if Germany got on her feet the day of revenge might be dreadful, even though France could draw upon African colonies for negro troops to help fight her battles. With Russia

[1] This whole matter is made very clear by Professor James T. Shotwell in *International Conciliation*, No. 208 (March, 1925). Professor Shotwell was chairman and one of the most influential members of the committee which was responsible for the American plan. This had a considerable influence upon later projects for peace.

out of the field, France had no powerful ally she could depend upon. On the other hand, Germany, disarmed and subjected to French invasion, was in a bad plight; and, bad as it was, it could be made worse if France and Belgium insisted on collecting reparations with bayonets.

Nor was the position of the new states to the east much better. They were nominally independent; but standing alone, as they did, they were weak against either Germany or Russia. It is true, as we shall see, that Czechoslovakia, Yugoslavia, and Rumania united in forming the "Little Entente" and that France and Poland joined them in special treaties; but at best such a union offered no assurance of peace to distracted Europe. In other words, the various nations of the Continent were busy making treaties and combinations looking to defense and war and were daily adding to their outlays for guns, munitions, forts, and armies. Even England, once safe on her island home and still mistress of the seas, stirred restlessly amid the new dangers. Her commerce was badly deranged by the turmoil on the Continent, and the growth of the French airplane service and submarine fleet for military purposes made her wonder whether her ancient sea power was any longer a guarantee of safety for her kingdom and empire. Clearly, unless something was done to restore confidence and assure security, a ruinous war might break out any time.

As Carlyle says, when it gets dark enough we can see stars. When Europe seemed on the edge of ruin, and after innumerable "conversations" and exchanges of notes, an important conference, called on the suggestion of Germany, was opened at Locarno in Switzerland on October 5, 1925. It was attended by the representatives of France, Belgium, Great Britain, Germany, Poland, Czechoslovakia, and Italy. Its purpose was to discuss the question of security which had been agitating Western nations since the close of the World War. For the first time since 1914 Germany became a party to an international conference for the maintenance of peace and was received on a friendly footing with the other nations in a common enterprise. To ease the strain the delegates took boat rides together on the neighboring lake and made automobile tours together in the surrounding country. At the end of twelve days' discussion Germany, Belgium, France,

Great Britain, and Italy signed a treaty of mutual guaranty, which is commonly called the Locarno Security Pact, and in addition, six bilateral arbitration treaties were made between Continental powers most likely to become involved in new controversies.

By the terms of the Security Pact of Locarno, the signatory powers bound themselves to maintain the frontiers between Germany and Belgium and between Germany and France, as provided in the Treaty of Versailles. They agreed also, in accordance with the provision of the treaty, to maintain the peace zone

FIFTY-KILOMETER ZONE

comprising German territory west of the Rhine and a strip, fifty kilometers wide, east of that river. In that "demilitarized zone" Germany is not to maintain armed forces nor mobilize troops. As a further guaranty, Germany and France pledged themselves not to attack each other, nor to invade each other's territory, nor to resort to war against each other. A similar pledge was made by Germany and Belgium. More than that: if a dispute arises between them, they are bound to settle it peaceably; if they cannot agree, they are to submit the question at issue to arbitration, and finally, if necessary, to the Council of the League of Nations.

Should one of these countries refuse to abide by the general agreement and actually make war on any of the others, then all the other signers of the Pact are pledged to come immediately to the aid of the party attacked. Furthermore, contestants agree to accept the decision of the Council of the League if all other countries are unanimous in their opinion. Article V deals with aggression which is not flagrant and is therefore the vital part of the treaty with respect to the prevention of war. It makes the test of aggression the refusal to accept the decision of the courts on legal matters or the decision of conciliation tribunals on other matters.

The Locarno Security Pact was supplemented, as we have said, by arbitration treaties between Germany and France, Germany and Belgium, Germany and Poland, and Germany and Czechoslovakia. These treaties provide that all disputes which cannot be settled by an exchange of views may be, and, in some cases shall be, submitted to a Permanent Conciliation Commission, to be composed of one citizen from each of the countries engaged in the dispute and three citizens from other countries not directly concerned in the quarrel. If no peaceful agreement can be reached by this Commission, then the case is to be submitted to the Permanent Court of International Justice, known as the World Court.

Another interesting departure was made in two other treaties signed at the same time. France and Poland openly agreed to aid each other if Germany violated the Security Pact and attacked either one, and France and Czechoslovakia made a similar promise. Thus, instead of secret treaties such as existed between France and Russia in the year 1914, concerning which Germany then knew very little, there are now public treaties giving Germany to understand just what she may expect in case another grave dispute arises.

The Locarno treaties marked a new era in international relations and were regarded by some observers as the beginning of a series of such conventions which might break down old barriers between nations and perhaps lead eventually to something like a federation of states of Europe. However this may be, the Locarno settlement was unique in many ways. In the first place, the Security Pact was notable for its simplicity and directness and for making no concessions to "national honor." The signatories pledged themselves to coöperate to maintain peace rather than to establish, as of old, a defensive alliance against a real or an imaginary enemy. This was not a secret treaty to preserve the "balance of power," but a frank and published agreement to "seek peace and pursue it." Furthermore, the parties chiefly concerned associated with themselves other nations as guarantors to see that their contracts are kept. Above all, they voluntarily promised to submit their disputes to a third party—a commission, a court, or a council—and to abide by the decision of this body.

By their terms the Locarno agreements were limited to the preservation of peace in specific regions of Europe, and thus left the rest of the world, including the United States, out of the circle. This was an obvious shortcoming, and on the tenth anniversary of the entrance of the United States into the World War, Aristide Briand, the French minister of foreign affairs, took advantage of the occasion to announce that "France would be willing to subscribe publicly with the United States to any mutual engagement tending 'to outlaw war' to use an American expression, as between the two countries." Later Briand transmitted to Washington the draft of a pact of perpetual friendship between France and the United States.

After a long delay the Secretary of State, prodded by prominent American citizens, replied by suggesting that, instead of drawing up a bilateral agreement between the two countries, an effort be made to obtain "the adherence of all the principal powers of the world to a declaration renouncing war as an instrument of national policy." As a result of these negotiations, on August 27, 1928, the representatives of Germany, the United States, Belgium, France, Great Britain, Italy, Japan, Poland, and Czechoslovakia signed in Paris the Pact of Paris, which has come to be known in the United States as the Kellogg treaty. A note was then addressed to forty-eight other powers inviting them to sign, and within a short time a large number of them, including Russia, responded favorably.

In Article I of the peace pact of Paris "the high contracting parties solemnly declare in the names of their respective peoples that they condemn recourse to war for the solution of international controversies and renounce it as an instrument of national policy in their relations with one another." In Article II they "agree that the settlement of all disputes or conflicts of whatever nature or of whatever origin they may be, which may arise among them, shall never be sought except by pacific means." By advocates of peace this action was hailed as marking a milestone in the history of international relations; but whether it did or not the future alone will determine.

As a matter of fact, by specific reservations and explanatory notes, most of the important signatories put limits on the scope of the pact, and in ratifying it the United States Senate, in an indirect manner, added American "interpretations." Under the terms of the pact, as explained by the signers, nothing "restrains or compromises in any manner whatsoever the right of self-defense"; and as every country claims that its wars are fought in self-defense, the loophole seems big enough for any eventuality. Furthermore, according to the interpretations, the resort to war by one party "would automatically release the other parties from their obligation to the treaty-breaking state." All agreements to resort to arms under the Covenant of the League of Nations and the Locarno treaties stood unimpaired. The belligerent implications of the "defensive" alliances made by France with Poland, Belgium, Czechoslovakia, Rumania, and Yugoslavia were declared "compatible" with the new convention. Supplementing the French reservations were the declarations of the British authorities. For the government in London the renunciation of war was to apply everywhere, except in "certain regions of the world which constitute a special interest for our peace and safety. . . . Interference with those regions cannot be suffered." Thus Great Britain may still employ war in areas which hold a special interest for her. And the Monroe Doctrine was, by a common understanding of the United States Senate, held to be still in full force. So it would seem that the government of the United States might, in spite of the Paris pact, carry on public and private wars in Latin America.

Whatever may be the significance of the League of Nations and the peace and security pacts, they did not prevent the governments of the Old World from entering into alliances and "conversations" designed to maintain or upset the existing balance of power. Czechoslovakia, Rumania, and Yugoslavia bound themselves together in the Little Entente by a series of treaties made in 1921–1922, later supplemented by conversations and conferences. Primarily this combination was directed against possible efforts of Hungary to recover any of her former dominions. When an attempt was made to restore Charles to the Hungarian throne in 1921, the Little Entente protested and forced an abandonment of the scheme. With these three states France definitely allied herself, and the treaty with Yugoslavia was concluded late in 1927, at a time when England and Italy were drawing together and tension was high. Besides rendering open aid to Poland in its war with Russia, France had entered into a formal alliance with that country in 1921 — a "defensive alliance," to be sure, and in accord with the principles of the Covenant of the League of Nations, but nevertheless a combination for coöperation in war if "either party should be attacked without provocation."

To these gravitations countermoves were made in other quarters. With respect to her aspirations in southeastern Europe,

Italy spun diplomatic threads with Hungary and Bulgaria, both of which had been stripped of valuable territory by the Treaty of Versailles and cherished hopes for a new redistribution. Although the treaty of friendship and arbitration concluded by Italy and Hungary in 1927 did not constitute a formal alliance, a shipment of arms from Italy to Hungary about the same time indicated that the friendship was to take substantial form. With Bulgaria, Italy's diplomatic relations were without immediate military implications, but Yugoslavia regarded the negotiations as directed against her. During the long tenure of power by the Conservative government in Great Britain, Mussolini and the British foreign minister made exchanges which were reported in the Italian press as "highly satisfactory," and aroused apprehension in France.

THE UNITED STATES AND WORLD AFFAIRS

With the huge complex of world affairs—economic, diplomatic, and political—which we discussed in Chapter VII, the government of the United States had closer and more numerous relations after the World War. It might refuse to join the League of Nations and proclaim its "splendid isolation," but it could not shut its doors and windows in the face of Europe and Asia. Indeed, on the morning after the "war to end war," it found itself involved in a dangerous naval rivalry with Great Britain and Japan, caught up in new perplexities in the Far East, and engaged in controversies over oil fields as far apart as Mesopotamia and Java. By no mere independent action could it solve such problems. Some kind of coöperation with the other great powers was inevitable. Accordingly, Senator William E. Borah, one of the leaders among the opposition to the League, proposed in Congress a resolution asking President Harding to call a conference of the nations at Washington to consider, among other things, the reduction of armaments. A resolution to this effect was carried, and the call duly went forth. On November 12, of the year 1921, delegates from the United States, Belgium, the British Empire, China, France, Italy, Japan, the Netherlands, and Portugal met in Washington. For nearly three months they discussed problems of armaments and international relations.

The results of the Washington Conference were embodied in several treaties and resolutions. A compact, known as the Five-Power Treaty, was made between the United States, the British Empire, France, Italy, and Japan, reducing the tonnage of their battleships and holding it at a fixed ratio for a period of ten years. By another agreement—known as the Four-Power Treaty—the United States, the British Empire, France, and Japan bound themselves to respect one another's insular possessions in the Pacific (not including the main islands of Japan) and to hold consultations whenever controversies should arise with respect to them. A third treaty pledged each of the powers represented at Washington to respect the sovereignty of China and to refrain from seeking special rights and privileges in that country to the detriment of the rights of citizens and subjects of other states. An arrangement was made for terminating the Anglo-Japanese alliance (p. 293 f.), which had long been a matter of grave concern to the government of the United States in its Far Eastern affairs. The Japanese and Chinese, whose relations were very strained, were brought together. A step was taken towards the settlement of the dispute over Shantung (p. 402), from which Japan agreed to withdraw after a time, on specified conditions—among them that China should pay for the property taken by Japan from the Germans. A number of additional decisions respecting the management of China's affairs were made by the Conference. Efforts to restrict the construction of submarines, cruisers, and other auxiliary ships and to prohibit the use of poison gas in warfare, however, came to naught.

All these arrangements, it is obvious, related to the settlement of specific matters. The sponsors of the Conference, President Harding and his Secretary of State, Charles E. Hughes, were careful to caution the American people against expecting general disarmament or any grand plan for universal peace. As President Harding pointed out in one of his addresses, with Europe prostrate and penitent, no one feared the likelihood of early conflict there. But the Pacific had its menaces, and they deeply concerned the United States. The Washington Conference, therefore, did not discuss any designs for universal peace, but sought to cut down the expenses for battleship-building and to settle disputes over territory and trade likely to involve the various nations in war. Whether this method of handling international affairs would be more successful than Hague conferences and other efforts of a general character, time alone could tell. All the world must at least have shared President Harding's hope that the new agreements had advanced international peace and reduced the chances of renewed hostilities, especially in the Pacific Ocean.

With rivalry over battleship construction and over certain Pacific questions allayed, temporarily at least, the government of the United States was in a position to take up the question of the European debts. After the declaration of war on Germany it had lent huge sums of money to the countries associated with it—in all to twenty different nations—particularly to England, France, Italy, Belgium, Poland, and Russia. These war loans were later supplemented by loans for relieving suffering and helping to restore industry. All in all these sums amounted to more than $10,000,000,000, which was procured by the United States government by selling Liberty bonds to its citizens and by taxing them.

Finally there came a day of reckoning. While a good many American citizens argued that these debts should be canceled, on the ground that the money was spent in a common cause, the Congress of the United States insisted that they should be collected. One or two loans were repaid in full; for example, Cuba had borrowed ten million and paid it off promptly. One

T

by one agreements were made with the other debtors, until by the opening of 1929 nearly all had made promises to pay a definite amount each year until a fixed sum was discharged. Russia, however, had not taken any steps looking towards settlement by that time, and the French parliament delayed until July of that year the ratification of a contract already drafted. Of all the debtors Great Britain agreed to meet her obligations most nearly; but in no case was any country called upon to pay the full amount with interest at the rate paid by the Federal government on most of its Liberty bonds—namely, $4\frac{1}{4}$ per cent. In fact, the rate of interest charged to Belgium was 1.8 per cent, to France 1.6 per cent, and to Italy 0.4 per cent. In this manner the United States canceled billions of dollars due under a legal interpretation of the original contracts.

Besides the debts owed by European governments to the government of the United States, new problems were raised by additional borrowings made in this country by European governments, cities, and business enterprises. These latter loans differ from the former, however, in that they were made by private American citizens who were willing to risk money in European bonds because such securities pay a higher rate of interest than domestic loans—in some cases 7 or 8 per cent. By the end of 1926 American citizens had over $2,000,000,000 invested in European stocks and bonds, and the amount was increasing rapidly. Indeed, there was hardly a country or important city on the continent of Europe that did not owe money to American citizens, to say nothing of European factory-owners, railways, and business firms. According to one reckoning, these private loans will, at the present rate of increase, reach the total of $6,000,000,000 by 1936. In any case, this investment of American capital in Europe and the distribution of foreign bonds all over America among small investors will form new ties of connection with European affairs during the coming years. What would happen, for example, to American interests if another war in Europe should end in a wholesale repudiation of debts, such as had actually occurred in the case of Russia, Germany, and Austria in 1917–1918?

Notwithstanding these multiplying ties of interest the government of the United States shrank from all official connections with the League of Nations. It would not offer to join the World Court without making a long list of reservations assuring its practical independence. It accepted the Paris peace pact, but that document contained no commitments requiring the United States to take any official action to preserve peace. The treaties drawn at the Washington Conference dealt mainly with regional, not world, affairs and involved no pledges beyond a promise to confer when difficulties arose in the Pacific Ocean. Although two American citizens, Charles G. Dawes and Owen D. Young, took prominent parts in the two great conferences, described above, to adjust German reparations, the government of the United States declined to participate officially and contented itself with giving its blessings to the American experts engaged in helping Europe to solve its problems.

Yet, as a matter of fact, Europe could not "manage its affairs" without the official coöperation of the United States. The Covenant of the League of Nations bound the signatory powers to proceed with schemes for disarmament, but even if they had been willing to do so, they could not have reached any conclusion without knowing the official attitude of the United States. Suppose the European powers were able to agree on a drastic reduction in naval and land armaments. Could England safely reduce her navy and yield undoubted superiority to the United States? Could the various countries curtail the manufacture of munitions if the United States would not forbid its citizens to make and sell arms to any and all possible belligerents? If in spite of such reductions war did break out and the nations having access to the sea could import munitions freely from the United States, they would at once have an overwhelming predominance. German reparations could not be finally adjusted without some reference to the position of the United States with respect to the debts owed by its late associates in the war.

Hence it seemed inevitable that the United States must have an official or unofficial, a front-door or back-door, relation to the League of Nations or, at all events, to the leading governments affiliated with it. "Isolation," however plausible as a theory, was restricted in fact by the necessity of coöperation. Even a stout advocate of this historic doctrine, Senator Borah, was reported as saying, with reference to the peace pact of Paris, "It is quite inconceivable that this country would stand idly by in case of a grave breach of a multilateral treaty to which it is a party." But he added that the government of the United States must be free to decide whether it will act or not in case the peace pact is violated, and what means it will choose. Thus it practices a limited coöperation with European countries without giving them any clear-cut, definite assurances on which they can count in arranging their affairs.

THE LEAGUE OF NATIONS

In the collection of "indemnities" and the maintenance of military control in a defeated country to enforce payment there was nothing new. Neither was there anything unfamiliar in endless parleys of diplomats, held to adjust disputes following an armed conflict. The novel feature in the European situation after the World War was the creation and existence of the League of Nations pledged to international peace as a system and to the solution of unsolved problems by peaceful methods. Although projects for some such institution were old, it was largely to President Wilson that Europe owed the actual establishment of a world council in 1919.

First among the purposes which he had in mind in summoning his countrymen to arms, President Wilson placed a device for putting an end to war. All through the United States people spoke of the "war to end war," and no slogan called forth a deeper response from the masses. As the conflict went on the President repeatedly declared that a general association of nations must be formed to guard the peace and protect all against the ambitions of the few. "As I see it," he said in his address on opening the Fourth Liberty Loan campaign, "the constitution of the league of nations and the clear definition of its objects must be a part, in a sense the most essential part, of the peace settlement itself."

Nothing was more natural, therefore, than the President's insisting at Paris that an international association should be formed, and Part I of the treaty with Germany—the Covenant of the League of Nations—was largely the outcome of his persistent labors. Within the League thus created were to be included at once all the Allied and Associated Powers lately at war with Germany, and nearly all the neutrals. Germany, Austria, Hungary, Bulgaria, Turkey, Russia, Mexico, and Costa Rica were temporarily excluded, but they might be admitted by action of the League itself. The agencies of the League were to be three in number: (1) a permanent secretariat, located at Geneva; (2) an Assembly consisting of one delegate from each country, dominion, or colony (including Canada, Australia, South Africa, New Zealand, and India); (3) a Council consisting of representatives of the United States, Great Britain, France, Italy, and Japan, and four other representatives selected from time to time by the Assembly of the League—a number later increased to five permanent members and nine elective members.

The duties imposed on the League and the obligations accepted by the members were numerous and important. The Council was to take steps to formulate a scheme for the reduction of armaments and to submit a plan for the establishment of a Permanent Court of International Justice. The members of the League on their part agreed to respect and preserve as against external aggression the territorial integrity and existing political independence of all members of the League. They bound themselves to submit to arbitration or inquiry by the Council all disputes which cannot be adjusted by diplomacy, and in no case to resort to war until three months after the award. Should any member disregard its agreements, its action would be considered as an act of war against the League, which would cut off the trade and business of the disobedient state and recommend through the Council to the several associated governments the military measures to be taken. In case the decision in any arbitration of a dispute was unanimous, the members of the League affected by it agreed absolutely to abide by it.

Such was the great program of international association with which President Wilson endeavored to redeem his pledges to his countrymen. Incorporated in the treaty of peace with Germany, it was formally presented to the countries concerned for their approval and laid before the Senate of the United States for ratification. Other nations rapidly set their seal upon it; but in the United States it was the subject of a long and acrimonious debate, in which the Democratic and Republican parties became gradually aligned on opposite sides. President Wilson took the field in defense of the treaty. In the midst of his arduous labors he experienced a physical breakdown from which he suffered until the end of his term. When the Senate of the United States refused to ratify the treaty, save with numerous reservations which President Wilson rejected, the whole question became an issue in the presidential campaign of 1920. Shortly after the inauguration of President Harding Congress declared the war with Germany and Austria at an end, and separate peace treaties were concluded with them. But the Covenant of the League of Nations remained unratified by the Senate.

According to the provisions of the Treaty of Versailles, the League of Nations was duly organized and in November, 1920, held its first session at Geneva. On this occasion there were

present the representatives of the forty-two nations then enrolled in the League. At the end of ten years the membership
had risen to fifty-four. In 1926 Germany was received into the
fellowship with great cordiality, leaving outside this "Parliament of Man" ten countries—Russia, the United States, Turkey, Egypt, Ecuador, Mexico, Costa Rica, Afghanistan, Hejaz,
and Irak, in addition to Argentina, which withdrew without
resigning. Since the establishment of the League its Assembly
has usually met annually and the Council, four times a year;
important matters have been decided, and numerous commissions appointed to make investigations and to carry out the
orders of the League.

In several ways the League promoted the peace of Europe.
In the first place, it was able to avert serious trouble between
its members by settling a number of controversies arising over
conflicting claims to territory. War between Italy and Greece
and between Greece and Bulgaria was fended off largely by
the intervention of the League. Relief work for refugees from
war-devastated areas was undertaken on a large scale by its
commissions, and aid and advice in financial reconstruction
were given, notably to Austria and Hungary. Permanent auxiliary departments for the prolonged study of important questions were organized. These departments were of two kinds:
technical bodies dealing with finance and economics, transit
and health; advisory committees occupied with military questions, disarmament, mandates, traffic in women and children,
opium, and intellectual coöperation. In addition two related,
but practically independent, bodies were established: the
Permanent Court of International Justice and the International Labor Organization.

An excellent example of the way in which the League may
work for peace in time of a crisis was afforded by the Bolivia-
Paraguay clash in 1928, which reached the point of an armed
collision and bloodshed and, if unchecked by outside powers,
might easily have ended in a war involving the interests of

three continents. Alarming reports of the affair reached the
Council of the League just as its fifty-third session opened at
Lugano. Immediately on the receipt of the news the Council
instructed its president, M. Briand, without waiting for an
appeal from either party, to cable both belligerents, reminding
them of their obligations as members of the League to seek
peaceful means of reaching a settlement and urging them to
come to terms by some pacific adjustment of their difficulties.
In a short time Paraguay sent a favorable reply, indicating a
willingness to reach a fair understanding with her neighbor;
but after some delay Bolivia, while employing conciliatory
language, accused Paraguay of aggression and asserted that she
had to "demand the satisfaction that is due in such cases and to
take military measures of a defensive character." Bolivia also
added that until this "satisfaction" was given, it did not seem
possible to allay public excitement sufficiently "to permit the
resumption of peaceful negotiations." In other words, the two
countries were in the kind of diplomatic deadlock that so often
eventuates in war.

Instead of withdrawing from the quarrel the League Council
now sent to both contestants a dispatch couched in vigorous
terms. After expressing the conviction that the two countries
would really respect their obligations as members of the
League, the note drew their attention to the fact that they
could not fail, under their solemn pledges, to resort to one of
the various procedures provided by the Covenant for the
peaceful settlement of disputes. It specifically informed Bolivia that the acts of Paraguay, if they were as alleged, constitute a breach of international law for which reparation could be
secured by judicial process. The note then urged them both to
refrain from any further steps likely to aggravate the situation
and warned them that the Council of the League would follow
events "with a view to any action that may be necessary."
This note, with other correspondence, was then sent by telegraph to fifty-four governments, at a cost of $26,000, so that

the whole world might know just what was occurring, and take notice of the conduct of both countries.

When this sharp but courteous note failed to have the desired effect, M. Briand invited the diplomatic representatives of the two powers at Paris and the representatives of the United States and Argentina to a conference and explained to them the nature of the transactions that had taken place. Interestingly enough, the United States did not regard the activities of the League in this instance as a violation of the Monroe Doctrine, but independently aided in heading off war. At this Paris conference, M. Briand informed the "near" belligerents that if the two governments did not accept mediation in some form within a few days a special session of the Council of the League would be held to consider the measures to be taken, "either because war has broken out—or because it is on the point of breaking out—between two members of the League."

This sharp warning helped to produce the desired effect; for on December 19, nine days after the dispute started, Bolivia and Paraguay agreed to choose a peaceful way of settling their quarrel. Thus, by prompt action the League Council had aided the two contestants in calming their fears and their anger and in coming to terms. At the same time it had demonstrated to the world the possibilities of the League as a stabilizing influence in time of excitement. It is difficult to believe that if there had been a League of Nations in 1914 the contest between Austria and Serbia would have been permitted to widen into a world conflagration.

On the other hand, the League has been unable to settle satisfactorily several disputes brought before it—although in no case has its failure led to war. For instance, in 1921 a controversy arose over a plebiscite taken in Upper Silesia to decide whether that territory should go to Poland or to Germany, and the vote in the region as a whole was overwhelmingly in favor of the latter. The Interallied Commission of Control then tried to draw a line separating the Polish communities from the

German; but it came to a standstill, because the French member of the commission favored the Polish side, and the British member the German side. As a result of the deadlock, the affair was taken to the Council of the League, which sought a middle ground by dividing the territory. As it happened, this pleased nobody, least of all the Germans, who thereby lost rich industrial districts developed by German capitalists and engineers. In this case the League made a decision, but did not solve the problem. Again, in 1928 the long dispute between Poland and Lithuania over the Vilna district (p. 454) was carried to the League, only to be sent back to the disputants without a settlement. By private negotiations and friendly counsel the League members were unable to make an adjustment, and so they did not venture to give a decision. Hence another troublesome problem remained as acute as ever. The League was equally powerless to reach a conclusion respecting a quarrel between Rumania and Hungary, laid before it in 1928, over the confiscation of estates belonging to Hungarian landlords in the former country.

Nor could it compel any of the states that had guaranteed equal rights to minorities within their borders to give serious heed to repeated complaints of violations of these rights. To millions of Germans scattered among neighboring countries by the Treaty of Versailles, this was a vital issue—one likely to disturb the peace of Europe unless fairly met by the League, under whose protection minorities were placed. The persistence with which the races concerned raised the question of their rights made it clear that sooner or later the League would have to face it or confess failure in the presence of one of the most obvious menaces to European security. Indeed, at its quarterly session held in June, 1929, the Council of the League again took the matter under consideration and made certain halting steps in the direction of clarifying the points in controversy, securing more accurate data, and giving wider publicity to cases of actual violation of rights.

Perhaps it is in the field of "fact-finding" that the League ordinarily does its most important work. Although its activities in this sphere do not make spectacular news, they are of the highest significance for peace and the smooth intercourse of nations. Through its various technical organizations, commissions, and bureaus the League is continually engaged in the study of economic, social, labor, race, health, commercial, and legal questions and is making its findings of fact available to the statesmen of all countries engaged in adjusting international relations.

It is impossible to overemphasize the value of this quiet, unobtrusive research. On second thought it is apparent that quarrels arise out of specific cases, usually out of differences of opinion as to what really constitutes the facts in dispute. As a rule an accurate statement of the facts removes many, if not all, the causes of a disagreement; in any event, it makes clear the sources of the controversy, informs the world as to the nature of the dispute, and throws on the aggressor the burden of proving that the facts as presented constitute a good reason for violent action. Publicity as to facts is an excellent check on hasty action. The opinion of mankind, when informed, is not to be ignored by the most belligerent government.

In connection with its technical work the League has served more and more effectively as an agency for the promotion of international conferences and treaties relative to the regular intercourse of nations. Before it was founded the various countries of the world had to hold periodical conventions of a special character to deal with such matters as international postal, cable, telegraph, railway, and shipping exchanges. Such special conferences have not disappeared, but, naturally, the League has seemed to be the most appropriate organization for arranging and managing such undertakings. It has its permanent seat, its offices, its library, its informed technical experts, and its various commissions continually dealing with the issues at stake. Owing to the multiplying machinery of modern life, international trade, travel, and exchange increase with amazing rapidity, constantly raising problems for governments to adjust; and the League offers to them the most convenient agency for calling the necessary conferences, working out the issues, collecting the facts, and arriving at satisfactory conclusions. In such activities there is little to encourage newspaper headlines; but the technical experts who plan and direct most of the world's work appreciate its significance, and in time an understanding of its importance will sink deep into the mind of the hitherto heedless masses.

In the course of the League's development the attitude of the United States to it gradually changed. If any American citizens thought that the problems raised by the creation of the League were disposed of for all time by the Senate's refusal to join it, they were doomed to disappointment. It is true that for a few months after President Harding's inauguration, in 1921, the government of the United States ignored communications from the Secretary-General of the League; but it soon adopted a more courteous course and at least replied to letters, if formally and negatively. When the League began to hold conferences to deal with serious problems in which the United States had an obvious interest, the American government began to send official representatives to act "in an unofficial and consultative capacity." Later this somewhat curious policy was followed by the practice of sending regular representatives to certain conferences held under League auspices. For example, in 1927 the government of the United States was officially represented at four League conferences—on economic affairs, transit and communications, import and export prohibitions and restrictions, and preliminary disarmament arrangements.

In 1924 Charles E. Hughes, Secretary of State, publicly declared that "there is no more difficulty in dealing with the organization of the League in this way for the purpose of protecting our interests or furthering our policies than there would be in dealing with the British Empire. Because several nations have formed an organization of which we are not a part is no reason why we cannot coöperate in all matters affecting our proper concern." Nor can the League proceed on important matters of its own concern without knowing what will be the attitude of the United States. Although the American government has tried to keep up separate conferences on certain subjects and has refused to participate in others, it has been forced by circumstances into closer coöperation with the League,— in its own interest, if for no other reason.

When a fair balance sheet of the accomplishments and failures of the League of Nations is struck, it will be generally admitted that it has justified the hopes of its sponsors. Under its auspices the representatives of more than fifty nations meet every year to discuss the outstanding problems in international relations. At the annual Assembly the grievances of the small powers against the great can be aired in the presence of the world, collected, so to speak, by the telegraph, radio, and cable at one spot. At the conferences of the Council of the League, held quarterly or oftener, the statesmen of the leading powers come together officially to discuss publicly and privately matters of common concern. An opportunity is thus given to the representatives of governments engaged in hot disputes to meet "unofficially" and thrash out their differences. More than once a foreign minister who had not dared to call on a neighboring minister for a heart-to-heart talk about some issue in controversy has "seen" him at Geneva in the ordinary course of League business and got into friendly relations with him. The League itself is a symbol of peace; its members are committed to peace; and it has permanent organs for discussion and bringing pressure to bear on disputants. It makes unnecessary and obsolete the kind of long-range debate which took place in the summer of 1914 and culminated in the World War.

One of the provisions of the Covenant of the League requires that all treaties made between members must be registered at the League; otherwise they shall be invalid. Over a thousand treaties and conventions have so far been deposited at Geneva, where they can be examined by everyone. "Open diplomacy," which President Wilson had especially at heart, is furthered by the frequent meetings of statesmen in Geneva; for their deliberations, instead of being filed away in various foreign offices, as formerly, are reported by the daily papers all over the world. In this way information is furnished upon topics hitherto not generally understood. All this works for the education of public opinion, for the promotion of peaceful adjustment and of a widespread sentiment against resorting to war.

Is War an Anachronism?

In the preceding pages the negotiations and compacts which mark the decade following the Peace of Versailles have been briefly reviewed. They are very impressive, and behind them lies an enthusiastic effort to put an end to war, which finds only a partial expression in the measures already taken to escape future conflicts. Before 1914 few had regarded warfare as a crime; and now—with the usual human reservations —it has been outlawed "as an instrument of national policy." This is at least a great concession to idealism, even if it should prove that wars continue to occur. Nothing like it has happened before in the history of mankind.

To very few does the World War seem a glorious affair—to most it appears an incredibly stupid, atrocious shame. When the birthday of the German Republic was celebrated in Berlin in 1929, the inscription on the cenotaph erected to the victims of the war read, *Allen Toten des Weltkrieges den Opfern der Republik und der Arbeit*. There was nothing said of heroes but only of those sacrificed. Where conscription prevails all the capable have to go (some as eager volunteers; many, on the other hand, with terrific apprehension), to face the bombs along the trenches rather than shame and punishment at home. Early in 1929 appeared a book by a German, Erich Remarque, called, in bitter irony, *All Quiet on the Western Front.* In seven months over 750,000 copies were sold in Germany. A German writer said of it: "It is unanswerable; it cannot be evaded. It does not declaim; it never accuses.... Out of his grave speaks the Unknown Soldier.... Let it make its way over the whole world." Thirteen editions of the translation were soon sold in England, and 250,000 copies in the United States. It is an account of the way the young men of all nations met the horrible situation, and their hopelessness in any attempt to explain to simple patriots at home what war meant. This is but an illustration of post-war literature. Many dramas and books have been written to make clear to all nations the nature of the *Journey's End* for those who were enmeshed in the ancient net of war.

The modern historian is chary of pronouncing moral judgments. He feels it to be his business to describe the past of mankind as truly as he can and let that speak for itself. It is, however, a historical fact that organizations to prevent war and to disseminate a knowledge and understanding of international relations have grown mightily since the bloody business which began in 1914. The Carnegie Endowment for International Peace has been keeping those who desire information supplied with authentic material in regard to international relations. The late Edwin Ginn established in Boston the World Peace Foundation. A stately quarterly, *Foreign Affairs,* is published under able auspices by the Council of Foreign Relations. *The New York Times* issues its monthly *Current History* (sold on the bookstands), to which well-known historians contribute. Various organizations, conspicuously the Foreign Policy Association, and many "institutes," such as that held annually at Williamstown, keep the problems of international understanding before the public by organizing discussions in which representatives of interested nations take part. All these enterprises take care to avoid narrow national considerations and endeavor to foster a sense of the comity of nations. The newspapers and the best weekly magazines give an increasing attention to foreign affairs, undreamed-of before the war.

The progress of democracy has brought with it the democratizing of war. We are one and all in it if it comes,—old and young. It is no longer, as has been abundantly shown, the marshaling of troops by a monarch with the hope of getting the better of another prince and his men. Its conspicuous camp followers are no longer dissolute women and sharpers, but the representatives of the Young Men's and the Young Women's Christian Association, the Red Cross, and the Salvation Army, together with a host of brave volunteer nurses.

Warfare today is, as was shown in an earlier section, an old name for strangely new operations. Modern scientific knowledge has so revolutionized military methods that fighting in our time is scarcely more like that of the Franco-Prussian War than the military procedure of 1870 resembled that of William the Conqueror. There is a justifiable suspicion that if another great conflict should be permitted to occur, the present means of destroying human beings and their property would be increased terrifically. The old kind of warfare is, then, an anachronism—it has, indeed, almost completely passed away in countries which have come under European influence. Consequently, those who would maintain peace have to face new problems and resort to unprecedented means if the age-long readiness to resort to arms is to be effectively checked, ultimately to die away like religious intolerance, the belief in witchcraft, and the institution of chattel slavery.

In a work called *War as an Instrument of National Policy and its Renunciation in the Pact of Paris*, Professor James T. Shotwell—a distinguished historical scholar who has devoted many years to plans for the prevention of international conflicts—endeavors to put war in its proper historical perspective. He says:

One thing is clear: the generation that has endured the realities of the World War will demand that the strategy of peace shall be real also. . . . Humanity cannot afford to trust its wistful hopes to anything, however promising, that may betray it in the hour of crisis; nor is it likely that the instrument of war so bravely denounced will be actually discarded if nations still believe that the use of this instrument is essential to them. The meaning of the Pact of Paris is, therefore, to be found not solely, or even mostly, in the text itself, but rather in the history of civilization and a survey of the practical politics of the immediate present. If war has been with us from the beginning of time, it will only yield to forces stronger than itself; whether these really exist in the world today or not is as much the subject of this inquiry as the story of the Pact itself.

Professor Shotwell points out that war is no longer a safe instrument for statesmanship. No one can any longer make a guess as to what will happen if war breaks out.

Victor and victim may suffer a common disaster. . . . In short, war which was once a directable instrument of policy has now changed its nature with the nature of modern society and ceases to be controllable and directable in the hands of statesmen. By reason of its all-embracing needs, it becomes a contagion among the nations; and one cannot safely use a contagion as an instrument.

T

CHAPTER XVIII

NEW CONCEPTIONS OF THE WORLD WE LIVE IN

THE FUNDAMENTAL RÔLE OF KNOWLEDGE IN HUMAN AFFAIRS

Many writers have compiled what they entitle the "elements," "essentials," or "foundations" of history, but few of them give any attention to the real basis of all civilization, whether primitive or advanced. It is at bottom *knowledge* and *skill based upon knowledge* that have gradually changed men from beasts, wandering in the woods and fields, to human beings such as we know today. This all-essential fact escaped the older historians, who, like most of their fellow men, took the knowledge of their period for granted and forgot that it had a history which really underlies all other history. *All discoveries and inventions are made by individuals of a rare type, not by peoples as a whole.* But tribes and nations will sometimes accept new ideas and arts when shown how to think or do; and the more thoroughly they assimilate new ways, the more likely they are to forget to whom they owe them.

The boastful patriot would find himself in a tragic predicament if from the supposed achievements of his own proud people were deducted those they really owed to other nations and to other times. This has been well set forth by Graham Wallas:

If every human being now alive were to lose all the knowledge and habits which he had acquired from preceding generations (though retaining unchanged all his own powers of invention and memory and habituation), nine-tenths of the inhabitants of London or New York would be dead in a month, and ninety-nine per cent of the remaining would be dead in six months. They would have no language to express their thoughts, and no thoughts but vague reverie. They could not read notices, or drive motors or horses. . . . Even in the country districts men could not invent, in time to preserve their lives, methods of growing food, or taming animals, or making fire, or so clothing themselves as to endure a northern winter.

Only the very lowest savage, far more ignorant than any on earth today, would be sufficiently animal-like to pull through if he lost what others had contributed to his resources.

In the United States the language commonly used is English. It is an importation, and, in spite of "Americanisms," remains much the same as it was before the colony at Jamestown or at Plymouth was founded. We can all easily read the writings of Shakespeare or Bacon, or the Authorized Version of the Bible, which belong to the earliest period of English colonization. English was originally brought into Britain from West Germanic countries, later to be modified and enriched by Norman French and especially by Latin. The Romans in their turn depended much on the Greeks in the development of their language and literature; the Greeks owed their alphabet to that of the Phœnicians, which came mayhap from the Egyptians; and the Egyptians based their writing on picture signs common to various savage tribes. Perfervid national pride and historical knowledge rarely go hand in hand, as we shall see later. A nation may perhaps repay its war debts in money or securities, but never its inescapable obligations to other nations for almost everything it has. It might, however, come to realize the stern fact that it is but a pensioner feeding at the table of accumulated human endeavor. And no more chastening lesson has history to impress than this.

The life of mankind is so complicated that it is no easy matter to describe it even in its simplest, most primitive forms; and no single historical writer can claim to trace the genesis and development of more than a very few of its present aspects. Nevertheless, it is possible to sketch the trend of modern thought about ourselves and the world in which we live.

In the first volume (Chapter II) some of the beliefs of the Middle Ages were recalled and then the questionings of these which became so conspicuous on the part of the bolder thinkers of the seventeenth century. Francis Bacon urged eloquently that inquiry be substituted for the accepted beliefs about nature which had been transmitted from the days of the ancient Greeks. He suspected not only that the old notions were wrong but that there was an indefinite amount to be found out which the Greeks and their disciples in the Middle Ages had never thought of investigating. He recommended a faith in doubt, as did Descartes. Abelard had said as early as the twelfth century that by doubting we come to question, and that by questioning we may come to the truth. This has proved very difficult for men to learn, and few have as yet mastered it; for we are by nature dogmatists. We are taught habits of belief by our elders when we are children—habits which were acquired by our parents and teachers when they themselves were young. This explanation of the persistence of old ideas is, as we shall see later, one of the important discoveries of modern times. It was formerly supposed that people accepted beliefs on their merits; but this is very rarely the case. Religious teachers have been particularly conspicuous in denouncing doubt as a temptation of the devil, to be resisted at all costs. But doctors, lawyers, and even philosophers and scientists themselves often refuse to consider novel suggestions.

Uncertainty is painful under most circumstances—a firm belief, faith, and confidence is refreshing and brings a sense of relief and safety. Yet a few individuals can doubt without being distressed. It is they who have curiosity and seek to satisfy it by exploration and research in the hope of rectifying old mistakes or unearthing hitherto unknown facts. It is noteworthy that only one ancient school of philosophy ever set changing one's mind, in view of increasing information and thought, as its goal. Cicero belonged to a group of Plato's followers who declared, "We pursue only what is probable and so are ready to debate with others without persistence and be refuted ourselves without vexation." He would be ashamed, he said, to believe next year just what he had believed last. He expected always to be learning and saw no justification for clinging to what he had happened to have accepted as possible in earlier days. This is the professed creed of scientific investigators in every field of research today, even if they find it hard to adhere to such a high standard. The respectability of doubt and its wide diffusion is certainly far greater now than when it was enjoined by Bacon and Descartes some four hundred years ago.

We saw that during the seventeenth century the confidence in alchemy and astrology was giving way, and that two departments of science—chemistry and astronomy—were being substituted for them. These branches of knowledge have grown rapidly and, as we shall see, have revolutionized our views of the whole cosmos and of the matter of which it is composed. We noted too the decline in the seventeenth century of witchcraft and the belief in the constant interference of the devil in human affairs. Along with this came suggestions on the part of the deists of a new conception of God and criticisms of the Bible and the miracles therein reported. Defenders of modern literature arose, who proclaimed it equal or perhaps superior to the writings of ancient times (Vol. I, pp. 42 ff.). Kingship based on the divine right of rulers as God's representatives was attacked, and the right was proclaimed by Milton and Locke of every man to speak out freely his opinions about religion and government so long as he engaged in no open sedition. Each should be free to publish his views in books and pamphlets without any preliminary censorship on the part of Church or State. These things form an impressive list of achievements belonging to the seventeenth and early eighteenth century upon which further progress has been based.

In Chapter VIII of the previous volume the increasing confidence in progress was illustrated in many ways. We recalled the criticisms suggested by Voltaire and the French *philosophes*; Montesquieu's novel analysis of government; Rousseau's denunciations of the highly artificial society of his days; his demand that children be saved from a vicious method of education, that the people be adjudged the sovereign power, and that there should be a return to "nature"; Beccaria's protest against the atrocities of the criminal law; Diderot's attempt in his *Encyclopedia* to bring knowledge up to date and make it easy of access; Turgot's and Adam Smith's treatises on the great matters of industry, commerce, and agriculture, and the question of how far the government should endeavor to control them. These and many other changes of thought and recommendations for reform characterized the decades immediately preceding the French Revolution.

The changes of thought and increase of knowledge in the seventeenth and eighteenth centuries were, however, but a foundation and starting-point for far more astonishing discoveries, inventions, and revolutions of opinion in the nineteenth century, to be followed by the deeper and wider questioning of the twentieth century, with answers impossible for previous thinkers to have suggested. While the practical inventions of the last fifty or sixty years far outrun those of any previous thousand years in man's existence and are obvious to all, the less obtrusive changes of attitude toward man and the world are quite as striking, and are inexpressibly impressive to one who takes pains to consider them.

The rapidity of change in man's ideas and surrounding may be illustrated by the history of the *Encyclopædia Britannica*. It first appeared in three volumes (1768–1771) not long after Diderot completed his far more comprehensive compilation. In 1910–1911 the eleventh edition was issued in twenty-nine volumes. Eleven years later three more volumes had to be added to catch up with increased knowledge and the striking developments of a decade. Four years later three more supplementary volumes were published. Then it was decided to recast the whole work, omitting much that had become obsolete and adopting a style of presentation which would appeal to a far greater number of readers than did the previous editions.

Those few who have the time and the disposition to engage in scientific investigation of man and his world often reach divergent conclusions. Most of them agree upon certain matters; but new discoveries are constantly being made, and there are always a good many highly important points upon which those who have studied hardest are not at one. Moreover, all new discoveries are tentative and subject to revision and amplification. No one familiar with the present trend of scientific research believes that we have as yet made more than the beginning of a beginning in learning about ourselves and the universe in which we are placed. Each new discovery reveals unforeseen mysteries and intricacies which stimulate further quest. So, in spite of all the progress in the past there now seems more to be discovered than Bacon and Descartes could have dreamed possible when they haled mankind into the path of modern research. It is a well-founded guess that in the matter of scientific information the encyclopedias of a hundred and fifty years hence will differ far more profoundly from those of the present day than the best of our time differ from that of Diderot.

As for the great mass of mankind, while they are profoundly affected by modern inventions, they still harbor a great part of those ideas which began to be vigorously called in question three hundred years ago. Most men are far too preoccupied with the immediate concerns of life to give much thought to the suggestions of scientists, scholars, and philosophers. So the old views of authority, heavenly and earthly, continue to prevail, with some slight modifications. There are always plenty of popular leaders to approve and encourage continued faith in the old beliefs, which they refuse to reconsider in the light of new knowledge. Those who teach children have to be cautious in imparting ideas which the scientifically minded might think true and important, lest these new views arouse the distrust of parents who cling to older and, to them, permanently settled conceptions of man's origin and duty. In reviewing the history of knowledge since the eighteenth century in this and the following chapter, only those great alterations of opinion are mentioned which the majority of the critically minded would accept today.

In the present chapter the modern discoveries in regard to the world in which man lives and his general position in the whole order of nature will be sketched; in the next chapter the modern ways of studying man himself, his nature, achievements, and possibilities, will be described; and finally, in the last chapter a new and curious development of the study of mankind through fiction will be illustrated. We shall begin with the newer discoveries in regard to the great age of our earth.

The Great Age of the Earth

Up until the middle of the nineteenth century practically everyone in Europe believed that the earth had existed for not more than five or six thousand years. This was the Christian tradition based upon the account of the generations of man in Genesis. St. Augustine declared confidently in his *City of God* that not six thousand years had elapsed since the creation of man. God, it was believed, had created not only the earth but the stars, together with all the species of plant and animal life, as well as the first man and the first woman, during the successive days of a single week. An Anglican prelate, Archbishop Usher, gave definiteness to this idea in his elaborate *Annals of the Old and the New Testament*, published in Latin in Cromwell's time (1650–1654). After a careful study of the Scriptures he reached the conclusion that the terrestrial animals and Adam were created on Friday, October 28, 4004 B.C. Eve too was made from Adam's rib on the same day, after Adam had given names to the animals. Usher's chronology was inserted by an unknown hand in the margin of the Authorized Version of the Bible and so became familiar to millions of readers, who accepted the glosses and the text as equally authoritative.

For this belief an entirely different one has been substituted by geologists, paleontologists, anthropologists, and astronomers. There is some difference of opinion as to how the earth originally came about [1] but none regarding its tremendous age from a human standpoint. While geologists do not all reach the same conclusions in regard to the period when the earth became suitable for plant or animal life, they agree that all things have come to their present state through a *gradual* process, extending through thousands of millions of years. There is no means as yet of settling this matter of geological dates. It may have required a hundred million or a thousand million years for the sedimentary rocks to be laid down in the beds of ancient seas. Many of these rocks contain fossils which indicate that plants and animals have existed on the globe from the very remote periods when some of the earlier strata were formed. Accordingly, it seems not unlikely that for at least a hundred million years the earth has had its seas and its dry land, differing little in temperature and geographical variety from the globe on which mankind wanders about today.

If we prudently reduce this conjectural period by one half, it is still impossible to form more than a faint idea of the time during which the simpler kinds of vegetable and animal life have possessed the earth. Let us imagine a record having been kept during the past fifty million years, in which a single page should be devoted to the chief changes occurring during each five thousand years (not much less than the whole age of the earth according to Usher). This mighty journal would now fill ten volumes of a thousand pages each; and scarcely more than the last page—Volume X, page 1000—would be assigned to

[1] For a short statement of modern theories of the earth's origin see *The Evolution of the Earth* (edited by R. S. Lull) or any good recent geology.

the whole recorded history of mankind from the earliest Egyptian inscriptions to the present moment.

As for the starry universe, of which our second-rate sun and his little following of planets form an infinitesimal part, that seems to our homely methods of reckoning in miles and years to have existed always and to be infinite in extent. Traveling with the speed of the fastest thing we know—light—at the rate of one hundred and eighty-six thousand miles a second, one might reach Neptune, on the outermost bounds of our solar system, in about four hours, whereas it would take over four years at the same speed to reach the star nearest us. By substituting photographic plates for the human eye, it has been found that, with long exposures, hundreds of millions of stars reveal themselves, too faint to be seen with the eye through the best telescopes. It is suspected that the very distant nebulæ are other vast systems of suns lying outside our whole stellar universe. All the heavenly bodies are moving with incredible rapidity; the earth not only revolves about its sun, but the sun travels through space like all the other stars. So far as the constitution of the stars throughout the universe is concerned, the spectroscope indicates that they are all made of the same chemical elements with which we are familiar on the earth: hydrogen, helium, oxygen, nitrogen, carbon, sodium, iron, nickel, and so forth. And such samples as fall on the earth in the form of meteoric dust or larger masses have so far proved on analysis to contain no materials strange to the earthly chemist.

As early as 1795 the Scotch geologist James Hutton published his conclusion that the earth had gradually assumed its present form by slow natural processes, and he roused a storm of protest by declaring that he found "no traces of a beginning and no prospect of an end." In 1830–1833 Sir Charles Lyell published his famous *Principles of Geology*, in which he explained at length the manner in which the gradual contraction of the globe, the action of rain and frost, had, through countless eons and without great general convulsions or cataclysms, formed the mountains and valleys and laid down the strata of limestone, clay, and sandstone. He showed, in short, that the surface of the earth was the result of familiar, everyday causes, most of which can still be seen in operation. The work of later geologists has served to substantiate Lyell's views.

THE THEORY OF EVOLUTION: DARWINISM

And just as the earth itself has slowly changed through the operation of natural forces, so plants and animals appear to have assumed their present forms gradually. Buffon, a French naturalist, who was busy on a vast *Natural History* at the time that Diderot's *Encyclopedia* was in course of publication, pointed out that all mammals closely resembled one another in their structure, unlike as they may appear to the careless observer. If a horse be compared point by point to a man, "our wonder," Buffon declares, "is excited rather by the resemblances than by the differences between them." As he noted the family likenesses between even widely divergent creatures he admitted that it looked as if nature might, if sufficient time were allowed, "have evolved all organized forms from one original type."

In other passages Buffon forecast the great theory of evolution, and in the opening decade of the nineteenth century his fellow countryman Lamarck published a work in which he boldly maintained that the whole animal world had been gradually developed from simpler forms. He was half a century in advance of his times in this conviction. He believed that traits acquired by an individual might be transmitted hereditarily to its offspring and that in this way successful adjustments would accumulate. Many modern biologists deny this "hereditary transmissibility of acquired characters," as the hypothesis is called. But the question becomes a very intricate one on inspection and cannot be said to be settled yet.

There appeared in England in 1844 a volume entitled *Vestiges of the Natural History of Creation*, by a writer who carefully concealed his name.[1] For the accepted idea of the instantaneous creation of all living species of plants and animals he substituted the notion of development through long periods:

The whole train of animated beings, from the simplest and oldest up to the highest and most recent are, then, to be regarded as a series of *advances of the principle of development*, which have depended upon external physical circumstances, to which the resulting animals are appropriate. I contemplate the whole phenomena as having been in the first place arranged in the counsels of Divine Wisdom to take place, not only upon this sphere, but upon all others in space, under necessary modifications, and as being carried on from first to last, here and elsewhere, under the immediate favor of the creative will or energy.

The writer urges that the emergence of more complex forms from simpler ones is not at all "more wonderful as a natural process than one which we never think of wondering at, because familiar to us; namely, that during the gestation of the mammals." Even the egg and the acorn give little promise of the hen and the oak which come from them. This argument from analogy is evoked down to the present day. The writer makes many moral reflections, calling attention, for example, to the fact that from this new standpoint so-called criminals are either the victims of bad social conditions or "are brought to error by tendencies which they are only unfortunate in having inherited from nature." This was a new solution of the problem of evil, now to be ascribed not to man's fall from an angelic state but to his rise from the unquestioning life of a wild animal (see below, pp. 638 ff.).

---

[1] In the twelfth edition of this book, published in 1884, it was finally admitted that it was written by Robert Chambers, who had died in 1871. The author dreaded the bitter controversy in which he would be involved if his name were known.

In 1852 Herbert Spencer, in one of his very earliest works, gave many reasons for supposing that the whole visible universe—the earth and all its plant and animal inhabitants, including even man himself and all his ideas and institutions—had slowly developed by natural processes.

Seven years later (1859) Charles Darwin's *Origin of Species by Means of Natural Selection*, the result of years of most patient study of plants and animals, finally brought the whole theory of evolution to the attention of the world at large. In his introduction he says:

Although much remains obscure, I can entertain no doubt, after the most deliberate and dispassionate judgment of which I am capable, that the view which most naturalists till recently entertained, and which I formerly entertained—namely, that each species has been independently created—is erroneous. I am fully convinced that species are not immutable, but that those belonging to what are called the same genera are lineal descendants of some other and generally extinct species.

The theologians knew little about zoölogical classification, and it was not hard for them to believe that all the kinds of animals and vegetables which they happened to have noticed existed in the Garden of Eden and were still to be found in exactly the same form in which God originally created them. If, however, one consults a botanical or a zoölogical handbook, one will discover that there are hundreds of thousands of kinds of organisms on the earth, differing from one another in physical characteristics and habits. Even of single-celled animals about sixteen thousand species have already been discovered. There are perhaps eighty thousand kinds of beetles and fifty thousand known species of flies. Then there are all the various mollusks, crustaceans, fishes, birds, and a relatively small assortment of mammals. The paleontologist discovers from the examination of the earth's strata that the species of animals and plants which happen to have left some record of themselves have often come and gone. He also finds that the so-called higher animals occur only in comparatively recent deposits, while the simpler creatures can be traced back tens of millions of years. It was considerations like these, together with experiments in breeding and hybridization, that led Darwin to accept the evolutionary hypothesis, which, as we have seen, did not originate with him. It was his attempt to *explain evolution* and the transmutation of one species into another that constitutes "Darwinism" in the minds of scientific workers, not the theory of evolution itself, as so many people still mistakenly suppose.

Darwin pointed out that if any species of animal or plant were left free under favorable circumstances to multiply, it would speedily fill the whole earth. For example, if a single pair of robins or sparrows were allowed to live and breed unmolested, they might increase to twenty million in ten years. This is a very moderate instance of the power of multiplication. Since the number of plants and animals shows no actual general increase, it is clear that by far the greater portion of the eggs of birds and fishes, the seeds of plants, and the young of mammals are destroyed before they can develop. Excessive heat and cold, rain and drought, are largely responsible for this destruction of potential life; but organisms destroy one another in all sorts of ways, often by merely crowding one another out and consuming all the available food. There is, consequently, a perpetual competition among all living things.

Darwin named this essential competition the "struggle for existence." But he is careful to say, "I use this term in a large and metaphorical sense, including dependence of one being upon another, and including (which is more important) not only the life of the individual but the success in leaving progeny." Those unfamiliar with animals and plants often get the idea that by "struggle for existence" is meant a sort of active warfare, conquest or defeat, devouring or getting devoured.

But Darwin was under no such illusion. Survival is in the overwhelming majority of cases a matter of seeming accident —the result of delicate adjustments, not by any means the outcome of a successful struggle in the usual sense of the word. For example, out of ten thousand winged milkweed seeds it is possible that one only may be wafted into a situation suitable to sprouting; of all the burs clinging to a herd of cattle but one may be detached at just the right point to perpetuate its kind. In any case, of all the seeds and eggs that are formed only a minute portion ever develop: one in five, in ten, in a thousand, in a million; of the young only a very small percentage reach maturity and reproduce their species.

These considerations lead to the great question whether reasons can be found which explain why some individuals and species survive while others decline or perish altogether. Alfred R. Wallace, a great admirer of Darwin (who had himself reached conclusions similar to Darwin's before the *Origin of Species* was published), thus summarizes the doctrine of *variation* and the *survival of the fittest*:

If all individuals of each species were exactly alike in every respect, we could only say that it [survival] is a matter of chance, but they are not alike. . . . We find that they vary in many different ways. Some are stronger, some swifter, some hardier in constitution, some more cunning. An obscure color may render concealment more easy for some; keener sight may enable others to discover prey or escape from an enemy better than their fellows. Among plants the smallest differences may be useful or the reverse. The earliest and strongest shoots may escape the slugs; their greater vigor may enable them to flower and seed earlier in wet autumn; plants best armed with spines or hair may escape being devoured; those whose flowers are most conspicuous may be soonest fertilized by insects. We cannot doubt that, on the whole, any beneficial variation will give the possessor of it a greater probability of living through the tremendous ordeal they have to undergo. There may be something left to chance, but on the whole *the fittest will survive*.

Darwinism may then be summarized as follows: It was the theory that animal and plant species do not endure indefinitely unchanged; but, owing to the "variations," or peculiar characteristics, which may be observed in every individual, no two of which are exactly alike, those best fitted to survive tend to have a better chance of escaping destruction in the bitter competition of life and of transmitting their advantageous characteristics to their offspring. In this way the increasing complexity of adjustment and the emergence of ever "higher" and more intricate creatures in the scale from the amœba to man seemed to be at least partly explained. Darwin also conjectured that "sexual selection" played a part in this process; by this he meant that the more vigorous, the better armed, or, in the case of birds, "the most melodious or beautiful" males would have the advantage of capturing or attracting the females and would consequently be more likely to have offspring than those individuals with poorer weapons and inferior charms. Darwin himself attached slight importance to this factor, although it caught the attention of the public.

Among the scientifically minded who heartily welcomed Darwin's book and approved his theories were Herbert Spencer, Alfred R. Wallace, Thomas Huxley, the American botanist Asa Gray, and the popular German writer Haeckel, all of whom devoted their expert knowledge and gifted pens to the explanation and defense of the new ideas.

The opponents of the evolutionary hypothesis were, however, very loud in their denunciations. Not only religious leaders but some distinguished men of science, like Alexander Agassiz, utterly refused to revise their opinions. The clergy, both Protestant and Catholic, could find no words too harsh to apply to the patient and careful Darwin, who seemed to them to contradict the express word of God in the Bible and to rob man of all his dignity by suggesting that he had originally sprung from lower animal forms. The new theory seemed to them an "attempt to dethrone God" and substitute mere gradual natural processes for the divine fiat which had called all things into existence. Pope Pius IX declared Darwin's theory to be the result of his natural depravity, and an absurd attempt to degrade man to the level of unreasoning brutes.

Some religious leaders, however, became gradually reconciled to the new conception of the development of all things. On further thought they recognized that God's ways were exhibited and illustrated in his works as well as in the Bible. A gradual process of creation might be quite as divine as a sudden one, as had been urged by the author of *Vestiges of the Natural History of Creation*, referred to above. Mankind, instead of suffering degradation by being included in the history of organic development, might be considered the goal toward which all nature's work from the origin of the globe had been directed. The works of John Fiske, the American historian and philosopher, and *Natural Law in the Spiritual World* (1883) by Henry Drummond, a devout Scotch Calvinist, as well as his *Ascent of Man* (1894), did much to remove the prejudice against evolution in the minds of thoughtful readers. Patrick Geddes wrote a little work emphasizing coöperation and a kind of inherent altruism in the process of evolution. And it seemed for a time that the original bitter antipathy to the evolutionary ideas was destined to pass away, as has that against the Copernican statement of the movement of the earth. But after the World War a well-organized effort was made, especially in the United States, to prevent the teaching of evolution in the schools, and two or three state legislatures were induced to pass laws forbidding teachers in public schools to present as true the scientific conception of man's origin (see page 631 below). Those who oppose the evolutionary view rarely have, or claim to have, any special knowledge of the ways of nature; it is enough for them that the new view seems opposed to the teachings of the Bible as they have been taught to understand it.

T

As for men of science, very few any longer doubt that if man's ancestry could be traced back far enough, it would be found to merge into that of the other higher animals, especially the monkeys and apes, although none of them believe man is *directly* derived from either of these groups. They accept the evolutionary hypothesis, but a great many feel that Darwinism as an explanation of the origin of species is inadequate and sometimes quite erroneous. For example, many assert that characteristics acquired by an individual cannot be transmitted hereditarily to its offspring, and that so-called sexual selection is based upon false assumptions. In short, further researches into the mysterious complications of natural processes has rendered the whole problem far more intricate and, as yet, more mysterious than it was believed to be even by the modest Darwin and his immediate followers. So it is sometimes said that "Darwinism is dead"; but this does not mean that scientific men are not all practically agreed that the higher plants and animals, including man himself, have a long lineage of simpler ancestors extending back to the first appearance of life on the globe.

The Study of Living Cells and its Results

While, as has been said, practically all biologists believe in evolution, the greater part of them are at present more concerned in studying the structure and workings of present-day creatures which are readily at hand in inexhaustible quantities. Fossil remains are very imperfect, although it has been possible to classify them into many families, genera, and species.

Without the modern compound microscope, which began to be improved about 1830 and reached a high degree of perfection in the latter half of the nineteenth century, our knowledge of the world of plant and animal life would remain slight. To illustrate this take a small pin and make a shallow indentation in a piece of paper. The spot will be about a hundredth of an inch in diameter. Now the overwhelming majority of animals and thousands of different kinds of plants are smaller, often much smaller, than the mark of the pin. The cells of which multicellular animals are formed are also less than a hundredth of an inch across, including the cell from which we all start. With the microscope a creature a hundredth of an inch in length can be studied as if he were a foot long, if one has lenses magnifying twelve hundred diameters, and these are common enough in any good laboratory.

About 1838 two German naturalists, Schleiden and Schwann, one of whom had been studying plants and the other animals, compared their observations and reached the conclusion that all living things are composed of one or many minute bodies which are called *cells*—a somewhat misleading name. For organic cells are not like those in a honeycomb or in a prison or in a monastery, but are minute masses of a gelatinous substance to which the botanist Von Mohl gave the name of *protoplasm* in 1846. All life, whether plant or animal, was shown to have its beginning in a tiny mass of protoplasm, and the old theory that simple organisms generated spontaneously from dead matter was finally shown to be a mistake. As Virchow, the famous German physiologist expressed it, only a live cell can produce another live cell (*omnis cellula e cellula*). The cell corresponds in a certain way with the molecules which make up inanimate substances.

The chemical elements of protoplasm are known, but, to judge from the miracles it performs, its still unknown structure and organization are complex beyond belief. There are a vast number of creatures, most of which live in the water, which consist of but one cell; but the microscope, although it reveals but few of their intimate secrets, shows them to be very complicated. These single-celled creatures are called *protozoans*, and they are not always very sharply differentiated from single-celled plants, since the animal and plant kingdoms merge into one another in their simpler forms.

All the forms of animal life we see about us—insects, fishes, birds, mammals—are composed of millions of cells. It is estimated that the human body contains many trillions, each of which is due to the division of a previous cell, and all of which spring, in the last analysis, from a single original cell (the ovum, or egg), in the same way that all multicellular animals and plants take their start.

All these cells are not alike, however, but just as in a social community one group of individuals devotes itself to the performance of one of the duties requisite to the well-being of the community and another group devotes itself to the performance of another duty, so too, in the body, one group of cells takes upon itself one special function and another, another.—McMurrich

In addition to the cells which form the skin, muscles, bones, and organs, the blood of vertebrates contains billions of cells (corpuscles, red and white), which circulate freely and act somewhat like protozoans, or unicellular animals.

Only two illustrations of the great importance of the microscopic study of cells need be mentioned here: (1) the investigations relating to the embryonic cell and its development into a full-grown creature, and (2) the discovery of bacteria and other single-celled and very minute creatures which play a great rôle in man's life both in health and disease.

Embryology—the science of germ cells and the ways in which parents transmit their characteristics to their offspring (heredity)—made rapid progress during the first quarter of the twentieth century. It has proved possible to follow somewhat closely the changes that occur in the egg after fertilization takes place and to describe the manner in which the contributions made by both male and female are combined in the building up of their progeny. There are incredibly small and numerous chemical packets called *genes*, which are combined into much larger packets (easily seen under the microscope) called *chromosomes*. It is quite impossible to describe in detail the current research in this fascinating field, but two or three conclusions of obvious importance in the readjustment of our older ideas may be noted.

In the first place, the mother and the father each contribute the same number of chromosomes or heredity-bearing packets, and both have an equal chance of transmitting their characteristics to their offspring. So the old genealogical tables, based on feudal ideas of *male* primogeniture are, from a modern standpoint, wholly unscientific and grotesque. One who proudly cherishes the fact that he had an ancestor in the *Mayflower*, perhaps ten generations back, and who traces his "direct" line back to someone living in 1620 is engaged in a purely fanciful operation. For all his ancestors, women as well as men, had had an equal chance of affecting his make-up, however stupid or ignorant or vicious they may have been. If intermarriages be neglected, each one of us living today had a thousand and twenty-four ancestors living ten generations ago, and in the interval a total of over two thousand forbears who may have helped to make or mar us.

In the second place, it is a well-known fact that brothers and sisters, with the same parents, differ widely in their physical and mental and emotional traits. The reason for this is now cleared up by the microscope. A new deal takes place when each of us comes into being as an individual. And the traits not only of our father and mother but of their parents and ancestors may happen to get into the new mixture which makes up any one of us. So each of us is unique in some respects, although the habits and conformities of life may make us seem more uniform than we are. This fact is discouraging to the so-called eugenists, who hope to improve mankind by precluding marriages between individuals whom they deem "undesirables." From the standpoint of heredity each of us has many fathers and mothers, and no one can control the shuffling of the chromosomes. Of course, all this does not call into question the fact that intelligent parents in a favorable position may exercise a great influence upon their children in rearing them advantageously, whatever their particular hereditary characteristics. But the problem of producing "well-born" human beings is shown to be far more intricate and difficult than many writers on eugenics seem willing to admit.

Lastly, there is much discussion nowadays about *heredity* and *environment*: some incline to attribute almost everything to the one; others, to the other. An eminent biologist[1] has pointed out that heredity and environment are equally important, since they always go together and cannot be thought of apart. This is the result of considering the cell from first to last. It can only live and develop as a result of its environment, and a change of environment will modify its behavior in all sorts of surprising ways, since it is very complicated and shows great powers of adaptation. Heredity consists in the chemical contents and organization of the cells; environment, in the circumstances in which the cells find themselves. So both are absolutely essential to life and development.

BACTERIA AND THE GERM THEORY OF DISEASE

As early as 1675 the simple microscopes of the day had revealed "little animals" (*animalcula*) in pond water and in milk, cheese, and putrefying meat. With the far more powerful microscopes of the nineteenth century these animalcula were found to constitute a vast world of tiny organisms differing from one another greatly in structure and in modes of life. Some of them belong to the one-celled protozoans; others are tiny plants; others form a large and varied group, extreme in their minuteness and having ways of life different from what are ordinarily called plants. These are now classed as *bacteria*.

A hundred years after the discovery of animalcula Pleincz of Vienna made the startling statement that he was firmly

[1] H. S. Jennings, *Prometheus, or Biology and the Advancement of Man.* This is a short and very interesting account of embryological discoveries.

convinced that both disease and the decomposition of animal matter were due to the activity of these minute organisms. But another century elapsed before Pasteur discovered in 1863 that the virulent ulcer called anthrax was due to the presence of little rod-shaped bodies which he named bacteria.

Pasteur (1822–1895) was a French chemist who made many important discoveries besides the treatment for hydrophobia, with which his name is most commonly associated. He proved that bacteria were very common in the air and that it was they that were at the bottom of physiological changes hitherto entirely unexplained. Pasteur was sent by the government to the south of France to study the disease of the silkworm, the ravages of which were impoverishing the country. He found the bodies and eggs of the silkworms full of bacteria and suggested the proper remedy. His study of fermentation enabled him to prevent great losses also among the winegrowers.

Koch of Berlin later discovered the *bacillus* of tuberculosis, one of the commonest as well as most deadly diseases. Other workers have found the germs which are implicated in diphtheria, lockjaw, the bubonic plague, etc.

Bacteria are rodlike, beadlike, or spiral in shape, often in rapid motion, and they multiply by dividing into two parts or by forming a germ or spore. They are very tiny. Four thousand of the larger kinds put end to end would extend only an inch; smaller ones are but one four-hundred-thousandth of an inch in length; and it is supposed that some diseases are due to those too small to be seen under the most powerful microscopic lenses. They would do little harm were it not for their tremendous powers of multiplication. Under favorable circumstances the offspring of a single bacillus dividing itself into two every hour would amount to seventeen million at the end of twenty-four hours. They are well-nigh everywhere: in air, water, milk, in and on the bodies of men and animals, and in the earth. Many kinds are harmless, and some even appear to be absolutely necessary for the growth of certain most useful plants. Only a few species cause infectious diseases.

The struggle against pathogenic, or disease-producing, germs had begun before the discovery of bacteria. As early as 1796 Edward Jenner tried vaccination to prevent smallpox, one of the devastating diseases of his time; this treatment gradually prevailed long before the modern germ theory could be worked out. In the same way better methods of dealing with surgical cases began to be suggested before bacteria were understood. Surgery was being greatly aided by the modern use of anæsthetics, a primitive knowledge of which had been widespread among the ancients. The Greeks and Chinese were aware that certain drugs would reduce or destroy pain. In 1800 Sir Humphry Davy, the famous English chemist, advocated the use of nitrous oxide (laughing gas). Some years later Faraday pointed out that the vapor of ether would produce insensibility. In 1847 Dr. Simpson of Edinburgh began to advocate the use of chloroform. American physicians (Dr. Long of Georgia, and Dr. Morton and Dr. Warren of Boston) tried successful experiments in this field in the forties; and from their time on, anæsthetics have been regularly used in operations.

The possibility of keeping a patient quiet and unconscious for a considerable period greatly increased the number and boldness of surgical enterprises. Many operations ended fatally, however, because blood-poisoning, erysipelas, gangrene, or inflammation of various membranes was pretty sure to set in. So to open the head or the chest or the abdomen usually meant a fatal outcome. Joseph Lister, an English professor of surgery, finally hit upon the remedy. By observing the utmost cleanliness and using certain antiseptics he greatly reduced the number of cases which went wrong. The reason for his success, however, was not yet understood in the early sixties, when his work first began to attract attention. Only when the minute and elusive causes of infection—namely, bacteria—

were submitted to careful study was it possible to take sufficiently complete precautions in the way of sterilization to insure the speedy and almost inerrant healing of a surgical incision. The hospitals and operating rooms of the middle of the nineteenth century would fill any contemporary doctor or nurse with consternation.

Our modern problem of healing is no longer witch-hunting and the exorcism of evil spirits but the struggle against bacteria. It would at first sight seem hopeless to attempt to avoid such minute and insidious enemies, whose forces increase each day by billions. But experience shows that bacteria can be fended off in surgical cases by the scrupulous sterilization of everything entering into the operation. It has been learned that typhoid fever comes generally from the use of impure water or milk, that tuberculosis is spread mainly through the dried sputum of those afflicted with it, that the germs of yellow fever and malaria[1] are carried by a certain kind of mosquito. These all suggest obvious precautions which would greatly reduce the chance of spreading disease. Moreover, various counteracting agents have been brought to light. Pasteur found that animals could be rendered immune to hydrophobia by the injection of the virus of the disease. So-called antitoxins, or counter poisons, have been discovered for lockjaw, diphtheria, and some other bacterial infections.

The Russian bacteriologist Mechnikov, working in Paris, demonstrated that the white blood corpuscles keep up a constant warfare with the bacteria and devour those which find their way into the body. Hence he called these corpuscles *phagocytes*; that is, "cells which eat." The study of these, of which there are a number of kinds, continues, and various means are suggested by which they may be increased and helped to make a good fight against the noxious bacteria. So

[1] Malaria, the sleeping sickness in Africa, hookworm disease, and certain other maladies are not caused by bacteria but are due to protozoans and various parasites.

the essential problem is being faced of hunting down, one by one, the microscopic foes of mankind and inventing ways to avoid them and means to counteract their poison or render our bodies immune to their attacks. Medicine would have forever remained a blind and blundering science had not the microscope and the consequent discovery of bacteria opened up hitherto undreamed-of possibilities in the treatment and prevention of disease.

THE CONSTITUTION OF MATTER: ATOMS AND MOLECULES

While living creatures were yielding some of their well-kept secrets to scientific investigators, those who busied themselves with what used to be called *inert* matter were discovering that its constituent parts are in a state of marvelous activity. Matter may be inanimate (which means "soulless"), but it is anything but inert. Familiar things like heat, light, and electrical currents are to be explained only by the incredible mobility of matter.

The notion that all things consisted of minute, indivisible particles, *atoms*, had been suggested in ancient Greece by Democritus, a contemporary of Socrates. The idea was taken up by the Epicureans and was later set forth, in the days of Cicero and Julius Cæsar, by a Roman poet, Lucretius, in his work *Concerning the Nature of Things*. This older theory can hardly be regarded as more than a shrewd guess, very ill supported by any experiments then possible.

Early in the nineteenth century an English chemist, Dalton, was led to revive the idea as a result of his careful consideration of the fixed proportions which entered into any chemical compound. He thought that all matter acted as if it were composed of atoms of the various elements and that these always combined in definite numbers to form the molecules, or least particles, of the innumerable compound substances. For example, he rightly guessed that an atom of carbon entered into combination with two atoms of oxygen to form what used to be called carbonic acid and is now called carbon dioxide. Moreover, as twelve parts by weight of carbon always combined with thirty-two parts of oxygen, he thought it might be inferred that the carbon atom weighed twelve units and the oxygen atom sixteen. This formed the basis of the modern atomic theory, which, after being very carefully worked out in relation to gases as well as solids by a long succession of celebrated chemists, has become the foundation of our conception of matter today.

For a good while the chemists believed the atom to be the smallest particle of matter of whose existence there was any evidence. They decided that theoretically there could be but ninety-two kinds of atoms (called *elements*), such as hydrogen, oxygen, carbon, nitrogen, calcium, silicon, sulphur, silver, gold, mercury, lead, and so on. With two or three dubious exceptions, these ninety-two have now all been discovered. Hydrogen is the lightest atom; uranium, the heaviest.

At the very end of the nineteenth century it began to become apparent to chemists that atoms were not *simple* but very *complex*, and during the first quarter of the twentieth century the most revolutionary discoveries were made. The ways in which physicists and chemists reach their conclusions are too complicated to be described here. The existence of "rays," beginning with X rays, to which Röntgen called attention in 1895, is one element in the situation. The X ray readily passes through substances which are opaque to light rays. Then in 1897 Monsieur and Madame Curie discovered radium and found that it, together with uranium and certain other very heavy atoms, emitted rays or particles *which were not atoms but small parts of atoms*. With subtle electrical devices and the spectroscope the analysis of the atom is progressing.

As atoms are now understood by physicists and chemists they are constructed each like a miniature solar system with a central body, the *nucleus*, around which revolve satellites called *electrons*. The electrons are negative charges of electricity attracted and held in their orbits by the nucleus, which contains positive charges, called *protons*. Hydrogen, the simplest atom and the lightest, has but one electron (as the earth has but one moon), which circulates about its center. Uranium, the heaviest known atom, has at least ninety-two electrons and is so complicated that some of its electrons break away from time to time, as is the case with the very heavy and insecure radium atom. It is supposed that the hydrogen electron is relatively as far from its nucleus as the earth is from the sun; but it whizzes about its nucleus at a rate of something like fourteen hundred miles a second, whereas the earth trundles round the sun at about eighteen miles a second.

If these general conclusions in regard to the constitution of matter are correct, it is to be noted that however quiet a mass of iron or stone may seem to us, its minute parts are electrical charges, negative and positive, in a state of incredible activity. Compact as iron and stone appear to the human hand, they are almost entirely emptiness—empty as the universe at large (p. 586). Professor Eddington says, indeed, that "the revelation by modern physics of the void within the atom is more disturbing than the revelation by astronomy of the immense void of interstellar space." He explains that "if we eliminated all the unfilled space in a man's body and collected his protons and electrons into one mass, the man would be reduced to a speck just visible with a magnifying glass."

Another physicist, Bazzoni, illustrates the matter as follows: if the nucleus of an atom of hydrogen were magnified to the size of a pea, its electron (which is much larger than the nucleus) would be some thirty feet in diameter and be revolving around its center at a distance of three hundred miles! Of course, what is called emptiness here is really an electric "field" which is essential to the very existence of the atom.

The stupendous littleness of protons and electrons and the tremendous magnitude of stars, the bewildering velocity of light, and of the distances which it traverses, overwhelm and stupefy the human mind used to its puny weighing machines and measuring rods and the snail-like records made by racing automobiles and airplanes. There is no chance here to say anything of the new ideas of "relativity," associated with the name of Einstein, which are revolutionizing the views of physicists and mathematicians in regard to space and time. The discovery that the shape and mass of a body alter with the rapidity of its motion throws out all older calculations and brings time in as a "fourth dimension" to be added to our old three dimensions. For it is now supposed that if a yardstick were flying through space endwise at a rate of 161,000 miles a second it would shrink to half the length it had at rest.[1]

No chemist has as yet learned to alter the constitution of an atom. Most elements remain permanent apparently, but radium and, in a less startling degree, some other elements tend to disintegrate into simpler atoms by successive explosions. There is evidently a vast amount of energy stored in the atoms, for radium will give out enough heat every hour to raise its own weight of water from the freezing point to the boiling point. It is supposed, however, to waste away only half its mass in fifteen hundred years. But so far this interatomic energy is in no way under human control.

It is *combinations* of atoms, not the atoms themselves, that lend themselves to human manipulation. For atoms cluster into *molecules*, which are usually made up of different elements. A molecule may contain only two elements, one atom of each; table salt, for instance, contains one atom of sodium and one of chlorine. On the other hand, molecules, especially those that plants and animals build up, may contain scores of atoms of several elements. And the change of a single atom may make all the difference in the world from a human standpoint.

[1] Perhaps the best and simplest account of the present views of matter is to be found in Eddington's *Nature of the Physical World* (1929). It reveals a new heaven and a new earth.

We breathe out every instant carbon dioxide (a combination of one carbon atom and two oxygen atoms), but a few whiffs of carbon monoxide will put us to sleep forever. Carbon is essential to life, and nitrogen forms four fifths of the air we breathe every instant; yet two atoms of carbon combined with two of nitrogen form a most deadly poison.

By juggling about the atoms so as to reproduce old kinds of molecules and create new ones, modern chemists engage in magical feats outrunning all the dreams of the alchemists. Substances such as alcohol, indigo, and various dyes and perfumes, which were formerly derived only from plants and animals, can now be made in the laboratory. Steel can be improved by adding certain atoms of other elements, and the soil can be rendered more fertile by rectifying its constituents. The most striking achievements have been accomplished in the utilization of coal tar. This contains a great number of complicated and valuable molecules, which have been turned into a multitude of dyes, perfumes, and medicines. A coal-tar product may be used to scent a handkerchief, to flavor a dish, to pull a tooth painlessly, or to construct a phonograph record. So the chemist is becoming more and more essential to manufacturers, mine-owners, farmers, health officers, and the public in general. This is because he has learned what substances are made of, and how to recombine their constituents so as to meet human needs and desires.

The molecules are in rapid motion, *for there is no rest in the universe.* As one inflates an automobile tire it would burst forthwith did not the molecules on the outside offset the beating of the molecules within. This explains the so-called "pressure" of gases. A sudden storm of wind may for the instant reduce the number of air molecules beating on the outside of our windows, in which case the air inside will burst the panes. Heat is produced by speeding up the molecules; cold, by reducing their velocity. If one puts his warm hand on a block of ice, the molecules of water will increase their speed, while the molecules of the hand will slow down in a painful way. *Everything is in motion; nothing is at rest.*[1]

Modern chemistry has supplied man with all sorts of novel conveniences: it enables him to carry on warfare on a far more destructive scale than ever before or, if so inclined, to enrich his fields with much the same things that he puts into his high explosives. It does much more: it explains to him his physical make-up and his bodily processes so that he may learn to increase his health and vigor and avoid or mitigate disease. The study of animal and vegetable processes is known as biochemistry, or the chemistry of life. This important branch of science has of late developed on a generous scale, and all biologists and trained physicians must reckon with its findings.

There is one special element, *carbon*, without which it is hard to conceive of life of any kind existing. It is the friendliest of atoms and can help toward building up very complicated molecules of great stability and at the same time very adjustable and plastic. One of the forms of chlorophyll in the leaves of plants is supposed to contain in each molecule thirty-four atoms of carbon holding together thirty-two atoms of hydrogen, five of oxygen, and four of the very unsociable nitrogen.

Among the most astonishing discoveries of biochemistry are the presence and essential workings of the vitamins, which in excessively minute quantities are necessary to maintain health. The secretions of the ductless glands are also being studied, with astonishing results. They play a marvelous and still inadequately understood rôle in the regulation of the body. These discoveries suggest new methods of treating old diseases and open the way for future advance in understanding the miracles which daily and hourly go on within us.[2]

[1] If the temperature could be reduced to 464 degrees below zero (by our common Fahrenheit thermometers), the molecules would cease to move, and it would be impossible to imagine anything colder. This point is called absolute zero, and has been nearly attained by ingenious devices.

[2] Some possibilities of human readjustment are suggested in *Dædalus*, by the well-known biochemist J. B. S. Haldane—a little book easy to understand.

CHAPTER XIX

NEW VIEWS OF MAN'S NATURE AND TRADITIONS

Influence of Natural Science upon the Study of Man Himself

Natural science deals with man's surroundings—the world in which he lives, and the animals and plants which share the earth with him. Since he has to make terms with his environment and—so far as he may to his own advantage—control it, his increasing knowledge of the ways of nature is of incalculable importance to him. This has been amply illustrated in the preceding chapter. Moreover, the attitude of mind of geologists, paleontologists, chemists, and biologists, who have been so successful in revealing the secrets of natural processes, has suggested new and more fruitful ways of investigating man himself.

In the first place, the student of nonhuman phenomena disclaims, and has long disclaimed, any confidence in merely traditional beliefs handed down in old books. He is not pledged to cling to any doctrines in his field of work just because they have long been accepted. He is at liberty to doubt or completely to reject the faith of the past in cases where it does not seem to fit the facts that he observes. He is always asking how, upon careful examination, things really are and how they really work, not how good men in the past have taught that they are. There is no place in science for dogma.

In the second place, it has become clear that there is no better way of understanding things and seeing how they really are and how they work than by going back and studying how they have come about. This is called the *genetic*, or developmental, approach to truth. By learning how animals once were, it becomes far easier to see not only how they came to be as they are but how they really are. For example, the examination of more primitive hearts and brains than those of the mammals serves to call attention to peculiarities in the higher animals which might otherwise be overlooked. The existence in man of vestigial muscles for moving his ears and wagging a tail can only be understood historically. The arrangement of his intestines and the weakness of his lower abdominal muscles —which often invite disease—take on a new aspect when one considers that his remote ancestors went on all fours. Moreover, embryology, or the history of individual development, has served to suggest explanations for important facts that were previously obscure.

Thirdly, the scientist constantly resorts to the *comparative* method. He collates, or lays side by side, so to speak, all sorts of animals and plants in order to note their resemblances and differences. He finds correspondences hidden under seeming diversity, differences disguised as resemblances, and curious methods of reaching the same essential ends in multitudinous ways. The pineapple and the so-called "moss" that hangs from trees in the South are nearly related; the wings of a bird and the forelegs of a frog are *morphologically* akin. On the other hand, objects which look alike to the casual observer often prove to be very different. What he takes for petals when he sees the brilliant poinsettia are really bracts; a sunflower or a daisy is not one flower but many.

Lastly, careful experimentation and "control" bring out a vast amount of information which would escape one who confined himself to observing merely what happened to happen when he was looking on. By arranging special conditions under which to watch occurrences the scientist places himself in a position better to judge causes and effects. For example, he makes lightning in his laboratory instead of waiting for a thunderstorm; or he devises methods of producing tremendous

T

pressure to see its effects on marble, instead of merely conjecturing the probable influence of geological pressure.

Man is at once the most important and the most difficult subject of scientific study. He has much in common with other animals; the chemist and biologist can tell us a great deal of ourselves, as has been indicated. But he is also a creature with the possibility of building up a mind and greatly altering his behavior; an animal subject to the most obscure emotional states and fluctuations, resulting from his multiform memories, his dependence on others, his ideals and his urgent longings for love, power, and honor, his hidden fears and resentments,— all of which perplex and frustrate those who try to explain his ways and thoughts scientifically. He combines all the chemical and organic problems of other forms of life with the mysteries of a consciously planning and conspiring creature persistently operating under misapprehensions about himself and others and in regard to his surroundings. He wants what he doesn't want; he doesn't want what he wants. As the Latin poet puts it, *Volo nolo, nolo volo.* A history could be written of the analysis of human misery and perversity from Buddha, Euripides, Koheleth (Ecclesiastes), Lucretius, and Seneca down to Schopenhauer and Von Hartmann; also of the various plans for deliverance or salvation recommended by each. But here we have no space to do more than suggest the influence which modern scientific methods have had upon the general conceptions of man's origin and nature.

The Newer Aims of Historical Study

History corresponds to the genetic, or developmental, approach in the natural sciences. But it is only recently that this has been realized. Formerly history was often defined as "a record of events." And so it is; but it is much more than that. The history of history is an interesting theme in itself. It was for many centuries a sort of "story agreed upon"; it dealt with conspicuous public events, especially wars, and no great pains were taken to secure adequate evidence for the alleged facts. It often had a definite bias, as when Orosius, a writer of the time of Augustine, wrote a history of the world to show that Christianity had made things no worse than they had been under paganism. Later examples are the controversial histories of Protestants and Catholics.

In the seventeenth and eighteenth centuries scholars began to collect the *sources* with some attempt to judge their authenticity, and this habit has continued down to the present day. In the middle of the nineteenth century the distinguished German historian Leopold von Ranke declared that his object was to describe *wie es eigentlich gewesen*; that is, to tell how things really had been regardless of any personal preferences or religious convictions of his own. This has been the scientific ambition of many scholars since, who believed the great danger lay in being misled by some purpose or partiality in presenting the past.

Gradually it became apparent that the older kind of history was not usually *historical,* in the sense of *developmental,* in its aims. It was a record of events; but the selection from the bewildering number of happenings was not made consciously with a view of showing how things had come about, but rather how they were in successive periods. So for Ranke's principle *Wie es eigentlich gewesen* was substituted *Wie es eigentlich geworden*—"How have things really *come about*"? It has been a constant reproach that history was trivial in spite of its solemn mien and did little more than satisfy a certain curiosity; that it recalled events which had little to do with getting a better hold upon man's nature and behavior. It can, however, be used to explain human conditions and problems by showing their origin and development. This has been the avowed and consistent aim in writing the present work. If one finds himself in a painful position, he can often seek enlightenment by reconsidering how he happened to get into his plight. Recalling the past, which is history, may even suggest means of escape from difficulties. This kind of history is not a perverted or biased statement, such as Ranke protested against. It has a purpose, it is true; but the purpose is scientific, and its goal is to reduce prejudice, not to fortify it. It is for the reader to judge how far the genetic method adhered to in these volumes has served to make existing conditions clearer than they would otherwise have been.

The scope of history has been greatly extended during the past fifty years by archæology. Former historians had to rely mainly upon written records, but the archæologist seeks under the accumulated dust of time other vestiges of man's past: his bones and primitive tools, remains of his buildings, his utensils and adornments. Prehistoric archæology has shown that man has been on the earth for several hundreds of thousands of years. Excavations in Egypt and Mesopotamia have made clear that a much higher civilization than was previously supposed existed in these regions long before the days of the Greeks. The whole history of the Greeks themselves has been put on a new foundation by researches in Crete and Asia Minor. If history did no more than furnish us with a new perspective of human development, it would have fully justified itself as a study essential to the understanding of mankind.

THE PERSPECTIVE OF HUMAN DEVELOPMENT

Before geological discoveries revealed the great age of the earth, it was assumed that the first man and woman were acquainted with both language and agriculture. As a distinguished American theologian explained in the early years of the nineteenth century:

God taught man to dress the garden of Eden; or, in other words, communicated to him the knowledge of agriculture, suited to the nature and circumstances of the spot in which he was placed. It was necessary for man to be employed. Idleness, even in Paradise, would

not improbably have proved fatal to his innocence and peace. . . .
God endowed him immediately with the power of speech, and the
knowledge of language to an extensive degree. This is clearly evinced
by the fact that he was able to understand the converse of God with
him. . . . Adam immediately after his creation gave names to every
beast of the field and fowl of the air—names suited to their respective natures, and conveyed down, as their appropriate names, to his
posterity. He also named Eve, when she was first brought to him;
and assigned a reason for the name which he had chosen. Both he
and she also conversed easily and freely, as appears abundantly
from the account given of them, notwithstanding its brevity.[1]

By the middle of the nineteenth century a few had begun
to doubt the sudden appearance on the earth of fully equipped
human beings. There seemed to be indications of the existence
of pre-Adamites, as they were once called. Stone tools were
discovered in geological strata, which indicated that they
greatly antedated the creation according to the estimates of
Archbishop Usher. More and more of these were found, as
well as skulls suggesting a lower order of humanity in the
matter of intelligence than those to be found on the earth
today. What Cotton Mather had accepted as thunderbolts
(*ceraunia*) turned out to be a rather recent variety of stone
hatchet. How long a kind of being who could make rude tools
of flint has lived on the earth, no one knows. Prehistoric
archæologists agree that a tool-making type of creatures existed from five hundred thousand to a million years ago. As
for skulls, it would seem that perhaps thirty thousand years
ago some were as capacious as can be found today. But these
ancient men, with seemingly good brains, were evidently what
we should call primitive savages.

There are now many scientific works on man before he
learned to write. When he learned to talk is a question which
will probably never be settled. When he came to use fire and,

---

[1] Timothy Dwight (president of Yale College, 1795–1817), *Theology Explained and Defended* (edition of 1850), Vol. I, pp. 395–396.

later, to make it, will probably never be discovered. Writing, whether with letters or with syllabic signs, seems always to go back to pictures, with which man must have begun. More and more is being discovered; and doubtless fifty years hence unexpected finds will have been made which will modify the general impressions of the prehistoric archæologists of today. But there seems no likelihood that they will reverse their present opinion that man slowly emerged from an animal life of nakedness, houselessness, and a precarious daily search for raw food. It seems clear that once upon a time he could not talk, or use fire, or *cultiver son jardin*, as Voltaire recommends to us all. All these things he had to discover and then teach to his offspring; and thus did civilization begin, according to the new gospel of those who busy themselves with prehistoric man.

In order to realize vividly the exceeding slowness of mankind's early progress in invention and how recently the conditions of life as we know them have come about, let us imagine the whole history of the halting and laborious accumulation of human culture compressed within the span of a single lifetime:

Let us assume that a single generation of men has in fifty years managed to accumulate all that now passes for civilization. They would have to start, as all individuals do, absolutely uncivilized; and their task would be to recapitulate what has occupied the race for, let us guess, at least five hundred thousand years. Each year in the life of a generation would therefore correspond to ten thousand years in the progress of the race.

On this scale it would require forty-nine years to reach a point of intelligence which could enable our self-taught generation to give up their ancient and inveterate habits of wandering hunters and settle down here and there to till the ground, harvest their crops, domesticate animals, and weave their rough garments. Six months later, or half through the fiftieth year, some of them, in a particularly favorable situation, would have invented writing and thus established a new and wonderful means of spreading and perpetuating civilization. Three months later another group would have carried literature, art, and philosophy to a high degree of refinement and set standards for succeeding weeks. For two months our generation would have been living under the blessing of Christianity; the printing-press would be but a fortnight old, and they would not have had the steam engine for quite a week. For two or three days they would have been hastening about the globe in steamships and railroad trains, and only yesterday would they have come upon the magical possibilities of electricity. Within the last few hours they would have learned to sail in the air and beneath the waters, and have forthwith applied their newest discoveries to the prosecution of a magnificent war on the scale befitting their high ideals and new resources.

This is not so strange, for only a week ago they were burning and burying alive those who differed from the ruling party in regard to salvation, eviscerating in public those who had new ideas of government, and hanging old women who were accused of traffic with the devil. All of them had been no better than vagrant savages a year before.[1]

The doctrine of the rise of mankind from an animal estate furnishes another set of explanations differing essentially from those offered by the earlier hypothesis of his fall from a state of original perfection. And when we add to this our present knowledge of the persistence of ancient custom and belief and the novelty of the conditions with which mankind has now to make terms, many things become clear that were formerly obscure. This, then, is in general the chief contribution that the historical method of dealing with humanity makes to our comprehension and understanding of its present ways and thoughts and conflicting ideals.[2]

THE COMPARATIVE STUDY OF MANKIND AND ITS FRUITS

Before the nineteenth century, in spite of much traveling and trafficking, European scholars had scarcely begun to study scientifically the extraordinary variety of customs and beliefs which merchants and missionaries came across in far-distant

[1] James Harvey Robinson, *The Mind in the Making*, pp. 83–84.

[2] A fuller account of all these matters of human development may be found in James Harvey Robinson's article entitled "Civilization," in the fourteenth edition of the *Encyclopædia Britannica*.

lands. Indeed, it was not until 1871 that the *Primitive Culture* of Edward Tylor opened up to English readers a new branch of human science, in somewhat the same way that Lyell and Darwin had earlier awakened them to the importance of their fields of research. Since the appearance of Tylor's volumes an extensive literature has grown up relating to primitive peoples. As an American anthropologist, William I. Thomas, points out, this attention to simpler civilizations shows that "the Savage is very close to us indeed, both in his physical and mental make-up and in the forms of his social life. Tribal society is virtually delayed civilization, and the savages are a sort of contemporaneous ancestry."

Primitive peoples, such as the Tasmanians (who died out only in the nineteenth century), the aboriginal Australians, the Eskimos, and some of the North American Indians, as well as many other groups, afford illustrations of how our ancestors got along without metals and writing. But every tribe on earth is found to have a spoken language, often very complicated and subtle, and often with a very copious vocabulary. The study of primitive tongues, religions, morals, customs, and institutions serves to explain many of our habits and ideas today. They underlie the great themes of anthropology in general and of comparative philology, comparative religion, and the history of morals. Sir Henry Maine used the comparative method in writing his impressive *Ancient Law* (1861). William Graham Sumner, who in early manhood had been an Episcopal clergyman and later became a professor at Yale, published in 1907 his *Folkways: a Study of the Sociological Importance of Usages, Manners, Customs, Mores, and Morals*. Quite conscious of the disturbing effect of anthropology upon conservative minds, he says in his preface, "I must add that if anyone is liable to be shocked by *any* folkways, he ought not to read about folkways at all."

The comparison of widely different plans of social organization, of customs having to do with birth, marriage, and death and with daily social intercourse, serves to call attention to various peculiarities of our own habits and proprieties which we should otherwise overlook on account of their very familiarity. Anthropologists show that great numbers of existing customs and beliefs are primitive "survivals," as Tylor first called them, and when we see them as such we are in a position to criticize practices of our own which we commonly take for granted. We are prone to assume that the way we do is the only right way, and that the ways of other peoples when they differ from ours are comical, perverse, or even horrible. Anthropology helps us to escape from this primitive illusion. Not infrequently other peoples, even primitive tribes, appear to have the advantage over us in some ways. A single instance of this will suffice:

Havelock Ellis[1] gives an account of the customs of the Lifuans, an island tribe living a thousand miles to the east of Australia. In former days, before they began to take on European habits, their ways in peace and war had many delightful characteristics.

The Lifuans were not acquainted with the civilized custom of making rules for warfare and breaking them when war actually broke out. Several days' notice must be given before hostilities commenced. Women and children, in contrast to the practice of civilized warfare, were never molested. As soon as a half a dozen fighters were put out of action on one side, the chief of that side would give the command to cease fighting, and the war was over. An indemnity was then paid by the conquerors to the vanquished, and not, as

[1] *The Dance of Life*, pp. 17–18. Mr. Ellis derives his information from a missionary, Mrs. Hadfield, in her book *Among the Natives of the Loyalty Group* (1920). Many examples could be given of ways in which so-called primitive or savage peoples reach far higher ideals of conduct than those with which we are familiar in so-called civilized society. Instances are cited here and there in Sumner's *Folkways*. The most astonishing and well-known description of a simple and remunerative life is by an American writer, Herman Melville, who visited the Marquesas Islands and wrote of his experiences in a charming little book, *Typee* (1846). A much later book may also be cited—Margaret Mead's *Coming of Age in Samoa* (1929).

among civilized peoples, by the vanquished to the conquerors. It was felt to be the conquered rather than the conqueror who needed consolation, and it also seemed desirable to show that no feeling of animosity was left behind.

The comparative study of the habits, customs, institutions, laws, and beliefs of various peoples has led to the modern use of certain terms which are now current in the discussion of conduct. The suggestion of Milton (Vol. I, p. 78), that *Custom* is man's chief teacher, is amply borne out by anthropological research. Our daily life is far more deeply influenced and determined by what are now called the *mores* than it is by laws, established institutions, or moral sanctions. When a European enters a church he customarily takes off his hat; when an Egyptian passes into a mosque he removes his shoes, as does a Japanese on going into a temple. This is a strict rule, but it would not be a violation of law nor a moral delinquency if it were neglected. Kissing, which is a sign of affection or respect in Western countries, is abhorrent in many lands. To smack one's lips as a proof that he is enjoying what his host puts before him is obligatory among certain peoples, but extremely vulgar with us.

There are everywhere various compulsive usages as to what women and men may wear on this occasion and that, and one who fails to conform may experience as much distress as if he had committed a sin or violated a law. It is quite as hard to alter the mores as the laws and the moral standards. European and American women had to have their skirts dangling down to their heels in 1900, in spite of the germ theory of disease. Those who disapproved the custom were helpless to alter it. For it is very characteristic of the mores that they are accepted as good and right and appropriate by practically everyone. They are *comme il faut*. Why they come and go is not easy to see; but it is clear that their causes are unconscious—very rarely the result of thinking or planning. "Conscious reflection is the worst enemy of the mores," as a German philosopher, Von Hartmann, remarks. So if they are to be controlled, it is intelligence and the spread of scientific knowledge rather than legal or religious measures that will forward their improvement. Anthropology has done much to make this apparent.

Primitive peoples commonly believe in what is called *animism*; that is, tend to ascribe souls and purposes to inanimate things, as well as to plants and animals. This is the *anthropomorphic*, or human, way of explaining natural phenomena. Against this the scientifically minded have always to be on their guard, for animism is shown to be a deep-seated and perennial tendency of mankind.[1] Our language constantly betrays in its use of verbs this ancient preconception. We say the branch *struck* him in the eye, the table *will not come* through the door, the key *refused* to turn. When we see in a newspaper "Vienna says," we may conjecture that this only means that the *Neue Freie Presse* published the opinion, and that it was really one man who hurriedly wrote it down. Our personifications of countries are survivals of animism. It is not *America* that refuses to permit a certain foreigner to land, but a few officials, perhaps one man in Washington or on Ellis Island. Accordingly, profitable thinking is still much hampered by the survival of savage modes of thought.

Taboo (originally a Polynesian word) is another term now commonly used to describe scruples and prohibitions which are traditional and for which no reason can be assigned. When we come suddenly upon the expression "Prohibited" (*Défendu* or *Verboten*), it may give us something of the feeling of a savage toward the taboos of his tribe. But our public prohibitions are usually based upon some law or ordinance; those of primitive peoples are not. This discovery has led writers to point out how much not only of our mores, but of our morality as well, consists in traditional avoidances and

---

[1] Poets are especially inclined to use animistic expressions in speaking of lakes and trees, the sun, the moon, and the stars.

scruples not so very unlike taboos. The Decalogue is made up mainly of what "thou shalt not" do. It is apparently easier to forbid than to furnish any positive guidance in conduct. Mankind seems more afraid that something wrong will be done than that something right may be left undone. Our morality is largely a matter of "do not's," from infancy onward. The more recent writers upon ethics have much to say of this ancient tradition of humanity. The mores and the taboos explain why the task of the reformer is so difficult when he tries to induce people to readjust their behavior in the light of new conditions and discoveries.

RACE PREJUDICE, NATIONS, AND NATIONALISM

Anthropological research has called attention to the confident feeling of uniqueness and superiority which all tribes and peoples enjoy.

When Caribs were asked whence they came, they answered, "We alone are people." The meaning of the name Kiowa [North American Indians] is "real or principal people." The Lapps call themselves "men," or "human beings." The Greenland Eskimo think that Europeans have been sent to Greenland to learn virtue and good manners from the Greenlanders. Their highest form of praise for a European is that he is, or soon will be, as good as a Greenlander. . . . As a rule it is found that nature peoples call themselves "men." Others are something else—perhaps not defined—but not real men. In myths the origin of their own tribe is that of the real human race.—W. G. SUMNER

This "pooled self-esteem," as an English writer well calls it, can be traced down through the ages. The Jews were the chosen people of God; to the Greeks all foreigners were barbarians; the name "French" means "freemen."

In recent times the loyalty which the savage tribe, the ancient city, the medieval lord, and the monarch by the grace of God formerly enjoyed in turn has been transferred to the national state. Each nation assumes with savage simplicity its own superiority and regards the loyalties and self-complacency of other peoples as strangely perverse, unfounded, and dangerous. It appears unpatriotic for a citizen to question in any way the obvious supremacy of his own particular country, whether he be an American, an Englishman, an Albanian, or an Estonian. Politicians and statesmen well know that if they are to retain their influence and position they must gratify national vanity. Newspapers must not come under the suspicion of hinting that the readers to whom they appeal are not *the* men of all the earth. The World War brought out the strength of existing national feeling, and impressed upon some minds the necessity of reducing it or at least curbing its more truculent and ambitious tendencies. Perhaps this problem may be clarified by making a distinction between an indiscriminate and oftentimes dangerous exaltation of one's own country and that enlightened public spirit which would improve one's nation by reckoning with the facts and with the rights and traditions of other peoples.

The investigation of races and peoples and their various contributions to the growth of civilization tends to weaken popular prejudices by showing that such prejudices have in general little foundation from a historical or anthropological standpoint. It is clear, as was said above, that existing nations owe an incalculable debt to other peoples, living in earlier times as well as today.

There are no pure races on the earth today—no aboriginal, or autochthonous, peoples. All nations are greatly mixed, and their ancestors have wandered into the regions they now occupy from other regions often unknown. Men and women of the most diverse race and circumstances are all sufficiently alike from a biological standpoint to be able to mate and have offspring. And the offspring will have an equal chance of inheriting traits from both father and mother. So if a king has a child by a foreign slave, it has no more chance of inheriting the traits of its father than those of its mother. The mores usually settle the status of the offspring without reference to the inexorable workings of embryology. In view of these considerations one must be suspicious of attempts to prove that one race is superior to another. Those who, like Stewart Chamberlain and others, would give the Germanic, or Nordic, peoples the highest place forget that they are gratifying a sentiment of "pooled self-esteem" by making assertions which, like those of Fichte (referred to in Vol. I, p. 406), are unsupported by anthropological, historical, and biological knowledge.

THE NEW METHODS OF STUDYING MIND

Comparative and genetic methods are being applied in the study of individual mental development with startling results. One could read the older works on psychology without learning much about himself. They were about *the* sensations, *the* passions, *the* faculties, *the* judgment, *the* eye, and *the* ear. But modern books make the reader feel that it is his own sensations, *his* passions, *his* eye and ear, that are in question. This is the result of taking into account the various discoveries which have already been mentioned, of considering how we each develop from childhood, and of comparing human behavior with the ways of animals, and the so-called normal mind with that of people adjudged unbalanced or insane. So it has been found that psychological research and the analysis of human behavior must be approached from many different angles. There are animal (or comparative) psychology, genetic psychology, abnormal psychology, experimental and behavioristic psychology, and analytical psychology. These all aim at the same thing: to cast light on man's still mysterious ways of feeling and acting and on his responses and adjustments to his surroundings.

In spite of the centuries during which philosophers have been thinking and writing about human beings, there has until recently been no concerted attempt to get at the facts regardless of traditional and moral considerations. It is obvious enough now that the earlier students of human nature did not know enough of man and his environment to approach the problem in a really scientific spirit. It would be out of place here to try to do more than put the recent and promising study of human "mind" in its general historic setting.

All through the Middle Ages the soul was regarded as something immaterial and indestructible which was imprisoned for a short time in the body, where it had to be as patient as possible and guard itself from the corruptions of the flesh. According as it succeeded in resisting the natural evil tendencies of the body or yielded to them, it was to be blessed or cursed when it put on the garment of immortality. The impenitent soul went straight to hell to suffer forever; the penitent, after a period of purification in purgatory, was admitted to eternal heavenly bliss. The anthropologists have discovered that the idea of the soul far antedates Christianity. It goes back to savage times when people found themselves conversing in dreams with the dead or moving from place to place when their bodies lay quietly asleep. Christians, following earlier ideas, came to feel that the body was a vile thing, which tended to degrade the soul within it owing to its low and evil appetites. So professional Christians, the monks and the nuns, retired from "the world" to escape the temptations of the flesh, which were those of the devil. The Christian ascetics strove to conquer their body and bring it into subjection by ill-treating it as the chief enemy of their highest good.[1]

As the body has been studied in modern times more and more carefully it proves to be the wonder of wonders in its incomprehensible intricacy and its incredible power of working miracles. It arouses a sense of reverence and mystery

[1] An admirable analysis of ascetic practices may be found in *The Varieties of Religious Experience* (pp. 259 ff.), by William James, with many first-hand reports of the attitude of the Christian saints.

rather than one of resentment and scorn. It seems to be something to cherish and aid, not to torture and debilitate. Moreover, our aspirations, high hopes, patience, and helpfulness to others—all that seems best in the soul—may be increased by bodily welfare. Some failure of a gland, owing to the lack of a single chemical—notably the appropriate action of the thyroid, which depends on a trifling supply of iodine—may make all the difference between idiocy and a decent degree of intelligence. An excess of urea in the blood may sap one's energy, sour one's temper, and degrade one's ideals. The constant interaction of what we call *body* and what we call *mind* may be illustrated in hundreds of ways. They cannot be clearly separated. Our bodily functioning constantly modifies our thoughts and feelings, and it seems equally clear that our thoughts influence deeply our circulation, our breathing, our digestion, and our available muscular strength.[1]

Those who cling to the older ideas of the soul have an unhappy habit of denouncing as "materialists" the scientists who reveal the bewildering competence of the body. This is an unfortunate old name handed down from times when matter, including the human body, was assumed to be evil.

IMPORTANCE OF CHILDHOOD; THE UNCONSCIOUS

At birth humankind are as helpless as the fledglings of a robin or the feckless progeny of a kangaroo. The baby cannot make terms with life from the start, like a caterpillar; it must be cherished by its elders and for a longer time than any other creature. This prolonged, pathetic dependence enables it very gradually to orient itself in its absolutely strange surroundings, to become civilized by learning the ways of man. An ant, a hen, or a colt starts off almost fully equipped. The

[1] Some physiologists and biochemists suspect that the messengers—*hormones* —sent out by the ductless glands always act as intermediaries in all our onsets and upsets, our hungers and rages, and, indeed, in the formation of our general character.

chick and the colt grow, it is true, become stronger, and can later reproduce their kind; but compared with a child they change little in their capacities. A calf is a little cow, but a baby is not just a little man or woman. He will, according to his circumstances, learn to talk any language on the face of the earth; he may became a holy man in India, a Chinese bandit, a Polish pianist, a farmer, a steamship captain, a biochemist, a Pennsylvania miner, an Episcopal bishop, a Wall Street broker, a district visitor, a portrait-painter, or a grocer. Each of these vocations, and of thousands of other possible careers, requires him to make innumerable adjustments and acquire special habits peculiar to his situation and object in life.

In order to establish points of departure in clarifying ideas about mankind, investigators have hit upon certain terms which have gained some currency among the laity. They try to distinguish between the original, or animal, tendencies of mankind and the traits acquired by being brought up in highly artificial conditions. They study the behavior of babies and the process by which they learn and adjust themselves. They use the terms *stimulus* and *response*, which are common to animal and human behavior. An amœba reacts to certain stimuli, and the range of its reactions has been studied. A cat and a nervous woman both react to the sight of a mouse, but differently. The dog on the hearth rug cares not whether his young master reads Cicero's *Tusculan Disputations* or a detective story, but father and mother may well make a sharp distinction between the two works. A pianist is susceptible to many stimuli which may leave a painter unmoved.

One of the most important of modern discoveries is that our behavior is by no means fully explained by the outward and manifest stimuli and reactions. Our susceptibility undergoes changes of which we are not conscious, and our reactions often surprise ourselves and others. We may have inexplicable dreads and aversions and mysterious longings and partialities for which we can give no reasonable explanation. This is not

T

strange, however, when we realize that before we were two years old we had many vivid experiences which we have wholly forgotten, and that our memory of the first ten years of life is very imperfect. We had shocks and frights; we made wrong guesses, established prejudices, came to love and hate, as a result of circumstances which later escape us. This produces what is called *the unconscious*. With scientific men it is not a mystical term, but a name for those potent factors in our responses which are due to our innate make-up, our early and forgotten experiences, or insensibly acquired habits which do not enter into our *conscious* thinking. Various ways have been devised for raising the unconscious factors into consciousness so that one may become aware of them and understand better why he does as he does and wants what he wants, and why he finds himself in various distressing *conflicts* with what he calls his better self.

There are thoughts and visions coming to us all day and all night which for one reason and another we usually keep to ourselves. We have a feeling that many of them would bore other people or would humiliate us. Our dreams by day and by night sometimes contain reflections, desires, and animosities which we should be loath to acknowledge; yet they are all a part and a most important part of ourselves, and modern methods of studying dreams and spontaneous mental associations help to make us clearer to ourselves. We can sometimes be led to recall early events in our lives which explain irrational fears and anxieties. Many physicians give much attention now to the state of mind of their patients and try to discover the psychic sources of worry, hidden remorse, or resentment. If one can throw off his "burdens," his physical vigor will often increase and his whole body function better. And this enlightenment may come from revealing unconscious or "repressed" factors in his thinking and emotions.

Many troubles are due to the conflict between one's desires and the rules prescribed by the mores, especially respecting the relations of men and women. In the Middle Ages passionate human love was thought to be an unclean thing. St. Augustine in his *City of God* declares that it was due to the fall of Adam; that no such disturbing element existed in man as he came from the hands of his Creator. The monks and the nuns abjured marriage and fled to monasteries to keep free from temptation or to cleanse themselves from past "sins of the flesh." So "sex" tended to become a disreputable and unholy subject, associated with impurity. So long as man's nature was called evil, and his body the enemy of his soul, this attitude was inevitable. Gradually, however, a more scientific view is beginning to prevail. The attraction of men and women for one another is, it is argued, a part of the natural order, which should be well understood and freed from the older associations. An understanding of it may better promote the chances of regulating an often troublesome urge than ignorance and suppression. It is not our business to discuss this matter here, but merely to note in passing why its consideration is so prominent today. It is the result of relinquishing medieval notions and striving for more scientific ones.

The general attitude toward childhood is altering as a consequence of the various discoveries which have been mentioned above.[1] Indeed, it is hardly too much to say that only recently has childhood been discovered. Once it was supposed that the duty of parent and teacher culminated in forcing the young to be obedient by fear and punishment and in keeping them properly ignorant of certain important matters. Modern teachers and parents have come to realize, however, that a child may be "spoiled" by harsh treatment as well as by

[1] There are other discoveries which, for lack of space, cannot be included here. Among these is the so-called *Gestalt-Theorie* formulated by Koffka, which makes it plain that there are no such things as isolated and simple sensations or ideas. Everything that "catches our attention" comes in a setting, or "configuration." Then it is clear that we are greatly influenced by "conditioned reactions," produced by the association established, let us say, by the ringing of a bell and the impulse to reënter the schoolroom or go to dinner. The eminent Russian physiologist Pavlov has made the most interesting study in this field by establishing conditioned reactions in dogs.

overindulgence. Fear may beget timidity and chronic anxiety and even result in later disorders of a very serious type. Ignorance may produce morbid curiosity, misapprehensions, and fatal errors. The terrible responsibility of bringing up the young is now impressively apparent. We know now that the character of men and women is much more completely and definitely formed in infancy and early childhood than was previously suspected.

It is curious to observe that not until about the middle of the nineteenth century did this fact dawn on story-writers. Dickens has much to say of children in his novels, of their maltreatment and sufferings under their stupid and even cruel elders. Daudet, in France, was impressed with the same thing. Nowadays there are very many of the leading novelists who write stories dealing wholly with childhood, or at least give great attention to the early and formative years of their chief characters (see next chapter).

The scientific investigation of the insane is the aim of abnormal psychology. It has been shown that those subject to obsessions, manias, melancholic states, delusions, and so forth are generally merely the victims of an excess of quite common and normal thoughts and emotions. They are not, as was formerly held, possessed by a devil, but have escaped from the usual balance of thought and conviction as determined by our daily surroundings and associations. The study of the exaggerations of the insane makes the workings of minds esteemed normal clearer than they once were.[1]

THE PROBLEMS OF EDUCATION

As knowledge increases, the problems of education become more and more difficult. Education is what chiefly distinguishes man from other higher animals. He can learn far more than any other creature and can change his habits on a vastly

[1] See Bernard Hart's book *The Psychology of Insanity*, a short and clear account of the newer ways of looking at both sane and insane.

more generous scale. Most that he learns comes to him informally as he grows up. His family, his companions, and his experiences are the great teachers. A recent writer has estimated that hardly more than a fifth of what is learned by the average person can be attributed to formal education in the classroom, even if one goes through college.[1] If one has educated parents, he may learn to read almost as soon as to speak. So most of our education lies outside the walls of the school. It consists in absorbing the prevailing mores, including the common run of information of the community in which we happen to be born, whether it be Tokyo, Belfast, Quito, or Plainfield, New Jersey. And this four fifths of education naturally greatly affects the other fifth, which may come to us in the way of systematic teaching and book-learning. In what is said here the term will be used in the sense of conscious, formal education.

In the medieval universities the so-called "arts course" was nominally confined to the seven liberal arts; that is, the studies regarded as suitable to a freeman (hence the term "liberal," derived from *liber*, "free"). These branches were grammar, rhetoric, logic, arithmetic, geometry, astronomy, and music. *As then taught*, the first three dealt with the rules for writing Latin in an elegant and logical fashion; the last four were essentially mathematical in form. So the tradition was established that Latin and mathematics are fundamental subjects. By the sixteenth century Greek was often added in the better schools. Only in the nineteenth century were courses introduced in the modern languages and literatures, the various natural sciences, and, lastly, the so-called social sciences, such as history, political economy, politics, anthropology, sociology. Philosophy, in various forms, had had a place in university education from the thirteenth century onward.

[1] John Palmer Gavit, in his excellent book *College*. It is of course quite impossible to establish any precise ratio between the results of formal and informal education. That adopted here is merely used for illustrative purposes.

As for the advanced professional subjects, these had been three in the Middle Ages: theology, law, and medicine. In the latter part of the nineteenth century and in the early years of the twentieth, schools of engineering (civil, mechanical, mining, electrical), education, and business were established to meet the demand for technical instruction in professions which had either not existed previously or had been learned outside the schools and universities. So it came about that not only was the variety of subjects included in high school and college as "liberal arts" greatly increased, but a wide range of professional departments, a few only of which were mentioned above, were organized to prepare students for their chosen life work.

While the teaching in professional or vocational schools is often severely criticized, it is certainly much easier to plan out a scheme of instruction suitable to a trade or a profession than to settle on what phases of human knowledge should be emphasized in school and college as best fitting one for life in general. Modern Western nations often require that their citizens should be forced to learn to read and write and deal with elementary arithmetic, and in this they have been astonishingly successful. The very recent constitutions of Russia, Turkey, and Egypt provide for elementary schools and propose to remedy the illiteracy which has hitherto prevailed in these lands, as it did everywhere, even in western Europe and America down to the middle of the nineteenth century. The further elements in a liberal education remain as yet doubtful and controversial. Some would still rely upon attention to the ancient languages of Greece and Rome and upon mathematics and formal logic. Others recommend a broad acquaintance with literature. Still others believe in natural science, in preparing for citizenship through a study of political economy and politics, or in religious education. This quandary and conflict of opinion is the outcome of the historical traditions and changes which have been recalled. Obviously, there is no simple answer to be looked for.

It may be pointed out that educational reformers have to consider the four fifths of education which they cannot easily control. All fundamental advance in education which changes opinion and begets enlightenment based upon fresh knowledge depends upon putting new discoveries in a form that will not seriously disturb prevailing ideas. As was pointed out in an earlier chapter, there has always been a sort of chronic, or endemic, conflict between the general human longing to feel that important matters are settled, and the conviction on the part of a few that much more is to be found out about everything. Teachers have to be prudent in calling the attention of their students to knowledge which seems to impugn beliefs and customs generally accepted as right and wrong—in short, the *mores* and *taboos*. This has always been the case; but the situation is rather more acute than it used to be, partly because education is so much more widespread.

In the Middle Ages there was a great dread of religious heresy, and teachers suspected of "novelties" in their teaching suffered harsh penalties. In 1819 Metternich, intent upon protecting the system of the divine right of kings, had laws passed in Germany providing that teachers who advanced ideas "subversive of existing governmental institutions" should be permanently deprived of their positions. In 1920 the so-called Lusk Laws, passed by the legislature of New York, disbarred teachers suspected of harboring socialistic or pacifist theories. In 1925 the legislature of Tennessee made it a punishable offense for any of the teachers in institutions receiving support from the state "to teach any theory that denies the story of the Divine creation of man as taught in the Bible, and to teach instead that man has descended from a lower order of animals." So whether the medieval church, monarchs by the grace of God, or democratically elected legislators be in power, there is the inevitable fear of subversive doctrine.

The arguments for liberty in the matter of teaching may be deduced from Milton's *Areopagitica*, supplemented by John

Stuart Mill's essay *On Liberty*, published over two centuries later (1859). Those who have tried to make abrupt or fundamental changes in mankind's ways of thinking have been subject to ill treatment by their contemporaries. It may well be, as Mill says, that "to discover to the world something which deeply concerns it, and of which it was previously ignorant; to prove to it that it has been mistaken on some vital point of temporal or spiritual interest is as important a service as a human being can render to his fellow creatures"; but to convince one's fellow creatures forthwith that one has made such a discovery is too much to expect! Those who are troubled with this incorrigible fact may comfort themselves and reënforce their patience and prudence with the following reflections of Mr. Mill:

Socrates was put to death, but the Socratic philosophy rose like the sun in the heaven and spread its illumination over the whole intellectual firmament. Christians were cast to the lions, but the Christian church grew up a stately and spreading tree, overtopping the older and less vigorous growths, and stifling them by its shade. Our merely social intolerance kills no one, roots out no opinions, but induces men to disguise them, or to abstain from any active effort for their diffusion. With us heretical opinions do not perceptibly gain, or even lose, ground in each decade or generation; they never blaze out far and wide, but continue to smolder in narrow circles of thinking and studious persons among whom they originate, without ever lighting up the general affairs of mankind with either a true or a deceptive light. And thus is kept up a state of things very satisfactory to some minds, because, without the unpleasant process of fining or imprisoning anybody, it maintains all prevailing opinions outwardly undisturbed, while it does not absolutely interdict the exercise of reason by dissentients afflicted with the malady of thought.

Teachers, especially those employed by governments, cannot hope to say always all that they think or to suggest all the inferences which may be drawn from scientific knowledge; but everywhere there is such liberty of expression that it is possible to put into books, if not always in the more widely diffused newspapers and magazines, any criticism, however harsh, of existing ideas and institutions.

Moreover, attempts to suppress ideas often advertise them, as was the case when the *parlement* of Paris had some of the works of Voltaire and Diderot burned. The action of the Tennessee legislature brought the arguments for the evolutionary theory to the attention of many who would otherwise have known little about the matter. The exclusion by the United States authorities of certain Europeans thought to be "dangerous radicals" results in a more effective dissemination of radical ideas by the newspapers than radicals could achieve themselves. So it becomes harder and harder for any group of people to stifle the publication of ideas which they dislike.

The ever-increasing insight into man's nature, setting, and workings which is coming with our modern scientific methods of studying him will no doubt have a great influence upon future historians. They will take note of essential matters which escaped their predecessors; their interpretation will be more profound and their perspective truer. The constant interplay between our knowledge of humanity in its past and in its present manifestations will be realized and emphasized, and history will no longer suffer under the imputations of superficiality and barrenness, but will emerge as an acknowledged instrument for the increase of human understanding.[1]

[1] To carry further one's knowledge of the overwhelming revolution that has overtaken man's ideas of himself and his world, one should do his best to understand Eddington's *Nature of the Physical World*, John Dewey's *The Quest for Certainty* (which describes a philosophy suitable to our new scientific knowledge and investigation), Pavlov's *Lectures on Conditioned Reflexes*, and C. Judson Herrick's *The Thinking Machine*. If one even partially comprehends these works, he will at least be trailing along in the wake of recent scientific and philosophical advance.

CHAPTER XX

THE STUDY OF MANKIND IN FICTION

HISTORICAL SIGNIFICANCE OF STORIES AND DRAMAS

We have spoken of the various ways which have developed of gaining deeper knowledge of man—his conduct, ideas, and institutions. These studies are called the social sciences. History, anthropology, psychology, sociology, political economy, and politics are now the most generally recognized. It might be better to call these not "sciences" but methods of approach in our attempts to understand humanity. They deal with different aspects of man and accordingly overlap and interlock in all sorts of ways, since their main subject is the same. Formal treatises on these subjects, however, tend to aspire to a scientific precision which ill suits the wayward creature with which they seek to make us acquainted. They may be said to be indispensable but insufficient, since, in spite of their various modes of approach, they usually are too general in their statements to describe actual living, doing, and feeling as we experience them and observe them in others.

The gaps left by the social sciences are being filled in more and more by literature, which is coming to be one of the most astonishingly successful methods of assessing ourselves and others. Although fictional and imaginative in form, the best stories, dramas, and poems are written by those who have a penetrating insight into human affairs, and who dare to depict them far more frankly than would be possible if they undertook to be "scientific," historical, or biographical. After all, everything said about humanity is said by a human being about human beings, whether he writes a treatise on sociology or a tale. A sociologist may happen to know far less about men and women than a dramatist and be far more constrained in presenting the knowledge he has. His collection of data may be imposing, and his theories and generalizations valuable. His books, however, rarely arouse such eager questioning and criticism when we contemplate our government, families, schools, churches, prisons, poorhouses, and insane asylums, as does a play of Ibsen's or a novel by H. G. Wells. Literature, which means works of imagination as distinguished from scientific, historical, philosophical, and practical books, should at its best be viewed not solely as an amenity or species of diversion but also as a source of knowledge of the tastes and interests of the period to which the writers happen to belong, and as a revelation of human perplexities and conflicts in meeting the crises of life.

Historians have, indeed, long relied on literature in their attempts to reconstruct the habits, beliefs, and aspirations of past civilizations. The Old Testament is an anthology of Hebrew religious literature from which a great part of our knowledge of the Hebrew people is derived. Homer and, later, the Greek dramatists are the foundation of much of our knowledge of Greek life. So with the Romans and the people of the Middle Ages. Without their fiction we should have a very much more inadequate idea of them, in a broad sense, than we now have. In short, fiction may have much historic fact hidden under its veil of imagination. In any case, it is in itself a highly significant element in the history of all periods when this type of writing has flourished. Imagination is one of the most persistent and omnipresent of human characteristics, and it is constantly affecting men's actions and belief.

Let no one think that an attempt is to be made here to sketch the history of literature during the period covered by this work. The object of this chapter is to illustrate the intimate relation of imaginative writing to men's other interests, habits, and changing views. Important names will remain unmentioned for lack of space, and works quite as remarkable as those here recalled will not be mentioned at all. Only those will find a place here which, especially during the nineteenth century, reflect general social conditions, fundamental alterations of interests, and the increasing tendency to criticize ruthlessly our prevailing notions of good and bad, right and wrong.

It will be convenient for various reasons to refer to English authors mainly in illustrating the historical significance of literature. It was in England that the first great flowering of modern imaginative writing occurred. The development of literature in other western European countries shows a striking parallelism. Books written in one country influenced those written in the others, and the startling changes which have been traced in these volumes affected the mood and determined the interests of authors wherever they might be living.

Even fairly informed persons would find it hard to recollect but one English writer before Shakespeare. Chaucer, two centuries before the days of Elizabeth, reveals the most charming insight into widely different characters, and his *Canterbury Tales* are as alive today as they ever were. As everyone knows, Shakespeare exhibited such genius in his best plays as to astonish the most exacting critics of all European countries for over three hundred years. Ancient tales and the crude *Chronicles of* Holinshed (died about 1580) gave hints for his plays, but the raw stuff disappears in the glorious metamorphosis which it underwent in his hands. He read Montaigne's *Essays*, an English translation of which appeared in 1601. Shakespeare and Montaigne had much in common—the same aloofness and toleration and distaste for committing themselves. The world seemed to both far too intricate to invite the quick and easy approval or condemnation so dear to the common run of us. Shakespeare often introduces a "fool" to make wise but indecorous comments on the behavior of his characters when they take themselves too seriously. Erasmus had adopted a similar device in his famous *Praise of Folly* (1511). We have a forecast here of the present-day outspoken jeering at the good and ultrarespectable members of society. In Bartlett's *Familiar Quotations* a hundred and forty pages are devoted to Shakespeare's sayings and thirty-seven to the most common citations from the Bible. One reading *Hamlet* for the first time is struck by such a multitude of current phrases that it seems to him impossible that one man could have sent them down the centuries. No psychoanalyst of our day could better define a "floating anxiety" than do the lines we find at the opening of the *Merchant of Venice*:

> In sooth, I know not why I am so sad:
> It wearies me; you say it wearies you;
> But how I caught it, found it, or came by it,
> What stuff 'tis made of, whereof it is born,
> I am to learn.

This loathsome affliction is now a theme of scientific scrutiny, but those subject to it, like Antonio, have still "to learn." Two plays of Shakespeare were recently given "in modern dress," and it was astonishing how very up to date they seemed. In order to make his appeal to theatergoers of his time the dramatist introduced much slang and silly punning and a good deal that austere judges would condemn as highly indecent. This precedent has by no means been lost sight of.

Milton towers beside Shakespeare as a poet, but his keen analysis of mankind is embedded in a theological romance the underlying ideas of which are growing obsolete. As we have seen (Vol. I, pp. 77 ff.), we must turn to his neglected prose works really to appreciate his keen arraignment of oppression whether found within the family or exercised by government censors.

After the return of Charles II a new school of comic dramatists arose, who, as Macaulay has said, chose for their characters "sharpers, bullies, hard-hearted impudent debauchees, and women worthy of such paramours." They remind one of the intrigues of Terence and Plautus. The plays turn on seductions, infidelities, cheating and revenge, and "devil take the hindmost." The playwrights of this period display what would now be called an "overcompensation" for the solemnities of the Puritans and the ostentatious godliness of the Commonwealth. Charles Lamb adjudged that their writers had fled the real world, and that to pass moral judgment on them was as absurd as to arraign a sleeper for his dreams. "They belong to the regions of pure comedy, where no cold moral reigns." However, Macaulay was probably right when he claimed that they dealt with certain kinds of people who are always to be found in large cities and elsewhere. The great majority of respectable citizens know little about them and may suspect that they do not exist. Today we have many stories and some dramas which differ from those of the Restoration not so much in the way the characters conduct themselves as in the attitude of modern writers. They can rarely keep out a suggestion of pathos quite different from the peals of "elvish laughter" which Congreve, Wycherley, and Farquhar expected to elicit. This is one of the great changes which have come since the days of Dryden. Sin and wickedness no longer seem such simple or diverting things as they once did.

The Problem of Evil

As writers gradually became more critical and observed the moral conflicts of life more sharply the problem of evil became a subject of discussion. Even the deists (see Vol. I, pp. 25 ff.) believed in a perfect, all-wise, and all-powerful God who had made all things. How could his goodness and wisdom be reconciled with the many horrible and unjust things to be observed in a world of his making? The Christians, who, unlike the deists, continued to accept the Bible as God's word with its account of man's "fall," had what they considered a full and final answer to the question. God had in the beginning created a lovely paradise free from sin and suffering. The first human couple had, however, wrought ruin by their disobedience and so lost their primal innocence, not only for themselves but for their offspring forever. No one had stated the case more poignantly than Calvin:

Such gifts as it pleased God to bestow on the nature of man he vested in Adam; and therefore when Adam lost them after he had received them, he lost them not only for himself, but also for us all. . . . Therefore from a rotten root rose up rotten branches, which sent their rottenness into the twigs that sprang out of them; for so were the children corrupted in their father that they in turn infected their children. . . . And therefore the very infants themselves, since they bring with them their own damnation from their mother's womb, are bound not by another's but their own fault.

Believing that the eating of the forbidden fruit "kindled the horrible vengeance of God on all mankind," Calvin could see no reason why the world should not be a sorry place. In the Anglican service it is still declared that "all men are conceived and born in sin." The Roman Catholic baptismal service assumes that the baby has a devil in him which must be cast out (*Rituale Romanum*, "De Sacramento Baptismi," opening responses).

God had, however, in his infinite mercy sacrificed his son, who offered up his life for man and the salvation of those who believed upon him. Theologians disagreed in regard to the conditions of salvation. Calvin, following the apostle Paul and St. Augustine, held that men were not created to like estate; but some by the eternal decree of God had been predestined to eternal life, and some to eternal damnation. The number is exactly fixed, according to the Westminster Confession of Faith drawn up by English Presbyterians in Cromwell's time. "It cannot be either increased or diminished." Those foreordained to salvation were chosen, before the foundation of the world was laid, by God's "mere free grace and love, without any foresight of faith or good works . . . or anything in the creature as conditions or causes moving Him thereunto, and all to the praise of His glorious grace." The damned sank to hell automatically under the weight of their original corruption.

Even in Calvin's city of Geneva there were those who murmured against this view of mankind's history and fate. They declared that if this was God's way, it seemed the willfulness of a tyrant. To those who made this criticism Calvin conceded their point. No wickedness could be fouler than to question God's decrees, "for the will of God is the highest rule of righteousness, that whatsoever He willeth, even for this that He willeth it, ought to be taken for righteousness." We have seen that Queen Elizabeth's theologians claimed for her the same godlike exemption from impudent inquiries (see account of *The Homilies*, Vol. I, pp. 50 f.). But in a few decades the divine right of sovereigns was repudiated in England by those very theologians who formulated God's despotism according to Calvin's ideas.

Most of the deistical writers appear to have been too busy trying to discredit revelation and miracles and substitute a universal natural religion to trouble themselves with the origin of evil. The problem was still there, but the whole doctrine of man's fall and possibilities of salvation had for them dropped out and with it the terrible emphasis on sin. Swift was contented in the main to satirize his fellow men, and his *Gulliver's Travels* (1726) describes various ways in which a race of very tiny beings or huge ones or even of highly virtuous horses could be used to set off the relativity of all human doings. Defoe used the marooned Robinson Crusoe to show the resources and reflections of one cut off from society. He also published many and varied "projects" for the betterment of mankind, on the assumption that reform was quite possible.

Bernard Mandeville, born in Holland, published in 1714 an inquiry into the origin of moral virtue under the title *The Fable of the Bees, or Private Vices Public Benefits*. The writer contends that without evil there can be no good. His book was condemned as a "nuisance" by the grand jury of Middlesex. Nevertheless, it is a penetrating analysis of the perennial compromise which goes on between man's talk of morality and his daily conduct. *The Fable* is in verse, then often used for didactic purposes.

This practice is well illustrated by Alexander Pope's *Essay on Man* (1733), which proved popular not only in England but also on the Continent. It was written during the deist controversy, and Bolingbroke, a prominent advocate of natural religion, was one of Pope's stanchest friends and advisers. The optimism,—which emerges from a seemingly cynical estimate of mankind,—the praise of God, the rapid flow of the verse, and the compact wisdom of some of the lines enchanted a wide range of readers. He opened up chasms of doubt, and so promptly closed them that one could flatter himself that all possible objections had been faced and that Wisdom had answered them all in a most decisive and charming way.

The German philosopher Leibnitz, a man of varied interests and with an uncommon knowledge of the world, had in Pope's early days proved to his own satisfaction that this was "the best of all possible worlds." Few could understand Leibnitz, but everyone could follow Pope with exultant applause:

> Of systems possible, if 'tis confest
> That Wisdom Infinite must form the best,—
>
> .   .   .   .
>
> Then in the scale of reas'ning life 'tis plain,
> There must be, somewhere, such a rank as man,
>
> .   .   .   .
>
> Respecting man, whatever wrong we call,
> May, must be right as relative to all.
> In human works though laboured on with pain,
> A thousand movements scarce one purpose gain;
> In God's, one single can its end produce;
> Yet serves to second too some other use.
> So man, who here seems principal alone,
> Perhaps acts second to some sphere unknown,

T

Touches some wheel, or verges to some goal;
'Tis but a part we see, and not the whole.
   When the proud steed shall know why man restrains
His fiery course, or drives him o'er the plains:
When the dull ox, why now he breaks the clod,
Is now a victim, and now Egypt's god:
Then shall man's pride and dullness comprehend
His actions', passions', being's, use and end;
Why doing, suff'ring, checked, impelled; and why
This hour a slave, the next a deity.

Not much more than a century after Leibnitz had tried to show that the idea of evil was only a lack of human insight, Schopenhauer published his system of philosophy called *The World viewed as Will and Idea* (1819). In this he sought to prove that our universe was one of hopeless, unceasing conflict and urgent but unsatisfied desire, which in man took the form of ideas of painful frustration. While he is the most celebrated "pessimist" and his chief work is rather hard to read, he became more cheerful in later years and wrote many attractive essays full of insight and learning. These may be had in an excellent English translation.

After reading the preceding chapters, one may guess that it is the problem of *good* rather than of *evil* that will in time arouse man's amazement. Robert Briffault exclaims that if we but consider the "self-creation" of man, once living as a wild creature

by the sole operation of his inherent qualities and powers, by the unfolding of what was in him, the ape, the brute, the beast, the savage, unaided by any external power, in the face of the buffets of hostile nature, of the intractabilities of his own constitution, into MAN, the demi-god, the thinker, the deviser, the aspirer after truth and justice, greater in his achievements and ideals than all the gods he is capable of conceiving—if there is a fact before which we may truly bow in solemn reverence and silent wonder, it is that.

As we proceed to call attention to the works of the novelists and dramatists it will be clear that they seem to take little stock in theories of man's "fall," in optimism or pessimism. Arnold Bennett, in his book *The Author's Craft*, advises his fellow writers to remember that "the world, without doubt, is a very bad world; but it is also a very good world." And most novelists now follow this advice.

ROMANTICISM

A number of novels of importance appeared in England in the first half of the eighteenth century which were not mere amusing stories but efforts on the part of the writers to describe and analyze the actual thoughts, feelings, and conduct of human beings. Among those who set standards for this type of literature was Samuel Richardson, who as a youth had been employed by young women to write their love letters. Many were too illiterate to write themselves. So it is not unnatural that his *Pamela, or Virtue Rewarded* (1740), the story of a highly virtuous maid servant, took the form of letters, as did his later *Clarissa Harlowe, or the History of a Young Lady*, in eight volumes of highly sentimental correspondence (1747–1748). He is called "the founder of the English domestic novel." Fielding set out to satirize *Pamela* in his *History of the Adventures of Joseph Andrews—the Tale of a Virtuous Man Servant* (1742). His much longer *Tom Jones* (1749) aims to describe human nature or, as has been said, John Bull in his actual procedure. The tale will seem rather coarse and common to many modern readers, but it has a sort of ruthless sincerity which recommends it to those who are sickened by the sentimentality of Richardson.

It is customary in the history of literature to distinguish between novels and romances. The distinction is rather vague but highly significant.

That prose fiction which deals realistically with actual life is called, in criticism and conversation, preëminently the *novel*. That prose fiction which deals with life in a false or fantastic manner, or represents it in the setting of strange, improbable, or impossible adventures, or idealizes the virtues and the vices of human nature, is called *romance.*—PROFESSOR WILBUR CROSS

Almost all the stories written by the ancient Greeks and Romans have been lost. It happens that of the two chief ones which we have, one is a novel, *The Banquet of Trimalchio*, by Petronius, and the other a romance, *The Golden Ass* of Apuleius. The first gives an account, full of colloquialisms, of the doings at a dinner given by a low-lived rich man in Nero's time. In the second the hero is transformed into an ass and has many marvelous adventures. So while there were "classical" models of poetic and dramatic compositions which could be used by later European writers, the story-tellers were left to follow their own tastes. The result was that when tales and narrative poems began to be produced in the twelfth and thirteenth centuries, they were all romances, for these are far more congenial to mankind at large than the sophisticated novel. Few care for a strict adhesion to the usual happenings of life and analysis of familiar characters. The great majority long for a good story, full of mysteries, horrors, lovers and villains, and virtue rewarded.

There had been a good deal said in the eighteenth century of Reason and the godlike supremacy of the intellect. Then Richardson, Fielding, Smollett, and Sterne told their stories in their various ways with an appreciation of a certain romantic or satirical or sentimental interest in human conduct under ordinary or unusual circumstances—for adventures are not uncommon or necessarily improbable. From both the worship of the intellect and the limitations of the novel there was a revolt which showed itself in a flood of romances and in a school of philosophers called the "romantic." The writers of stories and poetry discarded all attempts either to follow

classical models or confine themselves to reality and probability. The philosophers, especially Fichte, Schelling, and
Hegel, built up imposing structures with little regard to actual
human history or the advance of scientific knowledge. They
are romances of the Spirit, or aspiring Ego.

The romances which appeared in England in the late eighteenth century and early nineteenth are little read now. *The
Mysteries of Udolpho*, by Mrs. Radcliffe, appeared in 1794;
Matthew Lewis's *Ambrosio, or the Monk*, a year later. Tales
of the most elaborate horror were published by the dozen and
were eagerly devoured. There were haunted castles, tombs
and dungeons, rattling chains, secret passages, young women
caught in the toils of cruel seducers, and heroes appearing at
the right moment—all the devices of the lowest type of romance. While the devices have altered as time has gone on,
the romance persists. Our modern detective and mystery
stories, however, are sometimes written by authors of ability
and in an excellent style, and serve to give thoughtful readers
a respite from the tragic novels which flourish alongside them.

Of all the story-writers of this period Walter Scott (1771–
1832) gained the most solid fame. His poems, like *Marmion*
and *The Lady of the Lake*, were romantic but quite free from
the crude expedients of "Monk" Lewis. Scott lived on the
Scottish borderland and was an ardent antiquarian. There was
a ruined castle near his grandfather's farm which made a deep
impression on him. He had a vision of

> foragers who, with headlong force,
> Down from that strength had spurred their horse,
> Their southern rapine to renew,
> Far in the distant Cheviot's blue;
> And, home returning, filled the hall
> With revel, wassail-rout, and brawl.

His novels—appearing anonymously as the works of the "Author of Waverley" from 1814 to his death—are not novels but

romances. He wrote to amuse, not to instruct. His heroes and heroines are colorless, but he puts great spirit in his subsidiary, but really chief, characters. He had no tendency to dwell on the inscrutable pathos and mystery of life. To bring out the nature of romanticism one may recall the lines of Wordsworth, who had so little in common with his rather lukewarm friend Scott:

> The clouds that gather round the setting sun
> Do take a sober colouring from an eye
> That hath kept watch o'er man's mortality;
>
> .   .   .   .
>
> Thanks to the human heart by which we live,
> Thanks to its tenderness, its joys, and fears,
> To me the meanest flower that blows can give
> Thoughts that do often lie too deep for tears.

Contrast this with Scott's sense of Nature as a place for adventure or with the confidently didactic manner of Pope, who felt so little the

> Blank misgivings of a creature
> Moving about in a world not realized,
> High instincts before which our mortal nature
> Did tremble like a guilty thing surprised.

This sentiment of the well-nigh hopeless mystery of things has tended to deepen and is summarized in our own day by Housman in his

> A stranger and afraid
> In a world I never made.

Romanticism is what psychologists now call an "escape mechanism." Life is puzzling, painful, or boresome; thinking is tiresome. So we want to get away from everything that recalls its duties and responsibilities. Romantic stories, moving pictures, dramas, and even philosophies play us up in circumstances favorable to our longing for centrality. For we identify ourselves with such characters as we admire, and make a footstool of our enemies as they are recognized in the villains of the tale. Romanticism is not a study of man but a revelation of his deepest longings. Those who deal with mental diseases know that many people are so revolted by their experiences that they dwell in a romance or fantasy of what they would be, until they lose touch altogether with the real world. Romanticism may be regarded as a sort of reckless idealism which insists on asserting beauty and adventure, however scarce they may seem in practice.

During the period of flourishing romanticism, which exhibited itself especially in the verse of Keats, Shelley, and Lord Byron, a clergyman's daughter, Jane Austen (1775–1817), wrote six novels which are still read and cherished by the discriminating. She did no more than record with the insight of genius the daily happenings and conversation of the kind of people she knew best. Her great achievement was that she could make the commonplace seem romantic. She had no lessons to impart, no obvious resentments to satisfy, but set an example of story-writing with none of the improbable and exaggerated situations which had commonly been supposed essential to attracting and holding the reader's attention. She carefully avoided the sick souls and opened up no personal or social ulcers. Her realism is that of the parlor, ballroom, and country stroll. Many novels of this type were written during the Victorian period and many continue to be written.

In the middle of the nineteenth century several novelists appeared whose writings form substantial sets to be seen in the windows of booksellers today. The chief of these were Dickens, Thackeray, George Eliot, and the Brontë sisters.

Charles Dickens (1812–1870) introduced new and permanent features into his stories. Having spent a miserable boyhood, he appreciated the fact that the woes of childhood are fully as poignant as those of later years. He introduces us not only to mishandled youngsters but to all sorts of down-and-outers in whom he found a vivid interest. He was wont to course the streets and alleys of London at night in search of suggestions. He shows little of the "analytic" tendency so common in later novels but is bent on writing a good story. He rarely leaves the impression of hopeless tragedy, and one can be sure that there will be a "lived happily ever after" ending. He enriched the language with "in a Pickwickian sense," and the phrase often represents his own mood. His recurring satire on British institutions, especially the Court of Chancery, shows that he was not the victim of Victorian complacency. Thackeray was alive to hypocrisy and affectation as he saw it in the society of his time. His characters are chosen in general from the middle classes. The novels written by the Brontë sisters reflect life on the lonely moors of Yorkshire, and the fierce passions which might develop in solitude. George Eliot was a woman of philosophic training; and her characters, living mainly in the countryside, work out their destinies with a fatalism suitable to her philosophy. The best stories of all these writers can be read with greater interest if one considers them in relation to the estimate of human beings which they represent.

The term "Victorian" is now used to suggest prudishness, a smug acceptance of current mores and taboos. It is true that the writers mentioned above, even George Eliot, seldom raised religious questions or attacked social institutions overtly. The relations of men and women were dealt with in a manner which today seems cautiously superficial, but not necessarily prudish. In the latter part of the nineteenth century novels and dramas began to be frank exposures of the evil workings of those respectable ideas and customs which had in general been accepted by the mid-Victorian writers.[1] The signal for the revolution in playwriting was given by a Norwegian.

---

[1] The humanitarian stories of this period are mentioned on page 113.

The Quintessence of Ibsenism

Henrik Ibsen was born in a little Norwegian town in 1828. He worked as an apothecary's assistant and underwent every kind of discouragement in his early days. His first plays enraged his countrymen, and he left Norway to live in Rome, Dresden, Munich, and elsewhere; but he finally won admiration and returned to Christiania, where he spent his last years surrounded by adulation—a sort of public spectacle as he sat in a restaurant. As so often has happened, the public who scorned him in 1870 was ready to rear a bronze statue to him after he died, in 1906. But in such cases it must be remembered that it was not the same generation that scorned and then revered him, but one which had been influenced by him and the changing circumstances which had led him to write as he did. Ibsen's influence was so widely felt in England, the United States, and Germany, as well as in his own land, that we can use his dramas as a general illustration of the new type of play and novel which he promoted.

Passing over his earlier work, we come directly to his play *A Doll's House* (1879). This was his first important drama, destined in a few years to spread his reputation far beyond the limits of Scandinavia. It possesses many of the traits of those which followed. The whole play is carried to its end in the same room, the furnishings of which are very carefully specified by the author in his stage directions. There are four chief characters, together with three children and a porter. This economy of scene and actors is now very common. The whole drama consists of the talking that goes on in a sitting-room. Nora, Helmer's wife, comes in with the Christmas tree, and some parcels which she tries to hide from the children. Helmer gently upbraids her for extravagance. He does not know how she has to save in all sorts of secret ways to pay installments on a note she has forged with her father's name in order to give her husband a vacation he desperately needed. It was

Helmer's secretary who lent the money, and he wants a position in the bank of which Helmer has been made manager. Meanwhile a woman friend of Nora's turns up, also in dire need of employment. The secretary holds the forged note over Nora and threatens to tell all if she does not induce her husband to secure the position for him. In the last act Helmer, after he has learned the state of affairs, being a very "good" man, and cruelly nervous, above all, about losing his reputation, fiercely attacks his wife and makes no allowances for her having been treated as a doll —so ignorant of business that she had allowed herself to commit a crime to save his health. The forged note is magnanimously returned by its holder; and then Helmer, who has told his wife that she is too wicked to rear her children, now tries to make terms, since his conventional fear is gone with the burning of the note.

The terrific climax of the play is a final conversation between husband and wife. Nora had expected a "miracle"— that her husband, on knowing the facts, would say "I am the guilty one." It was her father's fault and his that she had been brought up such a fool. "I lived by performing tricks for you." Helmer accuses her of talking like a child, and of not understanding society. Nora replies that she does not, but will try to learn. "I must make up my mind which is right— society or I." When he says no man sacrifices his honor, even for one he loves, Nora replies, "Millions of women have done so." When Helmer tells her she is before all else a wife and mother, she replies, "That I no longer believe. I believe that before all else I am a human being, just as much as you are— or at least should try to become one. I know most people agree with you, Torvald, and that they say so in books. But henceforth I can't be satisfied with what most people say, and what is in books." She leaves him in the end as a stranger after eight years of marriage, to fare forth no longer a doll.

Ghosts appeared shortly after *A Doll's House* and created "a terrible uproar in the Scandinavian press," as its author reports. It is enacted in as confined surroundings as the former drama and has five characters—mother and son, pastor, carpenter, and maid. The boy, an artist, is represented as having inherited a disease from his father which speedily destroys his brain, and he commits suicide. The mother in the end shoots herself, because she feels that had she done better she might have prevented her husband's leading the disastrous life he did. The pastor manages to discredit himself in the reader's eyes by his conflicting commonplaces. When these two plays were given in England, they let loose a flood of virtuous indignation which went a good way to show that Ibsen was quite on the right track in displaying the weaknesses of society and the defenders of idealism. Bernard Shaw has collected from the newspapers of the day some of the epithets: "ugly, nasty, discordant and downright dull; . . . a gloomy sort of ghoul, bent on groping for horrors by night and blinking like a stupid old owl when the warm sunlight of the best of life dances into his wrinkled eyes." "Revolting, suggestive, and blasphemous," "garbage and offal."

However, Ibsen had three friends and ardent admirers in England who rode the tempest and quietly explained to their frantic fellow citizens that they were hasty in their condemnation. Edmund Gosse had taken the trouble to learn the Scandinavian languages; William Archer wrote introductions to the English translations of Ibsen's plays; and, most conspicuous of all, George Bernard Shaw explained *The Quintessence of Ibsenism* in a delightful little volume (1891), and then began to write plays of his own, which at least could not be called dull. He repeated over and over again all the shocking things that Ibsen had said.

Shaw turns to the question, Why are the plays of Ibsen so different from those of the first half of the nineteenth century? Those who could read the earlier writers from end to end "without the smallest intellectual or ethical perturbation" were unable to get through a play of Ibsen's without having their intellectual and moral complacency upset, their religious faith shattered, their "notions of right and wrong conduct thrown into confusion and sometimes reversed." Shaw asserts that before Dickens one finds "Poverty in rags is a joke, yellow fever is a joke, drunkenness is a joke, dysentery is a joke, kickings, floggings, falls, frights, humiliations and painful accidents are jokes. . . . The infirmities of age and the inexperience and shyness of youth are jokes; and it is first rate fun to insult and torment those who suffer from them. We take these jokes seriously enough now."

There are plenty of books, Shaw observes, that respond to our longing to be amused, to have the world dressed up "prettily" for us, and to see things going right, at least in stories. But to more and more people this seems cowardly, and we are willing sometimes to meet the efforts of those who bravely try to face current facts. And yet the popular moving pictures suggest often what Shaw calls "the laughter that African tribes cannot restrain when a man is flogged or an animal trapped and wounded." And as Ibsen makes plain, there are all sorts of floggings and trappings going on in family life and outside. In his *Wild Duck* (1884) Ibsen shows what a mischief-maker an idealist can be. He questions the old conceptions of the relations of husband and wife, of parents and children, and the pompous assumptions of *The Pillars of Society*, who are no better than they ought to be.

George Bernard Shaw introduced obvious humor and color into plays, much less austere than Ibsen's but better calculated to fascinate playgoers while they listened to his discussions of social evils. He was born in Dublin in 1856 of "genteel" parents, who found it hard to get a living. His mother delighted in music and had some ability as an amateur actress. So Shaw early became interested in music, pictures, and the theater. His first communication to the newspapers was an attack on Moody and Sankey, whom he had heard in Dublin. He horrified his pious relatives by confessing that if their gospel was religion he might be counted as an atheist. He had long to rely on his unsuccessful father and his mother to support him; no one would publish his novels. He read Marx, became a Socialist, joined the Fabian Society, and for years delivered addresses in various parts of London on the evils of capitalism. He declared poverty the worst crime, and he had had plenty of experience of how it hampered and degraded.

A fellow countryman of his, St. John Ervine, also a critic and dramatist, sums up Shaw's general conviction as follows:

The hatred of hypocrisy and pretentious respectability and irrational social cleavages and stupefying poverty and every kind of organized priestcraft, whether of the law or the Church or of medicine or of politics, which he acquired in Dublin as a boy and a youth, was poured out in his [early] novels and distilled from them into his plays.

Shaw's early socialist enthusiasm was supplanted by a general criticism of human ways, and he does not use his plays to promote the doctrine in any obvious fashion. He never forgot that he was born an Irishman and belonged to *John Bull's Other Island* (1907). He treats the English with somewhat sarcastic indulgence; but he has no partiality for the Irish.

Candida, one of Shaw's earlier plays, resembles Ibsen in being staged in a single room and having scarce half a dozen characters. A sentimental youngster, Eugene, is in love with the wife of a pompous, selfish, amiable clergyman, who has been the idol of his family and a vast care to his patient wife. When it comes to a showdown the wife says she will give herself to the weaker of the two. The youth immediately sees what she means, but her James accepts "his sentence." She then explains that the clergyman, "her boy," had been spoiled from his cradle. She has to "stand sentinel to keep the little cares out" while he writes his noble sermons. He is the weaker one. Shaw shows Ibsen's skill in this type of frugal drama, where there is just talk. Soon, however, he was giving great attention to the pictorial setting of his plays, whether laid in Africa, Spain, Egypt, America, England, or Ireland. He gives very elaborate stage directions, interlarding them through the dialogue, describing the character and appearance of the participants. He believed this to be essential to enable actors to interpret their rôles according to their various temperaments, by supplying them with ample information. Then he outfitted each play with a long introduction, in which he discussed anything it might suggest in the way of serious reflection.

With all this artistic and philosophic setting, he is in no way unfriendly to the extravagant. In *Androcles and the Lion*, a discussion of early Christianity, the beast follows its whimsical master about and is finally discovered in the Colosseum. He refuses to eat Androcles, and this miracle nearly converts the Emperor to the Christian faith. In *Cæsar and Cleopatra* the Egyptian queen nestles between the paws of the Sphinx. Cæsar is addressing the gigantic image, when Cleopatra calls out, "Old gentleman, don't run away." Cæsar replies, "Sphinx, you presume on your centuries. I am younger than you, though your voice is but a girl's voice as yet." Cleopatra says, "Climb up here, quickly, or the Romans will eat you." For some reason all this absurd playfulness does not stand in the way of a deeply serious impression, and Shaw knows this very well.

While modern story-writers make few references to God, Shaw has a sort of credo. His god, as reflected in the history of the world, is not prescient and all-wise but an experimenter, who destroys his works when they are not a success, as illustrated by many extinct animals and plants. He finally made man, capable of intelligent action and conscious ideals to aid him in the perfecting of his work. So far as men do aid him by abandoning falsehood and cruelty and do foster kindness, insight, and order, they are his servants. God may wipe out the race as he did the huge saurians if they prove too disappointing. This doctrine leaves Shaw quite free to criticize all religious beliefs and practices, while holding an inspiring faith of his own not easily upset by scientific discoveries.

H. G. WELLS ET AL.

Unlike his contemporary Mr. Shaw, H. G. Wells is greatly interested in the advance of science and its applications. He was born in Kent in 1866 of poor parents and has a great deal to say in his stories of the hard struggle of children to adjust themselves to the world with the ineffectual and hampering notions of education that prevail. He studied physics, chemistry, geology, and biology and graduated as bachelor of science from London University in 1888, with high honors; he later taught scientific subjects for a time. So his background was, in contrast with that of most novelists, *scientific* rather than literary and artistic. Like Shaw, he was a Fabian and continued to profess a sort of socialism, far, however, from the Marxian type. His early books turn on the future wonders of scientific discovery, including the navigation of the air, then unrealized in practice. In his novel *In the Days of the Comet* (1906) the world is regenerated by the addition of a small percentage of stimulating gas which gives people just enough more energy to banish depression and jealousy and impart a spirit of rapid reform.

Wells has described his outlook and dominating theme in the opening of *The New Machiavelli* (1911):

The things that might be done today! The things indeed that are being done! It is the latter that give one such a vast sense of the former. When I think of the progress of physical and mechanical science, of medicine and sanitation during the last century, when I measure the increase in general education and average efficiency, the power now available for human service, the merely physical increment, and compare it with anything that has ever been at man's disposal before, and when I think of what a little straggling, incidental, undisciplined, and uncoördinated minority of inventors, experimenters, educators, writers and organizers has achieved this development of human possibilities, achieved it in spite of the disregard and aimlessness of the huge majority, and the passionate resistance of the active dull, my imagination grows giddy with dazzling intimations of the human splendors the justly organized state may yet attain. I glimpse for a bewildering instant the heights that may be scaled, the splendid enterprises made possible.

Wells's novels *New Worlds for Old, The Research Magnificent, Modern Utopia, Men like Gods, The Dream*, are all aimed to point the way to Utopia and attempt to picture a regenerated world in which intelligence and good will shall prevail. There shall be no more misery and squalor, the superstition of clothes shall disappear, and all may think high and refreshing thoughts in bright, clean, gracious surroundings.

But all plans for improving human conditions are "entangled and mixed up with other, and more intimate things." When the old Machiavelli wrote his famous book *The Prince*, despots seemed the only hope of reformers. One no longer dedicates his treatises on betterment to them. They are for the most part gone, seemingly forever. On the other hand, half the human race are coming into the problems. Machiavelli "left the thought of women outside with his other dusty things when he went into his study to write, dismissed them from his mind. But our modern world is burdened with its sense of the immense, now half-articulate, significance of women."

So no consideration of how to achieve better things can be dissociated from the old and new troubles and discords between men and women. To this theme are devoted *The New Machiavelli, Marriage, The Wife of Sir Isaac Harman*, and *The Passionate Friends*. The perplexities of lovers and the ruin of lives wrought by efforts to escape the burden of ancient institutions and the current ideas of respectability are treated with great insight, delicacy, and sympathy.

Just after the close of the World War, Mr. Wells published his *Outline of History* in handsomely illustrated installments, to be sold on the bookstands in order to reach a great many readers. This book was a bold enterprise and was remarkably well done, considering the difficulty of getting sufficient information to give a sketch of human progress from the origin of the globe itself to the Treaty of Versailles. Tens of thousands of persons got their first insight into the overwhelming human drama from this work. It is a good thing for all those who propose to teach history or study it with care to take note of the following passage:

The need for a common knowledge of the general facts of human history throughout the world has become very evident during the tragic happenings of the last few years. Swifter means of communication have brought all men closer to one another for good or for evil. War becomes a universal disaster, blind and monstrously destructive; it bombs the baby in its cradle and sinks the foodships that cater for the non-combatant and the neutral. There can be no peace now, we realize, but a common peace in all the world; no prosperity but a general prosperity. But *there can be no common peace and prosperity without common historical ideas.* Without such ideas to hold them together in harmonious coöperation, with nothing but narrow, selfish, and conflicting nationalist traditions, races and peoples are bound to drift towards conflict and destruction. . . . Our internal policies and our economic and social ideas are profoundly vitiated at present by wrong and fantastic ideas of the origin and historical relationship of social classes. A sense of history as the common adventure of all mankind is as necessary for peace within as it is for peace between the nations.

Arnold Bennett, a year younger than Wells, has pictured the life into which he was born, the Five Towns in Staffordshire, gradually straggling out into the fields and much devoted to the manufacture of pottery. He is called a realist and describes with the greatest skill what he saw and how things go among the not so poor and by no means rich. *The*

T

Old Wives' Tale (1908) established his reputation. He deprecates the notion that he is trying to redeem mankind, but wrote two plays, *Milestones*, describing the changes from generation to generation, and *What the Public Wants*, an amusing comment on the expressed aim of the modern newspaper. His analysis of human motives is excelled perhaps by no other writer, and that gives him his importance in the contributions to a knowledge of men and women made by story-tellers.

John Galsworthy was born in the same year as Bennett, but under what are usually called more favorable circumstances. His works deal in the main with the often rough road traveled by the prosperous and educated. *The Forsyte Saga*, a sequence of novels, traces a family through three generations. His play *Strife* has to do with labor problems; his *Justice* with prisons, his *Loyalties* with conflicts of allegiance and responsibility which so often arise.

From the beginning of the twentieth century the number of distinguished women novelists has steadily increased. Even during the previous hundred years they had fairly held their own with the men. In subtle insight, breadth of sympathy, inexorable frankness, and sometimes beauty of style, their best works are indistinguishable from the finest of the man-made novels. So far they have not revealed an equal genius in either poetry or the drama.

Were there space available something might be said of the trend of the novel in America and the western countries of Europe. We should find developments similar to those in England. France had its romantic writers, like Victor Hugo, its attempts to depict life realistically as Zola tried to do, and its charming skeptics, like Anatole France. Then came Marcel Proust, with his volumes of introspection and analysis of the reverie, in whose eyes a day was as a thousand years. The German romanticists were succeeded by Hauptmann, Sudermann, and, later, Thomas Mann, who exhibited the transition from Ibsen-like stories to introspection.

In Russia the novel developed striking peculiarities. The shining lights of that land, so perturbing and mysterious to Western readers, were Turgeniev, Dostoievsky, and, above all, Tolstoy. All these felt that the Russian peasants constituted the true people—martyrs to oppression but possessing a species of noble dignity. They all harbored a distrust of the "higher classes." One seeking to understand the sentiments of poetic souls under the rule of the Tsars will find Turgeniev's *Fathers and Sons*, Dostoievsky's *Recollections of a Dead House* (the author's reminiscences of his cruel Siberian exile), *The Insulted and the Injured*, and *The Brothers Karamazov*, and Tolstoy's *War and Peace* and *Anna Karénina* worth volumes of what passes for Russian history.

Story-tellers have always been popular. A tale finds ready acceptance, for it is congenial to mankind. The drama is but a story designed to be acted out. The drama has a long history reaching from Æschylus to Bernard Shaw; the novel a short history, as we now conceive it, beginning in the middle of the eighteenth century. Its appearance was an historical event of the utmost importance. It is a device which enables sophisticated observers of man's conduct to illustrate human behavior, as the authors see it, in all its multiform manifestations. Its freedom from the exigencies of scientific classification permits its close approximation to actual experience.

The scope of the novel has widened so that it is no longer the diverting adventures of lovers but the romance of human existence. The child, the poor, and the humble are ever with us, and they are no longer neglected. Their story is often quite as absorbing as that of medieval knights and ladies. The discords of marriage and family disharmonies can be brought home to us far more vividly in a novel than in a treatise on domestic relations. How historians would rejoice could a Wells, Arnold Bennett, or Rose Macaulay be rediscovered in the age of Thutmose II, Alexander the Great, or Charlemagne!

EPILOGUE

It will be observed that the subtitle of this volume is "The Merging of European into World History." Only recently has it become apparent that we may be witnessing one of those expansions of civilization which have occurred on a less magnificent scale in the past. Egypt deeply influenced other lands, Greek civilization was carried into Asia by Alexander the Great and was disseminated in Europe by the conquests of Rome. From the twelfth century onward western Europe, on the basis of Christian ideas closely associated with survivals and revivals of Greek and Roman culture, began to develop a distinctive civilization of its own. At first it was largely reminiscent; but by the opening of the seventeenth century it began to become aggressive. The new element was *experimental science*, which had been heralded by Francis Bacon. This has altered not only man's whole conception of his world but also, as we have seen, his ways and his ideas of himself and his fellows. This new type of civilization originated and grew in that portion of Europe which lies to the west of Vienna; until recently the eastern portions of the Continent made no important contributions.

Among the applications of knowledge were unprecedented means of generating and distributing power—from the steam engine to the dynamo—and machines to use this power in the most diverse fashions. These resulted in previously undreamed-of methods of intercommunication, which have brought the whole globe into the compass of an old-time village. *Experimental science thus produced the means of spreading itself rapidly over the world*. The armies of Alexander and the legions of Rome were primitive and ineffective in comparison, and their range limited.

The nature and development of European civilization during the past three hundred years has been sketched in this work. It has been amplified in various ways by the United States, which has not hid in a napkin its talent transmitted to it from western Europe. The salient characteristics of Western civilization are experimental science, mass production,—with its great increase in daily conveniences and comforts,—highly developed financial organizations, democracy, popular education, and the growing tendency to criticize traditional religious, moral, political, and economic assumptions. As we have seen, the new means of communication and the urge of imperialism have carried these aspirations into Africa and Asia. The World War resulted in an international league devoted to insuring peace among the nations of the world—a World Council, a World Court, a World Bank.

Anthropologists, psychologists, economists, and novelists are busy trying to wean men from ancient illusions and encourage them in an effort to understand themselves and their neighbors in the light of ever-increasing knowledge. According to their findings, men and women are adjustable and amenable to new situations. Our situation is unprecedented in the history of mankind, but we have new resources which may enable us to meet it more successfully than any bygone generation.

SUGGESTIONS FOR READING

GENERAL REFERENCES

GOOCH, G. P., *History of Modern Europe, 1878–1919*, an excellent survey; KNIGHT, BARNES, and FLÜGEL, *Economic History of Europe*; ROSE, J. H., *Development of the European Nations, 1870–1914* (2 vols.) ; SLOSSON, P. W., *Twentieth Century Europe*. Constant use should be made of the new *Encyclopædia Britannica* (24 vols., including a volume with excellent maps and index).

CHAPTER I. THE HERITAGE OF THE TWENTIETH CENTURY

For the spirit and hopes of democracy there is nothing better than PAINE, THOMAS, *Rights of Man*, in many editions; WOLLSTONECRAFT, MARY, *The Rights of Woman* (in Everyman's Library) ; MILL, J. S., *The Subjection of Women*.

The technical revolution: MANTOUX, *The Industrial Revolution of the Eighteenth Century*; KAEMPFFERT, W. B., *Popular History of American Inventions* (2 vols.), with references to European origins ; BARNES, H. E., *Living in the Twentieth Century*; POUND, ARTHUR, *The Iron Man in Industry*.

For the critical spirit of the nineteenth century, BUCKLE, H. T., *History of Civilization in England* (2 vols.), is useful for its intrinsic merits and as a mirror of contemporary radical opinion.

Classical economy: RICARDO, *Principles of Political Economy and Taxation*; MILL, J. S., *Principles of Political Economy*. The *laissez faire* theory: SPENCER, H., *The Man versus the State* ; DONISTHORPE, W., *Individualism, a System of Politics*.

Socialism and social theories: LAIDLER, H. W., *A History of Socialist Thought*, is a valuable general survey and gives extensive bibliographies for each period. RUEHLE, O., *Karl Marx* (1929), excellent new life. MARX, *Capital : a Critique of Political Economy* (3 vols.), is the "Bible" of socialism. ENGELS, *Socialism : Utopian and Scientific*. RUSKIN, *Unto This Last*, the best statement of Ruskinian economics. CARLYLE, *Past and Present*, for Carlyle's critique of capitalism. O'BRIEN, *Medieval Economic Teaching*, a scholarly view of the Catholic heritage.

i

CHAPTER II. DEVELOPMENT OF GOVERNMENT IN THE NAME OF THE PEOPLE

BOURGEOIS, E., *Modern France* (2 vols.); COUBERTIN, *The Evolution of France under the Third Republic* ; HANOTAUX, *Contemporary France* (4 vols.) ; LOWELL, A. L., *Governments and Parties in Continental Europe*, Vol. I. HOWARD, B. E., *The German Constitution*, an analysis of the old Imperial Government. ROBINSON, J. H., *The German Bundesrath* (1891), a study in German federalism.

For the extension of the suffrage in general : PENMAN, J. S., *The Irresistible Movement of Democracy.* Political parties : LOWELL, A. L., *Governments and Parties in Continental Europe* and *The Government of England.* MAY, T. E., *The Constitutional History of England*, Vol. III, covers the period from 1860 to 1911. In this work the history of freedom of speech and of the press in England is traced in great detail. For a brief survey, BURY, J. B., *A History of Freedom of Thought* (Home University Library).

Misgivings about democracy : MILL, J. S., *On Representative Government*; MAINE, H. S., *Popular Government*; LECKY, W. E. H., *Democracy and Liberty.* MICHELS, R., *Political Parties* (1915), is a devastating criticism of democracy and the party system, especially in Germany.

An excellent guide to social and economic thinking in general is BARKER, E., *Political Thought in England from Herbert Spencer to the Present Day* (Home University Library), with useful bibliography at the end. INGRAM, J. K., *A History of Political Economy.* HANEY, L. H., *History of Economic Thought.*

CHAPTER III. CONFLICTS OF DEMOCRACY WITH KINGS, PEERS, AND PRELATES

FISHER, H. A. L., *The Republican Tradition in Europe*, traces the rise and decline of the republican movement to 1910. Tables of the ruling monarchs in Europe are to be found in the British annual, *The Statesman's Year-Book.* LUDWIG, E., *Wilhelm II*, a popular biography of the German emperor, especially useful for the democratic spirit ; also *Bismarck*, by the same author. The conflict between the old order and democracy in Austria can be traced in REDLICH, J., *Emperor Francis Joseph of Austria*, a scholarly biography by a competent authority. LOWE, *Life of Prince Bismarck* (2 vols.).

MARRIOTT, J. A. R., *Second Chambers*, a comparative study of upper houses in 1910. Detailed composition of each upper chamber given every year in the *Statesman's Year-Book.*

Popular movement in Russia: MILYOUKOV, *Russia and its Crisis*; MAVOR, J., *An Economic History of Russia* (2 vols.) ; PARES, B., *A History of Russia* (to 1927), with bibliographies; KENNAN, G., *Siberia and the Exile System* (2 vols.), based on personal observation; KORNILOV, *Modern Russian History* (2 vols.).

State and Church: MAY, T. E., *Constitutional History of England* (3 vols.), traces the relations in England in great detail. BOURGEOIS, E., *Modern France* (2 vols.). For a Lutheran view, NIELSEN, F., *History of Papacy in the Nineteenth Century* (2 vols.). Catholic views are to be found in the articles in the *Catholic Encyclopædia*. See also MACCAFFREY, *History of the Catholic Church in the Nineteenth Century* (2 vols.). CORNISH, F. W., *A History of the Church of England in the Nineteenth Century*.

CHAPTER IV. THE GROWTH OF STATE ECONOMIC CONTROL

Socialist programs are to be found in ENSOR, R. C. K., *Modern Socialism* (1910) ; SOMBART, W., *Socialism and the Social Movement*; KIRKUP, T., *A History of Socialism*; BEER, M., *A History of British Socialism* (2 vols.). For earlier phases of British factory legislation, HUTCHINS and HARRISON, *A History of Factory Legislation* (1903), a brief survey. HAYES, CARLTON J. H., *British Social Politics*, contains extracts from parliamentary debates on the Asquith–Lloyd George social and economic measures from 1906 to 1911. WEBB, S. and B., *The History of Trade Unionism* (in England). ELY, R. T., *French and German Socialism*. DAWSON, W. H., *The German Workman, Germany and the Germans* (2 vols.), and *The Evolution of Modern Germany*—all valuable for German social legislation and economic policy.

The state policies of France and Germany are briefly considered in CLAPHAM, J. H., *The Economic Development of France and Germany, 1815-1914*. HOBSON, J. A., *The Evolution of Modern Capitalism*. RUBINOW, I. M., *Social Insurance*. MOON, P. T., *The Labor Problem and the Social Catholic Movement in France*, with extensive bibliography in the appendix. MUIR, R., *Liberalism and Industry*, a short work, valuable for its account of the abandonment of *laissez faire* by Liberals. See also HOBSON, J. A., *The Crisis of Liberalism*. GUYOT, Y., *Where and Why Public Ownership has Failed*, an attack on state socialism by a French economist. For free trade see early history in MORLEY, J., *Life of Cobden* (2 vols.) ; ASHLEY, P., *Modern Tariff History* (1910); CUNNINGHAM, W., *Rise and Decline of the Free Trade Movement* ; DAWSON, W. H., *Protection in Germany*.

CHAPTER V. THE PROGRESS OF IMPERIALISM

The best general introduction is MOON, P. T., *Imperialism and World Politics*. For underlying economic forces, HOBSON, J. A., *Imperialism*; REINSCH, P., *World Politics at the End of the Nineteenth Century*. DAY, CLIVE, *History of Commerce*, for general development of trade. VIALLATE, A., *Economic Imperialism and International Relations*. DENNIS, J. S., *Christian Missions and Social Progress* (3 vols.). For Catholic missions in particular, consult *The Catholic Encyclopædia*. RECOULY, R., *The Third Republic*, especially useful for foreign and colonial policy of France. ROSE, J. H., *Development of European Nations*, Vol. II. TOWNSEND, M., *Origins of Modern German Colonialism* (2 vols.). TITTONI, T., *Italy's Foreign and Colonial Policy*. SKRINE, *Expansion of Russia* (3d ed., 1915).

KELTIE, J. S., *Partition of Africa* (1895); JOHNSON, H., *History of the Colonization of Africa by Alien Races* (1899); HARRIS, N. D., *Intervention and Colonization in Africa* (to 1913). For explorations see the writings of DAVID LIVINGSTONE, H. M. STANLEY, and SAMUEL BAKER. A full bibliography of all phases of African development is given in Appendix I to the work by N. D. HARRIS, cited above. ZIMMERMAN, E., *The German Empire of Central Africa*.

For the British occupation of Egypt : CROMER, EARL OF, *Modern Egypt* (2 vols.), tracing the history of British intervention from 1876 to 1908.

Detailed bibliography of all phases of imperialism in MOON, P. T., *Syllabus on International Relations*, Part III.

CHAPTER VI. THE BRITISH EMPIRE BEFORE THE WORLD WAR

EGERTON, H. E., *Origin and Growth of Greater Britain* and *A Short History of British Colonial Policy*; LUCAS, C. P., *Historical Geography of the British Colonies* (13 vols.); GUNN, H. (Ed.), *The British Empire* (12 vols.); ROBINSON, HOWARD, *The Development of the British Empire*; SEELEY, J. R., *The Expansion of England* (1883); DILKE, C., *Problems of Greater Britain* (2 vols., 1890); JENKS, *Government of the British Empire* (1923).

DUTT, R. C., *Economic History of India in the Victorian Age*; CROSS, C. M. P., *Development of Self-government in India, 1858–1914*. WITTKE, C., *A History of Canada*. EDGAR, *History of South Africa* (1923). SCOTT, E., *A Short History of Australia* (1916); JENKS, E., *History of the Australasian Colonies* (to 1897). DOUGLAS, A. P., *The Dominion of New Zealand* (1911). WISE, B. R., *The Making of the Australian Commonwealth*; MOORE, W. H., *The Constitution of the Commonwealth of*

Australia. PHILLIP, W. A., *The Revolution in Ireland, 1906–1923*; HAY-
DEN and MOONAN, *Short History of the Irish People* (from earliest times
to 1920).

CHAPTER VII. THE NEW WORLD AND THE OLD

DAMANGEON, *America and the Race for World Dominion*; PEEL, G.,
The Economic Impact of America; MATHEWS, J. M., *American Foreign
Relations*; DENNIS, A. L. P., *Adventures in American Diplomacy, 1896–
1906.* BISHOP, *Roosevelt and his Time* (2 vols.). DUNNING, W. A., *The
British Empire and the United States.* SCHIEBER, C. E., *Transformation
of American Sentiment towards Germany, 1870–1914.*

ROBERTSON, WILLIAM S., *Rise of the Spanish-American Republics* and
History of the Latin-American Nations; RIPPY, J. F., *Latin America in
World Politics*; SWEET, W. W., *A History of Latin America.* JAMES, H.
G., and MARTIN, P. A., *The Republics of Latin America*; GIBBONS, H. A.,
The New Map of South America. MARSH, M. A., *The Bankers in Bolivia*,
one of the Studies in American Imperialism edited by H. E. BARNES,
illustrating the advance of American business enterprise. HILL, H. C.,
Roosevelt and the Caribbean; USHER, R. G., *Pan-Americanism*; INMAN,
S. G., *Problems in Pan-Americanism.* GRUENING, E., *Mexico and its
Heritage.* DENNETT, T., *Americans in Eastern Asia* and *Roosevelt and
the Russo-Japanese War.* ROOSEVELT, N., *The Restless Pacific* (crucial
world issues now in the Pacific).

CHAPTER VIII. THE AWAKENING OF THE FAR EAST

GOWEN, H., *Asia: a Short History* (to 1927), one of the best brief
histories; TREAT, P. J., *The Far East*; DOUGLAS, R., *Europe and the Far
East.* GILES, *China and the Chinese.* WILLOUGHBY, W. W., *Foreign Rights
and Interests in China.* VLADMIR, *The China-Japan War.* UYEHARA, G.,
Political Development of Japan (to 1912). LATOURETTE, K. S., *Develop-
ment of Japan*; HERSHEY, A. and S., *Modern Japan*, excellent for eco-
nomic conditions. ASAKAWA, *The Russo-Japanese Conflict.* DENNETT, T.,
Americans in Eastern Asia and *Roosevelt and the Russo-Japanese War.*
CLEMENTS, P. H., *The Boxer Rebellion* (Columbia University Studies).
VINACKE, H. M., *History of the Far East in Modern Times*, mainly the
period after 1860, with excellent bibliographies for each topic; HORN-
BECK, S. K., *Contemporary Politics in the Far East* (1916; especially for
Manchuria). WEALE, B. L. P., *Fight for the Republic in China.* MILLARD,
T., *The Conflict of Policies in Asia.* MALLORY, W. H., *China, Land of
Famine.* McLAREN, W. W., *Political History of Japan.*

CHAPTER IX. ORIGINS OF THE WORLD WAR

The literature on the origins of the world war, in many languages, is enormous and is growing daily. A general bibliography of official documents and works is to be found in BARNES, H. E., *Genesis of the World War*. A continuing bibliography appears in *Foreign Affairs*, a quarterly journal published in New York. For a general background : GOOCH, G. P., *History of Modern Europe, 1878–1919*; *Franco-German Relations, 1871–1914*; and (with WARD, A. W.) *Cambridge History of British Foreign Policy* (3 vols.). BAKELESS, J., *Economic Causes of Modern Wars*. ONCKEN, H., *Napoleon III and the Rhine*. MOWAT, R. B., *A History of European Diplomacy, 1815–1914*. For a more extensive list of works see MOON, P. T., *Syllabus on International Relations*, Part Five.

For the origins of the war, FAY, S. B., *The Origins of the World War* (2 vols.), the standard, scholarly work. For a temperate German view, MONTGELAS, *The Case for the Central Powers*. GOOCH, G. P., *Recent Revelations on European Diplomacy*, a fair English survey. FABRE-LUCE, ALFRED, *The Limitations of Victory*, a moderate French review. RENOUVIN, P., *The Immediate Origins of the War*, judicial but not without sympathy for the official French view. BARNES, H. E., *Genesis of the World War* (2d ed.), a survey of the materials, with conclusions placing the main responsibility on Austria, Russia, and France.

Among the works by participating statesmen the following are of special value: VISCOUNT GREY, *Twenty-five Years* (2 vols.) ; ASQUITH, H. H., *Genesis of the War*; CHURCHILL, W. S., *The World Crisis* (2 vols.) ; POINCARÉ, R., *Origins of the War*; SEYMOUR, CHARLES (Ed.), *The Intimate Papers of Colonel House* (4 vols.) ; BAKER, R. S., *Woodrow Wilson, Life and Letters*; HENDRICK, B. J., *Life and Letters of W. H. Page* (3 vols.) ; ARTHUR, G., *Memoirs of Raymond Poincaré* (2 vols.) ; SAZONOV, S., *Fateful Years*.

SCHEVILL, F., *A History of the Balkan Peninsula*. SCOTT, J. F., *Five Weeks*, a study of the press on the eve of the war. PLAYNE, C. E., *The Pre-war Mind in Britain*. FULLERTON, W. M., *Problems of Power* (1913), an ingenious argument for the alignment of the Entente against Germany.

CHAPTERS X AND XI. THE WORLD WAR

Foreign Affairs and *The American Historical Review* publish quarterly surveys of the literature on the World War, which is already immense. A valuable introduction to the subject is to be found in *These Eventful Years* (2 vols.), published by the *Encyclopædia Britannica* in 1924. Various aspects, civil and military, are discussed by competent authorities. POLLARD, A. F., *Short History of the Great War*; HAYES, C. J. H., *A Brief History of the Great War*; FAYLE, C. E., *History of the Great War*; SIMONDS, F. H., *History of the World War* (5 vols.); EDMONDS, J. E., *History of the Great War*; JOHNSON, D. W., *Topography and Strategy in the Great War*. POTTER, P. B., *The Freedom of the Seas*. GRAHAME-WHITE and HARPER, *Aircraft in the Great War*. GIBSON, C. R., *War Inventions and How they were Invented*. For American participation: BASSETT, J. S., *Our War with Germany*, and McMASTER, J. B., *The United States in the World War*; SEYMOUR, CHARLES (Ed.), *The Intimate Papers of Colonel House* (4 vols.), a mine of information; HENDRICK, B. J., *Life and Letters of Walter Hines Page*; BAKER, R. S., *Woodrow Wilson, Life and Letters*.

For propaganda aspects: RUSSELL, BERTRAND, *Free Thought and Official Propaganda*; GIBBS, PHILIP, *More that Must Be Told*, an expression of the brilliant journalist's honest opinions after the war; JOHNSON, T. M., *Without Censor*, war news as it might have been; PONSONBY, A., *Falsehood in War-Time*, a collection of lies circulated during the war; LASSWELL, H. D., *Propaganda Technique in the World War*; COOK, E. T., *The Press in War-Time*; CREEL, GEORGE, *How we advertised America*; STUART, C., *Secrets of Crewe House*, on British propaganda; ANGELL, N., *The Public Mind*; LOWELL, A. L., *Public Opinion in War and Peace*; MARTIN, E. D., *The Behavior of Crowds*.

CHAPTER XII. A PERTURBING PEACE

The settlement at Paris: TEMPERLEY, H. W. V., *History of the Peace Conference* (British view in 6 vols.); *The Treaties of Peace, 1919–1923* (Carnegie Endowment); BARUCH, B., *The Making of the Reparation and Economic Sections of the Treaty*; SEYMOUR (Ed.), *Intimate Papers of Colonel House* (Vols. III and IV); BAKER, R. S., *Woodrow Wilson and World Settlement* (3 vols.); MILLER, D. H., *The Drafting of the Covenant*, inside history of the formation of the League of Nations; THOMPSON, C. T., *The Peace Conference Day by Day*, a lively account by a journalist; BOWMAN, I., *The New World* (4th ed., with 257 maps), valuable for territorial and economic settlement; BEER, G. L., *African Questions at the Peace Conference*; KEYNES, J. M., *Economic Consequences of the Peace* and *A Revision of the Treaty*, highly critical but informed.

Europe after the war: VANDERLIP, F., *What Next in Europe?* BOUTON, S. M., *And the Kaiser Abdicates*; NITTI, F. S., *The Decadence of Europe* and *Peaceless Europe*; BEARD, C. A., *Cross Currents in Europe Today*.

CHAPTER XIII. CHIEF FACTORS IN RECONSTRUCTION

For progress of socialism: McBAIN and ROGERS, *The New Constitutions of Europe*; *The Labour International Handbook* (British); and *The American Labor Yearbook*. LORWIN, L. L., *Labor and Internationalism*; RUSSELL, BERTRAND, *Prospects of an Industrial Civilization* and *Proposed Roads to Freedom*. TAWNEY, R. H., *The Acquisitive Society* and *Religion and the Rise of Capitalism*. HOBSON, J. A., *Democracy after the War* and *Problems of a New World*. WEBB, SIDNEY, and WEBB, BEATRICE, *A Constitution for the Socialistic Commonwealth of Great Britain*, together with their *Decay of Capitalistic Civilization*. MACDONALD, RAMSAY, *Socialism, Critical and Constructive*. BUELL, R. L., *Europe: a History of Ten Years* (1918–1928). BURNS, C. D., *A Short History of the World, 1918–1928*. BEARD, C. A., *Cross Currents in Europe Today*.

CHAPTER XIV. DEMOCRACY IN CENTRAL AND WESTERN EUROPE

HEADLAM-MORLEY, A., *The New Democratic Constitutions of Europe*. BRUNET, R., *The New German Constitution*. DANIELS, H. G., *The Rise of the German Republic*. DANTON, G. H., *Germany Ten Years After*. JAECHK, E., *The New Germany*. GUILLEBAUD, C. W., *The Works Council: a German Experiment in Industrial Democracy*, a study of labor control in industry. GRAHAM, M. W., *New Governments of Central Europe*. FOX, F., *Finland Today* (1926). OZOLIN, I. A., *Latvia in the Making*. KOROSTOWETZ, W. K., *The Rebirth of Poland*. GRUBER, J., *Czechoslovakia*. PHILLIPS, C., *New Poland*. RUTTER, O., *The New Baltic States and their Future*.

France: BUELL, R. L., *Contemporary French Politics* (1921); HUDDLESTON, S., *France* (1927); SAIT, E. M., *Government and Politics in France*.

Great Britain and her empire: HALL, W. P., *Empire to Commonwealth*, thirty years of British imperial history; NATHAN, M., *Empire Government* (British Commonwealth of Nations in 1928); CROSS, A. L., *A Short History of England and Great Britain* (edition of 1929); OGG, F. A., *English Government and Politics* (1929). MEECH, T. C., *History of Great Britain and Ireland*; GWYNN, D., *The Irish Free State* (1922 to 1927); O'CONNOR, J., *History of Ireland, 1789–1924*. TAWNEY, R. H., *The British Labour Movement*; WERTHEIMER, E., *Portrait of the Labour Party*, a vivid picture by an able German writer.

CHAPTER XV. STARTLING EXPERIMENTS IN GOVERNMENT

Russia: MARCU, V., *Lenin: Thirty Years of Russia*, an impressionist biography; MAVOR, J., *The Russian Revolution*, scholarly and critical; EASTMAN, MAX, *Marx and Lenin, The Science of Revolution*, a very interesting study of Marxian dialectic; NEARING, SCOTT, *Glimpses of the Soviet Republic*, favorable; PASCAL, P. (Ed.), *Selections from Lenin* (4 vols.); RUSSELL, BERTRAND, *Bolshevism: Practice and Theory*; PASVOLSKY, The *Economics of Communism*, for early phases; FARBMAN, M., *After Lenin*; WICKSTEED, *Life under the Soviets* (1928); DODD and STEVENS, *Russian Economic Development since the Revolution* (1928); CHASE, DUNN, and TUGWELL, *Soviet Russia in the Second Decade*; ZIMAND, S., *State Capitalism in Russia*; TROTSKY, L., *The Real Situation in Russia*, critical, by a former revolutionary leader.

Italian Fascism: SCHNEIDER, H., *Making the Fascist State* (1928), an excellent historical review and analysis of doctrines by an impartial scholar; *Mussolini as Revealed in his Speeches* (1924); VILLARI, L., *The Awakening of Italy*, the Fascist regeneration; GORGOLINI, P., *Fascist Movement in Italian Life*, favorable, by a Fascist "intellectual"; MUSSOLINI, *My Diary, 1915–1917*; SARFATTI, M., *Life of Benito Mussolini*, favorable.

Critical works: NITTI, F. S., *Bolshevism, Fascism, and Democracy*; SALVEMINI, G., *The Fascist Dictatorship in Italy*; STURZO, DON, *Italy and Fascism*, by a leader of the Catholic opposition.

Southeastern Europe: ARMSTRONG, H. F., *The New Balkans*; BEARD and RADIN, *The Balkan Pivot: Yugoslavia*; MILLER, W. R., *Greece*, recent developments to 1928.

CHAPTER XVI. INFLUENCE OF WESTERN IDEAS IN AFRICA AND ASIA

Africa: BUELL, R. L., *The Native Problem in Africa* (2 vols.), an indispensable work of present-day Africa; ELGOOD, F. G., *The Transit of Egypt*.

MILLER, W., *The Ottoman Empire and its Successors, 1801–1927*; ZWEMER, S. M., *Across the World of Islam*, the Moslem awakening.

GANDHI, M., *Young India, 1920–1926*; KRISHNA DAS, *Seven Months with Mahatma Gandhi*, a study of his teachings, by a disciple; ZIMAND, S., *Living India*, a good general survey; MAYO, K., *Mother India*, a severe indictment of conditions in India.

HARRIS, N. D., *Europe and the East* (to 1926), with bibliographies. VINACKE, H., *History of the Far East in Modern Times*. WHYTE, F.,

China and the Foreign Powers. MILLARD, T. F., *China: Where it is To-day*, especially the events of 1925–1927. NEARING, SCOTT, *Whither China* (from the socialist point of view; well informed). LATOURETTE, K. S., *Development of China* (1929). WEALE, B. L. P., *Why China Sees Red.* BROWN, A. J., *Japan in the World Today.* ALLEN, G. C., *Modern Japan and its Problems.* McGOVERN, W. M., *Modern Japan.* TSURUMI, Y., *Present-Day Japan* (1926). LATOURETTE, K. S., *The Development of Japan.*

CHAPTER XVII. QUEST FOR INTERNATIONAL PEACE AND UNDERSTANDING

Reparations: BERGMANN, *History of Reparations* (1925); MOUTON and McGUIRE, *Germany's Capacity to Pay*; DAWES, R. C., *The Dawes Plan in the Making*; SERING, MAX, *Germany under the Dawes Plan.*

League of Nations: BASSETT, J. S., *The League of Nations* (1928), by an impartial American scholar; MYERS, DENYS, *Nine Years of the League of Nations*; BAKER, P., *League of Nations at Work.*

The World Court: HUDSON, M. O., *The World Court, 1922–1928* (World Peace Foundation).

Plans for outlawing war: FABRE LUCE, A., *Locarno: the Reality*; MILLER, D. H., *The Geneva Protocol*, chapter in history of armaments reduction; BOECKEL, F. B., *Between War and Peace*, a general handbook on the peace movement; BUELL, R. L., *The Washington Conference*; ICHIHASHI, Y., *The Washington Conference and After*; ALEXANDER, F., *From Paris to Locarno and After*, a review of security efforts; NORTON, H. K., *Back of War*, a study of "danger spots" making for war; SHOTWELL, J. T., *War as an Instrument of National Policy*, especially the Kellogg Peace Pact, with an important introduction on the nature and uses of war; STEPHENS, J. S., *Danger Zones of Europe: a Study of National Minorities*; MOWATT, R. B., *A History of European Diplomacy, 1914–1925.*

American policy: MOUTON and PASVOLSKY, *War Debt Settlements*; SCHUMAN, F. L., *American Policy toward Russia*, a review of ten years; CARTER, J., *America's Painless Imperialism*; GIBBONS, H. A., *America's Place in the World*; FOX, F., *The Mastery of the Pacific* (Anglo-American rivalry); for a brief annual review of foreign relations see The American Year Book (Division II).

CHAPTER XVIII. NEW CONCEPTIONS OF THE WORLD WE LIVE IN

The Nature of the World and of Man (by various specialists) (University of Chicago Press), clear and excellent; WHETHAM, W. C. D., and WHETHAM, C. D., *Science and the Human Mind*; VEBLEN, THORSTEIN, *The Instinct of Workmanship*; BROWNELL, BAKER, *The New Universe*; SHAPLEY, HARLOW, *Starlight*, giving modern conception of the universe; LOCY, WILLIAM A., *Biology and its Makers*, excellently illustrated; BAZZONI, *Kernels of the Universe*; JEANS, *The Universe Around Us*; EDDINGTON, A. S., *The Nature of the Physical World*; LULL, R. S., *The Ways of Life*; DE KRUIF, PAUL, *Microbe Hunters*, popular in style; SLOSSON, *Creative Chemistry*, very interesting; CALDWELL and SLOSSON, *Science Remaking the World*; MARVIN (Ed.), *Progress and History* and *Recent Developments in European Thought*.

CHAPTER XIX. NEW VIEWS OF MAN'S NATURE AND TRADITIONS

BARNES, HARRY E., *History and Social Intelligence*; ROBINSON, JAMES H., *The New History* and *The Mind in the Making*; HART, JOSEPH K., *The Discovery of Intelligence*; BRIFFAULT, ROBERT, *The Making of Mankind*.

The Evolution of Man (Yale University Press), by various specialists; BOAS, F., *The Mind of Primitive Man*, excellent; SUMNER, W. G., *Folkways*; TYLOR, E. B., *Primitive Culture*; GOLDENWEISER, A. A., *Early Civilization, an Introduction to Anthropology*; OGBURN, W. F., *Social Change with Respect to Culture and Original Nature*; HAYES, C. J. H., *Essays on Nationalism*; THOMAS, WILLIAM I., *Source Book for Social Origins*.

TROTTER, WILLIAM, *Instinct of the Herd* (first two chapters); DEWEY, JOHN, *Human Nature and Conduct* and *Reconstruction in Philosophy* and *The Quest for Certainty*; LAY, *Man's Unconscious Conflict*; LEARY, DANIEL, B., *Modern Psychology, Normal and Abnormal*; WATSON, JOHN, *The Ways of Behaviorism*; WOODWORTH, R. S., *Dynamic Psychology*; HERRICK, C. JUDSON, *The Thinking Machine*.

The History of Christianity in the Light of Modern Knowledge, a collective work; BARNES, HARRY E., *The Twilight of Christianity*; McGIFFERT, ARTHUR, *The Rise of Modern Religious Ideas*; GUIGNEBERT, *Christianity, Past and Present*; LOWIE, R. H., *Primitive Religion*; CARPENTER, EDWARD, *Pagan and Christian Creeds*.

THOMAS, WILLIAM I., and THOMAS, D. S., *The Child in America*; RUSSELL, BERTRAND, *Education and the Good Life*; DEWEY, JOHN, and

T

DEWEY, EVELYN, *New Schools for Old*; HOBSON, J. A., *Free-Thought in the Social Sciences*. VEBLEN, THORSTEIN, *The Higher Learning in America*. JOHNSON, MARIETTA, *Youth in a World of Men*.

CHAPTER XX. THE STUDY OF MANKIND IN FICTION

The aim of this chapter is to show that literature is essential in following man's gradual understanding of himself. There are a great number of histories of literature; a few titles are given to help the reader to bring stories and dramas into relation with the other forms of human interest.

TAINE, H. A., *History of English Literature*, by a distinguished French philosopher and historian; BEERS, HENRY A., *A History of English Romanticism in the Eighteenth Century* and *A History of English Romanticism in the Nineteenth Century*; WARD, ALFRED C., *Twentieth Century Literature*, a delightful little book; THORNDIKE, ASHLEY, *Literature in a Changing Age*; CUNLIFFE, J. W., *English Literature during the Last Half-century*; CASAMIAN, LOUIS, *A History of English Literature, Modern Times (1660–1914)*; MAUROIS, ANDRÉ, *Aspects of Biography*, an ingenious short work; CROSS, WILBUR L., *Development of the English Novel*.

CURRENT HISTORY

The Statesman's Year-Book (British) is published annually. It contains a brief description of the governments of the world, and statistical information with respect to economic, religious, and social life. DAVIS and MALLORY's *Political Handbook of the World* (annual) is useful for parliaments, parties, and press. *Current History*, published by the New York Times Company, gives a monthly survey of world affairs, besides important articles and documents. *International Conciliation*, published monthly by the Carnegie Endowment for International Peace, gives the important documents in international relations and contains articles on the subject by competent authorities. *The Historical Outlook* (formerly the *History Teachers' Magazine*) (Philadelphia) contains current bibliographies for keeping up to date. Still more extensive bibliographies, with critical comment, are to be found in *Foreign Affairs*, published quarterly in New York City. Useful critical sidelights are furnished by *The Nation* (New York) and *The New Republic* (New York).

For special regions (in English): *The China Year Book* (Woodhead, editor); *The Japan Year-Book*; *The Near East Year Book*.

Survey of International Affairs, an annual publication by the British Institute of International Affairs. *The Annual Register* (British), an annual world review with documents and papers.

INDEX

Aaland Islands, 456
Abdul Hamid, Sultan of Turkey, 305
Abdullah Ibn Hussein, 521
Abyssinia, 157 f., 506
Adalia, 338
Adams, Henry, 246
Adams, John, 36
Adelaide, 194
Aden, 517
Adrianople, captured by Bulgarians (1912), 307; recovered by Turks (1913), 308
Afghanistan, 182 n., 185, 525 f.
Africa, 150, 164, 168, 507 f.; exploration and partition of, 151 ff., 162 ff., 402, 504 ff.
African Association, international, 168 f.
Agadir, 290 f.
Aggression and aggressor (in war), 551 f., 565 f.
Agrarian revolutions, 438 ff., 457, 478 f.
Ahmed Zogu, 503
Airships, 372, 520; in World War, 326 ff., 340, 358
Alabama claims, 240
Alaska, 228, 240
Albania, 305 f., 307 ff., 334, 503
Albert Nyanza, Lake, 167
Alberta, 190
Alexander I of Greece, 502
Alexander I of Yugoslavia, 441, 499 f.
Alfonso XIII of Spain, 497
Algeciras Conference, 171, 238, 288, 290
Algeria, 151 f., 166
Allenby, General, 523
All-Russian Congress of Soviets, 422
Alsace, 278 ff., 293, 322, 349, 392, 409, 459 f.
Amanullah Khan, 526
American Board of Foreign Missions, 148
American Peace Society, 240
"American plan" for outlawing war, 551 f.
American Revolution, 2, 4, 241 f.
Amherst, Lord, 251
Amiens, 354, 381
Amoy, 253
Amritsar, 529
Anæsthetics, 600
Anam, 154 f.
Anarchism, 27 ff., 34
Anglican Church, 91, 93; in Ireland, 209 f., 216 ff.

Anglo-French Alliance. *See Entente Cordiale*
Anglo-French "conversations" (1912), 295 f., 319
Anglo-Japanese alliance (1902), 264, 293 f., 560
Anglo-Russian convention (1907), 161, 294, 338, 524 f.
Anglo-Russian naval understanding (1914), 294 f.
Angola, 506
Angora, 514, 516
Angra Pequena, 156
Animism, 619
Anthropology, 615 ff., 620 ff.
Antwerp, 348
Apuleius, 644
Arabi, 173
Arabia, 401, 517 ff.
Arabs, nationalist plans of, 338, 517
Arbitration, international, 239 f., 302, 373, 554 ff.; and League of Nations, 566
Arbitration, Permanent Court of, 302, 548 f.
Archæology, 612 f.
Areopagitica, by Milton, 631
Argonne forest, 383
Armaments, competition in, 296 ff., 310 f., 313 f., 373 f.; numerical table, 298. *See also* Hague conferences; Naval armaments; Washington Conference
Armenia, 398
Arras, 352
Ashley, Lord, 114, 126
Asquith, Herbert, 68 f., 220, 427
Associations Law, 100 f.
Associations for Public Worship, 103 f.
Astronomy, 581, 586
Atoms, 602 ff.
Auckland, 195
Augustine, St., 584, 627, 639
Austen, Jane, 647
Australasia, 191 ff.
Australia, 191 ff., 351; in World War, 355
Australian ballot, 196
Austria, 5, 73; constitution of, 67; relations with Serbia, 306 ff., 311 f.; dissolution of, 392 ff.; republic of, 414, 452 f. *See also* Hungary; World War
Azerbaijan, 398
Azores, 366

Bacon, Francis, 15, 580 f., 660
Bacteria, 598 ff.
Bagdad, railway to, 310, 333, 351, 518;
  in World War, 352, 371; airplane serv-
  ice, 520
Bakunin, 28, 110
Baldwin, Stanley, 461 ff.
Balearic Islands, 160
Balfour, Arthur, 219, 522 ff.
Balfour Declaration, 522 ff.
Balkan states, conditions in the, 282 ff.;
  wars in, 304 ff.; relations with Aus-
  tria, Germany, and Russia, 304, 307,
  309 f.
Baltic states, 396, 456 f.
Baluchistan, 182 n.
Banat of Temesvár, the, 335, 441
Bank for International Settlements,
  544 ff.
Banquet of Trimalchio, The, by Petro-
  nius, 644
Baptists, 148, 218
Barnes, Harry Elmer, 311
Baruch, Bernard, 404
Bavaria, 387, 449
Bazzoni, 604
Beaconsfield, Earl of, 133, 204, 229 f.
Beccaria, 582
Bechuanaland, 167, 202
Behavior, animal and human, 625 f.
Beirut, 384
Bela Kun, 498
Belgian Congo, 168 ff., 506
Belgium, neutrality of, violated by Ger-
  man invasion, 314, 320, 322; in World
  War, 324, 348 f., 371, 376, 380; con-
  stitution, 447 f.
Benedict XV, Pope, 377
Benes, Edward, 457
Bennett, Arnold, 643, 657 f.
Benoist, Charles, 62
Berchtold, Count, 313
Berlin Conference (1884–1885), 169
Berlin, Congress of (1878), 304
Bessarabia, 335, 400 f.
Bethmann-Hollweg, Theobald von, 313
Biochemistry, 607
Biology, 594 ff.
Bishop, J. B., 238
Bismarck, 5, 9, 47, 49, 61, 70 f., 96 ff.,
  123 f., 129 ff., 146, 155 f., 297
"Black and Tans," 466
Black Hundreds, 82 ff.
Blockade in the World War, 356 ff.,
  364 ff.
Boer War (1899–1902), 201 f.
Boers, 166, 196 ff., 355 f.
Bohemia, 308, 371, 399
Bokhara, 160
Bolivia, 567 ff.
Bolsheviki, 369 f., 396, 398, 431, 471 ff.,
  525 n., 532, 534 f.
Bonapartists, 40, 43

Booth, Charles, 116 f.
Borah, William E., 559, 564
Bosnia, 52, 283 f., 290, 304, 306, 309 f.,
  371, 400, 440
Botany Bay, 193
Botha, General, 202
Boulanger, General, 43 f.
Bourbon, House of, 40, 43, 65
Bourgeoisie, 3, 7 f., 29 f., 135
Boxer rebellion, 228, 266 ff., 288 f.
Brazil, 226 f., 379
Brest-Litovsk, 339 f., 370 f., 376, 385,
  396
Briand, Aristide, 104, 556, 568 f.
Briffault, Robert, 642
Bright, John, 58 f., 115, 117, 128, 218,
  245
British Central Africa, 203
British Columbia, 190
British Empire, 166, 175 ff., 196 ff., 506,
  512 ff.; imperial federation in, 203 ff.,
  468 ff.
British Empire League, 206
British South Africa Company, 200 and
  note
Brontë, 647 f.
Brook Farm Colony, 23
Bryan, William Jennings, 241, 360
Bucharest, 355, 498
Bucharest, treaties of, 308, 339
Buffon, 587
Bukowina, 335, 371, 400
Bulgaria, 66, 304 ff., 334 f., 350, 371,
  384, 402, 501
Bülow, von, 238, 323
Bundesrat, German, 46 ff., 374, 420
Burke, Thomas, 220
Burma, 181
Business. See Capitalism, Investments

Cabinet system, 54 ff., 417 f.
Cable, Atlantic, 145
Cables, German, 406 f.
Calais, 348, 381
Caliphate abolished, 516
Calvin, 639 f.
Cambodia, 154
Cambrai, 380
Cameron, Lieutenant, 167
Cameroons, 356, 402, 505
Campbell, General Colin, 184
Campbell, Thomas, 478
Campbell case, 462 f.
Canada, constitutional acts (1774, 1791,
  1839, 1867), 187 ff.; rebellion under
  Mackenzie and Papineau (1837–1838),
  188 f.; relation to Great Britain, 191,
  207 f.
Canary Islands, 160
Canterbury Tales, 636
Canton, 250 ff., 532 f.
Cape Colony, 165 f., 196, 201
Cape-to-Cairo railway, 144, 202 f., 508

Cape Town, 201
Cape Verde Islands, 164, 366
Capitalism, 10 ff., 17 f., 29 f., 135 f.,
    145 ff., 224 f., 228 ff., 289, 434 f., 471,
    476
"Capitulations" (Turkey), 402, 516
Carbon, 606 f.
Carey, William, 148
Carl, Prince, of Denmark. See Haakon
    VII
Carlyle, Thomas, 20 f., 113, 243, 245, 553
Carnegie, Andrew, 549
Carnegie Endowment for International
    Peace, 575
Carniola, 400
Caroline Islands, 160, 288
Casablanca, 171
Castro, Cipriano, 234 f.
Catholic Emancipation Act, 92, 214 f.
Catholics, in England, 91 ff.; in Ger-
    many, 95 ff.; in Ireland, 209 ff.
Cavendish, Lord Frederick, 220
Cawnpore, 184
Cecil, Lord Robert, 118 f.
Censorship. See Press censorship
Central America, 229, 231
Ceylon, 177
Chamberlain, Joseph, 131, 205, 207
Chambers, Robert, 588, 593
Chambord, count of, 43
Chang Tso-lin, Marshal, 534
Charles I of Austria, 385, 498, 558
"Charter of Labor," 492
Château-Thierry, 382
Chaucer, Geoffrey, 636
Chemistry, 9 f., 330 f., 581, 602 ff.
Chiang K'ai-shek, General, 533 f.
Ch'ien Lung, Emperor, 255
Child Labor, 111 ff.
Childhood, importance of, 624 f., 627 f.
Chile, 380
China, 251 f.; relations with the United
    States, 227; with Europe, 248 ff.; re-
    lations with Russia, 262 ff., 281, 534 f.;
    anti-foreign movements, 266 ff., 289,
    533 f.; Republic of, 271 ff.; relations
    with Japan, 339, 371, 402, 537; and
    World War, 379; and Treaty of Ver-
    sailles, 402; revolutions in, 532 ff. See
    also Korea, Manchuria
Chosen. See Korea
Chromosomes, 596 f.
Chronology, historical, 614 f.
Church, and State, 36, 88 ff., 93 f.,
    443 ff.; in France, 98 ff., 460; in Italy,
    105, 495 f. See also Anglican Church;
    Clergy; Greek Church; Missions, for-
    eign; Pope
Churchill, Winston, 117, 121 f.
Cicero, 580 f.
City of God, The, Augustine's, 584, 627
Civilization, historical background of
    modern European, 1 ff., 578; diffusion

of western European, 149 ff., 660; re-
    lation of American to European, 222 f.
Clapham, J. H., 125
Clayton-Bulwer Treaty, 229 f.
Clemenceau, 390 f.
Clergy, position of, 89 f.; in Germany,
    98 f.; in France, 98 ff. See also Church
Clermont, the, 138
Cleveland, Grover, 233, 240
Coal-tar products, 606
Cobden, Richard, 58 f., 117, 128
Cochin-China, 151, 155
Colombia, 141
Combes, 102
Commerce, development of world, 135 f.;
    of Great Britain, 175 f.; early Amer-
    ican, 224 f.; of Latin America, 230;
    of Germany, 285 f.; after the War,
    413 f., 463 f.
Committee of Union and Progress, Turk-
    ish, 305
Communism, 431 f.; in Russia, 396, 398,
    425, 431 f.; in Germany, 449 f.; in
    France, 458; in Italy, 483; in Hun-
    gary, 498; in Bulgaria, 501; in China,
    533. See also Bolsheviki
Communist Manifesto, 26, 110, 431
Concessions in undeveloped countries,
    134, 228
Concordat of 1801, 101 ff.
Condorcet, 15, 241
Confucius, 268
Congo, French, 153; Belgian, 168 ff.,
    506; portion of French, ceded to Ger-
    many, 171, 290
Congo Free State, 168 ff.
Congregatio de Propaganda Fide, 147 f.
Conscription, adoption of, 207, 296 ff.,
    311, 354, 367
Constantine I of Greece, 336 f., 502
Constantinople, 281, 307 f., 310, 333,
    338, 351, 401, 514, 516
Constitutional Democrats in Russia, 77,
    84
Constitutions, post-war, of Europe, 415 ff.
Cook, Captain James, 193
Coolidge, Calvin, 549 f.
Copeland, Dr. Morris A., 432 n.
Corfu, 335, 350, 496
Corn Laws, 128
Cornwallis, Lord, 214
Corridor, Polish, 392, 455
Cortes, Spanish, 7
Crete annexed to Greece, 307 f.
Crimean War, 4 f., 281
Croatia, 310, 371, 399, 440 f., 500 f.
Cromwell, Oliver, 210 f.
Cross, Wilbur, 644
Cuba, 159 f., 229, 234, 243 f., 379, 561
Culebra, 160
Cunard Line, 138
Cunningham, William, 224
Curie, Marie, 603

Curie, Pierre, 603
Currency, in Germany, 50; inflation of European, after the War, 413, 451, 453
Curtis, George William, 23
Cushing, Caleb, 253
Cyprus, 333
Cyrenaica, 158
Czechoslovakia, republic of, 385, 395, 399, 417 f., 442, 457

Dahomey, 153 n.
Dail Eireann, 466
Dairen (Dalny), 269, 281
Dalhousie, Lord, 182
Dalmatia, 351, 371, 399, 485
Dalton, John, 602
Damascus, 384
Dana, Charles A., 23
Danzig, free city of, 392, 455
Dardanelles, 281 f., 351, 401
Darkest Africa, by Stanley, 168
Darwin, Charles, 33 f., 589 ff.
"Darwinism," 592, 594
Daudet, 628
Davy, Sir Humphry, 600
Dawes, Charles G., 541, 563
Dawes plan, 541 ff.
De Brazza, 153
Debts, European post-war, 412 f., 561 f.
Declaration of the Rights of Man (1789), 13 f., 36, 77
Defoe, Daniel, 640
Deists, 581, 640
Delcassé, 301 f.
Delhi, 184 f.
Democracy, 5 ff., 40 ff., 64 ff., 447 ff., 470, 504 ff.
Denmark, 53, 392, 447
Dennett, Tyler, 238
Dernburg, 55
Descartes, 580 f.
Deutschland, the, 362 n.
Dewey, George, 234
Dickens, Charles, 113, 628, 647 f.
Diderot, 2, 582, 587, 633
Dilke, Charles W., 204
Diplomacy, secret, 60, 237 f., 276, 294 ff., 332 ff., 338 f., 370, 374, 377, 427 f. See also London, secret treaty of
Discoveries, modern scientific, 578 f., 582 ff.
Disraeli, Benjamin. See Beaconsfield, Earl of
Dissenters, 91 ff.
Dobrudja, 402
Dodecanese islands, 159, 334, 496
Döllinger, J. J. I. von, 96
Dominicans, 100, 147
Dostoievsky, 659
Draft Treaty of Mutual Assistance, 551 f.
Drama, 659; English Restoration, 637 f.
Dreyfus, Alfred, 44 ff.
Drummond, Henry, 593

Du Bois, W. E. B., 509 ff.
Du Chaillu, 153
Ductless glands, 624
Duguit, Leon, 62
Duma, Russian, 52, 83 ff., 368
Durazzo, 307
Durban, 197
Durham, Lord, 189
Dutch, the, in Africa, 165. See also Boers
Dyer, General, 529

Earth, age of the, 584 ff.
East Africa, British, 203 n., 513 f.; German, 356; mandate over former German, 402, 505
East India Company, 184 f.
Ebert, Friedrich, 387, 429, 448, 451
Eddington, Professor, 604
Education, public, 88 f.; in France, 100 f.; in India, 186 and note; in China, 268; in Russia, 479 ff.; problems of, 628 ff. See also Universities
Edward VII, 64, 69, 238 f.
Egypt, Turkish conquest of, 163, 166, 171 ff.; British in, 173 f., 506 f.; independence of, established, 174, 507. See also Sudan
Einstein, 605
Eisner, Kurt, 449
Electricity, 6, 9 f.
Electrons, 604 f.
Eliot, George, 648
Elizabeth, Queen, 210, 640
Ellis, Havelock, 617
Embryology, 596 ff.
Emigration, European, to North and South America, 226 f., 231
Encyclopædia Britannica, 582 f.
Engels, Friedrich, 24, 431
English language, 579
English literature, 636 ff.
Entente Cordiale, the, 64, 295
Equality, doctrine of, 7 f., 28, 62 f.
Eritrea, 158, 506
Erzberger, Matthias, 450
Essay on Man, by Pope, 641 f.
Essex, Lord, 128
Estates General (1302), 7; (1789), 2 f.
Esterhazy, Major, 44
Eulenburg, Prince Philipp, 73
Eupen, 392
Evil, the problem of, in literature, 638 ff.
Evolution, theory of, 587 ff.; opponents of, 592 f., 631, 633

Fabian Society, 109
Fable of the Bees, The, by Mandeville, 640 f.
Factory system in England, 111 ff.
Faisal, Amir, 519 f.
Falkenhayn, General, 355
Far East, 248 ff., 371, 531 ff., 536 f.

Fascisti, 484, 486 ff.
"Fashoda incident," 153, 289
Fay, Sidney B., 319
Federation of states, modern, 469. *See also* British Empire
Fêng, General, 534
Fenians, 217, 220
Ferdinand of Bulgaria, 334 f.
Ferdinand of Rumania, 335, 400 f.
Ferghana, province of, 160
Feudalism, conquest of, by capitalism, 10 ff., 224
Fiction, study of mankind in, 634 ff.
Fielden, John, 112, 114
Fielding, Henry, 643 f.
Finland, 53, 76, 370, 383, 396, 456
Fisher, H. A. L., 65
Fitch, John, 138
Five-Power Treaty, 560
Foch, General Ferdinand, 280, 381, 384, 389
Ford, Henry, 247
Formosa, 262
Four-Power Treaty, 560
Fourier, Charles, 22 f., 26
Fourteen Points, 378 f., 386
France, revolutions of 1789, 1820, and 1848, 2 f., 7 f., 13, 38 f.; Third Republic, 40 ff., 51, 65, 67 f.; colonial expansion, 146, 151 ff., 153 n., 165 f., 171, 285, 288 f., 506, 509 ff.; alliance with Russia (1891), 280 f.; after the War, 458 ff.; treaty with Poland (1921), 555, 558. *See also* Church and State, World War
Francis Ferdinand, Archduke, 283, 311
Francis Joseph I, Emperor of Austria, 52, 73
Franco-Yugoslav Treaty (1927), 558
Frederick II (the Great) of Prussia, 4
Free trade, 17, 128 ff. *See also* Tariff
Freedom of the seas, 364 f. and note
Freedom of speech, 57 ff., 75 f., 428. *See also* Press, censorship of
French, Sir John, 331
Fuiton, Robert, 138

Galicia, 308, 350, 355
Gallipoli, 351
Galsworthy, John, 658
Gambetta, 43, 99
Gambia, 203 n.
Gapon, Father, 81
Garvin, J. L., 339 f.
Gas, poison, 325 f., 328, 331, 349, 352, 560
Geddes, Sir Eric, 404
Geddes, Patrick, 593
General Workingmen's Association, 106
Genes, 596
Geneva, 565 f., 573, 640
Geneva Protocol of 1924, 552
Geology, 586 f.

George II of Greece, 502
George V of Great Britain, 69, 462
Georgia, 398
Geraud, André, 445
Germ theory of disease, 598 ff.
Germany, army and navy, 30, 287 f., 297, 310, 375 f.; imperial constitution of, 46 ff., 54 f., 374; colonial expansion, 155 ff., 263 f., 286 f.; industrialization of, after 1870, 285 f.; republic of 1918, 387, 448 ff.; provisions of the Treaty of Versailles imposed on, 392, 405 ff., 413 f., 505; constitution of the Republic, 416, 418, 420 f.; monarchist *Putsch* and general strike (1920), 450. *See also* World War
Ghandi, 247, 528 ff.
Giolitti, 483
Gladstone, W. E., 9, 51, 64, 128, 199, 218, 220
Godwin, William, 27 f., 33
Gold Coast, 165, 203 n.
Golden Ass, The, by Apuleius, 644
Gompers, Samuel, 437
Gordon, General Charles, 174, 255
Gorky, Maxim, 82
Gosse, Edmund, 651
Grant, Ulysses, 140
Great Britain, revolutions in (1603–1688), 1; revolt of American colonies, 2, 4, 241 f.; social reforms in, 109, 111 ff.; relations with Ireland, 208 ff., 465 ff.; in the Far East, 251 ff., 264; Labor party government in, 461 ff., 465. *See also* British Empire, World War
Great Western, the, 138
Greece, war with Turkey (1897), 304 f.; war with Turkey (1912), 307; at war with Bulgaria (1912–1913), 307 f.; and World War, 335 ff., 379; republic of, 502 f.
Greek Church, in Russia, 76; disestablished, 472 f.
Grévy, Jules, 43, 99
Grey, Sir Edward, 294, 296, 312 ff., 316, 319 f., 427
Guam, 157
Guesde, Jules, 107
Guiana, British, 240
Guinea, French, 151, 153 n.; Portuguese, 166, 170 n.

Haakon VII of Norway, 65
Hague, peace conferences at the, 299 ff.; (1899), 302; (1907), 303, 325
Haiti, 230
Hamburg, 406
Hamilton, Alexander, 8, 242
Hankow, 265, 534
Harbin, 264
Hardenberg, 440
Hardie, Keir, 109

Harding, Warren G., 538, 549, 559 ff., 572
Harmsworth, Lord, 499
Harper, S. N., 473, 479
Hartmann, von, 610, 618 f.
Hauptmann, Gerhart, 658
Hawaiian Islands, 227 f.
Hay, John, 235
Hay-Pauncefote Treaty, 230, 235 n.
Hegel, 15 f., 25
Henry, Colonel, 44 f.
Henry, Prince, of Prussia, 266
Heredity, 587, 596 ff., 621 f.
Herriot, Edward, 458
Herzegovina, 52, 283 f., 290, 304, 306, 400, 440
Hill, Rowland, 144
Hindenburg, General von, 324, 348, 350, 355, 381, 386, 452
"Hindenburg" line, 380, 382
Hirohito, Emperor, 536
History, Hegel's interpretation of, 15 f.; developmental method of, 610 ff.
Hohenlohe-Schillingsfürst, Prince Chlodwig zu, 72
Hohenzollern, House of, 39, 387
"Holy Places," the, 338
Home Rule. See Ireland
Hong Kong, 253
Hoover, Herbert, 465
Hormones, 624 f.
Horthy, Nicholas, 498
Hötzendorf, Conrad von, 313
Houghton, Alanson B., 275 f.
House, Colonel E. M., 410 f.
House of Lords, 66 ff., 120, 122. See also Parliament, British
Housman, A. E., 205 f., 646
Hsien Fêng, Emperor, 253 ff., 255
Hudson's Bay Company, 190
Hughes, Charles E., 541, 549 f., 561, 572 f.
Hughes, W. M., 404
Hull, Jonathan, 138
Hung, 255
Hungary, in 1914, 73, 440; republic of, 385, 498 f.; communist revolution and restoration of monarchy, 416, 498 f.; treaty with Italy (1927), 559. See also Austria, World War
Husein, Sherif, 519
Hutton, James, 586
Hyderabad, 177

Ibn Saud, king of Hejaz, 519, 521
Ibsen, Henrik, 635, 649 ff.
Imperial conferences of British Empire, 207, 468 f.
Imperial Federation League, 206
Imperialism, 133 ff., 146 f., 150 f., 285 ff.
"Index of Prohibited Books," 460
India, British conquest and annexation in, 177 ff.; sepoy rebellion in, 183 f.; constitution of empire under British crown, 185 f.; nationalist movement in, 187, 526 ff.; in World War, 379; and Government of India Act (1919), 529; native states, 530
Indo-China, French, 155
Industrial Revolution. See Technological Revolution
Industrial Workers of the World, 434
Initiative and referendum, 421, 447
Institute of Pacific Relations, 538 f.
Institute of Politics, Williamstown, 575
Insurance Act, National (British), 122
International, First, 29, 110; Second, 110, 435 ff.; Third, 398, 436 f.
International Bank. See Bank for International Settlements
International conferences, promotion of, by League of Nations, 571
International Justice, Permanent Court of, 547 ff., 563, 565
International Labor Organization, 567
Invention, modern, 6, 9 f., 578 f., 582 ff.
Investments, foreign, 228, 230, 562 f.
Irak, 517 ff.
Ireland, relations with England, 208 ff.; land acts, 218 f.; demand for Home Rule, 219 ff., 465 f.; and World War, 221, 465 f.; creation of the Irish Free State, 466; "Government of Northern Ireland," 467; position of, in British Empire, 468 f.
Irkutsk, 263
Irredentism, Italian, 371, 484 ff.
Islands, former German, 339, 355, 371, 402, 531
Ismail I of Egypt, 172 f.
Italy, Kingdom of, 5; colonial expansion, 146, 157 f.; war with Turkey (1911–1912), 158, 306 f.; and World War, 315, 333 f., 351, 354 f.; dictatorship of Mussolini, 487 ff.; government reorganization of 1928, 493; diplomatic alliances with Hungary, Bulgaria, and Great Britain, 559
Izvolsky, A. P., 281

Jackson, Andrew, 242
"Jameson raid," 200
Janus, by Döllinger, 96
Japan, opening of, to Western trade, 227, 258 f.; adoption of Western civilization by, 248, 260 f.; early European missions in, 256 ff.; war with China (1894–1895), 262; in alliance with Great Britain, 264, 293 f., 560; at war with Russia (1904–1905), 268 ff.; in World War, 332 f., 339, 355, 383; development of commerce and industries, 535 f. See also Russo-Japanese War
Japanese-Anglo-American Understanding, 237 f., 294
Japanese language, 256 n.

Jay Treaty (1794), 239 f.
Jefferson, Thomas, 2, 7, 242
Jenner, Edward, 600
Jerusalem, "Holy Places" in, 338; in World War, 352, 371, 384; under British mandate, 523 f.
Jesuits, 96 f., 99 f., 147, 257 f.
Jews, massacres of, in Russia, 76, 84 f.; national home for, in Palestine, 521 ff.
Joffre, General, 310, 323
Johnson, Sir Harry, 168–169 n.
Junkers, 72 f., 375
Jutland, battle of, 358

Kaiser of Germany, powers of, 46 f., 374 f.; treaty provision for trial of, 408, 540
Kaiser Wilhelm's Land, 157
K'ang Hsi, Emperor, 254 f.
Kapital, Das ("Capital"), by Marx, 25 f.
Karageorgevitch, House of, 54
Karolyi, Count Michael, 498
Kellogg Peace Pact. See Pact of Paris
Kenya, 513
Kerensky, Alexander, 369
Khartum, 174
Khiva, Khan of, 160
Khokand, 160
Kiaochow, 263 f., 332, 355
Kimberley, 201
King of England, 64. See also Monarchy
Kipling, Rudyard, 205
Kishinev, 76
Kitchener, General, 174
Kluck, von, 323
Knowledge, rôle of, in human affairs, 578 f.
Koch, 599
Koffka, 627 n.
Kokan, 178
Korea, 79, 162, 238, 262, 268 ff., 271 n.
Koroshetz, 445
Kosciusko, 398
Kruger, Paul, 200
Kulaks, 476
Kultur, 344
Kuomintang, 534
Kurland, 370 f.
Kuropatkin, General, 270, 299
Kyoto, 259 f.

Labor, Charter of, 492
Labor legislation. See Social legislation
Labor party, British, 109, 432 f., 461 ff., 465
L'Action Française, 460
Lagos, 203 n.
Laissez faire, 16 ff., 20 n., 34, 37, 117, 430
Lamarck, 587
Lamb, Charles, 638
Land acts (Irish), 218 f.
Land League (Irish), 218 f.

Landholding, Germany, 72 f.; Austria-Hungary, 73, 284; Russia, 74, 86, 422, 472, 474 f.; Ireland, 210 ff., 215, 218 f.; Rumania, 442 f. See also Agrarian revolutions, Feudalism
Language and literature, 579, 635. See also Fiction
Lansing-Ishii agreement, 536 f., 538
Laos, 155
Lassalle, Ferdinand, 106
Lasswell, Harold D., 341 f.
Latin America, 222 ff.
Laurier, Sir Wilfred, 191
Lausanne, Treaty of, 401 f., 516
Lawrence, Colonel T. E., 519
League of Nations, 469, 564 ff., 661; mandates under the, 402; and projects for peace and security, 550 ff.; registration of treaties with, 573 f.
Leibnitz, 641
Lemberg, 350
Lenin, 76, 81 f., 369, 428, 436, 471
Lens, 380
Leo XIII, Pope, 98 f., 103 ff., 126 f.
Leopold II, 168 ff.
Lesseps, Ferdinand de, 139 ff.
Leviathan, the, 138
Lewis, Matthew, 645
Liaotung peninsula, 262 ff., 269
Liberal party in England, 68 f., 117 ff.
Liberia, 379, 506
Libya, 158, 504, 506
Liebknecht, Karl, 449
Life and Labor of the People in London, by Booth, 116 f.
Li Hung Chang, 255, 262, 268
Lille, 352
Lincoln, Abraham, 244 f.
Lipari Island, 488
Lister, Joseph, 600
Lithuania, 370 f., 454, 457, 570
"Little Entente," 498, 553; treaties of (1921–1922), 558
Livingstone, David, 167
Livonia, 370
Lloyd George, David, 68, 120, 220, 317, 378, 390 f., 403, 438 f., 461, 465 f.
Loans. See Debts, European; Investments
Locarno, treaties of, 451, 553 ff., 556
Locke, John, 581
Locomotive, 6, 9, 141 f.
Lodge, H. C., 239
London, Treaty of (1913), 307; secret treaty of (1915), 334, 485
Lords, House of, 68 f., 120, 122, 463. See also Parliament, British
Lords' Veto Bill (1911), 69
Lorraine, 278 ff., 293, 322, 392, 409, 459 f.
Loubet, 45
Louvain, 348
Lucknow, siege of, 184

Lucretius, 602
Ludendorff, General, 323, 351, 355, 385 ff., 429
Lüderitz, 156
Lusitania, the, 360 ff.
Lusk laws, 631
Lüttwitz, 450
Luxemburg, 349
Luxemburg, Rosa, 449
Lyell, Sir Charles, 586

Macao, 249 f.
Macaulay, T. B., 637 f.
MacDonald, Sir John, 191
MacDonald, Ramsay, 462 f., 465, 507
Macedonia, 305 ff., 334, 371, 402, 442
Machinery, introduction of, 6; in France, 176. See Technological Revolution
Mackensen, General, 350
Mackenzie, William, 188 f.
McKinley, William, 234
MacMahon, 42 f.
Madagascar, 154, 288
Madeira, 164, 366
Madison, James, 36
Mahan, Captain Alfred, 299
Mahdi, 174
Mahratta Confederacy, 177 ff.
Maine, the, 159
Maine, Sir Henry, 616
Majestätsbeleidigung, 61
Majuba Hill, 198
Malmédy, 392
Malthus, 33, 113
Mamelukes, 172
Man, scientific study of, 610, 615 ff.; in fiction, 634 ff.
Manchu dynasty, 248, 254 f., 271 f.
Manchuria, 79 f., 251, 262 f., 268 ff., 535
Mandarin, 251 n.
Mandates and mandated territories, 392, 402, 505
Mandeville, Bernard, 640
Mangin, General, 382
Manila, 159
Manitoba, 190
Maniu, Julius, 443, 502
Mann, Thomas, 658
Maoris, 192, 195
Marchand, 153
Marconi, 145
Marie, Queen, of Rumania, 400 f., 502
Markets, competition for foreign, 135 f., 145 ff.
Marne, battle of the (1914), 323
Martineau, Harriet, 243
Marx, Karl, 16, 24 ff., 34, 110, 245, 430 f.
Marx, Dr. Wilhelm, 452
Masaryk, Thomas, 399, 457
Matteotti, 488
Mauretania, the, 139

Maurras, Charles, 460
Max, Prince, of Baden, 386, 388, 429
Maximilian made Emperor in Mexico, 229, 233
"May laws," 97
Mehemet Ali, 172 ff.
Melbourne, 194
Mendelssohn-Bartholdy, Professor Albrecht, 318 f.
Mesopotamia, 338, 352, 371, 384, 401, 517 ff., 559
Metchnikov, 601
Methodists, 91, 148, 217 f.
Metz, 353
Mexico, 228 f., 231, 233, 235 f., 243, 380
Michael, Grand Duke, 368
Microscope, 594 f.
Militarism. See Armaments
Mill, John Stuart, 16, 37, 53, 61 f., 75 n., 632
Millerand, Alexandre, 108
Milton, John, 581, 618, 631, 637
Milyoukov, Paul, 75, 428
Minorities, protection of, 570
Missions, foreign, and imperialism, 147 ff., 228, 257 f.
Mohammed Ahmed, 174
Mohl, Von, 595
Molecules, 605 ff.
Moltke, General von, 323
Monarchy, perdurance of, 64 ff.
Monastic orders in Germany and France, 97 ff. See also Jesuits; Missions, foreign
Mongolia, 251
Monroe Doctrine, 232 f., 236, 558
Montenegro, 52, 307, 309, 350, 371, 400
Montesquieu, 66
Moon, P. T., 133 n., 136 n., 169 n.
Moore, John Bassett, 240, 549 n.
Moravia, 308, 399
More, Hannah, 18 f.
More, Sir Thomas, 21 f.
Mores, 618 ff., 622
Moresnet, 392
Morley, John, 115, 527
Morocco, 163, 166, 170 f., 236, 238, 288 ff., 295; Spanish, 497
Morse, Samuel F. B., 9, 144
Moscow, 82, 86, 396, 423 f.
Mozambique, 164, 504, 506
Mukden, 269 f., 532 ff.
Mussolini, 444, 483 f., 486 ff., 499, 559
Mustafa Kemal Pasha, 514, 516
Mutsuhito, Emperor, 259 f.

Nachtigal, Dr. Gustav, 156
Nagasaki, 259
Nagpur, 182
Nanking, 253, 255, 534 f.; Treaty of, 253, 255
Napier, Lord, 251
Napoleon III, 40, 129, 154, 229, 233, 243 ff., 253

Napoleon Bonaparte, 3, 39, 101 f., 139, 172, 277 f.
Natal, 197 f., 201
National Assembly, French (1789), 36; (1871), 40 ff.
National states, rise of, 5 ff.
Natural laws, 14 f. *See also Laissez faire*
Naval armaments, 207 f., 298 f., 409
Near East, secret understandings regarding partition of, 338
Negroes, democratic tendencies in Africa, 506, 508 ff.
Nelson, 172
"Nep," 475
Nepal, 180 f.
Nepmen, 476
Netherlands, 337, 447
New Brunswick, 189
New Guinea, 157
New South Wales, 193
New Zealand, 191 ff., 195, 351, 355
Newspapers. *See* Press, censorship of
Newton, Sir Isaac, 14
Nicaragua, 230
Nicholas II, Tsar, 39, 74 f., 80, 83 ff., 237, 246, 299 ff., 303, 313, 368 f.
Nigeria, 203 n.
Nogi, General, 269
North, Lord, 91
North America Act, British, 189
Northcliffe, Lord, 341
Norway, 53, 65
Nova Scotia, 189
Nyasaland, 513
Nyassa, Lake, 167

O'Connell, Daniel, 214, 219 f.
Oil fields, 517, 520, 559
Oku, General, 269
Olney, Richard T., 233
Ontario, 187 ff.
Opium War, 252 f.
Orange Free State, 198, 201
Orange River Colony, 166, 201
Origin of Species, by Darwin, 34, 589 ff.
Orlando, 390, 485
Orleanists, 40 ff.
Osaka, 536
Osman, House of, 516
Ottoman Empire. *See* Turkey
Oudh, 182
Owen, Robert, 23, 26, 114

Pacific islands, former German, 339, 355, 371, 402, 531
Pact of Paris, 557 f., 563 f., 576 f.
Paine, Thomas, 2
Palestine, 352, 384, 402, 521 ff.
Panama, 141, 379
Panama Canal, 140 f., 230, 235 n., 236
Pangalos, General, 502
Pan-Germanism, 310

Pan-Hispanic movement, 231 f.
Pankhurst, Mrs. Emmeline, 53 f.
Pan-Slavism, 309 f., 371
Papineau, Louis, 189
Paraguay, 567 ff.
Paris, count of, 43
Paris, in World War, 322, 348, 382; peace conference in (1919), 390 ff.; Pact of, 557, 563 f., 576 f.
Parker, Sir Gilbert, 346 f.
Parkes, Sir Harry, 259
Parliament, development of government by, 6 ff., 35; upper chambers of, 66 ff.; Australian, 194 f.; Austrian, 8, 67; British, 7, 68 f., 417; Bulgarian, 66; French, 42, 56, 67 f.; German, 374; Hungarian, 67, 498; Indian, 187; Irish, 209, 213; Japanese, 261; Prussian, 8; Serbian, 51 f., 66; Turkish, 52, 305 ff. *See also Bundesrat; Duma;* Lords, House of; *Reichstag*
Parliament Act (1911), 69
Parnell, Charles Stewart, 218 f.
Parties, political, 55 ff.; after the War, in Germany, 449 ff.; in Austria, 453. *See also* Constitutional Democrats; Labor party, British; Liberal party in England; Social Democrats
Pashitch, Nicholas, 500
Pasteur, 599, 601
Pavlov, 627 n., 633 n.
Peace conferences. *See* Hague, peace conferences at the; Paris, peace conference in (1919)
Peasants, in Bosnia and Herzegovina, 284; in Hungary, 440; in Ireland, 213, 215; in Rumania, 440; in Russia, 82 f., 86, 440 f.
Peel, Sir Robert, 128
Peking (Peiping), 251, 254, 265, 532 f.
Pelew Islands, 160
Pelloutier, Fernand, 434
Permanent Conciliation Commission, 555 f.
Permanent Court of Arbitration, 302, 548 f.
Permanent Court of International Justice, 547 ff., 555, 563, 565
Perry, Commodore, 227, 258, 260
Pershing, General John, 382
Persia, British and Russian spheres of influence in, 160 f., 338, 517, 524 f.
Peters, Dr. Karl, 157
Phagocytes, 601
Philippine Islands, 155, 159 f., 228, 234, 237 f., 536
Philosophes, 2, 14 ff., 582
Piave, second battle of the, 385
Picquart, Colonel, 44
Pilsudski, General Josef, 455 f.
Pius IX, Pope, 20, 90, 94 f., 97 f., 593
Pius X, Pope, 103 ff.
Plehve, Venceslas, 76, 79
Pleincz, 598

Pobyedonostsev, 75 ff.
Poincaré, Raymond, 280, 316, 320, 458 f.
Poland, in the World War, 324, 363, 370 f.; republic of, 395 f., 398, 417, 442, 454 ff.; "defensive alliance" with France (1921), 558; dispute with Lithuania, 570
Political economy, classical, 16 ff.; criticism of, 20 ff.
Pope, Alexander, 641 f., 646
Pope, Syllabus of Errors issued by the, 20, 94 f.; infallibility of, 95; position of (1870–1929), 105; grant of territory to, by Mussolini, 444 f., 487, 495 f.
Port Arthur, 80, 162, 262, 264, 268 ff., 281
Port Jackson, 193
Porto Rico, 159, 230
Portsmouth, Treaty of, 237 f., 271
Portugal, colonies of, 164, 166, 506; and World War, 337
Posen ceded to Poland, 392
Postal system, 144
Poynings's Act, 209, 213
Presidential system, American, 417; French, 41 f.; German, 418
Presidium, 424
Press, censorship of, 581; in England, 57 ff., 428, 462 f.; in France, 60; in Germany, 60 f.; in Italy, 488, 494 f.; in Russia, 75, 480 f.; in Spain, 497; in World War, 346 f.
Prince Edward Island, 190
Progress, idea of, 15 f.
Proletariat, 8; dictatorship of the, 396, 432, 471
Propaganda, in World War, 340 ff., 346 f., 540; in Russia, 480 f.
Proportional representation, 418 f., 447
"Protectorate," 134
Protoplasm, 595
Proudhon, 28
Prussia, in the eighteenth century, 31, 277; position in the German Empire, 47, 50 f., 72 f., 297; and Polish "corridor," 392, 455; constitution of republic of, 421
Psychology, modern, 622 ff.; study of abnormal, 628
Punjab, 181 f.

"Q-ships," 330
Quadruple Alliance, 351
Quebec (province), 188 f.
Quebec Act, 187
Queensland, 194
Quintessence of Ibsenism, The, 649 ff.

Race prejudice, 620 ff. See also Negroes
Radcliffe, Mrs., 645
Radio, 372
Raditch, Stephen, 500
Radium, 603

Railroads, development of, 141 ff.; in Africa, 144, 202 f., 508; in Canada, 190; in China, 264 f., 534 f.; in Germany, 32, 406; in India, 185; in Russia, 161 f., 474 f.
Ranavalona III, Queen, 154
Ranke, Leopold von, 611 f.
Rathenau, Walter, 450
Raw materials, quest for, 146, 224
"Red Sunday," 81
Redlich, 52
Reichstag, German, 47 ff., 420
Reims, 352, 382
"Relativity," 605
Remarque, Erich (pseudonym), 574 f.
Reparations by Germany, 404 ff., 448, 540 ff., 563 f.
Reparations Commission, 404 f., 407 f., 540 f.
Representative Government, Considerations on, by J. S. Mill, 62
Reunion Act (1839), 189
Reza Khan, Shah, 525
Rhine River, 338, 406 ff.
Rhodes, 159, 307, 496
Rhodes, Cecil, 200
Rhodesia, 202; Northern, 513
Ricardo, David, 16, 19, 23, 25 f., 113
Richardson, Samuel, 643 f.
Rivera, General Primo de, 497
Rivers, international, 406
Romanov, House of, 368
Romanticism, 643 ff.
Rome, 5, 487 ff.
Röntgen, 603
Roosevelt, Theodore, 141, 235 ff., 270 f., 303, 536
Root, Elihu, 241, 547 n., 550
Rosebery, Lord, 133 f.
Rossoni, Edmondo, 491
Rothermere, Lord, 499
Rousseau, Jean-Jacques, 2, 7, 66, 582
Rouvier, 102
Rowlatt Act, 527 f.
Rowntree, 117
Royal Colonial Institute, 206
Royal Geographical Society of England, 167
Ruhr valley, French and Belgian occupation of, 451, 541
Rumania, independence established, 304; in Balkan wars, 308; in World War, 335, 355, 363, 371; annexations by, 400 f., 501 f.; relations with Hungary, 498, 570
Rumelia, Eastern, 304
Ruskin, John, 20 f.
Russia, relations with Europe, 4 f.; under Nicholas II, 74 ff.; genealogical table, 74 n.; expansion of, in central Asia (1863–1886), 160 ff.; alliance with France (1891), 280 f.; revolution in (1905), 81 ff.; revolution of

March, 1917, 367 ff.; mobilization of (1914), 313 f., 320; in World War, 323, 349 ff., 355; Bolshevik revolutions in, 367 ff.; loss of territory, 370, 396 ff.; constitution of, 416, 419, 421 ff.; nationalization of land and industries in, 422, 430, 472, 474 f.; Soviet government in, 471 f.; recognition of the Soviet government by Great Britain, 462; failure of counterrevolution in, 474
Russian Socialist Federal Soviet Republic, 396, 398, 422
Russo-Japanese War, 79 f., 84, 236 f., 268 ff., 281, 290
Ruthenians, 308

Saar valley, 338, 407
Sadler, Thomas, 114
Saint Germain-en-Laye, Treaty of, 392 f., 453, 499
St. Mihiel, 383
St. Petersburg, 81 f., 86, 368 f.
St. Quentin, 380, 383
Saint-Simon, Comte de, 22, 26, 241
Sakhalin, 271
Salisbury, Lord, 131 f.
Salonika, 305, 308, 335 f.
Samoa Islands, 157, 228
Sand River Convention (1852), 198
Santo Domingo, 230
Sarajevo, 283, 290, 304, 311
Saskatchewan, 190
Savannah, the, 138
Sazonov, S. D., 281
Schäffle, Albert, 62
Scheidemann, Philipp, 450
Schleiden, 595
Schleswig, 392
Schlieffen, General, 323
Schmoller, 31, 122
Scholasticism, 14 f.
Schopenhauer, 642
Schwann, 595
Science, methods of modern, 608 ff., 660 f. *See also* Discoveries, modern scientific
Scott, Sir Walter, 645 f.
Secret treaties. *See* Diplomacy, secret
Security Pact. *See* Locarno, treaties of
Sedan, 383
Seeley, John R., 205
Seipel, Dr. Ignaz, 445, 453
"Self-determination," 396, 399, 409, 528, 537 f.
Senegal, 151, 153, 165 f., 504
Separation Law, 102 f.
Sepoy rebellion, 183 f.
Serbia, independence established, 5, 282 f., 304; relations with Russia and Austria, 304, 307, 309; in the Balkan wars, 307 ff.; constitution of, 51 f., 54, 66; in World War, 323 f., 335,

350, 363, 371, 384. *See also* Yugoslavia
Serbs, Croats, and Slovenes, kingdom of the. *See* Yugoslavia
Serfdom abolished, 260, 439 ff.
Sèvres, Treaty of, 401, 514
Sex, 627
Shaho River, battle of, 80
Shakespeare, 636 f.
Shanghai, 253 f.
Shantung, 263 f., 332, 339, 402, 531, 537, 560
Shaw, G. B., 109, 651 ff.
Shimonoseki, 259; Treaty of, 262
Shotwell, James T., 552 n., 576 f.
Shrámek, 445
Siam, 379
Siberia, 383, 396, 534, 537 f.
Siegfried, André, 247
Sierra Leone, 203 n.
Silesia, 399; plebiscite in, 392, 455, 569 f.
Simon, Sir John, 531
Sind, 181
Sinn Fein, 466
Sivaji, 178
Slave trade, African, 164 ff.
Slavonia, 310, 371, 399 f., 440 f.
Slovakia, 399
Slovenia, 310, 371, 400
Smiles, Samuel, 18
Smith, Adam, 25, 582
Smollett, 644
Smuts, General Jan, 202, 512 f.
Smyrna, 338, 401, 514 f.
Social democrats, in Germany, 55, 61, 71 f., 107, 429 f., 432 f., 448 f.; in Russia, 77 f.; in England, 109
Social legislation, 430; in Great Britain, 111 ff., 463; in France and Italy, 125 ff.; in Australia, 195 f. *See also* State socialism in Germany
Social sciences, 634
Socialism, Christian, 20; Guild, 433 f.; Marxian, 16, 24 ff., 63; Utopian, 21 ff.; in Germany and France, 106 ff.; in Great Britain, 109; after the War, 425 ff. *See also* State socialism; International, First, Second, Third
Socialist Revolutionary party in Russia, 78 ff.
Society for the Promotion of Christian Knowledge, 148
Society for the Propagation of the Faith, 148
Soissons, 382
Solomon Islands, 157
Somaliland, British, 203 n.; French, 153 n.; Italian, 158, 506
Somme, battle of the, 354
Sorel, Georges, 434
South Africa, Union of, 202, 355 f., 512 ff.

South America, 222 ff.
South Australia, 194
South Manchurian Railway, 537
Southwest Africa, German, 156 f., 356; administered by the Union of South Africa, 402, 505
Soviets, 81, 422; government of Russia by, 369, 396 ff., 421 ff., 471 ff.
Spain, constitution of, 51; war with United States (1898), 159 f.; loss of colonies of, 159 f., 289, 506; relations with Latin America, 231 f.; and World War, 380; dictatorship in, 497
Spanish-American War, 159 f., 234, 289
Spartacists, 449
Spencer, Herbert, 75, 589, 592
Stambolisky, 501
Stamp duties in England, 58 f.
Stanley, H. M., 136 n., 167
State socialism in Germany, 29 ff., 122 ff.
Steam engine, 6, 9, 137 ff., 176
Steamships, 137 ff., 190, 265 f.
Stefani, de, 490
Stein, 439
Stephens, 217
Stephenson, George, 6, 9, 142
Stettin, 406
Stevens, John, 138
Stolypin, 85
Strasbourg, 279
Stresemann, Gustav, 451
Strike, general, in Russia, 83 f.; in Great Britain, 464; in Italy, 492
Styria, 400
Subjection of Women, The, by J. S. Mill, 53
Submarines, 329 f., 358 ff., 365 f., 367 n., 373, 384 f., 560
Sudan, 172; French expedition to upper, 153; revolt of the Mahdi in, 174
Sudermann, 658
Suez Canal, 139 ff., 172, 507, 517
Suffrage, modern extension of, 7 f., 35, 51 ff., 61 ff., 73, 195, 242, 416, 420 ff., 424, 486, 492, 529, 536
Sumner, Lord, 404
Sumner, W. G., 616, 620
Sun Yat-sen, Dr., 272, 534
Swift, Jonathan, 640
Switzerland, constitution, 65, 447
Sydney, 193
Syllabus of Errors, 20, 94 f.
Syndicalism, 434; in Italy, 491 f.
Syria, 333, 338, 352, 371, 384, 401, 517

Taboo, 619 f.
Taft, W. H., 494, 536
Taipings, 255
Tadjikistan, 398, 423
Tanganyika, 513
Tanganyika, Lake, 167
"Tanks" in World War, 328, 354
Tariff, protective, 127 ff., 414; in the

United States, 31, 129, 245 f.; in Germany, 31 f.; in the British Empire, 207
Tasmania, 191 ff.
Technological Revolution, 9 ff., 26
Telegraph, 144 f., 265 f., 330, 372
Telephone, 372
Test Act (1673), 91 f.
Texas, 243
Thackeray, W. M., 648
Thiers, 40
Thomas, William I., 616
Thrace, Eastern, 401, 514, 516
Tibet, 251
Tientsin, 254, 534
Timbuktu, 153
Tocqueville, Alexis de, 242
Togo, Admiral, 270
Togoland, 156, 356, 402, 505
Tokugawa Iyeyasu, Emperor, 256, 258
Tokyo, 259 ff., 536
Toleration Act (1689), 91
Tolstoy, Leo, 29, 79, 528, 659
Tongking, 155
Tories, 55
Trade Disputes Act, British, 464
Trade unions, 437 f.; in Great Britain, 109, 464; in Russia, 481 f. See also Syndicalism
Transcaucasian Socialist Federal Soviet Republic, 398
Transjordania, 520 f.
Transportation and intercommunication, modern, 136 ff., 372
Trans-Siberian Railway, 143, 161 f., 264
Transylvania, 335, 355, 371, 399
Transvaal, 166, 197 ff., 202
Treasonable Practices Bill, 59
Treaties, registration of, with the League of Nations, 573 f.
Treitschke, Heinrich von, 61, 287
Trench warfare, 324 f., 349
Trent, 385, 395
Trepoff, General, 82
Trevelyan, Charles, 427 f.
Trieste, 355, 385, 395
Triple Alliance, 157 f., 291 f., 312, 315, 319
Triple Entente, 292 f., 312
Tripoli, 166, 306 f.
Tripolitania, 158
Trotzky, Leon, 81, 369, 428, 440, 476 f., 481
Tunis, 152, 157, 163, 166
Turgeniev, 659
Turkestan, Russian, 160
Turkey, Crimean War, 4 f.; loss of Greece and Balkan states, 5, 304 ff.; revolution of Young Turks (1908), 52, 305 ff.; war with Italy (1911–1912), 158, 306 f.; joins Central Powers in World War, 333, 350; and treaties of Sèvres and Lausanne, 401 f.; republic of, 514 ff.

Turkish language, 516
Turkmenistan, Eastern, 251
Turkmen Republic, 398
Twenty-one demands, 339
Tylor, Edward, 616 f.
Tyrol, South, 395
Tzu Hsi, "Dowager Empress" of China, 255, 266, 268

U-boats. *See* Submarines
Uganda, 203 n., 513
Uitlanders, 199 f.
Ukraine, 370, 383, 396, 398
Ulster, 221, 467
Unconscious, the, 626
Unemployment, English, 119
Union Congress of Soviets, 423
Union of Socialist Soviet Republics, 396, 423 f., 431
United Empire Loyalists, 187
United States, in 1815, 176; relations with Europe, economic, 222 ff.; diplomatic, 232 ff.; political, 241 ff.; relations with China, 228, 253; relations with Japan, 228, 237 f., 258 f., 294, 536 f.; neutrality in World War, 361 ff.; declares war on Germany, 366 f.; in World War, 380 ff.; peace treaties with Germany and Austria, 566; position as to League of Nations, 563 f., 566, 572 f.; position as to Permanent Court, 549 f., 563. *See also* American Revolution, Tariff
Universities, medieval, 629 ff.; in England, 93; in Russia, 75
Uranium, 603 f.
Usher, Archbishop, 584 f., 613
Usher, Roland G., 239
Utopians, 21 ff.
Uzbekistan, 398, 423 and note, 525 n.

Vaccination, 600
Valera, Eamonn de, 466
Valona, 334
Van Dieman's Land. *See* Tasmania
Vatican City, 495
Vatican Council (1869–1870), 95 f.
Venezuela, 233 ff., 240
Venizelos, 307, 336 f., 379, 502
Verdun, 352 ff.
Versailles, Treaty of, 391 f., 403 ff., 427; failure of United States Senate to ratify, 566
Vestiges of the Natural History of Creation, by Chambers, 588, 593
Veto Bill. *See* Lords' Veto Bill
Victor Emmanuel II, 5
Victoria, 194 ff.
Victoria, Queen, 64, 195; proclaimed Empress of India, 185
Victoria Nyanza, Lake, 167
Vieques, 160
Vienna, 452 f.

Vilna, 454, 570
Virchow, 595
Virgin Islands, 230
Vitamins, 607
Vladivostok, 263 f., 269, 383, 535
Voltaire, 2, 98, 614, 633
Voyvodina, 400

Wagner, 31, 122 f.
Wahhabis, 519
Waldeck-Rousseau, 100, 108
Wallace, Alfred R., 591 f.
Wallas, Graham, 109, 578 f.
War, 275, 317 f.; as an anachronism, 574 ff.; camp-followers of, 576; modern scientific, 576; plans for outlawing of, 372 ff., 551 ff., 574 f. *See also* Aggression and aggressor
"War guilt," 274 f., 315 ff., 403 f., 410
War loans. *See* Debts, European post-war
Warsaw, 350
Washington, George, 242
Washington Conference (1921–1922), 538, 559 ff., 563
Watt, James, 6, 9
Webb, Beatrice, 109
Webb, Sidney, 109
Weihaiwei, 264
Wells, H. G., 109, 635, 655 ff.
West Prussia, 392
Western Australia, 194
Weyler, General, 159
Whigs, 55
White Russia, 396, 398
Whitley Report, 434
William I of Prussia, first German emperor, 46 f., 297
William II, Emperor, 70 f., 124, 237, 288, 299 ff., 387 ff., 408, 540
William P. Frye, the, 359
Wilson, Woodrow, notes of, to Germany, 359 ff., 388; efforts of, for peace, 364, 377 ff., 420; address to Congress (April 2, 1917), 366 f.; Fourteen Points of, 378 f., 386; at the Peace Conference, 390 f., 404 f., 411; opposed Italian claims, 485; policy in Far East, 536 ff.; and the League of Nations, 564 ff.; quoted, 38, 277, 383, 399, 406, 410, 426, 528, 532, 537 f., 566
Wollstonecraft, Mary, 53, 417
Woman suffrage, 8, 52 ff., 195, 416, 447 f., 463
Women, employment of, 112; in World War, 331 f.; British laws regarding rights of, 417; novelists, 658
Wordsworth, 646
Workmen's Compensation Act, 118
World Bank. *See* Bank for International Settlements
World Court. *See* Permanent Court of International Justice

World Peace Foundation, 575
World War, origins of the, 277 ff.; nations at war, 274, 337, 379; neutrals in, 341 f., 357, 360, 379 f.; novel features of, science and technology, 321 ff.; mobilization of industries in, 331 f., 412; Austria's ultimatum to Serbia, 311 f.; efforts to preserve peace, 312 f.; first declaration of war, Austria to Serbia, 313; Germany declares war on Russia and France, 314; invasion of Belgium by Germans, 314, 322; Great Britain declares war on Germany, 314; the Western Front (1914–1915), 322 ff., 348 f., 352 ff., (1917–1918), 380 ff.; the Eastern Front, 323 f., 349 ff., 354 f.; the Balkan front, 350, 384; Dardanelles and Gallipoli campaign, 351 f.; British campaigns in Mesopotamia, Syria, and Palestine, 352 ff.; war on the seas, 356 ff., 365 ff.; peace proposals, 363 ff., 377; issues of the, 370 ff.; General Foch made commander in chief of Allied forces, 381; surrender of Bulgaria and Turkey, 384; surrender of Austria-Hungary, 385; armistice with Germany, 386, 388 f.; casualties, 412; national debts of participants, 412 f.; African and Indian native troops in, 504, 510 f.

X rays, 603
Xavier, Francis, 147, 257

Yokohama, 259, 536
Yoshihito, 536
Young, Owen D., 542 ff., 563
Young plan, 410, 469, 542 ff.
Young Turks, 52, 305 ff.
Ypres, 352
Yüan Shih-k'ai, 273
Yugoslavia (kingdom of Serbs, Croats, Slovenes), 395, 399, 499 ff.
Yugoslavs, 283, 308, 499

Zambezi River, 167
Zanzibar, 157
Zeebrugge, 380
Zeno, 27
Zeppelins, 326
Zionism, 521 ff.
Zola, Émile, 45
Zollverein, 176